The RoutledgeFalmer Reader in Psychology of Education

The editors of this essential Reader recognise the valuable and varied benefits of connecting the two fields of education and psychology, and have carefully selected contributions to reflect current trends in the subject and examples of how knowledge has an impact on practice.

This lively and authoritative book features parts on topics as varied as:

- assessment
- language
- motivation
- cognition and development
- intelligence
- memory.

Psychology and education have an entwined relationship, but one that is often complex and delicate. Day-to-day pressures of classroom life may often result in the negligence of the importance of child development. It is therefore crucial for students and practitioners to keep abreast of recent educational changes, which raise new questions for educational psychology.

With a specially written introduction from the editors, providing a much-needed context to the current education climate, students of educational psychology will find this Reader an important route map to further reading and understanding.

Harry Daniels and **Anne Edwards** are both Professors at the School of Education, University of Birmingham. They co-direct the Centre for Sociocultural and Activity Theory Research.

Readers in education

The RoutledgeFalmer Reader in Higher Education
Edited by Malcolm Tight

The RoutledgeFalmer Reader in Language and Literacy
Edited by Teresa Grainger

The RoutledgeFalmer Reader in Psychology of Education
Edited by Harry Daniels and Anne Edwards

The RoutledgeFalmer Reader in Sociology of Education
Edited by Stephen J. Ball

The RoutledgeFalmer Reader in Science Education
Edited by John Gilbert

The RoutledgeFalmer Reader in Multicultural Education
Edited by David Gillborn and Gloria Ladson-Billings

The RoutledgeFalmer Reader in Inclusion
Edited by Keith Topping and Sheelagh Maloney

The RoutledgeFalmer Reader in Teaching and Learning
Edited by Ted Wragg

The RoutledgeFalmer Reader in Psychology of Education

Edited by
Harry Daniels and Anne Edwards

 RoutledgeFalmer
Taylor & Francis Group

LONDON AND NEW YORK

First published 2004
by RoutledgeFalmer
11 New Fetter Lane, London EC4P 4EE

Simultaneously published in the USA and Canada
by RoutledgeFalmer
29 West 35th Street, New York, NY 10001

RoutledgeFalmer is an imprint of the Taylor & Francis Group

Typeset in Sabon and Futura by
Florence Production Ltd, Stoodleigh, Devon
Printed and bound in Great Britain by
TJ International Ltd, Padstow, Cornwall

British Library Cataloguing in Publication Data
A catalogue record for this book is available from the
British Library

Library of Congress Cataloging in Publication Data
A catalog record for this book has been requested

ISBN 0–415–32768–7 (hbk)
ISBN 0–415–32769–5 (pbk)

CONTENTS

ACKNOWLEDGEMENTS

Galloway, D., Rogers, C., Armstrong, D., Leo, E. and Jackson, C., 'Ways of understanding motivation' is reproduced from *Motivating the Difficult to Teach* (1998, London and New York) with the kind permission of Pearson Education Limited. © Pearson Education Limited.

Goswami, U., 'Cognitive development – no stages please – we're British' is reproduced from *British Journal of Psychology*, 92 (2001) with the kind permission of the British Journal of Psychology. © British Journal of Psychology.

Middleton, D. and Edwards, D., 'Conversational Remembering: a Social Psychological Approach' is reproduced from *Collective Remembering* (1990, London) with the kind permission of Sage Publications Ltd. © Sage Publications Ltd.

Slavin, R. E., 'When and Why Does Cooperative Learning Increase Achievement? Theoretical and Empirical Perspectives' is reproduced from *Interaction in Cooperative Groups: The Theoretical Anatomy of Group Learning* (1993, Cambridge) with the kind permission of Robert E. Slavin and Cambridge University Press. © Cambridge University Press.

All other articles and chapters are reproduced with kind permission of Taylor & Francis Group. http://www.tandf.co.uk.

INTRODUCTION

Harry Daniels and Anne Edwards

Psychology and education have an entwined relationship. It is most certainly not a one-way relationship in which psychology produces knowledge, for subsequent application in education. It is a complex and delicate two-way relationship. There is one sense in which some aspects of psychology need interaction with education. Arguably developments and advances take place as psychology responds to the field of education with its ever-changing tensions and dilemmas. Education could thus be seen as a spur to development in some aspects of psychology.

This is not the place to rehearse the analysis of the social and political pressures on psychology as a discipline. It is probably sufficient to note that the tendency of the discipline to present itself as the conveyor of scientific certainty has been enhanced by the opportunity, in the UK at least, to secure higher levels of funding as a science within universities. As a consequence, it may be reasonable to suggest that those aspects of Social, Cultural and Developmental Psychology which demand a close-to-the-field questioning of assumptions and the more reflective and participatory methods of the social sciences may struggle to flourish and expand within UK higher education.

At the same time, teacher training in England and Wales has been progressively stripped of accounts of child development, and even learning, so the intensity of the interchange between psychology and education has been diminished and impoverished. There is a need for renewal and not only in the UK. Education is struggling to come to terms with the peda-gogic implications of preparing young people and adults for the demands of a rapidly changing knowledge economy. The questions these societal changes invoke may well act to progress changes in psychology. For example, notions of situated and distributed cognition are invoked in speculations about the most appropriate way to conceptualise social and psychological processes in the collective production of knowledge in educational as well as work settings. As social change demands educational change so educational change raises new questions for psychology. These questions may, and perhaps should, act to change the conceptions and assumptions of psychology as it seeks to accommodate these new chal-lenges.

We are, therefore, not seeing psychology as a set of scientific certainties to be applied in education as a benign and passive field of study. Instead, we are suggesting that both areas of work benefit from mutual interaction. A particular contribution that psychology can make to education is to inform the intellectual tool kits of educationalists and sharpen thinking about the processes of teaching and learning. The contributions selected for this collection rarely offer clear-cut guidance. Rather, they demonstrate that the development of psycholog-ical knowledge is socially situated and slowly accumulative and that it frequently occurs in response to observations from the field that disconcert.

This book has, therefore, been planned to provide commentaries from psychology on issues of significance for education. In turn, these educational issues are challenging some of the suppositions of psychology and are giving rise to change. We suggest that particular value positions are associated with ways of understanding and approaches to explanation. These value positions in psychology are coming under what is, ultimately, social pressure.

We have selected contributions to reflect what, we think, are current trends in the usage of assumptions and development of new assumptions. The eternal verities and 'standards' of psychology have been published elsewhere. This is not an introduction to psychology that might be of interest to those working in education. Rather, it is a selection of examples of knowledge in use and development or knowledge that has been made available for development in practice. We are trying to show how psychology and education are shaping, and being shaped by, each other. We were invited by the publishers to draw largely on Taylor & Francis publications. This we have done in order to provide a set of readings that we think will be of interest and use to those working and studying in both psychology and education.

We do this at a time when education is being held increasingly accountable for its actions. At times it appears that the move to public account has restricted the gaze of some of those who work in the field. Narrowly defined targets, which become the metrics of standards and effectiveness can, if mismanaged, come to distort the service which they seek to protect. However, there are voices which seek to go beyond a retrospective account of knowledge as it appeared in schooling in the last century in order to reconceptualise the practice of education for the social and knowledge prospects of the current century (Bentley, 1998; Seltzer and Bentley, 1999; Brighouse, 2002). The promotion of learning in settings beyond the school gate, and conception of learning as a life-long activity make significant demands on the models, metaphors and theories of psychology.

Still, many practitioners operate in education with forms of craft knowledge which have been tacitly acquired through, and in, practice. They are also faced with, and comply with, explicit demands couched in terms of competence and performance. Yet, there is a growing recognition that in the future education for the knowledge society will require teachers who engage in deliberative action. The argument goes that knowledge-producing learners require teachers whose pedagogy is responsive. This is not a pedagogy of well-honed rituals. Rather, it is one which demands an informed ability to interpret complex learning situations and to select appropriate responses to those interpretations.

In order to do this teachers need to develop intellectual tools for action and reflection. These may be found in developments in psychology as it engages in the demands of practice. There is a significant challenge here. In the past psychological knowledge was often judged on the basis of its immediate practical utility by teachers. The relatively recent interest in the concept of pedagogy has not always been accompanied by a reference to psychology for knowledge on pedagogic development. There is a need to recognise the need for, and relevance of, certain forms of theoretical modelling, imagination and speculation on the part of practitioners. This calls on particular forms of expertise. Following Greeno (1991) we suggest that both parties need to learn to negotiate and interpret the knowledge landscape of the other. Rather than education moving away from the discipline of psychology there is a need to make it accessible and usable by practitioners. In the interplay, theories and practices may be developed.

It is with these issues in mind that we have selected the contents of this book. We see psychology as a cultural artefact that may be used in the analysis of educational problems and developments in which individual, interactional, systemic and historical influences weave together in the formation of what counts as a situated educational context (Cole, 1996).

Assessment

The part on assessment opens with a chapter by John R. Beech and Chris Singleton on the psychological assessment of reading. Their subtitle is 'theoretical issues and professional solutions' thus flagging an interplay between the two fields. They highlight the difficulties that may arise when research findings do not connect with the production of assessment materials. While the references to the Special Educational Needs (SEN) Code of Practice are now dated and some may disagree with their support for particular forms of assessment, they make an important general point that the haphazard approach to the assessment of specific reading difficulties may give rise to inappropriate placement and provision. They argue that educational practice is implicitly making demands that psychology has yet to answer.

In an important contribution to the field, Paul Black examines the ways subcultural influences are brought to bear on the development of assessment techniques. In Chapter 2 he identifies the roots, developments and prospects for four 'dreams' of assessment. He discusses the ways in which society and its specific practices appropriate and shape theoretical ideas and, in so doing, alters the prospects for those ideas.

Language

In the first of the two chapters in this part, Erica Burman traces the recent history of theoretical development and debate on issues of language development. She notes the irony of the ways in which theoretical development may work against its own best intentions. Attempts to take account of diversity and context have become constrained. Through reference to multilingual issues she illustrates a number of issues that are relevant to, but are underplayed by, theoretical accounts of language development. She argues that the shortcomings of the consequences of a theoretical move are highlighted when the theory that has developed is cast against specific forms of practice.

In Chapter 4, Neil Mercer and Rupert Wegerif discuss the investigation of the role of spoken language and joint activity in collaborative learning. Their concern is with the promotion of educationally productive talk. They develop theoretical and methodological tools as they investigate a form of speech they term exploratory talk. Here, the interplay between general developments in psychological theory and educational practice gives rise to specific advances in both. The development of the capacity to collaborate and use of language to reason in the classroom calls for the generation of more delicate theoretical accounts and methodological procedures than were previously available.

Motivation

The first chapter in this part is an introduction to a range of approaches to motivation which are of relevance to teachers working with learners who are difficult to engage. David Galloway and his co-authors work their way from a discussion of internally located, instinct-driven drive theory and on to the interactive and cognitive framework of attribution theory. Their emphasis on attribution theory and on a sensitivity to the motivational style of learners usefully informs the intellectual tool kits of teachers and has the potential to help practitioners to reflect analytically on their interactions with disengaged learners.

Chapter 6, by Margaret Carr and Guy Claxton, develops the focus on disposition hinted at in the chapter by Galloway *et al.* and builds on the work of both Carr and Claxton on disposition to engage as a key to successful learning. Here, they are concerned with both the development and assessment of those learning dispositions which, they suggest, can equip learners to function responsibly under conditions of complexity and uncertainty. Importantly, in the context of the present text, they argue that disposition as an analytic concept lies somewhere between a situation-specific response and a generalisable capability. Consequently, disposition may be best understood as a tendency to respond which has its origins both in the person in, for example, their resilience, and in the opportunities for response to be found in the situation.

Cognition and development

Work on cognition and development has a great deal to offer the field of education and much of the interesting work on these topics has, of course, been undertaken in educational settings. The first chapter in this part is extracted from Sarah Meadows' book *Child as Thinker*. It offers a detailed and comprehensive overview of the three models of cognition which have so far been most influential in education. She traces the within-person focuses of Piagetian developmental psychology and the extension of his work in a developmental account of cognition as information processing. Here, particular attention is given to the work of Robbie Case and his notion of child as problem solver. Meadows then compares the Piagetian and information-processing models with the approach of Vygotsky, Wertsch and others who follow in the sociocultural tradition. Acknowledging the sociocultural emphasis on the primacy of the social world in the shaping and making of minds, she makes a sharp contrast with the individual focus of the first two models. Finally, she points to the educational intent of Vygotsky's work by reminding us that the Vygotskian learner is assisted by more knowledgeable others in 'the guided reinvention of the accumulation of knowledge and ways of thinking which previous generations have constructed'.

The next contribution, from Usha Goswami, returns us to Piaget's influence on developmental psychology. But this is a challenging chapter for both psychologists and educationalists. Goswami argues for an increasingly interdisciplinary cognitive psychology which draws on genetics and molecular biology as well as on philosophy and behavioural science. This argument is illustrated with reference to her own studies of rime and reading and the wider body of work on theory of mind. Both areas of research certainly have much to offer teachers of young children. However, as Goswami reminds us, psychology, too, needs to enrich the conceptual base that underpins this work and to take advantage of technical developments arising elsewhere which allow, for example, detailed study of the developing brain.

Intelligence

This part provides an introduction to two directions in the development of the concept of intelligence. Both are strongly referenced to, and informed by, an understanding of the demands of educational practice.

In Chapter 9, Bruce Torff and Howard Gardner outline the case for multiple intelligences. At the time of writing they identified eight intelligences and outline a distinction between horizontal and vertical faculties and compare the theory of multiple intelligences to other vertical faculty theories. In their concluding sentence they affirm the restorative impact on theory of an attempt at a full consideration of the complexity of educational and cultural influence.

In Chapter 10, Lauren B. Resnick and Sharon Nelson-Le Gall open a rather different direction. Their point of departure is that of intelligence as a social practice. They contrast major strands in psychological theorising about intelligence and proceed to question how schools, as institutions, might be designed to socialise intelligence. They place particular emphasis on the impact of particular beliefs about intelligence in the practices of schooling. They argue that their research is planned as a series of cycles in which the design of schooling is 'actively merged with psychological theory and empirical research methods'.

Memory

Research on memory has a very long history in psychology. Part of that history has been traced in the first chapter in this part from Peter Morris. Morris takes us from the famous studies of Ebbinghaus in the 1880s through to the intentional and socially situated accounts of memory of, for example, Neisser in the 1970s and 1980s. He outlines the work that was starting to occur in the 1980s on the different functions of memory and the distinctions to be made between episodic memory (of personal events) and semantic memory (of factual knowledge no longer associated with specific events). He concludes that more work needs to be done on what memory is for.

The second chapter in this part provides one response to that question, by focusing on what Morris has described as episodic memory. This chapter, by David Middleton and Derek Edwards on collective remembering, locates the processes of remembering within socially situated narratives and owes a great deal to the contribution made in the 1930s by Bartlett to the idea of remembering as a process of knowledge construction. However, they extend Bartlett's analyses to focus more directly on how remembering can have a social function, such as when a teacher establishes with pupils a shared representation of work done in a previous lesson. The chapter also offers useful insights into how forms of discourse analysis can reveal how different ways of representing memories may serve different functions within texts. The authors conclude that remembering in conversation can be seen as 'organised social action' in which the past is 'reconstructed and contested'.

Cooperative learning

In the first chapter in this part, Robert E. Slavin draws on a career of detailed study of interactive group work, to offer what he describes as 'an integrative theory of cooperative learning and achievement'. Having examined six approaches to understanding cooperative learning, which include social cohesion, cognitive and motivational perspectives, he suggests that each strand has taken too narrow a line. He concludes that the next step has to be to think across the boundaries set up by each approach to produce a more integrated account of how cooperation actually does enhance learning.

Chapter 14, by Paul Light, tackles these issues head-on in his concern with what effects a 'collaborative mode of working might have on levels of achievement or learning outcomes'. This question has arisen from studies of children using computers which have suggested that there is a marked increase in children's socially interactive learning. The question is pursued by Light in an analysis of a number of studies of children's collaborative working with computers. His conclusion is guarded. There is, he suggests, evidence that the use of computers has the potential to enhance collaborative learning. But, he argues, we need to know much more about the role of classroom teachers and also how these interactions are mediated by conditions in wider social settings such as schools.

Activity theory

In this chapter, David R. Russell discusses two relative newcomers to the range of psychological theories that have been developed in and through education. He outlines the basic principles of activity theory and discusses learning in terms of Vygotsky's concept of the Zone of Proximal Development. He illustrates how activity theory may be applied in educational settings with carefully drawn examples from work in evaluating distributed learning, technical training, and a children's after school learning programme. He raises a number of important questions about the theory on the basis of speculations about practice.

Behaviour management

In this final chapter, Paul Cooper and Graham Upton discuss the origins of the ecosystemic approach to emotional and behavioural difficulties in schools. They draw on systemic theory and family therapy. They then proceed to outline the key components of the approach which was stimulated through a lack of satisfaction with other approaches to theorising such difficulties and designing intervention. In the conclusion they provide a discussion of the prospects for the approach in the context of particular political and psychological traditions as well as the suspected 'deskilling' of some teachers. Here is an example of a discussion of the cultural historical factors which may impact on the development of emergent theory.

References

Bentley, T. (1998) *Learning Beyond the Classroom: Education for a Changing World*, London: Demos and Routledge.

Brighouse, T. (2002) 'Comprehensive schools then, now and in the future – is it time to draw a line in the sand and create a new ideal', *The Caroline Benn, Brian Simon Memorial lecture*, 28 September 2002.

Cole, M. (1996) *Cultural Psychology: A Once and Future Discipline*, Cambridge, Mass.: Harvard University Press.

Greeno, J. (1991) 'Number sense: situated knowing in a conceptual domain', *Journal for Research in Mathematics Education*, 22 (3): 117–218.

Seltzer, K. and Bentley, T. (1999) *The Creative Age: Knowledge and Skills for the New Economy*, London: Demos.

PART 1

ASSESSMENT

CHAPTER 1

THE PSYCHOLOGICAL ASSESSMENT OF READING

Theoretical issues and professional solutions

John R. Beech and Chris Singleton

The Psychological Assessment of Reading, London, Routledge, 1997

Why do we need to assess literacy? Often because we, as professionals (either psychologists or specialist teachers), are called upon to do so. Usually it is because a child is experiencing (or is perceived by parents and/or teachers to be experiencing) some difficulties in learning to read, write or spell. We have to establish: (1) whether there really is a difficulty (not just an imagined problem); (2) the extent of the difficulty, should it exist; (3) the most likely cause, or causes, of the difficulty, and finally, (4) we are usually asked to recommend ways of putting things right. *Causes* are important, because they affect the recommendations one would make regarding appropriate help or support for the child. Many children with poor literacy skills are referred for assessment (whether privately or within the state system) on suspicion of dyslexia. Some are indeed found to have dyslexia, while others are often found to have been deprived of appropriate *teaching* (most commonly phonics tuition) or to lack the *practice* which is essential for basic literacy skills to become fluent. If the cause seems to be lack of appropriate teaching, simply recommending certain educational input may not be a sufficient remedy if the child's teacher does not have the appropriate skills or the child's school does not have the appropriate resources.

We could say initially that we need to assess children in order to monitor their level of achievement in literacy and we want to assess adults and adolescents because we need to see whether their achievement is sufficient to meet the requirements of whatever they are doing at work or in an educational setting. We assume here that assessment is in relation to the average literacy achievements of others of equivalent age. We might also implicitly assume that we are making the assessment in order to do something about it, if necessary.

Going deeper into this, we begin to get more controversial. Yes, we can monitor achievement in relation to others, but sometimes an assessor might say: 'I'm afraid that this level of achievement is to be expected given overall cognitive ability.' For example: 'This child's intelligence is predicting a level of performance in reading that is actually close to her actual level of reading.' This does not mean that we expect reading skill to be necessarily anchored firmly to expectation. For instance, a child on a par with expectation could probably still enhance reading skills. There may even be reciprocity so that improving reading skills gradually feeds back to improve intelligence (see Stanovich, 1986).

Returning to the adult or the adolescent, our problem is not just about potential cognitive processes in relation to literacy, but also about what we can do about it to compensate within an examination setting. Some might feel that it is a little late to tackle the problem in the examination room by allowing extra time, when the roots of the problem might have been tackled earlier. Another example might be that the adult is referred by the employer as the job requires an upgrade. Is the individual capable of handling more paperwork, perhaps taking down telephone messages, or entering information into a computer database? If not, could training be provided to improve the necessary skills?

These are some of the problems that permeate how we make an assessment in reading – and in writing as well. Assessment has grown in importance, due partly to the development of better techniques for assessment and to a change in political climate that requires more accountability. Not just politicians but parents are developing an increasing awareness of the issues involved. At the same time there has been a lot of publicity about the decline in standards in literacy. However, although there may be an impression of a decline, there is now little objective evidence for such a decline, simply because in the UK formal monitoring of standards was disbanded several years ago.

Dyslexia and associated controversies

Many people still believe that it is not possible to make a reasonable assessment of reading until the child is about 8 years of age. The reason given is that children differ in their rate of progress in their early years and as they have only started to learn to read at about the age of 5 years, it is difficult to tell reliably whether children are seriously behind in their reading development. Nevertheless, testing is reliable enough for it to be possible to use the WORD reading and spelling tests in conjunction with the Wechsler Intelligence Scale for Children (WISC-III), to work out if there is a significant disparity between observed and expected WORD scores down to the age of 6 years. The likelihood of finding a discrepancy and its reliability in the early years is probably lower compared with later. However, a bright child who can hardly write anything coherently and who cannot read and understand simple sentences would probably be a good candidate for testing at the age of 6 or 7 years.

These tests are psychometric tests that cannot be undertaken by the teacher but only by an appropriately qualified psychologist. Most teachers at present would not make an assessment concerning whether the child is reading significantly below potential, only that reading performance was below the child's peers. (If they desired they could use an *open* test of intelligence, a test that is unrestricted in use, and calculate centile or standard score discrepancy.) This is currently an important distinction in mode of operation between psychologist and teacher. It is also part of the controversy surrounding intelligence testing referred to earlier.

The basis of the reading discrepancy approach is to produce regression equations on large samples of reading and Intelligence Quotient (IQ) scores. This enables a prediction from the regression line of what the expected reading level would be for a given level of intelligence, allowing for chronological age. The important assumption is that there is a good linear relationship, or correlation, between the two variables. One area of debate has been to argue that the correlation with reading is less for full-scale IQ than for verbal IQ. Full-scale IQ involves the assessment of verbal and non-verbal processes or abilities in equal measure. It would therefore be better to base these regression equations on verbal IQ alone. One slight problem with this suggestion is that the mental arithmetic component of verbal IQ can be affected by poor verbal memory in the WISC-III. Mental arithmetic requires an involvement in verbal working memory, which can be problematic in dyslexia.

Another problem is a practical one. In a city like Leicester, for example, it would be difficult for the educational authority, responsible for more than 300 schools, to make a mass assessment of reading potential based solely on verbal intelligence as a substantial part of the community is of Indian, Pakistani, African and Afro-Caribbean origin. A proportion of these children are using English as a second language and testing their verbal intelligence on an English verbal intelligence test may be underestimating their intelligence. For example, Beech and Keys [. . . 1998] found that controlling for non-verbal IQ, there was a marked impairment in receptive oral vocabulary (a verbal IQ component) in a group of bilingual British Asian children of lower socioeconomic status aged 7–8 years compared with monolingual controls. This underestimate in verbal IQ would in turn reduce the proportion of such children who would be considered to be under-using their potential, because a lower predicted IQ in turn means a lower predicted potential in reading. An added complication is that the current data on the importance of phonology for early reading apply to an alphabetic language such as English in which letters approximately correspond to phonemes. This may not be so important in some other languages.

One alternative would be to produce special tests for each foreign language group, but this is also going to have the problem of being discriminatory. Clearly the issue has to be handled sensitively, but if one is too sensitive, many children may be forgoing appropriate skill learning.

If an education authority were to adopt the discrepancy approach there is the further problem that an application of an intelligence test, such as the WISC, has to be done individually by a qualified psychologist; this option is automatically ruled out for mass screening at present on the grounds of prohibitive cost.

The reading discrepancy approach can give rise to two different types of reading difficulty. First, there is the child with a specific reading difficulty, whose difficulties are confined to reading (and possibly other areas of literacy) but whose other skills and attainments are not significantly lower than expected. This is often referred to as 'dyslexia'.[1] In the context of reading, the term now generally refers to someone who from their full scale intelligence score is predicted to have a reading performance at a certain level, but who is statistically significantly behind this level of performance. Some authorities would argue that a 'discrepant' measure like this should be regarded as the defining characteristic of a *specific reading difficulty*, but not necessarily of *dyslexia*. There are many reasons why a child may be attaining in reading far lower than intelligence levels would predict. One reason might be that the child has not received appropriate teaching. If that were the sole reason for the child's difficulties one would not want to class this as a case of dyslexia, which usually implies a constitutional cause of some kind. Other authorities have sought to qualify a discrepancy approach by requiring several additional criteria, or impediments. However, to restrict the concept of 'dyslexia' to children who show no other difficulties (such as hearing problems) contradicts the fundamental concept of dyslexia being a *constitutional* condition. The same criticism may be levelled at those who in the past have adopted a view of dyslexia that has resulted in the condition being observed mainly among children from middle-class homes (see Critchley, 1970). This was an acknowledgement that there may be circumstances at home that may be responsible for a lack of literacy development. This is not necessarily to do with class, of course; it is thus difficult to make an assessment of this kind of influence. Similarly, a child may be emotionally affected in some way, perhaps manifesting substantial behavioural problems.

Another criterion used by some authors is that there has to be a minimum level of intelligence. For instance, Vellutino (1979) advocated an IQ more than 90 (the average, adjusting for age, is 100); Critchley refers to 'an adequate IQ'. However, given the use of the regression equation, one does come across children who have a lower IQ than 90, who still have a significant deficit in reading in relation to expectation. Realistically they should be referred to as having dyslexia. From the point of view of carrying out a research study on children with dyslexia one would normally use a cut-off point of something like 90. However, when testing an individual child for dyslexia, there should be no such limitation.

The second type of reading problem is often called 'poor reading', although in the past it has been referred to as 'reading backwardness'. This is usually where the child's intelligence is considerably below the norm. Using the same regression equation one would still be able to predict a certain level of reading performance. Because the child is at such a low level of IQ performance, the child is predicted to be low in reading as well. Thus this category of reader should be easily noticed in the classroom as reading performance would be poor on a standard reading test. The child with specific reading difficulties would not necessarily be noticed in the classroom, because the reading problem might be mild. However, in relation to potential it could be severe.

Do we treat the two types of children differently and should we treat them differently? The motivation of the teacher could be affected by this knowledge. One might think that learning is going to have to be at a slower pace for the poor reader. But this is not necessarily going to be the case. Yule *et al.* (1974) in a study of all the 9 and 10 year olds on the Isle of Wight found that children with specific reading difficulties actually made poorer progress. The main contrasts between the groups were that three-quarters of those with specific reading difficulties were boys and there were no organic disorders compared with 11% of the poor readers. There are interesting examples of children with low IQs who become very good readers, in the sense that their reading out loud becomes very accomplished.

Perhaps the major difference may be at the reading comprehension level. Brighter children with poor basic word reading skills often manage to compensate when reading text by making intelligent inferences about the gist of the text. They also use context more effectively, have a better knowledge of syntax and have a 'world knowledge' enabling them to make guesses that can compensate for specific word knowledge. By contrast, those who are less bright may have a better idea of word identification, but find it difficult to get to the appropriate meaning of the text. Another contrast is that those with specific reading difficulties tend to have problems more concentrated in terms of phonological difficulties (Jorm *et al.*, 1986).

Some have argued against using the intelligence test altogether, especially on the grounds that it is culturally biased. As far as assessing reading comprehension is concerned, some have advocated the use of listening comprehension as a simpler method of measuring the disparity between the potential to comprehend and actual level of comprehension by means of reading print. This is discussed further in Chapter 9 on reading comprehension. Listening comprehension is obviously going to be useful to assess reading comprehension potential, but for tests of accuracy of reading print we are still left with full scale IQ as all that is available at present.

To be even handed, there are researchers (e.g. Siegel, 1992) who have argued that the discrepancy definition of reading problems is unnecessary as poor readers (whose reading is consistent with their IQ scores) are not differentiated from discrepant readers as both have problems in phonology and verbal memory and other aspects. (This is in contrast to Jorm *et al.* cited earlier (1986).) Another argument against the intelligence test is that it is increasingly being recognised that dyslexia is a constitutional condition that is generally inherited (but which may be due to birth difficulties).

There is no reason why it should not occur among children of below average IQ. It could also (and probably will) co-occur with other disabilities (e.g. hearing impairment). The conventional definition of dyslexia rules out such children. Perhaps one day a definition of 'genetic dyslexia' will be devised.

The practical problem is that even if there were no difference in the difficulties of the two different types of problem readers, it does not preclude the importance of finding children who are underachieving. There could be large numbers of children who are discrepant in their reading and who are not being identified as having problems as such because their absolute level of reading and spelling performance is superficially indicating that nothing is seriously amiss. The situation at the moment is that such children are only coming to light if their parents make a fuss. Many LEAs do not explicitly tie specific learning difficulties to a *statistically* significant discrepancy between reading quotient and IQ, but to some *arbitrary* threshold (e.g. reading age two years behind chronological age). Often the child lags behind, but not enough to trigger specialist help. Then the gap steadily widens until the threshold is crossed and specialist help is eventually provided (but disappointingly late).

Miles (1994) makes a wider criticism of the notion that readers with dyslexia and poor readers should be lumped together, maintaining that, by contrast, there should be a separation of reading from other allied difficulties. Many individuals with reading problems also suffer from other difficulties such as slowness of processing, numeracy difficulties and difficulty in writing ideas that can be expressed much more easily verbally. The dyslexic versus poor reader distinction may be too simplistic, when there could be far more significant distinctions to be made, possibly with implications for future prospects in training.

So far we have only discussed the involvement of the psychologist in making an assessment of literacy. There could be other professionals implicated in this who at present have hardly any involvement. For example, speech and language therapists and optometrists ought to be involved in assessment. There is now plenty of evidence for the importance of phonology in reading [...]. Training children in establishing letter–sound connections can have positive benefits on their subsequent reading. Bradley and Bryant (1983) in a classic experiment trained children who were behind in phonology and showed that training such children in these skills, i.e. learning about letter–sound connections, significantly improved reading relative to other control groups. Many teachers would not be surprised in the least by these findings.

It could be helpful to involve speech and language therapists in assessments in phonology in relation to reading. There are simple initial tests that can be applied to see whether a referral would be useful. For instance, from about 6 or 7 years of age onwards a graded test of nonword reading could be a first filter to highlight children who are having problems with phonics. If it is clear that they have already been given extensive training in phonics by their teachers, they could be examined further by a speech and language therapist. This would be with a view to finding out if there is a problem with their underlying awareness of sound structure. If necessary, the therapist could be involved with appropriate intensive training to develop phonological and phonemic awareness further.

[...] One aspect related to reading is visual discomfort, for which at present we do not have very good ways of screening. However, it is potentially very important for the young child. It is clear that quite a number of children suffer from this problem (although we do not know how many) and it will inevitably affect their literacy acquisition from the beginning. When children are routinely screened in schools for eyesight, there is surely no reason why those who are also substantially behind in reading and spelling should not be given further tests for visual function that might relate to their current reading problems.

Types or levels of diagnostic literacy assessment

The assessment of literacy is usually equated with giving the child or adult a series of isolated words and asking them to read them aloud. However, reading aloud single words is just one of several skills that are important. Some would argue that an even more important skill is reading comprehension. It is possible to have a reasonably good reading vocabulary and yet have a poor reading comprehension, even though one would understand the same passage if one simply listened to it.

Beginning with single word reading, this in itself is not sufficient to determine if a child has reading problems, but it is a good start. Such tests typically begin with highly frequent, regularly spelled, short words and gradually move to the opposite poles of these dimensions ending with low frequency, irregular and long words. The writing also begins in large print and ends in a smaller font. The value of the test is that it is taking away all contextual cues and leaves the reader only with the letters of the word that they have to read.

This type of test can provide clues to the child's approach to reading. Does the child seem to have a long pause before making a pronunciation, and are there 'regularisation' errors (e.g. 'dread' being read as 'dreed')? Does the child 'sound out', i.e. produce a whispered phonetic pronunciation (e.g. 'duh-ruh-ee-duh: dreed')? These could all be indications of the use of phonics. This is usually a good sign, as it indicates an alternative route to reading is being developed. But beware of its overuse, so that even very familiar words are given the same treatment. This condition is sometimes referred to as 'developmental surface dyslexia'. Although such reading can become relatively fast, reading letters or small letter clusters representing phonemes (these letters or letter clusters, e.g. *sh*, are called 'graphemes'), then blending them to form words, is computationally a very demanding form of reading. The result is that such readers may rarely read for pleasure if they continue to do this for the majority of words (e.g. Hanley *et al.*, 1992).

Another test is a nonword test of reading. This is a more direct test of the use of the development of phonics in reading. The child is given a pronounceable nonword such as 'bleak' to read. This might be read by the use of letter–sound translation rules or by a mixture of analogy (with the words 'blank' or 'blend', perhaps) and phonics. Sometimes a child may be a poor reader, but be better developed in phonics. This could indicate a danger that phonics was being over-used in reading. The ideal is for a fast automatic response to familiar words.

A similar kind of test is one examining the efficiency of reading words that are regular and irregular in spelling. If there is a large disparity in performance, this can indicate that the child has an over-reliance on a phonic approach to reading. The irregular words are generating phonological codes that do not correspond to the correct pronunciation and therefore interfere with responses.

Another potential test of developmental surface dyslexia is to compare the reaction time to identify whether words which match vary according to length. This would normally be a laboratory-based task in which one is looking for an increased slope (the steepness of the angle of the line of best fit of the reaction times) as a function of word length relative to the slope of normal readers.

Little is known about what to do about an over-reliance on phonics. The first thing would be to try to produce an understanding of when it would be appropriate to use a phonics strategy, namely when a word is unfamiliar. However, fast automatised reading is far better for familiar words. For more inexperienced readers this might involve trying to work through a set of flash cards (containing individual words to be named aloud) against the clock. More experienced readers could be encouraged to speed read by tracing text with their fingers as quickly as possible.

Developmental phonological dyslexia is a condition when a child, or adult, is unable to read nonwords, or reads them with great difficulty. This inability does not present insuperable difficulties to learning to read, especially if the reader has someone to turn to who can supply the pronunciation of unfamiliar words (see the case studied by Campbell and Butterworth, 1985). From one perspective, many, if not most children with reading problems could be said to have developmental phonological dyslexia to varying degrees. They typically find it difficult to identify nonwords, but training in phonic skills can produce improvements in general reading performance (e.g. Adams, 1990). Therefore, poor nonword reading performance would normally be followed by the recommendation that the reader should be given training in phonics. This would not just be at a basic level of single letters to individual sounds, but would progress to more complicated grapheme–phoneme connections and further until pronounceable nonwords of sufficient length are tackled without difficulty. In this way, an efficient technique becomes available to help the reader over the hurdle of decoding difficult words. It has to be borne in mind that this technique will work better for regular words than for irregular ones. In addition, some children have such an impairment in their phonological processes that learning more than rudimentary grapheme–phoneme connections could be counter productive (Beech, 1994).

As the reader progresses, the reading comprehension test becomes increasingly important [. . .]. In the early years a lot of emphasis is given to learning to read and write and become numerate. Gradually these same skills are used more and more to acquire information about the curriculum. If a child fails to progress in literacy in these early stages there is a double burden: trying to learn these basic skills and trying to keep up with the curriculum. Understandably they can fall further and further behind. This is where the reading comprehension test becomes so important, as it might indicate the extent to which the child can cope with the curriculum.

As mentioned before, the single word reading test is valuable for examining skills in reading in the absence of context. Sometimes readers do very poorly on the single word test, but do well on the reading comprehension test. Although such children will get by in reading materials within their curriculum, there could still be problems ahead in situations in which the precise meaning of the text is crucial. A critical point can be when reading examination questions and understanding precisely what is required. Examiners are often told to award no marks to candidates who have not answered the question. Therefore, being able to read accurately can be crucial at certain times, often in situations of maximum stress. Children and young people with dyslexia find multiple choice examinations particularly difficult. The questions typically require attention to the subtlety in the wording of the question and to the alternatives.

One aspect to look out for if conducting a comprehension test involving silent reading, as in the WORD test, is to watch the lips of the child while reading to see if they are moving. This might suggest that fast automatised access to the meaning of the passage is still some way off.

A final point to note about reading comprehension is that there is evidence that frequent reading is related to improved reading vocabulary. Stanovich and

Cunningham (1992) have demonstrated that accuracy in the recognition of authors' names is related to reading performance. Like any skill, the more one uses it the better one becomes. It follows that a child with good reading comprehension has the facility to undertake a lot of reading. If this opportunity is used, reading skills should eventually be honed and accuracy in reading isolated words ought to improve as well.

Tests of reading speed are less common. There is a test of reading aloud accurately for one minute short, very common words. However, we do not know at this point how useful this is. At least it can show how automatised reading has become. It would probably be unwise to use it as evidence that a candidate needs extra time in examinations, as presumably slow reading can easily be faked. One problem with this test is that a line of words can be easily missed in the heat of the moment. The Neale Analysis test gives standardised measures of reading speed in terms of age equivalence up to 13 years of age (Neale, 1989).

The ideal test of reading speed and other allied elements would be to use eye monitoring equipment. This would allow an assessment of dysfunctional eye movements as well as scanning speed while reading, but this is not feasible for widespread use at the moment. [. . .]

Finally there are tests of literacy related to writing, including spelling [. . .]. There is perhaps not the same sense of urgency about problems in writing, and more particularly spelling, as there has been in the past. Massey and Elliott (1996) compared exam scripts from O level in 1980 with GCSE in 1994 and found significant declines in spelling, grammar, punctuation and powers of expression. For instance, exam scripts from 1994 had *three* times more spelling errors than those written in 1980. This could be due partly to significantly more candidates taking GCSEs, so it is difficult to make direct comparisons. In terms of priorities it is most important that the child approaching teenage years is able to read in order to acquire knowledge of school subjects. Being unable to spell correctly has not been considered to be so important. However, the importance of spelling is perhaps in the mind of the beholder. Poor spelling can be an impediment for job prospects. For instance, an employer does not want an employee to send out letters representing the organisation that appear 'illiterate'.

In the sphere of writing assessment, when the assessor is a psychologist the concern is most frequently with whether the writer is able to write normally under examination conditions. Poor spelling is often seen as an impediment to normal writing speed if the writer is having to stop at frequent intervals to review the correct spelling of words they are about to write. Content can also impede writing speed. Children whose spelling is poor often write in an immature manner because they are reluctant to use the vocabulary with which they can speak and understand but cannot spell correctly (e.g. 'big' versus 'enormous'). By having to continually stop and think about spelling when it should be automatic, the flow of thought is disrupted and writing thus becomes disjointed. When teachers are assessing children's (especially young children's) literacy development, they tend to be more concerned with legibility and whether the child can put down ideas and spoken thoughts accurately on paper.

As a footnote, it is important to observe whether the writer is using the appropriate tripod grip, holding the pen between the thumb and the first two fingers. An incorrect grip can lead to cramp or muscular fatigue, especially at crucial times in the examination room in later life. It is surprising how often a poor pen grip is overlooked in so many of our present reception classes. There are special triangular grips or triangular pencils which can be purchased to facilitate the tripod grip. (For detailed consideration of issues relating to assessment and teaching of handwriting see Alston, 1994, 1995, 1996; Alston and Taylor, 1985, 1987; Keily, 1996.)

Psychometric concepts

The first time we use a test we usually begin by looking at the test to give ourselves a rough idea of what the participant has to do. The next thing would be to examine the test manual to see how precisely the test is applied, how it is subsequently scored, and at what group the test is aimed. In the case of tests of reading and spelling, a major concern will be the age range of the test.

Another consideration is what information this test provides about the participant's skills. What is the rationale behind the test construction and what particular skills are being tested? Is there a sufficient range of skills being tested? For instance, a single word spelling test can inform about spelling vocabulary because it contains words that vary and are ordered in frequency of exposure and use. Thus, the inexperienced speller will only know how to spell words of a certain level of frequency of occurrence. However, does the test also inform about knowledge of those spellings that vary according to context (e.g. *weak* tea versus days of the *week*)?

Once satisfied at this level, check through the test's psychometric properties, which should be provided in the test manual. It is important not to skip this stage, even if the technical information may appear daunting at first. A good manual should provide information on reliability, validity and the distributions of the scores. It is less important to understand the statistical techniques that lie behind the actual test construction. The end result is that you will understand the test's purpose and have an impression of the extent to which you can trust its results. Do not be swayed too much by the tests used by other users. Form your own independent judgement.

One of the most important psychometric concepts is that of reliability. A measuring instrument should produce the same measurement on successive occasions. The extent of this consistency is known as the instrument's reliability. Reliability is going to depend to an extent on the stability of the underlying dimensions being tested, from one time to the next.

There are several kinds of reliability, all of which use the correlation statistic. This is a test of association in which a correlation of 1.0 indicates a maximum, or one-to-one, association and a correlation of zero indicates no relationship. Internal reliability or consistency measures the degree to which the scores on items correlate with other items. This is measured by computing how individual items correlate with the test as a whole. According to Kline (1990), internal consistency of a test should exceed 0.7. Stability measures (test-retest reliabilities) give correlations between successive testings, and equivalence measures provide the correlations in performance between different forms of the test.

Validity is another important concept that is really a matter of judgement. It goes to the heart of the matter as it queries what the test is actually measuring. For instance, is a test of reading comprehension really about the ability to extract information from print, is it about the accuracy of reading the individual words, or is it about both? Face validity refers to the test from the perspective of the person being tested. It is disconcerting for the testee if the tester appears to be applying tests that appear irrelevant to his or her particular problem. Content validity applies to validity as far as the professionals are concerned. Naturally, these two concepts overlap, but they differ insofar as content validity is about how well the test covers the breadth of the dimension under study. One concern here is whether the test items are sufficiently heterogeneous to measure the dimension.

Construct validity refers to the extent to which the test measures the theoretical construct underlying the test. Criterion-related validity is about the correlation between an assessment and an independent measure of a similar task. Concurrent validity refers to when the independent measure of the similar task is undertaken at the same time and is correlated with the test. Finally, predictive reliability is derived when the independent criterion test is carried out later. This would indicate the degree of association between the two tests and therefore the extent to which the assessment predicts performance of the future measure.

In the field of literacy testing face validity is usually high. Poor readers, for example, are asked to read aloud single words and to silently read passages of text. This is the kind of activity they do in everyday life when they experience difficulty in reading. When they are given tests that appear to be irrelevant, such as intelligence tests, the context of these needs to be explained.

Content validity can determine why one test is used in preference to another. Perhaps one relevant concern here is the age of the test; language use changes over time, so that some items may become inappropriate. A minority of professionals would criticise the content validity of using tests of single word reading because it is an unnatural test of reading, especially of children who are learning to read with the help of the context of pictures.

Comparing reliability and validity, reliability is necessary for validity, but not the other way round. It is possible to construct a test that is very reliable, but with no validity to the construction it is measuring. However, it is not possible to have a valid test that is at the same time low in reliability.

Finally, one has an outcome measure, such as a reading or spelling age equivalence, or a standard score. The standard score is in practice similar in distribution to the intelligence quotient, for which a score of 100 is the mean and the standard deviation is 15. They can have a mean of 50 and a standard deviation of 10, called T scores (e.g. as in the British Ability Scales). Technically, z scores are also 'standard scores'. Tables are available, even if not in that particular manual, in which the centile (or percentile) scores and confidence intervals can be checked. Centile scores have a range of zero to 100 and a mean of 50. Their main advantage is that a person's score can be viewed in relation to everyone else. A score on the 60th centile means that the individual is ranked in the 60th position out of 100 which is approximately equivalent to having 40 out of 100 individuals above that position in ranking. Another advantage is that they enable a comparison to be made across different test instruments that may themselves use different indices; for example, one might have an intelligence test (probably an IQ score), a reading test (a reading age) and a spelling test (perhaps a stanine score). Perhaps this Esperanto-like advantage should be used more often by all professionals involved in reading. Confidence intervals are an acknowledgement that there is imprecision in testing so that a standard score of 105, for example, provides a range in the tables between 100 and 110 where the true standard score lies on 95% of occasions. A more detailed account of the psychometric basis of testing may be found in Beech and Harding (1990).

Assessment and the Code of Practice

One powerful reason why we need to assess reading and other literacy skills is that schools and teachers now have legal responsibilities concerning the identification of children with special educational needs, that will frequently require the use of appropriate tests of literacy as well as of other abilities. The 1996 Education Act places a statutory duty on LEAs and on the governing bodies of schools to do their best to ensure that the necessary provision is made for any pupil who has special educational needs, and in so doing to have regard to the Code of Practice on the Identification and Assessment of Special Educational Needs (DFE, 1994). In particular, the Code of Practice states that the governing body's report should state the number of pupils with special educational needs and demonstrate the effectiveness of the school's system for identification and assessment. The importance of early identification, assessment and provision for any child who may have special educational needs is strongly emphasised, and the use of appropriate screening or assessment tools is advocated by the Code. A staged model of assessment and intervention is recommended, with five stages being suggested – the first three stages being school-based, while the last two are LEA-based. The fundamental principle is that the school should take primary responsibility for identifying and making provision for children's special educational needs during the first three stages. This approach contrasts with that of the 1981 Education Act, which located such responsibility primarily with the LEA, which then made provision largely through the means of a Statement of Special Educational Needs, and which in turn entitled the school to additional resources in order to meet that particular child's needs. The Code of Practice, as it is now being applied, generally means that access to the statementing procedure and the resources which that can release only becomes possible when a child has passed through the school-based stages of assessment and intervention, and has been shown to require support that is beyond the capabilities of the school using its own expertise or resources.

In the wake of the Code it is therefore now incumbent upon schools and their teachers to have effective procedures for identifying and assessing all types of special educational needs. Among the various types of information relevant to these procedures, the use of standardised tests is advocated by the Code. In deciding whether or not to make a statutory assessment at Stage 4 of the Code, the LEA will require satisfactory evidence of the school's assessment of a child's learning difficulties at Stages 1–3. Although school attainment is an important factor here, it is not the only criterion by which special educational needs are to be judged. The Code recognises that a child may have a learning difficulty even though school attainment is at an average or apparently satisfactory level because the child's attainment may fall short of what is expected. The Code suggests that assessment using standardised tests may be particularly relevant in determining such cases. Where specific learning difficulties are concerned (e.g. dyslexia), there is an expectation expressed in the Code that the school will be able to show clear recorded evidence of lack of progress in reading and spelling, demonstrated by results of appropriately applied tests of reading and spelling, and that in its own attempts to address the problem a structured reading programme has been followed, based on diagnostic assessment of the child's reading performance.

In recent years there has been a spate of legal cases brought by parents against LEAs on the grounds that the LEA failed to provide adequately for the special educational needs of certain children (Callman, 1996). In such cases, most of which have been common law actions for negligence, much has hinged on the expert evidence presented to the courts by psychologists and others, and on the adequacy or otherwise of the information (including information from standardised assessment) which either side has relied on. It is quite likely that in future in educational legal cases reference will increasingly be made to the Code of Practice when trying to establish what might reasonably be expected of a school or LEA in identifying and making provision for pupils with special needs. However, it should be stressed that the wording of the 1996 Education Act is that LEAs and schools should 'have regard to' the provisions of the Code of Practice. Otton (1996) reminds us that where such an expression has been used in other statutes it has not been taken to mean 'obey', 'apply' or even 'follow', and that consequently the legal scope of the Code may require definition by the courts on a case-by-case basis. Clearly there is considerable room for discretion. Nevertheless, the Code is a reflection of the fact that we are now in a political, legal, educational and social climate in which there is increasing expectation that children's educational difficulties will be identified and addressed in the school as swiftly and as effectively as possible. More and more of the education budget is being devolved to schools, and parents will inevitably blame the school when they feel that their child is not making satisfactory progress. Schools will be compelled to keep records which demonstrate that children's progress is being properly monitored and that all reasonable steps are being taken to detect learning difficulties as early as possible. Since school attainment is not the only criterion in this matter, the use of standardised tests will become ever more important. Finally, the objective evidence provided by standardised tests could become enormously important to schools which find themselves in the position of having to defend legal actions. Regardless of one's attitudes towards the growth of the 'litigious society', the future for teachers and educational psychologists is likely to be one in which standardised tests of literacy skills become more, rather than less, important. That being the case, it is imperative that, as professionals, we endeavour to ensure that test (and testing) standards are upheld, that the tests we use are the best possible for the job and that they are applied in the most appropriate way.

Assessment of bilingual pupils

There can be little doubt that the assessment of bilingual pupils, and those for whom English is not their first language, creates major problems for any psychologist or teacher. Non-English-speaking children may acquire 'surface' language skills within about two years of attending school, but adequate written language skills may take up to another five years to develop (Cummins, 1984). There are obvious obstacles to learning for these children in many areas of the curriculum when the medium of instruction is English. However, it is particularly difficult for the teacher or psychologist to know whether such a pupil is progressing in literacy in English as well as could be expected. By law, the Standard Assessment Tests (SATs) must be administered to all UK children at age 7, other than those who have been in Britain for less than six months (Education Act 1996). Since the bilingual 7 year old's English skills are likely to be very limited, it is difficult to see how SATs can be fairly administered and sensibly interpreted in such cases. Unlike children at school in Wales, who may be SATs tested in spoken Welsh, children from other minority language groups are forced to cope in English. Perhaps surprisingly, research suggests that fully bilingual children are not generally impeded in education, and can actually display linguistic, cognitive and social advantages over monolingual children. This may be because bilingual children have to work much harder – linguistically, cognitively and socially – than monolingual children in order to cope in school. However, bilingualism must be additive and not subtractive for these advantages to appear; i.e. the second language and its culture must be added to the first, not detract from them (Cummins, 1984). Gregory and Kelly (1992) point out that the thinking behind the National Curriculum and the SATs is based on the erroneous assumption that developing proficiency in the first language will interfere with development in the second, and so the emphasis is on developing fluency in English as rapidly as possible – if necessary, at the expense of the first language. In the UK, therefore, advantages that might derive from being brought up in a multilinguistic subculture tend to be swiftly eroded by the insistence of the educational system that proficiency in English (and knowledge of the cultural concomitants of English) should be the paramount goal.

It has often been argued (e.g. Bryans, 1992; Gipps, 1990; Gregory and Kelly, 1992; Joyce, 1988) that all educational experiences and the forms of assessment which accompany such experiences are culture-bound and hence 'unfair' when used with children from cultural, ethnic or linguistic minority groups. Standardised tests of the type used by educational psychologists (especially intelligence tests) are those most frequently singled out for criticism in this respect (Cummins, 1984). Standardised assessment instruments are applicable to the population on which they have been standardised and norm-referenced tests tend to be biased in favour of the majority group within that population (Joyce, 1988). It can be seen, therefore, that cultural, ethnic or linguistic minority groups will usually be at a disadvantage in educational and psychological assessment. Nevertheless, the law in the United States and Britain, as in many other countries, requires that children with learning difficulties are assessed so that appropriate educational provision can be made for them. If such children are from ethnic linguistic groups, how are the psychologists or teachers who have responsibility for assessment to discharge their duty? Note that a child in Britain cannot be regarded as having a learning difficulty solely because the language or form of language of the home is different from the language in which he or she is being taught (Education Act 1996). Similar regulations apply in other countries, such as the United States and Canada. Hence we have a dilemma: when a child from a cultural, ethnic or linguistic minority background is failing at school there is a legal duty to make a proper assessment of that child's learning difficulties and to make appropriate provision, but the forms of assessment available in such cases will generally be inadequate. In this situation, some educational psychologists would go so far as to reject the use of standardised assessment altogether. Bryans (1992), for example, contends that 'psychometric standardised assessment with most non-indigenous, non-white groups is irrelevant and misleading and should be discontinued' (p. 144). Furthermore, Bryans goes on to ask: if standardised assessment has to be discarded for some pupils, then why not for all? In the end, this particular debate boils down to the issue of whether or not we want assessment, as far as possible, to have a reliable scientific basis, or whether we are prepared to abandon reliability totally just because at present our scientific tools are inadequate for some cases. The abandonment of all standardised testing would surely be a retrogressive step that would leave education increasingly vulnerable to political prejudice, and the future of individual pupils at the mercy of 'expert' opinion unsupported by empirical evidence.

We will not pretend that a resolution of these complex issues can be offered here. However, teachers and psychologists working in a multicultural and multilingual society cannot turn their backs on the problems. Joyce (1988) suggests that criterion-referenced tests are preferable, and that these should be specific to the child's own progress and not involve comparison with other pupils. However, even criterion-referenced assessment may also be criticised since the criterion itself is inevitably derived from some teacher expectation which is itself norm-related, although perhaps not explicitly so (Pumfrey, 1991). For example, in applying a criterion such as 'Is the child able to read 100 Key Words?' the teacher must have some normative expectations. Otherwise, it is impossible to decide whether or not action should be taken following the answer to the question. If the child failed to achieve the criterion but was only aged 5½ the teacher would probably not see the need to intervene, whereas if that same child passed the criterion the teacher would probably regard the child as quite advanced in literacy development terms. On the other hand, if the child in question was aged 7½ and failed to achieve the criterion, the teacher probably would want to instigate exceptional steps to try to remedy the situation. In other words, there is an assumption being made on the part of the teacher that the 'norm' for acquisition of this criterion is somewhere between 5 years 6 months and 7 years 6 months. If that 'norm' is based on one particular cultural or linguistic group it will not necessarily be accurate when applied to any other.

Common sense dictates that before assessing the pupil's needs the assessor should always have an understanding of the child's cultural and linguistic background and should combine that understanding with observation of their behaviour in the learning situation. One possible way of avoiding the bias that can occur when a norm-referenced assessment instrument is administered to different cultural and linguistic groups is to have a variety of norms based on different groups, although creating or locating an appropriate set of norms may be tricky. A major advantage of computerised assessment [. . .] is that as children are tested, the computer is able to collect data which may then be used to construct 'local' norms. Under these circumstances the assessor would not be forced to use the norms that accompany the test – which may have been based on some other and entirely inappropriate cultural or linguistic mix of children – but instead can use norms based on the particular group in question.

Assessment of literacy in higher education

Assessment of literacy skills in adults is complicated by a number of factors. Chief among these is the dearth of appropriate tests. The vast majority of tests of reading and spelling have been designed for use with people age 16 years and under. One notable exception is the WRAT-3 (Wide Range Achievement Test; see Wilkinson, 1993) which comprises sub-tests of single word reading, spelling, and arithmetic. The norms are based on subjects in the United States, but in the absence of an equivalent British test it has become more widely used in the UK in the last few years. When carrying out assessment of students in higher education, testing of reading and spelling becomes even more problematic because of the lack of norms relating to this generally above average group. We do not know what are (or should be) acceptable limits of reading and spelling ability for undergraduates, and consequently a judgement of whether or not such individuals have a specific reading impairment which might be characteristic of dyslexia is highly uncertain.

Because of the lack of suitable tests (and perhaps also because most educational psychologists are more familiar with the assessment of children of 16 years and under) it is frequently found that psychologists administer to adults tests that were designed for use with children, a practice that is highly questionable (Singleton, 1994, 1995). Not only will the norms be inappropriate, but the content is likely to be as well. The Schonell Graded Word Reading Test (Schonell, 1950) and the Neale Analysis of Reading (Neale, 1989) are but two examples of tests which have been frequently misapplied in the past (Singleton, 1996), and there are some indications that the Wechsler WORD test is now being misused in this way (Singleton, 1993). It may be argued that provided the raw scores rather than the norms are used, then administration of child tests to adults is acceptable. However, all tests tend to be relatively poor discriminators at their extremes (i.e. near the 'floor' and 'ceiling' of the test) and when a child's test is used with an older subject (particularly one of above average ability) the person is likely to be scoring close to the ceiling of the test. Any differences found are likely to be due to the reading of a relatively small number of words which the person may not have encountered before – for example, words such as 'somnambulist' (Schonell) and 'antithesis' (WORD). The Schonell test is also likely to be unreliable because of its antiquity: it is now almost half-a-century old. At its upper extremes it contains examples of words which will be exceptionally difficult for today's readers because they are now almost archaic (e.g. 'sepulchre' and 'sabre') as well as words that might have been regarded as difficult fifty years ago but which are fairly commonplace today (e.g. 'statistics' and 'miscellaneous'). The Neale test is typically used because it is a well-constructed test and because there is not a suitable adult prose reading test available. However, the ceiling on this test is a reading age of 13 years. There are many students who attain the ceiling of this test but who nevertheless have reading skills which are inadequate for study at higher education level, because the Neale test has no sensitivity in this range. When the Neale test is misapplied in this way, it may result in students being unfairly excluded from special help or provision to which they might otherwise be entitled.

Hence the use of tests that are out of date in either their content or their norms, or with subjects for whom they were never intended, is unacceptable practice. Until recently, however, there was no great demand for literacy tests for use with adults. Demand was largely confined to assessment of adult basic literacy or of literacy impairment in cases of neurological damage, for example, in brain injury or stroke. In the case of adult basic literacy the Adult Literacy and Basic Skills Test (ALBSU) has most commonly been employed, whereas in cases of neurological damage the NART (National Adult Reading Test; see Nelson and Willinson, 1991). In the last few years, however, the demand for assessment for suspected dyslexia among students at A level, as well as in further and higher education has escalated and in these cases neither the ALBSU test nor the NART is suitable. Many psychologists are using the WRAT at this level, but the lack of an appropriate prose-reading comprehension test is a serious limitation in the assessment process (Singleton, 1996). The situation has become acute in higher education, where applications for the Disabled Students Allowance (DSA) by students who have dyslexia have increased substantially since 1990. The DSA provides funds to enable the disabled student to purchase a computer and other technological aids for their studies, as well as possibly financing special tutorial help in study skills. More than half of all students in higher education now in receipt of the DSA are cases of dyslexia (Computer Centre for People with Disabilities, 1996). The cost of DSAs is also rising. The Department for Education and Employment reported a threefold increase in overall costs of the DSA during the two-year period up to 1994 (DFEE, 1995). Furthermore, the assessment of students suspected of having dyslexia has become critical not only because the award of a substantial allowance hangs on the outcome, but also because such students usually obtain special provision in examinations, such as additional time. A recent national survey reported that the incidence of dyslexia in higher education in the UK is in the region of 1.3%. Many universities are reporting between 75 and 200 students applying each year for dyslexia assessments, and issues such as the qualifications of assessors as well as the assessment materials and methods used have come under intense scrutiny (Singleton, in press). Although there are no figures to go on, concern has also been expressed about possible abuses of the assessment procedure in which students may attempt to 'fake' dyslexia in order to obtain a DSA. However, there are as yet no nationally agreed standards or safeguards, although the National Working Party on Dyslexia in Higher Education (Singleton, 1993) is proposing some basic guidelines, including the use of appropriate tests by suitably qualified and experienced assessors. On the other hand, many high-ability students with dyslexia show extreme levels of 'compensation'. They have developed techniques for surmounting or circumventing many of their difficulties, often through immense personal effort, or they may camouflage their problems in various ways (McLoughlin *et al.*, 1994). Assessment in such cases is particularly tricky because the tests are insufficiently sensitive, and it may then be difficult for the students to obtain recognition of their dyslexia and access the support that they require and to which, arguably, they should be entitled. Unless there are agreed standards and appropriate tests, such a system (which has attractive financial and other benefits for students) will always be vulnerable to abuse by some and unfair to others.

The future

The way that we currently assess literacy is the result of an evolution in testing techniques over the years. In some ways, because the production of test materials is haphazard and costly, there is a growing gap between the findings that pour out of the research journals and the assessment materials that are available to practitioners. In more recent times interest has also been taken in case studies of unusual reading and writing problems, and publishing outlets such as *Cognitive Neuropsychology* are now available for researchers to submit such findings. There is a growing demand for children and adults to be tested, so what would be a likely scenario in the future?

Suppose we were on an all-powerful committee. What would be our wish list? A major consideration would be the amount of money available. A minimum step would be to make it national practice for all classes to be given national reading and spelling tests in about February or March of each year. This would be in place of the present haphazard system of identification of reading problems. The information from these tests would be collated with two purposes in mind: first, to examine national standards of literacy with a view to maintaining, if not improving standards. Second, it would help the identification of poor readers who were falling behind. As our previous discussion has shown, it would not identify all children with dyslexia, or specific reading difficulties, as this necessitates some form of diagnostic assessment, usually involving intelligence testing.

The next filter, to identify those with dyslexia in the remaining 'normal' body, would be to apply a group intelligence test. However, this would be expensive both in cost and in time, unless the test materials were quick to apply and reliable. Unfortunately, these two qualities do not normally go hand-in-hand.

Mass screening for literacy, one might argue, could be useful on the grounds of economy and efficiency. Identification of problems as they are developing can mean the focused training of the necessary skills at the appropriate time. For instance, perhaps a child is missing some prerequisite skills that need to be gained before progress can be made. Consider the child approaching his or her teens who is confronted with an expanding syllabus and with an unidentified substantial reading problem. Many such children now face this problem. Even if their problem is identified at this point, there is not enough time available to acquire basic reading skills as well as cope with curriculum subjects. These literacy skills should have been learned much earlier. [. . .]

At present our educational system fails many children, leading to early truancy. Furthermore, there is a high incidence of reading problems in young offenders, with consequent economic costs to society. For the many who struggle on with their literacy problems, there is a lot of misery, embarrassment and frustration that could probably have been averted if there had been sufficient resources available at the right time.

Turning to the professional assessor, there is a case for using tailored testing techniques in the future. For instance, the testing session should be an identification of as many aspects as possible of the area of the problem. At present there seems to be too much of a tendency to give the same battery of tests to all those being assessed no matter what their particular problem. Instead, it would be more efficient to conduct faster (but still reliable) testing of a range of candidate problems, but then to go through a hypothesis testing sequence of tests, in the same way that doctors would undertake a diagnosis of their patients.

In the (more distant) future this might involve a computerised assessment of various faculties including eye movements, some kind of brain scan, perhaps a genetic analysis, sophisticated optical and hearing tests, cognitive reactions and tests of affect. This might be followed by detailed programmes of computerised (virtual?) training that are already known to overcome these problems. If all this seems highly unlikely now, just think how far we have come, and just what knowledge about reading we are now acquiring. [. . .]

The classroom environment of the teacher has undergone many changes in recent years. Many teachers believe that they are now under a considerable amount of pressure due to the demands of the National Curriculum in the UK. This has meant that although there is now rudimentary testing of literacy in the new curriculum, time to hear children read (for example) has been squeezed because other subjects need to be covered as well. Nevertheless, regular assessment is steadily becoming an integral part of even the primary school curriculum, and is widely seen as funda-mental to the maintenance of educational standards and parental satisfaction. For example, in his report on the National Curriculum, Dearing (1993) quoted the Office for Standards in Education as saying:

> The assessment requirements of the National Curriculum have a vital role in raising the expectations of teachers, pupils and parents. In particular, assessment should ensure that individual learning is more clearly targeted and that short-comings are quickly identified and remedied, thus contributing towards higher standards overall.
>
> (p. 25)

Despite this, it is now possible for parents who think that their children are falling behind to pay for an assessment. If this shows that the child has a specific learning difficulty, it does not mean that the school is obliged to call in a psychologist for a Special Needs Assessment. However, teachers may feel pressurised into making a provision for the child that they believe is unnecessary or unjustified in financial terms, in relation to the problems they have to face elsewhere in the school. Not surprisingly, this can lead to resentment on the part of teachers and of parents who cannot afford such assessments.

On top of this, there has not really been much of an increase in resources, and as long as this continues it does not seem likely that there will be much scope for improvement in the classroom. In addition, in inner city schools in particular, prob-lems of vandalism can be serious; thus computer use is restricted.

The mass screening we advocated (in our dreams) to identify poor readers and those with dyslexia needs to be undertaken in the classroom. Involvement of teachers in the administration of this would be important. Many teachers might argue that the present National Curriculum fulfils this need, so why carry out additional testing? At present the Curriculum's precision in assessment, by means of SATs, leaves a lot to be desired. It does not give accurate diagnostic information. Psychologists often discover a mismatch between what National Curriculum SATs results are saying about a child and the conclusions that may be drawn from psychometric test results from that child. Clearly, much more research is needed on this, but there is empirical evidence of poor reliability of SATs measures (Davies *et al.*, 1995; James and Conner, 1993; Pumfrey and Elliott, 1991). It is not simply that SATs are assessing different things from psychometric tests. Rather, it is an issue that directly concerns the reliability and validity of the SATs measures themselves, for they provide only the crudest categorisation of performance in various educational skills that are in fact highly complex.

Dreams are all very well, but what in the near future would be feasible in literacy assessment? First, there is still much scope for improvement in test constructions. Many tests are still inefficient to apply. For example, in the worst examples one applies a test in which there is a criterion of, say, six consecutive incorrect responses and on the sixth response the respondent gets the answer correct, so one has to continue; the test never seems to end and the grading of difficulty appears to be poor. It should be possible to get to the appropriate level of achievement on the tested dimension as swiftly as possible. Computerised testing can aid this, so that the selection of the next item is determined by the previous response.

Second, we should have better models concerning the types of literacy problems (or skill deficits) that we are looking for. This would be allied to appropriate training experiments that could teach these particular skills. Unfortunately, although there is much theoretical speculation in reading, a consensus is comparatively all too infrequent. This is probably confusing for practitioners, who in any case have their own models of what they are looking for. Miles (1994) offers the beginnings of a taxonomy for dyslexia that falls into seven categories, of which only one, that of phonological deficiency, has received overwhelming research interest and consensus. Some (e.g. Wilding, 1989) might argue in contrast that individuals cannot be fitted into categories, but this is not necessarily a helpful attitude as an atheoretical stance can imply no practical advice for training.

Third, there is a need for research money to be available to fund research into assessment. This is one area of research from which research councils in the UK have largely steered clear. There appears to be some prejudice against such research as it is considered to be practically oriented and scientifically dull. Research on assessment, especially that coupled with appropriate training, is costly and time consuming. At present, the funding is mainly coming from commercial agencies, although some enlightened education authorities have given some modest funding as well. This lack of funding means that in this country most of the major psychometric tools have to be imported into the UK and then standardised to UK samples.

Note

1   It is preferable to refer to dyslexia in this way than to refer to someone as being 'dyslexic'. In the USA in particular, there is strong criticism of this use as it infers that a person or child *is* this category rather than implying that they are human beings who happen to have a condition called 'dyslexia'. We now shy away from calling a person 'a cripple' or 'a spastic' as there was a time when these were also used as terms of abuse. Some would argue that, as in all things, there needs to be a middle path between causing offence on the one hand and creating stylistically awkward passages of prose on the other. For example, 'dyslexic' ought legitimately (and without offence) to be used adjectivally (as in 'dyslexic student'). Many individuals with dyslexia in the UK refer to themselves as 'dyslexic' and regard this particular debate as pointless.

References

Adams, M.J. (1990). *Beginning to Read: Thinking and Learning about Print*. London: MIT Press.

ALBSU (1988). *Adult Literacy and Basic Skills Test*. London: Adult Literacy and Basic Skills Unit.

Alston, J. (1994). Written output and writing speeds. *Dyslexia Review*, 6, 6–12.

Alston, J. (1995). *Assessing and Promoting Writing Skills*. Tamworth: NASEN.

Alston, J. (1996). Assessing and promoting handwriting skills. In G. Reid (ed.) *Dimensions of Dyslexia*, Vol. 2. Edinburgh: Moray House.

Alston, J. and Taylor, J. (1985). *The Handwriting File: Diagnosis and Remediation*. Wisbech: LDA.

Alston, J. and Taylor, J. (1987). *Handwriting File: Theory, Research and Practice*. London: Croom Helm.

Beech, J.R. (1994). Reading skills, strategies and their degree of tractability in dyslexia. In A. Fawcett and R. Nicolson (eds) *Dyslexia in Children: Multidisciplinary Perspectives*. London: Harvester Wheatsheaf.

Beech, J.R. and Harding, L.M. (eds) (1990). *Testing People: A Practical Guide to Psychometrics*. London: Routledge.

Beech, J.R. and Keys, A. (1998). Reading, vocabulary and language preference in 7- to 8-year-old bilingual Asian children. *British Journal of Educational Psychology*.

Bradley, L. and Bryant, P.E. (1983). Categorizing sounds and learning to read: a causal connection. *Nature*, 301, 419–21.

Bryans, T. (1992). Educational psychologists working in a biased society. In S. Wolfendale, T. Bryans, M. Fox, A. Labram and A. Sigston (eds) *The Profession and Practice of Educational Psychology: Future Directions*. London: Cassell.

Callman, T. (1996). Negligent local education authorities? *Education, Public Law and the Individual*, 1, 3–6.

Campbell, R. and Butterworth, B. (1985). Phonological dyslexia and dysgraphia in a highly literate subject: a developmental case and associated deficits in phonemic processing and awareness. *Quarterly Journal of Experimental Psychology*, 37A, 435–75.

Computer Centre for People with Disabilities (1996). *Surveys into the Operation of the Disabled Students' Allowances*. London: University of Westminster Press.

Critchley, M. (1970). *The Dyslexic Child*. Springfield, Ill.: Thomas.

Cummins, J. (1984). *Bilingualism and Special Education Issues in Assessment and Pedagogy*. Clevedon: Multi-lingual Matters.

Davies, J., Brember, I. and Pumfrey, P. (1995). The first and second reading Standard Assessment Tasks at Key Stage 1: a comparison based on a five-school study. *Journal of Research in Reading*, 18, 1–9.

Dearing, R. (1993). *The National Curriculum and its Assessment*. London: School Curriculum and Assessment Authority.

DFE (1994). *Code of Practice on the Identification and Assessment of Special Educational Needs*. London: Department for Education.

DFEE (1995). *Further and Higher Education Review Programme: Interim Report, July 1995*. London: Department for Education and Employment.

Gipps, C. (1990). *Assessment – A Teacher's Guide to the Issues*. London: Hodder & Stoughton.

Gregory, E. and Kelly, C. (1992). Bilingualism and assessment. In G.M. Blenkin and A.V. Kelly (eds) *Assessment in Early Childhood Education*. London: Paul Chapman.

Hanley, J.R., Hastie, K. and Kay, J. (1992). Developmental surface dyslexia and dysgraphia: an orthographic processing impairment. *Quarterly Journal of Experimental Psychology*, 44A, 285–319.

James, M. and Conner, C. (1993). Are reliability and validity achievable in National Curriculum assessment? Some observations on moderation at Key Stage 1 in 1992. *The Curriculum Journal*, 4, 5–19.

Jorm, A.F., Share, D.L., Maclean, R. and Matthews, R. (1986). Cognitive factors at school entry predictive of specific reading retardation and general reading backwardness: a research note. *Journal of Child Psychology and Psychiatry*, 27, 45–65.

Joyce, J. (1988). The development of an anti-racist policy in Leeds. In S. Wolfendale, I. Lunt and T. Carroll (eds) *Educational Psychologists Working in Multi-cultural Communities*. Leicester: British Psychological Society Division of Educational and Child Psychology, Vol. 5(2).

Keily, M. (1996). Handwriting – skills, strategies and success. In G. Reid (ed.) *Dimensions of Dyslexia*, Vol. 2. Edinburgh: Moray House.

Kline, P. (1990) Selecting the best test. In J.R. Beech and L.M. Harding (eds) *Testing People: A Practical Guide to Psychometrics*. London: Routledge.

McLoughlin, D., Fitzgibbon, G. and Young, V. (1994). *Adult Dyslexia: Assessment, Counselling and Training*. London: Whurr.

Massey, A.J. and Elliott, C. (1996). *Aspects of Writing in 16+ English Examinations Between 1980 and 1994*. Cambridge: University of Cambridge Local Examinations Syndicate.

Miles, T.R. (1994). A proposed taxonomy and some consequences. In A. Fawcett and R. Nicolson (eds) *Dyslexia in Children: Multidisciplinary Perspectives*. London: Harvester Wheatsheaf.

Neale, M.D. (1989). *Neale Analysis of Reading Ability. Revised Version*. Windsor, Berks: NFER-Nelson.

Nelson, H. and Willinson, J. (1991). *National Adult Reading Test. Second Edition*. Windsor, Berks: NFER-Nelson.

Otton, Rt Hon Lord Justice (1996). A view from the Bench: an overview of the Education Act 1993. *Education, Public Law and the Individual*, 1(1), 1–2.

Pumfrey, P.D. (1991). *Improving Children's Reading in the Ordinary School: Challenges And Responses*. London: Cassell.

Pumfrey, P.D. and Elliott, C.D. (1991). National reading standards and Standard Assessment Tasks: an educational house of cards. *Educational Psychology in Practice*, 7, 74–80.

Schonell, F.J. (1950). *The Graded Word Reading Test*. Edinburgh: Oliver & Boyd.

Siegel, L.S. (1992). An evaluation of the discrepancy definition of dyslexia. *Journal of Learning Disabilities*, 25, 618–29.

Singleton, C.H. (1994). Issues in the diagnosis and assessment of dyslexia in Higher Education. *Proceedings of the International Conference on Dyslexia in Higher Education*. Plymouth: University of Plymouth.

Singleton, C.H. (1995). Dyslexia in Higher Education. *Dyslexia Contact*, 14(2), 7–9.

Singleton, C.H. [chair] (1996). Dyslexia in higher education: issues for policy and practice. In C. Stephens (ed.) *Proceedings of the Conference on Dyslexic Students in Higher Education*. Huddersfield: Skill and the University of Huddersfield.

Singleton, C.H. (in press). *The Report of the National Working Party on Dyslexia in Higher Education*. Hull: The University of Hull.

Stanovich, K.E. (1986). Matthew effects in reading: some consequences of individual differences in the acquisition of literacy. *Reading Research Quarterly*, 21, 360–406.

Stanovich, K.E. and Cunningham, A.E. (1992). Studying the consequences of literacy within a literate society: the cognitive correlates of print exposure. *Memory and Cognition*, 20, 51–68.

Vellutino, F.R. (1979). *Dyslexia: Theory and Research*. Cambridge, Mass.: MIT Press.

Wechsler, D. (1992). *Wechsler Intelligence Scale for Children. Third Edition*. London: Psychological Corporation.

Wilding, J. (1989). Developmental dyslexics do not fit into boxes: evidence from the case studies. *European Journal of Cognitive Psychology*, 1, 105–27.

Wilkinson, G.S. (1993). *WRAT-3: Wide Range Achievement Test*. Wilmington, Delaware: Jastak Wide Range.

Yule, W., Rutter, M., Berger, M. and Thompson, J. (1974). Over- and under-achievement in reading: distribution in the general population. *British Journal of Educational Psychology*, 44, 1–12.

CHAPTER 2

DREAMS, STRATEGIES AND SYSTEMS

Portraits of assessment past, present and future

Paul Black

Assessment in Education, Vol. 8, No. 1, 2001

Introduction

As reformers dream about changing education for the better they almost always see a need to include assessment and testing in their plans and frequently see them as the main instruments of their reforms. This is because assessment and testing are both ways of expressing aims and means to promote or impose them.

In this chapter I shall try to explore four projects for change in education in which assessment and testing have featured prominently. One of the four examples is the growth, from an origin in IQ testing, of the use of standardised tests, using mainly multiple choice techniques. Another is the development of national testing as an essential adjunct of, and support for, control of a nation's curriculum. Whilst these two have a long history, the other two are about hopes rather than achievements, one being the move for emphasis on classroom formative assessment, the other the vision that advances in psychology in the areas of cognition and social learning could transform school learning, particularly through an influence on assessment.

These examples will be used as sources for reflection about the functioning and effects of assessment and testing. Any such reflection has to examine the technical and instrumental features of the innovations involved. In this perspective a particular problem in all systems is the assumptions made about the relationship between the formative and the summative functions of assessment; the use of the terms 'assessment' and 'testing' partly reflects this duality. However, the need to give attention to both of these functions and to ways in which their mutual relationship is envisaged and may be developed is often overlooked.

It is also important to examine the 'dreams' from a broader perspective. Any serious educational reform is a piece of social engineering; the impetus to reform must be a dream about how things could be better and the criteria for 'better' rest on assumptions and beliefs about the good society. As in any other movement for reform, those promoting it can try to work at a variety of levels of influence in a social system, extremes being imposition from a centre of political power on the one hand and grass roots change developed and disseminated amongst practitioners on the other. Underlying the choice between such strategies will be assumptions about the most effective ways to achieve implementation, whether theoretical or pragmatic.

These various features interplay in diverse ways to give each of the four dreams its distinctive character, so they will have to be considered in the explorations developed here. The point of these explorations will be to inform reflections about the lessons that the cases can teach us. Do these converge, perhaps towards a millennial ideal, or do their mutual contradictions and inconsistencies simply make more clear to us that there are, and always will be, hard choices with far less room for manoeuvre than we imagine?

The IQ dream: social engineering by expertise

The story of this dream is a story of how an instrument developed for a modest purpose was harnessed to serve a vision of a 'scientific' basis for social engineering. After initial progress, this ambitious enterprise was stalled, except in the matter of selection for higher education, where it has burgeoned but is increasingly called into question.

The modest purpose of Binet in developing the first instruments to measure intelligence was to find ways to determine which children were so limited in their intellectual capacity that they could not benefit from normal education. However, other psychologists, notably Thorndike and Terman in the USA, saw that his development of the measurement of intellectual capacity would be of great value if the methods could be applicable to large numbers (see Hanson, 1993, ch. 7). The development of the multiple choice test made this possible.

By an accident of history, the first World War provided the research community in psychology with both the opportunity and the resources to carry the dream forward. The US army, having to recruit and train men in a very short time, needed a way to sort out its conscripts. The psychologists offered help and were thus enabled to develop multiple choice forms of the IQ instruments and try them out with large samples: they could claim that, for the first time, a scientific approach was being used in the selection of human beings. The so-called 'Army test' became a well-established instrument and the US military has used IQ tests ever since.

The new techniques were first applied in education to meet the needs of the admissions test agency of the Ivy League universities, the College Entrance Examinations Board (CEEB). They had worked with essay type tests to aid in selection, but Brigham, in an attempt to complement the traditional measures, adapted the 'Army Test', making it harder in order to discriminate at a higher level. Thus was born, in 1926, the Scholastic Aptitude Test (SAT). Further impetus was given by the president of Harvard, Conant, who wanted a way to select candidates for new scholarships which measured 'native intelligence' irrespective of the fortunes of strong or weak schooling. This project was entrusted to Henry Chauncey, who made the SAT the chief instrument.

From this point on the story of the dream can be described as of two main strands. One is about the larger vision of social engineering, the other about its particular implementation for college entrance through the SAT and Chauncey's eventual founding of the Educational Testing Service (ETS).

The dream of social engineering was reflected in Chauncey's intentions for ETS:

> He had agreed to run ETS because he thought mental testing was a scientific miracle that would soon reveal all the ancient mysteries of the mind, and as soon as it did, he wanted to mount the Census of all Abilities – to assess all Americans on all dimensions, and to use the information gained not just to place them in colleges and universities but to plot the whole course of their lives. That was his dream.

(Lemann, 1999, pp. 85–86)

To pursue this aim, Chauncey explored several novel tests. For example, tests of persistence, of creativity, of practical judgement and various personality tests were all tried, but could not satisfy his rigorous evaluation. He set up a Personality Research Centre and ETS staff formulated a new 'Test of Developed Ability' to replace the SAT, however, this cost $6 per candidate instead of $3 and was dropped after a few years. The economy of the SAT made it hard to beat.

This broader vision owed its origin, at least in part, to the involvement of both Chauncey and, particularly, Brigham as leading figures in the eugenics movement in the 1920s (Selden, 1999), which grew out of the Darwinism of the late 19th century. Another key figure was one of the main developers of the first IQ test, Terman, who believed that 'all feeble-minded are at least potential criminals' (see Hanson, 1993, p. 257). In this vision testing would be an instrument for a programme to improve society by scientific means, so that testing would determine each person's 'life chances'.

The eugenics vision never flourished as a political or social movement. The use in the USA of IQ-based testing during the Korean war could be seen as an example of its precarious survival. As that war called for more conscripts, there was a need to decide who could justifiably have their military service deferred. To serve this purpose, ETS devised intelligence tests which were taken by about one million college students. There was widespread public concern at the gruesome consequence, that the less 'intelligent' could be more readily risked on the battlefield. In this, as in other similar scenarios, it can be seen why the eugenics vision can never be acceptable in a democratic society.

The one part of the IQ dream that did flourish was the use of tests for college entrance in the USA. Conant's original programme, to select the most intelligent for the privileged universities, changed character, particularly after World War II, into a programme to promote equality of access for all. This led to the foundation of the ETS in 1947, which took over the work of the CEEB using only the SAT as its instrument. The size of the USA, the difficulties of communication, the multiplicity of curriculum influences in over 40 states and the heterogeneous background of a country still welcoming large numbers of immigrants, meant that test methods familiar elsewhere, notably in European countries, were unsuitable. The success was remarkable, for the numbers taking the SAT rose in the first 25 years of ETS from a few thousand per year to over two million.

More generally, the practice of multiple choice testing has burgeoned in the USA, where it has been estimated that between 140 and 400 million tests are taken each year. These range over the many varieties of standardised test, many claiming to test achievement rather than IQ or aptitude but yet being in multiple choice form and not directly related to the curriculum (Madaus & Raczek, 1996). Apart from education, tests are widely used by the military and by business. Some of these institutions have been leading innovators, notably in computer adaptive testing (McBride, 1998).

Despite its remarkable expansion and the lead that it gave to the growth of a major industry, the SAT has attracted a range of serious criticisms which call into question the whole basis of the IQ dream. Four of these attack the basic claims upon which the SAT is founded, as follows.

One claim that was essential to its reputation was that the previous experiences and education of candidates would not affect the measurement, so that no amount of coaching could enhance one's score on the test. This claim was severely dented very early in its history by private agencies who could raise the scores of their customers by *ad hoc* drilling with questions similar to those used in the test (although in some cases with the actual questions, obtained by subterfuge). The claim was abandoned by ETS in 1979. There is well-researched evidence that *ad hoc* test preparation does yield significant score increases (Bond, 1989).

A second claim is that tests should be free from bias, in that inequalities associated with irrelevant effects of the family origin, gender, race and so on of candidates will not affect their scores. A great deal of effort has been invested in exploring this problem in order to alleviate its effects, but it cannot be claimed that bias has been completely eliminated. There is a vast history of legislative battles in the USA over the problems of alleged bias in standardised tests and the SAT has endured its share of these (Cole & Moss, 1989; Heubert & Hauser, 1999).

A third claim is of particular importance for ETS, in that it has to be able to show its customers evidence of strong correlation between the SAT score of college applicants and their subsequent performance. Correlations between the SAT score and the performance of college students at the end of their first year are of the order of 0.5, which means that the SAT scores account for about 25% of the variance of college results. This is not very impressive and has usually been less than the correlation obtained with school grades (which can account for about 33% of the variance). The SAT scores do, however, add to the power of the school grades; the optimum combination of school grades and SAT can give correlations of more than 0.6, so accounting for about 40% of the variance (Morgan, 1989)[1].

A fourth, and more fundamental claim is that the IQ test, or the numerical and verbal parts of the SAT, measure well-defined, underlying and central components of human capacity and potential. Ironically, Brigham, the inventor of the SAT, who came to be one of its harshest critics, foresaw challenges to this claim when he wrote in 1929:

> The more I work in this field, the more I am convinced that psychologists have sinned greatly in sliding easily from the name of the test to the function or trait measured.
>
> (Quoted by Lemann, 1999, p. 33)

Most psychologists do not now accept the notion of the single unitary trait that the IQ claims to measure and argue for more complex measures of human thinking (Gardner, 1993; Sternberg, 1997). It may be, however, that for prediction of achievement in a particular sphere, notably tertiary level study, only a few aspects of this complex are relevant: the IQ test may then function usefully because it reflects a relevant combination of these aspects.

Alongside these challenges to the basic justifications of the SATs and similar tests, there have also developed serious concerns about their damaging effects on the practices of teaching and learning. The last 20 years have seen the emergence of increasingly severe criticism from teachers and educational researchers who deplore the narrowing and atomisation of learning (see for example Gifford & O'Connor, 1992). In this respect again Brigham foresaw the problems, in the following terms:

> If the unhappy day ever comes when teachers point their students towards these newer examinations, and the present weak and restricted procedures get a grip on education, then we may look for the inevitable distortion of education in terms of tests. And that means that mathematics will be completely departmentalised and broken into disintegrated bits, that the science will become highly verbalised and that computation, manipulation and thinking in terms other than verbal will be minimised, that languages will be taught for linguistic skills only

without reference to literary values, that English will be taught for reading alone, and that practice and drill in writing of English will disappear.

(Quoted by Lemann, 1999, pp. 40–41)

Some now argue that the cost and the undesirable effects of the SATs cannot be justified given that they do not add a great deal to the predictive power of school grades (Crouse & Trusheim, 1988). A British attempt to use a version of the SAT to check its predictive value for degree results against that of the UK A-level examinations showed that it was no better and that it added very little predictive power when added to the A-level results (Choppin & Orr, 1976). It may nevertheless have advantages in promoting equity: little attention has been given to effects of bias, particularly bias with social class, in the development of A-levels, whereas the SAT has been refined in an environment where such effects are taken more seriously and test developers have to have evidence that they have worked to reduce them.

Overall, it is clear Chauncey's wider dream has never been realised. The narrower programme has flourished, giving a powerful and wealthy (albeit not for profit) organisation, with many of the claims that justified its existence being open to doubt, but playing an important role in school education and in other areas of society. The damaging effects of its products are to be offset against their value in meeting a social and administrative need at minimal cost. In this respect, they resemble many of the products of 20th century technology.

Driving up standards: reform by imposition

State education was established to meet the needs of advanced societies for a literate population. The range and level of such aims has changed as new technologies have transformed society. The need to be able to handle numbers in addition to being able to read and write was evident from the outset. More recently, communication skills, IT skills, understanding of scientific, environmental and technological issues and education for citizenship have all claimed a place in the agenda of necessity. With such expansion has come a shift from primacy of emphasis on well-defined workforce needs to a more complex vision in which the rhetorics of workforce, flexibility, life-long learning, democracy and citizenship have all been stirred in. What distinguishes such movements is that they have not been driven solely by the dream of selection, but also by a competing need for success for all. Indeed, the dream of an efficiently selected meritocracy, albeit complemented by a workforce in which each member would ideally be content in the occupation that best suited them, has a downside in the spectre of an ill-educated and under-privileged majority seeing themselves as losers in an unjust society, which is thereby threatened by civil unrest (Young, 1959).

The problem here is that as the range and timespan needed for mass education have expanded, so has the cost. Thus, allied with the need to set and achieve new targets for all has been the need to check that the resources were being used effectively. The standards dream was a straightforward vision of a way to meet both these needs: the targets would be set and promulgated and external tests would show whether or not they were being achieved. With the addition of rewards and sanctions tied to test results the problem would then be solved.

The attraction of this approach is its simple appeal, particularly to those not in direct touch with the complexities of schooling. There is also more than a grain of truth behind the argument. There have always been some positive effects of examinations, particularly in motivating the learner. A don writing in 1855 about new written examinations in Cambridge saw this feature:

> The wonderful effect of these institutions (i.e. examinations) in exciting industry and emulation among the young men and exalting the character of the College, are such as may even have surpassed the hope of their promoters.
>
> (Quoted in MacLeod, 1982, p. 7)

Whilst such opinions are more commonly found in the press and in the writings from those outside the education system, it is also easy to find a wealth of opinions to the contrary in the academic and professional literature. Why is it that the promise of this dream is difficult to realise?

An enduring difficulty is illustrated by late 19th century development in Britain of the scheme for 'payment by results' (Sutherland, 1973; MacLeod, 1982). This scheme actually collapsed under its own internal tensions. The system became increasingly difficult to control and audit as numbers grew further and as attempts were made to include in it a wider range of subjects. Its abandonment after 30 years owed more to the UK treasury and the national audits than to any educational considerations.

Here one has to distinguish several features, evident in this early venture but basic in all that has followed. Later systems of this type have not collapsed so dramatically, but they have usually shared with it the negative effect of the tests on the quality of teaching. As one of the school inspectors subsequently wrote about payment by results:

> As profound distrust of the teacher was the basis of the policy of the Department, so profound distrust of the child was the basis of the policy of the teachers. To leave the child to find anything out for himself, to work out anything for himself, to think out anything for himself, would have been regarded as proof of incapacity, not to say insanity, on the part of the teacher, and would have led to results which, from the 'percentage' point of view, would probably have been disastrous.
>
> (Holmes, 1911, pp. 107–108)

The argument here is that such measures are bound to have a negative effect on the learning work in school classrooms. The pressures to do well almost inevitably lead teachers to teach to the test. The bad effects of such a response have been documented frequently (e.g. ASE Key Stage 3 Monitoring Group, 1992; Johnston *et al.*, 1995). The paradox is that this response, whilst natural, may not be the best way even to meet the demands of the external tests, i.e. the pressure is counterproductive. There is research evidence that pupils whose teaching is directly aimed at test perfomance do no better on the tests than those taught with an emphasis on understanding or on problem solving, and are at a disadvantage in that they may be unable to apply their knowledge and may subsequently have poorer long-term retention (Nuthall & Alton-Lee, 1995; Boaler, 1997).

The second difficulty is related to the first. It has been clearly expressed by Christie:

> A single dimension, the testing objective of the 1920s, is disastrous from the pedagogical point of view. How can teachers respond to such a score? It is a single number and all the teacher can endeavour to do is to make it larger. In these circumstances teaching to the test is the only sensible strategy but, as

Goodhart's law demonstrates in economics, attempts to manipulate a predictive variable, rather than to manipulate the performance that the variable predicts, immediately destroy the set of relationships which lent the variable predictive validity in the first place.

(Christie, 1995, p. 112)

Christie's point is illustrated by the evidence that whilst scores in any new high stakes test will rise over the first few years after its institution, the improvement is illusory. Linn (1994) quotes a striking example: one US state was using a particular standardised test (test A) on which, in common with almost all other US states, its scores were above the average (the 'Lake Wobegon' paradox; see Linn *et al.*, 1990). The state changed the test for a version from another supplier (test B). The scores immediately fell below average, but then rose to above average again over the next few years. Then, however, researchers tried using test A with a sample of pupils in that state and found that the scores that it now yielded had declined from their previous level and were now at the same low level as the scores for test B had been when it had first been used (Koretz *et al.*, quoted by Linn, 2000).

Thus, whilst they may lead to short-term and illusory gains in pupils' test performance, standards imposed by the pressure of external tests can be counter-productive in that they can damage classroom teaching and learning. It may still be asked whether there is evidence that pupil learning has been improved by large-scale reforms, notably in states in the USA and in the UK. There is no positive evidence to this effect and, indeed, it is hard to see how there could be: when both curriculum and methods of assessment are changed it is technically very difficult to measure overall losses and gains. It would be difficult even if matched experimental and control groups were set up to evaluate the reform process, but this has never been done for large-scale political reforms, given that politicians would not lightly support measures which might show up a failure of their reforms. International comparisons that can be made with the data from the TIMSS (Third International Mathematics and Science Study) do indicate that the overall performance of those countries with a prescribed national curriculum is no better than that of those without one (Atkin & Black, 1997).

Given the public and political confidence in testing as an aid to reform, there is thus a gulf in perceptions about the goods or the evils of large-scale external testing and, insofar as this might be recognised by those influential in public policy, it leaves them in a dilemma. There are two possible ways to escape.

Both ways were explored by the UK Task Group on Assessment and Testing (TGAT), and the fate of their attempt is an interesting case here (Department of Education and Science, 1988a, b). A group of professional educators expressed support for the positive effects of assessment as part of a system of external accountability, but set out conditions for such effects to be secured. One way was to design external tests so that they would be 'authentic', set in contexts familiar to the pupils, multi-dimensional and complex in character. The underlying aim was to ensure that teaching to the test would be good teaching for learning, so that the pressures of testing would be benign rather than harmful. This condition was taken seriously and tried: the novelty and complexity of the methods guaranteed that severe teething troubles would be encountered and these fuelled the opposition of those who could see no difficulty with simple tests: the verdict of the Minister responsible at the time was 'complicated nonsense'. The political perception of tests thus defeated an attempt to make them productive.

The second way, more ambitious and more positive, was to support efforts for the development of teachers' own assessments, so that they could yield trustworthy contributions to a national system of measurement. The fate of these proposals will be taken up in my next section, but it is worth noting here that this way ultimately sought to raise standards by a completely different approach. The point here was expressed by a US researcher:

> ... reforms so often debated in the media, in the White House, in Congress, and in statehouses across the country do not touch on the changes needed to fundamentally reform America's schools. ... These reforms ignore a basic truth. Student achievement cannot change unless America's teachers use markedly more effective instructional methods.
>
> (Slavin, 1996, p. 4)

The underlying fault in this dream thus stems from the fact that standards can only be raised by improved teaching. Testing can only help if ways can be found to resolve the tension between the demands of accountability testing and the requirements for tests to be valid in reflecting and reinforcing good pedagogy. It seems most unlikely that external tests which are short and affordable could ever be valid in this way and whilst teachers' summative assessments might do better, the use of these raises severe problems of trust and comparability. Different countries have struggled with, or ignored, this problem in different ways and it is clear that there is no 'quick fix' (see for example Noah & Eckstein, 1990). Insofar as a wholesale system reform is called for, the design and development would be a complex enterprise, requiring investment in a lengthy development which the politicians and their public seem unlikely to support because the need is not understood.

The standards dream has started in the wrong place; it looks to products without attention to the processes that produce those products. Yet those initiatives for which research has established significant learning gains have been concerned with the teaching and learning processes. To address those processes first is to start in a different place. Then the function of assessment is seen in a quite different perspective, which is the perspective of the next dream to be discussed.

The dream has also been flawed in failing to confront the problem of defining the criteria to which it should work. In the case of assessment for selection to higher education there is a fairly clear criterion, success in degree courses, and one can assess whatever turns out to correlate best with this criterion. But if this is no longer the main, let alone the only, criterion, then clarity of orientation is harder to achieve. For example, it is easy enough to proclaim a commitment to 'learning in the future': it is hard to see how criteria to operationalise this aim in assessment instruments could ever be validated (if they were they might well turn out to be concerned with learning process rather than with products).

The formative dream: interaction and involvement for all

This is a dream backed by evidence that it can improve the learning of pupils. However, its emergence to maturity has been a slow and tortured development, in part because its vision has been clouded repeatedly by the interference of summative testing, in part because it locates the functioning of assessment more closely within the complexities of pedagogy. These two features will be examined in turn.

In 1986 Harry Black reflected on the poor state of teachers' assessments that surveys in Scotland had revealed. He contrasted this with the wealth of resources devoted to external summative testing in the following passage:

Consider the amount of time, energy and money spent by both individual teachers, and schools in general, on setting and marking continuous assessment tests, end of session examinations and mock 'O' levels. Reflect on the money spent by examination boards and the number of assessment specialists employed by them. Read, if you can find a sabbatical term, the literature on the technology of assessment for reporting and certification. Compare these in turn with the complete lack of support normally given to teachers in devising and applying procedures to pinpoint their students' learning problems, with the virtual absence of outside agencies to develop formative assessment instruments and procedures, and the limited literature on the topic.

(Black, H. D., 1986, p. 7)

In a historical survey, Black's article goes on to quote work to develop formative assessment in the nineteenth century, but suggests that the growth of public examinations and, particularly, the use of various forms of standardised testing suppressed formative developments.

New impetus, however, came from programmed learning and the growth of mastery learning and these helped put the notion of 'criterion referencing' (Glaser, 1963; Wood, R., 1991, ch. 7) into the debate. Whilst this concept is central to both formative and summative assessment, attempts to use it in summative testing in the UK have encountered many difficulties, in part because, unlike in formative use, the necessary aggregation overrides the information and in part because it calls for quite new approaches to the design and marking of tests.

The growth of the use of assessment by teachers in Britain, particularly in the 1960s developments of the Certificate for Secondary Education, gave a different impetus, but one that was problematical:

In particular, teachers have developed skills which are appropriate to the construction of summative external examinations. We have also moved en masse towards the 'progressive' notion of continuous assessment. As a result, school assessment is dominated by staccato forms of the old end-of-session examinations. Continuous assessment in action means continual examination for reporting, and to make matters worse, many teachers are doing it rather well because of the skills they have picked up from the exam boards.

(Black, H. D., 1986, p. 10)

Thus it appeared, ironically, that investment in the quality and status of teachers' summative assessment had made it more, rather than less, difficult to develop formative assessment practices. One reason for this is that summative examinations demand a level of reliability which is unnecessary in classroom use and also raise problems of aggregation over the diversity of objectives encompassed in an external summative test. A teachers' formative work calls for criterion referencing focused on specific learning needs. It can be adjusted if there are misinterpretations and aggregation is not required. Thus, an underlying problem is that the requirement for a criterion referenced approach was not one that could be satisfied at that time by drawing on the experience of external certificate examinations (Black, H. D. & Dockrell, 1984).

In the UK the national view about formative assessment was shifted by the 1988 TGAT reports (Department of Education and Science, 1988a, b), which envisaged that formative assessment by teachers would be given prominence and support in a new national policy. The report also envisaged that teachers' summative assessments would be used for national assessments at the end of the Key Stages, in conjunction with external tests which would serve mainly to provide overall calibration for schools. One intention behind these proposals was that the new external testing should not dominate and undermine teachers' efforts to meet their main responsibility to promote the learning of their students.

In the event, matters worked out differently. The proposals about the involvement of teachers in the accountability tests were never accepted; the initial political decision on the TGAT proposals was that teachers' assessments and the results of external tests were to be kept separate, which ensured a fate of diminishing marginality for the status of teachers' summative assessments (Black, P. J., 1993b, 1997; Black, P., 1998).

National resources were devoted almost entirely to the development of external summative tests. The implementation of teachers' assessments in schools has subsequently shown all the signs of continuing the well-researched weaknesses of earlier practice, with little by way of training or of time for reflection which would be needed to stimulate and support any change. It was evident early on (see references in Black, P. J., 1993a) that teachers' assessments were mainly summative. Subsequent surveys have been equally negative in reporting that there was very little formative assessment to be seen in science work (Russell *et al.*, 1995; Daws & Singh, 1996).

In the TGAT reports the emphasis on formative assessment was not supported by any reference to evidence of the value of this aspect of teaching. In filling this gap a review of the literature by Black, P. & Wiliam (1998a) has provided new impetus. This review, initiated by the work of an assessment study group in the British Educational Research Association, showed that the research literature up until 1997 contained ample evidence that the strengthening of formative assessment could raise standards of pupil performance. The academic review was complemented by a 20 page booklet setting out the case for giving fresh support to this aspect of classroom teaching, but pointing out also that the present state of the art was very weak and that classroom application of the methods reported in the research literature would require careful development work in which teachers themselves would have to take a lead (Black, P. & Wiliam, 1998b).

The widespread interest in this argument (the booklet has sold over 14,000 copies to date and the authors have received numerous requests for talks and workshops on its message) was both welcome and puzzling. One possible explanation is that its message has struck a chord in stressing that standards can only really be raised by improvement in the classroom work of teachers, for which they are responsible. Other approaches to raising standards, notably setting targets or testing more frequently, impose pressures for which teachers are not responsible.

With its importance thus attested and its separate characteristics made clear, it is now possible for the formative assessment dream to develop and so mature. The vision as sketched out is that with better interaction in the classroom teachers will be in closer touch with their pupils' progress in understanding, pupils will become more active and responsible as they become involved in expressing their thinking to their teachers and to their peers, and pupils will be drawn into taking responsibility for their learning through self and peer assessment. All this should lead to enriched learning now and to pupils who are better equipped to learn in the future. Thus the promise is that standards will be raised in ways that are real rather than illusory and in ways that will yield benefits beyond performance in tests.

Recent experience has shown that work to develop their formative assessment practices can put teachers in touch with the state of their pupils' learning ideas and can lead them to give their pupils a stronger voice and a more active role in their own learning (Black, P. *et al.*, 2000). A process which develops in such directions is bound to open up a range of fundamental issues about teaching and learning. Examples of these are given below.

- If they are to elicit relevant and useful feedback for formative purposes, the tasks set and the questions asked by teachers have to be carefully designed so that they evoke aspects of understanding which are critical indicators of learning progress, a need which is underlined by the many researches into the problems of procedural and conceptual learning in several different subject disciplines (Pellegrino *et al.*, 1999).
- Such questions have to be set in a framework of goals, which will be open to amendment in the light of feedback, so that they are a challenge but are attainable by pupils; here the ideas link naturally with the concepts of the zone of proximal development and of scaffolding (Wood, D. *et al.*, 1976).
- Goals have to be clearly communicated to pupils and they can only learn if they can assess themselves in the light of those goals; these are the key features of any constructivist approach to learning (Sadler, 1989).
- In such a development the aims and criteria for learning become more clear and more salient; they have to be understood and used by the pupils, so that they begin to be able to evaluate and monitor their learning progress for themselves, i.e. they develop their powers of meta-cognition which cognitive research shows to be essential for effective learning (Hacker *et al.*, 1998).

Formative assessment, strictly defined, does not implement such developments directly, but experience in its implementation has shown that it can serve as a catalyst, perhaps as a Trojan Horse, for better learning practices. However, this opens up a far wider range of issues than those encompassed by the accepted notion of assessment and future maturing thus seems to lie in the embedding of concepts of formative assessment in broader theories of learning and pedagogy.

The changes being sketched out here are far from cosmetic and their power to evoke the need for radical approaches for pedagogy is also their weakness as agents for change. The lessons that they carry have to be worked on and owned for themselves by all teachers, for radical changes in everyday classroom practice cannot be imposed. Thus the main implementers of change here must be teachers themselves and they will need new tools for the work. Whether there can be a sufficiently strong and sustained drive to provoke such processes of change remains to be seen.

One factor inhibiting such change is that none of the recent developments in formative assessment has yet addressed the overlaps and tensions, between teachers' formative roles on the one hand and on the other the roles they have to play both in generating aggregated scores for their school and for parents and in assisting pupils to maximise scores on external summative tests. There are clear gaps of inconsistency and tension between these roles and it cannot be reasonable to expect that teachers will resolve the dilemmas that arise without policy changes which are designed to help with such dilemmas.

New theories in psychology: will they save us?

The core idea in this dream is that our test practices are unacceptable because they are based on 'application of 20th century statistics to 19th century psychology' (Mislevy, 1993, p. 19) and that the task now is to link assessment practices with current theories of cognition and instruction. This vision was first formulated by Cronbach (1957). Recent writers, notably Snow & Lohman (1989), Greeno *et al.* (1996), Mislevy (1996) and Pellegrino *et al.* (1999) have set it out in more detail, although all would admit that the vision has yet to be realised.

The analysis here starts from noting that traditional test theory is based on the notion of the trait, a single, stable and enduring cognitive property that is consistent across settings and contexts. A set of test items would be interpreted as measures of a trait confounded with random noise: the purpose of statistical analysis was to extract the measure from the noise to obtain a 'true score'. In the earliest versions a single trait was sought; later a multi-dimensional approach allowed for different traits matched to different types of tasks. This approach, the psychological roots of which are represented by Greeno *et al.* (1996) in labelling it as 'differential-behaviourist', called for task analysis to break down areas of interest into domains, each domain populated with questions which had in common their power to sample one single trait. Achievement would be defined as accumulation of increasing numbers of correct responses, so the numerical score would represent progress in the domain. Whilst adequate sampling of the domain could ensure reliability, validity would be inherent in expert judgements of the unity represented by the domain and, perhaps, also in the predictive power of the scores.

The breakdown of this paradigm was clearly set out by Snow and Lohman:

> The evidence of cognitive psychology suggests that test performances are comprised of complex assemblies of component information-processing actions that are adapted to task requirements during performance. The implication is that sign-trait interpretations of test scores and their inter-correlations are superficial summaries at best. At worst, they have misled scientists, and the public, into thinking of fundamental, fixed entities, measured in amounts.
>
> (Snow & Lohman, 1989, p. 317)

The central point here is that our understanding cannot be represented as a mere collection of fragments of knowledge and skill. The inter-connections and patterns are essential: cognition is characterised by structures in which principles, concepts and information are organised into schemas, where a schema:

> ... can be roughly thought of as a pattern of recurring relationships, with variables that in part determine its range of applicability. Associated with this knowledge are conditions for its use. While experts in various fields do command more facts and concepts than novices, and have richer interconnections among them, the real distinction lies in their ways of viewing phenomena and representing and approaching problems.
>
> (Mislevy, 1996, p. 389)

This argument is set out in detail by Pellegrino *et al.* (1999). The conclusion is that the results of tests fashioned and interpreted in the traditional psychometric tradition do not tell us about features that are of central significance in current theories of cognition because they are based on a model of independent 'traits'.

In this perspective the task of the teacher is first to start by taking account of the schema which pupils will deploy when faced with new tasks and ideas and then to help them to enrich, interrelate or, perhaps, reconstruct them. So the task of assessment has changed. As one review puts it:

> ... the field has moved from focusing on *how much knowledge someone has to providing adequate characterization of just what is the knowledge that someone has.*
>
> (Greeno *et al.*, 1996, p. 13, author's italics)

The shift has to be from accumulation of marks to yield scores to identification of models of the cognitive structure that a learner has. These models are then to be extended and may have to be reconstructed during learning, so that the quality and processes of a learner's reasoning may change. Responses to single questions cannot achieve such identification, the information required has to be extensive enough to support inferences about the learner's model, for if that model is not understood, the learner's reasons for a given set of responses cannot be understood. Moreover, this emphasis on the learner's power to integrate information has to be matched by assessment of the power to use these resources in dealing with new situations, i.e. the power to generate procedures and new structures of knowledge.

A further indicator of a learner's capacity is evidence of meta-cognition; a person with strong meta-cognition will have a clear overview of the goals of a task, will judge well when to abandon a line of attack on a problem when it is not working and try to attack it in a different way, will go back and check earlier steps when stuck with a task and can review his or her own writing in order to discern where it might not be clear to others.

Data for assessment should therefore be derived from a learner's responses to complex tasks as well as to simple tests of facts and skills. Moreover, such data mean little unless they can be analysed in terms of some model(s) of pupils' learning, otherwise it will be hard to draw valid inferences about learning needs or about future potential. Since both the integrative and generative aspects of a learner's cognitive powers work out differently between different learners (e.g. according to whether they adopt intuitive or analytical approaches to any task), the inference from the data to a model of the learner cannot be simple or direct. Ideally, assessment should be based on multiple complex tasks, with several aspects of the learner's response analysed by methods which allow for the inherent uncertainty in proceeding from data to a model. Whilst this seems formidable, examples of such analyses, in which probabilistic reasoning is used to optimise the fit between evidence of a learner's work and a proposed model of that learner's competence, already exist (see Mislevy, 1996). However, the increase in the complexity and range, both of the models required to give a fit to most learners and of the analyses of data, will be daunting. Glaser's vision, perhaps an over-optimistic one, gives a flavour of what is hoped for:

> As competence in a subject-matter grows, evidence of a knowledge base that is increasingly coherent, principled, useful and goal-oriented is displayed and test items can be designed to capture such evidence.
>
> (Glaser, 1991, p. 26)

The picture presented up to this point has focused on the learner as an individual who transcends the social context in which the learning has been situated. A further development in cognitive theory emphasises the centrality of situated cognition and the social dimension of learning (Greeno *et al.*, 1996). In this dimension what counts as knowledge is formulated and defined in social interactions, so that participation, with its accompanying shared meanings and symbols, is essential. The knowledge is situated in the discourse and practice of a community. The process of learning is thus seen as a process of enculturation and one's capacity to learn is seen, in this perspective, as a capacity to interact and participate effectively in such communities. It is not necessary to go as far as some, who would seem to claim that all learning is social and so leave no room for learning through the endeavours of the lone scholar (Bredo, 1994). Simply to accept that community participation is a focal element for almost all learning, that knowledge does not exist only in the minds of individuals and that learning proceeds by iteration between the individual and the communal is to accept a fundamental change in one's theory of learning.

From this situated view performance in any traditional test is seen as evidence of ability to participate in the lonely business of test taking and it cannot be assumed that such performance gives evidence of a capacity to participate in a learning community. Such evidence has to be obtained in situations where participatory abilities are being demanded, where the issue of how much an individual knows is subsumed into a capacity to contribute in getting the job done. Indeed, it can be argued that this view of cognitive ability subsumes, rather than replaces, the behaviourist and cognitive views (Greeno *et al.*, 1996). It follows that valid inferences about the learner's future can only be made from evidence which is interpreted in the light of a theory of the social nature of learning.

In many areas of employment, including research, the ability to participate and contribute in a community enterprise is an important determinant. Given that it usually turns out that surrogate assessments are not effective, it follows that there is no way to assess such competence except through recording the actual engagement in community endeavours, so such assessment would appear to be essential if, at the interface between schooling and employment, assessment results are to be good predictors of capacity to participate. This argument would have force even if the social nature of cognition were to be overlooked, but it acquires more fundamental significance if this social dimension is given prominence, for the social perspective then involves far more than the mere addition of some social skills to the skills of learning as an individual, because interactive functioning is now seen as an essential locus of the learning itself.

This development raises further challenges to assessment practice. A whole new technology for assessing group contributions will have to be developed. Then teachers will have to be trained both to find ways, with the aid of such technology, to promote and record participatory practices and to find means of collecting evidence to share with peers so that the process of inter-calibration of their methods and criteria (i.e. moderation) can be acceptably rigorous.

In summary, this dream looks to radical transformations in testing practices. It clearly has direct implications for formative assessment. Indeed, some of the relevant ideas about the requirements for good learning are already influential, for example in classroom innovations aimed at implementing constructivist principles, in giving pupils more responsibility for their own learning and in developing learning through group work. However, assessment developments to match such changes are not well developed, either for formative or for summative purposes: the apparatus of psychometric statistics will still be needed, but in the service of new endeavours, not as keeper and promoter of the old traditions.

Much of what is written does not make explicit whether programmes to rebuild the links between testing and cognition are primarily for formative or summative purposes. It is evident that much of what is proposed or implied bears directly on formative assessments, for the ways in which feedback is evoked from pupils, the contexts and practices within which evidence of learning is revealed and the interpretation of evidence in terms of learning needs are naturally required in formative work: the theories invoked here are theories of learning, not of assessment as such.

It now seems more evident than ever before that short episodes in the artificial contexts of the test hall are not suitable contexts for several important components of assessment work. The future envisaged is that traditional formal testing must at least be supplemented by assessment in the context of work on complex tasks and work in which interaction with others is integral and can be analysed in terms of a social theory of learning. However, because of obvious problems of cost and of provision of appropriate contexts and time, such assessment practices, now seen as essential for valid assessment, cannot be handled except within the normal timetabled work of the school and by the teacher. It follows that teachers may have to play two roles, one of planner and animator of the learning, the other as judge to pass verdicts on complex performances.

Conclusions

Each of these four stories carries lessons for the new millennium. The first started with a new tool for assessment, which, within the ideological context of its time, served to fuel the dream of scientific human selection. Its instruments served an important social purpose, which was a part, albeit a small part, of the vision of the dream. Its power in society derived from the power of higher education to select the élite and it has survived because it met this need for élite selection in a durable and inexpensive way. However, whilst the scientism of its dream has faded away, the approach and the instruments that it generated are still influential. Their serious shortcomings, particularly in their negative effects on learning, which are increasingly seen as unacceptable, are matters of great concern.

The second dream has taken as its starting point a conjunction between the need that society has for better education for all and an assumption that this goal is best pursued through prescription of the curriculum enforced by external testing. It has in common with the first, partly as an inheritance from it, that its strategic starting point is measurement, not the improvement of learning, but differs from it in that its power derives from the governments whose imagination it has captured. Because it has thereby led them to adopt an indirect rather than a direct route to their target of securing high standards, it has always been fragile. This fault has meant that its methods, whilst far broader (in most countries) than those of the IQ test, have been dysfunctional in that they have in part damaged the very teaching that they were meant to improve. This feature is linked to an ambiguity in the dream: its methods might be justified for the purpose of élite selection, but insofar as they both disadvantage and disappoint the large proportions who usually fail, they must undermine the aim of success for all.

The third dream comes from a completely different direction insofar as its starting point is direct improvement in the quality of teaching and learning. However, despite its strong claims, it has had to struggle for attention and it has the very restricted power of the adherence of academics and some professionals. It does not have the appeal to governments of the second dream, which is the promise of quick transformation through outside pressure, whilst its growth is inhibited by the conflicting pressures on teachers of external tests. So it faces three obstacles. The first is the difficulty of achieving a change in public and political understanding of the effects on teaching and learning of inexpensive external tests. The second is the need to build up a body of experience of its practice so that its dissemination, which involves radical changes in classroom practices for most teachers, can be effective. The third is the need to forge a new and positive relationship between the practice of formative assessment by teachers, their practice also of summative assessment and the demands of accountability for trustworthy evidence of pupils' attainments.

The fourth dream is a new feature. It shares some resemblances with the first, but is both more subtle and more complex, so that it is hard to see how its products could be recruited like those of the first to serve simple and appealing testing systems; it might even be objected that assessment could be very intrusive if this were to happen. The power of its ideas for teaching and learning is widely acknowledged, but implications for assessment are debated mainly in the academic community at present and, because of their complexity, it will be a long and difficult task to turn the ideas into classroom practice. As formulated at present, its first contribution would seem to be as a critique of the fundamental flaws in some current testing systems, but its second, and far more important, contribution will be to the enhancement of the quality of formative assessment. Indeed, to incorporate its lessons into external summative testing without any attempt at effects in the classroom would seem inconsistent with its focus on a deeper understanding of learning.

The approach in this paper overlaps with, but differs significantly from, those analyses which focus on the sociological and cultural determinants of assessment systems (Broadfoot, 1996). The intention is to supplement, rather than to call into question, such analyses. Indeed, there is strong overlap in the treatments here of the first two dreams; the way they have played out historically clearly illustrating the influence of social and cultural factors. It is not so easy to explore the influence of such factors for the formative dream, for although the power of political and public assumptions about assessment have clearly constrained its progress, the longer term influences are harder to discern because it has yet to emerge as an idea to be reckoned with. The same problem is even more evident for the fourth dream.

What is different here, and complementary, is signified by the notion of a 'dream'. This emphasises how the influence of innovations in the understanding of assessment and testing, and the development of new tools and analytical methods which accompany these, influence, or rather inspire, key individuals and groups to forge a vision to which their efforts and influence are harnessed. Without those personal and contingent visions, developments may have gone differently. Nevertheless, any attempt to forecast how the third and fourth dreams might affect practices in the future, however foolhardy, would have to take note of the sociological and cultural contexts which will fashion their progress.

Overall, the first dream is dead, the second is in need of redemption, the third is at best adolescent and in need of nurture, whilst the fourth hovers in the wings. What might be critical in the immediate future is the extent to which convergence can be achieved between the ways in which society might respond to two different pressures. The one is the pressure created by the new demands on education arising from the needs for mass education, which calls for all citizens and not just an élite to be equipped to adapt to the technological revolutions in the information society. The other pressure should arise from the implications of evidence and arguments to the effect that the second dream is selling it short and that only a quite new combination of the third and fourth can deliver what it will need.

Acknowledgements

I am grateful to my colleagues, Professor J. Myron Atkin at Stanford and Professor Dylan Wiliam at King's, and also to an anonymous referee, whose critical appraisals have helped me to improve this paper.

Note

1   The correlation coefficients quoted here were (in Morgan's analyses) adjusted to allow for attenuation of range. Thus, whilst the data available are, of necessity, limited to those who passed the admission hurdles set by the tests, a theoretical model is used to estimate what the correlation would have been if all had been admitted to college regardless of their test score.

References

Atkin, J. M. & Black, P. J. (1997) Policy perils of international comparisons: the TIMSS case, *Phi Delta Kappan*, 79(1), pp. 22–28.

ASE Key Stage 3 Monitoring Group (1992) Report on the monitoring of Key Stage 3, *Education in Science*, September, pp. 18–19.

Black, H. D. (1986) Assessment for learning, in: D. L. Nuttall (Ed.), *Assessing Educational Achievement*, pp. 7–18 (London, Falmer).

Black, H. D. & Dockrell, W. B. (1984) *Criterion Referenced Assessment in the Classroom* (Edinburgh, Scottish Council for Research in Education).

Black, P. (1998) Learning, league tables and national assessment: opportunity lost or hope deferred?, *Oxford Review of Education*, 24(1), pp. 57–68.

Black, P. & Wiliam, D. (1998a) Assessment and classroom learning, *Assessment in Education*, 5(1), pp. 7–74.

Black, P. & Wiliam, D. (1998b) *Inside the Black Box: raising standards through class-room assessment* (London, King's College). [Also published in *Phi Delta Kappan*, 80(2), pp. 139–148, October 1998.]

Black, P., Harrison, C., Lee, C. & Wiliam, D. (2000) The King's Medway Oxfordshire Formative Assessment Project, paper presented at the *British Educational Research Association Conference*, Cardiff, September 2000.

Black, P. J. (1993a) Formative and summative assessment by teachers, *Studies in Science Education*, 21, pp. 49–97.

Black, P. J. (1993b) The shifting scenery of the National Curriculum, in: P. O'Hear & J. White (Eds), *Assessing the National Curriculum*, pp. 57–69 (London, Paul Chapman).

Black, P. J. (1997) Whatever happened to TGAT?, in: C. Cullingford (Ed.), *Assessment vs. Evaluation*, pp. 24–50 (London, Cassell).

Boaler, J. (1997) *Experiencing School Mathematics: teaching styles, sex and setting* (Buckingham, Open University Press).

Bond, L. (1989) The effects of special preparation on measures of scholastic ability, in: R. L. Linn (Ed.), *Educational Measurement*, 3rd Edn, pp. 429–444 (New York, NY, Macmillan).

Bredo, E. (1994) Reconstructing educational psychology, *Educational Psychologist*, 29(1), pp. 23–45.

Broadfoot, P. M. (1996) *Education, Assessment and Society. A sociological analysis* (Buckingham, Open University Press).

Choppin, B. & Orr, L. (1976) *Aptitude Testing at 18+* (Windsor, NFER Publishing).

Christie, T. (1995) Defining the reading domain, in: P. Owen & P. Pumfrey (Eds), *Children Learning to Read: international concerns*, Vol. 2, *Curriculum and Assessment Issues: messages for teachers*, pp. 107–120 (London, Falmer).

Cole, N. S. & Moss, P. A. (1989) Bias in test use, in: R. L. Linn (Ed.), *Educational Measurement*, 3rd Edn, pp. 201–219 (New York, NY, Macmillan).

Cronbach, L. J. (1957) The two disciplines of scientific psychology, *American Psychologist*, 12, pp. 671–684.

Crouse, J. & Trusheim, D. (1988) *The Case Against the SAT* (Chicago, University of Chicago Press).

Daws, N. & Singh, B. (1996) Formative assessment; to what extent is its potential to enhance pupils' science being realised?, *School Science Review*, 77, pp. 93–100.

Department of Education and Science (1988a) *National Curriculum. Task Group on Assessment and Testing: a report* (London, Department of Education and Science and Welsh Office).

Department of Education and Science (1988b) *National Curriculum: Task Group on Assessment and Testing: three supplementary reports* (London, Department of Education and Science and Welsh Office).

Gardner, H. (1993) *Multiple Intelligences: the theory in practice* (New York, NY, Basic Books).

Gifford, B. R. & O'Connor, M. C. (Eds) (1992) *Changing Assessments: alternative views of aptitude, achievement and instruction* (Boston, MA, Kluwer).

Glaser, R. (1963) Instructional technology and the measurement of learning outcomes: some questions, *American Psychologist*, 18, pp. 519–521.

Glaser, R. (1991) Expertise and assessment, in: M. C. Wittrock & E. L. Baker (Eds), *Testing and Cognition*, pp. 17–30 (Englewood Cliffs, NJ, Prentice Hall).

Greeno, J. G., Pearson, P. D. & Schoenfeld, A. H. (1996) *Implications for NAEP of Research on Learning and Cognition. Report of a study commissioned by the National Academy of Education Panel on the NAEP trial state assessment* (Stanford, CA, National Academy of Education).

Hacker, D. J., Dunlosky, J. & Graesser, A. C. (Eds) (1998) *Metacognition in Educational Theory and Practice* (Mahwah, NJ, Lawrence Erlbaum).

Hanson, F. A. (1993) *Testing Testing: social consequences of the examined life* (Berkeley, CA, University of California Press).

Heubert, J. P. & Hauser, R. M. (Eds) (1999) *High Stakes; testing for tracking, promotion and graduation* (Washington, DC, National Academy Press).

Holmes, E. (1911) *What Is And What Might Be* (London, Constable).

Johnston, P., Guice, S., Baker, K., Malone, J. & Michelson, N. (1995) Assessment of teaching and learning in literature-based classrooms, *Teaching and Teacher Education*, 11, pp. 359–371.

Lemann, N. (1999) *The Big Test* (New York, NY, Farrar, Strauss & Giroux).

Linn, R. L. (1994) *Assessment Based Reform: challenges to educational measurement* (Princeton, NJ, Educational Testing Service).

Linn, R. L. (2000) Assessments and accountability, *Educational Researcher* 29(2), pp. 4–16.

Linn, R. L., Graue, E. & Sanders, N. M. (1990) Comparing state and district test results to national norms: the validity of claims 'That everyone is above average', *Educational Measurement: Issues and Practice*, 9(3), pp. 5–14.

MacLeod, R. (Ed.) (1982) *Days of Judgement: science examinations and the organisation of knowledge in late Victorian England* (Driffield, Nafferton Books).

Madaus, G. F. & Raczek, A. E. (1996) The extent and growth of educational testing in the United States: 1956–1994, in: H. Goldstein & T. Lewis (Eds), *Assessment: problems, developments and statistical issues*, pp. 145–165 (Chichester, John Wiley).

McBride, J. R. (1998) Innovations in computer-based ability testing: promise, problems and perils, in: M. D. Hakel (Ed.), *Beyond Multiple Choice: evaluating alternatives to traditional testing for selection*, pp. 23–40 (Mahwah, NJ, Lawrence Erlbaum).

Mislevy, R. J. (1993) Foundations of a new test theory, in: N. Frederiksen, R. J. Mislevy & I. I. Bejar (Eds), *Test Theory for a New Generation of Tests*, pp 19–39 (Hillsdale, NJ, Lawrence Erlbaum).

Mislevy, R. J. (1996) Test theory reconceived, *Journal of Educational Measurement*, 33, pp. 379–416.

Morgan, R. (1989) *Analyses of the Predictive Validity of the SAT and High School Grades From 1976 to 1985*, College Board Report no. 89–7 (New York, NY, College Entrance Examination Board).

Noah, H. J. & Eckstein, M. A. (1990) Trade-offs in examination policies: an international comparative perspective, in: P. Broadfoot, R. Murphy & H. Torrance (Eds), *Changing Educational Assessment: international perspectives and trends*, pp. 84–97 (London, Routledge).

Nuthall, G. & Alton-Lee, A. (1995) Assessing classroom learning; how students use their knowledge and experience to answer classroom achievement test questions in science and social studies, *American Educational Research Journal*, 32(1), pp. 185–223.

Pellegrino, J. W., Baxter, G. P. & Glasner, R. (1999) Addressing the 'two disciplines' problem: linking theories of cognition with assessment and instructional practice, *Review of Research in Education*, 24, pp. 307–353.

Russell, T. A., Qualter, A. & McGuigan, L. (1995) Reflections on the implementation of National Curriculum science policy for the 5–14 age range: findings and interpretations from a national evaluation study in England, *International Journal of Science Education*, 17, pp. 481–492.

Sadler, R. (1989) Formative assessment and the design of instructional systems, *Instructional Science*, 18, pp. 119–144.

Selden, S. (1999) *Inheriting Shame: the story of eugenics and racism in America* (New York, NY, Teachers College Press).

Slavin, R. E. (1996) Reforming state and federal policies to support adoption of proven practice, *Educational Researcher*, 25(9), pp. 4–5.

Snow, R. E. & Lohman, D. F. (1989) Implications of cognitive psychology for educational measurement, in: R. E. Linn (Ed.), *Educational Measurement*, 3rd Edn, pp. 263–331 (New York, NY, American Council on Education/Macmillan).

Sternberg, R. J. (1997) *Thinking Styles* (Cambridge, Cambridge University Press).

Sutherland, G. (1973) *Policy-Making in Elementary Education 1870–1895* (Oxford, Oxford University Press).

Wood, D., Bruner, J. S. & Ross, G. (1976) The role of tutoring in problem solving, *Journal of Child Psychology and Psychiatry, and Allied Disciplines*, 17, pp. 89–100.

Wood, R. (1991) *Assessment and Testing: a survey of research* (Cambridge, Cambridge University Press).

Young, M. (1959) *The Rise of the Meritocracy, 1870–2033: the new élite of our social revolution* (New York, NY, Random House).

PART 2

LANGUAGE

CHAPTER 3

LANGUAGE TALK

Erica Burman

Deconstructing Developmental Psychology, London, Routledge, 1994

[L]inguistic diversity is an asset. It provides an opportunity for pupils to gain first-hand experience, knowledge and understanding of other cultures and perspectives. It also helps to prepare pupils for life in a multicultural society by promoting respect for all forms of language. Variety of language is a rich resource which schools should use as they implement the National Curriculum.

(Linguistic Diversity and the National Curriculum,
circular 11, National Curriculum Council, March 1991)

David Pascal, the [National Curriculum] council chairman has signalled that he not only expects teachers to correct children who fail to use Standard English in any lesson or in the playground, but also that they should use Standard English when talking to each other.

(Guardian, 1 April 1993)

Research on language is one of the most vibrant and theoretically dynamic areas in developmental psychology. The process of children learning to talk, of entering language, poses in miniature the wider questions of social development. Moreover, some critical psychologists (and those in other disciplines) look to these developmental psychological accounts as the route to elaborate a socially and materially based theory of mind. As we shall see, the research does not always live up to this expectation. In failing to do justice to the variety and complexity of what it means to talk, not only does the research reproduce the familiar division between individual and social that it set out to transcend, it also maintains social and educational inequalities. This chapter reviews the forms which research on early language development has taken, focusing particularly on current functional approaches, and raises problems with these traditions. As we shall see, the same themes [. . .] about the relations between the structuring of developmental psychology and the regulation of women arise in particular ways within child language research.

Turning to language

The 'turn to language' within the social and human sciences has brought about an attention to issues of interpretation. Social constructionists such as Harré, Shotter and Gergen challenged positivist psychology to recognise the constructed basis of its 'data' by focusing on the accounting procedures of both psychologists and their research 'subjects' (Harré, 1983). But, paradoxically, while these developments precipitated a 'crisis' in social psychology (Parker, 1989), they have brought new credibility and invigoration to developmental psychology: social psychology's 'crisis' has boosted developmental psychology's status and profile. Now, as a new variant of the developmental myth (which sees what comes earlier as causally related to later events), psychology looks to parent–child communication in the hope of finding a solid grounding for social relations. As we shall see, in a bizarre way, in portraying adult–child interaction as the prototypical forum from which to elaborate psychological theories of social relations, social constructionism has thus brought about a new respect for empirical developmental psychology, with little reflection on the contexts and assumptions of its production. While this pretends to provide a socially and materially based model of psychology, it actually legitimates inadequate and oppressive psychological theories.

At the outset we should note that textbook accounts of developmental psychological child language research have not reflected the preoccupations of the recent research literature. They describe the sequence from babbling to the emergence of the first words, to the use of single word and gesture combinations to convey sentence-like meaning ('holophrases') and the emergence of condensed word combinations that display a rudimentary or 'telegraphic' grammatical structure. However, a restricted analysis of the role of language emerges from these accounts. If acquisition of language is taken to mark the graduation from infancy into early childhood, the role of language as the constitutive medium for the rest of development is ignored. As a topic, therefore, language appears within textbook chapters or subsections on early childhood, as if, once they have 'cracked the linguistic code', children's language learning consists of a simple accumulation of grammar and vocabulary. Seen in this way, the significance of language is limited and static. This view suppresses attention to language development (after all what is it that develops?), and divorces language from its contexts of use. It also fails to theorise qualitative shifts in the structure and use of language in later childhood (such as those arising from becoming literate), and it ignores variations in use arising from social positions and relations. Variation therefore becomes identified with departures from a standard, a standard which is itself a false construction.

Foundations and formalities

In part the preoccupation with acquisition derives from the legacy of both biological and structuralist approaches to language. In many respects the difficulty of locating language development research in relation to other disciplines instantiates the general problem of the place of developmental psychology. Explanations put forward for language and its course of development draw upon neurology, biology, linguistics, history, sociology and anthropology – to name a few. Rather than choose between competing explanations, as in most of the language debates, a more appropriate question is to resolve what it is developmental psychological accounts of language seek to explain. If we are interested in the specific patterns individual children exhibit in learning to talk, then no single theory or disciplinary model will suffice, nor can they simply be combined in an additive way.

Chomsky's structural analysis of language emphasised the creativity and generativity of (children's) language use which, he argued, could not arise from mere imitation of linguistic role models. Chomsky distinguished between the surface structure of the grammatical features of specific languages and (what he called) the deep structure of what he regarded as a universal grammar that underlies and is presupposed by all languages. It is this deep structure that, according to Chomsky, makes possible the acquisition of specific languages through transforming or realising the universal deep structure into a specific linguistic form. But Chomsky treated the child as a separate, isolated symbol manipulator, making it so difficult to envisage how the momentous achievements of language could occur that he invoked an innate mechanism (a Language Acquisition Device) to account for it. His claims that this was biologically pre-programmed and was specific to language have been challenged on both counts (see below). Most developmental psychology textbooks [. . .] outline Chomsky's (1959) critique of Skinner as the specific form in which the heredity and environment debate over language development has been played out.

What Chomsky offered was a formal model of the structure of language. He was not, however, suggesting that this could be taken as a psychological account of how children learn to talk. This conceptual confusion, made within much developmental psycholinguistic research, is tantamount to a variety of psychological essentialism, whereby form is treated as (an empirically investigable) property of mind. As Michael Silverstein (1991) notes:

> Noam Chomsky has himself frequently been at pains to point out the incoherence of assuming that the formalist 'linguistic organ', to repeat his metaphor, has anything to do, in realtime psychological processual terms, with language production/comprehension as studiable by empirical means of observational and laboratory psychology. Yet, of course many others have . . . attempted to study linguistic competence, or its development in children, by direct means without understanding the cluster of commitments that place such competence, as a conceptual construct, beyond the realm of the normal evidentiary modalities of psychology.
>
> (Silverstein, 1991: 151–2)

His argument is therefore that formal models of language structure have no direct bearing on the understanding of how children develop and exhibit these features, and the attempt to base a psychological investigation on this conceptual foundation appears misconceived (see also Sinha, 1989).

Increasing awareness of the limitations of formal, structural models of language has prompted the emergence of approaches which focus on the functions of language in context. But before we join the rush from structural to functional approaches (which themselves retain elements of these problems), we should recall that the problem is not formalism in itself but rather it is psychologists' failure to appreciate the limits of its applicability. What structuralist accounts do offer is an analysis of the specificity of language as a representational system which goes beyond mere substitution for, or reference to, objects to set up new possible domains of meanings. They pave the way for according language a privileged status as a conventionally agreed, public, symbolic system which not only represents but also communicates (and, social constructionists would add, *constitutes*) meaning. Moreover, regularities noted in the structure of language learning across cultures may be due to communicative universals rather than biology. Specific and less helpful legacies of Chomsky's work include a focus on structure rather than context and the separation of language from general communicative processes.

Actions speak louder than words: from structure to function

Critics of the formal, structural models of language and their associated claims of innateness treat the emergence of language as having continuities with non-linguistic developments, also highlighting prelinguistic precursors to language. By these accounts, meaning is not uniquely linguistic but arises from action. This seems a more promising route for a more socially based theory of individual language development. These so-called 'functional' approaches, called functional because they focus on language use (rather than structure), draw on a number of theoretical resources which include aspects of the work of Piaget, Vygotsky and some influence of 'ordinary language' philosophy.

Firstly, they refer to Piaget's (1953) account of sensorimotor cognition which relates communicative abilities to the development of more general cognitive structures and changes. Children's abilities to engage in purposive behaviour, understanding of cause–effect relations and means–end relations are all required for language (to want to communicate, to appreciate that words can produce effects, and to use words as the tool to produce those effects, respectively). Hence it is argued that the entry into language draws on other representational abilities, such as deferred imitation (reproducing a behaviour in another context – which is required for the learning of words) and object permanence (maintaining a representation of an object without external stimulus – necessary for remembering the word label).

Secondly, accounts highlight how in learning to talk a child needs not only to use a particular label to refer to a particular object, but also to use conventional labels or words in order to participate in a language community. Language is, after all, not only a symbolic system, but, in order to function communicatively, its signs have to be shared and understood. Work like Carter's (1978) documents the route by which children initially exhibit variable vocalisations which are linked to specific gestures, and later come to use the same vocalisation no longer tied to a particular action. This conventionalisation of sounds relies on their increasing decontextualisation.

In tracing the specific continuities between activity and the emergence of language, Lock's (1978) analysis of the changing meaning and use of sounds and gestures suggests how they come to be increasingly separated from the action or event they initially accompanied, thus paving the way for their use as symbols. He illustrates this through the example of a child raising its arms. As a response that was once a simple association elicited by a wide variety of cues, this comes to function as a gesture which has some detachment from the immediate context of its exhibition, and ultimately functions not in simple anticipation of being, but as a *request* to be, picked up. In these terms, the developmental path is correspondingly seen as a move from intention to convention via the transition from action, to gesture, to symbol.

Thirdly, accounts which highlight the emergence of language as arising within and from action emphasise how language is used to do things. The 'ordinary language' philosophy of Austin (1962) and Searle (1972) points out that language is not only used to name or label things, but also has non-descriptive functions (such as excusing or commanding) which constitute events, or 'speech acts', in themselves. When we speak we not only utter words, but in so doing our words constitute 'speech acts' and as such produce particular effects within the person(s) addressed (such as feeling pleased when being complimented) (Austin, 1962). Applied to early language development, this has been used to suggest that a complex social as well as linguistic knowledge is involved in learning to communicate. Learning to speak is also learning how to *mean* (Halliday, 1975), with all the semantic and pragmatic, as well as syntactic, understanding this involves. In particular, Bates *et al.* (1979) suggest that this speech act model can inform the exhibition and interpretation of children's early language. Like their gestures, children's utterances are initially *treated* as intentional, that is, as intended to produce effects. By this kind of model, it is only later that children understand the use of vocalisation to affect the behaviour of others.

Useful as these functional approaches have been in moving away from idealised or context-free models of language, they nevertheless retain some of the latter's guiding assumptions which they simply supplement rather than revise. In particular, the mapping of linguistic form on to psycholinguistic function and the failure to analyse the context of the production of the linguistic material under study invite the criticisms that they simply lapse into the same problems as exclusively formal models but in an inadvertent way. Moreover, the very term 'functionalist' harks back to an evolutionary framework that invokes biological (and social) adaptation and instrumentalism that is at odds with the ethos of most of this work. Concluding his critique of contemporary forms of 'functionalist developmentalism', Silverstein (1991) warns against the incoherence of a 'developmentalist "functionalism" mixed with non-developmental formalism' (Silverstein, 1991: 152). He comments:

> The irony may be that, in contrast to the mysterious pre-experiential, *sui generis* formal structure of committed formalist developmentalism, 'functionalism' of this sort always seems to appeal to mysterious, pre-experimental formal-functional transparency, commonsense naturalness, and analogy.
>
> (Silverstein, 1991: 179)

Hearing voices?

Emphasis on the emergence of language through activity, continuity of linguistic and prelinguistic development, and the general character of the prerequisites for language as common to all representational processes sets the stage for broader discussions of the relationship between language and thought. This issue also connects with questions about the individual–society relation and the social construction of subjectivity. In particular, textbook coverage presents this in terms of the debate between Piaget and Vygotsky over the status of 'egocentric speech'.

Despite his tendencies towards formalism in other areas (which is itself a source of other problems; see [. . .] Rotman, 1978), Piaget is called upon by functionalist child language researchers seeking to locate language within the context of child action and interaction. While his views on the status of language shifted over time and were sometimes contradictory (Flavell, 1963), Piaget is generally seen as having regarded language as reflecting (rather than more actively constituting) more general cognitive and representational processes. In this his views differ from those of Chomsky: while for Chomsky language and thought are independent, Piaget's ideas are used to treat cognitive development as the precondition for language development. Development consists of individual action on the world which gives rise to cognitive structures and thus representation, including language. Language is therefore simply one of various representational systems. In contrast, Vygotsky theorised language and thinking as originating separately but as coming to control each other. He saw language as fundamentally communicative (rather than solely action-oriented) and therefore social. As Cole and Cole put it in their Vygotskyan-informed textbook:

> In Vygotsky's framework, language allows thought to be individual and social at the same time. It is the medium through which individual thought is communicated to others while at the same time it allows social reality to be converted into the idiosyncratic thought of the individual. This conversion from the social to the individual is never complete, even in the adult, whose individual thought processes continue to be shaped in part by the conventional meanings present in the lexicon and speech habits of the culture.
>
> (Cole and Cole, 1989: 296)

The two theorists offer correspondingly divergent interpretations of young children's speech. Piaget regarded young children's speech as egocentric, or unadapted to the communicative context. His model of the egocentric character of young children's thinking was based on his analysis of children's speech (Piaget, 1926), and he treated egocentrism as an inability to take into account the perspective of, or interests of, others, which in turn confirmed his view of the unsocialised character of the child. By contrast, Vygotsky understood 'egocentric' speech as functioning as an intermediary between activity and thought, as an external aid or prop to problem solving. In one celebrated example, a child who was drawing a picture of a car when the pencil broke commented 'It's broken' and went on to draw a broken car. Vygotsky interpreted this as indicating that egocentric speech had modified the course of the activity and therefore plays a more integral role:

> The child's accidentally provoked egocentric utterance so manifestly affected his activity that it is impossible to mistake it for a mere by-product, an accompaniment to interfering with the melody.
>
> (Vygotsky, 1962: 17)

Thought, far from existing separately from speech, is rather a development from it as 'inner speech'.

> The older children in our experiments behaved differently from the younger ones when faced with obstacles. Often the child examined the situation in silence, then found a solution. When asked what he was thinking about, he gave answers that were quite close to the thinking-aloud operation of the pre-schooler. This would indicate that the same mental operations that the pre-schooler carries out through egocentric speech are already relegated to soundless inner speech in the schoolchild.
>
> (Vygotsky, 1962: 17–18)

Bridges and byways

Vygotsky has been taken up by developmental psychologists largely due to increasing recognition of the abstracted and asocial character of Piaget's model. In some senses, the functions played by Vygotsky's work to warrant more 'social' accounts of development are not unlike those played by that of G.H. Mead. Put (over)simply, for Piaget development is from the 'inside out' – a movement away from non-verbal (what he called 'autistic') thinking, first to egocentrism and then to inner speech (as thought). In contrast, for Vygotsky development is from the 'outside in', that is, from the social to the individual. The individual is therefore the end rather than the starting point of the process of development. As a Soviet developmental psychologist, albeit one very much in touch with and influenced by European psychology (Valsiner, 1988), Vygotsky was working within a theoretical framework which challenged the individualism of Western psychology, and treated the individual as constructed through the social. Vygotsky's cultural-historical perspective emphasises the differential meanings and values of biological and environmental factors according to the specific context, and here context is understood as including the historical development of culture (Vygotsky, 1978).

This emphasis on the socially mediated character of development contributes to Vygotsky's current popularity with social constructionists such as Harré and Shotter (e.g. Cole and Cole, 1989; Harré, 1986; Shotter, 1973). Despite hopes of building a thoroughly social model of the individual, the full implications of Vygotsky's ideas have not yet been reflected in developmental psychological theories. This is primarily due to the conservative readings of Vygotsky's work, which treat it largely as an educational technology, with the Vygotskyan notion of 'zone of proximal development' (what a child can do with help as indicative of what she will shortly be able to do unaided) being used to inform theories of instruction (e.g. Newman *et al.*, 1989). Although it can be used in more radical ways (Newman and Holzman, 1993), in part this exacerbates already existing tendencies within Vygotsky's work, due to the tendency to reduce the social world to the inter-individual, with its focus on small group, or dyadic, interaction. As James Wertsch (1991) comments:

> What is somewhat ironic for someone interested in formulating a Marxist psychology, he made precious little mention of broader historical, institutional, or cultural processes such as class struggle, alienation and the rise of commodity fetishism.
>
> (Wertsch, 1991: 46)

The arguments about the limitations of infancy research [. . .] are just as relevant to discussions of child language research. As we shall see, theorists – whether philosophers, psychoanalysts or social constructionists – who see the roots of social life in the selective analysis of early caregiver–child interaction currently on offer therefore risk screening out some of the most important aspects of its contemporary organisation.

Game playing and routines

Together with the influence of Vygotsky, the work on precursors has led to a focus on the characteristics of action in which children are seen as embedded in that action as well as exhibiting it. The particular focus here has been on how adults support children's language learning. This includes the role of specific contexts in the promotion and support for children's early communication. The influence of these ideas is mainly felt in developmental psychology through Margaret Donaldson's (1978) notion of embedded thinking and 'human sense' and (explicitly drawing on Vygotsky's ideas) through Jerome Bruner's notion of 'scaffolding'. Bruner's work is the one which is best known in developmental psychology in the US as well as Europe.

According to Bruner's conceptual framework, the scaffolding of early adult–child interaction originates in adults' attribution of communicative intention to the child, such that even young infants are treated as if they are conversational partners (Snow, 1977). In addition, the structure of conversation is seen to be prefigured by the structure of rhythmic games many adults play with infants. These set up contingent patterns of interaction which are held to involve, frame and structure the children's actions: from initially simply reacting to the game, the child begins to show anticipation of, for example, being tickled, and finally starts initiating turns. The turn taking that Kaye (1982) saw within infant feeding [. . .] now takes on a key role in setting up the pragmatic structure of dialogue through the reciprocal roles set up by the alternation between speaker and hearer (Bruner, 1975/6). This reversibility of roles is regarded as prerequisite to the use of deictic terms, that is those aspects of language that can be interpreted only in terms of the context of the speaker, such as 'this/that', 'here/there' and (especially important for communication) the pronouns 'I/you'. Joint activity, as the context in which early communicative interactions take place, forms the basis for joint reference or attention. This is indicated by mutual gaze, and from an early age the following and directing of gaze seems to be a reciprocal system (Scaife and Bruner, 1975). Joint attention and action is said to pave the way for, and is mirrored by, the topic–comment structure that characterises children's earliest words, and this structure forms the building block for the subject–predicate structure of linguistic propositions (Bruner, 1983). Functional continuities are therefore traced between the structure of adult–child activities and the conceptual demands presupposed by language.

But not only are these continuities subject to the claims of implicitly harking back to formalism (as already reviewed), they are also rooted in the assumption that language learning lies in dyadic interaction. As Lieven [. . . 1994] points out, the idea that all language learning is a dyadic process is a very particular cultural construction that reflects the Eurocentric and class biases of child language research. While most children learn to talk in polyadic situations (interacting with more than one adult, and with other children), and this may play a much more active role in the process by which children pair utterances with meaning, child language research routinely screens out all language partners other than the mother and child (see, for example, the Hoff-Ginsberg quotation below). While there is little research on the effects of siblings on children's language, Barton and Tomasello [. . . 1994] report that young children's language is more complex when their environment includes mother and an older sibling than when they are with mothers alone.

Bruner uses terms like 'routines', 'formats' and 'scaffolding' to describe the regular and rule-bound patterns of caregiver–child interaction which, he claims, enable adults to mark important features of the action gesturally or vocally and eventually to induct children into doing so too. These form established, familiar contexts within which children can first exhibit initial babbling sounds, then more differentiated vocalisations and then standard lexical words. Within this account, play is central to language development, since games provide the context for joint activity with others and 'tension-free' opportunities for the exercise and exploration of abilities. Routines set up shared action formats with clear sets of expectations and actions. These in turn set up a restricted and shared set of meanings that can help to provide references to which more advanced communicative signals are attached.

The context of book reading has attracted particular attention as a valuable context for the teaching of vocabulary. Pictures in early reading books, as two-dimensional representations of three-dimensional objects, are regarded as aids to decontextualisation, and the interactional pattern of query, answer and feedback plus label exhibited by mother–child pairs is seen as a prototypical instructional process (Ninio and Bruner, 1978). The value accorded to this activity has been extended to include not only other aspects of language development but also success in schooling (Tittnich et al., 1990). But here we need to step back to reflect on the terms and claims being elaborated.

Labelling and name calling

Despite the widespread focus on reading as instantiating the principal properties for language teaching, there are difficulties in treating it as the ideal-typical model. In the first place, it is a highly specific activity which has a structure that is not characteristic of adult–child interaction elsewhere. Indeed it was selected *because* of its idealised presentation of labels. It seems that different caregiving contexts (feeding, bathing, playing with toys, reading) all give rise to different patterning of adult–child talk (Hoff-Ginsberg, 1991). As Kevin Durkin (1987) comments:

Since language acquisition is universal and picture-book reading is culture specific, the causal potential of this situation is uncertain.

(Durkin, 1987: 116)

Secondly, the priority accorded to play divorces language learning from other everyday caregiving contexts, and presents a sanitised and idealised picture of women at home with no commitments other than to devote themselves to extending their child's vocabulary. While child language research follows in the footsteps of the developmental tradition of observation, most work is based on intensive analysis of relatively few 'case' studies, in fact often taking the form of diary studies of the researchers' own children. But far from simply recording what happens in homes, studies isolate the objects of study from their everyday contexts by excluding all parties other than mother and 'target' child, failing to document situations representative even of the participants. For example:

Because the children in this study were too young and because the mothers did not work outside the home, their spending several hours together at home was not a contrived situation except for the occasional exclusion of an infant sibling who would otherwise have been present.

(Hoff-Ginsberg, 1991: 786)

Thirdly, learning to talk is not the same as learning labels. It has, however, been suggested that children learn words and only later realise that words are names through the insight that actions name objects (McShane, 1980). This therefore calls into question the exclusive importance accorded both to labelling and to the promotion of adult–child interaction around contexts said to aid label learning. This links up with the regulation of women through the extension of criteria for adequate childcare into educational provision (Walkerdine and Lucey, 1989), exporting the discourse of 'sensitive mothering' from affectional to educative domains [. . .]. Rather, we should see the equation of language with naming as a reflection of the formalist emphasis on words as object names and on language as a referential activity, mapping concepts onto objects. What this does is to set up precisely the dualist division between language and thought that it aimed to resolve. Theoretically then this assumption harks back to the priority accorded to thinking by the philosopher Descartes, treating thought as private and divorced from language and social relations. It also presumes that language represents truths, rather than produces its own realities. In this sense the model of language on offer is profoundly and naively realist – unlike the constructionist and discourse analytic work emerging in social psychology (Parker, 1992; Burman and Parker, 1993). Politically, the fetishism within child language research on language as object rather than relationship can be connected to broader analyses of commodity fetishism within capitalism. Communicative processes are reduced to words which are treated as utterances by individuals, abstracted from their relations of production. These words acquire value as indices not only of children's competence but also of caring and teaching mothers [. . .]. Practically, this research pressurises children by treating vocabulary as the primary index of language development and oppresses mothers by demanding that they should devote themselves to accelerating this.

Fourthly, the reduction of language development to labelling bleaches all emotions out of contexts of meaning construction. To the extent that developmental psychology subscribes to a representational theory of language, it imagines that emotions are irrelevant, and, where it *does* admit their importance, it allows only the 'nice' emotions through. In particular, accounts present an overharmonious view of parent–child interaction. Subtle mismatches are a routine and perhaps necessary feature of adult–child interaction. Mention has [. . .] been made [. . .] of the differential evaluation of maternal and paternal communicational demands on children. Durkin (1987) cautions against the tendency of research to produce an idealised, sanitised representation of parent–child interaction. In a similar vein, Ben Bradley (Sylvester Bradley, 1983; Bradley, 1989) provides examples of the ways in which infant negativity and aggression are screened out of observational studies only to reappear as originating from the mothers. Using a Lacanian psychoanalytic framework, Urwin (1982, 1984) demonstrates how contexts of adult–infant play involve negotiations over and attributions of assertion and pleasure as well as identification:

> these playful interactions also provide the adult with occasions for playing with power and control, producing the baby as all-powerful one minute, and perhaps undercutting this the next, through breaking the baby's expectations, for example. In some instances the interactions may be highly erotic or sexualized. Here one would anticipate that the sex of parent and infant would produce differences, though not altogether predictable ones. The mother, for example, may conjure in fantasy the potential lover who controls or entices her, or project herself as the passive recipient of the desires of another, or as active and potent, a positioning which may not be available elsewhere. As for the baby in the mirror stage, these kinds of interactions act as a support to the adult's own narcissism. This is one of the reasons why relating to babies can be so pleasurable.
>
> (Urwin, 1984: 294)

The variety of fantasies and positionings available within adult–infant interaction make it unlikely that this would be as consistent and stable as current formulations of functionalist-constructivist work assume.

> much has been made of mothers 'interpreting' their baby's actions as if they signalled specific intentions or carried a particular meaning as an explanation for related changes in the babies' communications. . . . But by itself interpretation carries no magical properties. First . . . posing the problem in terms of meaning outside getting inside by-passes the issue of the infant's contribution. Second . . . one would anticipate that adults would normally show more inconsistency, more ambivalence, or contradiction than these studies seem to presume. For example, competing demands on the mother, her conscious and unconscious desires, will affect her subjective positioning and hence the particular discourse through which she reads the baby's behaviour at any one time.
>
> (Urwin, 1984: 298)

Finally, this focus on play moves away from a functional to a competence model since it treats the child rather than the interaction as the unit of analysis, thus illustrating a tendency for socially mediated models to collapse into more traditional socio-cultural evaluation. The focus on conventionalisation and labelling can lead to a suppression of the multiple forms of variation. While class variation in child language and mother–child language is measured against norms which are themselves based on samples of white, middle-class mothers (Lieven, [. . . 1994]), nowhere is the selective and regulatory structure of research more evident than in its treatment of multilingualism.

Native tongues: making multilingualism puzzling

There are two main questions that are thrown up by an attention to multilingual issues: the first is why it is largely absent from mainstream accounts and the second is why it is not treated as a topic of interest rather than as a problem. In contrast to sociolinguistic work (e.g. Chaika, 1982), there is an almost overwhelming assumption within accounts of early language development not only that this is unilinear, but also that children learn a single language. Books with titles like *A First Language* (Brown, 1973) or the journal title *First Language* suggest that children learn to talk one language, or at least one language at a time. Even now accounts of language learning sometimes omit all mention of bilingualism or, especially, multilingualism. More usually it appears as an extra chapter or 'issue' in a text. The editors of a recent volume on bilingual development comment on how little cross-over there is between researchers with a particular interest in bilingualism and those working on language development (Homel *et al.*, 1987). Bilingualism is effectively excluded from research as if it were a confounding variable, with studies littered with comments in sample sections or footnotes such as 'All of the participants were white, native speakers of English; all the families were monolingual' (Hoff-Ginsberg, 1991: 785), and 'All were white, British-born two parent families' (McGuire, 1991: 147), with no explanation about why or how the cultural background or family composition was relevant to the research aims. Moreover, multilingual issues often do not figure even in current books specifically designed for an applied professional audience (e.g. Tittnich *et al.*, 1990).

From this we might suppose that speaking more than one language is unusual. However, whatever the multiple forms and definitions of being multilingual (Baetens Beardsmore, 1982), the majority of the world's population are bilingual or multilingual. Once again we see the Anglo-centric samples of white, middle-class, monolinguals – majorities within their own countries, but a fraction of the world's population – which form the basis of research coming to function as the typical measure of development.

Not only is coverage of multilingualism conspicuous by its absence, but where it is discussed it is often in a negative light. Indeed current research on multilingualism is combating a tradition which treated it as a cognitive and educational handicap (cf. Hakuta, 1986). This is no surprise considering the methodological procedures by which these 'findings' emerged. Early twentieth-century studies attempted to correlate bilingualism and IQ (itself a culturally biased test) by comparing monolingual and bilingual performance on verbal tests in the bilingual child's *second* language. Even now, multilingual children are disadvantaged in assessment contexts which rely exclusively on verbal tests rather than also using non-verbal tests (McLaughlin, 1984).

The negative view of bilingualism arises from the investigation of linguistic minorities within a dominant culture, in which poverty and racism often confound the language issues. As Skutnabb Kangas (1981) makes clear, the linguistic and educational tasks facing those whose home language is that of the majority or minority group are very different, and language-teaching programmes correspondingly should reflect this. For a native speaker of a high-status majority language, learning a second language is an optional extra that current theories consider is best done through immersion programmes. For children whose home language is that of a minority, they have to learn the dominant language in order to have access to educational and employment opportunities. It is not surprising that children who are not yet proficient in the language in which they are learning curriculum subjects fail to achieve to the level of their native speaker counterparts. Moreover, as well as the historical treatment of bilingualism as a remedial educational issue, language difficulties are often confused with communicational problems by teachers (conversely also creating problems in identifying genuine learning disabilities). These factors contribute to bilingualism being seen as a 'special educational' issue, which is reflected in the over-representation of cultural minorities in education sectors associated with low academic achievement (CRE, 1992). In turn this both draws attention from the problem of an irrelevant curriculum being responsible for minority children's educational difficulties and reinstates cultural dominance:

> Developing from the notion of cultural deprivation, the immigrant children's special needs in education soon became the acceptable approach to cope with their alleged cultural and linguistic deficiencies. Gradually public attention was diverted away from the content of the curriculum and its dubious relevance to non-English children and directed towards evidence for their presumed cultural limitations and linguistic handicaps. The assumption was that the discontinuity between these children and their school was the result of the malfunctioning of the children themselves, not the school.
>
> (Tosi, 1988: 82–3)

Current theories take the position that disadvantaged cultural minorities should be taught through the medium of their home language, thus supporting and maintaining their cultural background, as well as facilitating the transfer of linguistic and reasoning skills from one language to the other. But, as the tensions between theory, policy and practice in the quotes at the beginning of this chapter suggest, even now multilingualism is often portrayed within assimilationist and compensatory models as a necessary evil to facilitate transition to the majority language. (For critiques and opportunities of the National Curriculum see Conteh, 1992; Savva, 1990.) It is in this context that Anglo-US developmental psychology textbooks continue to discuss bilingualism in terms of the educational disadvantage of minority children, with specific concern expressed at levels of provision for, and low rates of success of, English language programmes.

The complexity of the issues raised by multilingualism are rarely acknowledged. Discussions are often just in terms of bilingualism, yet rarely if ever is one an absolutely 'balanced' bilingual, or 'balanced' in all spheres (and what assumptions underlie this drive towards equilibrium?), since factors such as frequency and contexts of use, as well as cultural and familial identifications enter the definition. The relationship between methods of instruction and status of the speaker as part of a linguistic minority or majority has already been mentioned. But in some circumstances the meanings and relative importance accorded to bilingualism are not connected with majority or minority status. Treatments of multilingualism should be seen in their historical and class contexts. While currently most discussions of multilingual issues in Europe and the US are cast within a political framework of assimilation of minority groups (in terms of aiming either to promote or to prevent this), historically it has been cultural élites who have been multilingual while the colonised or subordinate groups have been denied access to other languages as a means of social control (as has happened recently in South Africa). To take a (less extreme and) contemporary example, in Catalunya at the moment the regional state administration are repudiating Spanish as their first language and promoting Catalan, which is seen as expressing resistance to rule from Madrid (Torres, 1992). In general, questions of power are integrally linked with those of rights to language, and the fact that Anglo-US dominated psychological research assumes a monolingual language learner itself speaks volumes about legacies of colonialism and imperialism – of both the territorial and the cultural varieties.

Given the association between language and cultural identity, and the history of colonialism (in which erosion of indigenous languages played a role crucial to the maintenance of political control), there is clearly an obligation on language researchers in general to dissociate themselves from that tradition and address properly theoretically informed questions which the study of multilingualism demands. More recently, surpassing a grudgingly corrective model, positive views are emerging of the role and importance of being bilingual, in terms of more flexible cognitive and problem-solving skills and more general benefits of being less tied to a particular world-view (Skutnabb Kangas and Cummins, 1988). Far from treating bilingualism as a problem, some researchers have subjected *mono*lingualism to scrutiny:

> Monolingualism is a psychological island. It is an ideological cramp. It is an illness, a disease which should be eradicated as soon as possible because it is dangerous for world peace.
>
> (Skutnabb Kangas, 1988: 13)

This disease metaphor has recently been taken up by the Instituto Central America to promote language schools with the slogan 'El monolingualismo es curable' ('Monolingualism can be cured'). Interestingly, this carries different implications for different audiences. While it functions as an invitation to Europeans and North Americans to learn (Latin-American) Spanish, it is also an exhortation to speakers of indigenous languages to learn international languages so that they can participate in the world scene directly.

Speaking with feeling

Consideration of multilingual language development therefore illustrates a set of general issues relevant to, but tending also to be eclipsed by, accounts of language development. Recognising language as a source of cultural or national identification invested with great emotional significance may, and should, inform the analysis of the origins and functions of individual differences in children's speech. Moreover, in spite of Bruner's benign notions of 'scaffolding', the initial context for learning language can also involve emotionally highly charged and conflictual situations. Roger Brown (1973) reports from his longitudinal study of the language development of a child, Eve, that she first used the time adverbials 'after', 'then' and 'first' after they were explicitly directed towards her in negotiating her request that she be allowed to drink milk from her baby sister's bottle. Further, it was only a considerable time later that she used these words in other contexts. Lieven (1982) discusses this account as highlighting how language learning takes place in particular contexts and that early language use displays that history. The conclusions she draws are that there is no single route to learning language, and that it is a continuous process. Children differ in the ways they construct speech and what they use speech for.

Related to this, it is also clear that the cultural context in which the child lives enters into the structure and style of, as well as the actual, language she speaks. Urwin (1984) too argues that descriptions of language development are so focused on whether or when a child has achieved possession of a particular linguistic or grammatical structure that they fail to attend to the emotional significance of the

development under consideration. The cognitivist interpretation of a child's extension of her linguistic repertoire is assumed to be determined by the salience of the
objects or actions they name. But, more than this, common first words like 'more'
or 'gone' 'are precisely those which are particularly likely to mark the child's own
control within predictable practices' (Urwin, 1984: 312). Salience here necessarily
takes on emotional meanings that remain untheorised within current accounts. It is
clear then that a more differentiated approach to language development is necessary,
one that attends to contexts of language use as well as structure. [. . .]

References

Austin, J.L. (1962) *How to Do Things with Words*, London: Oxford University Press.
Baetens Beardsmore, H. (1982) *Bilingualism: basic principles*, Avon: Multilingual Matters.
Barton, M. and Tomasello, M. (1994) 'The rest of the family: the role of father and
    siblings in early language development', in C. Galloway and B. Richards (eds) *Input
    and Interaction in Language Acquisition*, Cambridge: Cambridge University Press.
Bates, E., Camaioni, L. and Volyera, V. (1979) 'The acquisition of performatives prior
    to speech', in E. Ochs and B. Schieffelin (eds) *Developmental Pragmatics*, New York:
    Academic Press.
Bradley, B.S. (1989) *Visions of Infancy*, Oxford: Polity/Blackwell.
Brown, R. (1973) *A First Language*, Harmondsworth: Penguin.
Bruner, J. (1975/6) 'From communication to language', *Cognition*, 3: 355–87.
Bruner, J. (1983) *Child's Talk: learning to use language*, Oxford: Oxford University Press.
Burman, E. and Parker, I. (eds) (1993) *Discourse Analytic Research: repertoires and read-
    ings of texts in action*, London: Routledge.
Carter, A. (1978) 'From sensorimotor vocalisations to words: a case study in the evolu-
    tion of attention-directing communication in the second year', in A. Lock (ed.) *Action,
    Gesture and Symbol*, London: Academic Press.
Chaika, E. (1982) *Language: the social mirror*, Rowley, Mass.: Newbury House.
Chomsky, N. (1959) 'A review of B.F. Skinner's *Verbal Behaviour*', *Language*, 35: 26–58.
Cole, M. and Cole, S. (1989) *The Development of Children*, New York: Scientific American
    Books/Freeman.
Conteh, J. (1992) 'Monolingual children and diversity: the space in the centre', *Multicultural
    Teaching*, 11, 1: 27–31.
Council for Racial Equality (1992) *Set to Fail*, Oxford: Council for Racial Equality.
Donaldson, M. (1978) *Children's Minds*, London: Fontana.
Durkin, K. (1987) 'Minds and language: social cognition, social interaction and the acqui-
    sition of language', *Mind and Language*, 2: 105–40.
Flavell, J. (1963) *The Developmental Psychology of Jean Piaget*, New York: Van Nostrand.
Hakuta, K. (1986) *Mirror of Language: the debate on bilingualism*, New York: Basic
    Books.
Halliday, M.A.K. (1975) *Learning How to Mean: explorations in the development of
    language*, London: Arnold.
Harré, R. (1983) *Personal Being: a theory for individual psychology*, Oxford: Blackwell.
Harré, R. (1986) 'Steps towards social construction', in M. Richards and P. Light (eds)
    Children of Social Worlds, Oxford: Polity.
Hoff-Ginsberg, E. (1991) 'Mother–child conversation in different social classes and com-
    municative settings', *Child Development*, 63: 782–96.
Homel, P., Palij, M. and Aaronson, D. (1987) 'Introduction', to *Childhood Bilingualism:
    aspects of linguistic, cognitive, and social development*, New York: LEA.
Kaye, K. (1982) *The Mental and Social Life of Babies: how parents make persons*, London:
    Methuen.
Lieven, E. (1982) 'Context, process and progress in young children's speech', in
    M. Beveridge (ed.) *Children Thinking through Language*, London: Arnold.
Lieven, E. (1994) 'Crosslinguistic and crosscultural aspects of language addressed to chil-
    dren', in B. Richards and C. Galloway (eds) *Input and Interaction in Language
    Acquisition*, Cambridge: Cambridge University Press.

Lock, A. (ed.) (1978) *Action, Gesture and Symbol*, London: Academic Press.

McGuire, J. (1991) 'Sons and daughters', in A. Phoenix, A. Woollett and E. Lloyd (eds) *Motherhood: meanings, practices and ideologies*, London: Sage.

McLaughlin, B. (1984) *Second Language Acquisition in Childhood*, Vol. 1, Hillsdale, NJ: LEA.

McShane, J. (1980) *Learning to Talk*, Cambridge: Cambridge University Press.

Newman, D., Griffin, P. and Cole, M. (1989) *The Construction Zone: working for cognitive change in school*, Cambridge: Cambridge University Press.

Newman, F. and Holzman, L. (1993) *Lev Vygotsky: revolutionary scientist*, London and New York: Routledge.

Ninio, A. and Bruner, J. (1978) 'The achievement and antecedents of labelling', *Journal of Child Language*, 5: 1–15.

Parker, I. (1989) *The Crisis in Social Psychology and How to End It*, London: Routledge.

Parker, I. (1992) *Discourse Dynamics,* London: Routledge.

Piaget, J. (1926) *The Language and Thought of the Child*, London: Routledge & Kegan Paul.

Piaget, J. (1953) *The Origins of Intelligence in the Child*, London: Routledge & Kegan Paul.

Rotman, B. (1978) *Jean Piaget: biologist of the real*, New York: Academic Press.

Savva, H. (1990) 'The rights of bilingual children', in R. Carter (ed.) *Knowledge about Language and the Curriculum*, London: Hodder & Stoughton.

Scaife, M. and Bruner, J. (1975) 'The capacity for joint visual attention in the infant', *Nature*, 253 (5489): 265–6.

Searle, J. (1972) 'What is a speech act?', in P. Giglio (ed.) *Language and Social Context*, Harmondsworth: Penguin.

Shotter, J. (1973) 'Acquired powers: the transformation of natural into personal powers', *Journal for the Theory of Social Behaviour*, 3: 141–56.

Silverstein, M. (1991) 'A funny thing happened on the way to the form: a functionalist critique of functionalist developmentalism', *First Language*, 11: 143–79.

Sinha, C. (1989) *Language and Representation: a socio-naturalistic approach to human development*, Brighton: Harvester.

Skutnabb Kangas, T. (1981) *Bilingualism or Not: the education of minorities*, Avon: Multilingual Matters.

Skutnabb Kangas, T. (1988) 'Multilingualism and the education of minority children', in T. Skutnabb Kangas and J. Cummins (eds) *Minority Education: from shame to struggle,* Avon: Multilingual Matters.

Skutnabb Kangas, T. and Cummins, J. (eds) (1988) *Minority Education: from shame to struggle*, Avon: Multilingual Matters.

Snow, C. (1977) 'Mothers' speech research: from input to interaction', in C. Snow and C. Ferguson (eds) *Talking to Children*, Cambridge: Cambridge University Press.

Sylvester Bradley, B. (1983) 'The neglect of hatefulness in psychological studies of early infancy', unpublished ms.

Tittnich, E., Bloom, L., Schomberg, R. and Szekers, S. (1990) *Facilitating Children's Language: handbook for child-related professionals*, New York: Haworth Press.

Torres, P. (1992) 'Els Països Catalans, des del Sud', *Demà, Periòdic per la Revolta*, 10: 10–11.

Tosi, A. (1988) 'The jewel in the crown of the Modern Prince: the new approach to bilingualism in multicultural education in England', in T. Skutnabb Kangas and J. Cummins (eds) *Minority Education: from shame to struggle*, Avon: Multilingual Matters.

Urwin, C. (1982) 'On the contribution to non-visual communication systems and language to knowing oneself', in M. Beveridge (ed.) *Children Thinking through Language*, London: Edward Arnold.

Urwin, C. (1984) 'Power relations and the emergence of language', in J. Henriques, W. Hollway, C. Venn, C. Urwin, V. Walkerdine, *Changing the Subject*, London: Methuen.

Valsiner, J. (1988) *Development Psychology in the Soviet Union*, Brighton: Harvester.

Vygotsky, L.S. (1962) *Language and Thought*, Cambridge, Mass.: MIT Press.

Vygotsky, L.S. (1978) *Mind in Society: the development of higher psychological processes*, Cambridge, Mass.: Harvard University Press.

Walkerdine, V. and Lucey, H. (1989) *Democracy in the Kitchen: regulating mothers and socialising daughters*, London: Virago.

Wertsch, J. (1991) *Voices of the Mind: a sociocultural approach to mediated action*, Hemel Hempstead: Harvester.

CHAPTER 4

IS 'EXPLORATORY TALK' PRODUCTIVE TALK?

Neil Mercer and Rupert Wegerif

K. Littleton and P. Light (eds) *Learning with Computers: Analysing Productive Interaction*, London, Routledge, 1999

Introduction

This chapter is about the effective use of talk by children as a social mode of thinking and as a medium for their education. It also deals with the role of the classroom teacher and the use of computer-based activities in school. We put forward a characterisation of an educationally productive kind of talk, derived mainly from observational research on children working together at the computer in classrooms. This characterisation involves the concept of *exploratory talk*, a concept which we will explain in due course. We also deal with some issues of methodology, suggesting that new tools are needed for the investigation of the role of spoken language and joint activity in collaborative learning: tools which address the ways that intersubjectivity is pursued through dialogue, and which allow applied educational researchers to evaluate the quality of collaborative activity. The results of a recent classroom-based study are used to illustrate the utility of our conception of exploratory talk as educationally productive talk, and to demonstrate how qualitative and quantitative methods of analysis can complement one another in this field of investigation.

Sociocultural theory and intellectual development

Our theoretical approach has roots in the work of Vygotsky. But although he is celebrated as the founding father of a psychology of learning and cognitive development based on intersubjectivity rather than individuality, Van der Veer and Valsiner (1991) and others have suggested that the extent of Vygotsky's theoretical divergence from the individualistic developmental perspective of Piaget may have been overstated. Vygotsky saw what he called 'higher order thought' as an individual property (Wertsch, 1985, p. 201), at best 'quasi-social' (Vygotsky, 1991, p. 41), and produced through the individual's 'internalisation' of language use. His focus on the individual, albeit the individual in social and historical context, is reflected in his explanation of key Vygotskian concepts such as the zone of proximal development in terms of the supportive intervention of adults in the learning of *individual* children. Vygotsky reported no research carried out in normal classrooms, and most of the neo-Vygotskian developmental psychology which has followed in his footsteps has avoided or ignored both theoretically and methodologically – the social and cultural realities of classrooms, places where one adult is responsible for the learning of many children, in which specific educational goals are being pursued, and in which children may often (as in British primary schools) work in pairs or groups. It therefore seemed to us that in order to research the educational role of talk between children working together in classrooms we needed to go beyond Vygotsky and the neo-Vygotskians both theoretically and methodologically, to develop analytic tools which treat discourse and joint activity as intrinsic features of the educational process (not merely as factors in some stages of individual learning).

Some current psychological perspectives on language and social action show the influence of ideas which have emerged since Vygotsky's death, such as the pragmatics of Austin (1962) and Grice (1975), ethnomethodology (e.g. Garfinkel, 1967) and the related recent development of conversation analysis (e.g. Drew and Heritage, 1992). Thus some 'discursive psychologists' now propose that participation in social interactions is not distinct from the internalisation of social interactions (Harré and Gillet, 1994; Edwards and Potter, 1992; Forrester, 1992). A similar paradigm shift can be seen in Lave's suggestion that we conceptualise what Vygotsky called 'internalisation' in terms of the 'process of becoming a member of a sustained community of practice' (Lave, 1991, p. 65). These ideas resonate with recent social anthropological research which describes culturally based language practices in schools and other cultural settings (Heath, 1983; Street, 1993; Maybin, 1994), and with the work of Swales (e.g. 1990) and other linguists working with the concepts of 'genre' and 'community of discourse' to explain the functional variety of language in use.

The various lines of research described above provide resources for the development of a sociocultural perspective on learning, cognitive development and educational practice (as discussed in more detail by Mercer, 1995). The application of such a sociocultural perspective to the study of children's joint activity requires an appropriate methodology, and here other traditions of research, especially those of educational researchers expressly concerned with the quality of children's educational experience, have a great deal to offer. The sort of analytical tools we have been seeking must deal with the diversity of social contexts of formal education in which groups of children work together in classrooms, around computers or otherwise, and yet also have sufficient general applicability that they can be used to draw general comparisons between different educational events, programmes and activities. But before we put our own toolbox on display, we will briefly outline some of the methodological issues and problems which shaped its contents.

Methodological issues in the study of collaborative learning

There has been a great deal of research interest in collaborative learning in recent years. It has been investigated in various ways, of which most can be crudely categorised as either (a) experimental studies in which subjects carry out specially designed problem-solving tasks, their interactions are analysed using some sort of coding scheme yielding quantitative data, and this analysis is related to outcome measures of subjects' success with the set task; and (b) observational studies of the talk and interactions of children working together in their usual curriculum-based classroom activities, in which researchers use qualitative, interpretative methods to describe and explain the processes observed, with little attention usually being given to outcomes. We will briefly review some of the methodological benefits and problems which these very different kinds of enquiry have generated, as they are relevant to our interests here.

Experimental methods based upon coding

There are methods for analysing talk and interaction in which talk data is reduced to coded categories which are then statistically compared. (There is in fact a well-established methodological tradition, commonly called 'systematic observation', of studying the classroom talk of teachers and children in this way: see for example Croll, 1986.) The particular set of categories employed varies according to the focus of the research study. Teasley (1995) offers a recent example of this type of method, applied to the study of collaborative learning. In Teasley's study the talk of children working in pairs on a problem-solving task was transcribed and each utterance attributed to one of fourteen mutually exclusive categories. These categories included such functions as 'prediction' and 'hypothesis'. Transcripts were coded independently by two coders and the level of agreement measured to ensure reliability. A count of categories of talk in different groups was correlated with outcome measures on the problem-solving activity in order to draw conclusions about the kinds of utterances which promote effective collaborative learning. There have been many other studies of collaborative learning which have used some version of this coding approach to analysing talk. King (1989), for example, used measures such as length of utterance as well as pragmatic functional categories to investigate variables affecting the success of collaborations. Kruger (1993) counted utterances considered indicative of 'transactive reasoning' and correlated their incidence with measures of the success of children's problem solving. Barbieri and Light (1992) similarly measured the incidence of plans and explanations expressed in talk, while Azmitia and Montgomery (1993) looked for talk features indicative of scientific reasoning. And, drawing on the neo-Piagetian concept of 'sociocognitive conflict' (Doise and Mugny, 1984; Perret-Clermont, 1980), Joiner (1993) counted the number and type of disagreements in interactions and related these to problem-solving outcome measures.

These and other studies using similar coding methods have produced interesting and valuable results. Their strength, as opposed to the qualitative methods discussed below, lies in their capacity to handle large corpora of data, to offer explicit criteria for comprehensively categorising the whole of a data set, to offer a basis for making systematic comparisons between the communicative behaviour of groups of children and to enable researchers to relate this behaviour to measures of the outcomes of collaborative activity. However, the use of coding methods in studies of talk and joint activity has encountered serious criticisms. Edwards and Mercer (1987, p. 11) note that in reports of such studies the coded analysis is often presented as a *fait accompli*, so that the original observational data is lost and the coded information appears as if it were the data; the prior interpretative analysis that generated the codes from the data is commonly obscured or forgotten. Focusing on the analysis itself Draper and Anderson (1991) identify four specific kinds of problem that coding methods must encounter in dealing with language in use:

1   Utterances are often ambiguous in meaning, making coding difficult or arbitrary.
2   Utterances may have – indeed often have – multiple simultaneous functions, which is not recognised by most coding schemes which normally involve the assignment of utterances to mutually exclusive categories.
3   The phenomena of interest to the investigator may be spread over several utterances, and so any scheme based on single utterances as the unit of analysis may not capture such phenomena.
4   Meanings change and are renegotiated during the course of the ongoing conversation.

It might be thought that using two or more independent coders and measuring their level of agreement overcomes the first problem. Indeed, coding schemes are often used in preference to other discourse analysis methods because they appear to offer a more 'objective' basis for validity claims. But, as Potter and Wetherell (1994) point out, this widely held belief confuses the reliability of a measure with its validity. That two or more coders can consistently agree on how to code different classes of ambiguous utterances tells us only that they have a shared way of interpreting utterances – it tells us little if anything about the validity of their way of interpreting utterances. If, as Edwards and Mercer (1987) suggest, such researchers frequently offer no examples of the utterances they have coded in their original discursive contexts, readers of their research reports have to take the validity of any interpretations entirely on trust. Moreover, Potter and Wetherell argue that talk is inevitably and necessarily ambiguous in its meanings because it is a means by which shared meaning is negotiated. Crook (1994) suggests that coding methods encounter particularly serious problems when applied to the study of collaborative learning, because the process under study is one of the development of shared knowledge, through language use and joint activity, over time. Because coding schemes for talk fail to capture this crucial temporal dimension of co-operative activity, and tend to reduce collaborations into atemporal 'inventories of utterances' (*ibid.*, p. 150), their value for such research is necessarily limited.

As mentioned above, coding schemes are often used to search for correlations between the incidence of some kinds of talk and particular outcomes of joint activity (for example, success or failure in solving problems). But while coding methods can show a statistical relationship between two events in time, i.e. that event B generally follows event A, they are not good at demonstrating causal relations between two events, i.e. how and why event A led to event B. For example, King's (1989) finding that there is a statistical correlation between the incidence of task-focused questions and group success in problem solving is interesting, and suggestive of a causal link; but that kind of analysis does not in itself explain how such a link is achieved. To explain such a relationship, a researcher would have to show exactly how asking questions helped the groups of learners to solve the problems.

Interpretative approaches to the analysis of talk and collaborative activity in classrooms

Douglas Barnes (Barnes, 1976; Barnes and Todd, 1978, 1995) was amongst the first researchers to devise an analytic method for studying collaborative learning in classrooms which was sensitive to context and to the temporal development of shared meanings. In contrast to the coding approaches described above, Barnes has used detailed classroom observation and the interpretation of transcribed talk of children engaged in normal classroom tasks to explore the processes through which knowledge is shared and constructed. His approach is allied to ethnography in that it incorporates intuitive understanding gained through discussions with teachers and children and participation in the contexts described. His usual method of reporting his research is to demonstrate and illustrate his analysis by including transcribed extracts of talk, on each of which he provides a commentary. Since Barnes's pioneering work, many other educational researchers have developed similar methods of discourse analysis, and some have applied them to the study of children's talk and joint activity (e.g. Lyle, 1993; Maybin, 1994; Mercer, 1995).

In their comprehensive review of methods for researching talk in classrooms, Edwards and Westgate (1994, p. 58) argue that the strength of Barnes's early work lay in making 'visible' aspects of classroom life which are easily taken for granted and so making them available for reflection and that the value of this can be seen in the recognition his insights gained immediately from many teachers. However, they also quote many critics of such 'insightful observation' methods (*ibid.*, p. 108). It is easy, they write, to pull transcript evidence out of context in order to illustrate a case already made and so to offer 'only the illusion of proof'. Stubbs (1994) similarly argues that while studies based on the presentation of fragments of recorded talk can be insightful and plausible they raise 'problems of evidence and generalisation'; it is often not clear how such studies could be replicated and results compared. While we are not convinced that Stubbs's own methods of sociolinguistic analysis are appropriate for the investigation of collaboration and the development of shared understanding, his criticisms of fragment-based discourse analysis are particularly relevant to our concerns here and all the more so because they lead him to advocate the use of computer-based text analysis.

Qualitative discourse analysis in the tradition of Barnes must rely on presenting short selected texts. Yet educational research often seeks generalisations, and evaluative comparisons, which cannot rest only on these samples. This is why, as Hammersley (1992) has argued, qualitative analysis can be effective for generating theories but not so effective for rigorously testing them. In contrast, the quasi-experimental research designs which are often associated with the use of coding schemes and other quantitative measures can offer explicit tests of hypotheses and systematic comparisons between the communicative behaviour and outcomes of 'target' and 'control' groups.

Because quantitative and qualitative methods have such different strengths and weaknesses, they might well seem to offer complementary approaches to the study of collaborative activity, approaches which could be combined in one research design. However, as Snyder (1995) points out in her discussion of integrating multiple perspectives in classroom research, different methodologies embody different views of the nature of meaning. To engage in the act of coding a text into a limited number of discrete categories, for example, would seem to imply that researchers view the meaning of utterances as relatively unambiguous, and that 'types' of utterance (as identified by their surface features) will always fulfil the same pragmatic functions independent of context. But, as noted above, many language researchers insist otherwise, arguing instead that the meaning and function of any utterance depends upon the way it is interpreted by participants in the collaboration and so is not only highly sensitive to historical and contemporaneous context but also necessarily always ambiguous (Potter and Wetherell, 1994; Graddol *et al.*, 1994; Mercer, 1995).

All these considerations suggest that any successful combination of such different kinds of method needs to be underpinned by a practical theory of discourse and the construction of knowledge, one which can enable researchers to transcend such positions and make a systematic, selective, complementary use of particular methods. It must enable researchers to move between the de-contextualised units measured by coding schemes and the highly context-sensitive descriptive accounts of the more qualitative approaches. It must deal with both processes and outcomes, allowing researchers to explore the development of intersubjectivity over time through actual classroom events, while also enabling them to make some useful generalisations about the process of collaborative activity in classrooms and its observable consequences.

Three types of talk

In this section of the chapter we will describe some findings of our continuing study of children's talk and joint activity. We will focus on the conventions, or 'ground rules', operating in talk in classrooms and consider how these ground rules affect children's use of language as a way of thinking together – language as a social mode of thinking (Mercer, 1995). Drawing on the various theoretical approaches and research traditions mentioned earlier in the chapter, we are attempting to provide an explanation of how children learn to reason in terms of their induction into genres of language use.

The work described emerged mainly from the SLANT project (Fisher, 1992; Dawes *et al.*, 1992; Mercer 1994) in which many hours of videotape of children talking together at computer-based tasks in British primary school classrooms were taken and analysed in search of patterns in the talk. In analysing this wealth of data, the SLANT team found it useful to typify three distinct types of talk. These (as presented by Mercer, 1995, p. 104) were as follows:

- Disputational talk, which is characterised by disagreement and individualised decision making. There are few attempts to pool resources, or to offer constructive criticism of suggestions. Disputational talk also has some characteristic discourse features – short exchanges consisting of assertions and challenges or counter-assertions.
- Cumulative talk, in which speakers build positively but uncritically on what the other has said. Partners use talk to construct a 'common knowledge' by accumulation. Cumulative discourse is characterised by repetitions, confirmations and elaborations.
- Exploratory talk, in which partners engage critically but constructively with each other's ideas. Statements and suggestions are offered for joint consideration. These may be challenged and counter-challenged, but challenges are justified and alternative hypotheses are offered. Compared with the other two types, in exploratory talk *knowledge is made more publicly accountable and reasoning is more visible in the talk.*

'Disputational', 'cumulative' and 'exploratory' are not meant to be descriptive categories into which all observed speech can be neatly and separately coded. They are nevertheless analytic categories because they typify ways that children observed in the SLANT project talked together in collaborative activities. We continue to find this typology a useful frame of reference for understanding how talk (which is inevitably resistant to neat categorisation) is used by children to 'think together' in class. The following three short sequences of talk, taken from SLANT data, illustrate something of the kind of variation with which we are concerned. All three sequences come from activities in which pairs or groups of girls (aged 10–11 years) were working together at the computer, writing dialogues between fictional characters. (Note: the fictional dialogue they generate is presented in inverted commas; any talk which was unclear is in brackets and additional contextual information is in brackets and is italicised. The transcripts have been punctuated to make the talk more intelligible to a reader.)

Sequence 1 shows talk which has some obvious 'disputational' features:

Sequence 1

Carol: Just write in the next letter. 'Did you have a nice English lesson'.
        (Jo typing on computer)
Jo: You've got to get it on there. Yes that's you. Let's just have a look at that. 'Hi, Alan did you have a nice English lesson. Yes thank you, Yeah. Yes thank you it was fine.'
Carol: You've got to let me get some in sometimes.
Jo: You're typing.
Carol: Well you can do some, go on.
Jo: 'Yes thank you'
Carol: *(Mumbles)*
Jo: You're typing. 'Yes thank you' 'I did, yeah, yes, thank you I did.'
Carol: You can spell that.
Jo: Why don't you do it?
Carol: No, because (you should).

In the next sequence, where two other girls are involved in this joint writing task, a more 'cumulative' style of talk is apparent:

Sequence 2

Sally: Yeah. What if she says erm erm 'All right, yeah.' No, just put 'Yeah all right.' No, no.
Emma: *(Laughs)* No. 'Well I suppose I could . . .'
Sally: '. . . spare 15p.' Yeah?
Emma: Yeah.
Sally: 'I suppose . . .'
Emma: 'I suppose I could spare 50p.'
Sally: '50?'
Emma: Yeah. 'Spare 50 pence.'
Sally: '50 pence.'
Emma: '50 pence.' And Angela says 'That isn't enough I want to buy something else.'
Sally: Yeah, no no. 'I want a drink as well you know I want some coke as well'.
Emma: 'That isn't enough for bubble gum and some coke.'
Sally: Yeah, yeah.

In the third sequence, three girls are working together. One of their fictional characters is a teenage girl, who has to explain to her angry father why she has stayed out so late. Here we can see talk which is more 'exploratory': ideas are explicitly debated, requests for ideas and justifications for challenges are made, and alternative suggestions are offered.

Sequence 3

Kris: 'I was only at the disco with Gemma.'
Fiona: No.
Helen: No.
Kris: That's too nice.
Helen: That's too um . . .

Fiona: Outrageous! *(laughs)*
Helen: Yeah.
Kris: It's got to be really silly.
(Brief interruption from some other children outside the group: the girls then resume.)
Fiona: What can we say?
Helen: Um, what is a totally innocent place?
Fiona: The park?
Helen: No, it's late, remember?
Fiona: Oh yeah.
Kris: Yes, exactly.
Helen: It's dark.
Kris: Oh no, she's not the brainiest of people, is she?
Fiona: Where, where can it be? Um, um, no, she could be staying at school.

The intellectual and educational significance of exploratory talk

Our conceptualisation of the different types of talk is generated by a theory of language and cognition which is essentially sociocultural, and which identifies a developed capacity for the joint creation of knowledge between contemporaries and across generations as a crucial and distinctive psychological characteristic of our species (Mercer, 1995). This theory incorporates a strong interpretation of the significance of *context*, which here means that we believe that talk which resembles any one of the three types – disputational, cumulative, and exploratory – may be socially appropriate and effective in some specific social contexts. But the theory also suggests that the kind of talk which (following Barnes and Todd, 1978, 1995) we call 'exploratory' represents a *distinctive social mode of thinking* – a way of using language which is not only the embodiment of critical thinking, but which is also essential for successful participation in 'educated' communities of discourse (such as those associated with the practice of law, science, technology, the arts, business administration and politics). Of course, there is much more involved in participating in an educated discourse than using talk in an 'exploratory' way: the accumulated knowledge, the specialised vocabulary and other linguistic conventions of any particular discourse community have to be learned, and account has to be taken of members' relative status and power. And such language is essentially situated and context-sensitive, not 'context-free' or 'de-contextualised' as some (e.g. Donaldson, 1978, 1992; Wells, 1986) have suggested. There are limits on how explicit members of a discourse community need to be to make meanings clear: they can share new ideas effectively enough by implicitly invoking the community's shared knowledge and understanding. The key judgement made by effective communicators within a discourse is about what needs to be made explicit to any particular audience on any particular occasion. Our conception of exploratory talk embodies qualities that are a vital, basic part of many such educated discourses. Encouraging an awareness and use of that kind of talk may help learners develop intellectual habits that will serve them well across a range of different situations.

Exploratory talk and effective collaboration in the classroom

'Exploratory talk', then, in the sense we use the term, is a communicative process for reasoning through talk in the context of some specific joint activity. Participants in exploratory talk offer reasons for assertions and expect reasons from others as they pursue some common goal. The ground rules for exploratory talk as a language practice facilitate the production and the critical examination of varied ideas in such a way that the proposal best supported by reasons will be accepted by all. Participants must therefore recognise each others' rights to participate and respect the potential validity of each others' contributions, and so there are implications for the social order of a collaborative pair or group. This requirement can be related to the results of studies of collaborative activity which have found that socially symmetrical pairs or groups reason together better and produce a better learning outcome than asymmetrical groups (Light and Littleton, 1994), and that friendship is an important factor in supporting explicit reasoning (Azmitia and Montgomery, 1993).

The cumulative educational implication of all these ideas is that pupils should be encouraged and enabled to practise exploratory talk in the classroom. There are, however, some difficult problems to be faced in transforming this proposal into educational practice. Barnes's early advocacy of the educational importance of talk of an 'exploratory' kind (Barnes, 1976; Barnes and Todd, 1978) found official endorsement in British education, in *The Bullock Report* (DES, 1975), through the National Oracy Project (Open University, 1991; Norman, 1992) and eventually in the orders for the National Curriculum (DFE, 1995). But recent studies of British primary classrooms indicate that children still have very little opportunity to engage in open and questioning enquiry through talk (Bennett and Dunne, 1990; Galton and Williamson, 1992). One reason for this could be the dilemma that teachers face in combining free and open discussions with their professional responsibility to teach a set curriculum. The role of the teacher in guiding students into explicitly rational discussions is a difficult one. The teacher–student relationship is, by definition, asymmetrical. Research has shown that teachers' questions commonly constrain pupils' contributions and discourage extended responses (Dillon, 1990; Wood, 1992). And as Douglas Barnes noted:

> the very presence of a teacher alters the way in which pupils use language, so that they are more likely to be aiming at 'answers' which will gain approval than using language to reshape knowledge. Only the most skilful teaching can avoid this.
>
> (Barnes, 1976, p. 78)

In modelling and coaching exploratory talk teachers have to simulate a situation of symmetry. How can this be done? The teaching of 'exploratory talk' in schools may also face a second problem. This is the issue of how well children can adapt and apply ways of talking or thinking that they have learned to the demands of subject-specific areas of the curriculum. We believe that the computer can help with both these problems.

The role of the computer

In their classic discourse analysis research, Sinclair and Coulthard (1975) proposed that the basic exchange structure for classroom discourse had the following form:

- Initiation (by the teacher)
- Response (by the pupil)
- Feedback (by the teacher)

It is generally accepted that the IRF exchange is a fundamental feature of teacher-centred education, and one associated with teachers' power to direct, shape and control the learning of students (see e.g. Mehan, 1979; Edwards and Westgate, 1994; Edwards and Mercer, 1987; Mercer, 1995).

Fisher's (1992) analysis of SLANT project data suggested that some types of exchanges occurring between students and computers also have an IRF structure (see also Crook, 1994, p. 11). She argued that this exchange type occurred where the computer–user dialogue structure was relatively 'closed' and directive. That is, the computer programme initiated exchanges (I) and acknowledged responses (F). Pupils' responses (R), according to Fisher, could be assigned to one of the following three categories:

1   a key press
2   a key press accompanied by an oral description of what is being done by the operator
3   some discussion of what should be done followed by a key press

This observation is valuable, and can be developed to serve our current interests. We wish to distinguish exchanges in which some discussion between children takes place from those in which computer initiations are merely followed by key presses or some other 'action-response'. We therefore find it useful to identify an exchange structure IDRF, as follows:

- I   –   Initiation (by the computer)
- D   –   Discussion (between the children)
- R   –   Response (by the children acting together)
- F   –   Follow-up (by the computer)

The IDRF structure combines two very different kinds of interaction: the IRF inter-action between computer and users, and the D which is discussion between the users. The IDRF exchange structure also potentially combines two very different educational genres. In terms of the basic IRF sequence, users are passive and the computer plays a role similar to that of a teacher who directs and evaluates the responses of learners. But the computer does not have the same social role and authority status as a teacher: children are much less inhibited in their discussions by its presence (Dawes *et al.*, 1992; Mercer, 1995). The computer–user interaction frames their discussion and can direct it towards specific areas and outcomes (Wegerif, 1996a, 1996b). In discussion mode, on the other hand, users are potentially active, deciding together what answers they will test out on the computer and so pushing the computer into the passive role of a learning environment.

To maximise the educational potential of group work around computers, children must talk together effectively before responding to computer prompts. For educationally valuable talk to occur there must be a switch in mode after the computer's 'initiation', putting active engagement with the software on hold while pupils reflect on their current situation and what their next move should be.

Applying the concept of exploratory talk

The SLANT project analysis suggested that the quality of children's discussion could be influenced by both the design of the software factors and the input of teachers. The largest amount of exploratory talk between children was observed when off-computer teaching of effective ways of talking together in groups was combined with the use of software which encouraged discussion (Mercer, 1994; Wegerif, 1996a). Other research (for example, that discussed by Crook, 1994 and Light and Littleton, 1994) supports the view that one of the most effective ways of using computers for teaching and learning in school is through classroom activities which integrate (a) the instructional and supportive involvement of a teacher with (b) software expressly designed to elicit discussion and (c) opportunities for pupils to work together without constant teacher supervision. In the next part of the chapter, we describe how these observations were used to design, implement and evaluate a small-scale experimental teaching programme with both off-computer and on-computer components. We will use this account to illustrate the points we have made about the need for concepts which can be used with rigorous 'objective' comparisons and generalisations while remaining sensitive to the cumulative and temporal nature of the development of shared knowledge in productive talk.

The intervention programme

The intervention programme consisted of a series of lessons focusing on exploratory talk (further information on this is given in Dawes, 1995; Wegerif and Mercer, 1996). A central feature of this programme was the promotion of a set of ground rules for exploratory talk which could be accepted by the children and then taught through modelling and learned through practice. The specific ground rules which the children and a teacher agreed upon were as follows:

Ground rules for talk

1 Everyone should have a chance to talk
2 Everyone's ideas should be carefully considered
3 Each member of the group should be asked: what do you think? and why do you think that?
4 Look and listen to the person talking
5 After discussion, the group should agree on a group idea

This list was displayed prominently on the wall and referred to throughout the programme. The programme also included software designed to support exploratory talk within curriculum areas. (More detail on the design of this software and the principles behind it can be found in Wegerif, 1995, 1996b.)

The evaluation

The evaluation of this intervention programme also applied the concept of exploratory talk in a way that combined classroom observation and detailed discourse analysis with the use of a pre- and post-intervention comparison. The pre- to post-intervention comparison used scores from a group reasoning test and pre- to post-intervention comparisons of the recording talk of videotaped groups of children doing this reasoning test. A control class of same-age children in a neighbouring school were also given the group reasoning test both before and after the intervention. The use of video made it possible to relate the talk to the answers given to particular problems in the test. With this research design it was possible to relate changes in test score measures to changes in linguistic features, in a similar way to many coding and counting studies; but it

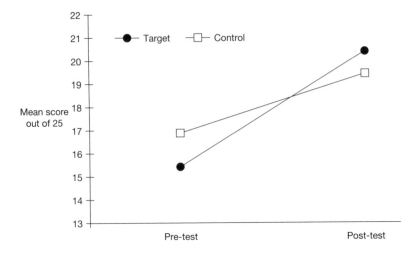

Figure 1 Pre- to post-intervention change in the mean scores of the target and control
classes on the group reasoning test.

was also possible to relate the talk of groups to their work on specific problems, as is
normally done in the qualitative discourse analysis tradition.

Assessing the 'educational productivity' of talk

Using problems from an established test of reasoning, Raven's Standard Progressive
Matrices (performance on which correlates well with educational achievement), we
devised a simple way of investigating the productivity of the children's talk. Graphical
problems from the Raven's test were given to the children who were asked to work
together in groups of three coming to joint answers. The same test was given to the
target class (who had received the training) and to the control class (who had not).
Children in both classes were in the same school year, and were 9–10 years old.
Each class was divided up into groups of three, and each group in each class was
tested at the beginning of the intervention programme and again at the end.

All the group scores in both target and control classes increased over the period
of the intervention programme. As illustrated in Figure 1, the target class group
scores increased by 32 per cent while the control class group scores increased by 15
per cent. The differences between the pre- and post-intervention test scores for all
groups in the target class were compared to the differences between the pre- and
post-intervention test scores for all groups in the control class and it was found that
this difference was significant ($Z = -1.87$ $p = 0.031$. One-tailed Mann-Whitney test,
corrected for ties).

An analysis of the quality of children's talk during the reasoning test

The test results show that the groups of children in the target class became more effective in solving problems together. However, these results do not in themselves provide
evidence of the intervention programme leading to the increased use of exploratory
talk by children. To find out if this indeed was the case, we analysed videotapes of

groups in the target class working together on the same reasoning problems during the initial pre-intervention test and during the post-intervention test. From these it was possible to isolate and compare the talk of groups successfully solving problems on the later occasion with their talk on the earlier occasion when they had failed to solve exactly the same kinds of problem.

It was generally found that problems which had not been solved in the pre-intervention task and were then solved in the post-intervention task (leading to the marked increase in group scores) were solved as a result of group interaction strategies associated with exploratory talk and coached in the intervention programme. The following two transcribed sequences (taken from the activity of one group) illustrate the findings of this discourse analysis. The problem they are facing is shown in Figure 2.

Group 1: pre-intervention talk in the reasoning test

John:	*(Rude noise)*
Elaine:	How do you do that?
Graham:	That one look.
All:	It's that. *(Elaine rings 1 as answer for A9)*
Elaine:	No, because it will come along like that. *(Elaine rings 5 as answer for A11)*
John:	Look it's that one. *(Elaine rings 2 as answer for B1)*

Group 1: post-intervention talk in the reasoning test

John:	Number 5.
Graham:	I think it's number 2.
John:	No, it's out, that goes out, look.
Graham:	Yeh, but as it comes in it goes this.
Elaine:	Now we're talking about this bit, so it can't be number 2 it's that one.
Elaine:	It's that one, it's that one.
Graham:	Yeh 'cos look.
Elaine:	4.
Graham:	I agree with 4. *(Elaine rings 4 as answer for A11)*

Commentary

In the pre-intervention task question A11 was answered wrongly in the context of a series of several problems which were moved through very rapidly. The other problems in this short series were answered correctly. Elaine's second utterance 'No, because it will come along like that' implies that one of the other two group members had just pointed to a different answer on the page. She gives a reason to support her view and this is not challenged. There is no evidence that agreement is reached before the answer is given. The group move on to the next problem. An examination of the full transcript suggests that the children do not take the task set very seriously and much of their talk is off-task.

In the post-intervention task episode much more time is spent by the group on A11. Two alternatives are considered and rejected before the right answer is found and agreed on. This is crucial. In the pre-intervention task example only one alternative was considered and rejected before a decision was reached. The structure of the problem is such that, to be sure of a right answer it is necessary to consider at

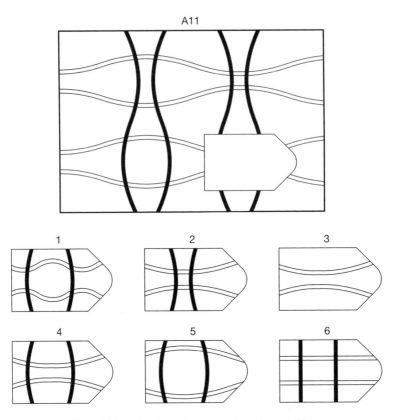

Figure 2 Problem A11 of the Raven's Progressive Matrices Test.

least two aspects of the pattern. John first spots the pattern of the dark vertical lines moving outwards and so suggests answer 5. Graham then spots the pattern of the lighter horizontal lines moving inwards and so contradicts John saying the answer must be 2. Just as Graham's reason means number 5 is wrong so John's reason means that number 2 is wrong. Elaine apparently sees this and so turns to number 4. Graham sees that she is right and points to confirming evidence on the page. In the context of John's vocal objections to previous assertions made by his two partners his silence at this point implies a tacit acceptance of their decision. Both episodes contain talk of an 'exploratory' kind: challenges are offered, reasons are given and the group appear to be working together. However, the second episode includes a much longer sustained sequence of exploratory talk about the same shared focus.

We had also wanted to know if computers could be used effectively to enable children to apply, develop and practise exploratory talk in curriculum-related activities. The effectiveness of the intervention in achieving this was assessed by analysing the talk of children doing the specially designed computer-based tasks on science and citizenship. This analysis (reported in more detail in Wegerif, 1995, 1996b) showed that children in the target class were able to apply exploratory talk effectively in dealing with these tasks. Moreover, we were able to make systematic comparisons between the talk of children in the target class (who had taken part in the off-computer component of the programme) and the talk of children in the control class (who had not) working at the computer, and between the talk of children working at the computer and those working on off-computer tasks. The evidence of this analysis supports the view that when children experience the off-computer teaching about talk combined with the use of the specially designed computer tasks of the programme, this is especially effective in both expanding the amount of discussion which takes place at the computer (the D of the IDRF exchange) and encouraging more exploratory talk.

Changes in word usage studied through the use of computer-based text analysis

The brief analysis of episodes of talk above illustrates how the concept of exploratory talk applied to educational practice through our intervention programme generated productive talk. This sort of analysis can show how, through applying the ground rules of exploratory talk which they have been taught, children find solutions to problems and construct knowledge together over time. But by being based on very short extracts of transcript, they face the criticism commonly made of ethnographic and similar interpretative studies, that it is difficult to draw general or comparative conclusions from them. One way to overcome this is to supplement interpretative studies with the use of computer-based text analysis programmes. Devised mainly for lexicographical work and literary analysis, such programmes allow researchers to investigate (amongst other things) the relative occurrence and co-occurrence (or 'concordance') of selected linguistic features through and across texts. One such programme has been designed by our Open University colleague David Graddol to serve the particular needs of discourse analysts; it is called !KwicTex (Graddol, [. . . 2000]). The use of this programme brings with it some of the advantages of coding schemes in terms of a capacity to deal with large amounts of transcribed talk data, to generate quantitative results and do so with rigour and 'objectivity', and yet it does so without the disadvantage of losing the contexts of the actual words spoken.

Used in conjunction with our characterisation of types of talk and with more detailed interpretative studies, a text analysis of linguistic features can show changes in the kind of talk being used over time and between conditions. For example, we used our qualitative analysis to identify a number of linguistic features which appeared to be indicative of exploratory talk. We then used !KwicTex to determine the relative occurrence of these throughout the data, and check whether or not their relative incidence was indeed associated with the use of talk of an 'exploratory' kind. We then compared their relative occurrence in the talk of the target class groups doing

Table 2 The relative occurrence of linguistic features associated with exploratory talk in the pre- and post-test talk of the three target-class groups

Linguistic features	Pre-test				Post-test			
	Gp1	Gp2	Gp3	Total	Gp1	Gp2	Gp3	Total
Questions	2	8	7	17	9	33	44	86
Because/'cos	12	18	9	39	21	34	40	95
So	6	3	1	10	6	5	7	18
If	1	1	0	2	13	8	14	35
Total words	1460	1309	715	3484	2166	1575	2120	5761

the reasoning test before and after the teaching programme. We found that the incidence of some of these features – children's use of questions, and their use of 'because' and 'if' – increased dramatically after the teaching programme (see Table 2).

The same sort of results were obtained for counts of word usage in talk around the software. It must be stressed that, unlike coding schemes, this kind of text analysis works with the actual words spoken and reveals their occurrence in their linguistic context. By looking at key words in their linguistic context, it is possible also to explore differences and changes in the ways in which particular words are being used. For instance, in the talk of one group the use of 'because/'cos' shifted from primarily co-occurring with 'look' (as an appeal to, say, information on a computer screen) to being found more in passages of elaborated verbal reasoning.

Exploratory talk revisited

The findings of the study we have described lead us to conclude that the combination of specially designed software and intervention programme succeeded in both expanding the amount of discussion and enhancing its quality; there was more talk, and more of it was 'exploratory'. Moreover, it seems reasonable to infer that increased use of exploratory talk was a key factor in improving the problem-solving performance of groups of children. These findings therefore provide some support for a sociocultural theory of language and cognition because they show that exploratory talk is indeed productive talk, in terms of children's capacity to solve reasoning problems.

However, the concept of exploratory talk and the three-part typology from which it emerged should not be judged as finished products. Rather, they are provisional and tentative attempts to provide the kind of concepts that are needed if we are to understand the ways that pupils' talk in classrooms functions as a social mode of thinking. Our intention is to relate talk to cultural practices, or genres, based on cultural conventions or ground rules. In this way we attempt to overcome the weaknesses of more usual qualitative approaches by providing a framework for comparison and evaluation. Nevertheless, we know that actual talk is not reducible to such typifications, and requires contextualised interpretation by some method of qualitative discourse analysis. We have therefore described how such a qualitative analysis can be combined with the use of computer-based concordancers or text analysis programmes to explore the way patterns of language use emerge and re-emerge in different contexts and at different times. It is worth noting that we have only provided a glimpse of what such text analysis programmes offer the discourse analyst.

Summary and conclusions

This chapter has described our attempt to develop theoretical and methodological tools for the investigation of collaborative talk, and in so doing we have elaborated the concept of a particular way of using language as a social mode of thinking, called *exploratory talk*. We have suggested that this concept, when embedded in a sociocultural theory of language and cognition, is particularly useful for the study of collaborative activity in educational settings. We described a role the computer might play in prompting and sustaining children's use of exploratory talk, and of doing so in a way that integrated the role of a teacher as a crucial mentor for children's initiation into culturally based discourse practices, and which also took account of curriculum constraints and imperatives. By combining selected qualitative and quantitative methods, we were able to evaluate the success of an experimental programme for encouraging exploratory talk. We find the results of our small-scale classroom-based research encouraging, not only because of the support provided for our developing theory and methodology, but also because the research indicates how classroom activities could be designed to deal more directly with the development of children's capacities for collaborating and using language to reason. At the time of writing, we are embarking on a new school-based project which will allow us to pursue this work on a much larger scale.

References

Austin, J. (1962) *How to Do Things with Words*, Oxford: Oxford University Press.

Azmitia, M. and Montgomery, R. (1993) 'Friendship, transactive dialogues, and the development of scientific reasoning', *Social Development* 2(3): 202–221.

Barbieri, M. and Light, P. (1992) 'Interaction, gender and performance on a computer-based task', *Learning and Instruction* 2: 199–213.

Barnes, D. (1976) *From Communication to Curriculum*, Harmondsworth: Penguin Books.

—— (1992) 'The role of talk in learning', in K. Norman (ed.), *Thinking Voices*, London: Hodder and Stoughton.

Barnes, D. and Todd, F. (1978) *Communication and Learning in Small Groups*, London: Routledge and Kegan Paul.

—— (1995) *Communication and Learning Revisited*, Portsmouth, NH: Boynton/Cook Heinemann.

Bennett, N. and Dunne, E. (1990) *Talk and Learning in Groups*, London: Macmillan.

Croll, P. (1986) *Systematic Classroom Observation*, Lewes, Sussex: The Falmer Press.

Crook, C. (1994) *Computers and the Collaborative Experience of Learning*, London and New York: Routledge.

Dawes, L. (1995) 'Team talk', *Junior Education* March: 26–27.

Dawes, L., Fisher, E. and Mercer, N. (1992) 'The quality of talk at the computer', *Language and Learning*, October: 22–25.

DES (Department of Education and Science) (1975) *The Bullock Report*, London: HMSO.

—— (1990) *Curriculum Guidance, 8*, London: HMSO.

DFE (Department For Education) (1995) *The Orders of the National Curriculum*, London: HMSO.

Dillon, J. T. (1990) *The Practice of Questioning*, London: Routledge.

Doise, W. and Mugny, G. (1984) *The Social Development of the Intellect*, Oxford: Pergamon Press.

Donaldson, M. (1978) *Children's Minds*, London: Fontana.

—— (1992) *Human Minds*, London: Allen Lane.

Draper, S. and Anderson, A. (1991) 'The significance of dialogue in learning and observing learning', *Computers and Education* 17(1): 93–107.

Drew, P. and Heritage, P. (eds) (1992) *Talk at Work: Interaction in Institutional Settings*, Cambridge: Cambridge University Press.

Edwards, A. D. and Westgate, D. (1994) *Investigating Classroom Talk* (second edn), London: The Falmer Press.

Edwards, D. and Mercer, N. (1987) *Common Knowledge*, London: Methuen/Routledge.

Edwards, D. and Potter, J. (1992) *Discursive Psychology*, London: Sage.

Fisher, E. (1992) 'Characteristics of children's talk at the computer and its relationship to the computer software', *Language and Education* 7(2): 187–215.

—— (1993) 'Distinctive features of pupil–pupil talk and their relationship to learning', *Language and Education* 7(4): 239–258.

Forrester, M. A. (1992) *The Development of Young Children's Social-Cognitive Skills*, New Jersey: Lawrence Erlbaum Associates.

Galton, M. and Williamson, J. (1992) *Group Work in the Primary Classroom*, London: Routledge.

Garfinkel, H. (1967) *Studies in Ethnomethodology*, Englewood Cliff, NJ: Prentice Hall.

Graddol, D. (2000) '!KwicTex – a computer-based tool for discourse analysis', *CLAC Occasional Papers in Language and Communications*, Centre for Language and Communication, The Open University.

Graddol, D., Maybin, J. and Stierer, B. (1994) *Researching Language and Literacy in Social Context*, Clevedon: Multilingual Matters.

Grice, H. (1975) 'Logic and conversation', in P. Cole and J. Morgan (eds) *Syntax and Semantics 3: Speech Acts*, New York: Academic Press.

Hammersley, M. (1992) *What's Wrong with Ethnography*, London: Routledge.

Harré, R. and Gillet, G. (1994) *The Discursive Mind*, London: Sage.

Heath, S. B. (1983) *Ways with Words: Language, Life and Work in Communities and Classrooms*, Cambridge: Cambridge University Press.

Joiner, R. (1993) 'A dialogue model of the resolution of inter-individual conflicts: implications for computer-based collaborative learning', unpublished Ph.D. thesis, IET, Open University, Milton Keynes.

King, A. (1989) 'Verbal interaction and problem solving within computer aided learning groups', *Journal of Educational Computing Research* 5: 1–15.

Kruger, A. (1993) 'Peer collaboration: conflict, cooperation or both?', *Social Development* 2(3): 165–182.

Lave, J. (1991) 'Situated learning in communities of practice', in L. Resnick, J. Levine and S. Teasley (eds) *Perspectives on Socially Shared Cognition*, Washington, DC: American Psychological Association.

Light, P. and Littleton, K. (1994) 'Cognitive approaches to group work', in P. Kutnick and C. Rogers (eds) *Groups in Schools*, London: Cassell.

Lyle, S. (1993) 'An investigation into ways in which children "talk themselves into meaning"', *Language and Education*, 7(3): 181–197.

Maybin, J. (1994) 'Children's voices: talk, knowledge and identity', in D. Graddol, J. Maybin and B. Stierer (eds) *Researching Language and Literacy in Social Context*, Clevedon: Multilingual Matters.

Mehan, H. (1979) *Learning Lessons: Social Organisation in the Classroom*, Cambridge, MA: Harvard University Press.

Mercer, N. (1994) 'The quality of talk in children's joint activity at the computer', *Journal of Computer Assisted Learning* 10: 24–32.

—— (1995) *The Guided Construction of Knowledge: Talk Amongst Teachers and Learners*, Clevedon: Multilingual Matters.

Norman, K. (ed.) (1992) *Thinking Voices: The Work of the National Oracy Project*, London: Hodder and Stoughton.

Perret-Clermont, A-N. (1980) *Social Interaction and Cognitive Development in Children*, London: Academic Press.

Potter J. and Wetherell, M. (1994) *Discourse Analysis and Social Psychology*, London: Sage.

Sinclair, J. M. and Coulthard, R. M. (1975) *Towards an Analysis of Discourse*, Oxford: Oxford University Press.

Snyder, I. (1995) 'Multiple perspectives in literacy research: integrating the quantitative and qualitative', *Language and Education* 9(11).

Street, B. (ed.) (1993) *Cross-Cultural Approaches to Literacy*, Cambridge: Cambridge University Press.

Stubbs, M. (1994) 'Grammar, text and ideology: computer-assisted methods in the linguistics of representation', *Applied Linguistics* 15(2): 202–223.

Swales, J. (1990) *Genre Analysis: English in Academic and Research Settings*, Cambridge: Cambridge University Press.

Teasley, S. (1995) 'The role of talk in children's peer collaborations', *Developmental Psychology* 31(2): 207–220.

The Open University (1991) *Talk and Learning 5–16: An In-Service Pack on Oracy for Teachers*, Milton Keynes: The Open University.

Van der Veer, R. and Valsiner, J. (1991) *Understanding Vygotsky: A Quest for Synthesis*, Oxford: Blackwells.

Vygotsky, L. (1991) 'The Genesis of Higher Mental functions', in P. Light, S. Sheldon and M. Woodhead (eds) *Learning to Think*, London: Routledge.

Wegerif, R. (1995) 'Computers, talk and learning: using computers to support reasoning through talk across the curriculum', unpublished Ph.D. thesis, Open University, Milton Keynes.

—— (1996a) 'Collaborative learning and directive software', *Journal of Computer Assisted Learning* 12(1): 22–32.

—— (1996b) 'Using computers to help coach exploratory talk across the curriculum', *Computers and Education* 26(1–3): 51–60.

Wegerif, R. and Mercer, N. (1996) 'Computers and reasoning through talk in the class-room', *Language and Education* 10(1): 47–64.

Wells, G. (1986) *The Meaning Makers*, London: Hodder and Stoughton.

Wertsch, J. V. (1985) *Vygotsky and the Social Formation of Mind*, Cambridge, MA: Harvard University Press.

Wood, D. (1992) 'Teaching talk', in K. Norman (ed.) *Thinking Voices: the Work of the National Oracy Project*, London: Hodder and Stoughton.

PART 3

MOTIVATION

CHAPTER 5

WAYS OF UNDERSTANDING MOTIVATION

David Galloway, Colin Rogers, Derrick Armstrong,
Elizabeth Leo, with Carolyn Jackson

Motivating the Difficult to Teach, London and New York, Longman, 1998

Introduction

Evaluation of children's successes and failures at school almost invariably includes reference to motivation. Sir Ron Dearing (1994) has recognised the importance of enhancing pupils' motivation within the national curriculum. School effectiveness research acknowledges the relevance of motivational factors such as self-concept, attitudes to school and to learning, behaviour and attendance as influences on school performance. Yet despite the political and educational consensus, the reality is that motivation is an elusive concept. The extent to which theoretical approaches to the study of motivation can help teachers to clarify the concept of motivation and use it in their professional practice is not altogether encouraging.

[. . .] motivation is not independent of context: to understand children's motivation we must take account not only of their own personality but also of the social psychology of teaching and learning. The distinction has obvious importance for teachers. Teachers cannot reasonably expect to exert a profound influence on the personality of each of their pupils, but they clearly do have an influence on their progress and behaviour at classroom level. To see the extent of this influence we can draw on three sources of evidence. First, teachers know from their own professional experience that *the same children* make better progress and behave better with some teachers than with others. Second, this professional knowledge is confirmed by research on school effectiveness (e.g. Mortimore *et al.*, 1988). Third, Ofsted has repeatedly drawn attention to unacceptable variation within and between schools (e.g. Ofsted, 1993). Motivation is unlikely to be the only factor in these differences, but it would be odd to deny its potential importance.

This chapter traces the development of ways of understanding motivation from its early focus on personality to more recent work emphasising how pupils may respond to the classroom environment. We will discuss the relevance of concepts such as ability and under-achievement, and conclude by arguing that more attention is needed to contextual influences on motivation. The interaction between these, for example teacher and school subject, and between these and pupils' individual characteristics, for example cognitive ability and educational attainment, needs to be elucidated.

Changes in thinking about motivation

P. Marsh *et al.* (1978) have reported an intriguing study of a group of pupils who would be difficult to teach by anyone's standards. The subjects were a group of adolescent boys who saw themselves as having been written off by the educational system, and the aim of the research was to describe their perspectives on schooling and on football. Any casual observer of classrooms containing these pupils might instantly sympathise with the teachers who had done the writing off. The pupils were badly behaved in the extreme, constantly challenged the authority of the teacher and disrupted lessons on a regular basis and with a great intensity. This disorderly behaviour was also evident when the same young people attended their local football team's home matches on a Saturday, for here too they would appear to the outsider to be committed to establishing disorder and disruption.

The book reporting this research achieved some notoriety in its time due to the argument it put forward about the appropriate ways of dealing with the problem of football hooliganism which at the time was a matter of growing public, media and political concern. The authors' basic premise was that the apparent disorderly behaviour was indeed just that, apparent, and was actually based on a clear and well-structured definition of what was and what was not acceptable. Intervention by other authorities, for example the police, was unnecessary and indeed likely to be counter-productive. Leaving to one side the furore caused by this latter recommendation, the significant point to emerge from the research was that Marsh and his colleagues were arguing that the pupils' behaviour within the classroom was guided by what they referred to as the need to mark out a 'moral career' for themselves. The notion of 'moral career' is clearly a motivational one. The thesis advanced by Marsh and his colleagues was that pupils are looking to school, in its formal sense, to provide them with an opportunity to develop a moral career, an opportunity to make their mark, to be noticed. If they conclude that school is not, in fact, going to make this possible because a moral career within the formal school context requires academic success and that does not seem to be possible, then they turn to an informal school culture of their own making for the same ends. [...] these difficult to teach pupils are not lacking in motivation: they may if anything be too well motivated and thereby unwilling to accept failure in the school system in a resigned way.

A similar argument has also been developed by David Hargreaves (1967, 1982). He argued that anti-school and anti-authority behaviour act as a self-protective strategy to maintain pupils' self-esteem. Like adults, children and teenagers need to feel valued as contributing members of a social group; if the school and classroom do not meet this need they will look elsewhere.

Implicitly, Marsh and Hargreaves both see motivational problems at least partly as a product of the failure of teachers to meet pupils' need for recognition. This view threatens the self-concept of teachers as competent professionals. Moreover, it recognises motivation as a potentially negative force; it is not just that some pupils may lack motivation; they may be actively motivated against the school's goals. Before taking the argument any further, though, we must look at some of the earlier conceptions of motivation. These were perhaps less challenging to teachers, but also proposed a more limited role for them.

Drive theories

Most famously represented by Hull (1943), the notion of drive was developed from the concept of instinct and was seen as the source of energy for human behaviour.

Hull distinguished between drive and learning. Whereas learning would explain the direction of children's behaviour, for example a mathematics or English task, drive would explain both the intensity and the duration of their behaviour, i.e. how long and how hard they concentrated on it. As drive was linked to basic needs, it would wax and wane as these needs were met to a greater or lesser extent. Hull also saw behaviour as being affected by habit, i.e. how accustomed children were to behaving in a particular way. Because drive and habit stood in a multiplicative relationship to each other (behaviour = drive × habit), it followed that a very low or zero drive level would ensure that no appropriate behaviour was carried out.

According to this theory, in as much as drive is equated with motivation, the pupil's progress is determined both by drive level and by the learning that takes place. The latter determines the direction and shape of the behaviour but the former the degree of energy that is exerted.

Such a mechanistic, or quantitative view of the nature of motivation does not preclude teachers from having a significant influence, but it is limited by the drive level brought into the learning situation by the pupils. The distinction between drive and learned responses is one that teachers often find attractive. According to the theory, their role is to encourage and facilitate learning by providing the right type of classroom learning experiences; the degree to which the pupils respond to these is likely to be determined by their drive level, or motivation. Drive has also been regarded as a 'pooled energy source' (Weiner, 1992) in that it is non-directive and does not necessarily lead to the channelling of behaviour in any particular direction. This energy source will be subject to variations over time, for example, a drive associated with hunger rises and falls in intensity with the passage of time since the last meal.

The teacher's role is then one of directing the available energies of the pupil. Teachers often talk of the need to channel a particular pupil's energies in appropriate directions or of having to re-establish an interest in an activity. These notions are close to the notions of drive and habit which were central to some of psychology's earliest contributions to an understanding of motivation. The prime point to make here is that the notion of drive serves to separate the notions of motivation and learning in a way that encourages teachers to regard learning as something which they might well be able to influence, but motivation, or drive, as something which is much more difficult for them to influence.

Differences between pupils are likely therefore to be understood primarily in terms of the *degree* to which they are motivated (the level of drive strength they currently possess) rather than the direction of that motivation. Motivation thus becomes a concept that can be readily used to divide the population of pupils into the relatively good and the relatively bad. Good pupils are those with strong drive levels who are therefore responsive to the teachers' efforts at teaching. The good teacher will be more effective at directing these energies in desired ways, but even the best teacher has no hope with the pupils who lack the basic motivating drive. These unmotivated pupils will be the difficult to teach. This drive-based conception of motivation perhaps helps us to understand why motivation often seems to be used to explain why some pupils are difficult to teach rather than why other pupils seem to be good learners. The presence of high drive levels provides the necessary, but not sufficient, conditions for learning to take place. Given a high drive level it is now up to the teacher to make the most of this. Learning problems for these pupils become a problem of ineffective teaching, classroom or school management. However, the presence of a lower drive level means that a necessary condition for successful learning has not been met. It is then likely that many teachers will see this as a problem that resides within the pupil, and one over which they themselves can have relatively little influence.

This does, however, raise a fundamental question about whether the assumed distinction between drive and learning is valid. An alternative conception sees motivation as an integral component of learning, with both being affected by the quality of teaching. Moreover, the development of other approaches will make clear that understanding motivation may be as important for high-achieving as for low-achieving pupils. These alternative conceptions enable us to see individual differences in motivation more in terms of how children adapt to a particular situation than in terms of their level of motivation. If this argument is valid, then the development of effective or adaptive motivation should be seen as an educational objective in its own right.

Behaviourism

Behaviourist theories offer one line of approach. The central tenet of behaviourism is that all motivation arises from basic drives, instincts or emotions in ways that are predictable. Therefore, teachers can plan what they wish children to learn and condition their learning accordingly; the question of whether children see the point in learning is irrelevant. From a behaviourist perspective, the amount of time children appear to be 'on task' indicates their level of motivation. An important implication here for teachers is that motivation is essentially an observable and quantifiable variable. Through appropriate reinforcement, teachers can increase children's motivation. Classroom interventions designed to increase 'on task' behaviour are readily accessible to teachers and presuppose teacher efficacy. However, Deci (1975) highlighted the potentially detrimental effects of external rewards and reinforcement upon children's interest in learning and continued (intrinsic) motivation to engage in classroom tasks. There is also evidence to suggest that competition for rewards promotes a surface approach to learning where children attempt to maximise their rewards at the expense of time and effort invested in learning (Condry and Chambers, 1978). That does not, however, imply that reward systems inevitably lead to a superficial approach to learning. Cameron and Pierce (1994) have documented circumstances in which they can have motivational benefits.

Another problem with this approach is that behaviour is *not* always predictable. Further, in its more naive forms it assumes that teachers condition children's learning, and overlooks the ways in which pupils and teachers interact in the classroom, with each influencing the other's behaviour. We need, therefore, to look at less deterministic approaches.

Towards qualitative conceptions of motivation

Achievement motivation

Probably the most influential advance on the early drive theories was Atkinson's (1964) concept of achievement motivation. Atkinson's theory retains a belief in basic tendencies which children bring with them to the classroom and which dispose, or rather predispose, them to respond in a certain way. These 'dispositional' elements are unlikely to be easily influenced by the actions of other people such as teachers. Atkinson did however introduce an important new element into his theory, namely that motivation can vary depending on how far success or failure are seen as relevant and important outcomes. In the classroom, success can be measured against a defined standard, and this provides a criterion for deciding whether or not that standard has been achieved. The standard can, of course, be set by pupils themselves or by teachers. This may affect the interpretation of success or failure but the basic definition of performance as successful or otherwise remains the same.

Any task requiring a pupil to achieve a certain standard can thus be seen to be double-headed. It offers both the prospects of success and the prospects of failure. Indeed, one cannot properly be considered to be present without the other. Any outcome obtained where failure literally was not possible could not be considered to be a success, and vice versa. Atkinson's theory recognised two different motivational strands each related to one of the two facets of achievement-related activity.

First, he considered the nature of a motive to succeed. He regarded this as a basic personality characteristic related to the degree to which individuals have a capacity to experience pride and other positive emotional reactions consequent upon success. Such feelings may also be aroused by the anticipation of a success experience. While everyone will experience some degree of pride following success, some will feel more than others. This extra capacity to experience such an emotion under appropriate circumstances leads to a greater degree of motivation to engage in activities which could provide a sense of achievement. It is important to note that this motivation is related to the intrinsic satisfaction consequent upon a success. It is not directly related to extrinsic sources of satisfaction, which may include the praise we receive from others, the approval of our peers, the increase in our pay packet or the gold star from the teacher. These all act as additional inducements.

Atkinson also recognised that people with the same disposition will not always respond in the same way to all instances of success. Some successes are more satisfying than others. (Again this is with reference to the intrinsic satisfaction that accompanies the success, not any extrinsic rewards that might be associated with it.) Similarly, the anticipation of some successes will be more likely than others to give rise to a positive desire to engage in the task. For Atkinson a key component in the determination of these differences between situations was the individual's perceptions of their chances of succeeding at the task. Atkinson expressed his theory as a series of algebraic formulae but essentially the perceived probability of succeeding has a direct effect on motivation and also has a further effect through influencing the value that would be attached to the success should it be obtained.

One of life's less kind tricks is to lead us to attach a greater value to those successes that we are less likely to obtain and a lesser value to those successes that we are most likely to obtain. The most readily obtainable successes are of course those on which pupils, and teachers, believe they have the highest chance of succeeding, and the least readily obtained are those they regard as the most difficult. On the one hand, then, we are most likely to find attractive a task where the probability of success is considered to be high. Such an easy task is attractive because it gives us the greatest probability of obtaining the successes that enable us to experience the good feelings that will follow success. Similarly we will be least attracted to those tasks where the chances of success are considered to be low. Difficult tasks can be unattractive because these naturally give us the lowest chance of gaining the good feelings that will follow success. However, a consideration of the value that would be attached to these different tasks complicates the situation. The easily obtained success offers a low value (essentially because it is easy to obtain) while the greatest value is attached to success in the hard tasks. There is a conflict, then, that has to be resolved. The resolution is obtained by looking for the point that gives us the most favourable combination of a decent chance of actually being successful and a decent value attached to the success should we get it. *Atkinson therefore predicts that the motive to success leads us to find tasks of an intermediate difficulty level most attractive.* These offer a reasonable chance of success, but as they are not too easy, they also offer a decent value. The success is still worth striving for.

However, this is only one of the conflicts with which we have to deal. The second major conflict arises from the motive to avoid failure which is itself associated with the prospect of failure. As stated above, any task which offers a genuine success opportunity must also, by definition, offer a prospect of failure. As Atkinson had argued for the existence of a basic dispositional force relating to the prospects of, and the experience of success, so he argued for a complementary dispositional force associated with failure. Pupils' motivation to avoid failure is essentially determined by the level of anxiety they experience as a result of failure. The greater the anxiety experienced as a result of failure, the less attractive any achievement-related situation will appear to be. The motive to avoid failure is so named because it is argued that the most effective way of reducing anxiety associated with failure is simply not to undertake achievement-related activities in the first place: *nothing ventured nothing lost.* A fuller account of Atkinson's work would demonstrate how pupils with a strong motive to avoid failure would generally be expected only to engage in achievement-related tasks where the extrinsic system of rewards and punishments provides a net inducement to start and remain engaged in an activity. Atkinson argues that individuals with a stronger motive to avoid failure than their motive to achieve success will be most attracted to tasks that are perceived to be either very easy or very difficult. The individual with the stronger motive to succeed, as noted above, is primarily attracted to tasks of intermediate difficulty level.

The easy and difficult tasks can be understood as being most attractive (or more accurately least unattractive) to the anxious pupil as they provide relatively safe havens. Anxieties can be reduced when confronted with a particularly easy task by the reassurance that failure (while it would be terrible if it did occur) is unlikely. The relatively difficult task also provides a haven of sorts in that while failure is clearly likely, the very difficult nature of the task provides a source of comfort. It cannot be so bad to fail at something that is clearly very difficult. We can see here that Atkinson is arguing that failures have their value too. Easy tasks carry a high negative value (failure under these circumstances is particularly damaging and anxiety provoking), while failures on hard tasks carry a low value (the sheer difficulty of the task itself provides some comfort).

This summary of Atkinson's work is perhaps sufficient to introduce some important notions that have guided our own thinking. First, and perhaps most importantly, it is suggested that individuals' first concern in achievement-related settings is not always with the prospect of gaining success. There are combinations of situations and people which produce an overriding concern with the need to avoid failure. This is an active motivating force in its own terms; it is not just the absence of a positive desire to be successful.

Second, dependent, as Atkinson sees it, on the relative strength of various basic motivational forces, people will be inclined to demonstrate either 'adaptive' or 'maladaptive' motivational patterns. The quotation marks around the terms adaptive and maladaptive need to be heavily emphasised. Adaptiveness is a relative concept. One's behaviour is adaptive in respect to some particular set of criteria. It is quite possible for behaviour to be judged as adaptive by one criterion but as maladaptive by another. Thus it is with motivation. Judged against the criterion of gaining success in the formal educational system, the predictions made for Atkinson's individual who is relatively high in the motive to achieve success are suggestive of an adaptive style. Being intrinsically most attracted to tasks of an intermediate level of difficulty is likely to lead to the maximising of learning over a period of time. Alternatively, the motivational pattern which makes these intermediate tasks the least attractive is likely to lead to patterns of behaviour that would be judged as maladaptive relative to the concerns of the educational system. A more detailed examination of some of the predictions derived from Atkinson's work further illustrates the compatibility of the two approaches. For example, Atkinson predicts that pupils with a relatively high motive to achieve are likely to want to move on to more difficult tasks following success and to backtrack to easier ones following failure. Pupils with the alternative motivational pattern, however, are predicted to display so-called atypical shifts under certain circumstances. This might, for example, involve moving to even more difficult tasks following a series of failures at tasks judged initially to be easy. Again the former pattern is likely to be widely regarded as more adapted to the needs and concerns of schooling.

However, adaptiveness can also be considered in terms of how it relates to criteria set by the individuals themselves rather than the school system. In this light, the actions and reactions of the pupil motivated to avoid failure can be interpreted as adaptive. If one's concern is to avoid the most personally damaging and anxiety-provoking aspects of failure then it is adaptive, under the right circumstances, to avoid tasks of intermediate difficulty level and to make atypical shifts after success and failure like the one described above. It is essential to remember that Atkinson is arguing that for such pupils the gaining of success, and the making of progress towards the gaining of success, is not the prime concern in achievement-related settings. If the most damaging consequences of failure, or the anxieties produced by the anticipation of failure, can be reduced or avoided altogether by taking action that perhaps severely reduces the chances of gaining success, then so be it. The risks involved in attempting success are simply perceived as too great to make the effort worthwhile.

The final point to note here is that Atkinson's predictions are not simply based upon the assumption that the motive to achieve success is low. Rather they are based on the assumption that these behaviour patterns are what follows when the need to avoid failure is high. Apparently maladaptive patterns of motivation are not just the result of a lack of motivation. Consequently, we should not assume that they will be found only in pupils perceived to lack motivation, nor that they will be dealt with by simply trying to increase motivation. It is the quality not simply the quantity of the motivational forces in operation that is important.

Before turning to the limitations of Atkinson's work we need to recognise that his approach was not the only one under development at this time. Richard De Charms (1968, 1976) developed a theoretical approach to motivation which also placed an emphasis on both cognition and the environment. De Charms starts with a nicely intuitive distinction between people acting as 'origins' or as 'pawns'. People acting as pawns feel themselves to be essentially under the control of external forces. They are pushed around by other people and it is those others who ultimately decide what happens, how it happens, and when it happens. When acting as an origin, however, individuals feel themselves to have control. One's actions originate from within oneself. In the following section of this chapter we shall see how these ideas have a number of similarities with the work of Weiner and the attribution theorists.

De Charms, however, is also concerned with the influence which different contexts may have on motivation. Some situations seem to induce pawn-like behaviour while others encourage a more origin-like response. De Charms is clear that it is better to act and feel as an origin rather than as a pawn. His school improvement work (De Charms, 1976) indicated that successful attempts to encourage origin-enhancing classrooms can have clear educational benefits for the pupils. This work also demonstrated that the effectiveness of his interventions was related to the extent to which he and his colleagues changed the context in which pupils worked and learned rather than seeking to influence directly the pupils themselves.

De Charms developed simple research instruments to assess the ways in which pupils perceive their classroom environments. [. . .] De Charms would argue that if pupils move from an environment which they perceive to be pawn inducing to one which they perceive as origin inducing, motivation should improve. Our own interest in this related to the motivational consequences of transfer from primary to secondary school and of different curriculum subjects. For present purposes, this very brief reference to the work of De Charms serves to remind us that the classroom clearly can and does make a difference to the sense of control which pupils see themselves as having. As we turn now to the work of Weiner it is important to bear this simple point in mind as it is too easy to interpret much of Weiner's work as suggesting that it is the cognitive processes of the individual which count rather than the context in which they work. De Charms gives us an early hint that both individual cognitions and contextual forces need to be taken into account.

Weiner and the attributional approach

Atkinson's theoretical ideas have proved to be important. However, Bernard Weiner's (1986, 1992) useful surveys of the available work on motivation have drawn attention to the failure of evidence fully to support Atkinson's claims regarding task preferences (Weiner was, incidentally, a previous PhD student of Atkinson). While there is widespread support for the prediction that tasks of intermediate difficulty levels will be preferred by pupils who are high in the motive to achieve success, there has not been much support for the prediction that pupils who are high in the motive to avoid failure will express preferences for tasks of either a very easy or very difficult nature. However, it does seem to be clear that they have a lower preference for tasks of an intermediate level of difficulty. In explaining the pattern of findings produced by this body of research Weiner suggests that the information pupils obtain from learning situations are more important in determining their responses than the particular dynamics with which Atkinson was concerned.

Attribution theory holds that people *attribute* causes to events. It is concerned with analysing the ways in which people make decisions about the causes of events, and the ways in which those decisions might then affect a person's reactions to those events. It is possible to regard attribution theorists as presenting people as engaging in a relatively dispassionate analysis of the causes of events in much the same way as a scientist supposedly studies the phenomena in which he or she is interested (Kelley, 1972). A series of rules, or at least rules of thumb, are acquired as a part of the socialisation process and the application of these rules to particular sets of information will largely determine the attributions made, which in turn will help to determine the way in which the event in question is responded to.

The experiences of success and failure will help to clarify the nature of these concerns (see also Rogers, 1982). Consider two pupils who have each experienced a failure which appears to the outside observer to be equal. One pupil decides that her failure has been caused by a lack of effort, while the other attributes failure to a lack of ability. Weiner's analysis of attributions and motivation suggests that the first will be more optimistic about the possibility of success in the future. Both have seen the failure to reside within themselves, but one has attributed the failure to the 'stable' cause of ability and the other to the 'unstable' cause of effort. Differences in the degree of stability of the reason for an outcome are held to affect expectations for the future. Stable causes give rise to more expectations for the same or similar outcomes. Unstable causes lead to greater uncertainty in terms of what is thought likely to follow. It would follow, then, that a pupil who typically attributes failure to stable causes and success to unstable causes will have lower expectations for the future than one who typically attributes success to ability and failure to lack of effort. This would be true even if the actual pattern of success and failure were the same.

Weiner's analysis includes a role for emotion in the determination of patterns of motivation. Emotions are held to be determined by the outcome itself (we feel good if we succeed and bad if we fail) but the precise emotion experienced can also be influenced by the attributions made for the success or failure. Failures attributed to controllable causes are more likely to give rise to feelings of guilt than failures attributed to uncontrollable causes. Successes attributed to internal causes, i.e. something to do with us, are more likely to lead to feelings of pride than are those attributed to external causes.

The classic Weinerian position sees the perceived causes of success and failure being arranged along a network of dimensions (internal–external, stable–unstable, controllable–uncontrollable, global–specific, leading to intended–unintended consequences) with the implications of the success or failure being influenced by the location, on this network of dimensions, of the causes held to be responsible. Motivational differences are thus seen to be the result of differences in attributions. The attributions operate on behaviour via their effects on expectations and affect or emotion. In this way Weiner's work can be seen to be a continuation of the themes begun by Atkinson. Motivation represents the interaction between expectations and the value attached to those expected outcomes. However, in Weiner's case the expectations and the affect-laden values are seen as being a product of the attributional judgements that have been made earlier.

Thus Weiner moves thinking about the nature of motivation more clearly into the cognitive arena. The fundamentals of motivational differences are to do with the ways in which available information is noticed, interpreted and analysed. People with clearly different histories of success and failure might then be expected to demonstrate different motivational patterns (the more failure has been experienced in the past the more likely it is to be attributed to a stable cause and therefore the more it will be expected in the future). However, the relationship between personal history and motivation will not be a perfect one as attributions are also seen to be influenced by the individual's vested interests and their particular perspective.

In a sense, then, the personality component that was a clear factor in the theoretical system of Atkinson is replaced in Weiner's system by an information processing component. Expectations and emotions are still regarded as important but they are now seen as being only an indirect response to a particular stimulus. The mediating role of attributions is held to be of paramount importance.

Implications for teachers

Weiner's work raises interesting questions about classroom practice. The distinction between the task and the individual pupil's reaction to the task is clearly crucial. Thus, feedback which focuses on the difficulty of the task, ('Yes, it *was* hard,'), without suggesting a way of overcoming the difficulty would be likely to discourage effort in the future. Similarly, praising children for effort may simply strengthen their belief that effort is futile: even though I tried I *still* failed. Clearly, well-intended encouragement can backfire. That, however, raises important questions about teachers' attributions.

Galloway (1995) has summarised evidence that home background appears to exert relatively little influence on pupils' behaviour in school *provided evidence is collected by independent observers*. Evidence based on independent observations using time- or event-sampling methods consistently fails to show higher rates of disruptive behaviour in schools with high rates of social disadvantage in pupils' homes than in schools with low rates. In contrast, when the research relies on teachers' reports, high rates of disruption are more likely to be reported in schools with higher rates of social disadvantage. This evidence supports the view that teachers may attribute behavioural and, perhaps, learning difficulties, to the children's home background. To the extent that home background is felt to be beyond the control of both teacher and pupil, the potential consequences for teachers' attributions for pupil achievement are clear.

Yet there is another even more damaging attribution which teachers can offer for pupils' progress, or lack of progress. This is that they lack the ability to do better. If children believe they have failed on a task due to lack of ability their motivation to attempt the same task again is likely to be low. If teachers believe children have failed due to lack of ability, *their* motivation to encourage children to continue working on similar tasks is likely to be low.

Ability and learning

The attributional account of achievement motivation emphasises the importance of attributions for success and failure being made to causes that vary along a number of dimensions. One of the more important of these dimensions is held to be that of stability. According to Weiner (1979), stable causes, such as ability, give rise to a more confident expectation of more of the same than do unstable causes, like effort. Ability is frequently given as an example of a stable cause and most adult readers are generally happy to accept this. However, one of the contributions made by Nicholls (1989) has been to demonstrate that this view of the nature of ability is not one that is shared under all circumstances. Nicholls argues that young children are less likely to hold the view that ability is stable. For the young child ability, like effort, is held to be extendible. In other words, abilities can increase with practice and application (Nicholls, 1978; Nicholls and Miller, 1983).

Nicholls' work on the concept of ability led him to argue that pupils can hold three relatively independent orientations to achievements. First, they vary in the degree to which they are 'task oriented'. Task orientation is concerned with a focus on achievement itself; it is reflected in feeling pleased when learning and progress have taken place. Progress and learning are valued for their own sakes, and not for the advantages which they might offer in other respects. Some of these 'other respects' would be covered by Nicholls' notion of 'ego orientation'. The highly ego oriented are concerned with their standing in relation to other people. Doing better than others is what makes one feel good about school. Progress is measured by how far ahead of the pack one might be, rather than by how much of the task has been accomplished and mastered. Finally, Nicholls identifies 'work avoidance'. Here what makes people feel good about their experience in achievement-related settings is getting away with doing as little as possible. Work avoidance is the orientation of the skiver.

Nicholls' work complements that of Carol Dweck who has been one of the most influential of the North American motivational researchers. She has been concerned particularly with an attributional analysis of learning difficulties, to which we shall turn shortly, but in doing this she has helped to develop further an understanding of the nature of other fundamental motivational processes. Dweck (1985) identifies two fundamental sets of cognitions which, she argues, help to exert a strong influence on the motivational patterns which will be displayed in a variety of contexts. These are to do with beliefs about the nature of ability, and the goals with which a person is operating.

Ability, argues Dweck, can be conceptualised within either an incremental or an entity framework. Within the incremental framework ability can be extended or increased, while within the entity framework it is perceived as fixed. At the same time a person can operate in achievement-related settings with either a learning or a performance goal. As with the orientations derived from Nicholls, the essential difference here is between a focus on the task itself and the progress being made with it, and a focus on one's performance in relation to other people.

The important point made by Dweck, for our current purposes, is that if children hold an incremental view of ability then pupils with either high *or* low levels of confidence in their present level of ability can display positive forms of motivation to meet their learning goals. However, if an entity view of the nature of ability is held then it is likely that *only* those with high levels of confidence in their ability will be positively motivated. This leads us to the notion of motivational style and the work for which Dweck is best known.

The notion of motivational style

It should be clear by now that there is no consensus about the nature of motivation, nor even about the most appropriate way to analyse it. The notion of motivational style is even more contentious. Often, when we have lectured to groups of academic psychologists they have been preoccupied with it to the exclusion of any consideration of the results of our work. Ames (1987) has defined motivation as the systematic, qualitative response which people make to the various challenges and threats arising from situations in which either success or failure is possible. The problem for some psychologists seems to rest with the word 'style'. They have a legitimate point in preferring to talk about motivational *responses*. Yet if, within a particular context, responses are systematic, as opposed to arbitrary or random, the notion of style does not seem unreasonable. We start by identifying two motivational styles emerging from the attributional analysis presented above.

Learned helplessness

Learned helplessness is probably the best known maladaptive motivational style. It's maladaptive from the point of view of the school system in that it is likely to prevent pupils from making the most of whatever talents they possess. From an attributional perspective (Abramson *et al.*, 1978) learned helplessness arises from a strong propensity to attribute a lack of success to a lack of ability, and to see that lack of ability as being beyond personal control. Seligman's (1975) initial formulation of learned helplessness sought to demonstrate the wide range of situations to which the concept could be applied, and it is a concept that clearly seems meaningful to teachers. Learned helpless pupils will simply assume that they are unable to complete tasks successfully. If work becomes difficult, the learned helpless pupil will abandon rather than increase effort. Attempts to cajole them into applying themselves in order to achieve success are as likely to be effective as similar attempts to cajole the very depressed person into cheering up. (Seligman sees acute depression as often deriving from learned helplessness.) Attempts by teachers and others to offer help and assistance are likely to be interpreted as confirmation of the pupil's essential lack of competence. Once established, the learned helpless pattern is one that can be very difficult to break as the pupil has a view of the world which overly assimilates events into the learned helpless schema. Attempts at enhancing this view through deliberately seeking to change attributional patterns, rather than changing the pattern of success and failure itself, have met with some success (e.g. Andrews and Debus, 1978; Craske, 1988) indicating the appropriateness of regarding attributions as an important part of the process.

Mastery orientation

The concept of mastery orientation has been examined by several writers but most notably by Dweck (1986, 1991; Dweck and Leggett, 1988) whose ideas have been introduced above. All too often this positive and adaptive form of motivation is simply referred to as a yardstick against which other less favoured and less adaptive forms of motivation may be compared. As mastery orientation is in many senses the ideal goal for the teacher, this relative lack of explicit attention is unfortunate. However, mastery orientation can be understood as a motivational style characterised by a concern with achieving success, rather than with avoiding failure, by reasonable and realistic levels of self-esteem, and by a concern to achieve mastery over the subject matter rather than a concern with showing oneself to be better than others. This latter point is important, for it has implications about the ways in which a lack of success at any point in the learning process will be interpreted. Failure is not necessarily taken to imply a lack of ability that precludes future success. Instead, present failure is more likely to be regarded as a temporary setback which can almost be seen as presenting opportunities for developing more effective learning strategies. It will be appreciated that the mastery oriented ought to be more likely to display task orientation and incremental views concerning the nature of ability.

Limitations

While the concepts of learned helplessness and mastery orientation have a certain validity for teachers, they also have limitations. It is not clear that lack of motivation does always result from lack of belief in one's own ability as assumed in the concept of learned helplessness. In a most eye-catching title for a research paper Nicholls (1976, 'Effort is virtuous but it's better to have ability') neatly sums up the problem. Yet as Covington (1992) has gone on to argue, it may not be the success or failure *per se* which are critical, but their implications for the individual's sense of self-worth. Success can indicate the presence of ability; failure can indicate its absence. In Western culture, ability is a highly valued commodity and a sense of self-worth will be tightly bound up with the degree to which one can believe in one's own competence. Clearly, if one experiences a relatively high degree of success the preservation of a sense of self-worth will be easier than if one does not. However, as Covington (1992) discusses at some length, much of the success that is available in the formal educational context is competitively defined. As demonstrated in a variety of research programmes (Ames, 1987; Slavin, 1983; Johnson and Johnson, 1987; Rogers and Kutnick, 1990; Kutnick and Rogers, 1994) the effects of competition on the interpretation of success are powerful. Competition seems to have the effect of increasing the degree to which success is linked with ability. Competition also decreases sharply the number of people who can experience success. In the classic zero-sum game there is only one winner, everyone else loses. Covington (1992) argues that even those who would seem to be enjoying a relatively high level of success can experience high levels of anxiety because they are not being ultimately successful, i.e. they are not number one.

However, is it not the case that those who are currently number two try harder? The traditional view of competition as a motivator, which seems to underlie much of government educational policy throughout the 1980s and early 1990s in both the UK and the USA, suggests that this is believed to be the case. However, Covington's analysis of self-worth suggests that it will not always be so. At this point we can return again to a consideration of the role of attributions, but from a somewhat different perspective to that developed by Weiner.

Weiner's own research (1986) has demonstrated how people are able to make use of *causal schemata* in making judgements about the role played by different possible causes in bringing about a given event. Two people have enjoyed an equal degree of success at the same task. One has tried harder than the other. Who has the most ability? All other things being equal we would find it hard to resist coming to the conclusion that the person who tried less hard had the greater ability. Ability and effort are related to each other in predictable ways. The more effort exerted in order to bring about a given level of performance, the less ability is assumed to be present. The truly brilliant generally impress us by apparently achieving their outcomes without needing to break into a sweat! It is due to our understanding of these relationships (even though the understanding may be only implicit rather than explicit) that Covington concludes that effort can sometimes be dangerous. If we and others know that a higher degree of effort has been exerted, then our outcomes may reveal more of our ability levels than would otherwise be the case. If the outcome equals success, then the personal implications are likely to be acceptable. However, if the outcome equals failure then it becomes difficult to avoid reaching the conclusion that our ability must be limited. When threats to a sense of self-worth are experienced, therefore, we are less likely to feel comfortable about exerting the maximum effort. The notion of maladaptive behaviour once again comes to the fore.

Self-worth motivation

As was argued above, however, in relation to the work of Atkinson, the notion of maladaptiveness has to be understood relative to the individuals' goals. If the goal is concerned with maximising performance and learning, then any feeling that the exertion of effort might be personally dangerous is clearly maladaptive. While Covington would recognise the Yerkes-Dobson law (which states that too much arousal, as well as too little may undermine performance) most teachers would argue that insufficient effort was a greater problem with the difficult to teach than too much. However, Covington is able to demonstrate that insufficient effort can itself be a consequence of too much arousal.

High arousal, or anxiety, inhibits performance in at least two ways. First, the anxiety itself can prevent pupils from demonstrating what they have, in fact, already learnt. However, anxiety can also bring into play self-defensive mechanisms where the reduction of effort, and possibly therefore the diminution of performance, is strategic. It is this strategic use of defensive mechanisms (which may include the reduction of effort, but also procrastination, aiming too high, aiming too low and cheating (Covington, 1992)) that is the essence of the self-worth motive. Behaviours which are maladaptive in respect to improving performance may be highly adaptive in respect to maintaining the best possible sense of self-worth when failure threatens. It is what one is aiming to do that counts.

In common with learned helplessness, the individual's confidence in their own level of ability lies at the heart of the self-worth motive. However, whereas learned helpless pupils have effectively abandoned hope as far as their ability level is concerned, individuals governed by the self-worth motive still have the belief that they have, or may have, the necessary degree of competence, but are not certain. This does, however, indicate a limitation in Covington's theory. It is based on the twin premises: (a) that academic success is a culturally valued commodity; (b) that pupils protect their self-esteem from possible failure to achieve academic success. These premises may not always be valid. For example, some pupils may reject the goal of academic success in order to maintain their status in their peer group, not because they fear academic failure. This argument has obvious links with the work of P. Marsh *et al.* (1978) and Hargreaves (1982) mentioned earlier in the chapter. Nevertheless, Covington's work has shown how defensive strategies may often be seen as necessary in order to protect self-esteem against the possible or anticipated effects of failure. We have also seen how these self-defensive strategies, including procrastination and devaluation of the task will often be maladaptive from the point of view of enhancing progress. Individuals who demonstrate the self-worth motivated style are simply those who most clearly demonstrate this particular pattern of behaviour and concerns.

Conclusions

This chapter has provided a brief review of the work of the principle motivation theorists, such as Atkinson, Weiner, Nicholls, Dweck and Covington. We have noted Nicholls' distinction between task orientation, ego involvement and work avoidance and have identified three motivational styles based largely on the work of Dweck and Covington: mastery orientation, learned helplessness and self-worth motivation. While these should not be seen as all-inclusive, the contrast between adaptive and maladaptive motivational styles, and also between two maladaptive styles, offers a useful framework for further investigation of motivation in relation to pupils who are difficult to teach. Before any further investigation is possible, though, we need to show that each of the broad types of theory with which the researchers have been associated carries with it a different set of assumptions about the nature of motivation.

Ames' (1987) definition (see p. 113) implies that motivational style is a recognisable and consistent pattern of responses to particular contexts. However, Ames' definition does not make it clear whether consistency is a function of the individual who is displaying the style, or of the context within which the display takes place. In other words style can be considered to be a property of the pupil, something which he or she brings into the situation and which determines the way in which they respond. The style would belong to the person and would be expected therefore to show some degree of consistency over different times and contexts. Alternatively, motivational style, although of course displayed by individual people, can be regarded as a prime function of the context. Some situations will be likely to produce a greater display of one style than others almost irrespective of the nature of the individuals within them.

Thirdly, both of the above may be possible and style is best understood as the outcome of interactions between individuals and contexts in which both play a part but in which neither on its own determines the styles displayed. Let us then briefly consider how the various broad theoretical positions discussed above might have a bearing on the nature of motivational style.

Possible bases for beliefs concerning the determinants of motivational style

1 Personality

The theoretical approach to achievement motivation provided by Atkinson and Raynor (1974, 1978) offers one starting point. As we have seen, Atkinson's position is one that gives a prominent role to the nature of relatively stable and deep-rooted personality traits. The adoption of the view that motivational style stems from differences in such personality traits would encourage the view that motivational style is established relatively early in life and is brought into the classroom with the child. There would be little that the classroom teacher could do to effect change. Such a conception would therefore imply relatively low levels of teacher efficacy with regard to developing more adaptive forms of motivation than those already found in the classroom. The child's home background and significant early experiences would be judged to be more important determinants of motivational style than would current school-based experiences. It should also follow that such a conception would lead to the view that a child would show similar motivational patterns across a range of situations, both within school and between school and non-school settings.

2 Information processing

Strongly associated with the attributional approach of Weiner is the view that motivational style reflects the culmination of the child's exposure to given patterns of information. When conceived in information processing terms, the attributional approach to motivation suggests that individuals will each apply essentially the same sets of rules (these being perhaps culturally determined) to varying sets of information. Persistent failure in an area of work will give rise to different attributions from those produced by intermittent or very occasional failure. Motivational style develops as the pattern of information, for example about success or failure, becomes more clearly established and begins to interact with the attributional process in order to produce a consistent and repeated response to given situations.

Such a conception suggests that changes to the pattern of information may succeed in producing changes to the underlying motivational style, but that one would have to attend to the attributional responses as well. For example, changing a teaching method to enable pupils to achieve success more frequently *may* produce a change in motivational style, but this will not necessarily be the case if they attribute their success to luck or to the task having been made too easy. However, it can be noted that the degree to which effective change is judged to be possible will depend largely on the extent to which the informational and attributional patterns have become entrenched. Thus, the more a teacher believes that a well-established pattern has been created, the less she/he is likely to accept that effective remedial action is possible. Secondary school teachers might therefore produce less optimistic prognoses in terms of the changes that might be possible than will primary school teachers. This in turn might help to produce greater stability in the motivational styles of older children in addition to the effects of an accumulating history of given levels of success and failure.

3 Goals and related cognitions

The final example of a basis for motivational style can be taken from the work of Dweck, Nicholls and Covington examining the various cognitions associated with

104 David Galloway et al.

the styles of learned helplessness, self-worth motivation and mastery orientation. These authors are each essentially arguing that the pattern of motivation displayed by an individual is a function of the beliefs and goals that a person adheres to *at that time*. The emphasis is important, for it is quite possible under this conception that the style of an individual will be subject to change as they move from one context to another. The work of H.W. Marsh and his colleagues (1988) in connection with the self-concept in educational contexts is increasingly making it clear that self-directed beliefs are variable across different parts of the education system. Specifically Marsh has argued that self-concepts in English need not have a simple and direct relationship to those held in mathematics. So it may well be with the self-beliefs and goals associated with motivational style. A set of beliefs that apply in one subject, or even more likely in one school or with one teacher, need not apply when the context changes. Such a view offers the prospect of concluding that motivational styles can indeed be influenced by the behaviour of teachers and offers a useful additional perspective on the debate concerning effective schools and effective teachers.

In essence, then, motivational style need not be characterised simply as a property of the individual pupil. Style *may* be a function of personality and may therefore, once established, become stable across different contexts. Style *may* be a function of the context itself, so while that context typically produces, say, a mastery oriented response, those same people will not necessarily carry that positive style with them into other, less favourable, contexts. Style *may* be the result of interactions between personal and situational influences. Individuals bring with them orientations which might dispose them towards one style or another, but those orientations are subject to the influence of the relevant parameters of the situation in such a way as to make the prediction of style on the basis of information concerning the individual alone a hazardous process. [. . .]

References

Abramson, L.Y., Seligman, M.E.P. and Teasdale, J.D. (1978) Learned helplessness in humans: critique and reformulation. *Journal of Abnormal Psychology*, 87, 49–74.

Ames, C. (1987) The enhancement of student motivation. In M.L. Maehr and D.A. Kleiber (eds) *Advances in Motivation and Achievement. Vol.5: Enhancing Motivation*. Greenwich, CT: JAI Press.

Andrews, G.R. and Debus, R.L. (1978) Persistence and the causal perception of failure: modifying cognitive attributions. *Journal of Educational Psychology*, 70, 154–66.

Atkinson, J. (1964) *An Introduction to Motivation*. Princeton, NJ: Van Nostrand.

Atkinson, J. and Raynor, J. (1974) *Motivation and Achievement*. Washington, DC: Winston.

Atkinson, J. and Raynor, J. (eds) (1978) *Personality, Motivation and Achievement*. Washington, DC: Hemisphere.

Cameron, J. and Pierce, W.D. (1994) Reinforcement, reward and intrinsic motivation: a meta-analysis. *Review of Educational Research*, 64, 363–423.

Condry, J.D. and Chambers, J. (1978) Intrinsic motivation and the process of learning. In M.R. Lepper and D. Greene (eds) *The Hidden Costs of Reward: New Perspectives on the Psychology of Human Motivation*. Hillsdale, NJ: Erlbaum.

Covington, M.V. (1992) *Making the Grade: A Self-worth Perspective on Motivation and School Reform*. Cambridge, MA: Cambridge University Press.

Craske, M.L. (1988) Learned helplessness, self-worth motivation and attribution retraining for primary school children. *British Journal of Education Psychology*, 58, 152–64.

De Charms, R. (1968) *Personal Causation*. New York: Academic Press.

De Charms, R. (1976) *Enhancing Motivation: Change in the classroom*. New York: Irvington.

Dearing, R. (1994) *The National Curriculum and its Assessment. Final Report*. London: SCAA.

Deci, E.L. (1975) *Intrinsic Motivation*. New York: Plenum Press.

Dweck, C.S. (1985) Intrinsic motivation, perceived control and self-evaluation maintenance: an achievement goal analysis. In C. Ames and R.E. Ames (eds) *Research on Motivation in Education. Vol.2: The Classroom Milieu*. London: Academic Press.

Dweck, C.S. (1986) Motivational processes affecting learning. *American Psychologist*, 41, 1040–8.

Dweck, C.S. (1991) Self-theories and goals: their role in motivation, personality and development. *Nebraska Symposium on Motivation, Vol. 38*: University of Nebraska Press.

Dweck, C.S. and Leggett, E.L. (1988) A social-cognitive approach to motivation and personality. *Psychological Review*, 95, 256–73.

Galloway, D. (1995) Truancy, delinquency and disruption: differential school influences. *Education Section Review (British Psychological Society)*, 19, 2, 49–53.

Hargreaves, D.H. (1967) *Social Relations in a Secondary School*. London: Routledge and Kegan Paul.

Hargreaves, D.H. (1982) *The Challenge for the Comprehensive School: Culture, Curriculum and Community*. London: Routledge and Kegan Paul.

Hull, C.L. (1943) *Principles of Behaviour*. New York: Appleton-Century-Crofts.

Johnson, D.W. and Johnson, R.T. (1987) *Learning Together and Alone*, 2nd Edition. Englewood Cliffs, NJ: Prentice-Hall.

Kelley, H.H. (1972) Causal schemata and the attribution process. In E.E. Jones, D.E. Kanouse, H.H. Kelley, R.E. Nosbett, S. Valins and B. Weiner (eds) *Attribution: Perceiving the Causes of Behaviour*. Morristown, NJ: General Learning Press.

Kutnick, P. and Rogers, C.G. (1994) *Groups in Schools*. London: Cassell.

Marsh, H.W., Byrne, B.M. and Shavelson, R.J. (1988) A multifaceted academic self-concept: Its hierarchical structure and its relation to academic achievement. *Journal of Educational Psychology*, 80, 366–80.

Marsh, P., Rosser, E. and Harre, R. (1978) *The Rules of Disorder*, London: Routledge.

Mortimore, P., Sammons, P., Stoll, G., Lewis, D. and Ecob, R. (1988) *School Matters: The Junior Years*. Wells: Open Books.

Nicholls, J.G. (1976) Effort is virtuous, but it's better to have ability: evaluative responses to perceptions of effort and ability. *Journal of Research in Personality*, 10, 306–15.

Nicholls, J.G. (1978) The development of the concepts of effort and ability, perception of academic attainment, and the understanding that difficult tasks require more ability. *Child Development*, 49, 800–14.

Nicholls, J.G. (1989) *The Competitive Ethos and Democratic Education*. Cambridge, MA: Harvard University Press.

Nicholls, J.G. and Miller, A.T. (1983) The differentiation of the concepts of difficulty and ability. *Child Development*, 54, 961–9.

Office for Standards in Education (Ofsted) (1993) *Curriculum Organisation and Classroom Practice in Primary Schools: A Follow-up Report*. London: Ofsted.

Rogers, C.G. (1982) *A Social Psychology of Schooling*. London: Routledge and Kegan Paul.

Rogers, C.G and Kutnick, P. (1990) *The Social Psychology of the Primary School*. London: Routledge.

Seligman, M.P. (1975) *Learned Helplessness: On Depression, Development and Death*. San Francisco, CA: Freeman.

Slavin, R.E. (1983) *Cooperative Learning*. New York: Longman.

Weiner, B. (1979) A theory of motivation for some classroom experiences. *Journal of Educational Psychology*, 71, 3–25.

Weiner, B. (1986) *An Attributional Theory of Motivation and Emotion*. New York: Springer-Verlag.

Weiner, B. (1992) *Human Motivation: Metaphors, Theories and Research*. London: Sage.

CHAPTER 6

TRACKING THE DEVELOPMENT OF LEARNING DISPOSITIONS

Margaret Carr and Guy Claxton

Assessment in Education, Vol. 9, No. 1, 2002

Introduction

There is a growing consensus that 'learning to learn' is, as Burgogne (1998) has put it, the 'ultimate life skill for the 21st century'. In a world of rapidly developing technology, radical changes in the nature of work, the melding of cultural and moral frameworks in pluralistic societies and the proliferation of lifestyle images and models in the media, it is an increasingly vain hope that education can provide young people with the knowledge, skills and understanding they will need to function well in adult life. As Boud (1998) asks, 'how can we teach what we don't know?' Instead, the focus of education is shifting to a concern with the development of aptitudes and attitudes that will equip young people to function well under conditions of complexity, uncertainty and individual responsibility: to help them become, in other words, good real-life learners.

Crudely, we might say that this real-life 'learning power' (Claxton, 1999a) consists of two inter-related facets: capabilities and dispositions. Capabilities are the skills, strategies and abilities which learning requires: what you might think of as the 'toolkit' of learning. To be a good learner you have to be able. But if such capabilities are necessary, they are not of themselves sufficient. One has to be disposed to learn, ready and willing to take learning opportunities, as well as able. Just as there is a big difference between being able to read and having the disposition to be a reader, being able to listen and being disposed to listen (Katz, 1993), so is there with learning more generally. Of course, the two aspects interact. Developing ability breeds success and success may tend, all other things being equal, to make a person more inclined to engage in the successful activity. Conversely, the disposition to learn about something tends to lead to greater engagement and thus to the development of ability. But the relationship is an uncertain one: capability does not always produce disposition, nor *vice versa*. Education for lifelong learning has, therefore, to attend to the cultivation of positive learning dispositions, as well as of effective learning skills.

But what exactly do we mean by 'dispositions'; what distinguishes those that are particularly crucial for learning; and how is their development to be tracked and evaluated? Considerable headway has been made in elucidating the nature of dispositions and their role in effective learning, and we summarise this work in the next section. But if the development of positive learning dispositions is to be accepted as a legitimate and feasible educational aim, then these ideas have to be translated into workable methods for their assessment. As Broadfoot (see for example Broadfoot,

1996) has continually stressed, forms of assessment, whether we like it or not, are the most powerful drivers of forms of teaching and learning. In the latter part of this paper we briefly review some of the currently mooted candidate assessment methods. We then offer an outline of a method for tracking the development of learning dispositions that overcomes some of the shortcomings of the other methods, retains and combines their strengths and sites the assessment of dispositions within a particular dimension of 'situated' learning.

What are dispositions?

Though the word 'disposition' is necessarily imprecise, it points very usefully at a domain of human attributes that are clearly different from 'knowledge, skill and understanding'. Katz (1988), for example, says that 'dispositions are a very different type of learning from skills and knowledge. They can be thought of as habits of mind, tendencies to respond to situations in certain ways' (p. 30). She cites curiosity, friendliness and being bossy as examples of dispositions. Carr (1999) suggests that dispositions also guide the interpretation and editing of experiences in characteristic ways, while Perkins (1995) argues that 'dispositions . . . are the proclivities that lead us in one direction rather than another, within the freedom of action that we have' (p. 275). Perkins *et al.* (1993), following Resnick & Klopfer (1989), argue that a disposition has three aspects: skill, inclination and sensitivity to occasion. For them, to be disposed to act in a certain way involves being competent to do so and aware of when it is appropriate to do so. Thus, Perkins and colleagues include the idea of 'capability' within the notion of disposition. However, particularly in the context of discussions about assessment, we prefer to keep the ideas of capability and disposition distinct. Perkins *et al.* (1993) also tend to take a very intellectual and scholastic view of learning, often treating 'learning' and 'thinking' dispositions as if they were the same thing. Again, we prefer to treat 'thinking' as one important kind of learning, but to hold open the possibility that there are other kinds of learning that do not depend on conscious rationality (Claxton, 1997).

Where are learning dispositions 'situated'?

There has been some debate recently about the validity of such generalisable personal qualities. Authors interested in 'situated learning', such as Lave & Wenger (1991) for example, argue that human behaviour is so situation specific that the traditional vocabulary of psychological traits and processes itself becomes highly questionable. And it is true that much research over the last 20 years has shown that human learning and performance are indeed much more situation specific than had often been presumed. What people appear to be able to do and how they seem to go about things is highly dependent on a large number of interwoven factors: how they are feeling, what the setting is, their presumptions about the task and their assessment of their own resources, to mention just some of these factors. Even small, apparently incidental details of the way a task is described or instantiated can make a huge difference to performance (see for example Donaldson, 1978; Ceci & Bronfenbrenner, 1985). And we know, too, that putatively abstract measures of general purpose 'intelligence', for example, do not in fact predict how intelligently people behave in specific, real-life settings (Ceci, 1996; Perkins, 1995).

But the fact that we cannot presume that people's traits are completely general does not imply that they may not vary along dimensions of relative 'disembedding' (Donaldson, 1978). Some dispositions may be, at least initially, tied very closely to particular kinds of tasks, contexts and materials. But this does not mean that, over time, they may not come to appear in an ever-increasing number of domains and situations. Whether they do so will, of course, depend on the practices and intentions of people who may be framing learners' environments and on the opportunities to deploy a particular disposition and thus discover its value. Some environments 'afford' and encourage the deployment of 'playfulness' or 'persistence', for example; others do not. One of the goals of 'education for real-life lifelong learning' must surely be the creation of educational milieux that afford such possibilities [see the discussion of Meier (1995) later in this chapter and, for example, Brown *et al.* (1993)].

Concomitantly, one of the considerations in designing methods for tracking and assessing the development of these dispositions must be the extent to which the 'testing' situation itself affords or invites the expression of the dispositions in question. As students progress through school, for example, successive classes may well be differentially 'friendly' towards the expression of different learning dispositions, thus creating the appearance, but only that, when dispositions are being tracked, of discontinuities in the individual's development. [Broberg *et al.* (1997) have documented the existence of such 'sleeper effects'.] Nor does the evidence for situated cognition imply that dispositions themselves remain fixed in their nature: they may well grow in their complexity and subtlety and in their likelihood of being deployed in situations that are novel or which cannot readily be pigeon-holed as belonging to any particular domain.

From a sociocultural point of view, learning is seen as transacted or 'jointly composed in a system that comprises an individual and peers, teachers, or culturally provided tools' (Salomon, 1993, p. 112; see also Wertsch, 1991). In this view, disembedding is more difficult to establish because the 'surround in a real sense holds part of the learning' (Perkins, 1992, p. 135). We are required to pay close attention to the relationship between the learner and the 'surround' and accept that the manifestation of learning dispositions will be very closely linked to the learning opportunities, affordances and constraints available in each new setting. Assessment from this position would focus on participation in relationships, activity systems or discourses or communities of practice (Wenger, 1998) where the learner edits, selects from and adapts artefacts, roles and scripts. Learning and performance take place within a shifting landscape and their assessment has to be concerned with the process of participation. If we are to think of education in terms of 'the development of mind', rather than merely as the accumulation of knowledge, skill and understanding (see for example Bruner, 1996), then terms such as 'disposition' usefully describe the most salient aspects of this developmental process.

Our idea of a disposition is therefore intermediate between the highly situated sociocultural notion of a community of practice and highly abstracted, decontextualised psychological notions such as 'ability' or 'intelligence'. A disposition is neither unique to a specific situation nor generally manifested across all situations. It is a tendency to respond or learn in a certain way that is somewhat, but incompletely, 'disembedded' from particular constellations of personal, social and material detail. Specifically, on the basis of the above considerations, we argue that dispositions may vary in their robustness (the extent to which they persist as situations become less familiar or auspicious and spontaneously generalise across different domains of experience) and their sophistication (how rich and differentiated they have become). By defining dispositions in this developmental fashion, we may be able to get a more powerful handle on their assessment.

What are the key learning dispositions?

Not all dispositions are equally relevant to learning power. The inclination to be bossy, for example, is probably less crucial to learning in general than the tendency to persist with learning in the face of confusion or frustration. However, there is no clear agreement about what the 'key' learning dispositions might be. Several authors have offered candidate lists of learning dispositions. Bronfenbrenner (1979) describes 'educational competence', for example, in terms of dispositions to think, to persist in tasks, to give opinions and contribute ideas and to work collaboratively. Goleman's (1996) list of what he describes as the seven key ingredients for the capacity to know 'how to learn' (p. 193) comprises disposition-like terms: confidence, curiosity, intentionality, self-control, relatedness, communication and cooperation. Defining a disposition as a tendency to edit, select, adapt and respond to the environment in a recurrent, characteristic kind of way, we have separately produced our own lists of current favourites. Carr (1999) derives a number of learning dispositions from the strands of Te Whaariki, the New Zealand national early childhood curriculum, which she refers to as courage, curiosity, playfulness, perseverance, confidence and responsibility. Claxton (1999b) describes what he refers to as 'learnacy' (by analogy with literacy and numeracy) as comprising curiosity, mindfulness, selectivity, resilience, experimentation, reflection, opportunism and conviviality. Clearly there is both overlap and diversity between these preliminary attempts to identify 'key' learning dispositions.

Part of the problem is that the above candidate dispositions are at different levels of generality. Some might properly be seen as subordinate to or component parts of others. Katz (1993) reminds us that for a list of learning dispositions to be of practical utility it should be manageable.

> Much research is needed to determine which dispositions merit attention, and whether dispositions of a general or specific focus should be addressed by educational goals. If the desirable dispositions listed among the goals are very specific, the list is likely to be unmanageably long. ... However if dispositional goals are too general, they become too difficult to observe and therefore to assess. Ideally, educational goals should include dispositions that strike an optimal balance between generality and specificity.
>
> (Katz, 1993, p. 20)

It is also the case that, while we might be able to draw conceptual distinctions between different learning dispositions, in practice they tend to be dynamically interwoven and therefore hard to tease apart. Furthermore, and more fundamentally, any list of learning dispositions reflects a particular set of culturally determined values. In Carr's case, for example, dispositions are firmly linked to a bicultural early childhood curriculum that is specifically appropriate to the history, culture and geographical location of New Zealand (New Zealand Ministry of Education, 1996).

In this chapter we make no claim to be offering a definitive array of learning dispositions. Instead, we have chosen three that seem to us to be prime candidates to underpin and illustrate our discussion of assessment. In selecting these three learning dispositions, we have favoured ones which seem to us to be: (i) at a suitably intermediate level of generality; (ii) relatively independent of each other; (iii) commonly afforded by educational settings; (iv) useful from the point of view of exploring the 'assessment question'. For example, we see 'curiosity' as a portmanteau disposition, one which emerges from a conjunction of others, and too general for the purposes of assessment. Claxton's (1999b) 'opportunism', on the other hand, the disposition to scan the environment for resources that are potentially relevant to a current problem or learning challenge, we judge to be too specific for present purposes. In what follows we shall focus on the learning dispositions we refer to as resilience, playfulness and reciprocity.

Resilience

One of the key learning dispositions must surely be the inclination to take on (at least some) learning challenges where the outcome is uncertain, to persist with learning despite temporary confusion or frustration and to recover from setbacks or failures and rededicate oneself to the learning task. Dweck (1991) and others have identified resilience as a central characteristic of those with 'learning' (Dweck, 1991), 'mastery' (Ames, 1992) or 'task-involvement' (Nicholls, 1984) goals, as opposed to 'perform-ance' or 'ego involvement' goals. This disposition is markedly influenced by people's previous learning history and, especially, the kinds of attributions they have learnt to make subconsciously for their own successes and failures. People who believe that experiencing difficulty is a reflection of a generally or innately low level of 'ability' tend to select less challenging learning situations and to become defensive much more quickly in the face of frustration than those who believe that through effort it is possible for them to develop their 'learning muscles' (Dweck, 1999). Kagan (1994) has shown marked differences in the resilience of children of little more than a year old, for example, which cannot be satisfactorily accounted for on the basis of heredity, while Smiley & Dweck (1994) have shown that many 4-year-olds are sacrificing valu-able learning opportunities in order to 'look good'. The opposite disposition to resilience we might call 'brittleness', a tendency to get upset at the first sign of diffi-culty and to shift from 'learning mode' into a defensive, self-protective stance. The key indicators of resilience might be taken to be: sticking with a difficult learning task; having a relatively high tolerance for frustration without getting upset; being able to recover from setback or disappointment relatively quickly.

Playfulness

Being playful, in the present context, means being ready, willing and able to perceive or construct variations on learning situations and thus to be more creative in inter-preting and reacting to problems. In our current conceptualisation we identify three different types of playfulness, which we refer to as mindfulness, imagination and experimentation. Mindfulness is a kind of perceptual openness which relies upon the inclination to notice the unfamiliar or to 'read the situation' in different ways (Langer, 1991, 1997). The opposite pole to mindfulness is 'mindlessness': the inclination to see only in terms of familiar categories and ignore details that are incidental to the process of categorisation or inconvenient to it. Mindlessness 'is marked by a rigid use of information during which the individual is not aware of its potential novel aspects', whereas mindfulness is characterised by 'active distinction-making and differ-entiation' (Langer & Piper, 1987, p. 280).

Imagination is mental playfulness: the inclination to generate alternative inner scenarios and fantasies, to draw on different analogies and spot unlikely connections. Children who are more imaginative 'seem to manage their school lives with more persistence, self-control, and enjoyment' (Singer & Singer, 1992, cited in Sutton-Smith, 1997, p. 154). The opposite of being imaginative is, of course, being unimagin-ative: not being able to see beyond an initial interpretation and being stuck with it as the 'literal truth' of the situation. Experimentation refers to the ability to play with or explore physical material and conditions so as to discover their latent properties and possibilities. Often just 'messing about', without a clear goal or purpose, reveals new affordances and thus makes both new means and new goals possible. (What one might want to do emerges from an open-minded exploration of what one can do.) The opposite of being practically playful in this way we might call being 'conventional', or suffering from what Maier (1945) famously called 'functional fixedness': seeing only familiar uses for objects and being unable to shift categories when it might be useful to do so. In her study of playfulness, Lieberman (1977) identifies the disposition in terms of physical, social and cognitive spontaneity, a sense of humour and a kind of joyful, exuberant or even mischievous attitude, a 'glint in the eye'.

Reciprocity

The third of our illustrative learning dispositions we call 'reciprocity', and this term again embraces a number of more specific variants. The most valuable learning resources, especially for the young, are, of course, other people. Those who lack the awareness to articulate their own learning processes and problems, the ability to communicate these to others or the inclination or the courage to do so are inevitably handicapped as learners. Reciprocity, to us, has both expressive and receptive and verbal and non-verbal dimensions. We assume that effective learners need the confidence and inclination to give opinions and contribute ideas (Bronfenbrenner, 1979, p. 192) through any or several of a range of communicative and expressive means. Ecological and sociocultural approaches to learning (Vygotsky, 1978; Lave & Wenger, 1991; Bruner, 1996; Cole, 1996) have convincingly demonstrated just how much of our psychological learning toolkit begins life in the context of interaction between people. Constraints on the disposition to interact with others in learning situations deprives learners of this powerful medium of enculturation into the learning strategies and attitudes of their milieu. Learning to learn has been shown to flourish in the context of 'reciprocal and responsive relationships' (Carr, 1998, p. 2) with others and this requires a willingness and an ability, on both sides, for 'joint attention' (Moore & Dunham, 1995; Smith, 1999), participation (Rogoff, 1990, 1997; Kantor *et al.*, 1992) and taking account of 'the opinions and needs of others' (New, 1993, p. 219).

A classroom can be characterised by the degree and kind of reciprocity that is typically encouraged or afforded. Filer (1993), comparing a Year 2 with a Year 1 classroom, observed that: 'in Year 2 there was a much more volatile classroom atmosphere with emotions more on the surface ... the Year 2 teacher interacted with pupils in a much greater variety of situations than was the case in Year 1' (p. 203). In the Year 1 classroom one of the children, Peter, had been assessed as poor at speaking and listening (although he talked freely to the researcher and could expand on the topic of conversation). In the Year 2 classroom, in contrast, Peter was assessed as 'good in groups' and it was noted by his teacher that he was often the one in his group to come up with all the ideas.

The opposite of reciprocity is a kind of 'epistemic solipsism' in which the existence of others, both as resources and as learning partners with needs and goals of their own, is ignored. Characteristics of the disposition for reciprocity will include a willingness to engage in joint learning tasks, to express uncertainties and ask questions, to take a variety of roles in joint learning enterprises and to take others' purposes and perspectives into account.

Reciprocity clearly resides in a transactional relationship between the individual and the context. But there are important senses in which resilience and playfulness do as well. Resilience depends upon beliefs about the relationship between the learner's capacities and the nature of the challenges which he or she is facing. The ability to persist in the face of difficulty depends critically on the nature of these transactional beliefs. Rutter (1990, p. 184, cited by Howard & Johnson, 1999) comments that 'resilience cannot be seen as a fixed attribute of the individual. If circumstances change, the risk alters' (Howard & Johnson, 1999, p. 15). The willingness to show playfulness likewise depends on the setting: perhaps on a degree of trust and on the capacity for unreserved involvement which such trust may permit. Csikszentmihalyi (1991, 1996) sees very clear connections between the capacity for and the experience of 'flow' or involvement and creativity. Trust and involvement are obviously key parts of the relationship between the individual and the context.

Why is assessment of learning dispositions important?

There are a number of reasons why it is important to generate valid and reliable methods for assessing learning dispositions and thus for tracking their development. First, if we are to help young people develop learning-positive dispositions, we need kinds of diagnostic and formative assessment that will enable us to relate to them appropriately. Though this need may well be relevant across their entire educational careers, such methods are particularly vital in early childhood, for it is here that the foundations of learning are being laid. Without some systematic way of keeping track of students' progress in this regard, it is all too easy for parents', teachers' and students' attention to be captured by the traditional goals of achievement and to lose sight of the more slippery, but even more important, development of dispositions.

Second, assessment of learners' progress is necessary in order to evaluate the efficacy of the educational programme and the 'dispositional milieu' (Carr, 2001a) which schools offer. Without some systematic tracking of learners, educators cannot know whether their good intentions are being translated into the desired outcomes. Third, it is a truism that what is assessed is what is valued, by teachers, families and learners themselves. If the goal of developing positive learning dispositions is to be translated into practice, then there have to be assessment instruments which serve to keep teachers' and learners' eyes on this particular ball and prevent attention sliding back onto the mastery of content, with its long tradition of assessment. Fourth, it is necessary to be able to demonstrate the efficacy of 'education for the development of learning dispositions' in the face of either scepticism or a simplistic 'back to basics' agenda that, whatever its shortcomings, can at least point to (what appears to be) hard data about educational achievement. If it is to be effective, the rhetoric of learning to learn has to be backed with convincing evidence.

What constraints are there on an effective system of dispositional assessment?

In order to evaluate possible ways of trying to keep track of dispositional development, it is necessary to have some criteria against which to judge them. We suggest the following. First, any assessment procedure has to be manageable and practical. It has to be capable of being administered, interpreted and recorded by busy educational practitioners. Second, any procedure needs to be, in the conventional senses, reliable and valid. We need to agree that resilience, playfulness and reciprocity are indeed being captured by the assessments and that sequential assessments are capturing the same thing. As Moss (1994) comments:

> A growing number of educators are calling for alternative approaches to assessment that support collaborative inquiry and foreground the development of purpose and meaning over skills and content in the intellectual work of students ... and teachers. ... We need to find ways to document the validity of assessments that support a wider range of valued educational goals.
>
> (p. 6)

These issues are discussed in detail in Moss (1994), Messick (1994), Black (1995), Black & Wiliam (1998) and Gipps (1999), and we will not go into them in detail here. Moss warns that less standardised forms of assessment present serious problems for reliability across readers and tasks (and, we would add, places and time) (Moss, 1994, p. 6). Less standardised forms of assessment are often appropriate for complex aptitudes and attitudes. Moss gives the following as examples of high stakes assessments that are not standardised: making decisions about whether submitted papers will be published, hiring people, decisions in law courts and groups of teachers reviewing children's portfolios. Later in this paper we describe an example of teachers reviewing children's portfolios for learning dispositions (or 'habits of mind') (Meier, 1995).

Third, and closely related to the second, an assessment procedure needs to contain some built-in flexibility, so that teachers at every level can adapt it to suit the realities of their own seminar rooms, classrooms or early childhood centres without losing the central features of the developmental 'trail'. If we want assessment procedures to cover a span of years, i.e. from early childhood at least to the end of compulsory schooling, then one of our purposes is summative: we are seeking to provide a trail of evidence concerning the growth of some aspect of mind. But we are likely to run into different definitions of validity for local (classroom) formative purposes. High levels of reliability are needed for tracking dispositions across contexts, but they may inhibit the connection to local opportunities for learning (the local dispositional milieu) that formative work needs.

Finally, assessment procedures must, formatively, support the development of learning dispositions. The assessment procedures themselves must form part of a dispositional milieu that affords resilience, playfulness and reciprocity and encourages and values their development. And they will be situated in episodes of joint attention and reciprocal, responsive relationships. Messick (see for example Messick, 1994) expanded the definition of validity to include a consideration of social consequences, adding consequential to construct validity. Related to this, Ames (1992) argues that certain structures within the classroom make different goals salient. Her primary interest is in the development of resilience, but her analysis would apply equally well to playfulness and reciprocity. She identifies three characteristics of the relationship between the individual and the environment that affect how students approach and engage with learning: the evaluation (assessment), the authority pattern and the tasks. Writing about assessment, she concludes that: 'when evaluation is normative, emphasizes social comparison, is highly differentiated, and is perceived as threatening to one's sense of self-control, it contributes to a negative motivational climate' (Ames, 1992, p. 265). In other words, such features of assessment adversely affect the development of resilience, playfulness and reciprocity.

Candidate methods for the assessment of learning dispositions

We might divide possible methods for assessing learning dispositions into three groups: those based on direct observation of learners 'at work'; those based on information derived through interviews or questionnaires with teachers, parents or peers who know the learner; those based on self-report or self-assessment by learners themselves. In addition, portfolio approaches may combine a number of different methods. In this section we briefly outline some examples of each of these approaches to the assessment of learning dispositions, in the light of the criteria outlined above. To recapitulate: is the assessment manageable; does the assessment give a valid handle on the constructs of resilience, playfulness and reciprocity; is it flexible enough to reflect local conditions but also capable of being more broadly ecologically valid, longitudinal and reliable? And is it consistent with theory and practice that values learning dispositions and sees their early development as consequential on relationships between the learner and the social and material learning environment?

Observational methods

These methods infer learning dispositions from observations of how people behave when actually confronted with learning challenges. We have ordered these examples in terms of the extent to which they are predetermined and 'experimental', on the one hand, and responsive to the particular worlds the children inhabit ('authentic'), on the other.

Dynamic assessment

There has been a long sub-tradition, we might call it, within the psychometric testing of 'intelligence' that has concerned itself with the assessment of learning ability. Thorndike (1922), for example, defined intelligence itself as 'the ability to learn', saying that estimates of intelligence 'should be estimates of the ability to learn. To be able to learn harder things or to be able to learn the same things more quickly would then be the single basis for evaluation' (Thorndike, 1922, p. 17 quoted in Guthke & Stein, 1996, p. 1). In recent years this approach has reappeared under the name of 'dynamic assessment', and it basically involves the assessor setting 'examinees' a task that is too hard for them and observing how they respond and how they make use of standardised prompts and hints as they are offered. This approach has been developed in detail by Feuerstein *et al.* (1979), using what they call their Learning Potential Assessment Device (LPAD), primarily with children who have special educational needs and are taking part in Feuerstein's programme of 'instrumental enrichment'. Different versions of dynamic assessment are being developed by Guthke & Stein (1996), Haywood *et al.* (1990) and others, some of which draw explicitly on Vygotskian notions of the 'zone of proximal development' (ZPD). An individual's 'learning power', in this latter conception, is indexed by the nature and extent of the ZPD that that person is capable of generating through scaffolded interaction with the assessor. Comprehensive reviews are to be found in Lidz (1987) and, more recently, in Grigorenko & Sternberg (1998).

Though dynamic assessment is generally acknowledged to be an interesting and potentially fruitful development, it is also recognised that this potential is yet to be fully realised (Grigorenko & Sternberg, 1998) and that there are unresolved problems in terms of the criteria we laid out above. Most obviously, administering and scoring the sessions is complicated and time consuming. There is no way that a busy classroom teacher, for example, could devote the time to each student which these instruments currently require. And so, although they may potentially reveal a great deal of information about the student-as-learner, these tests at the moment lack the power to influence standard educational practice.

Most forms of dynamic assessment currently target specific age and ability groups and thus lack the flexibility which we think is desirable to track development across spans of years. However, there is no reason in principle why such versions could not be produced. For this to happen, though, a more differentiated theoretical base (an explication of what learning-to-learn actually involves) would be required that could underpin different versions of the test appropriate to different levels of age and experience in terms of, for example, the learning capabilities and dispositions being targeted. At present the measure of learning power that dynamic assessments produce is a global one: we may expect developments in the future as the traditions of dynamic assessment and learning dispositions make more fruitful contact with each other.

It would not be hard to see how we might make a start on this project. For example, how well and how long people persist in the face of difficulty may be taken as a mark of their resilience. How effectively and imaginatively they grapple with the problem and how creatively they make use of the hints that are offered provides an index of playfulness, as we have defined the term. How learners engage with the assessor, how willing they are to explore their uncertainty through conversation and what kinds of questions they ask may be taken as an indicator of the development of reciprocity, though, as these tests are usually conducted in one-to-one sessions, there is no opportunity to see how well learners interact with their peers or under less formal conditions.

Explorations of the validity and reliability of dynamic assessment methods are under way. Feuerstein *et al.* (1979) have shown that their LPAD gives a more valid measure of children's learning potential than traditional 'static' intelligence tests. Guthke & Stein (1996) have discovered correlations ranging from −0.35 to −0.50 between their 'learning test' and complex problem solving performance on, for example, implicit learning tasks (Berry & Broadbent, 1984). On the other hand, many dynamic assessments use abstract puzzles and materials similar to those found in traditional static intelligence tests and there is considerable evidence that performance with such materials is not a valid indicator of 'real-life' intelligence (Ceci, 1996). It remains to be seen if the use of such materials in the context of dynamic testing leads to greater 'ecological validity'.

Overall, therefore, while dynamic assessment is a promising line of development, its current dependence on abstract materials leaves a question mark over its construct validity; while its time consuming and complicated procedures for administration and scoring render it too cumbersome for large-scale use in everyday educational settings.

Experimental and customised challenges

Experimental tasks have been used by researchers to investigate children's learning dispositions and some of these may be adapted as customised challenges for assessment purposes. Jigsaw puzzle solving was used by Smiley & Dweck (1994) to investigate young children's resilience, for example. Children completed a puzzle task that involved first working on three insoluble puzzles and then on one solvable puzzle. They made self-ratings of their emotion for each of the puzzles (using a face scale of five faces from 'very sad' to 'very happy'), responded to a question about future success on this task and were asked to indicate whether they preferred to work again on one of the insoluble puzzles or on the solvable puzzle and to give a reason for their choice. This experiment tapped into their tendency to seek or to avoid challenge after an experience that included failure. Two groups emerged from these two measures: a group of 38 children who sought challenge (providing evidence of learning goals) and one of 40 that avoided it (providing evidence of performance goals). Role plays with pretend story lines about failure provided additional data (Dweck, 1991, p. 213).

Research has also been carried out by Ellen Langer and her colleagues that could be developed to assess the aspect of playfulness that we have referred to as 'mindfulness' (and its converse, 'mindlessness'). She maintains (Langer, 1991) that the teaching of facts as the absolute truth can lead to mindlessness and she has assessed mindlessness in a number of experiments. In one of them she and her colleagues introduced a collection of different objects to one group of subjects in an ordinary, unconditional way and to another in conditional terms. To the first group they said, for instance, This is a dog's chew toy', to the second group 'This could be a dog's chew toy'. After the objects had been introduced, they asked subjects to fill out some forms with pencils, gave them instructions and then announced that they could not finish the study because the instructions had been wrong, the forms had been filled out incorrectly and they had none spare. They had created an urgent need for an eraser. Those subjects who had not been given the conditional cue were much more likely to be assessed as approaching the task in a mindless or unimaginative way. Both of these paradigms, solving jigsaw puzzles and detecting novel uses for objects, could easily be incorporated with a 'dynamic assessment' protocol.

Learning dispositions could also be assessed in specially arranged situations where the learning activity is less clearly prescribed. Such situations might include 'playing' with materials provided by the assessor, where the students are effectively given carte blanche to create their own learning activities (see for example Duckworth, 1987). Similarly, Project Spectrum (Krechevsky, 1994) makes use of an early childhood assessment format, designed to assess learning style and domains of interest or talent, based on Gardner's taxonomy of 'multiple intelligences' (Gardner, 1983). Features of the child's open-ended 'play' in each of Gardner's seven domains are observed and recorded. Of interest to the topic of this paper is the assessment of 'working style' to describe a child's interactions with the tasks and materials from various content areas.

> These working styles are intended to reflect the 'process' dimension of a child's work or play, rather than the type of product that results. They address indices of affect, motivation and interaction with materials, as well as more stylistic features, like tempo of work and orientation toward auditory, visual or kinesthetic cues.
>
> (Krechevsky, 1994, p. 203)

A Working Styles checklist lists a number of 'stylistic features' of the children's approach to the tasks and materials. Sixteen of these are written as opposites: for example, playful or serious, persistent or frustrated by activity. Definitions include the following for the 'playful' child: 'delights in materials or activity; easily uses materials, frequently making spontaneous comments or playful extensions of the activity (e.g. the child talks to the pieces of the grinder, telling them to stay on, move, etc.)' (Krechevsky, 1994, p. 207).

However, experiments and customised challenges, although designed to reveal generalised traits, may not predict behaviour in the everyday world of the classroom and many of them were not developed as formative assessment instruments. As Cole (1991) points out,

> the crosscultural literature is replete with discussions of the methodological dilemmas that arise once one suspects that experimental cognitive tasks are special kinds of culturally mediated social interaction and not privileged windows on the mind.
>
> (p. 408)

These specially designed challenges largely rely on activities that are very different from many of those involved in normal curriculum implementation and, therefore, are less manageable by teachers because they have been separated from the process of teaching. Many of them look and feel like 'tests' and, therefore, run the risk of falling foul of Ames' (1992) criticisms of the formative or consequential validity of assessments that emphasise comparison, are highly differentiated (their criteria inflexibly defined) and normative. In their use, such tests are unlikely to advance the development of dispositions such as resilience, playfulness and reciprocity. They have, however, been useful for clarifying our understanding of such complex constructs. Dweck's and Langer's work has provided us with vivid exemplars for discussion.

On the other hand, however, we must admit that some structured classroom tasks may frequently look very similar to experimentally manipulated 'non-authentic' challenges (cf. Lave & Wenger, 1991). In the early days of the National Curriculum in the UK, for instance, practically based Standard Assessment Tasks (SATs) attempted to explore the ways in which children were using fundamental principles and elementary concepts (James & Gipps, 1998); Wiliam (1994) analysed assessment schemes based on classroom tasks in mathematics and English. And with 'thinking' dispositions in mind, Norris (1992) has used open-ended yet focused problem situations, such as a search for living creatures on another planet, in which students' responses to opportunities to derive hypotheses, interpretations and conclusions were analysed. It may be possible to use classroom tasks that are rich in dispositional potential for both curriculum implementation and assessment; ways to enhance the reliability of these local task assessments would have to be devised.

Learning stories

'Learning stories' have been developed as an assessment tool for use with the New Zealand early childhood education curriculum (Carr, 2001b). Learning stories are structured observations in everyday or 'authentic' settings, designed to provide a cumulative series of qualitative 'snapshots' or written vignettes of individual children displaying one or more of the target learning dispositions. The five key learning dispositions highlighted by Te Whaariki are translated into observable actions: 'taking an interest', 'being involved', 'persisting with difficulty', 'expressing an idea or a feeling' and 'taking responsibility or taking another point of view'. The latter two ('expressing an idea' and 'taking another point of view') roughly correspond with our 'reciprocity', 'being involved' has elements of 'playfulness' and 'persisting with difficulty' looks like 'resilience', but the correspondence between the two sets of dispositions is not exact. Practitioners collect 'critical incidents' that highlight one or more of these dispositions and a series of learning stories over time, for a particular child, can be put together and scanned for what Carr has called emerging 'learning narratives': what we might call, in the present context, 'developmental trajectories' of learning dispositions (Carr, 2000a, b). Children's stories are kept in a portfolio; often they include photographs or photocopies of children's work and children's comments.

> For example: Sean is four years old, and his portfolio includes a polaroid photo of him using the carpentry drill. Attached to the photo is a short 'story', written by Annette, one of the teachers, which describes a situation in which Sean displays resilience, persevering with a difficult task even when he gets 'stuck'.

> Comment included: 'The bit's too small Annette, get a bigger one'. We do, drill a hole and then use the drill to put in the screw. 'What screwdriver do we need?' 'The flat one'. Sean chooses the correct one and tries to use it. 'It's stuck'. He keeps trying even when it is difficult.

There is just enough detail in the text and the photograph for this to provide a discussion point for Sean and the teacher next day and the story is filed with others that tell of similar occasions when Sean has completed a difficult task of his own choosing. Practitioners in Carr's (2001b) study had significant freedom to define each of the five dispositions in their own way, in order to reflect the priorities of their centres and their communities. In Sean's kindergarten, for instance, examples of persisting with difficulty included: following a plan (and adapting the plan), persevering with (choosing, persisting with and perhaps completing) a difficult or complex task, acknowledging an error or problem (and planning to solve it or actually solving it). The dimension of dispositional strength that we have called 'sophistication' is indicated by the elaborations in parentheses: children who both followed and adapted their plans for making things could be described as having a higher level of sophistication in their perseverance or resilience. Learning stories, unlike experimental challenges, can retain the 'richness, complexity, and interdependence of events and actions in the real classroom' (Salomon, 1991, p. 16). Construct validity has been enhanced by the discussions that the stories generate: they encourage staff to ask themselves 'Is this really an example of perseverance?' The flexibility, however, raises questions about reliability across settings: we cannot be sure that resilience is 'the same thing' in each setting or that Sean will be described as resilient when he goes to school and the opportunities for resilience are very different. But when the same sort of learning story appears in different areas of the programme, even in the one setting, the disposition begins to appear more robust.

The system has proved manageable and interesting for early childhood teachers and it has the consequential benefit of including families and children in the assessment story discussions. We know that teacher and parent expectations can be a powerful influence on children's learning (see for example Frome & Eccles, 1998) and the 'credit' approach of the learning story format in comparison with 'deficit-based' checklist alternatives has addressed this aspect of the formative potential of an assessment practice: its consequential validity.

Outsiders' questionnaires and interviews

Where the methods in the previous section aimed to track the development of learning dispositions through observations of specific learning episodes, those in this section rely on more cumulative, perhaps more impressionistic, judgements made by those who have had experience of learners over a period of time. For example, Lieberman

(1977) devised an instrument through which teachers could make and record judgments about a student's disposition towards playfulness. A rating scale asked such questions as: 'How often does the child show joy in or during his/her play activity' or 'While playing, how often does the child show flexibility in his/her interaction with the surrounding group structure?' (We should perhaps pass quickly over the fact that Lieberman's scale also included the question: 'How attractive is the child?') She produced differently worded, but essentially similar, versions of her rating scale that were appropriate to different ages from kindergarteners up to college students and school teachers themselves. While some of the indices of playfulness obviously vary with age (adults typically are less physically exuberant and expressive than 5-year-olds), others, such as those she called 'manifest joy' and 'a sense of humour', seemed to show considerable consistency over different age groups. However, such rating scales do not encourage the detailed observations of learners by their assessors that are required by, for example, learning stories. They do not necessarily serve as effectively to draw adults' attention to the kinds of activities which will lead to the development of learning dispositions.

A New Zealand longitudinal study of children from age five, the Competent Children's Project (Wylie *et al.*, 1996, 1999; Wylie & Thompson, 1998) has attempted to assess what the authors called 'being' competencies (communication, inquisitiveness, perseverance, peer social skills, social skills with adults and independence) over time by asking the children's teacher to describe the child on a five point Likert scale. The child's teacher was asked to judge to what extent a given description matched the child. There were, for example, four descriptions for inquisitiveness: 'asks a lot of questions and/or likes to take things apart'; 'explores and asks about people, animals, plants'; 'likes to play with things that fit together/build'; 'gets excited about new books, places, toys, experiences'. And there were four descriptions for perseverance, which is close to our 'resilience': 'keeps trying till resolves problem with puzzle/toy'; 'persists in problem-solving when creating'; 'good concentration span on things of interest'; 'makes an effort, even if unconfident'.

As an indication of the longitudinal reliability, and the inter-item agreement, correlation coefficients were computed at ages 5, 6 and 8. At age 5, correlations between the four descriptions of perseverance were not high: 0.31 between 'has good concentration span on things of interest' and 'makes effort, even if unconfident'; 0.58 (the highest correlation) between 'keeps trying till resolves problem with puzzle/toy' and 'persists in problem-solving when creating'. By age 8 the correlations between items had increased and all correlations ranged from 0.56 to 0.72. At age 5 teachers rated 25% of children as low on 'makes effort even if unconfident'; for the same cohort that figure dipped to 14% at age 6 and went up again to 25% at age 8. The same group of children were apparently more resilient in their first year of primary school than in either their second year or the last year of early childhood experience. This may reflect the changing nature of the children's 'dispositional milieu': the context of activities with which one can persevere in the 'new entrant' (first year of school) classroom. Structured reading, writing and arithmetic tasks may perhaps have provided clear and interesting new objectives for children (on average) to 'keep trying' with. And it may also be that perseverance may have been easier to score in this setting.

In general, outsiders' questionnaires and interviews have the capacity to provide comparable data across settings, if respondents are given good guidance and the reliability of the questions or descriptions has been confirmed. Construct and local validity is threatened, however, as the essential connection to context is usually lost too. If there is too much reliance on 'check-lists', alternative sources of data, necessary to confirm the assessment and to build up a richer picture of the learning, will be neglected (a point made cogently by Delandshere & Petrosky, 1998; James & Gipps, 1998). Projects like the Competent Children Project that use Likert scales are not attempting to provide rich and situated descriptions of the learning of individuals; they aggregate the scores for a cohort. But they are nevertheless helpful for framing construct discussions by teachers. While these kinds of surveys are relatively quick and easy for teachers to fill in, they probably have a much weaker effect in terms of encouraging parents and teachers to change their own education practice and priorities.

Self-reports

In the third category of assessments it is the learners themselves who offer a summary picture of their own learning styles, abilities and dispositions.

Questionnaires

Self-report assessments are exemplified by the California Critical Thinking Dispositions Inventory (CCTDI) (Facione & Facione, 1992) where students respond to 75 items using a six point Likert scale. Burden's (1995) 'Myself as a Learner' (MALS) test invites schoolchildren to respond to a simple 20 item questionnaire that gives a single measure overview of their self-image as learners. Claxton's (1998) more elaborate 'Effective Lifelong Learning Inventory' (ELLI) is intended to offer an indication of learners' views of their learning power in terms of a number of key learning dispositions, such as those we have chosen to focus on here. This instrument, though more comprehensive, is still in development. It has the potential both for use as a formative tool and as a summative measure that describes a learning path or trajectory across settings, but much of this potential is as yet unexplored.

Situated projective interviews

Carr (2000b) devised an interview based around observations in an early childhood centre. An observer or a teacher uses children's own developing 'learning narrative' to construct an open-ended storybook that played back their own learning style and strengths to them and asks them for an ending and any comments. It was especially devised to find the children's perspective on resilience and tackling difficulty and it was initially constructed from episodes of learning in one particular context. The procedure is obviously time consuming and very specific to one context. However, like many narrative-based assessment methods that might be seen as impracticable, this open-ended storybook provoked a valuable reflective discussion between the assessor and the children that illuminated the construct of interest from the children's point of view. In this case, the context-specific nature of resilience was very apparent when the kindergarten children went on to describe those activities they perceived as 'difficult' (and therefore demanding resilience): 22 of the 36 responses referred to situations at sites away from the kindergarten. The children's responses also painted a rich picture of domains of resilience or challenge for these 4-year-olds: physical (e.g. doing hand stands), symbolic (drawing, reading and writing), social ('telling Emily that I don't want to play with her') and cultural (the challenging task that Matt aspired to was to go by himself 'up the street to get the eggs'). Some of these domains were very specific: one child reported that she was practising the difficult task of 'drawing noses properly'. It is at this level, the specific and the concrete, that resilience, playfulness and reciprocity make sense to young children;

it is at this level therefore that they can evaluate their own endeavours, and such discussions gain high marks for formative value.

Self-created learning stories

A number of educators have recently been exploring the educational value of students' keeping reflective 'learning logs': a kind of informal diary or journal within which they are encouraged to reflect regularly on their ups and downs as learners. Sometimes these logs are private, sometimes seen by the teacher and sometimes used as the basis for an interactive oral or written conversation between teacher and student around the topic of the students' developing learning power. For example, Kate Drew, a primary school teacher from the UK with whom one of us (G.C.) has been working, has 10-year-olds write regular entries in their 'Journey into the Unknown' journal, which is a mixture of private and 'open to comment'. Students may mark pages with a cross, in which case Kate undertakes not to read them. Other pages may form the basis of a reflective dialogue. Mahn (see Mahn & John-Steiner, 2002) has shown how the use of such interactive journals facilitates students' second language development. Though such journals clearly offer great potential as cumulative records of students' learning progress, this remains unexploited, not least, perhaps, because of the tension between their formative value as private, heavily situated, unsystematic documents and their use as public testaments of progress. Here again is a potentially fruitful area for the tracking of learning that has yet to be explored.

Interviews

A collaborative project in South Australia between the Salisbury Plains Coalition of Schools and the Faculty of Education at the University of South Australia has focused on issues of student resilience within an ecological framework (Dryden *et al.*, 1998), using student interviews. The study initially investigated how children and their teachers constructed and understood the notion of childhood resiliency. 'Themes of resilience' emerged (two of the most prominent were relationships and beliefs). Based on the information gathered from the children, their teachers and the literature, the researchers constructed a screening device to help teachers identify children displaying resilient and non-resilient behaviours. Teachers identified 55 9- to 12-year-olds who were experiencing 'tough lives' and, using the researchers' screening device, 30 of them were described as displaying 'non-resilient' behaviour, 25 displaying 'resilient' behaviour. They then designed a longitudinal study that would track the 55 children over several years. To do this, the researchers talked to the children individually twice, one year apart, using a This Is Your Life format for the interview. The findings are reported in Howard & Johnson (1999), who provide case studies of children who have shifted to more resilient behaviour, displayed the same non-resilient behaviour or continued to display resilient behaviour. The methodology here was not specifically developed as an assessment tool; researchers interviewed the children and these interviews were lengthy, one-to-one and often private. But the value of this example is its longitudinal nature, its inclusion of the learner's perspective and its connection to the changing circumstances in the children's lives. Similarly, Bloomer & Hodkinson (2000) interviewed secondary school pupils in the north-west and south-west of England over a 3 year period to investigate continuity and change in dispositions to learning.

There are two great advantages of self-report methods. Firstly, the learner-self is common over time and across settings. The data tend to be idiosyncratic, but the

Australian material indicates that, given some framing themes for the interview and the analysis, the development of dispositional behaviour of individuals can be tracked across time. The second advantage is that self-report methods can tap into the student's point of view and, as in the open-ended storybook example, this can highlight domains and sites for resilience, playfulness and reciprocity that are not obvious to adults but are of great interest to the learners. The learners' stories can build up a picture not only of the dispositions, but of the dimensions of strength: what sophisticated and robust examples of each disposition might look like. They encourage reflection by the learners and, hence, they can be part of educational practice that encourages learning dispositions. Focused interviews and conversations highlight the reciprocal nature of both curriculum and assessment; questionnaires are less able to do this (but are, of course, more easily administered and scored).

Portfolios

Students' portfolios can potentially include data from any or all of the above methods. For example, in a multi-cultural public secondary school in Harlem described in Meier (1995), five desirable 'habits of mind' are listed on almost every classroom wall, discussed every week in a newsletter, used to organise curricula and are the base criteria that teachers use for judging students' portfolios on graduation. (Such taxonomies of educational dispositions or 'habits of mind' have been adopted by a number of school programmes in the USA and form the basis of curricula and the portfolios that are used to assess them.) The habits of mind, together with the questions that each is designed to pursue, are: evidence (what's your evidence?); viewpoints (what viewpoints are we hearing?); connections (how are things connected to each other?); voice (can we imagine alternatives?); conventions (who cares?). In order to graduate with a high school diploma, every student must complete requirements in 14 different 'portfolio' areas, literature, history, ethics, science, maths and so on, and present seven of them to a Graduation Committee for questioning and defence. The Graduation Committee includes at least two assigned teachers, another adult of the student's choice and a student. As Meier says (1995, p. 42) 'The whole thing is like a series of doctoral orals!' She also adds: 'It's a form of assessment that builds standards, examines teaching practice, and raises issues of curriculum – all at one and the same time'.

In the Central Park East early childhood, primary and secondary schools described by Meier, assessment is absolutely part of curriculum processes. Developed over a number of years and continually being discussed and adapted, it has become manageable within a uniquely designed disposition-oriented school system. And, because of a consistent curriculum, a compatible portfolio system and a democratic form of organisation that comprises small schools with a high level of teacher autonomy, the assessment is both locally valid and reliable across schools.

Tracking learning dispositions across place and time: how are we to do it?

All of the above methods of assessing resilience, playfulness and/or reciprocity score well on some of our criteria of merit. They variously provide methods that: (i) are manageable for busy teachers to implement; (ii) attend to construct validity; (iii) are locally flexible but longitudinally reliable; (iv) support a curriculum in which learning dispositions are integral. But no method so far scores highly on all these desiderata. We conclude that the best way forward lies in combining different approaches and, in this concluding section of the paper, offer some preliminary suggestions about what such an approach might look like. We describe this approach as the LDA: Learning Disposition Assessment. There are two arms to this approach: the Learning Disposition Grid (LDG), and the Learning Disposition Portfolio (LDP).

The Learning Disposition Grid

Both learning and assessment are situated within social contexts. 'Assessment' is not a special kind of process or event that stands outside the normal cultural life of a classroom (seminar room, workplace, etc.). Attempts to mark assessment as 'different' from learning may serve only to confuse learners and reduce the power of assessment to drive learning in desirable directions. As the 'assessment' of learning dispositions can only fairly take place in a context that welcomes their expression, our starting point, in thinking about the kind of integrated practice that we wish for, is to site assessment in nominated classroom situations in which the available artefacts and activities afford (but do not demand) resilience, playfulness and reciprocity. Participation in these activities or situations involves the kinds of learning that are of interest. Writing about reading and mathematics understanding, Greeno (1997) comments:

> In contrast to the behaviorist and cognitive views, where a domain of skills needs to be sampled, the situative view requires sampling across a domain of situation types in which participation involves the kinds of knowing that are of interest.
>
> (p. 8)

We offer an example of a composite assessment format within a matrix framework (see Figure 3) for the evaluation of the potential of activities or situations. There are two axes on the matrix: dispositions (resilience, playfulness and reciprocity, our present examples of learning dispositions) and dimensions of strength (sophistication and robustness). Teachers collect exemplars of positions that can be along a five point scale, from 1, 'the disposition is absent', to 5, the appearance of dispositions which are so robust and sophisticated, they have become such a pervasive part of a person's 'being' as a learner, that the learner in effect functions as a role model of that disposition for others. Indicators and exemplars are not the same thing, although indicators can be treated as exemplars rather than as a prescriptive scheme. Research has suggested that performance indicators, useful for some purposes, are too prescriptive for complex performances such as the display of learning dispositions. Writing about assessing authentic tasks in mathematics in the UK, Wiliam (1994) points out that where teachers were guided by schemes that used general criteria of progress across tasks, they used only coursework tasks that conformed to that model of progression; as a result the tasks became 'stereotyped' (p. 53). He adds

> What is required is a way of assessing authentic tasks on their own terms – in terms of what the student set out to do, but it does not seem as if any kind of explicit assessment scheme can achieve this.
>
> (p. 54)

He recommends a move away from criterion- and norm-referenced assessment to the idea of 'construct-referenced' assessment, where 'the domain of assessment is holistic, rather than being defined in terms of precise objectives' (p. 59). A 'holistic'

Learning dispositions Dimensions of strength	Resilience	Playfulness	Reciprocity
Sophistication	1. 2. 3. 4. 5.	1. 2. 3. 4. 5.	1. 2. 3. 4. 5.
Robustness	1. 2. 3. 4. 5.	1. 2. 3. 4. 5.	1. 2. 3. 4. 5.

Figure 3 Learning disposition grid.

or 'hermeneutic' method (Moss, 1994) depends on collaborative interpretations of collected performances. This collaboration is easy and manageable in early childhood with its tradition of team teaching; teachers of older learners will need to gather a small group together from other staff, interested researchers, parents and/or students for this purpose. The UK experience with 'agreement trials' for assessing pieces of work for GCSE English indicate that it can be made reliable (Wiliam, 1994, p. 60). Not all activities will be eligible; many activities are primarily designed to teach basic skills.

We provide an example from early childhood (Carr, 1998, 2001b). A kindergarten has decided to design their curriculum around a 'project' approach and they have settled on 'gate making' as a focus activity since a builder has recently built a fence to divide the kindergarten playground into a front and a back yard and left a space for a gate. The teachers have provided a rich array of materials for the children to use for this purpose and the builder has demonstrated drawing up a plan, following a plan and problem solving with carpentry tools. On the LDG, this activity rates highly for its potential resilience. The teachers have anticipated (and observations will confirm and add to this) several levels of sophistication. There are a number of interesting problems that the children face: following a plan, holding it all together, measuring the parts so that they fit together, devising hinges and latches and so on. The teachers also predict a range of degrees of robustness that are possible: the gate construction is fairly firmly sited in a technology/construction domain and for many children this is not a familiar activity (for some of the boys perseverance at carpentry is already routine, but making a gate provides new and unfamiliar challenges).

The teachers also rate this activity highly for playfulness. They can think of several levels of sophistication for playfulness: although the gate idea developed as an addition to the playground fence and they have walked around the neighbourhood looking at how this problem has been solved in their local area, they indicate that the children may develop imaginative designs for themselves. Teachers have also read a number of stories that involve gates of various kinds and they anticipate that the story lines the children develop will stray beyond the purpose of the playground gate (to keep children in the front yard where they can be supervised) and that this straying into unfamiliar purposes will contribute to the robustness of the disposition towards playfulness. Observations will confirm this and provide them with a number of exemplars.

Finally, the project scores well on its potential for reciprocity: although the children typically make their own individual products, gates are big enough to warrant group activity and, therefore, sophisticated negotiation and conjoint problem solving. As exemplars are collected, so they will add to the collective definition of reciprocity that is emerging: borrowing ideas from each other and evaluating each other's designs, might be added, for example. The teachers are aware that the boys usually work with boys on construction tasks and girls with girls; they are hoping to increase the robustness of the children's reciprocity by encouraging children to work in mixed gender groups and with unfamiliar peers.

The Learning Disposition Portfolio

The Learning Disposition Grid forms the framing device for the second arm of the LDA: the Learning Disposition Portfolio, or LDP. This portfolio stays with the learner from early childhood to whenever. Participation in a number of activities that score highly on the LDG is written up each year by either the adult or the learner (depending on the age of the child) or a combination of both. The write-up is framed around the specified learning dispositions and the two dimensions of strength. A negotiation on the level of sophistication and robustness is reached and the rationale is recorded and included in the LDP. Perhaps a committee of peers or an outsider adult is involved in this assessment, and the examples that established the LDG are used here for guidance. Wiliam (1994) comments of the Graded Assessment in Mathematics scheme developed at King's College during the 1980s:

> Attempts to communicate standards were consistently most successful when actual samples of students' work for each of the levels of the system, annotated to illustrate important points, with several different approaches to each task at each level, were used.
>
> (p. 63)

The ratings are firmly embedded in the detail of the learning stories, the comments of the learners (perhaps emerging from a questionnaire like the ELLI, referred to earlier, with additions that allow the students to refer to the task currently being assessed) and the annotations by the teacher. Ratings can be problematical. Writing of the assessment of teachers for certification, Delandshere & Petrosky (1998) warn that ratings encourage readers to 'bypass careful, elaborate documentation' (p. 15); they also ask 'Are numerical ratings of these diverse performances credible?' (p. 15). However, since we are interested in tracking over time, it seems worthwhile to trial a system of ratings.

Here is another example from the kindergarten. The activity comes from data in Carr (1998), but the analysis using the LDG as a framing device has been added for this paper. One morning, 4-year-old Chata drew a plan for what came to be called the 'party gate'. This design included a number of vertical lines, a cross bar at the top and a series of happy faces drawn along the cross bar. She then worked with three other 4-year-olds (her sister being one of them) to make this gate out of cardboard tubes. They joined the tubes into a grid, using masking tape, then added faces made from shells and feathers. When Jenny joined the group Chata includes her and says 'I'm your friend now eh'. A teacher and the researcher talked with them about the activity: Chata tells the adults that she and the other children are making 'a gate for our people'. She comments that the 'people are standing up' and if they fall off 'in the water, they die when they open they mouth'. She adds that 'It's a party'.

Using the LDG as a framing for the analysis, the portfolio for Chata would include an account of this activity together with her drawings, photos of the project in progress and transcripts of conversations, if they were available. There were two events going on: an imaginative story line and a complex construction. Annotated notes would indicate a high level of sophisticated playfulness. For Chata and her sister (recent immigrants) the notion that if the children ('our people') fall off the gate they will drown appeared to be of great significance and the children were working at a complex level of imagination, 'reading the situation' of making a gate in personal, unusual and elaborate ways. The final gate was an elaborate structure with smiling faces attached to the top (faces were drawn on large white shells that they found at the kindergarten, with small feathers attached as hair or hats). This story line appeared new; the children were not playing out a routine story line, so there is clearly evidence of playfulness being imported into a situation of some novelty and, therefore, of some robustness.

Three of the children had frequently worked together, but Jenny was a new member of the team and Chata welcomed her and gave her a role: evidence of reciprocity. We have no notes from the observation about the level of negotiation and group planning during this activity; more observations or tape recordings would have assisted with the analysis of the sophistication of this disposition. The children persevered for a sustained period on a moderately difficult task. To an adult's eyes this was a difficult task that involved construction, patterning and measuring. Developing a sustained story line that linked to the construction was also a challenge. Thus, resilience is also showing a fair degree of robustness. And so on.

The teachers would discuss these additions to the portfolio and agree on ratings for the three dispositions along each of the two dimensions, using examples from other children in this activity to guide them. A few months later, the teachers, in consultation with Chata and perhaps others, would write up participation in the same activity or participation in another activity that had achieved equivalent rating on the LDG. In the meantime, they would have notes from other assessments on the domains of interest for Chata (and her friends) so that their commentary about the robustness of dispositions in unfamiliar circumstances would be informed and well documented. (At the same time, and using the same activities supplemented by other work, the teachers are documenting Chata's increasing skill in her second language, as well as in mathematics – in this task, the measuring and patterning – technology, drawing, socio-dramatic play and story telling.) When Chata leaves for school, she takes her LDP with her and she and the teachers at school continue the process. As she gets older, her own contribution to the LDP (the reflection, the write-up and the assessment) becomes greater.

Experience in early childhood settings with 'learning stories' and in primary schools with 'reflective journals' suggest that this kind of approach would appear to be manageable for teachers interested in learning dispositions as a feature of their classrooms or early childhood programmes. The assessment is based on 'authentic' tasks and is increasingly shared with the learner and, perhaps, with peers and an outside assessor. The method combines dialogue and reflective journals with structured learning stories in a portfolio format to maximise local validity of complex performances in complex environments. Validity is enhanced by the exercise of the teachers having to come to agreements about scoring activities on the LDG. Reliability is enhanced by the same process, as well as the involvement of the learner throughout, in much the same way as reliability was nurtured in the longitudinal Australian study of resilience. The trail of evidence, an aspect of reliability (or accountability; see for example Smagorinsky, 1995) in an interpretive research project, remains accessible. The examples of dimensions of strength developed for each classroom are shared with teachers or tutors in the next classroom, contributing to reliability as well. It is anticipated that the process would both contribute to and be a consequence of a dispositional milieu that includes assessment, relationships and activities that reflect resilience, playfulness and reciprocity.

Final comment

This sort of integrated assessment combines a number of formats that are already in the literature: dynamic assessment, customised challenges or activities, learning stories, teacher or researcher scales and self-reports. Although we have made some suggestions, further longitudinal research across one community of linked educational settings is needed to establish a method for tracking learning dispositions across time and settings. We have outlined some criteria for the evaluation of such projects. Further research will most usefully come from the work of teachers and of researchers who are teachers as well. As Cole (1997) says:

> I have been particularly struck by the impact on my ways of theorizing development that ensued when I climbed down out of the researcher's booth and began to take responsibility, as a teacher, for implementing the theories I was proposing and helping the children I was working with.
>
> (p. 261)

We can offer the following as possible focus points for such research. The first is for a consortium of teachers to evaluate tasks and activities for their capacity to enhance resilience, playfulness and reciprocity (and whatever other learning dispositions may attract a consensus) using an LDG (grid). This would describe a range of equivalent or commensurable learning situations across place and time and provide examples of different dimensions of strength for each disposition of interest. As examples accumulate, these evaluations may need to be reviewed and adapted. A second focus for research would then be for the same consortium of teachers to develop the LDP (portfolio) with the same cohort of children across a range of settings and age groups.

Our discussion has highlighted the tension, in devising assessment procedures, between local validity and beyond-local reliability and between the notion of a learning outcome as 'in-the-head' and as situated in the environment, or dispositional milieu. It has also highlighted an area of interest (dispositions) in which interpretive, authentic and reciprocal methods of assessment are clearly particularly appropriate, methods that demand new ideas about validity and reliability. As Perkins *et al.* (1993) comment, 'dispositions inevitably include reference to things that are genuinely hard to pin down: motivations, affect, sensitivities, values and the like' (p. 18). We have sited them in practice, in the relationships between the individual learner and the environment, so we also see them as situated and distributed. For these reasons they may stretch our capacity for assessment to its limit. But we have suggested that they are important building blocks for life-long learning and that educational settings can provide environments that exemplify and encourage their development. We also maintain that documenting the development of learning dispositions is an important aspect of feedback and reflection for the community that is involved: teachers, children and families. We argue for more research on ways to trace their development beyond a single setting.

References

Ames, C. (1992) Classrooms: goals, structures, and student motivation, *Journal of Educational Psychology*, 84 (3), pp. 261–271.

Berry, D. C. & Broadbent, D. E. (1984) Interactive tasks and the implicit-explicit distinction, *Quarterly Journal of Experimental Psychology*, 36, pp. 209–231.

Black, P. (1995) Can teachers use assessment to improve learning?, *British Journal of Curriculum and Assessment*, 5 (2), pp. 7–11.

Black, P. & Wiliam, D. (1998) Assessment and classroom learning, *Assessment in Education*, 5 (1), pp. 7–74.

Bloomer, M. & Hodkinson, P. (2000) Learning careers: continuity and change in young people's dispositions to learning, *British Educational Research Journal*, 26 (5), pp. 583–598.

Boud, D. (1998) How we teach what we don't know, Inaugural Professorial Lecture, University of Technology Sidney, Australia.

Broadfoot, P. (1996) Liberating the learner through assessment, in: G. L. Claxton, T. Atkinson, M. Osborn & M. Wallace (Eds.), *Liberating the Learner: lessons for professional development in education*, pp. 32–44 (London, Routledge).

Broberg, A. G., Wessels, H., Lamb, M. E. & Hwang, C. P. (1997) Effects of day care on the development of cognitive abilities in 8-year-olds: a longitudinal study, *Developmental Psychology*, 33 (1), pp. 62–69.

Bronfenbrenner, U. (1979) *The Ecology of Human Development* (Cambridge, MA, Harvard University Press).

Brown, A. L., Ash, D., Rutherford, M., Nakagawa, K., Gordon, A., & Campione, J. C. (1993) Distributed expertise in the classroom, in: G. Salomon (Ed.), *Distributed Cognitions: psychological and educational considerations*, pp. 188–288 (Cambridge, Cambridge University Press).

Bruner, J. S. (1996) *The Culture of Education* (Cambridge, MA, Harvard University Press).

Burden, R. (1995) Assessing children's perceptions of themselves as learners and problem-solvers, *School Psychology International*, 19 (4), pp. 291–305.

Burgogne, J. (1998) A declaration on learning, *People Management*, 1 October, pp. 28–29.

Carr, M. (1998) *Assessing Children's Experiences in Early Childhood: final report to the Ministry of Education* (Wellington, Ministry of Education).

Carr, M. (1999) Being a learner: five learning dispositions for early childhood, *Early Childhood Practice*, 1 (1), pp. 82–99.

Carr, M. (2000a) Technological affordance, social practice and learning narratives in an early childhood setting, *International Journal of Technology and Design Education*, 10, pp. 61–79.

Carr, M. (2000b) Seeking children's perspectives about their learning, in: A. B. Smith & N. J. Taylor (Eds.), *Children's Voice: research, policy and practice*, pp. 37–55 (Auckland, Addison Wesley Longman).

Carr, M. (2001a) A sociocultural approach to learning orientation in an early childhood setting, *Qualitative Studies in Education*, 14 (4), pp. 525–542.

Carr, M. (2001b) *Assessment in Early Childhood: learning stories in learning places* (London, Paul Chapman).

Ceci, S. J. (1996) *On Intelligence: a bioecological treatise on intellectual development* (Cambridge, MA, Harvard University Press).

Ceci, S. J. & Bronfenbrenner, U. (1985) Don't forget to take the cupcakes out of the oven: strategic time-monitoring, prospective memory and context, *Child Development*, 56, pp. 175–190.

Claxton, G. L. (1997) *Hare Brain, Tortoise Mind: why intelligence increases when you think less* (London, Fourth Estate).

Claxton, G. L. (1998) Assessing progress towards effective lifelong learning: the Effective Lifelong Learning Inventory (ELLI), unpublished paper, University of Bristol Graduate School of Education.

Claxton, G. L. (1999a) *Wise Up: the challenge of lifelong learning* (London, Bloomsbury).

Claxton, G. L. (1999b) A mind to learn: education for the age of uncertainty, invited keynote paper to *Motivation as a Condition for Learning* conference, University of London Institute of Education, March.

Cole, M. (1991) Conclusion, in: L. B. Resnick, J. M. Levine & S. D. Teasley (Eds.), *Perspectives on Socially Shared Cognition*, pp. 398–417 (Washington, DC, American Psychological Association).

Cole, M. (1996) *Cultural Psychology: a once and future discipline* (Cambridge, MA, Harvard University Press).

Cole, M. (1997) Cultural mechanisms of cognitive development, in: E. Amstel & K. A. Renniger (Eds.), *Change and Development: issues of theory, method, and application*, pp. 245–263 (Mahwah, NJ, Lawrence Erlbaum).

Csikszentmihalyi, M. (1991) *Flow: the psychology of optimal experience* (New York, NY, HarperCollins).

Csikszentmihalyi, M. (1996) *Creativity: flow and the psychology of discovery and invention* (New York, NY, HarperCollins).

Delandshere, G. & Petrosky, A. R. (1998) Assessment of complex performances: limitation of key measurement assumptions, *Educational Researcher*, 27 (2), pp. 14–24.

Donaldson, M. (1978) *Children's Minds* (New York, NY, W. W. Norton).

Dryden, J., Johnson, B., Hoeard, S. & McGuire, A. (1998) Resiliency: a comparison of construct definitions arising from conversations with 9 year old–12 year old children and their teachers, paper presented at *AERA*, San Diego, April 13–17.

Duckworth, E. (1987) *'The Having of Wonderful Ideas' and Other Essays on Teaching and Learning* (New York, NY, Teacher's College Press).

Dweck, C. S. (1991) Self-theories and goals: their role in motivation, personality, and development, in: R. A. Dienstbier (Ed.), *Nebraska Symposium on Motivation 1990*, pp. 199–235 (Lincoln, NB, University of Nebraska Press).

Dweck, C. S. (1999) *Self-theories: their role in motivation, personality and development* (Philadelphia, PA, Psychology Press).

Facione, P. A. & Facione, N. C. (1992) *The California Critical Thinking Dispositions Inventory* (Millbrae, CA, California Academic Press).

Feuerstein, R., Rand, Y. & Hoffman, M. B. (1979) *The Dynamic Assessment of Retarded Performance: the learning assessment potential device, theory, instruments and techniques* (Baltimore, MD, University Park Press).

Filer, A. (1993) The assessment of classroom language: challenging the rhetoric of 'objectivity', *International Studies in Sociology*, 3, pp. 193–212.

Frome, P. M. & Eccles, J. S. (1998) Parents' influence on children's achievement-related perceptions, *Journal of Personality and Social Psychology*, 74 (2), pp. 435–452.

Gardner, H. (1983) *Frames of Mind*, 2nd edition (London, Fontana).

Gipps, C. (1999) Socio-cultural aspects of assessment, in: A. Iran-Nejad & R. D. Pearson (Eds.), *Review of Research in Education*, pp. 355–392 (Washington, DC, American Educational Research Association).

Goleman, D. (1996) *Emotional Intelligence* (London, Bloomsbury).

Greeno, J. G. (1997) On claims that answer the wrong question, *Educational Researcher*, 26 (1), pp. 5–17.

Grigorenko, E. L. & Sternberg, R. J. (1998) Dynamic testing, *Psychological Bulletin*, 124 (1), pp. 75–111.

Guthke, J. & Stein, H. (1996) Are learning tests the better version of intelligence tests?, *European Journal of Psychological Assessment*, 12 (1), pp. 1–13.

Haywood, H. C., Brown, A. L. & Wingenfeld, S. (1990) Dynamic approaches to psychoeducational assessment, *School Psychological Review*, 19 (4), pp. 411–422.

Howard, S. & Johnson, B. (1999) Tracking student resilience, *Children Australia*, 24 (3), pp. 14–23.

James, M. & Gipps, C. (1998) Broadening the basis of assessment to prevent the narrowing of learning, *The Curriculum Journal*, 9 (3), pp. 285–297.

Kagan, J. (1994) *Galen's Prophecy: temperament in human nature* (New York, NY, Westview Press).

Kantor, R., Green, J., Bradley, M. & Lin, L. (1992) The construction of schooled discourse repertoires: an interactional sociolinguistic perspective on learning to talk in preschool, *Linguistics and Education*, 4, pp. 131–172.

Katz, L. G. (1988) What should young children be doing?, *American Educator*, Summer, pp. 29–45.

Katz, L. G. (1993) *Dispositions: definitions and implications for early childhood practices*, Perspectives from ERIC/ECCE: a monograph series (Urbana, IL, ERIC Clearinghouse on ECCE).

Krechevsky, M. (1994) *Project Spectrum: preschool assessment handbook* (Cambridge, MA, Harvard Project Zero, Graduate School of Education).

Langer, E. (1991) *Mindfulness* (Reading, MA, Addison-Wesley).

Langer, E. J. (1997) *The Power of Mindful Learning* (Reading, MA, Addison-Wesley).

Langer, E. J. & Piper, A. I. (1987) The prevention of mindlessness, *Journal of Personality and Social Psychology*, 53 (2), pp. 280–287.

Lave, J. & Wenger, E. (1991) *Situated Learning: legitimate peripheral participation* (Cambridge, Cambridge University Press).

Lieberman, J. (1977) *Playfulness: its relationship to imagination and creativity* (New York, NY, Academic Press).

Lidz, C. S. (1987) *Dynamic Assessment: an interactional approach to evaluating learning potential* (New York, NY, The Guilford Press).

Mahn, H. & John-Steiner, V. (2002) Developing the affective zone of proximal development, in: G. Wells & G. L. Claxton (Eds.), *Learning for Life in the 21st Century: sociocultural perspectives on the future of education*, pp. 46–58 (Oxford, Blackwell).

Maier, N. R. F. (1945) Reasoning in humans III: the mechanisms of equivalent stimuli and reasoning, *Journal of Experimental Psychology*, 35, pp. 349–360.

Meier, D. (1995) *The Power of their Ideas* (Boston, MA, Beacon).

Messick, S. (1994) The interplay of evidence and consequences in the validation of performance assessments, *Educational Researcher*, 23 (2), pp. 13–23.

Moore, C. & Dunham, P. J. (Eds.) (1995) *Joint Attention: its origins and role in development* (Hillsdale, NJ, Lawrence Erlbaum).

Moss, P. A. (1994) Can there be validity without reliability?, *Educational Researcher*, 23 (2), pp. 5–12.

New, R. S. (1993) Cultural variations on developmentally appropriate practice: challenges to theory and practice, in: C. Edwards, L. Gandini & G. Forman (Eds.), *The Hundred Languages of Children: the Reggio Emilia approach to early education*, pp. 215–232 (Norwood, NJ, Ablex).

New Zealand Ministry of Education (1996) *Te Whāriki. He Whāriki Mātauranga mō ngā Mokopuna o Aotearoa: early childhood curriculum* (Wellington, Learning Media).

Nicholls, J. G. (1984) Achievement motivation: conceptions of ability, subjective experience, task choice, and performance, *Psychological Review*, 91 (3), pp. 328–346.

Norris, S. P. (1992) Testing for the disposition to think critically, *Informal Logic*, 2/3, pp. 157–164.

Perkins, D. (1992) *Smart Schools: better thinking and learning for every child* (New York, NY, The Free Press).

Perkins, D. (1995) *Outsmarting I.Q.: the emerging science of learnable intelligence* (New York, NY, The Free Press).

Perkins, D. N., Jay, E. & Tishman, S. (1993) Beyond abilities: a dispositional theory of thinking, *Merrill-Parker Quarterly*, 39 (1), pp. 1–21.

Resnick, L. G. & Klopfer, L. E. (1989) *Toward the Thinking Curriculum: current cognitive research* (Alexandria, VA, American Society for Curriculum and Development).

Rogoff, B. (1990) *Apprenticeship in Thinking: cognitive development in social context* (Oxford, Oxford University Press).

Rogoff, B. (1997) Evaluating development in the process of participation: theory, methods, and practice building in each other, in: E. Amstel & K. A. Renniger (Eds.), *Change and Development: issues of theory, method and application*, pp. 265–285 (Mahwah, NJ, Lawrence Erlbaum).

Rutter, M. (1990) Stress research: accomplishments and tasks ahead, in: J. Rolf, A. Masten, D. Cicchetti, K. Neuchterlein & S. Weintraub (Eds.), *Risk and Protective Factors in the Development of Psychopathology*, pp. 181–214 (New York, NY, Cambridge University Press).

Salomon, G. (1991) Transcending the qualitative-quantitative debate: the analytic and systemic approaches to educational research, *Educational Researcher*, 20 (3), pp. 10–18.

Salomon, G. (1993) No distribution without individuals' cognition: a dynamic interactional view, in: G. Salomon (Ed.), *Distributed Cognitions: psychological and educational considerations*, pp. 111–138 (Cambridge, Cambridge University Press).

Singer, D. & Singer, J. L. (1992) *The House of Make-believe* (Cambridge, MA, Harvard University Press).

Smagorinsky, P. (1995) The social construction of data: methodological problems of investigating learning in the zone of proximal development, *Review of Education Research*, 65 (3), pp. 191–212.

Smiley, P. A. & Dweck, C. S. (1994) Individual differences in achievement goals among young children, *Child Development*, 65, pp. 1723–1743.

Smith, A. B. (1999) Quality childcare and joint attention, *International Journal of Early Years Education*, 7 (1), pp. 85–98.

Sutton-Smith, B. (1997) *The Ambiguity of Play* (Cambridge, MA, Harvard University Press).

Thorndike, E. L. (1922) Practice effects in intelligence tests, *Journal of Experimental Psychology*, 5, pp. 101–107.

Vygotsky, L. S. (1978) *Mind in Society: the development of higher psychological processes* (edited by M. Cole, V. John-Steiner, S. Scribner & E. Souberman, translated by A. R. Luria, M. Lopez-Morillas, M. Cole & J. Wertsch (Cambridge, MA, Harvard University Press).

Wenger, E. (1998) *Communities of Practice: learning, meaning and identity* (Cambridge, Cambridge University Press).

Wertsch, J. V. (1991) *Voices of the Mind: a sociocultural approach to mediated action* (Cambridge, MA, Harvard University Press).

Wiliam, D. (1994) Assessing authentic tasks: alternatives to mark-schemes, *Nordic Studies in Mathematical Education*, 2 (1), pp. 50–70.

Wylie, C. & Thompson, J. (1998) *Competent Children at 6: families, early education, and schools* (Wellington, NZCER).

Wylie, C., Thompson, J. & Lythe, C. (1996) *Competent Children at 5: families and early education* (Wellington, NZCER).

Wylie, C., Thompson, J. & Lythe, C. (1999) *Competent children at 8: families, early education, and schools* (Wellington, NZCER).

PART 4

COGNITION AND DEVELOPMENT

CHAPTER 7

MODELS OF COGNITION IN CHILDHOOD

Metaphors, achievements and problems

Sarah Meadows

The Child as Thinker, London and New York, Routledge, 1993

I will begin my discussion of models of cognition in childhood by picking out two themes which have run through most of our discussion of children's thinking. One is the general question of how far children's thinking is different from adults' thinking. Here we can see a wide range of beliefs, from St Paul's eloquent assumption that children's thought is different from and inferior to adults' thought –

> But when that which is perfect is come, then that which is in part shall be done away.
>
> When I was a child, I spake as a child. I understood as a child, I thought as a child: but when I became a man, I put away childish things.
>
> For now we see through a glass, darkly; but then face to face: now I know in part; but then shall I know even as also I am known.
>
> (Corinthians 13: 10–12)

– to the contemporary emphasis on the structure and process of children's thought being similar to adults' from the very earliest years of schooling onwards, and the differences being due to children's ignorance of relevant material and their lesser practice at meditating on and describing their own thinking. [. . .] the general question of degree of difference and of development is [. . .] very much a theme in the wider models of cognition surveyed in this chapter. The second theme is in many ways an even more fundamental one. It is the question of what models are appropriate for cognition: is it more helpful to think of ourselves as 'in essence limited capacity manipulators of symbols' (Siegler 1983: 129) very similar to slow and inaccurate computers; or as biological organisms with a long evolutionary history which has led to us having a brain which functions in particular ways and leads to particular cognitive activities just as we have evolved lungs, livers and a thumb articulated with fingers so that fine grasping is possible; or as members of social groups taking part in relationships and cultures, and using and developing our cognition within them and inseparable from them? Different models of human nature make different assumptions about the relative importance of the social and the biological, of cognitive processes and physiological structures and problem context. Which metaphors seem appropriate arises from these assumptions and also constrains what questions will be asked and what answers will be seen as possible. I will argue that though we may learn a great deal about cognition by thinking of it as computation, as adaptation or as acculturation, we must be clear and explicit about our basic assumptions and remain aware of how our chosen metaphor may obscure important points which another model would have clarified. The discussion of several models of cognitive development which follows will include some assessment of how adequately the models match up to these demands.

Piaget's model of cognitive development

We begin with a model which set out its basic assumptions far more elaborately than any other and which took into account a uniquely wide range of biological and philosophical considerations. Piagetian theory was a tremendous intellectual achievement, and for all its faults, and despite all the idiocies committed on data by people who misunderstood what was important about it, has shaped the field in quite remarkable ways. It gives an account of cognitive processes which is still influential and is in certain respects probably basically correct, and needing mainly testing and specification; and an account of cognitive structure which has been more popular (because less abstract), but is clearly too rigid and does not deal adequately with the influence of cognitive material or cognitive context.

It would take several volumes larger than this to describe and evaluate Piagetian theory fully; here I will focus on a few of his most important ideas. For fuller accounts of Piaget's work, I would suggest 'beginner readers' begin with Donaldson 1978, Flavell 1985, and Brainerd 1978 (in ascending order of difficulty), and those who already have some acquaintance with his work might address themselves to his own classic account (Piaget 1983) and to important discussions of his last work by Gelman and Baillargeon (1983), Beilin (1992) and Vuyk (1981).

At the core of Piaget's model is the idea that cognition is one form of the adaptation between organism and environment which is seen through all the living world. The child, or indeed the adult, is all its life actively trying to make sense of the world, just as any organism must try to adapt to its environment. I have discussed the implications of evolutionary theory and brain research for cognitive development theory elsewhere (Meadows 1983 [. . .]; see also Young 1987); Piaget's main work on this, *Biology and Knowledge* (1971) is still an important book. He said that 'adaptation' in cognition proceeded by means of 'assimilation', or relating new information to pre-existing structures of knowledge and understanding, and 'accommodation', or by developing the old structures into new ones under pressure from new externally-given information or problems or from the pressure of internal contradictions by incompatible structures. These two cognitive processes or twin 'functional invariants' work together throughout the whole of cognitive life (the assimilation of new information must lead to some degree of accommodation in the old system of knowledge, if only to the minor degree of 'ah, here's another *X*: I've seen at least a hundred of those in my time, so now I've seen at least a hundred and one'), and together with the equally innate tendency to organise knowledge into coherent systems and smooth routines they give rise to a series of 'structures' of cognition, that is, ordered rules, categories, procedures and so forth which eventually amount to unified organisations of logical operations.

An example may help to clarify what 'assimilation', 'accommodation' and 'organisation' might look like at the level of observable behaviour. I devised it originally to make a number of points in a criticism of Piagetian theory, but I do not think it is in any way unfair to Piaget's intentions. The protagonist is an experienced cook. He or she has successfully cooked carrots and potatoes, carrots by boiling them, grating them raw for salads, and making carrot soup, potatoes by boiling, roasting, frying, mashing and making chips. The initial state of knowledge of ways of cooking carrots and potatoes could be represented as in the first matrix.

Method	Carrots	Potatoes
Boiling	✓	✓
Chipping	not tried	✓
Frying	not tried	✓
Grating, for salad	✓	not tried
Mashing	not tried	✓
Roasting	not tried	✓
Soup	✓	not tried

The cook now meets parsnips for the first time. The new vegetable is *assimilated* to the carrot repertory, perhaps on the basis of similarity of shape and texture. Parsnips boil very well, make a rather bland soup (Grigson (1980) recommends adding curry powder), and although they taste quite pleasant raw are not a visually attractive ingredient in salad. The cook also assimilates parsnips to the potato repertoire; parsnips need careful chipping or frying, mash well and are delicious roasted. The knowledge matrix after assimilation of parsnips would have one further column, as shown in the second matrix.

Method	Parsnips
Boiling	✓
Chipping	possible
Frying	possible
Grating, for salad	maybe
Mashing	✓
Roasting	✓
Soup	maybe

Assimilation is always accompanied by accommodation, however. The schema 'vegetables you can mash' is augmented with parsnips, for example, and the importance of butter is emphasised. The cook may accommodate further by extending the mashing schema to carrots, and hence to the full range of vegetable purées. Since roast potatoes and roast parsnips are successful, the schema 'roasting' may be tried out on carrots, with success. A fully developed knowledge system for cooking carrots, potatoes and parsnips might look something like the final matrix.

Method	Carrots	Potatoes	Parsnips
Boiling	✓	✓	✓
Chipping	no	✓	possible
Frying	no	✓	possible
Grating, for salad	✓	no	maybe
Mashing	✓	✓	✓
Roasting	✓	✓	✓
Soup	✓	maybe	maybe

This sort of procedure is obviously infinitely extendable. The same basic principles of assimilation, accommodation and organisation leading to a thoroughly developed knowledge structure will apply whatever new vegetable the cook encounters: turnips, celeriac, Jerusalem artichokes, and so forth.

Assimilation and accommodation are fundamental but abstract concepts which are at one and the same time immensely plausible and hard to tie down to specific behaviour, let alone specific brain activity or specific educational practice. They are almost certainly essential basic components of a good model of cognitive development, though they need considerably more specification (Beilin 1992, Gelman and Baillargeon 1983, Meadows 1983, 1986). Piaget's own main account was given in two books published in English in 1978, where he distinguishes between different sorts of assimilation. He postulated that there is a sort of natural instinct to assimilate: 'any scheme of assimilation tends to feed itself, that is, to incorporate outside elements compatible with its nature into itself' (Piaget 1978), thus driving development on. This happens at three levels. The first is assimilating objects to schemes, as the infant does when grasping a new object, or as scientists had to when a new planet's existence was discovered. The second is assimilation between different schemes, for example eye–hand co-ordination or the sort of alternation between writing and critically reading one's own writing which is achieved by the secondary school pupil [. . .]. The third and highest level is assimilation between subschemes and the totality which integrates them into a coherent whole; the concept of 'gravity', for example, is at the core of physicists' accounts of many quite different localised events, from the motion of the planets round the sun to the falling of Newton's apple. These assimilations are said to involve the scheme 'finding' or 'distinguishing' characteristics which match the scheme or are near neighbours to it, as opposed to others which negate or contradict it, though these too must in the end be co-ordinated into the total scheme. Thus both affirmations and negations are important. A balance between affirmations and negations is necessary for development, just as a balance between assimilation and accommodation is.

While this account of assimilation and accommodation is of great interest, a number of problems arise. Some cluster around the 'drive to assimilate'. It is not clear to me at what point this drive would be satisfied: the model appears to imply that there could always be further assimilation and accommodation, that the 'natural' state of cognitive development is progress towards a highly developed, subtle, sophisticated, intricately integrated, perfectly balanced cognitive system. Is this an empirical account of what is really done, or a rational reconstruction of ideal cognition? There is room for real doubt about whether most people really do go in for this sort of thorough thinking-out of everything (Boden 1982, Mischel 1971); perhaps here Piaget was using himself as a prototype and forgetting that the rest of us are, probably, sloppier thinkers, content with localised understanding, not pushing its limits outwards, and quite capable of believing contradictory things?

There are problems also over the question of what is or can be assimilated to a scheme, and how this is done. What degree of match, on what dimensions, means that a new object or event affirms a pre-existing scheme? What mismatch negates it? For example, suppose that I initially believed that every word of the Bible was literally true, and that, therefore, we knew the world was created in exactly seven days (in late October of 4004 BC, if I also believed Archbishop Ussher's biblical commentary). What would then be my adaptation to the theory of evolution and the evidence of geology and the fossil record? I could refuse to assimilate science and stick to creationism, or accommodate to science and reject the literal truth of the Bible: or, like some unhappy nineteenth-century scientists, suggest that God during his seven days' work created new rocks and animals containing evidence of an evolutionary history which had never actually happened. Of these three adaptations, the last is inherently unstable, leading for example to a pretty odd sort of God; the first is adaptation by restriction, like the amoeba who successfully protects itself against the drying up of its pond by retreating into a shell-like skin; only the second is likely to lead to further cognitive development and better understanding of the world. Whether it also leads to better adaptation in a wider sense depends on the socio-cultural context; for someone living amongst fundamentalists it might well lead to blasphemy trials and outright persecution.

This is an extreme example (though one which has occurred quite frequently – and violently – in both [. . .] [the nineteenth and twentieth centuries]), but it is a real problem [. . .]. Piaget's examples tend to be *post hoc*, and no one else has yet done better. We may also doubt whether affirmations and negations are equally readily dealt with by the thinker, as negations in logic, and in scientific theory building, seem to be so difficult to manage (see Kuhn 1962, Wason 1977). Further, in many areas it is extremely hard to see whether a new event affirms or negates a scheme; the concept is hard to apply in questions of moral or political judgement, for example, or in the visual arts. Russell (1978) argues that one of the important things we have to learn is, precisely, which kinds of knowledge have to be consistent and which do not.

Assimilation, accommodation and organisation, functioning together, were held together by an even more important (and mysterious) process called 'equilibration', Piaget believed. He saw equilibration as central to evolution, to all biological functioning and to cognition in particular. It was a central theoretical concept from the beginning to the end of his career, but it is hard to define it precisely, not least because Piaget's own account of it developed over the years. Essentially, perhaps, it marks his belief that although assimilation, accommodation and organisation functioned incessantly to deal with the information and the problems that continually impose themselves on the organism's attention, there was none the less stability in cognition to a considerable degree, not the constant shifting of cognitive structures which constant change – the maturation of the organism, its second-by-second experience of the environment, the pressures of the social world – might seem to force during development. 'Equilibration' is clearly a force for stability, via a self-regulation that balances external and internal changes. In some cases it works by restoring the previous stable state; in the cases which are more interesting for development, successful adaptation calls for a more radical and pervasive shift if balance is to be regained, an 'equilibration majorante' (Piaget 1978).

Why did Piaget believe that cognition was an equilibrated system? He clearly believed that organisms *need* to maintain a stable internal equilibrium within the changes and uncertainties of the outside world, a belief which one can sympathise with. There are a number of biological systems of self-regulation which serve precisely this sort of need: the regulation of body temperature in warm-blooded animals is one example. If our blood temperature varies too far, our bodies automatically work to correct this, and if necessary set up conscious actions which change the temperature of our surroundings. Receptor cells in the hypothalamus, pre-set at a level of about 38.4°C by our genes, are activated when the blood temperature rises or falls beyond narrow limits, and signals from these receptors initiate sweating, shivering, panting, increased metabolism of fat from the liver and so forth. Sensory cells in the skin provide conscious sensations of heat or chilliness. These cells generate signals which activate the cerebral cortex and initiate programmes of activity such as taking off clothes or lighting the fire, which prevent further rise or fall in body temperature before it has changed substantially. The receptors in the hypothalamus innately and precisely signal deviation from the pre-set temperature level, and innately set in train effective responses, but are not conscious: the receptors in the skin, reporting to the cortex, inform it whether the skin is getting hotter or colder rather than indicating absolute temperature, and while we may or may not be conscious of our need and what to do about it, we have learned the appropriate conscious actions and can choose amongst them (see e.g. Young 1987). If something goes wrong with either the automatic or the behavioural self-regulation of body temperature, we lose our physiological equilibrium and may become quite seriously, even fatally, damaged, as in cases of heat stroke or hypothermia. 'Durable disequilibria constitute pathological organic or mental states' (Piaget 1968: 102).

The other root of Piaget's belief in cognitive equilibria must surely be related to the coherence, closure and self-structuring properties of logico-mathematical systems. The number system, for example, or the rules of formal logic, structure reasoning so as to lead on every occasion to true and non-contradictory answers. It is always true that '2 + 2 = 4', for example, and excludes the possibility that '2 + 2 = 5' or '2 + 1 = 4'; if 'every dog will have his day' then there can be no dog anywhere who has neither already had his day nor cannot legitimately look forward to it today or sometime in the future. The main question here, [. . .], is whether such perfectly clear and consistent systems of knowledge are representative of knowledge as a whole and whether we use them easily; Piaget seems to have seen them as at least pre-eminently important and desirable.

Equilibration relies extremely heavily on the assumption of invariant regularities and consistencies in thought. It explains *how* cognitive development occurs in terms of 'need' for a coherently organised and consistent way of thinking. The changes and demands of the outside world produce in the thinker small 'perturbations' or 'conflicts' which lead the cognitive system to small automatic adjustments (of assimilation and accommodation) to cope with the conflicts and return either to the original cognitive equilibrium or to a new and better one. It is the momentary non-functioning of a cognitive scheme which both signals the presence of a 'perturbation' and is the sole motivator of efforts to seek a new equilibrium, but the non-functioning does not of itself indicate what the conflict is or how to solve it. Even in his most detailed account (1978) Piaget did not succeed in specifying what contradictions are noticed or resolved or exactly which lead to cognitive progress. He warned that not all contradictions are fruitful, and speculated that structural contradictions are more relevant to cognitive development than are momentary contradictions due to perception or historical accident. A theory of effective spurs to cognitive change would be very useful, but is not available at present. In order to resolve disequilibrium in the direction of cognitive growth, you must be able to recognise (not necessarily consciously) that there is a disequilibrium, and as Rotman (1977) points out this is not unproblematic; you must similarly recognise at least approximately what has caused it; you must *want* to resolve it, rather than deciding to live with the contradiction (like the White Queen in *Through the Looking Glass* who deliberately practised believing impossible things before breakfast). There may also be, in many cases, alternative equally valid resolutions of the contradiction, and in other cases no resolution may be possible (as in various logical and mathematical paradoxes (Hofstadter 1979)). Bryant (1982) argues that confirmation by two schemes leading to the same conclusion may lead to development more effectively than conflict.

Piaget did discuss (1978: 30–8) what makes one state of cognitive equilibrium 'better' than another; better equilibria can cope with more elements or dimensions, they are both more differentiated and more integrated, they co-ordinate and complete earlier equilibria, they are more flexible, and they provide more possibilities for interacting with a wider environment. This is a plausible description of a cognitive system but hard to translate into behavioural terms, and there are some problems in founding 'betterness' on increased complexity or width of application. It *is* obvious that adults do interact in more varied ways with their environment than infants do, and with more different aspects of it, and similarly that human–environment interactions are wider and more differentiated than amoeba–environment interactions. It should not be taken as obvious however that this makes humans or adults 'better' or 'better equilibrated' or 'better adapted to their environment' than amoebae or infants are (Midgley 1985, Ruse 1986). Nor does this account explain why 'lower' forms of life (such as amoebae) or of cognition are prevalent and apparently well adapted to the world. Would we have tabloid newspapers, for example, if equilibration really pushed cognition ever on?

Piaget somewhat compounded this problem by his insistence that cognitive development formed a single invariant sequence of stages. He insisted that these were a result of individual equilibratory construction, not due to an innate teleology of development, though he was clearly sympathetic to the work of biologists such as Waddington who demonstrated how much of embryological development and physical growth was pre-programmed while still under the influence of the organism's experience of the environment. 'Preformationism' has been a non-respectable position in much thinking about cognition (Mischel 1971), but in far more subtle, specific and limited forms is now appearing to be more viable as a basis to theories of cognition [. . .]. We need to understand a great deal more than we do at present about the nature and mechanisms of genetic programming and central nervous system functioning (and about the nature and mechanisms of the effects of life experiences, which are if anything less well understood and no less complex), but modern biology, as Piaget was perhaps the earliest to see, has a great deal to offer to those concerned with cognition (see e.g. Young 1987). Nevertheless, the claim that the Piagetian sequence of stages is invariant and universal is not unproblematic. Significant problems remain in the diagnosis of stages whose internal consistency is not clear (see Gelman and Baillargeon 1983, Meadows 1975, Klausmeier and Sipple 1982), but the cross-cultural evidence suggests that besides these there are a number of significant variations not just in rate of development, which would have only marginal relevance to the validity of Piaget's theory, but in whether the later stages develop in the sort of form Piaget described. The sort of schooling the culture provides and the sorts of concepts it values seem to be the main determining factors (Dasen 1977, Laboratory of Comparative Human Cognition 1983). The evolutionary analogy would itself suggest that a single invariant sequence is less likely than a branching tree-like pattern: certain cognitive adaptations are developed but other possible adaptations remain potential rather than actualised, or are even given up. The time and resources required to develop mathematical or musical ability to the full, for example, might preclude even the normal development of other areas of cognition, let alone developing them too to their full potential. Post-Piagetian researchers, particularly in the United States, seem to be more concerned with domain-specific developments at present, and with emphasising the crucial role of acquired information, than with the general universal and relatively content-independent sorts of structures which make up the Piagetian stage sequence.

Piaget's use of 'structures' has been very influential, both at the basic conceptual level, where, as we will see, there are problems, and even more at the level of descriptions of behaviour, where his stage descriptions have caught many psychologists' imaginations. I think that much of this influence is now declining, and Piaget's own interest shifted towards an emphasis on 'procedures' towards the end of his life. (To some extent, this is a shift in level of description. 'Structures' are the timeless, abstract, universal laws of transformations and relations between objects or concepts, such as the mathematical system of real numbers; 'procedures' are the goal-directed behaviours which, occasion by occasion, we use. For example, commutativity $(8 + 2 + 7 = 7 + 2 + 8 = 2 + 7 + 8$, etc.) is part of the structure which underlies our successful procedures for adding up our bills, top to bottom or bottom to top, pence and pounds together or separately.) Nevertheless, some discussion of 'structures' and 'stages' is appropriate here.

It would be hard to deny that human thought, at least after infancy, is in some senses structured. It has rules, legitimate procedures and hierarchies of concepts. We are not completely bound by these structures, we may not be aware of them, and we do not, on the whole, have adequate descriptions of them, but generally we work within their system. So far, this is commonplace, a very vague description applicable to language, Piaget's formulations, number systems and even the extreme behaviourists' associative networks (Feldman and Toulmin 1976). As we become more detailed, problems start to arise, and I want to discuss the forms some of these take in Piaget's work (see particularly Piaget 1970, 1971).

The first problem is that of the ontological nature of 'structures', what sort of existence they have. The slightest sort of existence would be that of theoretical construct; thus we make no claims about whether there are such structures in the child but we describe his thinking in terms of organisations and properties which exist only in our theoretical analysis. If we keep to it, this is a fairly safe position, though it may look trivial – but it is all too easy to forget that the 'structures' are in our description not in the child's thought, and be carried away by our metaphor. Locating the structures in the child reifies them a degree beyond descriptive constructs, and serious problems arise. One is the question of *where* they are in the child, thinking, mind or brain all being possibilities. There are too many controversies about the relationship between these three to go into here [. . .]; Piaget's position was ultimately reductionist, that thinking is firmly centred in a neuro-physiological base, but also that it must have an abstract description, the two levels being isomorphic. His description of the earliest stage of thought was primarily biological, that of the later stages primarily abstract and in terms of formal logic. This general position is a reasonable avoidance of the dilemma, though what the isomorphisms are remains as yet unknown.

A second problem is that we do not directly observe thinking or other cognitive processes, we infer them from observable behaviour. Inhelder and Piaget (1979), discussing the relationship between procedures and structures, reiterate that the best evidence for the existence of structures in the child's mind is what the child considers possible, impossible, or necessary, and some very interesting and ingenious research is being done in this area (see e.g. Russell 1981a,b, 1982). However, unless we are extremely careful, clever and scrupulous, we may make the wrong inferences, and this is particularly likely when we are studying people different from ourselves or comparing groups different in age, class, or culture. Cole and Means (1981) discuss this question very thoroughly. Their strictures apply to much of Piaget's account of the inadequacies of young children's thought, which we will come back to. Piaget's formulation, which slides (often almost within a chapter) between structures which are in the theorist's description and identical or virtually identical structures which are in the child, was inadequate.

There is one further possible sort of existence for structures of thought, not incompatible with those already described. This is that they exist in some sense outside the individual, as in what Popper calls 'World 3' (Popper 1967, Popper and Eccles 1977). I know of no comment by Piaget on this idea, but it would not seem to be a part of his formulation of cognitive development. This sort of existence, though not entirely easy to understand, might be more easily related to Vygotsky's theory than to Piaget's (see later in this chapter).

Piaget was, then, not so precise as one could wish about the ontological status of structures, and his position was fraught with similar difficulties over his treatment of the relation he believed there to be between 'structures' and observable behaviour. It is often problematic to go from performance (which is comparatively observable) to competence (which has to be inferred from a sample of performance and from a theory of what competence is like). I have found myself in difficulties over the validity of the transition in much of the work on cognitive development [. . .]; but Piaget's treatment of the problem has seemed to many psychologists to be peculiarly unsatisfactory. Behaviour is an important source of data for the theory, but it has to be *interpreted* before its degree of support for his theoretical claims can be assessed. This was clearly his procedure in most of his published 'experiments': a deliberately artificial situation is presented to the child and his thinking about it is probed and then interpreted by the experimenter, this 'thinking' being manifested primarily in the child's talk about the situation and secondarily in his manipulations of the material. The theory arises from the interpretations, not from the overt behaviour; and the behaviour is reported, selectively, as supporting illustration of the theory. Thus it can be for the reader a matter of considerable doubt and difficulty to relate what the child can be observed to do or, very often, say, and the abstract formal mental structures that are said to explain the child's activities, and this I will come back to when I discuss some questions of the empirical validity of Piagetian structures. It was, presumably, not a problem for Piaget, but then he was neither a psychologist nor an empiricist. The elucidation of thought by the examination of language does not seem to have struck him as particularly problematic. He believed that language was unable to convey what was not already established in thought. This would seem to imply that language is, at least slightly, retarded compared with thinking. Unless the lag is very small, this would mean that there would be occasions when the child's language was too underdeveloped to express the greater sophistication of his thinking. Using language to diagnose thought would in these cases give rise to false diagnoses of immature thinking; and there are indeed many demonstrations of 'failure of thinking' which appear to be due primarily to language difficulties (e.g. Donaldson 1978). Nor is the interpretation of children's language necessarily unproblematic.

There is one further central problem in Piaget's use of structures, which we must deal with before discussing the empirical validity of his work. This is two characteristics of structures which appeared very early in his work on them (Piaget 1952) and which relate to both his biologism and his description of structures in formal and abstract terms. Cognitive structures tend to form structured wholes (*structures-d'ensemble*), and this is what, once they are fully established, the concrete operational stage, the formal operational stage and other logico-mathematical systems consist of. 'Stages' are periods of relative equilibrium in the development of the child's thought, which is said to resemble the development of thought in the human species (this resemblance being one reason for Piaget's interest in children's thought, it being impossible to investigate the thought of, say, Australopithecus or Neanderthal Man). There are a number of points here which need a brief comment on a theoretical level; some we will return to, as they raise empirically answerable questions.

Both *structure-d'ensemble* and 'stage' imply the existence of a fairly tight relationship amongst a set of cognitive structures. On the whole, we would expect the structures which form a *structure-d'ensemble* to develop and appear together, and to react one upon the other. Piaget's theory also suggests that they form at each stage qualitatively different structures, being not just bigger but better (in terms of coherence, complexity and field of application, as we said earlier). Again, at a very general level this would appear really rather likely, but the detail of Piaget's models of *structures-d'ensemble* turns out to be unsatisfactory. Both concrete operations and formal operations are described in terms of logical systems which logicians regard as of poor quality (see e.g. Boden 1979: 80–6, Ennis 1978), and which are inferred from behavioural (largely verbal) data in ways that turn out, at least in the case of formal operations, to be quite simply wrong (Bynum *et al.* 1972).

In addition to these difficulties Piaget's model of stages has changed with development. The earlier model implied a stage sequence where transitions from stage to stage are the disequilibrated periods and are relatively brief, so that there are fairly abrupt changes from stage to stage. It is this model of clearly contrasted stages that dominated most popular accounts of Piagetian theory. In the later model there is a considerably less step-like development, and the preparation, achievement, consolidation and superseding of, say, concrete operations flow into one another smoothly and cover a period of several years. If this is the better picture (and, as I describe below, the empirical evidence is for the later more complex model not for the earlier one) the descriptive value of stage and *structure-d'ensemble* concepts begins to look very slight indeed. There are indications that psychologists studying cognitive development are moving away from their use (e.g. Beilin 1992, Flavell 1963, 1977, 1985).

In Piagetian theory the structures of thought are applicable to virtually any area of knowledge; they are seen as abstract content-free ways of reasoning. Piaget described them as fitting together into a succession of coherent and qualitatively different stages; the major ones are the sensori-motor, pre-operational, concrete operational and formal operational stages, and there are sequences of substages within the sensori-motor stage and within areas of operational thought, such as conservation of quantity. The structure of each stage is such that thought at any given moment is relatively consistent in its level across different content areas; consistency is especially to be expected at the times when concrete operations and, later, formal operations are fully developed, as both these stages are based on logical models. While logical systems are being constructed, temporary inconsistencies and fluctuations are to be expected, but an emphasis on differences between stages and similarities within them remains. In a child behaving according to the Piagetian model, performance on one test of, say, conservation predicts performance on other conservation tests and on other tests of concrete operations. Furthermore, the stage structure limits the possibilities of improving performance by instruction. The child cannot assimilate or accommodate to events which are too incompatible with his or her whole coherent system of understanding, and instruction can at best produce only a limited and possible temporary advance, isolated in the area being trained.

The sensori-motor stage develops over the first two years or so of the child's life [. . .] for an interesting review of it see Harris 1983. The school years begin late in the 'pre-operational' period, cover 'concrete operations', and end during 'formal operations'. It is therefore appropriate to provide a very brief account of each stage. The pre-operational stage is described (1) as the period when children begin to use semiotic systems such as language and imagery, and (2) as a time when they lack operational thought, that is, flexible reversible reasoning which allows them to conserve, classify, seriate, co-ordinate perspectives, overcome misleading perceptual impressions, etc. Concrete operational children have these abilities: they can think much more systematically and quantitatively and their thinking is described in terms of formalised logical structures (the 'groupings') relating to classifications and relations in quantity and in space. The final formal operations stage is a more integrated and more abstract development from concrete operations, less tied to content and more capable of dealing with hypothetical material. Formal operations receive a more abstract holistic and rigorous description from Piaget. Logicians as well as psychologists have queried the models given for both the concrete operations and the formal operations stages (Vuyk 1981), and they remain controversial.

With this account of stages, Piagetian theory puts up a challenge which has attracted a good deal of research response. As I have said, direct evidence on the reality of assimilation, accommodation and equilibration has been hard to get: testing the stage model has been somewhat easier, though not altogether unproblematic. Sequences of stages are fairly well confirmed, though there have been some suggestions that their order is logically necessary (e.g. Smedslund 1980) and so of no empirical interest. Rate of progress through the sequence seems to vary somewhat between individuals, but this is far from crucial to Piagetian theory, which is concerned with the idealised 'normal' epistemic subject, not with individual differences. Rate also varies between cultures, degree of schooling and less formal educational experience being one of the main relevant variables; in some cultures there is little sign of formal operations. This finding is mildly embarrassing for a model which has been taken as claiming that formal operations is a universal high point of human cognition, but in fact Piaget's main account does not explicitly make such a claim (Inhelder and Piaget 1958). The role of social and environmental experience in cognitive development is an important issue which needs more investigation than the main stream of Piagetian thought provided. [. . .]

The behaviours typical of different stages appear in a fairly constant order, then, if not at a constant rate. Their appearance can certainly be accelerated by training (Brainerd 1983). Contrary to the predictions of the Piagetian account, training does produce improvement in performance which can be considerable, long-lasting and pervasive [. . .]. A variety of training methods have been seen to succeed, and it is not the case that 'neo-Piagetian' models, which conjure up equilibratory mechanisms or provoke discovery, are any more successful than methods involving imitation, didactic interaction, or the following of verbal rules. Initial stage level does not seem to predict the possibility of training or limit how effective it will be. Pre-schoolers have successfully been trained on the concrete operations tasks which they would not be expected to get right for another three or four years, and their performance after training appears as competent as that of untrained 8-year-olds (Brainerd 1983, Gelman and Baillargeon 1983). This has been interpreted as showing that there are minimal differences between the cognitive structures of pre-school children and those of primary school children. It does seem to be clear that Piaget painted far too negative a picture of children's thinking in the pre-operational stage (Beilin 1992, Vuyk 1981), and we might prefer a model of cognitive development which described more pre-school competence and (perhaps) a less complete later stage competence, with a gradual consolidatory transition rather than a qualitative shift during the school years (Braine and Rumain 1983, Donaldson 1978). However, there seems at present to be some danger of arguing away a developmental change in cognition rather than carefully analysing the extent and nature of the change.

One of the differences between younger and older children is in the degree and type of within-stage consistency they show, or how many *décalages*, that is, slips in level of performance, there are. The question here is how the different areas fit together as structured stages. The usual research design has been the obvious one of seeing how children's performances correlate across a number of tasks which each involve the same logical principles (e.g. conservation) or belong to the same stage (e.g. measure of class inclusion, weight conservation and perspective-taking, which all belong to the concrete operations stage). It is not always altogether clear how large a correlation is required to support the theory of within-stage consistency, and the statistical complexities are considerable. If, accidentally, one test is slightly more difficult than another, for example, this may lead to misleading patterns of synchrony (Brainerd 1978). On the whole, research studies have found less consistency between different areas of concrete operations than a simple model of logical structures which are constructed quickly and underlie all tasks would suggest (Gelman and Baillargeon 1983, Klausmeier and Sipple 1982, Meadows 1975). There have also been numerous inconsistencies between different measures of ostensibly the same operation, for example, conservation tests using materials which seem obviously equivalent to the adult but produce obstinately different responses from children (e.g. Beard 1963, Miller 1982, Uzgiris 1964). Some of these *décalages* are due to the 'figurative aspect' of the test situation; for example, if the transformed material in a conservation test looks very different from the original, then children will be less likely to give a conserving response than if the change in appearance is slight. Similarly, various changes in the social situation or in the language used help young children to conserve or manage class inclusion (e.g. Light *et al.* 1979, Siegel *et al.* 1978). Some *décalages* receive only a last resort explanation: that the objects involved offer more 'resistance' to the thinker. Piaget never dealt with the problem of *décalages* thoroughly. He was less interested in them than in how children managed the general principles underlying operational thought, for example how they had a feeling of certainty despite appearances which suggested otherwise. He thus had little to say about *décalages* except where they were common to all children, hence characteristic of his 'epistemic subject'. Recent work by Longeot (1978) starts to deal with this omission, and with some of the problems of low correlations within stages, with a model which predicts when consistencies and *décalages* will occur. Longeot points again to the possibility that there may be discrepancies between the logico-mathematical structures of the epistemic subject and the natural thinking of children solving adaptive problems in real life: the distinctions between 'knowing' and 'doing' and between various degrees of 'having a concept' that I mentioned earlier. This work has also shown that there may be alternative paths to the same outcome, and such individual differences need to be accounted for. One possibility raised relates Piagetian concepts to psychometric ones: the suggestion is that there are different and partially independent sorts of intelligence (cf. Gardner 1983). There is interest also in the possibility that cognitive development is domain-specific rather than, as in Piagetian theory, general across domains. Investigation here obviously requires detailed descriptions by domain and comparison between them; this is very much what Piaget and Inhelder did in the series of studies which are still acknowledged as brilliant investigative observation.

Information-processing models of cognitive development

Introduction

Psychologists using the information-processing approach to the study of cognition and cognitive development describe cognition as largely a matter of handling information in order to solve problems. They are primarily concerned with how information is selected, represented, stored, retrieved, transformed, and so forth. The focus is on what mental processes are used to deal with information, with how they are organised, and with how they change during learning or development. Computation is seen as the basis for human cognition, and sometimes computers are used to test hypothetical accounts of the information-processing that goes into solving a problem. Even if they are not, some attempt is made to specify the hypothetical cognitive processes sufficiently precisely for them to be tenable by experiments with people if not by computer simulation. The cognitive tasks investigated tend to be fairly tightly defined also, and they quite often have a Piagetian or psychometric pedigree. Siegler (1978, 1983, 1984, 1989), for example, has done extensive analyses of a balance task, as I describe below, and Klahr (Klahr and Wallace 1976, Klahr 1984) of conservation and class inclusion. More recently, Anderson (1992) combines psychometrics and information-processing in an interesting model of cognitive development and intelligence. The basic assumption is that 'people are in essence limited capacity manipulators of symbols' (Siegler 1983: 129) and that analogies with the ways in which computers process information will be helpful. Just as computers operate by combining a number of microlevel distinct operations in an appropriate sequence, so humans are seen as using a fairly small number of elementary cognitive processes in a structured way over a period of time. Mental processes which mediate in varying ways between stimulus and response are emphasised, and in many aspects human cognition is seen as active and constructive, unlike the passive S-R models of classical behaviourism, or indeed the run-of-the-mill computer.

Like Piagetian models, information-processing approaches to cognitive development seek to describe children's cognitive capabilities and limitations at successive points in their development, and to explain how a later and more advanced understanding emerges from an earlier less adequate one, that is, these models too are concerned with 'what develops' and with 'how does this development occur'. They deal with these questions by trying to specify what cognitive processes the child applies to what information, which processes in which order for how long, and what information, how represented, and when in the processing sequence. They also seek to specify how development occurs, what components of processes and representations are self-modifying, or can be modified by outside influences, or are resistant to change. They assume that knowing about adult information-processing (or computer information-processing) can lead to illuminating comparisons with children's information-processing (and vice versa).

In order to clarify issues which will arise in my later discussion of information-processing models of cognitive development, I will outline some concepts which have proved important in models of adults' information-processing. The first is derived from the work of Atkinson and Shiffrin (1968) whose account of the memory system has proved useful [. . .]. They distinguish between memory structure and the control of memory; the former is analogous to computer hardware and constrains speed of operation and memory capacity, the latter is like the computer's software, specifying what processes should be carried out when for this particular task. They propose that memory includes several different stores; the details are not universally agreed but it seems to be helpful to think in terms of there being a sensory register, a short-term memory store and a long-term memory store, each of which could be divided up according to whether the incoming information is visual, auditory, olfactory or whatever. These memory stores are linked [. . .]. Each uses certain basic processes (which can only run at up to a certain maximum speed), and the sensory register and short-term memory stores are also limited in the amount of information they can take in and how long it lasts for. Atkinson and Shiffrin suggest that these memory structures are universal: all adults have them, and all children, and they may perhaps be 'wired-in' to the brain [. . .].

Memory control, however, can be changed by development or by learning. Control processes, such as rehearsal, operate on information within memory stores, and allow people to overcome the structural limitations of the system. Information is processed in the sensory register, which can only hold it for a fraction of a second, and then moves to the short-term memory store or 'working memory', which is analogous to the central processor of a computer. It is here that conscious and strategic processes operate. We can be conscious of what is in our working memory even though we are not conscious of what is in our sensory register or our long-term memory. Memory strategies mediate the transfer of information between working memory and the other memory stores. Using verbal rehearsal, for example, keeps information in working memory longer than its normal time limit of less than a minute and also makes it more likely that the information will be transferred to the permanent store of long-term memory; organising information into larger meaningful chunks overcomes the normal limited capacity of working memory. A case-study by Ericsson, Chase and Faloon (1980) illustrates this. The normal quantity of unrelated bits of information which can be held in working memory is about seven items, seven randomly ordered digits, for example. However given a few hours' daily practice for a year or so the student who was the subject of the case study could remember strings of 75 digits! He was able to do this because he organised groups of the random numbers into meaningful items. He happened to be an experienced cross-country runner who could encode numbers as race times; '3492' for example was encoded as a speed for the mile, as '3 minutes 49.2 seconds, near world record time'. With practice he could group such meaningful chunks into larger 'super groups'. His knowledge provided him with a strategy, which practice perfected, so that he could transcend the structural limitations of memory, at least for strings of numbers which could be grouped into patterns which resembled race times.

This study illustrates a point about information-processing which has been made by other theorists, for example Herbert Simon (1981). It is important to analyse the demands of the task if we are to understand the performance of people working on it. What they do is constrained by their own cognitive limitations, but it is also directed by what they think the task requires. A strategy may be used because it is adaptive for them on that task, not because it is the best strategy available. This is important developmentally for a number of reasons. What strategy of processing information is used will depend on what the task is seen to require, hence its familiarity will affect performance. It will also depend on what relevant information is available, and again children may lack information which older problem-solvers would have. The 'costs' of the strategies which could be brought to bear on a task may also be different for children: less easily assessed, in the first place, and less easily leading to a cost-benefit analysis. We may perhaps be, unlike computers, problem-solvers who are willing to settle for a 'good enough' near-solution to a problem if it would be very laborious to give up our not-quite-adequate strategy and replace it with a more efficient but more expensive one. [. . .]

Information-processing models, then, are concerned with the encoding and transformation of information in the solving of cognitive problems. The core constructs are that there must be internal representations of information which cognitive processes act upon, generating, manipulating or transforming the initial representation. Representations and processes together make up the knowledge base, and it is assumed that this is large and rich in interconnecting links, so a particular piece of information can be accessed in many different ways from strong association to indirect inference. Although the knowledge base is to all intents and purposes infinitely large, some of its content may be difficult or impossible to reach on occasion, and only a very small subset of knowledge can be acted on at any one time, as there is only a limited quantity of attentional resources available to bring knowledge and processes into an active state and maintain them there. Some activation is automatic and requires little or no attention; other processes needing more immediate control make heavy demands on attentional resources. Automatic processing tends to be fast and to make minimal demands on resources, but it is not under voluntary control so it cannot easily be modified. Controlled processing is slower and uses up many more attentional resources, and may be less efficient, but it is easier to modify and fit flexibly to task demands and other varying aspects of each situation.

There is considerable and often heated debate about the ways in which people are able to represent knowledge (Block 1981, 1983, Boden 1988, Cooper and Shepard 1984, Pylyshyn 1980). The issues under debate include whether we have visual image representations of knowledge or solely verbal propositional ones, whether knowledge is declarative or procedural, explicit or inferred, and so on. Most of the debate is at the level of the formal and abstract description of the structure of knowledge, and it is not often linked with our increasing understanding of how the brain works [. . .]. Siegler (1983, 1986) discusses a number of different ways of representing knowledge and information-processing, and makes the point that these models will be useful for analysing different tasks. Semantic networks, for example, seem to be most useful for pinning down a set of linked meanings, and thus for modelling a person's store of facts about the world or part of it, say facts about the music of Tchaikovsky. Production systems are more like knowledge about procedures, set up as smoothly executable routines for the performance of tasks such as addition, speaking, skiing, playing the violin and so forth. They may be harder to access and discuss than the semantic network of declarative knowledge, and seem to be organised for effective action rather than for self-awareness. Scripts represent generalised events: they are accounts of situations where both procedural and declarative knowledge are involved (Nelson 1986 [. . .]), such as playing in an orchestral concert.

These different ways of representing knowledge are more likely to be useful simplifications, which make it easier to analyse the information-processing demands of a task, than to be true reflections of genuinely separate ways of representing knowledge. In order to play the violin in an orchestra, for example, one certainly needs to have procedural knowledge, to get fingers and bow to the right places in a staggeringly rapid succession. But one also presumably follows a script of co-operating with other players and the conductor, and one may have available declarative knowledge about the style of the piece, its composer, other interpretations by other musicians, and which critics or talent-spotters are in the audience. These different sorts of knowledge are not independent, and even on a simplified task, such as would be used in a laboratory investigation, may be strong influences on behaviour. Where the subject's 'irrelevant' representations are not what the experimenter would expect, as may often be the case when the subject comes from a different culture (Cole and Means 1981) or different age group, performance may be adversely affected and the wrong cause for this failure inferred.

Issues in information-processing

Information-processing models of cognition could be seen as tending towards the same two separate categories as other accounts of children's cognition, the first category being those which focus on the cognitive system *per se* and describe the very basic structures and processes which underlie all cognitive functioning, a largely syntactic approach, and the second category taking much more account of how the general system is applied to particular tasks.

This sort of polarisation can be seen in the AI literature, where some models are of General Problem Solvers and some are of more limited Expert Systems, as well as in the developmental literature reviewed here. On the whole the current trend seems to be towards working on the details of cognition in particular limited fields, on how the content of a task affects the ways in which a person (or a computer) adapts general processes in order to get the task done, and researchers have discovered a great deal of flexibility in how processes common to several tasks are used in each case. This has led to description of cognitive strategies and a recognition of the complexities of the interaction between cognitive activities, the skills, knowledge and attitudes of the learner or problem-solver, and the task demands. Strategic descriptions tend to be set out at a different level from the syntactic processes descriptions, as a comparison between, for example, the models of class inclusion proposed by Klahr and Wallace (1976) and by Case (1985) suggests. The former looks closer to a computer program, the latter to a common-sense account such as might be usefully taught to and understood by a child. As they stand, neither accounts for the 'horizontal *décalages*' documented in the literature. For example, in Siegel *et al.* (1978) class inclusion of different sorts of sweets was facilitated by a particular form of question ('Would you rather eat the sweets or the toffees?') and no doubt also by the motivation of gastronomic interest and understanding of the social setting of food distribution.

John Searle has argued very strongly that a computer that only used syntactic rules could not be said to have a mind. His argument (Searle 1984: 39–41, 1990) is as follows. Minds are entirely caused by processes going on inside the brain: 'brains cause minds'. 'Syntax is not sufficient for semantics', that is, form alone is conceptually different from meaning. 'Computer programs are entirely defined by their formal, or syntactical, structure' and 'Minds have mental contents; specifically, they have semantic contents'; mental activities refer to or concern things in the world. The conclusion which follows from these four premises is that 'No computer program by itself is sufficient to give a system a mind. Programs, in short, are not minds, and they are not by themselves sufficient for having minds.' Further, 'the way that brain functions cause minds cannot be solely in virtue of running a computer program': the computational properties of the brain are not enough to explain its functioning to produce mental states. As Searle asserts, brains are biological engines, their biology matters. An artificial brain, if it were to be able to do all the human brain can do, must have powers equivalent to those of the human brain, not just the power to implement computer programs.

AI specialists, and indeed other philosophers interested in AI (e.g. Boden 1988, 1989, Churchland and Churchland 1990, Gregory 1987, Haugeland 1985), do of course dispute these conclusions. Searle himself would not deny that computational descriptions may be interesting, though he is strongly sceptical about their long-term usefulness: 'The computer is probably no better and no worse as a metaphor for the brain than earlier mechanical metaphors. We learn as much about the brain by saying it's a computer as we do by saying it's a telephone switchboard, a telegraph system, a water pump, or a steam engine' (Searle 1984: 55–6). For my purposes [. . .], I want merely to underline his point that there are two levels of description of cognition which are quite incontrovertibly important: the neurophysiological workings of brains, and the psychological level of behaviours like recognising faces, understanding language, social cognition and so forth. Adequate neurophysiological and behavioural descriptions and theories may make computational information-processing ones redundant. Since the information-processing metaphor still, for good and bad reasons, dominates the field, I will discuss it further here, but readers may wish to take my discussion in the light of the fact that I am much more impressed with the exciting findings that are coming out of recent brain research [. . .], and feel that the future lies there and in studies of cognitive behaviour in the real world rather than in abstract computational models of cognition. To see people as 'in essence limited capacity manipulators of symbols' (Siegler 1983: 129) is one possible view, but perhaps a misleadingly narrow one.

Boden discusses current computer models of learning and cognitive development, and the difficult conceptual questions involved. How are 'learning' and 'development' to be distinguished for example? What are the prerequisites for learning? Are there distinctions to be drawn between types of learning, and how relevant is the content and structure of what is learned? Can the human learner be modelled by a computer system? These questions do not have simple obvious answers, and Boden believes that so far computer models of learning have been only partially successful (1988: 190–201). One model she discusses is a system designed by J. R. Anderson (for a full account see Anderson 1983). This system, ACT*, can perform a variety of tasks, using a repertory of cognitive skills, and it can gradually incorporate its items of declarative knowledge into procedures for solving problems. It is also capable of 'transfer' to new problems (Singley and Anderson 1989). The successful use of rules leads to their being strengthened, and being more likely to be used in future; their failure has the opposite effect. New rules are created in three main ways. In 'proceduralisation' an item of declarative knowledge which has been used in the same procedure several times comes to be represented as an integral part of the procedure as well as being part of the semantic network. In 'composition' a well-used sequence of operations is collapsed into one cohering package which gradually comes to be utilised in the place of its separate constituents. In 'tuning' successful and unsuccessful procedures are adjusted to work better. Analogies with rules which worked on similar problems are made; generalisation combines the rules which worked on two similar problem-solutions and derives a more general rule; discrimination introduces differentiations into a rule which has been applied to different problems; and, again, composition tidies procedures into smooth-running combinations. The computer instantiation of these rules provides a good analogue of human learners in Anderson's experiments. Boden however criticises it as being somewhat '*ad hoc*', lacking sufficient task-analysis and a full underlying theory of what learning is. These problems amount to a 'vagueness' such that, Boden says, 'it is highly doubtful whether Anderson has a clear understanding of *just what his system can and cannot do*, and *why*' (Boden 1988: 207, her emphasis). As the ways in which ACT* learns seem very similar to those which developmentalists have suggested (see the next section), Boden's criticisms would seem to apply there too, with perhaps added force as the developmental models are even less closely tied to a systematic instantiation.

While constructs about representation, processes, knowledge base, attentional resources and executive control are to be found in most of the many information-processing models of cognition, these vary in detail and particularly in their attention to cognitive development. I will provide here an outline of the changes models try to account for, some description of typical information-processing models of cognitive development, and some discussion of possible developmental mechanisms. These should be read as the comments of someone outside the information-processing camp who has reservations about the metaphor of 'man-as-computer' and feels that the approach would benefit from detailed attention to the instantiation of minds as brains. Information-processing *aficionados* would no doubt take a different line (see e.g. Boden 1987, 1988 for a clear and fair account).

Information-processing accounts of 'what develops'

Like other approaches to cognitive development, information-processing accounts seek to establish *what* develops, and *how* the development takes place. As to what develops, the candidates are basic capacities, strategies, metacognition, the knowledge base, or combinations of these.

By 'basic capacities' is meant processes such as recognition, scanning for information, categorisation, associating correlated events, learning, co-ordinating different modalities and integrating information. There is a vast literature on these processes (for useful reviews see Haith and Campos 1983, and for a brief introduction see Meadows 1986, chapter 2). Summarising it ruthlessly, it would appear that the rudiments of recognition, scanning, categorical perception, and various associations between different modalities, events and pieces of information can be observed even in very young children; but that each of these shows experience-related and age-related changes in speed, exhaustiveness and flexibility (e.g. Kail 1991a, 1991b). For example, even new-born infants show habituation to some stimuli, which requires some retention and recognition of the stimuli (Harris 1983 reviews the literature), but there are developmental improvements in how well stimuli are encoded, how much time is necessary for recognition and how much time recognition lasts for, what the effects of distractors are and what errors of inference are made, and so on. One controversial aspect of these developmental improvements is whether they relate to increases in the size of the information-processing capacity (see my discussion of Case's model, elsewhere in this chapter) or to changes in the strategic use of capacity whose size changes little (Kail 1986, 1988, Stigler *et al.* 1988). The two are not easily distinguished; evidence on how brains work will perhaps help to solve this question as well as clarifying how different inputs are integrated [. . .]. Meanwhile it is now clear that extreme empiricism, the belief that the infant mind is a completely clean slate on which anything could be written, is not an acceptable position. Evidence from infants' behaviour (Haith and Campos 1983), from neuroscience (Young 1978, 1987) and from computational psychology (Boden 1988) shows that there is much inbuilt psychological structure from birth (for some recent discussion see Anderson 1992, Carey and Gelman 1991, and a special issue of *Cognitive Science* (vol. 14, 1990)). Unstructured learning systems can learn little of any interest, indeed Fodor (1976) argues that to learn a new concept one must already have a conceptual system capable of representing the 'new' item, and this pre-existing system must have been, ultimately, innate. This degree of nativism probably is too much (see e.g. Boden 1988, Haugeland 1985, Johnson-Laird 1983), both because its view of concept learning does not include all the processes by which concepts develop and because it omits full consideration of conceptual development as a process influenced by others who have already developed the concepts in question. However, learning and development – whether of skills or concepts – do clearly depend on cognitive structures which are complex from the start. They may also be constrained by the structure of the domain of knowledge involved, including the language used to talk about it (e.g. number systems, Longuet-Higgins 1987). Task analysis, as I've already said, may be crucial.

There are clearly developmental changes in cognitive strategies, the second candidate for an important role in cognitive development. [. . .] In particular, it is clear that young children show less evidence of using deliberate strategic approaches to problems (at least of an academic rather than social or practical sort), and have smaller and less flexible repertoires of strategies than older children. To give a well-documented example, pre-school children rarely show deliberate efforts to remember information, may not allocate their resources efficiently to a memory task, and do not seem to notice that their non-strategic attempts to remember have led to poorer performance than they can achieve when they are taught to use a mnemonic technique (see e.g. Brown *et al.* 1983). There are considerable improvements in memorising strategies, particularly over the primary school years. Changes in life's task demands, such as the requirements of the school curriculum and the need to co-ordinate home and school worlds, may contribute to this change. Awareness of one's own achievements and activities in remembering seem important also.

Such awareness, knowledge about and use of cognition are the concern of the field known as 'metacognition', or cognition whose own subject-matter is cognition. There is some debate over whether metacognition is separate from cognition that is about other aspects of the world, and about the role of conscious awareness; but it seems to be fairly clear that there are changes in children's knowledge about and control of their cognition as they get older. [. . .]

There is even less doubt that the knowledge base available to children increases as they get older. Theories which concentrated on universal cognitive processes set this sort of developmental change aside as uninteresting, just as studies of learning in adults tried to rule out knowledge as a contaminating variable. Recently there has been more interest in cognitive development within specific domains of knowledge, and these studies have suggested that the amount of knowledge available and the ways in which it is organised may have important effects even on universal cognitive processes, and may be one of the major components of cognitive development (e.g. Chi and Ceci 1987, Keil 1989). Just as we do not yet understand how metacognition and cognition interact, we do not really understand how content knowledge affects cognitive processes or how knowledge systems should be modelled. [. . .] this seems likely to be a busy area for some time, as researchers seek to picture knowledge and cognition in an increasing number of domains. Studies which investigate the sources of knowledge and how it is organised and used will no doubt make more contribution to psychological theory than those which merely describe age difference in content.

As I said earlier, there have been a number of developmental models of general information-processing as well as the specific and detailed accounts of the information-processing which is involved in various levels of success or failure on a particular task, such as predicting the movement of a balance or answering a class inclusion test. The next section briefly describes the models proposed by Case (1974, 1984, 1985), Kail and Bisanz (1982), Keil (1984), Klahr (1984), Klahr and Wallace (1976), Siegler (1983, 1984, 1986, 1989) and Sternberg (1984, 1985) [. . .].

Case's theory

The first model I will outline is that proposed by Robbie Case (Case 1974, 1984, 1985). Case's work has roots in Piagetian theory and is similarly anattempt at a general theory of intellectual development. He tries to describe the complexity of infants' and children's cognition while differentiating them fromadults'; to integrate cognitive, linguistic and social development while also allowing for (and accounting for) developments which are specific to different domains;and to use recent more sophisticated modelling techniques derived from cognitivepsychology and computer science. The theory deals with the structure of children's thinking, with its successive stages, and with how transitions from stage to stage are made.

Case's central metaphor is of the child as a problem-solver,

> an organism that is endowed with certain natural desires, and that encounters
> certain natural barriers to their realization, but which also has the capability for
> overcoming these barriers by refining and re-combining the inborn procedures
> with which it comes equipped.

(1985: 59)

Despite the use of the words 'organism' and 'natural' there is far less biological reference and discussion here than in Piagetian theory: Case's account of cognition is
more mechanistic than organismic. The basic level of the model is of mental schemes,
either *figurative* schemes which represent patterns of stimulation that the child has
encountered several times and recognises, or *operative* schemes, which represent rules
which can be used to transform the figurative schemes in various ways. For example,
a child might recognise a picture, assimilating it to a figurative scheme, and be able
to use an operative scheme representing relative size to say which object in the picture
is biggest. The model also has, very importantly, *executive* schemes, which are representations of how to use figurative and operative schemes over a period of time to
solve a particular problem or reach a particular goal. It is the executive schemes
which determine what temporal sequence of figurative and operative schemes is called
up. If, for example, the task is to say how many windows there are in the back of
your house, you may need to call on a figurative representation of how the house
looks and then an operative scheme to count the windows; if the task is to say
whether or not the house is burglar-proof, the figurative and operative schemes called
on will be rather different. Because of its problem-solving character, cognition has
an affective character: from infancy onwards people are motivated to solve problems, to be pleased at their success and unhappy at their failure. Active problem-solving
is an innate human characteristic, and even infants are capable of some control over
both its cognitive and its affective aspects, though it is perhaps the nature of such
control that changes most as development proceeds.

Case suggests that even neonates have figurative and operative cognitive schemes,
and executive schemes have very early roots. Schemes are co-ordinated and form
four major structured stages, each of which develops over a number of years into a
stable system which then, differentiated and co-ordinated, serves as the building
blocks for the next stage. These stages are recognisably Piagetian. In the first 'sensori-
motor operations' stage, the child uses sensory representations (e.g. seeing a frightening
face) and motor responses (e.g. leaving the room, hiding the eyes). In the second,
'representational operations', stage, the child's representations include durable concrete
internal images and their responses can produce additional representations (for
example using a mental image of a scary face to draw a monster). In the stage of
'logical operations' representations are more abstract and more open to transformation though still on a simple level. The fourth, 'formal operations', stage involves
complex representations and complex transformations of abstract information.

The stages differ in terms of the sort of executive schemes or control structures
which are available. Minor shifts occur within a stage as executive schemes which
are similar in complexity, form and function are co-ordinated; major between-stage
shifts occur when schemes whose form and function differ are co-ordinated into
overall structures with new emergent properties. There is a sequence of types of
control structures within each stage, creating the sort of 'vertical *décalage*' or repetitions at new levels which Piaget described. The sequence within each stage shows
an increasing number of simple schemes being put together: first the various schemes
are consolidated separately, then two are co-ordinated, then these are elaborated as

additional elements are incorporated. Case (1985, chapters 7–11) analyses behaviour on a variety of tasks achieved from infancy to adulthood in these terms, and in terms of the sort of operations involved, and uses his analysis to justify his claim of strong vertical *décalage* or repetition. It is not entirely clear to me (nor to Flavell 1984), however, that the analysis is really justified by the data rather than necessary for the claim. There is not always a completely obvious reason why a particular response to a task is analysed as made up of exactly this particular number of unitary schemes, nor whether schemes are all equal in the demands they make. Case's characterisation of substages emphasises similarity but does not dispel suspicions that development may show more differences than he allows, both in the sequence of development within different stages and in the levels of thought about different areas within the same stage ('horizontal *décalage*'). A precise measure of 'scheme demands' and a firm distinction between schemes which are truly indivisible units and those which are composites might be useful, but it is hard to see how they could be arrived at. Computer simulation might tell us what they were for computers, but it is not altogether clear how we can extrapolate from computers to people. And if information-processing ideas about developmental processes are correct, the demands which schemes make, and how separable they are, will change as they become more practised.

For all that his structural account seems at present less than perfectly justified (though an improvement in many ways on earlier structural models), Case has some interesting suggestions to make about developmental *processes*. He postulates innate capabilities for setting goals, formulating strategies to meet these goals, and for integrating different strategies into more complex and effective ones. He begins (1985, chapter 12) by pointing out that children have four general regulatory processes which orchestrate their mental activity. These are a tendency to problem-solving, a tendency to exploration, a tendency to imitation, and a capacity for mutual regulation with other people. Problem-solving involves searching for an operation which bridges the gap between the state of affairs which is to be found now, and a more desirable goal state. The child, faced with a less than optimum present situation (such as not being able to reach the toy on the floor from his or her seat in the high chair) and able to envisage a more desirable situation (having the toy to hand), searches for a strategy which will transform the former into the latter, and calls for help (or leaps out of the chair, or pulls the string that ties the dropped toy to the chair's arm, or whatever is possible). The first step in problem-solving is to search for operations which will transform the less pleasant, less desired state of affairs into the more pleasant, more desired, perhaps by matching the particular features of the problem and the goal ('distant toy', 'I can't move to get it') with features of schemes in the repertoire ('Mummy gets things for me', 'pulling strings moves distant things') and computing some sort of best fit. Next the proposed sequence of operations ('Get Mummy's attention, point out toy, show I want it back, accept toy') is evaluated for its effectiveness, either after actually being enacted or after an imagined 'dry run'. This can then lead to 'retagging' of the sequence so that it can be more easily accessed if it has succeeded ('when I said "Dolly please" Mummy gave me Dolly *and* a biscuit') or avoided if it has led to a negative outcome ('jumping out of the high chair really hurts'). Finally the schemes used become consolidated, or hierarchically integrated, as essential components run more automatically and inessential ones are dropped, and as separate components come together to form larger invariant units. Our child in the high chair might give up leaning over to stretch out an arm for the toy which is beyond arm's length, but begin to incorporate automatic 'please' and 'thank you' as parents demand an explicit acknowledgement of their services.

Case's second natural developmental process is exploration. Here the child does not have an explicit goal but does have a situation to which several possible schemes could apply. What happens here is a sort of 'suck it and see' procedure: the child tries out various schemes and notes their results. Schemes are chosen because they have features applicable to the starting situation, not because they are relevant to any particular goal, and typically several schemes will be applied in succession. As in problem-solving, the results are evaluated and the schemes retagged, and because several schemes have been tried out freely and in rapid succession they can be con-solidated, their components varied, automated, integrated and so forth. Exploration is a 'bottom-up' process, while problem-solving is a 'top-down' one; it is also, in Piagetian terms, heavily assimilatory.

The third natural general developmental process is imitation. Often young chil-dren do not know what to do or what results could possibly be obtained, but more experienced people do have this knowledge and may act on it in the child's presence. Children can observe what those around them do and seem to have a strong natural tendency to imitate the actions of others, to get the same result, or for the sake of being like another person, or just for fun. The adult, or more skilled person, models both possible strategies for dealing with the situation and the goals that these strategies can achieve in this case. The child may focus on the action or on the goal; as in the cases of problem-solving and exploration which do not involve modelling themselves on other people, the schemes the child uses are evaluated, retagged and consolidated.

Case's final process is 'mutual regulation', or the adaptation of the child and another person to each other's feelings, cognitions and behaviour. This may be done to serve emotional or social ends, as in attempts to comfort or please, or to achieve dominance through assertion or aggression, or it may be task-oriented as when chil-dren and adults co-operate to solve a problem or instruct each other. The same common subprocesses of accessing schemes and experimenting with novel sequences, evaluating the consequences, retagging the schemes and consolidating them, apply. Case's main example here (1985: 270–1) is of what happens during deliberate instruction of a less skilled person by a more skilled one, and he does not elaborate on his brief nomination of affective mutual self-regulation as a means to intellectual development. Nevertheless, it seems to me to be a helpful advance for an information-processing model to make an explicit recognition of social facilitation of development and of cognition's affective roots. Both mutual regulation and imitation are Vygotskian learning processes.

All these four general learning processes are seen as arising early in infancy, and as occupying a considerable proportion of young children's time. Both their early emergence and their high frequency suggest that they are quite strong candidates for important developmental processes. Case believes they would give rise to the sort of stage transitions described earlier because they would produce a hierarchical inte-gration of what were previously separate control structures. The subprocesses of activation, evaluation, retagging and consolidation are invariant and resemble Piaget's functional invariants of assimilation, accommodation and equilibration, but in the cases of imitation and mutual regulation are put to use in ways more reminiscent of Bruner and Vygotsky: the child inherits the cultural tools used by adults and, first by mutual regulation then in more and more internalised ways, can use them as his or her own independent strategies and skills. Case has said that the child has a more or less innate and invariant set of capacities – for setting goals, for activating existing schemes in novel sequences in pursuit of these goals, for evaluating the results, and for reworking or 'retagging' sequences that have been evaluated positively so that they can be generated intentionally in future, and for recalling such reworked structures and consolidating them so that they form smoothly functioning executive structures (Case 1984: 27–8). It is not clear how strongly he means these to be seen as literally invariant over the course of development; as Flavell (1984) points out it may be misleading rather than helpful to suppose that, for example, the 'goal-setting' of the neonate is very like the 'goal-setting' of the adolescent. Some sort of 'goal-setting' process is indeed likely to be useful both as a means to development and as a means to minute-by-minute survival, but we need more details of what 'goal-setting' is available at different points in development – and in different ecological settings and for individuals with different histories – than Case's reliance on functional invariants provides.

Consideration of this sort of issue might be very relevant to some of the problems that Case sees for his theory (1985: 282–8). One of these is that cognitive development takes such a long time. If it were solely a matter of the integration of subprocesses and substages, it should surely proceed faster than it does. Laboratory training studies suggest to Case that it should be possible to progress from the early sensori-motor structures to adolescent structures in about 250 half-days, or about a year, allowing for weekends off! Since the ordinary time-span required is about fifteen years, despite the claim Case made earlier that pre-school children are spending at least half their waking hours exploring, solving problems, imitating and so forth, the slowness of children's development is puzzling.

Further, if children have differing amounts of experience in different domains, as they presumably do, it is not clear why there seem to be (in Case's judgement) developments which are general and cross domains (Case 1984). Theorists who de-emphasise such shifts would not find them the problem that Case does, of course. He acknowledges that he cannot account for this. His two main suggestions are, essentially, that he has underestimated the complexity of interdependences between different content domains (and he certainly has not dealt thoroughly with the acqui-sition and organisation of content as opposed to process) or that there may be maturational limits to the rate of cognitive change (which was of course Piaget's position), though quite why training can often transcend these, while normal devel-opment does not, remains unclear. It is however a maturational-limit model that he goes on to elaborate, though as a default option rather than as the basis for a research programme that could expand our understanding of cognitive development.

The main maturational constraint which Case discusses is the size of the short-term storage space (STSS) which a child has available for information-processing. He is picking up the idea (which appeared in neo-Piagetian theory and is common-place in information-processing work) that human beings have limited attentional resources, which have to be divided between the current execution of operations, 'operating space', and storing or retrieving the results of operations which have just been carried out. There is a trade-off between these two: if a great deal of mental space or resources must be used for difficult operations, then less is available for storage, and vice versa. Short-term storage is seen as active, not just as dumping the results of operations in boxes, incidentally. A new cognitive acquisition can only be made if it demands no more working memory capacity than the child has avail-able; if the child's working memory is too full for the new cognition, it will not be acquired. [. . .] Case proposes that the capacity of STSS increases with development, but at a slow speed which restricts the overall rate of cognitive development. STSS increases because with the greater operating efficiency that comes with prac-tice, the requirements of operating space decrease, and more of the total attentional resources are available for use as the STSS. Total resources do not change during development, but their distribution between operating and storage does: operating needs fewer resources as operations become more practised, more consolidated and more integrated, so that more space is available for holding their results ready for operation. Operations continue to develop and to become more and more slick for as long as they are practised. This implies that the major cognitive difference between adults and children is the amount of practice they have had on basic cognitive operations, and also on cognitive operations specific to a particular domain. Adults will almost always have had more practice on the general basic operations, but there may be some domains where the child has had more practice than the adult (new topics in the maths curriculum, for example, or childhood crazes such as puns and other word play) and may be the quicker and better thinker.

As I have discussed elsewhere (Meadows 1986), it is not going to be easy to distinguish whether there are changes in the totality of attentional resources available or merely, as Case (1984, 1985) suggests, in how they are distributed between operation and storage, because these two necessarily interact both in observable behaviour and within the model. Performance on a task will be a function of the strategy sequence used, the demands which that sequence makes on operating space and short-term storage space, and the size of the available attentional resources. We know that for many tasks there are developmental changes in strategies and in their demandingness, and in the existence and accessibility of relevant knowledge. Attempts to measure total resources or total available cognitive space have to hold these developmental changes constant if they are to distinguish between changes in the size of total space and changes in the way a space of unchanging size is used. A very precise analysis of tasks, of learner activities, of how tasks and learners change with practice, and of the interdependences between knowledge, strategies and processing, is required; and this is not going to be easy to achieve. Meanwhile the 'best guess' seems to be that developmental changes in absolute amount of processing space, if they exist at all, are less important than changes in how they are used. Changes in what information is stored and how it is accessed, and a wider range of more sophisticated processing possibilities which can gather and act on information, seem to be more important. Case does maintain, however, that these changes, which could obviously be very domain-specific, are held together so that cognitive development is homogeneous across domains, the 'homogenising' factor being maturational limits such as the degree of myelinisation of the central nervous system. [...]

Kail and Bisanz's theory

Kail and Bisanz (1982) provide another account of the mechanisms of cognitive development. They see development as being generally in the direction of increasingly having rules and processes which are *sufficient*, in that they allow a wider scope of proficient problem-solving, as in the case of Siegler's balance scale task or Karmiloff-Smith and Inhelder's balancing objects task (e.g. Siegler 1978, Karmiloff-Smith and Inhelder 1974/5), where young children have only one strategy, which works excellently but only over a very limited range of situations, and older children have developed more complex and conditional rules, which lead to success in most predictions of balancing. They suggest that development also leads to a shift towards more *efficient* information-processing, to using procedures which are more powerful and require less slow and error-prone rote repetition. Using such procedures frees attentional resources for other cognitive activities. There is also development in the knowledge base, which incorporates more elements and organises them into larger and more meaningful units, which are increasingly linked on the basis of conceptual relationships not just perceptual similarities.

These developments are supported by increases in attentional resources, in total capacity or in use of the same capacity, or in increasingly effective and flexible use of a capacity which is itself increasing, and through processes which modify both declarative and procedural knowledge. These include processes which add or delete 'nodes' in the associative network (for example adding 'mammal' in between 'dog' and 'cat' on the one hand and 'animal' on the other) and processes which strengthen or weaken links (a visit to the slums of India, or to a kennel full of pit bull terriers, might weaken the association between 'dog' and 'pet'). There are also processes which compare procedures with other procedures or with goals or other external events, detecting either inconsistencies or regularities. Inconsistencies, as in Piagetian theory, need to be resolved by changes in the cognitive system; regularities which recur and demand resources lead to packaging and streamlining of procedures and to chunking of knowledge elements. They also contribute to the possibility of higher level organisation of knowledge and processes, and perhaps to one's confidence in the correctness and adequacy of one's processing (cf. Bryant 1982). While these monitoring processes play an important part in cognitive development, they make heavy demands on attentional resources, and if these are not available to a sufficient extent the processes of consistency and inconsistency detection and consequent reorganisation cannot reach fruition. Resources become available through increased automatisation of cognitive processes, or through growth in the total information-processing capacity (if such growth occurs), or through changes in the knowledge base which alter the ways in which the cognitive system investigates and interprets its environment, hence altering the feedback which is monitored by the detector processes. That is, changes in the declarative and procedural knowledge base can enable the identification of regularities and inconsistencies which were previously undetectable. The modifications consequent on the detection of inconsistencies tend to generate more *sufficient* representations and processes, allowing cognition to apply to a wider range of phenomena without giving rise to too many exceptions and anomalies; modifications following the detection of regularities tend to generate more *efficient* representations and processes as links between elements and processes become smooth and automatic. Altogether there is a fairly steady development towards more complex and more hierarchically integrated cognition.

Other accounts

A certain similarity will already have emerged from my accounts of the models proposed by Case and by Kail and Bisanz. Some of it is no doubt due to my interpretation; but it deters me from providing equally long accounts of other available information-processing models. In brief, Sternberg's model (Sternberg 1984, 1985) is an information-processing analysis of intelligence with developmental implications. [...] The main developmental mechanism is strategy construction based on the use of knowledge-acquisition components, performance components (which are processes such as encoding, drawing inferences, mapping relations between similar contents) and metacomponents which select and monitor performance, these last being 'the major basis for the development of intelligence' (Sternberg 1984: 172). Klahr and Wallace (1976, Klahr 1984) have 'generalisation' at the core of their developmental model. They focus on regularity detection and redundancy elimination, like Kail and Bisanz, and on the 'time-line' record of cognitive processing. The time-line contains the data on which generalisation is based. It is a record of how the cognitive system encountered and dealt with problem-solving situations. For example, a time-line concerned with the balance scale problem would have a record of what previous balances had looked like, what the child had therefore predicted and which side had in fact gone down. If these are retained in detail, generalisations useful to the setting up of an effective production system may subsequently be made, by detecting regularities and eliminating redundancies. It is thus important that all the relevant information should be accurately encoded, otherwise the self-modifying cognitive system could not work. Siegler's model (Siegler 1983, 1984, 1986) stresses that much of children's knowledge is rule-governed, using 'if . . . then' question–answer patterns. Some aspects of these rules are quite broadly applicable, for example there may be fall-back rules which are resorted to in several different situations when information-processing demands overwhelm the cognitive system. He sees encoding as central to cognitive development, since if the crucial features are not adequately represented automatisation, generalisation and strategy construction cannot proceed fruitfully. A comparison of the accounts I have described is set out in Table 3. [. . .] Sternberg (1984) includes essays on the mechanisms of cognitive development and further references. Anderson (1989a, b, 1992 [. . .]) provides a recent and interesting model.

It seems to me that there are very similar models under discussion in these papers. Learning proceeds by association of new information with old information, either through the two occurring together in a regular way (contingency) or through the two being similar on some dimension (with infants perhaps having an innate preference for similarity on some dimensions, where similarity on others will be ignored); this is of course the assumption that has dominated information-processing work (and its predecessors in Learning Theory). The various theorists' proposed processes for change, for example, seem to form at least overlapping sets, with a frequent emphasis on self-monitoring and processes for automatisation and the detection of consistencies and inconsistencies. They take different positions on the role of the knowledge base; Case, for example, assumes it is minimally relevant to processing and Keil sees it as the main arena for cognitive change, and there seem to be parallel assertions about whether development is general across all domains and uniform in rate between them, or whether it varies very much from one domain to another. Similarly there is a degree of disagreement about how far development is influenced by the outside world, particularly by interaction with other people; Keil and Case specify instruction as a means to cognitive development, Klahr's model is primarily internally motivated, system-driven, not taught. Finally, the models centre on a similar range of tasks, problems derived from the cognitive psychology literature, though Case tries to extend his discussion in social and affective areas and Keil's focus is on knowledge systems which seem closer to semantic network studies. Indeed, the same data serve more than one model as evidence: Siegler's documentation of the balance task is used by other theorists for their own purposes.

Flavell (1984), reviewing the models described in Sternberg (1984), finds all of them interesting but none, as yet, convincing. His final comment is that 'there is more variety in *what* gets developed and also more variety in *how* these varied developments get accomplished' (p. 206) than the models, as yet, allow. The more interesting part of this comment refers to the possibility that different sorts of learners have different sorts of cognitive processes available to them, for example, that the developmentally early ways of processing information give rise to new mechanisms for processing information so that cognitive development proceeds in new ways. Becoming able to process language for discrepancies and agreements between literal meaning and the message that the speaker intends to convey, or to analyse words into phonemes, to give two examples, changes current understanding of discourse and of spelling respectively *and* gives tools for further developments. Flavell likens this to technological development: things are possible now that we have satellites or laser beams or non-stick cake tins which were impossible or very difficult before. Changes in information-processing mechanisms may be one of the sources of differences between novices and experts, or between the gifted and the ungifted; however, like Keil, I think we should not forget the probability of different knowledge bases here.

One further point to be made about these models is that they do not use biological evidence. Though several theorists stress that they see their subjects as organisms produced by evolution, the models are mechanistic rather than organismic, even if the machine is an active, constructive and self-modifying one. What is being discussed is also, on the whole, 'cold' cognition rather than 'hot'; the sort of dispassionate, detached, cognition which is brought to bear on formal well-defined 'academic' tasks of not much immediate relevance to the desires of the problem-solver, let alone his or her survival. The cognitive processes described here are not closely linked to affect (except in Case's model, where goals are set by unrealised desires). This may reflect the models' origins in 'cognitive science', where computers and affect are incompatible, and affect is very hard for artificial intelligence to cope with. In view of the increasing amount of evidence that in the human brain there are strongly structural links between cognition and affect [. . .] the disassociation may be unfortunate.

New models of information-processing and cognitive development

It may be that some of these difficulties with information-processing models centred on analogy with the serially-operating digital computer will be reduced or even eliminated by new accounts of cognition, which put forward a rather different account of the architecture of cognition. The work on information-processing which I have discussed so far conceives of the mind as a system which represents information as syntactic symbols, operates on these symbols according to logical rules, and stores the resultant symbols in specified localities in a long-term memory store: just like a digital computer which takes in symbolic information into particular locations in its memory, retrieves them to be operated on by a central processing unit, and stores them again in appropriate places in memory. This metaphor for cognition has worked well for tasks which require conscious effort and strategic thought when human beings do them, such as playing chess or doing complex arithmetic to predict whether a beam will balance; it has not succeeded anything like so well with cognitive tasks which human beings perform without conscious or strategic effort, such as building a tower out of blocks or recognising an object in the environment. New models of information-processing which stay closer to the way we know brain neurones work may provide a better account of this sort of cognition.

These new approaches to cognition are creating a great deal of excitement. They are referred to in different ways, as 'parallel distributed processing', 'neural networks', or 'connectionism'. The work of James McClelland and David Rumelhart and their colleagues (McClelland and Rumelhart 1986, Rumelhart and McClelland 1986) is perhaps the best known example. For discussion of the approach see Bechtel and Abrahamsen 1991, Clark 1989, Minsky 1988. What is proposed varies from model to model, but the basic hypothesis is that information-processing involves a large number of units working contemporaneously in parallel, with units, like neurones, stimulating or inhibiting each other through networks of connections. These units process very small pieces of information, smaller than a meaningful symbol and so often called 'subsymbols'. Information is not stored in a localisable place but exists

Table 3 Information-processing accounts of cognitive development: some comparisons between models.

Source	Change in knowledge base?	Change in attentional resources?	Knowledge modification processes	Domain-specific or general cognition?	Other features
Case 1984, 1985	Not emphasised.	In use, not in total capacity; Short Term System Storage increases.	Differentiation and hierarchical integration, executive control structures become more complex. Goal setting, search, evaluation, retagging and consolidation.	Emphasis very much on general parallels across wide range of domains; processes universal, even evolution-based.	Stages: natural processes of problem-solving, exploration, imitation and mutual regulation, including instruction. Affective motives for cognition.
Kail and Bisanz 1982	Number of elements increases; so does amount in chunks. More conceptual links, perceptual less salient.	Increase, possibly in total capacity, possibly in effective use related to knowledge.	Addition or deletion of knowledge nodes, strengthening and weakening of links. Inconsistency and regularity detectors. Chunking, automatisation and speed increases.	Model applies across domains but need not be uniform development.	
Keil 1979, 1984	Main source of cognitive change. Structure of knowledge determines processes.	Not emphasised.	Increasing differentiation of knowledge and awareness of links. Higher order relations, coherence and juxtaposition in semantic field. Current knowledge and structural constraints on processing and learning. Processes cannot be independent of structure of knowledge involved.	Specific to domain. Expect experience to affect level.	Emphasis that there is less evidence for complex processing than for complex representation or structure from which processing is derived. Instruction may be important.

Table 3 (continued)

Source	Change in knowledge base?	Change in attentional resources?	Knowledge modification processes	Domain-specific or general cognition?	Other features
Klahr 1984, Klahr and Wallace 1976	Knowledge includes time-line record of own cognitive processing.	Better chunking, representation, production.	Self-modifying production systems (equivalent to Piagetian 'reflective abstraction'). Includes conflict resolution rules, selection of better strategies, elimination of redundancies, generalisation etc.	Global structural reorganisations from local incremental modifications.	Development mainly internally system-driven, spontaneous not externally taught. Stages, at least in rules.
Siegler 1983, 1984, 1986, 1989, Klahr and Siegler 1978	Constitutes rules for specific and general problem-solving. Adequate encoding essential.		Encoding, combination processes, monitoring. Synthesis becomes more accurate and efficient. Negative feedback in evaluation and selection of features.	Some processes biologically given, some learned. Experience is important. Analogies with evolution.	This is a process model at an early stage of generalisation from its origins in fine analysis of a limited range of tasks.
Sternberg 1984, 1985	Knowledge acquisition central; selective encoding, and combination comparison. Increase in knowledge and changes in efficiency of its use lead also to more sophisticated later acquisition and easier performance.	Limited capacity, especially meta-components.	Feedback from performance and acquisition components to metacomponents, which are self-monitoring and deal with feedback. Automatisation, repeated activation leading to detection and use of regularities and inconsistencies. Metacognition important.	Development of local subsystems of knowledge, general global system used in default of good local system.	Includes novice–expert and gifted–retarded descriptions.

as a pattern of excitation and inhibition between units; thus instead of there being a slot in memory in which information about Piaget is stored, the system has information about Piaget only when particular sets of units are active and stimulating or inhibiting each other in particular connection patterns.

Units that are active together have their excitatory connections strengthened and their inhibitory connections weakened; for units that are not active together the reverse happens. This means that over time a network that repeatedly receives the same input will develop a strong set of excitatory connections and inhibitory connections; the units that have repeatedly been active together will come to excite each other more reliably and strongly than ever. Even if only some of the units are activated, the whole configuration will come into play; no single subsymbol of information is crucial and the configuration will be activated even if a few incorrect or irrelevant pieces of information are included in the generally correct package of incoming stimulation. There is no information store, no knowledge of rules, no metacognition, independent of the activated connections.

Connectionist models appear to have a number of very positive advantages. They seem to be in principle compatible with what we know about the nervous system [...], where neurones activate and inhibit each other in complex networks, carrying out basic processing so incredibly rapidly that parallel processing must be involved. The connectionist networks are not strongly deterministic in their functioning, so they can deal with conflicting information and find the best or most probable possible outcome. Thus they can use connections developed over old experiences to deal with new ones, or handle cases which are an exception to the usual rule. When their limits are reached, they do not crash suddenly and completely, but begin to perform less well; just like human brains they show gradually failing performance or 'graceful degradation'. They show 'content addressable memory', where a variety of different cues which are linked to the memory may summon it up: if enough of the units of a particular network are properly activated, the whole circuit comes to function. There is feedback, or 'back propagation', from later stages of processing back to earlier ones. Finally, connectionist networks can learn from experience by changing the weights of connections, the strength of the excitatory or inhibitory links between units; this would be the sort of gradual learning over many trials which is probably what we do when developing our coherent knowledge of language or arithmetic.

These characteristics suggest that connectionist network models may be very useful for some of the most crucial and problematic areas of cognitive development. They might provide a basis for the conceptually and practically difficult distinction between maturation and learning, between the development and the acquisition of cognition. Maturation changes in development might change characteristics of the network such as the maximum number of units that could be involved and the general and threshold activation levels, that is, they would involve the architectural structure of the system. Learning would change the fine-tuned detail of weights of connections between units and of connections between networks. Connectionist models might provide a mathematically based account of the phases of neurological development where there is a rapid proliferation of synapses followed by a period of weeding many of them out [...]. They may provide a much more specific account of assimilation and accommodation than Piagetian theory has done. They may clarify, whether development is sensibly described as 'stage-like', whether development is from one distinct, well-integrated and general across domains to another separate one, or whether there is continuity across a succession of small and gradual changes. Models of a normally functioning system may be tampered with to model impaired development or the effects of damage, and to suggest how problems might be remedied. It seems likely that current enthusiasm for connectionist models may lead to notable advances in our understanding of these and related issues.

Vygotsky

The third major model of cognitive development to be discussed is that associated with the name of L. S. Vygotsky. I say 'associated with' for three reasons. First, Vygotsky died prematurely in 1934, his work unfinished, and his successors have developed his ideas, a development which has included disagreement (Kozulin 1986, 1990, Zinchenko 1985). Second, similar points were made contemporaneously by other theorists, notably Pierre Janet, G. H. Mead and J. M. Baldwin, and had appeared a century earlier in Hegel's philosophy (Markova 1982), and the developmental theory which is currently being used perhaps incorporates some of their insights too (Broughton and Freeman-Moir 1981, Van der Veer and Valsiner 1988). The third reason is a practical one. Vygotsky wrote in Russian and it is only comparatively recently that his writings have been translated into English. I am not one of the small minority of students of cognitive development who read Russian, so in order to approach Vygotsky's work I have to use it in translation into English. Sutton (1983) has shown that there are severe and pervasive problems in Vygotskian translation and that readers of translations must proceed with caution. However free from linguistic errors a translation may be, the labours of translator and editor, working perhaps thirty or more years after Vygotsky, mediate between the reader and what he wrote; how each of us understands his text is affected by our knowledge of current, post-Vygotskian, developmental psychology. (I remember seeing a performance of an early play by Chekhov in which he seemed to anticipate twentieth-century psychology with extraordinary specificity, forty or fifty years before these ideas occurred to psychologists. While literature (especially in the hands of Chekhov) may indeed be far more advanced in conveying understanding of human behaviour than psychology is, it has to be said that in this instance Chekhov's play had been newly translated into English by a woman who was very well read in twentieth-century psychology). Thus my access to Vygotsky is less immediate and less direct than my access to Piagetian psychology or to information-processing psychology, which I can read in the original with only occasional doubts about whether my mental translation into English has really captured the meaning. So far as presenting 'Vygotsky's theory' here is concerned, I have tried to focus on those ideas which are regarded as central by several English language commentators. To do so means that my description will be an introduction to current English language neo-Vygotskian writing rather than to the original work, whose exact extent and content is unknown to me, as to most developmental psychologists. However it is clear that a number of important themes emerge, which both point to a significant contrast between the Vygotskian approach and the other models described in this chapter, and suggest important issues for the development of cognitive skills, [. . .]. A useful introduction is provided by the Laboratory of Comparative Human Cognition (1983), and Tharp and Gallimore (1988) and Wood (1988) use Vygotskian ideas in suggesting educational programmes.

Both the Piagetian model and the information-processing approach are based on one key idea: there are psychological structures (formal operations, concepts, working memory, intelligence, for example) in people's minds which explain their behaviour, which are invariant across cultures, settings and tasks, and which are essentially independent of the individual's relations to other individuals, to social practices, and to the cultural environment. Psychology is thus the study of the individual mind's inner workings, which are seen as developing through individual maturation or learning, or individual construction of an internal model of outside reality, or some combination of such factors in the individual mind. At the centre of Vygotskian theory is a radical challenge to this key idea: far from being internal and individualistic, cognitive abilities and capacities are formed and built up in part by social phenomena, they are public and intersubjective, created through interaction with the social environment. Any description of cognition which isolates it from the social interaction that constitutes it is seriously incomplete and may provide a distorted and misleading picture. In particular, it is essential to study the development of cognition if its mature forms are to be properly understood. Thus Vygotskian theory rests on quite different philosophical bases from other theories of cognitive development.

For our present purposes, the central idea in Vygotsky's theory of cognitive development is summed up in this frequently cited passage:

> in the process of development, children begin to use the same forms of behaviour in relation to themselves that others initially used in relation to them. Children master the social forms of behaviour and transfer these forms to themselves. . . . Logical argumentation first appears among children and only later is united within the individual and internalized. Child logic develops only along with the growth of the child's social speech and whole experience. . . . it is through others that we develop into ourselves and . . . this is true not only with regard to the individual but with regard to the history of every function. . . . Any higher mental function was external because it was social at some point before becoming an internal, truly mental functioning.
> . . . Any function in the child's cultural development appears twice, or on two planes. First it appears on the social plane, and then on the psychological plane. First it appears between people as an interpsychological category, and then within the child as an intra psychological category.
> (Vygotsky 1981, in translation by Wertsch 1981)

This emphasis on the primacy of the social world in cognitive development is very different from the emphases of the Piagetian and the information-processing approaches. Piaget, as we have seen, gave comparatively little attention to social interaction other than social disagreement on judgements, mainly between peers; and this he saw as only a minor source of the internal disequilibrium which may lead the individual to reflection and cognitive advance. The Piagetian thinker creates his or her own individual new ways of thinking and new concepts, and what these new thoughts are like stems from the individual's own experience of the logico-mathematical and physical worlds and perhaps from maturation, not from the social world or the language the thinker uses. This account left Piaget at something of a loss as to why individual constructivism should give rise to cognitive structures which were so highly similar across individuals (Meadows 1983, Rotman 1977). His explanation was based in the logical necessity of operational thought, not in the social or physical common ground of individuals' experience. Information-processing models, with the partial exception of Case's, say even less about anything except the individual thinker and his or her intellectual problem; they provide a distinctly non-social body of work, though this omission is remedied to some extent in some of the work on their practical application (e.g. Brown *et al.* 1983).

Vygotsky's assertion that cognitive development involves the internalisation, transformation and use of routines, ideas and skills which are learned *socially*, from more competent partners, thus forms a unique contrast to the individualistic cognitivist approach.

His account also solves, perhaps almost too completely, what has been called (Williams 1989) the 'bootstrapping problem' of explaining how more sophisticated cognitive competences can arise from less sophisticated ones. It is to all intents and purposes impossible to lift yourself up using the straps of the boots you are wearing; similarly it has been hard to see how a child might solve everyday cognitive problems such as realising that a word picks out a particular aspect of an object, without previously having a whole complex of concepts about that object and what can be done with it. 'Red' is intended by the knowledgeable speaker to refer to an object's colour: but how are naïve listeners to know that colour is what is meant, not location, size, function, ownership or name, or any combination of these, unless they have a prior notion of colour as a characteristic which can be separated out and commented on? A word can become a name, or a label, for an object only against a background of beliefs about which is being picked out by the word.

Both the origins of these beliefs, and their mapping on to language, will be problematic for those who assume that cognitive development is by individual construction. One solution is to say that cognitive processes and concepts are, ultimately, innate (e.g. Fodor 1981); a second is to seek precursors of the problematic skills in the hope that a full enough sequence will have small enough steps between successive levels of skill that the transition from one to the next will look easy to explain. Vygotsky's solution makes the innate ideas solution unnecessary, and moves the other to the realm of description not of explanation. It is that children develop more sophisticated cognitive competences despite only having simpler ones in their own repertoire, because adults (that is, older, more skilled persons available as teachers or models) have the more sophisticated competence and guide the child repeatedly through the relevant behaviour. The child as an individual does not have the resources necessary for the higher level of cognitive functioning, but the teaching adult does. Adult and child interact, the adult providing the structured context within which the child can act as though he or she was competent to solve the problem, and by so acting in such a context, the child can indeed reach the solution successfully. To begin with, the adult has to provide almost all the cognition necessary for the task, but as the child becomes more and more familiar with it the adult can leave more and more for the child to do, until at last the child can undertake the entire task successfully. Repetition of this 'scaffolding' of learning on related tasks extends the child's competence and eventually leaves him or her able to take on new examples with minimal adult support, or alone. The child's independent cognitive behaviour has developed from less sophistication and expertise to more, and the medium of development has been social interaction, apprenticeship to another, more skilled, person. Cognitive development is to be understood in terms of the child being trained to behave in ways which the culture has developed as cognitively useful. By so behaving, and by practising and reflecting on what is done, the child internalises the cognitive skills of the culture and can develop them and pass them on to the next generation.

Thus, for the neo-Vygotskian, there is no bootstrapping problem; rather the child is helped by the adult in the 'guided reinvention' of the accumulation of knowledge and ways of thinking which preceding generations have constructed. The skills required of the child are of observation and imitation, and of generalisation and decontextualisation, but even these fundamental skills develop under the fostering support of social interaction. Some of the skills learned from adults are what Bruner has called 'cultural amplifiers', cognitive tools which make thinking jobs easier. The Arabic number system which we now use has, I would imagine, made mathematical computation easier than it was for the Romans, with their more cumbersome way of writing numbers, while later inventions such as logarithms and electronic calculating machines have made computation easier still. Other cultural habits of thinking may impede cognitive development, although they are highly serviceable within their particular cultural domain. To give one ideologically delicate example, belief in the literal truth of the Book of Genesis precludes understanding evolutionary theory, which has proved a most useful cognitive amplifier in its organisation and explanation of biological phenomena; and to give one less delicate but less clearly documented example, some educational policy-makers have argued that the use of calculators impedes children's understanding of numbers in ways which reliance on traditional computation methods would facilitate. Whether helpful or not, the culture's ways of thinking surround children, are modelled to them by other users and discussed with them, and they may structure their language, their play, their schooling and their social interaction. The developing thinker does not have to create cognition out of an unpeopled vacuum, but may adopt and eventually internalise some of the cognitive content and processes provided by others.

Vygotsky suggested that in the course of development the child's own activities are shaped by the culture, or, more immediately, by the reactions of other people, and thus they move beyond what he admitted was to some extent a biological origin. Pointing, for example, is initially an unsuccessful reach for a too-distant object, which is responded to by the baby's mother as a sign that the baby wants the object. The child's movements are interpreted by the mother as an indicatory gesture. As she comes to the child's aid, the movement that was a gesture 'in-itself' becomes a gesture 'for-others'. The child, with some awareness of the communicative power of the movement, comes to use it as a deliberate gesture: the 'reaching' becomes reduced to movements which signal need but could not themselves achieve the desired object even if it were within reach, and other signals (such as cries, looks at the mother, and eventually words) are added. The child now addresses the gesture to adults who might bring about the desired result of grasping the object, rather than to the object itself which was the focus of interest in the first place. It also becomes possible to use the gesture for oneself: to point out, or touch, an object as part of directing one's own attention to it, as in counting a set of objects or as in [. . .] memory tasks [. . .]. A similar sequence appears in the development of the 'higher mental functions', both processes such as selective attention, logical memory and concept formation, and language, writing, counting, drawing and other 'external' cultural skills (Vygotsky 1978, and see Lock 1978).

At the heart of this development is one of the most important concepts in Vygotskian theory: 'internalisation'. It has been one of the returning difficulties of philosophy and psychology to understand the relationship between the external and the internal, whether these are contrasted as completely different and unrelated phenomena, or one reduced to the other, or some other relationship between the two postulated, as we see in, for example, the various solutions to the mind–body problem [. . .]. Vygotsky gives an unusually precise answer to how external and internal relate, emphasising above all that it is a developmental relation where cognitive processes external to an individual are transformed to create a plane of internal processes. Uniquely, he stresses that internalisation is primarily seen in the context of social interactions, and he analyses it in terms of the systems of meaning (semiotic systems) which mediate social functioning, of which language is the most familiar. Internalisation is part of the construction of consciousness through human social interaction: the child takes on self-consciousness and self concept through social experiences (cf. Lewis and Brooks-Gunn 1979, Mead 1934), and cognitive consciousness and competence also arise socially.

> All higher mental functions are internalised social relationships. . . . Their composition, genetic structure, and means of action – in a word, their whole nature – is social. Even when we turn to mental processes, their nature remains quasi-social. In their own private sphere, human beings retain the functions of social interaction.
>
> (Vygotsky 1981: 164; see also Wertsch and Stone 1985: 166)

Thus Vygotsky is stressing a close and complex relationship between external social processes and internal psychological ones. The example of memory may help to illuminate this relationship. Cultures have developed their own mnemonic techniques, and these are normally made available to the members of the culture. The very young and the uneducated, who have not yet learned to use the culture's technique, may have ways of remembering which combine a biological basis with the effects of early learning; Vygotsky called these 'mneme' (Kozulin 1990). These ways of remembering may be very effective for the informal and repetitive experiences of the young child; [. . .] we are discovering more and more cognitive effectiveness in young children working on 'ecologically natural' tasks. As the individual is taught the culturally-mediated ways of remembering that the culture has developed ('mnemo-techniques'), these may displace the 'natural' processes so that they play a subordinate role in memory, and the memory skills of an acculturated adult represent a complex functional system which will be used more deliberately, more flexibly and with more self-awareness than the child's. To begin with, the child's biologically based memory is the centre of his or her own skill, and the culture's memory skills are an external world; as the cultural skills are learned they become internalised, take over much of the child's memorising and recall, and become integrated with skills of inference, concept use, and story-telling. Non-cultural memory processes remain essential for remembering, as the memory disorders found in patients with various sorts of brain damage show (Mayes 1988), but culturally learned skills may enhance these processes or make up for their deficiencies.

Internalisation changes the complexity of what is done, ultimately for the better but initially, perhaps, for the worse. Culturally provided skills are generally more sophisticated than the skills which they replace, and so the learner cannot usually manage them easily and well. The learner's version of a culturally provided skill will be cruder than the expert's; and it may indeed be cruder than the learner's own pre-existing skills. The small girl trying hard to learn to be 'a ballerina' may move more awkwardly in her ballet lesson than she does normally; the adult writer may resist learning word-processing because text compiles itself more smoothly with pen and paper than with keyboard and screen. 'Functional regression' may be part of the internalisation of any complex skill: it may be one of the reasons why cognitive development can seem slow and effortful (cf. Karmiloff-Smith and Inhelder 1974/5).

Internalisation, however, transforms the social process into the psychological, and thereby changes its structure and functions. This inevitably happens because the central process in internalisation is the gradual emergence of control over external processes, including control over external signs and systems of communication. Children perform actions, or use words and signals, without having a full understanding of their significance. They may know from their past successful usage that a particular action is a necessary part of getting the desired result (for example they may always wash their hands and display their cleanness before meals) without understanding *why* the action is important (because washing hands decreases the possibility of infection from dirt, a goal highly valued by their hygienic mothers). Similarly a child may know that a word refers to a particular object but not appreciate the full range of meaning it connotes. Social interaction necessarily involves the use of sign forms, including words, which have acquired a rich meaning over the generations of their use. Initial use, which may only involve a fragment of this meaning, progresses through generalisation to include more and more connotations. Vygotsky states that the

> basic distinguishing characteristic of the word is the generalised reflection of reality

and that

> in order to transmit some experience or content of consciousness to another person, there is no other path than to ascribe the content to a known class, to a known group of phenomena, and as we know this necessarily requires generalisation.
>
> Thus it turns out that social interaction necessarily presupposes generalisation and the development of word meaning i.e. generalisation becomes possible with the development of social interaction. Thus higher, uniquely human forms of psychological social interaction are possible only because human thinking reflects reality in a generalized way.
>
> (Wertsch and Stone 1985: 168)

It is not entirely clear to me whether this passage is asserting that generalisation is an intrinsic part of human thinking irrespective of generalisation being a necessary part of learning from other people's experience, or whether practice in generalising about what other people teach you leads to habitual generalisation. Of course the two interpretations are by no means incompatible, as Vygotsky is stressing a complex developmental pattern of relationships between internally-arising and externally-given generalisation. So far as developmental psychologists' concern with diagnosing children's competence is concerned, two important points arise. The first is that agreement between child and adult as to meaning at one point must not be taken as showing that they have the same full range of generalised meaning. Child and adult may agree on the referent of a word but not on the full meaning, or the child may know that an object is a member of a particular category by virtue of its possessing a particular attribute but not understand whether that attribute is merely characteristic or a defining property (Keil 1981, Vygotsky 1986). Nor will the child initially use word or concept in an adult way. While the child or novice's understanding of words may be based on relatively simple and context-bound relationships between word and object, adults will understand them in terms of a complex system of meaning that involves relationships between words. 'Interested', 'curious', 'inquisitive', 'nosey', 'enthralled', 'absorbed', for example, carry subtly varied social and linguistic connotations. Children's difficulties with figurative language provide other examples [. . .].

The second point, [. . .], is that individuals may differ in their ability to provide generalisations for themselves or for others, and to profit from them. Some individuals may set up for others fertile situations of 'mediated learning' (Feuerstein *et al.* 1980), giving them experiences which an expert has framed, selected, highlighted and scaffolded in such a way that appropriate learning and transfer are facilitated. Some individuals, lacking such cognitive functioning, may fail to generalise even when to do so would prevent them from having to learn to solve each problem from the very beginning. Internalisation itself can presumably be more specific or more general, depending on the characteristics of child, adult, their interaction and the cultural content.

As well as an emphasis on the role of inter-psychological experience in intra-psychological cognitive development, on the importance of learning with and from other people, Vygotsky's theory has at its core the notion of 'mediation', the use of psychological 'tools' or 'signs', which allows a qualitative change in mental (or socio-historical) life. Language, for example, changes the relations of human beings to each other and to the non-human world from what those relations are in those who cannot use language. Mediation, or the use of communicable systems for representing reality as well as acting on it, is at the foundation of cognitive processes, which there-fore cannot be reduced to automatic links between stimulus and response (as the Behaviourist psychology dominant in the West during Vygotsky's lifetime, and import-ant also in Russia, would have argued). Signs, like artefact-type tools, are a product of the history of the culture. (Vygotsky's historical interests are, unfortunately, beyond the scope of this chapter, but see Kozulin 1986, 1990, Scribner 1985.) We have developed and grown up with a whole collection of symbols and of ways of problem-solving which shape our thinking. If we want to remember something, we can use writing as an *aide-mémoire*, or knots tied in a piece of string such as the Incas used, or rote learning of phrases and rules of rhyme and rhythm which together allow the near-verbatim recall of material such as long traditional stories (Lord 1960) or nursery rhymes. Signs can be used for communication between people or for communication with oneself, in thinking. They are embedded in activity, constructed through the subject's interactions with the world (and particularly, perhaps, with the other people in the world). And the sign systems one has available have a marked effect on the sort of consciousness and degree of cognitive organisation one has. Young children might operate on a practical level of intelligence and on a symbol system level independently, but adults would in most of their experience integrate the enactive and the symbolic levels. Language, the 'psychological tool' *par excellence*, is perhaps the most potent means of integrating practical (or procedural?) and symbolic (or declarative?) knowledge.

> [The child] plans how to solve the problem through speech and then carries out the prepared solution through overt activity. Direct manipulation is replaced by a complex psychological process through which inner motivations and inten-tions, postponed in time, stimulate their own development and realisation.
>
> (Vygotsky 1978: 26)

Activity is mediated by the use of language for planning (and for monitoring and evaluating and other metacognitive activities), using (because language has social roots) a socially created and socially determined system of symbols and rules. The interweaving of thought and language, and their use within social interactions with more skilled partners who wish the child to learn, allow the child to move from fragmentary use without understanding to a coherent and flexible mastery of repre-sentational systems and cognitive skills. There is an increasingly profitable dialectic between the child's actions and the child's representations, and also between the child's understanding and other people's (Vygotsky 1986).

Here Vygotsky is placing far more emphasis on the origins and characteristics of representational systems than Piagetian or information-processing approaches do, though both of course are very much concerned with how problems are represented. His discussion of these semiotic issues is no more complete than the rest of his work could be, but it includes some points which have emerged as important from our earlier discussion of cognitive skills. Among them are the developmental course of language (and other forms of representation and of thinking) from social roots to a mature form which also incorporates internal communication; the dialectic inter-action between the use of procedural knowledge, or 'activity', and declarative know-ledge, which become increasingly interdependent as development proceeds; the role of metacognition and symbolic control of behaviour; and the effects on cognition of different cultural tools.

Much of Vygotsky's account of cognitive development focuses on the role of language. He saw it as one of the most important of 'psychological tools', cultur-ally developed ways of behaving towards objects which allow high level cognitive functioning. Other psychological tools include counting systems, mnemonic tech-niques, writing and diagrams and maps. Integrating any of these into a psychological function such as memory or spatial perception transforms the mental functioning, in Vygotsky's view. The psychological tools are not merely facilitators or auxiliaries: their use allows (or even requires) qualitatively different functioning, 'revolutions' in thinking associated with changes in psychological tools. Kozulin (1998: 134–5) uses as an example different ways of measuring the passing of time. Early devices for measuring time used natural processes occurring steadily over time to record the passing of time intervals: for example, the shadow moving across the sundial, sand falling from top to bottom of an egg-timer, or water running to a marked height in a water-clock. Clockwork clocks provide a less immediate representation of passing time: the movements of the cogs, weights, pendulum, springs and so forth are too complex to show us the amount of time that has passed, even if they are visible, and we have to use the 'symbolic time' of the position of the hands on the dial; this means we have to learn to read the clock-face. Electronic digital watches provide a purely symbolic measure of time, and require us to use arithmetical knowledge to judge whether more time has elapsed between one pair of times than between another, as no physical analogue at all remains for the time.

Individuals 'appropriate' psychological tools from their social and cultural milieu. They do not inherit them as instincts or reflexes, they do not normally reinvent them from scratch, they do not discover them in their independent interactions with the nat-ural world. In particular they learn to use tools through face to face communication and social interaction with other people who are also using psychological tools. Thus the tools have communication among their functions. Development involves, as we have said, initially interpersonal use of psychological tools, which increasingly become available for intrapersonal use.

> Social life creates the necessity of subordinating the individual's behaviour to social demands and in addition creates complex signalisation systems – the means of connection that direct and regulate the formation of conditional connections in the brains of individual humans.
>
> (Vygotsky 1960, translated by Wertsch (1985a))

Language is of course pre-eminent amongst the 'complex signalisation systems' which Vygotsky considered, and the relationship between language and thought was perhaps his central interest (Kozulin 1990, Vygotsky 1962, 1986). He proposed a distinction between pre-intellectual speech and pre-verbal thought. Children under 2 use vocal activity as a means of social contact and emotional expression, and are capable of systematic and goal-directed activity which does not require verbal operations. This first 'primitive' stage is followed by a stage of 'practical intelligence' in which the child's language uses syntactic and logical forms which have parallels in the child's practical problem-solving activity but are not linked to them in any systematic or useful way. In the third stage the child starts to use external symbolic means, such as language or other cultural tools, to help with internal problem-solving. It is at this stage that children can be heard to talk themselves through problems or to count by using their fingers as aids. Finally, such aids are internalised and problem-solving thought uses internal dialogue, while language can be used more to reflect on and develop thought than as a prop to support problem-solving.

Thus Vygotsky saw speech as beginning to have social functions very early in the child's life, developing amongst the child's 'complex and rich social contacts' into an increasingly powerful tool. Expression of emotions and maintenance of social contacts are followed by the use of language to communicate, to make reference, to represent ideas, to regulate one's own actions, initially within a context of social interaction and shared knowledge but increasingly independently of social partner and of supportive context. The child who talks to himself or herself is regulating and planning mental activities, not, as Piaget suggested, failing to communicate with others because of an overwhelming egocentricity (Vygotsky 1986). The child's private monologue is a precursor of the completely 'in the head' talking oneself through a problem (such as composing a sentence or working out the consequences of a particular chess move) which may facilitate solution for adults. Regulation of and by others using language, self-regulation by language; communication with others using language, communication with oneself using language: these merge within the developing individual, as he or she takes part in social interactions within the culture, into mature verbal thought. Language becomes more and more useful as a tool for abstract reflection. It also changes immediate perception and action, which become more and more integrated into a cognitive system which is to a large extent represented through language and expressed in language. The internalisation of perception leads to language mediation, which leads to greater cognitive freedom and flexibility (Lee 1985); cultural development fuses with organic development as the culture's higher mental functions are extended to and internalised by individuals. Internalisation brings about the socio-cultural determination of the human mind as the culture's 'psychological tools' become involved in controlling one's own mental processes (Davydov and Radzikhovskii 1985).

Vygotsky's emphasis on social interaction entails two important consequences which his own interest in education and in mental handicap (defectology) developed (Kozulin 1986, Sutton 1983, Vygotsky 1978). The first is that more complex cognitive functioning will be possible in a dialogue between two individuals than is possible for those individuals alone, or at least for the less skilled individual, though at a late stage in development an individual may be able to provide his or her own interlocutor. The other consequence is that instruction could be a facilitator of cognitive development, not, as Piaget would have it, at best irrelevant and at worst a distortion (see, especially, Vygotsky 1986, chapter 6). 'Learning by transaction' is at the heart of cognitive development.

[. . .] [B]y no means all the evidence which is relevant to these issues comes from Vygotskian researches [. . .]. It will suffice here to mention a few observational studies in which children have been set to solve a problem with and without an interlocutor. David Wood (Wood 1980, 1988, Wood *et al.* 1978) observed mothers and 4-year-olds working together to construct a wooden pyramid. James Wertsch (1978, 1979, 1985a, 1985b, Wertsch *et al.* 1980) recorded children working with their mothers on constructing a copy of a 'model' puzzle. Ellice Forman (Forman and Cazden 1985) made a longitudinal study of pairs of children solving problems such as chemistry experiments. On a rather larger scale, Vygotskian theory underpins the Kamehameha Elementary Education Project (Tharp and Gallimore 1988, Tharp *et al.* 1984). The data from these studies, and from others which are, for example, Piagetian in origin (e.g. Doise and Mugny 1984, Perret-Clermont and Brossard 1985), show that inter-nalisation can be observed in children's use of tutorial interchanges, social interaction may facilitate performance on a task, and the improvement may transfer to similar tasks done alone later. If the limited quantity of focused interaction typically provided in these studies can produce such effects, how much more might day-in, day-out learning from mother? We lack naturalistic data on cognitively-productive social inter-action in children's daily lives, [. . .] but I will mention here that Ernst Moerk [. . .] argued (Moerk 1989) that the LAD which Chomsky postulated to explain language development is most probably a LADY, the unfairly undervalued mother whose chatter and listening seems to him to be excellently fitted to producing an expert speaker. Given the Soviet (and indeed Marxist) context of this section, I will not restrain the exhortation 'Mothers of the world unite, you have nothing to lose but your deprecators!'

One important Vygotskian concept which has not yet been mentioned is the 'zone of proximal development' or ZPD. He presents it as part of a discussion of the inter-action between 'learning' and 'development' (Vygotsky 1978: 79–91). Here he argues that if we are to provide learning opportunities which will enable the child to develop we must determine at least two developmental levels. The lower of these is the sort of thing which the usual psychological and educational test measures, what the child can do independently; the higher is what the child can do with such assistance as demonstrations, prompts or leading questions.

> The zone of proximal development . . . is the distance between the actual devel-opmental level as determined by independent problem solving and the level of potential development as determined through problem solving under adult guid-ance or in collaboration with more capable peers.
>
> (Vygotsky 1978: 86)

Independent unaided problem-solving indicates what cognitive functioning the child has already mastered; problems which the child can only solve with assistance suggest what functions are not yet mature but are in the process of maturation. 'What a child can do with assistance today she will be able to do by herself tomorrow' (Vygotsky 1978: 87). Diagnosis of the ZPD is necessary both for a full assessment of the child's abilities and for the optimum targeting of instruction. There is little profit from teaching aimed below the bottom of the ZPD because the child's func-tioning here is already mature, or from teaching aimed above the top of the ZPD, because the difference from the child's actual present functioning may be too great: 'the only "good learning" is that which is [slightly] in advance of development' (Vygotsky 1978: 89); teaching is good only when it 'awakens and rouses to life those functions which are in a stage of maturing, which lie in the zone of proximal devel-opment' (Wertsch and Stone 1985: 165).

How does progress through the ZPD come about? In particular, how can 'good learning' be in advance of development? In one sense, we are back at the 'boot-strapping problem' here, and Bruner offers the 'teacher lifts the boot straps' answer. The teacher (adult or more competent peer)

> serves the learner as a vicarious form of consciousness until such a time as the learner is able to master his own action through his own consciousness and

control. When the child achieves that conscious control over a new function or conceptual system, it is then that he is able to use it as a tool. Up to that point, the tutor in effect performs the critical function of 'scaffolding' the learning task to make it possible for the child, in Vygotsky's word, to internalise external knowledge and convert it into a tool for conscious control.

(Bruner 1985: 25)

During the earliest periods of learning in the ZPD a child may have a very limited degree of understanding of what the task involves; the teacher offers a model or successive precise and simple directions, and the child merely observes or imitates. Gradually, as the child becomes able to cope with more components of an activity, and has more understanding of how they fit together, an understanding which will include more appreciation of what the goal is and how the means to it work, the adult reduces the assistance given and changes from very directive help to suggestion and encouragement. The adult needs to take less and less responsibility for the successful performance of the activity as the increasingly competent learner takes it on. The developmental task is to move from other-regulation to self-regulation (Brown *et al.* 1983); eventually the child provides his or her own scaffolding.

Here Vygotsky's observations on 'egocentric' speech are relevant (Vygotsky 1962, 1986). As is well known, he criticised Piaget's notion of egocentric speech as being a product of the child's inability to understand the world without solipsism (absolute egoism, exclusion of all knowledge except of oneself). Piaget believed that children's immature use of language was due to their lack of understanding of how to communicate with others who did not share their own knowledge, and that it disappeared as they became socialised. Vygotsky argued that 'egocentric' speech was speech used for overt self-regulation but produced in potentially communicative settings. Initially, the child's speech is purely social and communicates to others; gradually, adults' communicative and regulatory speech is internalised and as the child comes to be a cognitive self-regulator 'egocentric' speech is produced, which functions as part of the child's self-regulation but can also be seen (by listeners and by the child) as communicating to others, though in fact, being self-directed in origin, it does so inefficiently. Children at this age of course have difficulties in telling whether the speaker or the listener is responsible for a communication breakdown (Robinson and Robinson 1977, 1980, 1981). With further development 'egocentric' speech becomes 'inner speech', and the self-regulator's problem-solving dialogue with self is no longer observable. It may only become examinable when the task is difficult, or when an outsider asks for explicit 'talking-through' the problem. Self-regulation is overt during the early stages of achieving mastery of a task; once the task can be executed smoothly and independently, once it is 'automatised', self-consciousness may be disruptive and self-regulation will only be noticeable when task difficulty is great. Very great task difficulty may force recourse to other regulation; finding another helpful text, or seeking out an expert to answer one's questions or provide further training, for example.

If there is, as this account implies, a gradual transition from other-regulation to self-regulation as the child moves towards the upper part of the ZPD and becomes able to do independently what previously could only be done with assistance, it follows that there will be changes in the best form for assistance and other-regulation to take. Early in the learning cycle, assistance will be elaborate, explicit and frequent, as when the child is instructed through a close sequence of small steps. Later, assistance will be more abbreviated, less explicit and less frequent, with hints such as 'OK, what else could you look for?' rather than instructions such as 'Get the big yellow one that's over there'. Optimum assistance adapts itself to the learner's successes and failures (Bruner 1983, Tharp and Gallimore 1988, Wertsch 1978, 1979, 1985a, Wood 1980, 1988). [. . .]

Finally, I must make some reference to the fact that Vygotsky saw his work as a 'socio-cultural' theory of psychological processes. He emphasised that children pick up the socially constructed psychological tools that are available to them, and that these, superimposed on organic development, 'form a single line of socio-biological formation of the child's personality' (in Lee 1985: 74). Thus there will be both cultural and historical patterns in cognition. He used the ethnographic material on cultures which was available to him to investigate these issues, but also used parallels between development in the child and socio-historical development. His colleague A. R. Luria, for example, went in the early 1930s to remote parts of central Asia where the mechanisation and collectivisation of agriculture were transforming the traditional peasant economy and way of life (Luria 1976). His intention was to compare the cognitive processes used by nonliterate 'unreformed' peasants and those who were participating in more modern ways of life. He did find some of the differences predicted by Vygotsky, for example illiterate and uneducated peasants sorted objects by their appearance and use (as young children do) while schooled respondents preferred more taxonomic sortings, but considerable controversy arose over the extent of the differences (see e.g. Cole and Griffin 1980), and even more over their interpretation (it was politically unacceptable to 'denigrate' the peasants by saying their thought was 'childlike'). Part of the problem was the lack of a detailed theory of the cognitive structure and processes provided by and required by the traditional peasant culture. A functional sorting of local artefacts is not self-evidently less useful than a taxonomic one. The sufficiently successful basis for the arrangement of objects in my kitchen cupboards, for example, is largely based on functional attributes such as 'vulnerable to mice', 'not to be got at by my small daughter', 'used here together', and taxonomic classifications (except those isomorphic with the perceptual characteristics of size and weight) are secondary. It seems quite likely that many of the cognitive processes which we take for granted as part of the normal repertoire of skills have become so as a result of us having been schooled in them, and using them in our everyday activities (see e.g. Cole and Means 1981 for discussion of this).

The concept of 'activity', which appears in Vygotsky's writings but has been developed since by Soviet psychologists, is of importance here (Davydov and Radzikhovskii 1985, Kozulin 1986, Wertsch 1981, Zinchenko 1985). Socially meaningful activity must be an explanatory principle and a basic unit of analysis in psychology. It is also seen to be a generator of consciousness, and activity mediated by psychological tools and interpersonal communication produces the higher mental functions. The analysis of activities must include consideration of their goals, and their embedding in the social context, for as social structures and processes influence what practical activities are engaged in, and these activities determine cognitive development, ultimately social consciousness and the modes of production (Vygotsky's was an explicitly Marxist theory) determine psychological development. Different cultures (and subcultures) have different activities and different goals; an individual's cognitive activity operates within both cultural constraints and cultural amplifiers, including cultural differences in the way the ZPD operates (see Cole 1985, Rogoff 1990, Stigler, Schweder and Herdt 1990, Valsiner 1988a, 1988b, Winegar 1989).

As Hundeide (1985), Mellin-Olsen (1987) and other educators have pointed out, the pupil's definition of an activity may differ radically from the teacher's, with resultant difficulties in their learning. As Tharp and Gallimore (1988) argue, the who, where, what, why and when of activity settings need to be considered. It may be more important to examine patterns of differences in cognition than the generalised and abstract models of Piaget and the information-processing theorists have supposed.

Thus Vygotsky's work contrasts with the approaches of Piaget and the 'information-processors' in its insistence on the relevance of the social, cultural and historical milieu to the individual's cognitive development. It also makes a far more incisive analysis of the learning process, and so is of great importance to educators, both in and out of school. [. . .] but I will just mention here an apparent paradox. If neo-Vygotskian 'scaffolding' of socially meaningful activity is the best way of helping learning, and schools do rather little of it (not least because it requires a teacher–pupil ratio of approximately one to one, a pretty detailed diagnosis of what skills exist, which are potential, and how to teach each one, and a very sensitively implemented teaching programme over an extended period of time – not the conditions that the ordinary school provides), how is it that schools are at all successful?

One obvious way out of the paradox is to say that schools are in fact *not* at all successful, and certain reviewers of the educational process do indeed take this position, though their proposed remedies range from de-schooling (e.g. the argument associated with Ivan Illich) to a far more authoritarian and didactic use of school time (e.g. various pronouncements by MPs), via an increase in neo-Vygotskian schooling (e.g. Tharp and Gallimore 1988). I have no sympathy with this position: schools seem to me to be remarkably successful under difficult conditions, though they might indeed be more successful if they could be more Vygotskian. Another solution of the paradox is to assert that there are ways of learning which involve less scaffolding by a teacher, and indeed there obviously are, in the various 'conditions of learning' described in so many classic educational textbooks (e.g. Gagné 1985). The 'Piagetian' model used in early childhood education (see Meadows and Cashdan 1988 for a critical discussion) and the traditional rote learning which Tharp and Gallimore 1988 attack so intensely are, in their contrasting ways, methods of learning, and even of facilitating cognitive development. What is interesting here is the relationship between different ways of learning. Might it possibly be the case, for example, that an early history of good scaffolding so to speak 'sets up' learners to become their own scaffolders, so that they can both take their own rote learning and mechanical information-processing 'beyond the information given', and act in a Piagetian mode as never-ceasing equilibrators, continually seeking a deeper and broader and more flexible understanding of their worlds? [. . .]

References

Anderson, J.R. (1983) *The Architecture of Cognition*, Cambridge, Mass: Harvard University Press.

Anderson, M. (1989a) 'New ideas in intelligence', *The Psychologist* 2(3): 92–4.

Anderson, M. (1989b) Letter, *The Psychologist* 2(8): 331.

Anderson, M. (1992) *Intelligence and Cognitive Development*, Oxford: Blackwell.

Atkinson, R.C. and Shiffrin, R.M. (1968) 'Human memory: a proposed system and its control processes', in K.W. Spence and J.T. Spence (eds) *Advances in the Psychology of Learning and Motivation*, vol. 2, New York: Academic Press.

Beard, R. (1963) 'The order of concept development: studies in two fields', *Educational Review* 15: 105–17, 228–37.

Bechtel, W. and Abrahamsen, A. (1991) *Connectionism and the Mind: an Introduction to Parallel Processing in Networks*, Oxford: Blackwell.

Beilin, H. (1992) 'Piaget's enduring contribution to developmental psychology', *Developmental Psychology* 28: 191–204.

Block, N. (ed.) (1981) *Imagery*, Cambridge, Mass.: Bradford Books/MIT Press.

178 Sarah Meadows

Block, N. (1983) 'Mental pictures and cognitive science', *Philosophical Review* 92: 499–541.

Boden, M. (1979) *Piaget*, London: Fontana.

Boden, M. (1982) 'Is equilibration important? A view from artificial intelligence', *British Journal of Psychology* 73: 165–73.

Boden, M. (1987) *Artificial Intelligence and Natural Man*, Brighton: Harvester.

Boden, M. (1988) *Computer Models of Mind*, Cambridge: Cambridge University Press.

Boden, M. (1989) *Artificial Intelligence in Psychology*, Boston, Mass.: MIT Press.

Braine, M.D.S. and Rumain, B. (1983) 'Logical reasoning', in J.H. Flavell and E.M. Markman (eds) *Handbook of Child Psychology*, vol. 3, series ed. P.H. Mussen, New York: Wiley.

Brainerd, C.J. (1978) *Piaget's Theory of Intelligence*, Englewood Cliffs, NJ: Prentice Hall.

Brainerd, C.J. (1983) 'Modifiability of cognitive development', in S. Meadows (ed.) *Developing Thinking*, London: Methuen.

Broughton, J.M.B. and Freeman-Moir, D.J. (1981) *The Cognitive-developmental Psychology of James Mark Baldwin: Current Theory and Research in Genetic Epistemology*, Norwood, NJ: Ablex.

Brown, A.L., Bransford, J.D., Ferrara, R.A. and Campione, J.C. (1983) 'Learning, remembering and understanding', in J.H. Flavell and E.M. Marman (eds) *Handbook of Child Psychology*, vol. 3, *Cognitive Development*, series ed. P.H. Mussen, New York: Wiley.

Bruner, J.S. (1983) *Child's Talk*, New York: Norton.

Bruner, J.S. (1985) 'Vygotsky: a historical and conceptual perspective', in J.V. Wertsch (ed.) *Culture, Communication and Cognition*, Cambridge: Cambridge University Press.

Bryant, P.E. (1982) 'The role of conflict and of agreement between intellectual strategies in children's ideas about measurement', *British Journal of Psychology* 73: 243–52.

Bynum, T.W., Thomas, J.A. and Weitz, L.J. (1972) 'Truth-functional logic in formal operational thinking', *Developmental Psychology* 7: 129–32.

Carey, S. and Gelman, R. (eds) (1991) *The Epigenesis of Mind*, Hove: Erlbaum.

Case, R. (1974) 'Structures and strictures, some functional limitations on the course of cognitive growth', *Cognitive Psychology*, 6: 544–73.

Case, R. (1984) 'The process of stage-transition: a neo-Piagetian view', in R.J. Sternberg (ed.) *Mechanisms of Cognitive Development*, New York: Freeman.

Case, R. (1985) *Intellectual Development: Birth to Adulthood*, New York: Academic Press.

Chi, M.T.H. and Ceci, S. (1987) 'Content knowledge: its role, representation and restructuring in memory development', in *Advances in Child Development and Behavior*, vol. 20, New York: Academic Press.

Churchland, P.M. and Churchland, P.S. (1990) 'Could a machine think?' *Scientific American*, January 1990: 26–31.

Clark, A. (1989) *Microcognition: Philosophy, Cognitive Science, and Parallel Distributed Processing*, Cambridge, Mass.: MIT Press.

Cole, M. (1985) 'The zone of proximal development: where culture and cognition create each other', in J.V. Wertsch (ed.) *Culture, Communication and Cognition,* Cambridge: Cambridge University Press.

Cole, M. and Griffin, P. (1980) 'Cultural amplifiers reconsidered', in D.R. Olson (ed.) *The Social Foundations of Language and Thought*, New York and London: Norton.

Cole, M. and Means, B. (1981) *Comparative Studies of How People Think: an Introduction*, Cambridge, Mass.: Harvard University Press.

Cooper, L.A. and Shepard, R.N. (1984) 'Turning something over in the mind', *Scientific American* 251 (6) (December): 106–14.

Dasen, P. (1977) 'Are cognitive processes universal? A contribution to cross-cultural Piagetian psychology', in N. Warren (ed.) *Studies in Cross-cultural Psychology*, London: Academic Press.

Davydov, V.V. and Radzikhovskii, L.A. (1985) 'Vygotsky's theory and the activity-oriented approach in psychology', in J.V. Wertsch (ed.) *Culture, Communication and Cognition*, Cambridge: Cambridge University Press.

Doise, W. and Mugny, G. (1984) *The Social Development of the Intellect*, Oxford: Pergamon.

Donaldson, M. (1978) *Children's Minds*, London: Fontana.

Ennis, R.H. (1978) 'Conceptualization of children's social logical competence: Piaget's prepositional logic and an alternative proposal', in L.S. Siegel and C.J. Brainerd (eds) *Alternatives to Piaget*, New York: Academic Press.

Ericsson, K.A., Chase, W.G. and Faloon, S. (1980) 'Acquisition of a memory skill', *Science* 208: 1181–2.

Feldman, C.F. and Toulmin, S. (1976) 'Logic and the theory of mind', in *Nebraska Symposium on Motivation*, Lincoln, Nebr.: University of Nebraska Press.

Feuerstein, R., Rand, Y., Hoffman, M. and Miller, R. (1980) *Instrumental Enrichment*, Baltimore, Md.: University Park Press.

Flavell, J.H. (1963) *The Developmental Psychology of Jean Piaget*, Princeton, NJ: Van Nostrand.

Flavell, J.H. (1977) *Cognitive Development*, Englewood Cliffs, NJ: Prentice Hall.

Flavell, J.H. (1984) 'Discussion', in R.J. Sternberg (ed.) *Mechanisms of Cognitive Development*, New York: W.H. Freeman.

Flavell, J.H. (1985) *Cognitive Development*, 2nd edn, Englewood Cliffs, NJ: Prentice Hall.

Fodor, J.A. (1976) *The Language of Thought*, Hassocks, Sussex: Harvester.

Fodor, J.A. (1981) *Representations: Philosophical Essays on the Foundations of Cognitive Science*, Brighton: Harvester.

Forman, E.A. and Cazden, C.B. (1985) 'Exploring Vygotskian perspectives in education: the cognitive value of peer interaction', in J.V. Wertsch (ed.) *Culture, Communication and Cognition*, Cambridge: Cambridge University Press.

Gagné, R.M. (1985) *The Conditions of Learning and Theory of Instruction*, New York: Holt, Rinehart & Winston.

Gardner, H. (1983) *Frames of Mind: the Theory of Multiple Intelligences*, London: Heinemann.

Gelman, R. and Baillargeon, R. (1983) 'A review of some Piagetian concepts', in J.H. Favell and E. Markman (eds) *Handbook of Child Psychology*, vol. 3, *Cognitive Development*, series ed. P.H. Mussen, New York: Wiley.

Gregory, R.L. (1987) 'In defence of artificial intelligence – reply to John Searle', in C. Blackmore and S. Greenfield (eds) *Mindwaves*, Oxford: Blackwell.

Grigson, J. (1980) *Jane Grigson's Vegetable Book*, Harmondsworth: Penguin Books.

Haith, M.M. and Campos, J. (eds) (1983) *Handbook of Child Psychology*, vol. 2, *Infancy and Development Psychobiology*, series ed. P.H. Mussen, New York: Wiley.

Harris, P.L. (1983) 'Infant cognition', in M.M. Haith and J.J. Campos (eds) *Handbook of Child Psychology*, vol. 2, New York: Wiley.

Haugeland, J. (1985) *Artificial Intelligence: the Very Idea*, Cambridge, Mass.: MIT Press.

Hofstadter, D.R. (1979) *Godel, Escher, Bach: an Eternal Golden Braid*, Harmondsworth: Penguin Books.

Hundeide, K. (1985) 'The tacit background of children's judgement', in J.V. Wertsch (ed.) *Culture, Communication and Cognition*, Cambridge: Cambridge University Press.

Inhelder, B. and Piaget, J. (1958) *The Growth of Logical Thinking from Childhood to Adolescence*, New York: Basic Books.

Inhelder, B. and Piaget, J. (1979) 'Procédures et structures', *Archives de Psychologie and Society*, London: Macmillan.

Johnson-Laird, P. (1983) *Mental Models*, Cambridge: Cambridge University Press.

Kail, R. (1986) 'Sources of age differences in speed of processing', *Child Development* 57: 969–87.

Kail, R. (1988) 'Reply to Stigler, Nusbaum and Chalip', *Child Development* 59: 1154–7.

Kail, R. (1991a) 'Processing time declines exponentially during childhood and adolescence', *Developmental Psychology* 27: 259–66.

Kail, R. (1991b) 'Developmental change in speed processing during childhood and adolescence', *Psychological Bulletin* 109, 490–501.

Kail, R. and Bisanz, J. (1982) 'Information processing and cognitive development', in *Advances in Child Development and Behaviour*, New York: Academic Press.

Karmiloff-Smith, A. and Inhelder, B. (1974/5) 'If you want to get ahead, get a theory', *Cognition* 3: 195–212.

Keil, F.C. (1979) *Semantic and Conceptual Development*, Cambridge, Mass.: Harvard University Press.

Keil, F.C. (1981) 'Constraints on knowledge and cognitive development', *Psychological Review* 88: 197–227.

Keil, F.C. (1984) 'Mechanisms on cognitive development and the structure of knowledge', in R.J. Sternberg (ed.) *Mechanisms of Cognitive Development*, New York: Freeman.

Keil, F.C. (1989) *Concepts, Kinds and Cognitive Development*, Boston: MIT Press.

Klahr, D. (1984) 'Transition processes in quantitative development', in R.J. Sternberg (ed.) *Mechanisms of Cognitive Development*, New York: Freeman.

Klahr, D. and Siegler, R.S. (1978) 'The representation of children's knowledge', in H.W. Reese and J.P. Lipsitt (eds) *Advances in Child Development and Behaviour*, New York: Academic Press.

Klahr, D. and Wallace, G. (1976) *Cognitive Development: an Information-processing View*, New York: Erlbaum.

Klausmeier, H.J. and Sipple, T.S. (1982) 'Factor structure of the Piagetian stage of concrete operations', *Contemporary Educational Psychology* 7: 161–80.

Kozulin, A. (1986) 'Vygotsky in context', in L.S. Vygotsky, *Thought and Language*, A. Kozulin (ed.), Cambridge, Mass.: MIT Press.

Kozulin, A. (1990) *Vygotsky's Psychology*, Brighton: Harvester.

Kozulin, A. (1998) *Psychological Tools: A Sociocultural Approach to Education*, Cambridge, Mass., and London: Harvard University Press.

Kuhn, T.S. (1962) *The Structure of Scientific Revolutions*, Chicago: Chicago University Press.

Laboratory of Comparative Human Cognition (1983) 'Culture and cognitive development', in W. Kessen (ed.) *Handbook of Child Psychology*, vol. 1, *History, Theory and Method*, New York: Wiley.

Lee, B. (1985) 'Intellectual origins of Vygostky's semiotic analysis', in J.V. Wertsch (ed.) *Culture, Communication and Cognition*, Cambridge: Cambridge University Press.

Lewis, M. and Brooks-Gunn, J. (1979) *Social Cognition and the Acquisition of Self*, New York: Plenum Press.

Light, P.H., Buckingham, N. and Robbins, A.H. (1979) 'The conservation tasks as an interactional setting', *British Journal of Educational Psychology* 49: 304–10.

Lock, A. (ed.) (1978) *Action, Gesture and Symbol: the Emergence of Language*, London: Academic Press.

Longeot, F. (1978) *Les Stades operatoires de Piaget et les facteurs de l'intelligence*, Grenoble: Presses Universetaires de Grenoble.

Longuet-Higgins, H.C. (1987) *Mental Processes: Studies in Cognitive Science*, Cambridge, Mass.: MIT Press.

Lord, A.B. (1960) *The Singer of Tales*, Cambridge, Mass.: Harvard University Press.

Luria, A.R. (1976) *Cognitive Development: its Cultural and Social Foundations*, Cambridge, Mass.: Harvard University Press.

McClelland, J.L., Rumelhart, D.E. and the PDP Research Group (1986) *Parallel Distributed Processing: Explorations in the Micro-structure of Cognition, vol. 2, Psychological and Biological Models*, Cambridge, Mass.: MIT Press.

Markova, I. (1982) *Paradigms, Thought and Language*, New York: Wiley.

Mayes, A.R. (1988) *Human Organic Memory Disorders*, Cambridge: Cambridge University Press.

Mead, G.H. (1934) *Mind, Self and Society*, Chicago: University of Chicago Press.

Meadows, S. (1975) 'The development of concrete operations: a short-term longitudinal study', Ph.D. thesis, University of London.

Meadows, S. (ed.) (1983) *Developing Thinking: Approaches to Children's Cognitive Development*, London: Methuen.

Meadows, S. (1986) *Understanding Child Development*, London: Hutchinson.

Meadows, S. and Cashdan, A. (1983) *Teaching Styles in Nursery Education: Final Report to SSRC*, Sheffield: Sheffield City Polytechnic.

Mellin-Olsen, S. (1987) *The Politics of Mathematics Education*, Dordrecht: Reidel.

Midgley, M. (1985) *Evolution as a Religion: Strange Hopes and Stranger Fears*, London: Methuen.

Miller, S.A. (1982) 'On the generalizability of conservation: a comparison of different kinds of transformation', *British Journal of Psychology* 73(2): 221–30.

Minsky, M. (1988) *The Society of Mind*, New York: Simon & Schuster.

Mischel, T. (ed.) (1971) *Cognitive Development and Epistemology*, New York and London: Academic Press.

Moerk, E.L. (1989) 'The LAD was a lady and the tasks were ill-defined', *Developmental Review* 9(1): 21–57.

Nelson, K.E. (1986) *Event Knowledge: Structure and Function in Development*, Hillsdale, NJ: Erlbaum.

Perret-Clermont, A.-N. and Brossard, A. (1985) 'On the interdigitation of social and cognitive processes', in R.A. Hinde, A.-N. Perret-Clermont and J. Stevenson-Hinde (eds) *Social Relationships and Cognitive Development*, Oxford: Clarendon Press.

Piaget, J. (1952) *The Child's Conception of Number*, New York: Basic Books.

Piaget, J. (1968) *Six Psychological Studies*, London: University of London Press.

Piaget, J. (1970) *Genetic Epistemology*, New York: Columbia University Press.

Piaget, J. (1971) *Biology and Knowledge*, Edinburgh: Edinburgh University Press.

Piaget, J. (1978) *The Development of Thought: Equilibration of Cognitive Structures*, Oxford: Blackwell.

Piaget, J. (1983) 'Piaget's theory', in W. Kessen (ed.) *Handbook of Child Psychology*, vol. 1, series ed. P.H. Mussen (previously published 1970 in P.H. Mussen (ed.) *Carmichael's Manual of Child Psychology*, 3rd edn, vol. 1, New York: Wiley.

Popper, K.R. (1967) *Objective Knowledge*, Oxford: Clarendon Press.

Popper, K.R. and Eccles, J.C. (1977) *The Self and its Brain*, Berlin: Springer-Verlag.

Pylyshyn, Z.W. (1980) 'Computation and cognition: issues in the foundation of cognitive science', *Behavioural and Brain Sciences* 3: 111–34.

Robinson, E.J. and Robinson, W.P. (1977) 'Development in the understanding of the cause of success and failure in verbal communication', *Cognition* 5: 363–78.

Robinson, E.J. and Robinson, W.P. (1980) 'Egocentrism in verbal referential communication', in M.V. Cox (ed.) *Are Young Children Egocentric?* London: Batsford.

Robinson, E.J. and Robinson, W.P. (1981) 'Ways of reacting to communication failure in relation to the development of children's understanding about verbal communication', *European Journal of Social Psychology* 11: 189–208.

Rogoff, B. (1990) *Apprenticeship in Thinking*, Oxford: Oxford University Press.

Rotman, B. (1977) *Jean Piaget: Psychologist of the Real*, Hassocks, Sussex: Harvester Press.

Rumelhart, D.E. and McClelland, J.L. (eds) (1986) *Parallel Distributed Processing: Exploration, in the Microstructure of Cognition*, Cambridge, Mass.: MIT Press.

Ruse, M. (1986) *Taking Darwin Seriously: A Naturalistic Approach to Philosophy*, Oxford: Blackwell.

Russell, J. (1978) *The Acquisition of Knowledge*, London, Macmillan.

Russell, J. (1981a) 'Dyadic interaction in a logical reasoning problem requiring inclusion ability', *Child Development* 51: 1322–5.

Russell, J. (1981b) 'Why "socio-cognitive conflict" may be impossible: the status of egocentric errors in the dyadic performance of a spatial task', *Educational Psychology* 1: 159–69.

Russell, J. (1982) 'Propositional attitudes', in M. Beveridge (ed.) *Children Thinking Through Language*, London: Edward Arnold.

Scribner, S. (1985) 'Vygotsky's use of history', in J.V. Wertsch (ed.) *Culture, Communication and Cognition*, Cambridge: Cambridge University Press.

Searle, J.R. (1984) *Minds, Brains and Science*, Harmondsworth: Penguin Books.

Siegel, L.S., McCabe, A.E., Brand, J. and Matthews, L. (1978) 'Evidence for the understanding of class inclusion in preschool children: linguistic factors and training effects', *Child Development* 49: 688–93.

Siegler, R.S. (ed.) (1978) *Children's Thinking: What Develops?* Hillsdale, NJ: Erlbaum.

Siegler, R.S. (1983) 'Information processing approaches to development', in W. Kessen (ed.) *Handbook of Child Psychology*, vol. 1, series ed. P.H. Mussen, New York: Wiley.

Siegler, R.S. (1984) 'Mechanisms of cognitive growth: variation and selection', in R.J. Sternberg (ed.) *Mechanisms of Cognitive Development*, New York: Freeman.

Siegler, R.S. (1986) *Children's Thinking*, Englewood Cliffs, NJ: Prentice Hall.

Siegler, R.S. (1989) 'Mechanisms of cognitive development', *Annual Review of Psychology* 40: 353–79.

Simon, H. (1981) *The Sciences of the Artificial*, Cambridge, Mass.: MIT Press.

Singley, M.K. and Anderson, J.R. (1989) *The Transfer of Cognitive Skills*, Cambridge, Mass.: Harvard University Press.

Smedslund, J. (1980) 'Analyzing the primary code: from empiricism to apriorism', in D.R. Olson (ed.) *The Social Foundations of Language and Thought*, New York and London: Norton.

Sternberg, R.J. (ed.) (1984) *Mechanisms of Cognitive Development*, New York: Freeman.

Sternberg, R.J. (1985) *Beyond IQ: a Triarchic Theory of Human Intelligence*, New York: Cambridge University Press.

Stigler, J.W., Nusbaum, H.C. and Chalip, L. (1988) 'Developmental changes in speed of processing: central limiting mechanism or skill transfer?' *Child Development* 59: 1144–53.

Stigler, J.W., Schweder, R.A. and Herdt, G. (1990) *Cultural Psychology: Essays on Comparative Human Development*, Cambridge: Cambridge University Press.

Sutton, A. (1983) 'An introduction to Soviet developmental psychology', in S. Meadows (ed.) *Developing Thinking*, London: Methuen.

Tharp, R.G. *et al.* (1984) 'Product and process in applied developmental research: education and the children of a minority', in M.E. Lamb, A.L. Brown and B. Rogoff (eds) *Advances in Developmental Psychology*, vol. 3, Hillsdale, NJ: Erlbaum.

Tharp, R.G. and Gallimore, R. (1988) *Rousing Minds to Life: Teaching, Learning and Schooling in Social Context*, Cambridge: Cambridge University Press.

Uzgiris, I. (1964) 'Situational generality of conservation', *Child Development* 35: 831–41.

Valsiner, J. (ed.) (1988a) *Child Development within Culturally Structured Environments*, vol. 1, *Parental Cognition and Adult–Child Interaction*, Norwood, NJ: Ablex.

Valsiner, J. (ed.) (1988b) *Child Development within Culturally Structured Environments*, vol. 2, *Social Co-construction and Environmental Guidance in Development*, Norwood, NJ: Ablex.

Van der Veer, R. and Valsiner, J. (1988) 'Lev Vygotsky and P. Janet: on the origin of the concept of sociogenesis', *Developmental Review* 8: 52–65.

Vuyk, R. (1981) *Overview and Critique of Piaget's Genetic Epistemology, 1965–1980*, vols 1 and 2, London: Academic Press.

Vygotsky, L.S. (1960) 'The development of higher mental functions', quoted in J.V. Wertsch (1985a) *Vygotsky and the Social Formation of Mind*, Cambridge, Mass.: Harvard University Press.

Vygotsky, L.S. (1962) *Thought and Language*, Cambridge, Mass.: MIT Press.

Vygotsky, L.S. (1978) *Mind in Society: the Development of Higher Psychological Processes*, ed. M. Cole, V. John-Steiner, S. Scribner and E. Souberman, Cambridge, Mass.: Harvard University Press.

Vygotsky, L.S. (1981) 'The genesis of higher mental functions', in J.W. Wertsch (ed.) *The Concept of Activity in Soviet Psychology*, Armonk, NY: M.E. Sharpe.

Vygotsky, L.S. (1986) *Thought and Language*, new edn, ed. A. Kozulin, Cambridge, Mass.: MIT Press.

Wason, P.C. (1977) 'On the failure to eliminate hypotheses', in P.N. Johnson-Laird and P.C. Wason (eds) *Thinking*, Cambridge: Cambridge University Press.

Wertsch, J.V. (1978) 'Adult–child interaction and the roots of metacognition', *Quarterly Newsletter of the Laboratory of Comparative Human Cognition* 2(1): 15–18.

Wertsch, J.V. (1979) 'From social interaction to higher psychological process: a clarification and application of Vygotsky's theory', *Human Development* 22: 1–22.

Wertsch, J.V. (ed.) (1981) *The Concept of Activity in Soviet Psychology*, Armonk, NY: M.E. Sharpe.

Wertsch, J.V. (1985a) *Vygotsky and the Social Formation of Mind*, Cambridge, Mass.: Harvard University Press.

Wertsch, J.V. (ed.) (1985b) *Culture, Communication and Cognition*, Cambridge: Cambridge University Press.

Wertsch, J.V. and Stone, C.A. (1985) 'The concept of internalisation in Vygotsky's account of the genesis of higher mental functions', in J.V. Wertsch (ed.) *Culture, Communication and Cognition*, Cambridge: Cambridge University Press.

Wertsch, J.V., McNamee, G.D., McLane, J.B. and Budwin, N.A. (1980) 'The adult–child dyad as a problem-solving system', *Child Development* 51: 1215–21.

Williams, M. (1989) 'Vygotsky's social theory of mind', *Harvard Educational Review* 59(1): 108–27.

Winegar, L.T. (ed.) (1989) *Social Interaction and the Development of Children's Understanding*, Norwood, NJ: Ablex.

Wood, D.J. (1980) 'Teaching the young child: some relationship between social interaction, language and thought', in D.R. Olson (ed.) *The Social Foundations of Language and Thought*, New York: Norton.

Wood, D.J. (1988) *How Children Think and Learn*, Oxford, Blackwell.

Wood, D.J., Wood, H.A. and Middleton, D.J. (1978) 'An experimental evaluation of four face-to-face teaching strategies', *International Journal of Behavioural Development* 1, 131–47.

Young, J.Z. (1978) *Programs of the Brain*, Oxford: Oxford University Press.

Young, J.Z. (1987) *Philosophy and the Brain*, Oxford: Oxford University Press.

Zinchenko, V.P. (1985) 'Vygotsky's ideas about units for the analysis of mind', in J.V. Wertsch (ed.) *Culture, Communication and Cognition*, Cambridge: Cambridge University Press.

CHAPTER 8

COGNITIVE DEVELOPMENT

No stages please – we're British[†]

Usha Goswami

British Journal of Psychology, Vol. 92, 2001

One hundred years ago, James Sully, Grote Professor of Philosophy of Mind and Logic at University College London and in some senses the founder of the BPS, wrote a book entitled *Studies of childhood* (Sully, 1905). He suggested the importance of a scientific and empirical approach to the study of cognitive development, noting 'it is the human psychologist ... who has a supreme interest and scientific property in these first years of a human existence' (p. 7). Some 30 years later, Susan Isaacs, a Fellow of the BPS and Head of the Department of Child Development, University of London Institute of Education, addressed the BPS on 'Recent advances in the Psychology of Young Children' (in 1938, published in Isaacs, 1948). One of Isaac's themes was the need to apply psychological findings to the physical and mental well-being of children. These examples show that the trio of founding influences on the BPS noted by Edgell (1947) – philosophy, physiology and the experimental method – were notable even in the earliest British approaches to studying the mental development of children. British cognitive developmental work today is similarly strongly empirical, with an emphasis on rigorous experimental methods. It also demonstrates a healthy respect for underlying philosophical questions and plausible physiological mechanisms. British work in cognitive development during the next millennium seems set to continue in these traditions, coupling them with an active awareness of the importance of adopting an interdisciplinary approach to the study of mental development.

A quick survey of the symposia titles from the early years of the BPS reveals the extent of the continuities. For example, the discussion 'Can there be anything obscure or implicit in a mental state?' (1913) could be the title of a symposium for a Millennium meeting, with participants such as Uta Frith, James Russell, Norman Freeman, Liz Robinson, Simon Baron-Cohen and Francesca Happé (and many of their colleagues). All of these scientists have made significant contributions to our understanding of the development of mental states. The symposium on 'Instinct and Intelligence' held in 1910 could be repeated today in 2001, perhaps in the MRC centre for Social, Genetic and Developmental Psychology (MRC SGDP) created by Michael Rutter, Robert Plomin and Judy Dunn and now headed by Peter McGuffin.

[†] This article is dedicated to the memory of George Butterworth, whose enormous contribution to British developmental psychology was cut short by his untimely death on 12 February 2000.

This unit has produced important work on the interactions between genes and environment in cognition. Emerging evidence on the importance of the maturation of the frontal cortex for cognitive development suggests that a developmental debate on 'The Function of the Frontal Lobes' (1903) would still be topical in 2001, perhaps between infancy researchers such as Mark Johnson, Alan Slater, Gavin Bremner and Annette Karmiloff-Smith, all of whom have made significant contributions to our understanding of early development. Finally, 'The Fundamental Forms of Mental Interaction' (1906) could characterize British developmental research into how perception, language and cognition interact in the development of basic cognitive skills such as reading, science and mathematics, and also in the development of more general cognitive skills such as working memory, deductive reasoning and the understanding of transitive relations. Landmark research in these areas has been carried out by Peter Bryant and by the late Rosalind Driver, and by many other respected British laboratories including those at Bristol (Baddeley, Gathercole and Freeman), Nottingham (Wood and O'Malley), Oxford (Bishop, Harris and Plunkett), Sussex (Perner, Oakhill, Ruffman and Yuill), Warwick (Brown and Lewis) and York (Ellis, Snowling and Hulme).

Other important influences on British cognitive-development psychology include Jean Piaget, Jerome Bruner, Neil O'Connor and Beate Hermelin. Piaget has of course had a profound worldwide influence on the progress of cognitive developmental psychology as a discipline, and he had a hand in training a number of today's outstanding developmental researchers in the United Kingdom (e.g. Peter Bryant and Annette Karmiloff-Smith). When Jerome Bruner was at Oxford he attracted many young people who have since gone on to do important work in cognitive development in other countries, including Andy Meltzoff, Chris Pratt, Alison Gopnik, Alison Garton, Roy Pea, Anat Ninio and José Linaza. Other of Bruner's students and post-docs remained in the UK, for example Kathy Sylva, David Wood, Paul Harris and (until recently) Alan Leslie. Neil O'Connor established the MRC Developmental Psychology Unit in London (which closed in 1982), and both Peter Bryant and Uta Frith were his and Ati Hermelin's doctoral students. Both Frith and Bryant in turn have trained a number of distinguished British developmentalists, including the late George Butterworth, Paul Harris, Gavin Bremner, Vicky Lewis and Charles Hulme for Bryant, and Maggie Snowling, Simon Baron-Cohen and Francesca Happe for Frith. The MRC then established the Cognitive Development Unit (MRC CDU) under the directorship of John Morton, which pioneered a modular approach to cognitive development in the UK, and has only recently closed (in 1998). Both MRC units recognized the importance of studying disorders of development and then formulating theories about normal development from these studies, another characteristically British approach to cognitive development. Notable former members of both units other than those already mentioned include Barbara Dodd, Linda Pring, Peter Hobson, Alan Leslie (now in the USA), Mike Anderson (now in Australia) and James Blair. Finally, it is important to mention John Bowlby, the pioneer of attachment theory and the study of social and emotional development (e.g. Bowlby, 1969). Social and emotional development, of course, affects cognitive development, and significant contributions to understanding social and emotional development have been made by British researchers such as Robert Hinde, Joan Stevenson-Hinde, Rudolph Schaffer and Colwyn Trevarthen. Finally, there is a strong British tradition of research on the development of drawing, led by researchers such as Maureen Cox, Norman Freeman and John Willatts.

Looking back, it is clear that the BPS's philosophical and empirical roots are flourishing in much of the cognitive development work that typifies current British research.

British cognitive developmental psychology is known for its interest in philosophical questions (e.g. the development of a theory of mind in children, the relationship between nature and nurture), and for its preference for linking basic research to applied issues in education and cognitive disorders (e.g. why the development of adequate phonological skills might be important for reading and spelling progress, or why the development of a theory of mind might be important in explaining some aspects of autism). It is also known for its willingness to learn both methodologically and theoretically from work in animal psychology and in physiology more generally (e.g. in using work with animals to inform approaches to understanding the development of deception and imitation in children, and by using physiological tools such as event-related potentials (ERPs) as a basis for studying cognitive development). However, cognitive developmental psychology is a discipline in many respects founded by the work of Jean Piaget.

Piagetian cognitive developmental psychology and UK research

Piaget was originally a biologist. This led him to translate the notion that organisms adapt themselves to their environments to the study of children's thinking. Piaget suggested that cognitive development was caused by three processes: accommodation, assimilation and equilibrium. Accommodation is the process of adapting cognitive 'schemes' for viewing the world (general concepts) to fit reality. Assimilation is the complementary process of interpreting experience (individual instances of general concepts) in terms of current cognitive schemes. The goal of the child is cognitive equilibrium. However, as every cognitive equilibrium is only partial, every existing equilibrium must evolve towards a higher form of equilibrium – towards a more adequate form of knowing. Piaget argued that this process of ontogeny drove cognitive development. When one cognitive scheme became inadequate for making sense of the world, it was replaced by another, requiring fundamental cognitive restructuring on the part of the child.

Piaget suggested that there were four major cognitive stages in logical development, corresponding to four successive forms of knowledge. During each of these stages, children were hypothesized to think and reason in a different way. These stages, and their approximate ages of occurrence, were:

1   The sensory-motor period: 0–2 years.
2   The period of pre-operations: 2–7 years.
3   The period of concrete operations: 7–11 years.
4   The period of formal operations: 11–12 years on.

However, Piaget recognized that the acquisition of each new way of thinking would not necessarily be synchronous across all the different domains of thought. Instead, he argued that the chronology of the stages might be extremely variable, and that such variability might also occur *within* a given stage. Thus the ages of attainment that Piaget gave for the different cognitive stages are only approximations.

'Sensory-motor' cognition was based on physical interaction with the world. One of Piaget's fundamental notions was that thought developed from action. In his view, a 'logic of action' existed prior to, and in addition to, the representational logic of thought (sensory-motor behaviours *became* thought). For example, one of the hallmarks of this period was the attainment of 'object permanence'. The development of object permanence refers to the understanding that objects continue to exist even when they are hidden from view. A complete understanding of object permanence was said to emerge only between 15 and 18 months, marking the attainment of a *cognitive representation* of the object. If it were true that cognitive representations do not emerge until the final stage of sensory-motor cognition, then babies would have to wait a long time before they could engage in any meaningful cognitive activity. Learning, memory, reasoning and problem-solving abilities would all be seriously constrained.

Between around 18 and 24 months, the beginning of the internalization of action was thought to occur, although the results of such internalizations (called 'compositions') could only support limited forms of thought as they were not yet mentally reversible. A full understanding of the properties and relations of concrete objects was thought to develop very gradually during the pre-operational stage. During this period, children's solution of problems concerning objects and their relations (e.g. class inclusion problems, conservation problems) displayed modes of thought that were egocentric. The child perceived and interpreted the world in terms of the self. Pre-operational thought also displayed centration, in that the child tended to fix on one aspect of a situation or object and ignore other aspects. Finally, it displayed a lack of reversibility, in that the child was unable to reverse mentally a series of events or steps of reasoning. The pre-operational child was thus seen as pre-logical, having a subjective and self-centred grasp of the world. Nevertheless, via the transition from sensory-motor to pre-operational forms of thought, the practical logic of relations and classes in terms of sensory-motor action were the precursor of the representational logic of relations and classes used in the concrete operational stage.

During 'concrete operational' cognition, the compositions of internalized actions became reversible, making the beginning of mental operations such as class inclusion, transitivity and conservation. Piaget developed tests of the attainment of each of these operations which have become classic tasks in the cognitive developmental literature. The acquisition of concrete operations was marked by the gradual waning of egocentricity, by the ability to 'decentre' or consider multiple aspects of a situation simultaneously, and by 'reversibility' or the ability to understand that any operation on an object simultaneously implied its inverse. The child's growing logical insights were thought to lead to the development of concrete operational mental 'structures', such as classification, seriation and conservation. Piaget's idea was that mathematical logic could be used to describe the psychological reality of the logical structures developed by the child, and the reversibility of those structures. These mathematical groupings described operations such as class inclusion ($A + A' = B$) and transitivity ($A > B$, $B > C$, therefore $A > C$).

During 'formal operational' cognition, certain concrete operations became linked together, marking the onset of scientific thought. 'Formal operational' reasoning depended on the ability to take the results of concrete operations, to generate hypotheses about their logical relationships and to represent alternative hypotheses and their deductive implications. Piaget described this level of reasoning as 'operating on operations', or 'second-order' reasoning. He conceptualized this mathematically, in terms of the ability to apply a formal system such as propositional logic to the elementary operations concerning classes of objects and their relations. Many of Piaget's tests for the presence of formal operational structures involved tasks requiring scientific thought, such as discovering the rule that determines whether material bodies will float or sink in water, discovering the rule between weight and distance that will enable a beam to balance, and discovering the rule that governs the oscillation of a pendulum.

British research in the Piagetian tradition

The writings of researchers such as Kenneth Lovell, Eric Lunzer and Wolfe Mays helped to introduce Piaget's theory of cognitive development to British developmental psychology (e.g. Lovell, 1961; Lunzer, 1965). It has since been appealing to researchers and educationists at a number of levels. For example, Piaget's notion that children learn about the world via the means that they have available to them, and that their sensory and motor experiences are crucial to this learning, has been very influential in guiding approaches to preschool education and in devising enrichment programmes for children perceived to need extra stimulation. Some of Piaget's views about the connections between mathematical and cognitive logic seem quite futuristic if viewed from the perspective of computer modelling of certain aspects of cognition and the pressure that such modelling brings for fairly mathematically precise descriptions of cognitive behaviours. However, Piaget's overall theory of cognitive development has been displaced increasingly over the last 20 years by a more broadly knowledge-based view of cognitive development. This knowledge-based perspective has challenged the idea that certain cognitive milestones (e.g. conservation and transitivity) are the hallmarks of particular ways of thinking. Researchers in the UK have made a significant contribution to the displacement of the Piagetian perspective, with particularly notable contributions from the laboratories of Margaret Donaldson and Tom Bower in Edinburgh and Jerome Bruner and Peter Bryant in Oxford (e.g. Bower, 1973; Bremner & Bryant, 1977; Bruner, 1974; Bryant, 1974; Bryant & Trabasso, 1971; Butterworth, 1977; Donaldson, 1978; Harris, 1974). Because of space constraints, three examples of this British contribution will have to suffice, concerning object permanence (Stage 1), conservation (Stage 3) and analogical reasoning (Stage 4).

A great deal of British infancy research has shown that babies perceive the world quite adequately before they go through all six of Piaget's substages of sensory-motor cognition (e.g. Bower, 1966; Trevarthen, 1974; Wishart & Bower, 1982). A particular British interest has been the development of object permanence. Work by Gavin Bremner, George Butterworth and Paul Harris suggested that by 9 months of age, infants had a fairly well-developed notion that objects are permanent. These researchers all focused their experimental tasks on the 'A-not-B' search error that occurs during the development of object permanence. This error occurs in simple hiding-and-finding tasks that involve more than one location. Imagine that an object is hidden at one location (location A) for a number of trials. The infants retrieve the object without difficulty. The hiding location is then moved to another location (location B). Although this switch in hiding location occurs in full view of the infants, the infants persist in searching at location A. This is the 'A-not-B' error. Piaget argued that the infants believed that the object was associated with the first location (i.e. location A), and that they could egocentrically re-create the object at A simply by deciding to look there.

Perhaps the most comprehensive experiment rejecting this view was conducted by Bremner (1978). He devised a methodology in which the infant was moved rather than the hiding location (see also Bremner & Bryant, 1977). For example, an infant seated at a fixed point in front of a table who must search for an object that is now hidden at location B must reach to a new location in order to retrieve the toy. An infant who is moved around the table to search at location B must reach to the same side as previously: an 'egocentric' reach (see Fig. 4). Bremner showed that infants could search correctly after being moved, wherever the object was hidden, as long as the hiding locations were differentiated by distinctive cues (covers of different colours). In separate experiments involving perspex boxes as locations A and B (Butterworth, 1977) and perspex doors to locations A and B (Harris, 1974),

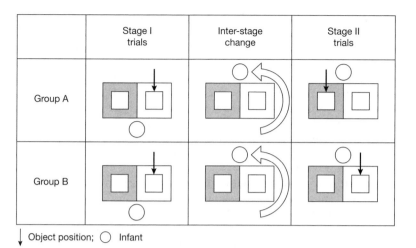

	Stage I trials	Inter-stage change	Stage II trials
Group A			
Group B			

↓ Object position; ◯ Infant

Figure 4 The experimental set-up used by Bremner and Bryant (1977), in which the infant was physically moved around the table.

Butterworth and Harris showed that infants would also search at visibly empty locations. They argued therefore that the disappearance of the objects *per se* could not be driving search errors in the A-not-B task. For example, the infants may be as interested in the containers used in the task as in tracing the location of the objects that have been hidden. More recently, the importance of frontal cortex maturation in the A-not-B error has been demonstrated (e.g. Diamond, 1991). The maturation of the frontal cortex is now known to be important for cognition more generally, and British researchers have played a key role in demonstrating the importance of 'frontal' or 'executive' functions in cognitive development in slightly older children (e.g. Hughes, Dunn, & White, 1998; Russell, 1996).

Regarding concrete operations (Stage 3), a key logical concept is conservation, which is the ability to conserve quantity across changes in appearance. This logical operation underpins the understanding of invariance, an important logical insight that in turn underpins the number system. Piaget's conservation task measured children's understanding of invariance by asking them to compare two initially identical quantities, one of which was then transformed. For example, a child could be shown two rows of five beads arranged in 1:1 correspondence, or two glasses of liquid filled to exactly the same level. An adult experimenter would then alter the appearance of one of these quantities while the child was watching (e.g. spreading out the beads in one of the rows so that the row looked longer). Most children below the age of around 7 who were given the conservation task told the experimenter that there were now more beads in the spread-out row.

In a seminal monograph, Donaldson (1978) raised the possibility that the adult's actions towards the conservation materials might lead the child to answer the conservation question on the basis of the attribute that he or she *thought* the adult intended to ask about rather than the actual attribute specified linguistically. To test her idea she devised the ingenious 'naughty teddy' paradigm (McGarrigle & Donaldson, 1975), which has since become a classic. The children were told that they would play a special game, and were shown a cardboard box containing a teddy bear. They were told that the teddy was very naughty and escaped from his box from time to time to try to 'mess up the toys' and 'spoil the game'. Conservation materials were then brought out (e.g. two rows of counters in 1:1 correspondence). The child was asked, 'Are there more here or more here or are they both the same number?' All of a sudden, the naughty teddy appeared and altered the length of one of the rows by shoving the counters together. The teddy received the appropriate scolding, and the children were then asked the conservation question again. Under these conditions of an 'accidental' transformation of the arrays, the majority of 4- and 5-year-old children in the experiment gave conserving responses. Many different types of accidental or 'incidental' transformations of the conservation materials have since demonstrated similar conservation abilities in so-called 'pre-operational' children (e.g. Light, Buckingham, & Robbins, 1979).

A task characteristic of formal operational reasoning is reasoning by analogy. Solving analogies requires children to reason about similarities *between* the relations between objects ('second-order' relations). The standard test for analogical reasoning (used in IQ testing) is the 'item analogy' task. In item analogies, two items, A and B, are presented to the child. A third item C is presented, and the child is required to generate a D term that has the same relation to C as B has to A. The relations between A and B and between C and D are first-order relations. The relation that links A–B to C–D is the second-order relation. For example, in the analogy 'Bicycle is to handlebars as ship is to . . .?' the correct response is 'ship's wheel'. When Piaget gave a pictorial version of the item analogy task to children aged from 5 to 12 years, the younger children offered solutions like 'bird', giving reasons like 'both birds and ships are found on the lake' (Piaget, Montangero, & Billeter, 1977). Piaget concluded that younger children solved analogies on the basis of associations (see also Sternberg & Nigro, 1980).

However, a key methodological problem was that Piaget did not check whether the younger children in his experiments understood the relations on which his analogies were based (e.g. the relation 'steering mechanism' in the bicycle : handlebars :: ship : ship's wheel analogy). This means that the younger children's apparent failure to reason by analogy could have arisen from a lack of knowledge. One way to test this possibility is to design analogies based on relations that are known to be highly familiar to younger children from other cognitive developmental research. For example, simple causal relations such as melting, wetting and cutting are known to be acquired early in development, and to be available for use in picture-based tasks by the ages of 3 and 4 years (Bullock, Gelman, & Baillargeon, 1982),

Goswami and Brown (1989) thus devised a series of pictorial item analogies based on these physical causal relations (see Fig. 5). Children aged from 3 to 6 years were given analogies like 'chocolate is to melted chocolate as snowman is to . . .?' and 'playdoh is to cut playdoh as apple is to . . .?'. Knowledge of the causal relations required to solve the analogies was measured in a control condition. The results showed that both analogical success and causal relational knowledge increased with age (3 years: 53% correct for the analogies and 52% for the control sequences; 4 years: 89% analogies and 80% control sequences; 6 years: 99% analogies and 100% control sequences). There was also a significant *conditional* relationship between performance in the analogy condition and performance in the control condition. Analogical reasoning in children is thus highly dependent on relational knowledge. Even children as young as 3 years of age are able to reason by analogy – as long as they have the requisite relational knowledge. The recent literature on analogical reasoning provides a perfect example of how a 'knowledge-based' approach has exposed key weaknesses in Piaget's stage theory (e.g. Goswami, 1992, 1998).

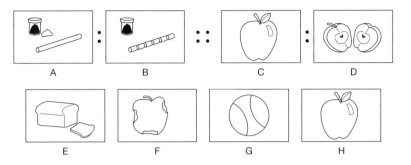

Figure 5 The stimuli in the pictorial item analogy 'playdoh is to cut playdoh as apple is to . . .?' (Goswami & Brown, 1989). The distractor pictures represent a new item with the correct causal transformation (E), the correct item with an incorrect causal transformation (F), an appearance match for the C term (G), and an identity match for the C term (H).

Cognitive developmental psychology in the late 20th century

At least three trends can be discerned in recent years in the explanatory frameworks devised to describe cognitive development. One is an ongoing debate between 'domain-general' versus 'domain-specific' or 'modular' theories of cognitive development. A second concerns the respective roles of genes vs. environment in cognitive development. The third debates the contributions of qualitative vs. quantitative change to describing cognitive development. All three trends have been influenced by research conducted within the UK.

Domain-general and domain-specific theories of cognitive development

Piaget's theory is widely regarded as a domain-general explanation of cognitive development. Domain-general theoretical accounts are based on the idea that key logical developments are acquired and are then applied across all cognitive domains. However, in the last 20 years or so the notion that cognitive development is domain-specific or even modular has been gaining in popularity. Strictly domain-specific theoretical accounts postulate that the development of logical thought depends on the domain, with different mechanisms being applied in different domains. Related accounts argue that not all concepts are equal, and that the structure of knowledge is different in important ways across distinct content areas. Thus logical tools such as inferences may be used differently depending on whether a child is attempting to understand why another child is upset (the domain of psychological causation), why animals usually have babies that look like them (the domain of biology), or why objects fall when they are insufficiently supported (the domain of physical reasoning).

According to modular accounts, cognitive development can be described in terms of distinct kinds of knowledge (e.g. theory of mind) developing independently of all other knowledge in almost encapsulated form (Fodor, 1992). The potential explanatory power of 'modules' in cognitive development has largely been demonstrated by scientists from the MRC CDU, and has had a major impact on the international scene. For example, the notion of a 'theory of mind mechanism' (ToMM) originated in the CDU with the work of Alan Leslie, and has been built upon in various forms by researchers such as Frith, Happé and Baron-Cohen (e.g. Baron-Cohen, Leslie, & Frith, 1985; Frith, Happé & Siddons, 1994; Leslie, 1994).

These two kinds of theory (domain-general vs. domain-specific) are not necessarily developmentally mutually exclusive. Some parts of the cognitive system may rely on domain-general processes and others on domain-specific ones. Alternatively, something that may appear domain-specific may in fact be domain-general. For example, while the ability to make deductive inferences *per se* may be available early, the use of this kind of reasoning may appear to be domain-specific, appearing in different domains in different forms, because children may need sufficient *knowledge* in order to use their deductive abilities in these domains and this knowledge may be very different in kind between domains. Similarly, cognitive development may appear to be modular once a certain degree of specialized knowledge has been attained within a given domain, because the general learning mechanisms required to 'kick-start' the domain are now being applied to such specific kinds of information that the knowledge that they represent appears to 'stand alone'. This has been shown by recent research by ex-MRC CDU scientists such as Karmiloff-Smith and Johnson. For example, in his recent work on the development of face recognition in infancy, Johnson has demonstrated that the module for face processing is better described as cortical specialization and localization for face processing, which develops as a result of specialized early learning during the first months. Even in such a biologically important domain, there is apparently no innate cognitive module (Johnson, 1997; see also Karmiloff-Smith, 1992). However, the documentation of exceptional abilities in the face of general retardation, such as the exceptional drawing abilities of the autistic child Nadia documented by Lorna Selfe (1977), or the skills of 'idiots savants' (O'Connor & Harmelin, 1988), suggest that domain-general theories of development are by themselves insufficient.

Genes and environment in cognitive development

A related theoretical issue is that of nature vs. nurture. The nature/nurture debate was inherited from British empirical philosophy, with its notion of the infant mind as a 'blank slate' upon which experience can write. This notion has been long discredited, but recent research demonstrating the relative sophistication of infant cognition has led to a renaissance of strong nativist views in some quarters (see Turkewitz, 1995, for discussion). However, genes cannot be thought of as 'coding' psychological traits in any fixed or hard-wired fashion, as in a single 'gene' for reading or a single 'gene' for intelligence. Genes and their protein products are important in determining the patterns of interconnections between neurones in the brain and their functioning, but the transcription process through which the protein-making machinery is regulated can be affected by external environmental factors such as stress or learning as well as by internal environmental factors such as the sex hormones (see Skuse, 2000). Knowing whether a particular ability is present at or near birth does not help us to understand its developmental source. Rather, it is a starting point for the investigation of its causes and consequences. The real question for cognitive developmental psychology is how genes and environment *interact* to produce development. One approach to this question is to take advantage of naturally occurring genetic anomalies in the natural population of human beings (e.g. Skuse *et al.*, 1997). Another is to conduct twin studies, and one of the earliest pioneers of the twin approach was the British psychologist Sir Cyril Burt, whose controversial conclusions concerning the high heritability of intelligence are now increasingly being supported (see Mackintosh, 1995). One of the largest twin studies in the world is currently under way in the UK, involving 16,000 twin pairs and led by the researchers at the MRC SGDP headed by Robert Plomin. Important discoveries from this project concerning gene–environment relationships in a number of areas of cognitive development look extremely likely (e.g. Dale *et al.*, 1998; Perrill *et al.*, 1998; Plomin & Rutter, 1998). Theoretically related projects such as Michael Rutter's recent studies of the cognitive outcomes of the Romanian orphans adopted into UK families address a similar theme, and suggest that some 'cognitive catch-up' is possible despite the most adverse of early environments (e.g. Rutter, 1998).

Qualitative vs. quantitative change: dyslexia and autism

The third theoretical issue alluded to above, that of qualitative vs. quantitative change in cognitive development, is strongly linked to the first, as domain-general accounts of cognitive development are essentially qualitative change accounts. Qualitative change in cognitive development refers to the emergence of qualitatively new modes of thinking which are then applied to all relevant domains. Quantitative change theories attribute key importance to the gradual acquisition of relevant knowledge and strategies, which may vary between domains. A useful way of thinking about qualitative vs. quantitative change accounts within a UK framework is to consider how disorders in development can inform theories about normal progression. Our understanding of at least two major developmental disorders, namely dyslexia and autism, has developed markedly because of work conducted within the UK. This work has suggested important roles for *both* qualitative and quantitative aspects of development. For example, children with dyslexia are seen as representing the lower end of the normal curve that describes reading development. If reading development is thought of as a continuum, with some children performing exceptionally well, others performing exceptionally poorly, and still others (the majority) performing at an average level, then those children with dyslexia are all at the lower end of this continuum, but there is no enlarged 'lump' at this bottom end. The 'symptoms' of dyslexic children in terms of reading-related deficits cannot be distinguished from those of other 'garden variety' poor readers, who have difficulties with all aspects of the curriculum (see Rodgers, 1983; Stanovich, 1986). However, given the close relationship between progress in reading and the development of phonological processing skills, it seems likely that there may be *qualitative* differences in the ways that dyslexic children process phonology compared to normally progressing readers and 'garden variety' poor readers (e.g. Swan & Goswami, 1997).

Much of the most influential research in terms of demonstrating a linguistic basis to dyslexia originated in the UK. Snowling and Frith in London, Bryant and Bradley in Oxford, Miles, Ellis and colleagues in Bangor and Seymour in Dundee all made important discoveries concerning the dyslexic child's difficulties with phonological processing (the ability to process the sound patterns of the language) and the consequent/related difficulties in phonological memory. For example, Snowling was one of the first researchers to propose that the phonological representations of speech underlying word production and recognition might be compromised in dyslexia (Snowling, Goulandris, Bowlby, & Howell, 1986), and Bradley and Bryant (1978) were the first to argue for the importance of a reading level match control group in studies of cognitive deficits in dyslexia. Whether these phonological difficulties are conceptualized theoretically as a deficit in a phonological 'module' (e.g. Morton & Frith, 1995) or in auditory organization in general (e.g. Bradley & Bryant, 1987), the explanatory power of a phonological processing deficit explanation of dyslexia is now clearly recognized (see Goswami, 2000).

Similarly, influential research suggesting that autistic children have specific deficits in acquiring certain aspects of social cognition that 3- and 4-year-old children acquire

Figure 6 Schematic depiction of the series of events in the 'Sally Ann' task.

with ease originated in the UK. Whereas typically developing 3- and 4-year-olds can understand that protagonists can have 'false' beliefs that cause them to act in certain ways, autistic children appear selectively impaired in tasks requiring an understanding of false beliefs, and appear incapable of even quite unsophisticated deceptions. An experimental task for assessing preschooler's understanding of false belief, the 'Sally Ann' task invented by Wimmer and Perner (1983), was first extended to autism in the UK and this lead has been followed worldwide (see Fig. 6). In the Sally Ann task, the child is introduced to two dolls, Sally and Ann. Sally has a marble, which she puts in her basket. She then leaves the scene. While Sally is away, Ann transfers the marble to her box. Sally returns, and the child is asked where she will look for her marble. Children who understand that protagonists can have false beliefs (most 4-year-olds) answer correctly that she will look in her basket. Children who do not, such as many autistic children, answer that Sally will look in Ann's box. Again, whether this deficit is conceived of in terms of a damaged 'module' (Leslie, 1994), a more general problem in social cognition (Mitchell, 1997) or even in terms of a lack of centralized 'coherence' in processing certain kinds of cognitive events (Frith, 1989), the explanatory and potential diagnostic power of a 'theory of mind' deficit description of autism is widely recognized (e.g. Charman, 2000).

The next millennium?

Taking these theoretical questions into the 21st century is demanding that psychologists adopt an increasingly interdisciplinary and precisely specified approach to the study of cognitive development. Expertise in many disciplines is required to produce a truly developmental model of any of a number of cognitive processes (e.g. working memory) or cognitive skills (e.g. reading). Cognitive developmental psychology will need input from geneticists and molecular biologists as well as behavioural scientists and philosophers in order to flourish in this century. This is being recognized by the increasing number of cross-disciplinary research groupings that are emerging within UK universities. The study of cognition in general is also relying increasingly on the notion that psychologically plausible cognitive theories should be implementable as computer models. Again, British scientists have been quick to recognize this need, and have produced computer models of varying degrees of power of aspects of cognitive development such as past-tense acquisition and object-oriented behaviours in infancy (e.g. Mareschal, [. . . 2001]; Mareschal, Plunkett, & Harris, 1999; Plunkett & Marchman, 1996).

Distinctively British contributions to cognitive developmental psychology: rhyme, reading and theory of mind

To end this chapter, I would like to select some aspects of cognitive development in which a distinctively British contribution has been made that the rest of the world has followed. Two examples spring most readily to mind: one is the demonstration of the importance of rhyme for reading development in English; the second is the notion of the development of a theory of mind in preschoolers.

Rhyme and reading

The popularity of the ubiquitous 'nursery' rhyme among English-speaking children suggests that it may have developmental importance. Why would children devote so much energy and enthusiasm to rhymes and rhyming if these activities had no developmental significance? More recently, research studies have confirmed that rhyming (and language play in general) have an important linguistic function (e.g. Crystal, 1998) and that rhyme is also related to reading and spelling development (e.g. Bradley & Bryant, 1983). Bryant and his team have shown that knowledge of nursery rhymes at age 3 predicts reading development at age 6, that the ability to detect rhyme measured via an 'odd man out' task (child detects odd man out from *cat, fit, pat*) at ages 4 and 5 is related to reading and spelling progress at ages 8 and 9, and that rhyme is related to reading both via a direct developmental pathway and via an indirect route through phoneme awareness (Bradley & Bryant, 1983; Bryant, Maclean,

Bradley, & Crossland, 1990; Maclean, Bryant, & Bradley, 1987). These findings have since been replicated in a number of studies conducted with English-speaking children around the world (see Goswami, 1999a, for a summary).

Rhyme seems to be related to reading for both linguistic and lexical-statistical reasons. The robust finding that phonological awareness predicts reading development has already been mentioned. Linguistically, the rhyme is a very salient phonological unit, and seems to have an organizing function for English phonology. One word rhymes with another because it shares the linguistic unit (called the 'rime') comprising the vowel phonemes and any final consonant phonemes (e.g. tea–tree; light–kite), and it differs from that other word because the phonemes before the vowel (the 'onset') are distinctive (e.g. /t/ in tea, /k/ in kite). Prior to being taught about phonemes, children seem to organize their mental lexicons of known spoken word forms in terms of syllables, onsets and rimes (see Goswami, 2000). Child phonologists have proposed that the need to compare and contrast words that differ by a single phoneme during language acquisition (phonological 'neighbours': 'cop', 'cat', 'dot' are all equal neighbours of 'cot') is one of the major sources of pressure for the representation of segmental phonology (which is what pure phonological awareness tasks measure). It turns out that the majority of phonological neighbours for many English words are rhyme neighbours (see Goswami, 1999b, 2000). When Lynette Bradley described the oddity task as a test of 'auditory organization', she was anticipating this finding by about 20 years (Bradley, 1980).

The other reason that rhyme is related to reading is to do with the spelling system of English, which is not strictly alphabetic. Statistical analyses of large lexical databases can provide information about the level of consistency of grapheme–phoneme combinations in different languages. In a truly alphabetic orthography, a particular initial consonant (C_1) should always map to the same sound across all single-syllable words, a particular final consonant (C_2) should always map to the same sound across all single-syllable words, and a particular vowel (V) should always map to the same sound across all single-syllable words. In English, although the pronunciation of initial and final consonants is reasonably consistent ($C_1 = 96\%$, $C_2 = 91\%$ (e.g. 'c' in cat, cup, cone etc.; 'p' in cup, rope, cheap etc.), the pronunciation of vowels is very inconsistent across different words (51%, e.g. 'a' in cat, saw, care: see Treiman, Mullennix, Bijeljac-Babic, & Richmond-Welty, 1995). When the spelling-sound consistency of larger spelling units in CVC words is considered, namely the onset-vowel (C_1V) and rime (VC_2) units, there is a clear advantage for the rime. Whereas only 52% of CVC words sharing a C_1V spelling have a consistent pronunciation (e.g. 'bea' in beak and bean), 77% of CVC words sharing a VC_2 spelling have a consistent pronunciation (e.g. 'eak' in peak and weak).

This statistical analysis shows that the spelling–sound consistency of the English written language is greatest for initial consonants (onsets), final consonants and rimes. It indicates that the context of the final consonant or consonants can disambiguate the pronunciation of the vowel (e.g. 'a' makes a different sound in cat, ball, car, day, saw, cake and care, but these different phonemic correspondences are consistent within rhyming groups: cat, mat, bat; ball, fall, wall; care, dare, stare; and so on). McGuinness (1998) has shown that vowel sounds in English have the largest number of spelling alternatives (up to seven for some sounds). Treiman *et al.*'s (1995) analysis shows that many of these alternative spellings become highly predictable if the rime is considered as a unit. A child with good onset-rime awareness may well be in a better position to discover the stability of vowel phonemes within rimes. Such a child is also more likely to make analogies between spelling patterns for rimes (e.g. using 'beak' as a basis for reading 'peak'; Goswami, 1990), and analogy is important in building a visual-orthographic lexicon in English (Goswami & Bryant, 1990; Goswami, Gombert, & de Barrera, 1998). Connectionist simulation models of reading development, which attempt to provide plausible simulations of the architecture of the brain, seem to learn grapheme–phoneme correspondences in English faster when they are taught to segment words at the onset-rime boundary (e.g. Zorzi, Houghton, & Butterworth, 1998). It appears that rhyme is important for reading, both because it corresponds to a salient linguistic unit for young children (the rime), and because this linguistic unit has functional significance in the spelling system of English (Goswami, 1999a, 1999b).

Theory of mind

The importance of developing a theory of mind (ToM) for normal social-cognitive development was first highlighted in a landmark study by the Austrian psychologists Heinz Wimmer and Josef Perner (1983). Their work was to have a profound impact on British developmental psychology in the 1980s and 1990s (Perner worked at Sussex from 1979 to 1994). ToM can be defined as the ability to impute mental states to oneself and others (Premack & Woodruff, 1978). The ability to make inferences on the basis of what other people *believe* to be the case is important for predicting what they will do. ToM is thus an essential aspect of social-cognitive development, and as Wimmer and Perner pointed out, it critically involves *meta-representation*. Meta-representation refers to the ability to represent any representation, although it was initially tied to the ability to represent a person's thought about another person's thought (Perner & Wimmer, 1985). The development of knowing that other people want, feel, know or believe things was argued to begin during the second year in life, but to undergo a major shift between the ages of 3 and 4 years in normally developing children. This was when the ability to understand 'false beliefs' was thought to develop.

The ToM approach to the understanding of representation and minds has generated a great deal of productive British cognitive developmental research into theoretically related areas such as children's pretence (an extension pioneered by Alan Leslie), children's general awareness of mental phenomena, their understanding and employment of deception, their ability to engage in joint attention, their ability to adapt their language and communications to a listener's needs and their perspective-taking abilities (see Lewis & Mitchell, 1994; Mitchell, 1997; for useful overviews). Influential parts of this research have been carried out in the UK. For example, Baron-Cohen, Leekam, Charman and colleagues have demonstrated that joint attention behaviours are an important precursor of ToM; Robinson, Mitchell and colleagues have demonstrated the involvement of counterfactual reasoning in false belief tasks; and Russell, Hughes, Jarrold and colleagues have demonstrated the involvement of executive functions in some tests of deceptive ability (e.g. Charman *et al.*, 1997; Hughes, 1998; Leekam, Baron-Cohen, Perrett, Milders, & Brown, 1997; Riggs, Peterson, Robinson, & Mitchell, [. . . 2001]; Russell, Jarrold, & Potel, 1994).

British researchers have also been active in demonstrating that 3-year-olds can succeed in false belief tasks in certain conditions (e.g. when videotapes are used to help the child to go through the ToM story, when children have to 'post' a representation of the critical object (e.g. a marble) into a toy letterbox, when a hide-and-seek script is used, and when they are asked where Sally will 'look first' for her marble; see e.g. Appleton & Reddy, 1996; Freeman, Lewis, & Doherty, 1991; Mitchell & Lacohée, 1991; Surian & Leslie, 1999). Such demonstrations have been challenging for stage theorists who ascribe great importance to the 'watershed' in ToM at 4 years (see Surian & Leslie, 1999, for a discussion). Broadly speaking, there are currently two popular accounts of the development of ToM. According to the modular account of ToM development, which originated in the CDU with the work of Alan Leslie, the ToM mechanism (ToMM) is a specialized learning device which enables preschool children to attend to and learn about mental states and their causes. The ToMM is an innate domain-specific prestructured representational system, and underlies both early-emerging abilities linked to ToM such as pretend play and later-emerging abilities such as false belief. An alternative theoretical account, which originated in the Sussex/Salzburg partnership of Josef Perner and Heinz Wimmer, suggests that young children find it difficult to represent the fact that a proposition (such as where the marble is) can be given a different truth value to the one that it has been assigned by the children themselves (its current location in Ann's basket; see e.g. Perner, 1991). Between the ages 3 and 4 years, a major shift occurs, and children discover that mental states are really representations. They then become able to succeed in false belief tasks. The 'shift' view of development and the modular view both have strengths and weaknesses, and are still the subject of hot debate. ToM research has somewhat dominated British cognitive developmental psychology in the last decade. As discussed above, it is currently broadening its perspective and making important links with more general aspects of cognitive development. As such, it seems likely to continue to play a leading role in shaping British cognitive developmental research in the next century.

A crystal ball?

Cognitive development and adult cognition are usually treated as separate topics in psychology, despite the fact that the two are necessarily linked. My own prediction is that future research in both disciplines will increasingly feel the need to recognize this intimate connection, especially as techniques in functional brain imaging become more sophisticated and suited to use with children. This intimate connection is already being recognized in areas of cognition that are sufficiently well-specified to allow computer modelling of cognitive processes. For example, in the field of reading the demand for psychologically appropriate models of skilled reading has driven researchers who study reading in adults to look more closely at developmental processes, and interesting continuities are being discovered (e.g. concerning the importance of time units in both reading development and skilled reading: see Goswami, 1986; Ziegler & Perry, 1998). In reasoning by analogy, it has been pointed out that the process of drawing analogies has important similarities to the process underlying the computation of categories and concepts, and that the processes governing conceptual development might thereby provide important insights for modelling reasoning by analogy (Ramscar & Pain, 1996). In conceptualizing developmental disorders, it has been argued cogently that end states in adulthood are not a useful guide to initial states in infancy (e.g. Bishop, 1997; Karmiloff-Smith, 1997). Rather than using adult neuropsychological models of intact and impaired modules as a framework for studying development, truly developmental frameworks must recognize that even very subtle differences in the start state can give rise to huge differences in developmental outcome (e.g. Karmiloff-Smith, 1998; Oliver, Johnson, Karmiloff-Smith, & Pennington, 2000). Similarly, the developing brain has enormous plasticity, and regions that subserve particular functions in adulthood are not necessarily pre-wired to do so (e.g. Vargha-Khadem *et al.*, 1997).

A second promising direction is the technical developments that enable the study of foetal development and imaging of the developing brain. Even foetuses have some form of cognitive life, as learning and memory are functioning in rudimentary form in the womb. For example, memory for the mother's voice is developed during the final trimester, and there is also evidence for foetal learning of particular pieces of music (such as the theme tune of the soap opera *Neighbours* in babies whose mothers regularly watch this programme; Hepper, 1988, 1997). The period of foetal development is also a critical one as far as genetic expression is concerned. Although cognitive development begins in earnest when the infant enters the everyday world of people and objects, when vision becomes possible, and when auditory input is no longer mediated by amniotic fluid, an understanding of how the brain is shaped by environmental contingencies during foetal life (e.g. substance dependency in the mother) cannot fail to inform our understanding of cognitive development. Similarly, if advances in brain imaging technology fulfil their promise of enabling imaging of the developing brain, psychologists may be able to study the effects of different environmental contingencies (such as different nutritional regimes for IQ, or different teaching regimes for dyslexia) by direct observation and measurement of their effects on and their interactions with developing brain systems.

Acknowledgements

I would like to thank George Butterworth, Annette Karmiloff-Smith, David Skuse, Tony Charman and an anonymous reviewer for insightful comments on this chapter.

References

Appleton, M., & Reddy, V. (1996). Teaching three-year-olds to pass false belief tests: A conversational approach. *Social Development, 5*, 275–291.

Baron-Cohen, S., Leslie, A. M., & Frith, U. (1985). Does the autistic child have a 'theory of mind'? *Cognition, 21*, 37–46.

Bishop, D. V. M. (1997) Cognitive neuropsychology and development disorders: Uncomfortable bedfellows. *Quarterly Journal of Experimental Psychology, 50A*, 899–923.

Bower, T. G. R. (1966). The visual world of infants. *Scientific American, 215*, 80–92.

Bower, T. G. R. (1973). *Development in infancy*. San Francisco: Freeman.

Bowlby, T. G. R. (1969). *Attachment and loss*. London: Hogarth Press.

Bradley, L. (1980). *Assessing reading difficulties*. London: Macmillan.

Bradley, L., & Bryant, P. E. (1978). Difficulties in auditory organisation as a possible cause of reading backwardness. *Nature, 271*, 746–747.

Bradley, L., & Bryant, P. E. (1983). Categorising sounds and learning to read: A causal connection. *Nature, 310*, 419–421.

Bremner, J. G. (1978). Egocentric versus allocentric coding in 9-month-old infants: Factors influencing the choice of code. *Developmental Psychology, 14*, 346–355.

Bremner, J. G., & Bryant, P. E. (1977). Place versus response as the basis of spatial errors made by young infants. *Journal of Experimental Child Psychology, 23*, 162–172.

Bruner, J. S. (1974). *Beyond the information given: Studies in the psychology of learning*. New York: Norton.

Bryant, P. E. (1974). *Perception and understanding in young children*. London: Methuen.

Bryant, P. E., Maclean, M., Bradley, L., & Crossland, J. (1990). Rhyme, alliteration, phoneme detection, and learning to read. *Developmental Psychology, 26*, 429–438.

Bryant, P. E., & Trabasso, T. (1971). Transitive inferences and memory in young children. *Nature, 232*, 456–458.

Bullock, M., Gelman, R., & Baillargeon, R. (1982). The development of causal reasoning. In W. J. Friedman (Ed.), *The developmental psychology of time* (pp. 209–254). New York: Academic Press.

Butterworth, G. (1977). Object disappearance and error in Piaget's stage 4 task. *Journal of Experimental Child Psychology, 23*, 391–401.

Charman, T. (2000). Theory of mind and the early diagnosis of autism. In S. Baron-Cohen, H. Tager-Flusberg, & D. Cohen (Eds.), *Understanding other minds: Perspectives from autism and developmental neurosciences* (2nd ed. pp. 422–441). Oxford: Oxford University Press.

Charman, T., Swettenham, J., Baron-Cohen, S., Cox, A., Baird, G., & Drew, A. (1997). Infants with autism: An investigation of empathy, pretend play, joint attention and imitation. *Developmental Psychology*, 33, 781–789.

Crystal, D. (1998). *Language play*. London: Penguin.

Dale, P. S., Simonoff, E., Bishop, D. V. M., Eley, T. C., Oliver, B., Price, T. S., Purcell, S., Stevenson, J., & Plomin, R. (1998). Genetic influence on language delay in two-year-old children. *Nature Neuroscience*, 1, 324–328.

Diamond, A. (1991). Neuro-psychological insights into the meaning of object concept development. In S. Carey & R. Gelman (Eds.), *The epigenesis of mind: Essays on biology and cognition* (pp. 67–110). Hillsdale, NJ: Erlbaum.

Donaldson, M. (1978). *Children's minds*. Glasgow: William Collins.

Edgell, B. (1947). The British Psychological Society. *British Journal of Psychology*, 37, 113–132.

Fodor, J. A. (1992). A theory of the child's theory of mind. *Cognition*, 44, 283–296.

Freeman, N. H., Lewis, C. N. & Doherty, M. (1991). Preschoolers' grasp of a desire for knowledge in false belief prediction: Practical intelligence and verbal report. *British Journal of Developmental Psychology*, 9, 139–158.

Frith, U. (1989). *Autism: Explaining the enigma*. Oxford: Blackwells.

Frith, U., Happé, F. G. E., & Siddons, F. (1994). Autism and theory of mind in everyday life. *Social Development*, 3, 108–124.

Goswami, U. (1986). Children's use of analogy in learning to read: A developmental study. *Journal of Experimental Child Psychology*, 42, 73–83.

Goswami, U. (1990). A special link between rhyming skills and the use of orthographic analogies by beginning readers. *Journal of Child Psychology and Psychiatry*, 31, 301–311.

Goswami, U. (1992). *Analogical reasoning in children*. Part of series 'Developmental Essays in Psychology'. London: Erlbaum.

Goswami, U. (1998). *Cognition in children*. Hove: Psychology Press.

Goswami, U. (1999a). Causal connections in beginning reading: The importance of rhyme. *Journal of Research in Reading*, 22, 217–240.

Goswami, U. (1999b). Phonological development and reading by analogy; Epilinguistic and metalinguistic issues. In J. Oakhill & R. Beard (Eds.), *Reading development and the teaching of reading: A psychological perspective* (pp. 174–200). Cambridge: Cambridge University Press.

Goswami, U. (2000). Phonological representations, reading development and dyslexia; Towards a cross-linguistic theoretical framework. *Dyslexia* 6, 133–151.

Goswami, U., & Brown, A. (1989). Melting chocolate and melting snowmen: Analogical reasoning and causal relations. *Cognition*, 35, 69–95.

Goswami, U., & Bryant, P. E. (1990). *Phonological skills and learning to read*. Hillsdale, NJ: Erlbaum.

Goswami, U., Gombert, J., & deBarrera, F. (1998). Children's orthographic representations and linguistic transparency: Nonsense word reading in English, French and Spanish. *Applied Psycholinguistics*, 19, 19–52.

Harris, P. L. (1974). Perseverative search at a visibly empty place by young infants. *Journal of Experimental Child Psychology*, 18, 535–542.

Hepper, P. G. (1988). Foetal 'soap' addiction. *The Lancet* (11 June), 1347–1348.

Hepper, P. G. (1997). Memory in utero? *Developmental Medicine and Child Neurology*, 39, 343–346.

Hughes, C. (1998). Finding your marbles: Does preschoolers' strategic behaviour predict later understanding of mind? *Developmental Psychology*, 34, 1326–1339.

Hughes, C., Dunn, J., & White, A. (1998). Trick or treat? Uneven understanding of mind and emotion and executive dysfunction in hard-to-manage preschoolers. *Journal of Child Psychology and Psychiatry*, 39, 981–994.

Isaacs, S. S. (1948). *Intellectual growth in young children*, London: Routledge.

Johnson, M. H. (1997). *Developmental cognitive neuroscience*. Oxford: Blackwell.

Karmiloff-Smith, A. (1992). *Beyond modularity: A developmental perspective on cognitive science.* Cambridge, MA: MIT Press/Bradford Books.

Karmiloff-Smith, A. (1997). Crucial differences between developmental cognitive neuroscience and adult neuropsychology. *Developmental Neuropsychology, 13,* 513–524.

Karmiloff-Smith, A. (1998). Development itself is the key to understanding developmental disorders. *Trends in Cognitive Sciences, 2,* 389–398.

Leekham, S., Baron-Cohen, S., Perrett, D., Milders, M., & Brown, S. (1997). Eye-direction detection: A dissociation between geometric and joint attention skills in autism. *British Journal of Developmental Psychology, 15,* 77–95.

Leslie, A. M. (1994). ToMM, ToBY and Agency: Core architecture and domain specificity. In L. A. Hirschfeld & S. A. Gelman (Eds.), *Mapping the mind* (pp. 119–148). New York: Cambridge.

Lewis, C., & Mitchell, P. (1994). *Children's early understanding of mind: Origins and development.* Hove: Erlbaum.

Light, P., Buckingham, N., & Robbins, A. H. (1979). The conservation task as an interactional setting. *British Journal of Educational Psychology, 49,* 304–310.

Lovell, K. (1961). A follow-up study of Inhelder & Piaget's 'The Growth of Logical Thinking'. *British Journal of Psychology, 52,* 143–153.

Lunzer, E. A. (1965). Problems of formal reasoning in test situations. In P. H. Mussen (Ed.), *Monographs of the Society for Research in Child Development*: Vol. 30 (2), *European research in child development* (pp. 19–46).

Mackintosh, N. J. (1995). *Cyril Burt: Fraud or framed?* Oxford: Oxford University Press.

Maclean, M., Bryant, P. E., & Bradley, L. (1987). Rhymes, nursery rhymes and reading in early childhood. *Merrill-Palmer Quarterly, 33,* 255–282.

Mareschal, D. (2001). Connectionist methods in infancy research. In J. Fagen & H. Hayne (Eds.), *Progress in infancy research* (Vol. 2, pp. 112–131). Hillsdale, NJ: Erlbaum.

Mareschal, D., Plunkett, K., & Harris, P. (1999). A computational and neuropsychological account of object-oriented behaviours in infancy. *Developmental Science, 2,* 306–317.

McGarrigle, J., & Donaldson, M. (1975). Conservation accidents. *Cognition, 3,* 341–350.

McGuinness, D. (1998). *Why children can't read.* London: Penguin.

Mitchell, P. (1997). *Acquiring a conception of mind.* Hove: Psychology Press.

Mitchell, P. & Lacohée, H. (1991). Children's early understanding of false belief. *Cognition, 39,* 107–127.

Morton, J., & Frith, U. (1995). Causal modelling: A structural approach to developmental psychopathology. In D. Cicchetti & D. J. Cohen (Eds.), *Developmental psychopathology: Vol. 1. Theory and methods* (pp. 357–390). New York: Wiley.

O'Connor, N., & Hermelin, B. (1987). Visual and graphic abilities of the idiot savant artist. *Psychological Medicine, 17,* 79–90.

Oliver, A., Johnson, M. H., Karmiloff-Smith, A., & Pennington, B. (2000). Deviations in the emergence of representations: A neuro-constructivist framework for analysing development disorders. *Developmental Science, 3,* 1–23.

Perner, J. (1991). *Understanding the representational mind.* Cambridge, MA: MIT Press.

Perner, J., & Wimmer, H. (1985). 'John thinks that Mary thinks that . . .': Attribution of second-order beliefs by 5- to 10-year-old children. *Journal of Experimental Child Psychology, 39,* 437–471.

Petrill, S. A., Saudino, K., Cherny, S. S., Emde, R. N., Fulker, D. W., Hewitt, J. K., & Plomin, R. (1998). Exploring the genetic and environmental etiology of high general cognitive ability in fourteen- to thirty-six-month-old twins. *Child Development, 69,* 68–74.

Piaget, J., Montangero, J., & Billeter, J. (1977). Les correlats. In J. Piaget (Ed.), *L'abstraction reflechissante* (pp. 115–129). Paris: Presses Universitaires de France. [Analogies, Abstractive reflection].

Plomin, R., & Rutter, M. (1998). Child development, molecular, genetics, and what to do with genes once they are found. *Child Development, 69,* 1223–1242.

Plunkett, K., & Marchman, V. A. (1996). Learning from a connectionist model of the acquisition of the English past tense. *Cognition, 61,* 299–308.

Premack, D., & Woodruff, G. (1978). Does the chimpanzee have a theory of mind? *Behavioural and Brain Sciences, 4,* 515–526.

Ramscar, M. J. A., & Pain, H. (1996). Can a real distinction be drawn between cognitive theories of analogy and categorization? In *Proceedings of the 18th Annual Conference of the Cognitive Science Society*, (pp. 346–351). San Diego, CA.

Riggs, K. J., Peterson, D. M., Robinson, E. J., & Mitchell, P. (2001). Are errors in false belief tasks symptomatic of a broader difficulty with counterfactuality? *Cognitive Development*, 13, 34–52.

Rodgers, B. (1983). The identification and prevalence of specific reading retardation. *British Journal of Educational Psychology*, 53, 369–373.

Russell, J. (1996). *Agency: Its role in mental development*. Hove: Psychology Press.

Russell, J., Jarrold, C., & Potel, D. (1994). What makes strategic deception difficult for children: The deception or the strategy? *British Journal of Developmental Psychology*, 12, 301–314.

Rutter, M. (1998). Developmental catch-up, and deficit, following adoption after severe global early privation. With the English and Romanian Adoptees (ERA) study team, London, England UK. *Journal of Child Psychology and Psychiatry*, 39, 465–476.

Selfe, L. (1977). *Nadia: A case of extraordinary drawing ability in an autistic child*. London: Academic Press.

Skuse, D. H. (2000). Behavioural neuroscience and child psychopathology: Insights from model systems. *Journal of Child Psychology & Psychiatry*, 41, 3–31.

Skuse, D. H., James, R. S., Bishop, D. V. M., Coppins, B., Dalton, P., Aamodt-Leeper, G., Bacarese-Hamilton, M., Creswell, C., McGurk, R., & Jacobs, P. A. (1997). Evidence from Turner's syndrome of an imprinted X-linked locus affecting cognitive function. *Nature*, 387, 705–708.

Snowling, M. J., Goulandris, N., Bowlby, M., & Howell, P. (1986). Segmentation and speech perception in relation to reading skill: A developmental analysis. *Journal of Experimental Child Psychology*, 41, 489–507.

Stanovich, K. E. (1986). Matthew effects in reading: Some consequences of individual differences in the acquisition of literacy. *Reading Research Quarterly*, 21, 360–407.

Sternberg, R. J., & Nigro, G. (1980). Developmental patterns in the solution of verbal analogies. *Child Development*, 51, 27–38.

Sully, J. (1905). *Studies of childhood*. London: Longmans.

Surian, L., & Leslie, A. M. (1999). Competence and performance in false belief understanding: A comparison of autistic and normal 3-year-old children. *British Journal of Development Psychology*, 17, 141–156.

Swan, D., & Goswami, U. (1997). Picture naming deficits in developmental dyslexia: The phonological representations hypothesis. *Brain and Language*, 56, 334–353.

Treiman, R., Mellennix, J., Bijeljac-Babic, R., & Richmond-Welty, E. D. (1995). The special role of rimes in the description, use and acquisition of English orthography. *Journal of Experimental Psychology, General*, 124, 107–136.

Trevarthen, C. (1974). Conservations with a 2-month-old. *New Scientist*, 2, 230–235.

Turkewitz, G. (1995). The what and why of infancy and cognitive development. *Cognitive Development*, 10, 459–465.

Vargha-Khadem, F., Gadian, D. G., Watkins, K. E., Connelly, A., van Paesschen, W., & Mishkin, M. (1997). Differential effects of early hippocampal pathology on episodic and semantic memory. *Science*, 277, 376–380.

Wimmer, H., & Perner, J. (1983). Beliefs about beliefs: Representation and constraining function of wrong beliefs in young children's understanding of deception. *Cognition*, 21, 103–128.

Wishart, J. G., & Bower, T. G. R. (1982). The development of spatial understanding in infancy. *Journal of Experimental Child Psychology*, 33, 363–385.

Ziegler, J. C., & Perry, C. (1998). No more problems in Coltheart's neighborhood: Resolving neighborhood conflicts in the lexical decision task. *Cognition*, 68(2), 53–62.

Zorzi, M., Houghton, G., & Butterworth, B. (1998). The development of spelling–sound relationships in a model of phonological reading. *Language and Cognitive Processes*, 13, 337–371.

PART 5

INTELLIGENCE

CHAPTER 9

THE VERTICAL MIND – THE CASE FOR MULTIPLE INTELLIGENCES

Bruce Torff and Howard Gardner

M. Anderson (Ed.) *The Development of Intelligence*, London, Psychology Press, 1999

Horizontal and vertical faculties of the human mind

Playing the guitar, solving a physics problem, throwing a baseball, fixing a car – these are among the challenges of life in a modern industrial society. Elsewhere in the world, people face different yet no less daunting tasks. For example, Trobriand Islanders have an elaborate scheme, one that involves no notation system, for determining ownership of land and for negotiating disputes (Hutchens, 1980). Individuals attaining a high level of competence in these activities can surely be said to be exhibiting intelligent behaviour. The question is: How is the mind set up to handle these diverse chores? Does the mind have a single, centralised system, or a set of separate cognitive mechanisms geared to particular kinds of information or tasks?

Befitting so fundamental a question, there is long-standing and widespread debate about the propriety of dividing human intellect into parts. Many disciplines feature 'horizontalists' who believe in a single faculty and 'verticalists' who favour a set of specialised faculties. In what follows, we describe and argue for a vertical approach: Howard Gardner's (1983/1993a) theory of multiple intelligences (hereafter 'MI'). We begin with a summary of MI and then compare MI to other vertical faculty theories. In making comparisons among the conceptually diverse verticality theories, we will continue to use the neutral terminology – 'horizontal faculties' refer to centralised structures or processes, and 'vertical faculties' refer to sets of separate mechanisms (e.g. modules, domains, intelligences).

The theory of multiple intelligences

In the late 19th century, as psychology struggled to become a scientific discipline in the manner of biology or physics, a heavy premium was placed upon the accumulation of quantitative 'hard' data about human behaviour. The emergent 'classical' view of human intelligence came to focus on psychometric tests – instruments designed to reveal individual variation in intellectual competence on the basis of numerical score on a standardised instrument.

The theory of multiple intelligences contrasts pointedly with the test-based approach. Concerned with the intellectual skills that were never considered in the development of test instruments, Gardner endeavours to account for the wide range of intelligent performances that are valued in different societies. As a result, MI theory is not so much concerned with explaining the results of tests than with accounting for the variety of adult roles (or 'end-states') that exist across cultures. MI is an attempt at a comprehensive theory of intellect, one that not only charts the realm of maturation but also addresses educational and cultural issues.

Accordingly, MI theory puts forth a broad definition of intelligence: the ability to solve problems or fashion products that are of consequence in a particular cultural setting or community (Gardner, 1983/1993a). Intelligence is a term for organising and describing human capabilities in relation to the cultural contexts in which those capabilities are developed, used, and given meaning. Drawing on diverse sources of evidence, Gardner defined eight criteria which must be met by a candidate's intelligence. This analysis has yielded a list of eight intelligences. Next we describe the sources of evidence, criteria, and resulting intelligences.

Sources of evidence

Before examining MI's sources of evidence, it is important to note that MI theory is empirical though not 'experimental' in the usual sense of the term. It is not the kind of theory that can be proved or disproved by crucial experiment. (It is worth noting that no other theory of intelligence has proved susceptible to such a 'thumbs up' evaluation.) The subjective factor analysis on which MI is predicated works by establishing a set of criteria for what constitutes an intelligence. Additional information, experimental or otherwise, could have an impact on the resulting list of intelligences. For example, Rauscher, Shaw, and Ky (1993) have provided evidence that training in music can improve performance on certain spatial tasks. These data are limited at present; however, if replicated and elaborated, these new findings would weaken the claim that spatial and musical intelligences are autonomous and would thus suggest a reconfiguration of the intelligences. Rauscher's work serves as a reminder that MI theory is empirical and is subject to supporting or invalidating evidence. In what follows, we summarise in brief the eight criteria that must be met if candidate ability is to be judged as a human intelligence (Gardner, 1983/1993a).

Potential isolation by brain damage.   Gardner finds strong support for MI in studies of once-normal people who have become brain damaged due to stroke or injury. Evidence for autonomy is seen in the sparing or breakdown of a capacity after brain damage. For example, brain-injured musicians may have impaired speech yet retain the ability to play music (aphasia without amusia). In other cases, language is spared and musical ability lost (amusia without aphasia) (Hodges, 1996; Sergent, 1993). That these two abilities can be isolated from each other suggests that music and language are based on relatively autonomous intelligences – 'autonomous' in that one cannot predict strength or weakness in one intelligence from strength and weakness in another intelligence, and 'relative' in that intelligences make use of some of the same processes (e.g. musical rhythm has mathematical components). In our view, it is unnecessary and misleading to suggest complete autonomy.

The existence of idiots savants, prodigies, and other exceptional individuals.   Studies of special populations – prodigies, savants, and other exceptional individuals – also lend support for MI. Prodigies are individuals who show high levels of achievement in a discipline (e.g. chess, music) at a young age but who are unexceptional in other areas. *Savants* are individuals of low attainments, sometimes classified as retarded, who demonstrate remarkable skills in one 'island' of ability. For example, an individual may be able to play the piano by ear, perform calculations with large numbers instantly, or draw with great accuracy. Among these special populations, certain capacities operate in isolation from others. The appearance of high-level abilities in people who are otherwise unexceptional suggests that the intelligences involved are relatively autonomous (Winner, 1996). It is noteworthy, however, that *savants* often are skilled in only a small part of a discipline (e.g. there are people who cannot add but can calculate prime numbers). Findings as such suggest that the 'core operations' (counting in mathematics, tonal apprehension in music) of the intelligences may be more autonomous, and some of the ancillary operations (such as phrasing in music) are somewhat less autonomous.

Support from experimental psychological tasks. Research in experimental psychology also points to autonomous intelligences. For example, studies in which subjects are asked to carry out two tasks simultaneously indicate that some abilities operate autonomously, whereas others appear to be linked by the same underlying mental operations (Brooks, 1968). Findings such as these suggest that certain musical, linguistic, and spatial information-processing operations are carried out independently.

Support from psychometric findings. Psychometric findings also provide some support for MI. Gardner has criticised psychometric assessment as taking too narrow a sample of human abilities. Certain abilities within the province of these tests have proven relatively autonomous, however. For example, factor analyses generally support the existence of two 'big group' factors – verbal and spatial. Other researchers of intelligence have also put forth a multiple interpretation (Gould, 1996; Guilford, 1967; Thurstone, 1938).

A distinctive developmental history, along with a definable set of end-state performances. Another source of evidence for an intelligence is a characteristic developmental trajectory leading from basic and universal manifestations to one or more possible expert end-states. For example, spoken language develops quickly and to great competence in normal people. In contrast, while all normal individuals can count small quantities, few progress to higher mathematics even with formal schooling.

An evolutionary history and evolutionary plausibility. Evolutionary biology is an additional if more speculative source of evidence for MI. Gardner looks for origins of human intelligence in the capacities of species which predate humans. The existence, for example, of bird song suggests the presence of a separate musical intelligence, and there are strong continuities in the spatial abilities of humans and other primates. Other intelligences, such as intrapersonal and linguistic, may be distinctly human.

An identifiable core operation or set of operations. Each intelligence must have one or more basic information-processing operations or mechanisms which can deal with specific types of input. As a neurally based computational system, each intelligence is activated by certain kinds of internally or externally presented information. The intelligences are not input systems *per se*; rather, the intelligences are potentials, the presence of which allows individuals to activate forms of thinking appropriate to specific forms of content. Hence, MI theory is not inconsistent with an information-processing account of human cognition. Indeed, each intelligence presumably has its distinctive modes of information processing.

Susceptibility to encoding in a symbol system. An intelligence must also be susceptible to encoding in a symbol system – a culturally created system of meaning which captures and conveys important forms of information (e.g. language or mathematics).

The relationship of a candidate intelligence to a cultural symbol system is no accident. The existence of a core computational capacity anticipates the existence of a symbol system which exploits that capacity. 'Symbol systems have evolved in just those cases where there exists a computational capacity ripe for harnessing by culture. A primary characteristic of human intelligence may well be its "natural" gravitation toward embodiment in a symbol system' (Gardner, 1993b, p. 66).

The eight intelligences

These criteria and their attendant sources of evidence converge to support a set of eight candidate intelligences. We now describe these, along with end-states that exemplify them.

1   Linguistic intelligence describes the ability to perceive or generate spoken or written language. Linguistic intelligence is exemplified by poets, lawyers, and journalists.
2   Logical/mathematical intelligence involves using and appreciating numerical, causal, abstract, or logical relations. It is exemplified by mathematicians, scientists, and engineers.
3   Spatial intelligence describes the ability to perceive visual or spatial information (large-scale or more local), to transform and modify this information, and to recreate visual images even without reference to an original physical stimulus. Spatial intelligence is used in visual art, drafting, and navigation.
4   Musical intelligence refers to the ability to create, communicate, and understand meanings made out of sound. It can be seen in musicians and music critics but also outside the musical sphere (e.g. auto mechanics and cardiologists make diagnoses based on careful listening to patterns of sound).
5   Bodily/kinesthetic intelligence involves controlling all or part of one's body to solve problems or fashion products. It can be seen, for example, in athletics, dance, and hiking.
6   Interpersonal intelligence involves the capacity to recognise and make distinctions among the feelings, beliefs, and intentions of other people. Interpersonal intelligence enables people such as Martin Luther King and Mao Zedong to communicate with others and do their work effectively.
7   Intrapersonal intelligence enables individuals to form a mental model of themselves and to draw on the model to make decisions about viable courses of action. Among the core operations are the capacity to distinguish one's feelings and to anticipate reactions to future courses of action.
8   Naturalist intelligence involves the ability to understand and work effectively in the natural world (Gardner, 1999). A recent addition to the list of intelligences, naturalist intelligence is exemplified in biologists, zoologists, and naturalists.

Horizontal and vertical faculties

An intelligence has automatic and fast mechanisms at its core, but it also involves slow and contemplative ones. The intelligences grow out of sensory systems, but more than one sensory system can lead into or feed an intelligence (e.g. linguistic intelligence can grow out of audition, vision, gesture; spatial intelligence can draw on visual and kinesthetic information). Since they grow out of sensory systems, intelligences inevitably involve sensory cortical microcircuitry; at the same time, the intelligences themselves involve association or cross-modality cortexes (parietal lobe, frontal lobe), not just primary sensory ones. In essence, the intelligences are involved in higher-level computation as well as sensing and discriminating.

Hence, the intelligences are not, in normal adults, 'encapsulated' or 'cognitively impenetrable' (that is, cut off from the other modules). The intelligences are loosely coupled and penetrable sets of information-processing devices of which only the core processes are encapsulated.

Vertical faculties that communicate enable MI theory to downplay the need for a prominent central processor or executive. One possibility is that there is no executive at all – the intelligences simply coordinate as is necessary to engage in a task, and the effectiveness of this coordination constrains task performance. It is also possible that there exists a 'dumb' executive which coordinates the intelligences but which has little intellectual import in its own right. Gardner has also speculated that intrapersonal intelligence may come to function as an executive, as this intelligence is involved in the individual's self-knowledge and deliberate deployment of knowledge and skill.

Development of the intelligences

The intelligences are universal, in that all normal people exhibit some capacity for each, but there is considerable individual variation in initial profile of intelligences. Individuals begin life with a particular profile of intelligences, and this starting profile will have some influence on the achievements of the individual, but the profile will change in the course of development as a result of the history of experiences in particular cultural contexts.

Combining fast and slow mechanisms, MI draws a distinction between two different kinds of verticality, each with its own developmental path. We call these 'early developing' and 'later developing' verticality.

'Early developing' verticality.   At the core of an intelligence is a computational system (or a set of such systems) activated by certain kinds of internally or externally presented information. These computational systems form the basis for early developing verticality.

The core processes of the intelligences can be characterised in four ways. First, they are innately specified. The human genome endows normal individuals with a complement of core processes that are present at birth or emerge early in life (Zentner & Kagan, 1996). Second, the core processes are probably sensory-linked – that is, they operate in accordance with particular types of sensory input. For example, the core processes in musical intelligence include mechanisms for tonal discrimination that work only in relation to sensory input from hearing. Third, the core processes are encapsulated – a particular core process does not accept output from other ones. Finally, the core processes are not easily perturbed. It would be difficult to argue, for example, that stereoscopic vision used in spatial intelligence develops over time in the sense that its underlying architecture is altered. Rather, the core processes of the intelligences are unlikely to be significantly changed in the course of normal development.

'Later developing' verticality.   'Later developing' verticality refers to a later evolving, prototypically developmental form of verticality, that emerges because of years of practices that correlate with one another. For example, a smoothly operating reading faculty comes about because of the ways in which individuals handle sound and grapheme discrimination and combine sounds and graphemes into chunks. Such a

faculty would not be present in individuals in nonliterate cultures, and the development of a reading module depends on the cultural milieu – the domains and disciplines organising the reading-oriented activities that are valued by the ambient culture.

Early in life, the child encounters a world of cultural forms – languages, concepts, roles, values, and so on. Different cultures entail different disciplines or 'domains' that require the intelligences to be used in particular ways. The intelligences are transformed and combined in ways that relate directly to the culturally devised activities that the individual is called upon to perform. It is noteworthy that disciplinary activities typically require a combination of intelligences. The concert pianist draws on musical intelligence to be sure, but also on logical-mathematical (interpreting the score), linguistic (following verbal directives in the score and responding to coaching), spatial (orienting one's self to the keyboard), interpersonal (responding to the audience), and intrapersonal (playing expressively) (Torff, 1996). The range of intelligences involved in an activity is often greater than it appears at first sight. It may seem, for example, that mathematicians work solely in the logical-mathematical realm, but they must also draw on interpersonal intelligence to function in the field of mathematics, get their work published, and function smoothly in a university setting.

The activities required in disciplines such as music and mathematics require a blend of intelligences. The fact that several intelligences working in concert are utilised in a single activity underscores that an intelligence is not the same as a domain or discipline. There is no one-to-one correspondence, for example, between musical intelligence and music as a discipline.

Unlike early developing modules, later developing modules draw on multiple sources of sensory input. The concert pianist, for example, relies on not just hearing but also vision (e.g. following the conductor) and touch (responding to the feel of the keyboard). Accordingly, later developing modules are unencapsulated, interconnected sets of information-processing devices. These later emerging forms of verticality may be what is being captured in 'parallel distributed processing' systems, which slowly evolve and sometimes reach a stable state of functioning.

In sum, MI draws a distinction between two kinds of verticality with separate developmental paths. Hard-wired into the nervous system, the core processes of the intelligences emerge early in life. These early developing forms of verticality have a distinctive developmental path which features little in the way of sweeping developmental changes or cultural differences. Later developing verticality is very different. Combining various senses and intelligences, later developing vertical faculties emerge in response to the particular demands made by culturally organised activities. As a result, this later developing form of verticality involves significant developmental changes and cultural variation. In order to understand cognitive development, it seems necessary to examine the relations between earlier and later forms of intelligence – as Gardner has done previously with earlier (naive) and later (expert) forms of intuition (Gardner, 1991).

MI's stated aim – to frame an account of human intellect that encompasses the range of intelligent performances seen cross-culturally – raises the issue of how mental abilities in such diverse settings are to be assessed. We remain sceptical that tests provide a suitable window on many human mental abilities. In our view, it is not possible to create a valid 'knowledge-free' test to measure the core ability of an intelligence. A central implication of MI theory, then, is the need for 'intelligence-fair' assessments which allow participants to engage in real-world activities and use relevant background knowledge to solve problems. Thus, we have joined researchers and educators in developing 'performance' assessments (e.g. scoring of participants' work on discipline-based projects) and techniques of 'portfolio' assessment (process-tracing collections of participants' work). Alternative assessments enable the intelligences to work in assessment as they do in real-world activity (Gardner, 1993b).

Comparing MI to other vertical faculty theories

Recent vertical faculty theories emphasise such diverse elements as processing speed and cultural context. The conceptual and methodological diversity of these approaches means that comparing them is no straightforward task (Hirschfeld & Gelman, 1994). At the same time, in our view, any vertical faculty theory confronts a set of issues: (1) description and role of vertical faculties; (2) description and role of horizontal faculties, if any; (3) treatment of cognitive development; and (4) connection to cultural roles.

In this section, we look at these issues to compare MI to contemporary vertical faculty theories. Three lines of such theories have emerged in recent years: (1) the modularity theory of Fodor (with its intellectual indebtedness to Chomsky's 1988 notion of 'mental organ'); (2) vertical faculty conceptions of intelligence; and (3) domain-specific approaches to cognitive functioning. In what follows we compare MI to three prominent vertical faculty theories, one from each group. These include models put forth, respectively, by Fodor (1983), Anderson (1992), and Karmiloff-Smith (1992).

Jerry Fodor's 'modularity of mind'

Fodor (1983, 1985) has strongly argued for the modularity of mind while retaining an explicit focus on horizontal faculties (Fig. 7).

Description and role of vertical faculties:
To describe the genetically specified structure of cognition, Fodor posits a set of modules based on input systems: hearing, sight, taste, smell, touch – plus language. Patterned after reflexes, modules are fast-acting, mandatory, automatic, and hardwired. Modules are informationally encapsulated – they do not accept input from each other or from the central processor.

Description and role of horizontal faculties:
A central processor is responsible for higher-order processes of thought ('fixation of belief'). It uses a particular 'language of thought' and accepts output from modules and from itself.

Treatment of cognitive development:
Neither the modules nor the central processor 'develop' in the sense that there are developmental changes in the structure of cognition. Modules remain fully encapsulated throughout the lifespan. Additional modules (e.g. reading) may emerge.

Connection to cultural rules:
Culturally devised artefacts such as language provide content (and triggering mechanisms) for learning, but cultural products have no effect on underlying cognitive structure.

Figure 7 Fodor's 'modularity of mind'.

Fodor's model, like Gardner's, represents a challenge to the predominant domain-general approaches found in psychology, linguistics, and elsewhere. However, Fodor and Gardner put forth significantly different notions of vertical faculties. By emphasising input mechanisms, Fodor provides a finer-grained analysis than does MI. In essence, while modules are posited to account for what the nervous system is doing (processing sensory input), intelligences are broader faculties that draw from multiple perceptual systems. The intelligences contain core information-processing mechanisms that are similar to Fodor's modules. However, unlike modules, the intelligences are involved in the comparatively slow-acting, deliberate, and reflective processes of thought.

From our perspective, the criteria Fodor establishes for his list of modules seem idiosyncratic. Fodor compiles his list combining logical (e.g. domain-specifying) and empirical (e.g. fast-acting) criteria. If language is a module, why not music as well? MI theory explicitly states eight criteria for an intelligence (restricted to empirical considerations) and seeks to survey the evidence for each candidate intelligence in a systematic manner.

Fodor has argued that theories positing modularity of thought – such as MI – represent 'modularity theory gone mad' (Fodor, 1985, p. 27). Indeed, the role of a central system is also a point of disagreement between Gardner and Fodor. Since Fodor's modules are encapsulated, his model requires some mechanism for enabling input from the different modules to be drawn together. Thus, a central processor is necessary for Fodor. MI's appeal to interconnected vertical faculties that need no central processor is implausible, according to Fodor, because there is no 'unmonitored, preestablished harmony of the modules' (1985, p. 36). According to this argument, too many modules would be required and the coordination problems would be too difficult.

In contrast, Gardner argues that the intelligences have the potential to account for the range of human cognitive achievements and that it is crucial to account for these achievements using a vertical approach. In arguing against a central processor, Gardner differs with Fodor's interpretation of neuropsychological evidence. Gardner finds ample evidence of patterns of breakdown of capacities that suggests that the capacities are not as equipotential or central as Fodor suggests (e.g. Luria, 1976). Another argument against a central processor involves a non-empirical point. On grounds of parsimony, an analyst should favour one cognitive system over two. A second system makes it necessary to trace two evolutionary paths, two forms of hardware, and so on. Twin systems as such involve considerable, and perhaps implausible, theoretical and modelling complications. And the central processor, with its 'wisdom', raises the spectre of a homuncular solution to human cognitive complexity.

Before a central processor is invoked, and the attendant theoretical baggage taken on, cognitive scientists ought to examine the extent to which human cognition can be accounted for by a vertical faculty account. Gardner believes that such an enterprise should obviate the need for a central processor. In general, MI works to blur the distinction between modules and central systems. Gardner posits that there are module-like processes at the centre of the intelligences, but there is also some degree of penetration or cross-talk between intelligences. As elements become more susceptible to automatisation (incomprehensible shapes come to be seen as letters), their processing seems encapsulated. But, as elements become the subjects of special scrutiny (the typographer critically compares the fonts) they seem less modular. In place of a dichotomy, there emerges a continuum with relatively modular mechanisms (e.g. pitch discrimination) at one end and relatively isotropic mechanisms (e.g. musical composition) at the other.

Such a continuum points out the need for developmental perspective – another point of friction between Gardner and Fodor. The nativist thesis of *The modularity of mind* (Fodor, 1983) provides little room for developmental change. For Gardner, it is important to trace the evolution of the principal forms of thought from the relatively modular and encapsulated forms of processing, which can be observed in infancy, to the far more open or 'isotropic' forms characteristic of mature individuals, and ultimately to later developing verticality. Every intelligence has a developmental history, which after the first year of life involves engagement of the symbol systems of the surrounding culture, and which culminates in the mastery of entire cultural domains by adolescence or thereafter. Thus we may begin life with a proclivity to analyse sounds or to parse phrases in certain ways, but these processes undergo perceptual reorganisation in light of the experiences encountered by the individual over the course of life. A non-developmental account of modularity moves away from what is distinctive about human cognition.

A further consequence of Fodor's stance against development is that cultural factors are posited to have little influence on cognitive activities. Cultural products like language are posited to produce learning (new knowledge) but not cognitive change (alteration in underlying cognitive structure). Fodor assumes that each of his modules simply unfolds, independently of the interpretive frameworks provided by culture. Gardner believes that vertical faculties that are isolated as such are visible only in exceptional cases (e.g. *savants* or autistic children). Even phoneme perception and sensitivity to visual illusions are affected by the kinds of sounds and sights that are present or absent in a particular culture. Fodor, like many nativists, does not deny the triggering effect of the environment. However, he sidesteps the question of how the modules are fashioned by the ambient culture and, indeed, how the entire gamut of human cognitive and cultural achievements can be explained.

The modularity of mind has a somewhat ironic title, because the book attributes all higher-order cognitive activities to centralised processes (Sperber, 1994). Like other recent theories (e.g. Karmiloff-Smith, 1992), MI theory holds that thought, as well as perception, is best explained by vertical processes. MI theory, though admittedly more tentative, has the virtue of suggesting ways of explaining human behaviours that transcend reflexes. Fodor's work has been highly influential, however, and much recent productive domain-specific work (e.g. Carey & Gelman, 1991; Hirschfeld & Gelman, 1994; Keil, 1989; Spelke, 1990) bears the Chomsky/Fodor stamp.

Mike Anderson's theory of intelligence

Anderson (1992) focuses on a single level of explanation, the computational or information-processing level, in an attempt to account for a pattern of findings in the experimental literature on intelligence (Fig. 8).

Anderson and Gardner marshal similar sources of evidence – including neuropsychological research, studies of *savants* and prodigies, and psychometric research – but they reach different conclusions. At first blush, Anderson's specific processors appear similar to the intelligences – they are broad-based, slow-acting, unencapsulated, and connected to multiple sources of input. However, a closer look reveals differences between intelligences and specific processors. Beyond the obvious discrepancy between eight faculties and two, there are other incompatibilities. Anderson's specific processor 'propositional thought' encompasses language and mathematics, which are handled separately in MI theory. The autonomy of these two faculties is, in our view, supported in the neuroscientific literature. For example, there is evidence

Description and role of vertical faculties:
To account for universal human abilities that show no individual differences, a set of 'modules' is posited: perception of 3-D space, language functions, various 'constraints on induction' and/or 'naive theories', and possibly others that result from automatisation. To account for 'specific cognitive abilities' that are constrained by the basic processing mechanism and thus show individual differences, two 'specific processors' are posited: propositional thought (in language and logic) and spatial cognition.

Description and role of horizontal faculties:
To account for *g*, Anderson posits a basic processing mechanism (BPM). The BPM varies across individuals in speed – increased speed means more knowledge acquired by specific processors. Individual variation on intelligence tests stems from differences in knowledge, the acquisition of which depends on BPM speed.

Treatment of cognitive development:
Intelligence constrains development, in that BPM speed and functioning of specific processors constrain knowledge acquisition. Intelligence does not develop; speed or structure of BPM does not change over time. Developmental changes in intellectual competence are attributable to addition and elaboration of new modules.

Connection to cultural roles:
Cultural products like language provide content for knowledge acquisition mechanisms used by modules and specific processors. Cultural participation facilitates the addition and elaboration of new modules but does not influence the underlying architecture of cognition.

Figure 8 Anderson's 'minimum cognitive architecture of intelligence'.

that individuals may lose (through brain injury) the ability to reason in mathematics but retain language skills, or vice versa (Gardner, 1983/1993a).

Anderson provides no criteria by which specific processors are nominated: Specific processors are simply posited to account for a particular pattern (and interpretation) of findings. The absence of criteria is significant, in that it allows Anderson's vertical faculties to be justified in an *ad hoc* manner. For example, specific processors and modules are proposed because some individuals demonstrate particular cognitive deficits; elsewhere, Anderson ascribes these disorders to impaired mechanisms.

The second area of contention between Gardner and Anderson concerns the notion of modules. Many of the comments made in relation to Fodor's modules apply as well to Anderson's. Anderson's modules may be similar to the information-processing components that comprise the core of the intelligences. Unlike modules, the intelligences are involved in higher processes of thought; they undergo complex developmental changes; and they are influenced by the cultural environment. Moreover, Anderson's claim that modules show no individual differences lacks evidence. Some modules specified by Anderson (e.g. syntactic parsing) may well show individual differences (Pinker, 1994). We think it unlikely that there are significant systems in which individual variation is nil.

Gardner also differs with Anderson in the need to posit a centralised processor like the BPM, and he has criticised the psychological construct *g* which Anderson's BPM endeavours to explain. According to Gardner, *g* is a construct that has been encouraged by use of intelligence tests. However, in a non-testing environment, *g* would either not exist at all or it would consist of different abilities which correlate with different outcomes. If reliable assessments could be constructed for different intelligences, and these assessments did not rely solely on short answers, often through paper-and-pencil presentations, but instead used the materials of the domain being measured, the correlations that yield *g* would greatly diminish. Indeed, estimation of *g* can go up or down depending on the population examined and statistical procedures used (Ceci, 1996; Gould, 1996). From a societal point of view, a focus on *g* is biased and often unproductive.

Turning to the issue of development, Gardner differs with Anderson's Fodorian position in that cognitive development is limited to the appearance of new modules. According to Gardner, sweeping stage-like change cannot be explained as simple maturations of new modules; if so, all normal people would achieve changes such as the formal operations described by Piaget. Rather, schooling and other aspects of culture strongly affect such development (e.g. Bruner, 1990; Newman, Griffin, & Cole, 1989; Vygotsky, 1978). On a related point, Anderson and Gardner provide somewhat different views of the mechanisms that account for individual differences in intelligence(s) and developmental changes in intellectual competence. Like Anderson, Gardner believes that individual differences in intelligence(s) are inevitably a joint product of genetic factors and experiential ones (although, as noted, Gardner does not share Anderson's view that the genetic influence is constrained primarily by speed). Unlike Anderson, Gardner believes that developmental changes result both because of epigenetic factors (including brain development) and because of experiences with culturally devised systems.

Indeed, the role of cultural factors constitutes the final point of dispute between Anderson and Gardner. Like Fodor, Anderson suggests that cultural explanations have held too much sway in recent years. Laudable as is the pursuit to explain human behaviour at a single level of description (in Anderson's case, the computational level), we are unpersuaded that the question of culture is so easily sidestepped. We take the view that intelligence does not operate in a vacuum; it is influenced by the experience of the individual in particular cultural contexts (Ceci, 1996). Strict adherence to the computational perspective gives Anderson's model a certain coherence but at the cost of failing to account for much of what is interesting about intellectual development and achievements.

Anderson's vertical faculties are posited to explain 'exceptions' to the general pattern that supports *g*. This stance is reminiscent to that of Piaget, who put forth the concept *décalage* as a 'fudge factor' to explain observed variations across tasks which appear to contradict the theory of domain-general structures. For many psychologists, *décalage* proved more the rule than the exception. We believe that vertical functions, not centralised processes with attendant fudge factors, ultimately yield the more parsimonious and evolutionarily plausible model of intellectual development.

Annette Karmiloff-Smith's 'representational redescription' model

Karmiloff-Smith (1992) has heroically attempted to reconcile Piaget's notion of development with the nativism of Fodor and Chomsky (Fig. 9).

Karmiloff-Smith's model has much in common with Gardner's. Each posits a set of vertical faculties in the absence of a prominent central processor (although they

Description and role of vertical faculties:
To account for observed variation in cognitive development in different content areas, Karmiloff-Smith posits a set of domains – sets of representations sustaining a particular area of knowledge. Candidate domains describe the child as linguist, physicist, mathematician, psychologist, and notator.

Description and role of horizontal faculties:
No central processor is discussed; cognition is assumed to have a fundamentally domain-specific character. However, to account for observed commonalities in cognitive development across domains, Karmiloff-Smith posits a universal developmental process, called representational redescription (RR).

Treatment of cognitive development:
Taking a developmental-constructivist perspective, the RR model describes development in terms of three phases of representational character of knowledge in a domain: (1) implicit; (2) explicit level 1 (not available to verbal report); (3) explicit level 2 (available to verbal report). Development is seen in terms of two parallel processes: progressive modularisation and progressive explicitation.

Connection to cultural roles:
Culture provides the environment for the constructivist interaction that drives the process of representational change, but the character of that change is fundamentally regulated by endogenous factors. Cultural roles and products are built up on domain-specific cognitive mechanisms.

Figure 9 Karmiloff-Smith's 'representational redescription' model.

present somewhat incompatible sets, as we discuss later). Unlike Fodor (and to lesser extent, Anderson), Karmiloff-Smith and Gardner agree on the importance of development. Furthermore, Gardner concurs with Karmiloff-Smith that at least one strand of development moves in the direction of systems which are increasingly modular. What we are calling 'later developing' verticality is consistent with Karmiloff-Smith's notion of modularisation. Finally, Karmiloff-Smith and Gardner share the belief that human intellect must be explained in relation to the ambient cultural context.

In a number of ways, however, Karmiloff-Smith's model is incongruent with the notion of multiple intelligences. There is some overlap in the candidate vertical faculties put forth by Gardner and Karmiloff-Smith – in the areas of language, mathematics, and perhaps psychology (interpersonal intelligence). However, there are some significant differences between Karmiloff-Smith's domains and Gardner's intelligences. An intelligence is a biopsychological construct – the sets of capacities that the species has evolved to realise, given cultural support. A domain is a culturally defined activity or set of activities, which can be arrayed in terms of expertise (Csikszentmihalyi, 1988; Feldman, 1980). A single intelligence can thus be activated for various domains and will be mobilised differently in different societies and different epochs. Conversely, domains involve combinations of intelligences. The domain of physics, for example, involves primarily logical-mathematical and spatial intelligences. Physicists also use a wider range of intelligences in the course of gaining funding, collaborating with colleagues, and disseminating findings.

A second difference concerns the existence of innately specified modules. Karmiloff-Smith (1992, p. 5) has written that 'development involves a process of gradual modularisation rather than prespecified modules'. This account differs from the notion of 'early developing' presented earlier, which holds that a set of innately specified and early developing modules constitute the core processes of the intelligences.

Third, Gardner and Karmiloff-Smith offer contrasting views of the role of domain-general developmental processes such as representational description. According to Gardner (1995), the RR model captures an important process in some domains, but evidence for it is weak in other domains. Gardner believes that the RR model works better for skills that people master over time, like playing the piano or using irregular verbs, than it does for conceptual understandings such as those arrived at by the young physicist, mathematician, or theorist-of-mind. In general, MI downplays the importance of commonalities in information-processing across intelligences. Each intelligence is thought to have a separate, if not unique, developmental history. There may be some overlapping qualities between the various developmental histories, and these would be fruitful to uncover, but it is vital to look as well, and perhaps first, at processes unique to particular intelligences.

Overall, we find much to recommend in Karmiloff-Smith's model. Her stated aim is a laudable one – to specify the processes that account for how vertical faculties develop and interconnect. Whereas we remain unpersuaded that a domain-general model such as RR will turn out to be the most felicitous description of development of domains, or of intelligences, we admire Karmiloff-Smith's attempt to integrate nativist and constructivist approaches to intellectual development.

Placing MI among vertical faculty theories

The most striking aspect to emerge from our survey of recent vertical faculty theories is that MI theory presents the most extreme form of verticality. Among the four theories, only MI opts not to appeal to centralised processes or structures – Fodor and Anderson posit prominent central processing mechanisms, and Karmiloff-Smith puts forth a domain-general developmental process. MI is, in a sense, the radical among the vertical faculty theories. Perhaps appropriately, MI theory also presents the most clearly delineated criteria for selection of candidate vertical faculties.

Full-blown verticality is supported by a number of key features of MI theory. First of all, the intelligences present a qualitatively different analytic unit from other vertical faculty theories. Clearly, the intelligences operate at a 'higher' level than the modules modelled after reflexes posited by Fodor and Anderson. There are probably module-like mechanisms at the core of the intelligences, but the intelligences also mediate the higher-order processes of thought, not just the reflexive intelligence built into the hardware. The intelligences function at a biopsychological level, while the domains discussed by Karmiloff-Smith are inherently cultural constructions. It turns out that several intelligences are needed to account for operations lumped together in one domain. The intelligences are reminiscent of 'specific processors', but Anderson posits only two of these, and there are competing views of how these faculties work – whereas specific processors are constrained by the basic processing mechanism, intelligences operate under no such constraint. Overall, the intelligences stand alone as a necessary and sufficient set of analytic devices.

As a second consideration, MI posits vertical faculties that are penetrable, inter-communicating, and, in a sense, collaborative. MI thus accounts for the fact that individuals can represent knowledge of something in a number of ways and compare those representations. For instance, the fact that people can encode an experience linguistically or spatially and then compare the results of these encodings is a positive human capacity. MI accounts for this capacity not by resorting to a mysterious executive or homunculus, but by positing that the intelligences are able to communicate. Quite possibly, different intelligences serve as a *lingua franca* for different individuals, much as different sections can take the lead in the performance of a musical work.

MI is sometimes called a 'modular theory of central processes' (e.g. Anderson, 1992; Sperber, 1994), apparently to distance the intelligences from lower-level mechanisms like modules. This characterisation is somewhat ironic, given that MI is such a strong statement of verticality. At the same time, we accept the characterisation if it helps to keep the locus on interconnected vertical faculties working in the absence of a prominent horizontal processor.

Third, MI theory provides a unique view of the nature of cognitive development. The nativist Fodor has little interest in development – modules are encapsulated and remain so throughout the life span. Anderson concurs and adds that intelligence is a function of speed (which does not change), and thus cognitive development is limited to the addition of new modules. Karmiloff-Smith offers a more comprehensive developmental view but assumes that development proceeds toward modularisation. Only MI describes development in terms of twin systems. Whereas the early developing core processes of the intelligences probably do not involve significant developmental changes over the lifespan, later developing cognitive skills are highly sensitive to developmental changes, cultural influences, and the individual's own personality, motivation, and goals.

Finally, perhaps MI's most significant contribution (to the vertical faculty movement, at least) is its insistence that human intellect be explained in relation to ambient cultural contexts. MI seriously examines the role played by cultural products in the development of the individual mind. Stepping aside from the assumption that cognitive functioning is fundamentally endogenously regulated, MI is consistent with the developmental theory of Vygotsky (1978; see also Rogoff, 1990). Like Vygotsky's theory, MI endeavours to draw together the universal, genetically specified human potentials (c.f. the 'genetic method') with the cultural roles and artefacts that organise activity and guide the development of the individual mind (c.f. the theory of internalisation from a 'zone of proximal development').

At the heart of any theory is the explanatory goal of the theorist (with resulting implications for how the theory is constructed and how research proceeds). Fodor's goal is to explain the genetically specified structure of input systems. Anderson attempts to account for a particular pattern of experimental findings obtained largely in the psychometric tradition. Karmiloff-Smith endeavours to reconcile Piaget's horizontalist and constructivist notion of development with Chomskian modularity and nativism.

MI has a rather different set of objectives, ones with parallels to the recent history of research on human memory. Earlier in this century, memory research was dominated by laboratory tasks in which subjects memorised strings of nonsense syllables. In recent decades, researchers became dissatisfied with the limitations of this approach and began to use lengthy and substantive texts, resulting in a reinvigoration of memory research and a reconceptualisation of what memory is (Neisser, 1982; Schacter, 1996). Classic intelligence theory has, in its own way, maintained a focus on something like the nonsense syllables. Research on intelligence has been oriented toward its test instruments, many of the dry, brief, paper-and-pencil variety. In essence, classic intelligence theory has tried to lay intelligence bare, and, in the process, may have obscured much of what is distinctive and human about it.

We suggest that MI has contributed to a kind of reinvigoration of investigations of the intellect, one reminiscent of the changes in memory research. Rather than simply using test instruments to make inferences about human intelligence, Ml theory works chiefly in the other direction – from the world back to the theory. Examining the skills demonstrated by, say, rock guitarists and Trobriand islanders, MI attempts to frame an account, based on clear criteria, of the universal intellectual faculties needed – alone and in combination – to carry out these tasks. Directly confronting the complexity of cultural and educational influences, MI attempts to restore range and passion to research on intelligence.

References

Anderson, M. (1992) *Intelligence and development: A cognitive theory*. Oxford, UK: Blackwell.

Brooks, L. (1968). Spatial and verbal components of the act of recall. *Canadian Journal of Psychology*, 22, 349–350.

Bruner, J. (1990). *Acts of meaning*. Cambridge, MA: Harvard University Press.

Carey, S. & Gelman, R. (Eds) (1991). *The epigenesis of mind*. Hillsdale, NJ: Lawrence Erlbaum Associates Inc.

Ceci, S. (1996). *On intelligence . . . more or less*. Cambridge, MA: Harvard University Press.

Chomsky, N. (1988). *Language and problems of knowledge*. Cambridge, MA: MIT Press.

Czikszentmihalyi, M. (1988). Society, culture, person: A systems view of creativity. In R.J. Sternberg (Ed.), *The Nature of creativity* (pp. 325–329). New York: Cambridge University Press.

Feldman, D. (1980). *Beyond universals in cognitive development*. Norwood, NJ: Ablex Publishing.

Fodor, J. (1983). *The modularity of mind*. Cambridge, MA: MIT Press.

Fodor, J. (1985). The modularity of mind. *Behavioral and Brain Sciences*, 8, 1–42.

Gardner, H. (1991). *The unschooled mind*. New York: Basic Books.

Gardner, H. (1993a). *Frames of mind*. New York: Basic Books. (Original work published 1983.)

Gardner, H. (1993b). *Multiple intelligences: The theory into practice*. New York: Basic Books.

Gardner, H. (1995). Green ideas sleeping furiously [Review of S. Pinker, *The language instinct*; A. Karmiloff-Smith, *Beyond modularity*; J. Bruner, *Acts of meaning*]. *New York Review of Books*, 42(5), 32–38.

Gardner, H. (1999). Are there additional intelligences?: The case for naturalist, spiritual, and existential intelligences. In J. Cain (Ed.), *Education: Information and transformation* (pp. 111–132). Englewood Cliffs, NJ: Prentice Hall.

Gould, S. (1996). *The mismeasure of man* (2nd ed.). New York: Norton.

Guilford, J. (1967). *The nature of human intelligence*. New York: McGraw-Hill.

Hirschfeld, L., & Gelman, S. (1994). *Mapping the mind: Domain-specificity in cognition and culture*. Cambridge, UK: Cambridge University Press.

Hodges, D. (1996). Neuromusical research: A review of the literature. In *Handbook of music psychology* (2nd ed.). New York: IMR Press.

Hutchens, E. (1980). *Culture and inference*. Cambridge, MA: Harvard University Press.

Karmiloff-Smith, A. (1992). *Beyond modularity*. Cambridge, UK: Cambridge University Press.

Keil, F. (1989). *Concepts, kinds and cognitive development*. Cambridge, MA: Harvard University Press.

Luria, A. (1976). *Cognitive development: Its cultural and social foundations*. Cambridge, MA: Harvard University Press.

Neisser, U. (1982). *Memory observed*. San Francisco: Freeman.

Newman, D., Griffin, P., & Cole, M. (1989). *The construction zone*. Cambridge, UK: Cambridge University Press.

Pinker, S. (1994). *The language instinct*. New York: Morrow.

Rauscher, F., Shaw, G., & Ky, K. (1993). Music and spatial task performance. *Nature*, 365, 611.

Rogoff, B. (1990). *Apprenticeship in thinking*. Cambridge, MA: Harvard University Press.

Schacter, D. (1996). *Searching for memory*. New York: Basic Books.

Sergent, J. (1993). Music, the brain and Ravel. *Trends in Neurosciences*, 16, 5.

Spelke, E. (1990). Principles of object perception. *Cognitive Science*, 14, 29–56.

Sperber, D. (1994). The modularity of thought. In L. Hirschfeld & S. Gelman (Eds), *Mapping the mind: Domain-specificity in cognition and culture*. Cambridge, UK: Cambridge University Press.

Thurstone, L.L. (1938). *Primary mental abilities*. Chicago: University of Chicago Press.

Torff, B. (1996). Into the wordless world: Implicit learning and instructor modeling in music. In V. Brummett (Ed.), *Music as intelligence*. Ithaca, NY: Ithaca College Press.

Vygotsky, L. (1978). *Mind in society*. Cambridge, MA: Harvard University Press.

Winner, E. (1996). *Gifted children: Myths and realities*. New York: Basic Books.

Zentner, M., & Kagan, J. (1996). Perception of music by infants. *Nature*, 383, 5th September, 29.

CHAPTER 10

SOCIALIZING INTELLIGENCE

Lauren B. Resnick and Sharon Nelson-Le Gall

L. Smith, J. Dockrell and P. Tomlinson (eds) *Piaget Vygotsky and Beyond: Future Issues for Developmental Psychology and Education*, London, Routledge, 1997

In this chapter, we want to explore a conception of intelligence that is founded in part on the cultural and developmental theories of Vygotsky but that can find full expression only through joining with the constructivist lines of epistemological theory, for which we are indebted to Piaget. We argue for a view of *intelligence as social practice*, a conception rooted at least as much in theories of social development and social competence as in theories of cognitive development. It is also grounded in our efforts to make sense of and actively contribute to educational programmes aimed at raising the overall cognitive competence and academic achievement of the least educationally advantaged populations of children in our formal educational systems.

Our argument addresses one of the central social and political, as well as scientific, debates of our time: what intelligence is, who has it, and the role of social institutions in developing and sustaining it. *Intelligence* is one of the great constructs of scientific psychology. Perhaps no concept has garnered as much attention from psychologists. Yet after a century of fundamental and applied research on intelligence, there is no single definition of the construct to which all psychologists would agree. And, in the USA at least, fierce battles continue to rage concerning the social and political implications of differences in measured intelligence, without adequate attention to what the measurements mean and how intelligence actually functions in the world (Herrnstein and Murray, 1994).

We present our argument in four parts. First, we argue that interpreting intelligence as a social practice requires a critical expansion of the definition of the construct to include not just the cognitive skills and forms of knowledge that have classically been considered the essence of intelligence, but also a cluster of social performances such as asking questions, striving to master new problems and seeking help in problem solving. One's likelihood of engaging in these social practices of intelligence, furthermore, is as much a matter of how one construes his or her rights, responsibilities and capabilities as of purely cognitive capacities. To put it in oversimplified form (we elaborate later), if you believe that you are *supposed* to be asking questions and learning new things all the time, you *will* ask lots of questions and strive to keep learning.

Second, we show that important individual differences exist in people's beliefs about intelligence and that these beliefs are related to people's tendency to engage in the social practices of intelligence that we define in the first section. Perhaps the most important differences, we argue, relate effort and ability – whether people believe that effort can actually create ability or only compensate for limitations in ability. There are also important differences in what *kind* of effort people put out under conditions of challenge, depending in great part on their beliefs about the nature of intelligence.

Third, we argue that the beliefs and habits that constitute the social practice of intelligence are acquired through processes more akin to what developmentalists have studied as *socialization* than to what they have studied as either cognitive development or learning. Vygotsky's (1978) theory of cognitive development as a process of internalizing socially shared actions and of the role of language in enabling and constraining overall cognitive development forms a point of contact between our notion of intelligence as socialized and the more traditional views of intelligence as a purely cognitive competence.

Fourth, we ask how schools and other institutions charged with promoting human development might function to socialize intelligence as we define it here. In the concluding section, we lay out a set of hypotheses that go well beyond individual development to embrace concepts of social design and mechanisms of cultural change.

(Re-)defining intelligence

We begin this section by briefly reviewing several major strands of psychological theorizing about intelligence, from individual difference and mental measurement theorists through Piaget. We then present our own definition of intelligence as social practice, a view that extends Vygotsky's interpretation of learning and cognitive development as inherently social and builds on more recent sociocultural theories as well.

Intelligence as individual mental abilities

Individual difference psychologists – from Binet to modern psychometricians – can be roughly divided into two camps. One, launched by Binet (Binet and Simon, 1905) himself, defines intelligence very loosely and pragmatically: some people seem to learn more quickly and behave more adaptively than others. Rather than trying to define precisely the mechanisms that make for this adaptive capacity, Binet collected a broad band of questions that children might be expected to learn to answer as they grew up. He used the collection as a whole, scaled according to empirically derived age expectations, to compare the relative intelligence of children. This general knowledge criterion, presumably reflecting speed and ease of learning, was carried into pencil-and-paper intelligence testing by Terman (1916, 1919) and others who developed measures of *general intelligence*, which largely became known as IQ.

Historically, IQ was understood to point to differences in mental ability, not to social competence or performance (although many intelligence tests do contain some items that test knowledge of appropriate social behaviour). It was also assumed to be largely determined genetically and to set firm limits on how much learning could be expected of an individual. This question of intelligence as limiting learning is an issue to which we return later. For now, what is important to note is that measurers of general intelligence essentially gave up on defining intelligence, except to insist that it is a mental capacity of some kind.

Another group of individual difference psychologists – for example, Thorndike (1926), Thurston (1938), Carroll (1966), Guilford (1967), Sternberg (1977) – kept looking for differentiated components of intelligence, often using increasingly sophisticated techniques of factor analysis and cluster analysis. For the most part, this research has focused on purely cognitive capabilities, but there have been persistent efforts to broaden the concept of what counts as intelligent, as in Howard Gardner's (1993) concept of 'multiple intelligences', which encompass such abilities as music and the visual arts. Some theorists have also expanded the term *intelligence* to cover more social competencies, for example, Robert Sternberg's efforts to define, measure and even teach 'practical intelligence' (Sternberg and Wagner, 1986). Even these theories, however, treat intelligence as an attribute of the individual, not as a set of practices in which individuals adapt and tune their behaviours to immediate contexts of performance.

Intelligence as structures for reasoning

Piaget's interest in human intelligence was entirely different in kind from any of the mental measurers. Uninterested in individual differences, he focused an entire research career on the question of what underlay the adaptive mental capacities of the human species (Piaget, 1960, 1970a, 1970b). His answer, [. . .], was that humans are biologically prepared to develop certain logico-deductive structures. Piagetian theory holds that each individual develops these structures, along with certain fundamental mathematical and scientific concepts for which the logical structures are essential, through interactive engagement with the world. Piaget himself was never very clear about the nature of this interaction. Some 'social Genevans' (e.g. Doise and Mugny, 1984; Perret-Clermont, 1980) have argued that social interaction, especially the cognitive conflict created by certain forms of disagreement with peers, is an essential engine of the development of intelligence. For most of these theorists, however, intelligence itself remained an essentially individual, biologically founded construction.

Intelligence as acquisition of cultural tools and practices

Vygotsky is the first modern theorist of cognitive development to place social interaction at its heart. In fact, many of Vygotsky's interpreters (e.g. Cole and Scribner, 1974; Rogoff, 1990; Wertsch, 1985), along with other theorists of *situated cognition* (e.g. Lave, 1988; Suchman, 1992; see also Resnick *et al.*, [. . . 1998]), have argued that learning and cognitive development are a matter of absorbing appropriate cultural practice through (scaffolded) participation in activities important in the society.

Vygotsky (1978, p. 88) proposed that the development of human mental functioning 'presupposes a specific social nature and a process by which children grow into the intellectual life of those around them'. In each sociocultural context, children participate in both formal and informal instructional exchanges that bring about their adaptive functioning within those contexts. Through reciprocal processes of social interaction, children develop a system of cognitive representations as interpretive frameworks and make a commitment to the common value system and sets of behavioural norms promoted in their sociocultural context. This process of socialization thus incorporates the acquisition and use of knowledge, ways of representing that knowledge, and ways of thinking and reasoning with that knowledge. These, along with language, are the 'cultural tools' that might be said to constitute intelligence.

Intelligence as habits of learning

The idea of cultural tools for reasoning and thinking takes us part of the way towards the redefinition of intelligence that we are seeking. We would like to go further, though, to connect the cultural practice conception with the notion of general intelligence as the ability to learn well and easily. This is important, we believe, because *our* culture particularly rewards certain patterns of learning – those connected with success in school and other closely related institutions – and provides socially and economically disfavoured places in society for those who do not engage in these favoured ways of learning. It is for these social justice reasons, as well as the hope of confirming theories of what makes people good learners (i.e. 'smart'), that the prospect of *teaching intelligence* has fascinated many psychologists.

Different theorists of intelligence have tried teaching the cognitive skills that have been central in their theories: the skills that are directly tested on IQ tests, such as techniques for recognizing or generating analogies (e.g. Pellegrino and Glaser, 1982), Piagetian logical structures (e.g. Shayer and Adey, 1981) and metacognitive strategies (see Brown *et al.*, 1983). There is a repeated pattern in the results of these experiments. Most of the training experiments were successful in producing immediate gains in performance on the kinds of tasks taught. But, with the exception of the recent Shayer and Adey work (which involved a much more extended and ambitious intervention than the laboratory training studies), subjects in the studies ceased using the cognitive techniques in which they had been trained as soon as the specific conditions of training were removed. In other words, they became *capable* of performing the skill that was taught, but they acquired no general *habit* of using it and no capacity to judge for themselves when it was useful.

This repeated finding is just what one would expect from an intelligence-as-cultural-practice perspective. Cognitive activity and intelligent behaviour occur in a socially organized environment. Culturally organized environments produce constraints on what affordances can be utilized by whom and when (Goodnow, 1990a, 1990b; Reed, 1993). The objects and situations experienced in an environment provide affordances because they possess specific characteristics or properties. These particular properties are not intrinsic; rather, they are properties that exist with respect to agents who will perceive or utilize them. Reed (1993) observes that learning affordance properties of objects, events and places requires practice and experience that are typically gained through consistent encouragement and even instruction from other individuals.

Subjects in the cognitive skill training experiments learned to engage in a particular practice (e.g. rehearsing, forming mnemonics) in a particular environmental situation. In a new situation, the learned practices appeared to have no relevance. The practices were tuned to the affordances and environmental presses of the training situation. When those affordances and presses were not perceived in the new situation, the learned practices disappeared.

This analysis suggests that, if we want to see a general 'ability to learn easily' develop in children, we need a definition of intelligence that is as attentive to robust *habits of mind* and how they are nurtured as it is to the specifics of thinking processes or knowledge structures. As we show in the next section, there is reason to believe that people's habits of thinking are heavily influenced by their beliefs about intelligence. For now, we want to propose a working definition of intelligence that will structure the remainder of our chapter.

Intelligence as a social construction

Our definition of intelligence treats intelligence as a social construction, as much a matter of how individuals construe themselves and their action in the world as of what specific skills they have at a given moment. *People who are intelligent-in-practice*:

- *believe they have the right (and the obligation) to understand things and make things work.* Goodnow (1990a, 1990b) observes that people do not merely acquire knowledge, cognitive skills and strategies, or learn to apply that knowledge or skill in problem solving. They also learn that we are expected to acquire some pieces or forms of knowledge and skill and that some domains of knowledge or skill 'belong' more to some people than to others. Our intelligence-as-cultural-practice view of intelligence treats acquiring knowledge and new skills as the responsibility of each individual.

- *believe that problems can be analysed, that solutions often come from such analysis and that they are capable of that analysis.* This belief in one's efficacy to acquire valued knowledge and skills and to use these in solving valued problems can be socialized through the tacit messages embedded in the routines of daily practices.
- *have a toolkit of problem-analysis tools and good intuitions about when to use them.* These might be metacognitive skills, analogical reasoning skills, quantitative analysis skills or a host of other specific learnable capabilities.
- *know how to ask questions, seek help and get enough information to solve problems.* In this definition of intelligence, making use of the social environment is an integral part of the understanding process.
- *have* habits of mind *that lead them to actively use the toolkit of analysis skills and the various strategies for acquiring information.* None of the cognitive skills and social strategies that are elements of intelligence-in-practice are functional unless the individual routinely uses them and seeks occasions to use them.

Patterns of belief and behaviour: relating effort and ability

We are concerned in this section with habits of mind, the tendency to use one's toolkit of analysis skills and one's strategies for gathering information. We turn to a body of research that has been examining the factors that seem to shape these habits, factors that have much to do with people's beliefs about the relations between effort and ability. People differ markedly in these beliefs, and their beliefs are closely related to the amount and above all to the kinds of effort they exert in situations of learning or problem solving.

Most research on these differences has been carried out by social developmentalists interested in *achievement goal orientation*. Different kinds of achievement goals can affect not only how much effort people put into learning tasks but also the *kinds* of effort. Several classes of achievement goals have been identified that are associated with different conceptions of success and failure and different beliefs about the self, learning tasks and task outcomes (Ames, 1984; Dweck and Leggett, 1988; Nicholls, 1979, 1984). Two broad classes of goals have been identified: *performance-oriented* and *learning-oriented* (these are the terms used by Dweck and her colleagues; Nicholls used the terms *ego-involved* and *task-involved*).

People with performance goals strive to obtain positive evaluations of their ability and to avoid giving evidence of inadequate ability relative to others. Performance goals are associated with a view of ability as an unchangeable, global entity that is *displayed* in task performance, revealing the individual either to have or to lack ability. This view of ability or aptitude has sometimes been termed an *entity theory of intelligence*.

In contrast, people with learning goals generally strive to develop their ability with respect to particular tasks. Learning goals are associated with a view of aptitude as something that is mutable through effort and is *developed* by taking an active stance towards learning and mastery opportunities. Learning goals are associated with a view of ability as a repertoire of skills continuously expandable through one's efforts. Accordingly, this view of aptitude has been labelled an *incremental theory of intelligence* (Dweck and Leggett, 1988).

People who hold incremental theories of intelligence tend to invest energy to learn something new or to increase their understanding and mastery of tasks. But brute energy alone does not distinguish them from people with entity theories. Incremental theorists are particularly likely to apply self-regulatory, metacognitive skills when they encounter task difficulties, to focus on analysing the task and trying to generate and execute alternative strategies. In general, they try to garner resources for problem solving wherever they can: from their own store of cognitive learning strategies and from others from whom they strategically seek help (Dweck, 1988; Nelson-Le Gall, 1990; Nelson-Le Gall and Jones, 1990). In general, these individuals display continued high levels of task-related effort in response to difficulty. Thus performance goals place the greater effort necessary for mastering challenging tasks in conflict with the need to be regarded as already competent, whereas learning goals lead to adaptive motivational patterns that can produce a quality of task engagement and commitment to learning that fosters high levels of achievement over time.

The achievement goals that individuals pursue also appear to influence the inferences they make about effort and ability. Performance goals are associated with the inference that effort and ability are negatively related in determining achievement outcomes; so high effort is taken as a sign of low ability (Dweck and Leggett, 1988). Learning goals, by contrast, are associated with the inference that effort and ability are positively related, so that greater effort creates and makes evident more ability.

This body of research on achievement goal orientation shows that the beliefs and the habits of mind that we have defined as the practices of intelligence are associated. It shows, furthermore, that there are individual differences in beliefs about the nature of intelligence and, therefore, in associated practices. Where do these beliefs come from? How are the habits of practice acquired? We address these questions in the next section.

Acquiring habits of mind through socialization

Persistent habits and deeply held beliefs about the self and human nature in general are not the kinds of things that one learns from direct teaching and certainly not from school-organized lessons. They are, instead, acquired through the processes that developmentalists usually call *socialization*. The term *socialization* refers to the incorporation of the individual as a member of a community. As soon as a child is born, adults and other knowledgeable individuals begin to contribute to the child's socialization by arranging the environment and the tasks encountered in it and by guiding the child's attention to and participation in the community's valued practices. Socialization is the process by which children acquire the standards, values and knowledge of their society.

Socialization proceeds not so much through direct formal instruction of the young or novice individual, although there are instances in which direct instruction or tutoring occurs. Rather, it proceeds via social interaction, through observation and modelling, cooperative participation and scaffolding. It depends, furthermore, on the negotiation of mutual expectations, that is, intersubjectivity. We readily acknowledge the socialization process, its function and products in informal, everyday out-of-school settings such as the family. But, with few exceptions, psychologists fail to recognize its role in intellectual functioning in more formally organized contexts such as schools.

Individual differences in beliefs about effort and ability are, we assume, socialized by different patterns of family belief and practice. But there are also broad societal differences. In the USA, most adults recognize ability as an inherently stable characteristic of individuals, one that is unequally distributed among the human population and not subject to being increased by personal or environmental influence (Nicholls, 1984; Weiner, 1974). Most also tend to hold the view that effort and ability are distinct, negatively related causes of achievement outcomes. In other words, the dominant cultural norm in the USA is an entity theory of intelligence.

These assumptions about ability and effort are shared throughout our society and promulgated by our societal institutions (Howard, 1991); it is not surprising, therefore, to see them clearly manifested in most traditionally structured formal schooling settings. In such classrooms, direct comparisons of one student's work and learning outcomes with another's are frequent and often public. Teachers and students find it 'normal' that some students do not learn what is taught and do not achieve as well as others. When the emphasis in the classroom or the school is on relative ability and (presumptively associated) performance outcomes, and when instructional policies and practices seek to sort students by aptitude, students and teachers alike are more likely to focus on *performance* than on *learning* goals.

In other cultures, however, effort and ability are not viewed as independent dimensions. It has been reported, for example, that, in several Asian cultures (e.g. Chinese and Japanese), people are typically socialized to espouse and act on the belief that high effort and perseverance are the keys to successful performance; indeed, perseverance is even a moral obligation. The positive orientation towards hard work and effort that Japanese people are socialized to adopt conveys a shared belief that ability can be changed and that it refines and enhances the self (Holloway, 1988; Peak, 1993; Stevenson and Lee, 1990). People in such cultures behave as if they pursue learning goals. This alternative view about the relation of effort and ability is likewise reflected in these societies' educational philosophies and is promulgated by their educational institutions.

In their extensive comparative studies of US, Japanese and Chinese education systems, Stevenson and Stigler (1992) have described in substantial detail a very different pattern of beliefs and practices in Chinese and Japanese schools than in ours. Differences in organization, expectation and practice can be detected as early as preschool (Peak, 1986, 1993; Tobin, Wu, and Davidson, 1989). These differences in motivational orientation and their associated institutional support may have much to do with the generally higher academic achievement in these countries.

In Japan, folk beliefs place more emphasis on social competence as a component of intelligence than is the case for laypersons in the USA (Holloway, 1988). Being an effective speaker and listener, being good at getting along with others and taking another person's point of view are all aspects of social competence that tend to be viewed as controllable by the individual. This emphasis on the quality of interactions and relations between individuals and their social environment reinforces the development of a sense of connectedness and collective identity that is important, in that failure in performance becomes a failure for others as well as the individual.

Institutional designs for socializing intelligence

In this final section, we consider how schools might be organized to deliberately socialize learning goal orientations in children. We focus our attention on American schools – the only ones we know well, the ones in which we have an opportunity to test the hypotheses that we outline here.

The possibility that effort actually creates ability, that people can become smart by working hard at the right kinds of learning tasks, has never been taken seriously in America (Resnick, 1995). Certain educational initiatives and programmes have instantiated some aspects of a learning-oriented motivational design, a design in which practices assume that well-directed effort can create ability and not just reveal its limits. For example, Edmonds and his associates (1979) described characteristics of schools in which poor and minority students were succeeding beyond normal expectations. Among the features of these schools were the setting of high expectations for achievement and frequent assessment of children against these expectations. Jaime Escalante, a mathematics teacher in Los Angeles, succeeded in teaching advanced placement calculus to some of the poorest and, supposedly, most difficult to teach students in California's schools (Escalante and Dirmann, 1990).

Jaime Escalante, educators working within the Effective Schools movement and others who have been able to raise achievement levels among traditionally low-achieving populations of students, worked on motivational characteristics of teaching and learning. They did this by changing fundamental institutional norms, expectations and practices (in Escalante's case, within a classroom; in Effective Schools, within a whole school). Working with students judged by others, and often by themselves, as weak or even candidates for remediation, they placed students in honours programmes or held out expectations for above-normal achievement. Although the organizers of these programmes did not speak explicitly to theories of personal motivation, they all implicitly depended on changes in the mediating motivational characteristics of students. That is, the greater the level of effort invested by students in all programmes, their persistence in courses that were – at least initially – difficult for them, and the subsequent greater learning and achievement that they showed were presumably partly a function of changes in their motivational orientations.

Each of these programmes and others like them, however, have had to work against beliefs widely held in American society and influential in its educational institutions: namely, that what individuals can learn and what schools can teach are largely determined by ability, and that ability is largely unalterable by effort or environmentally offered opportunities (Howard, 1991, 1995). The existence of cultures that appear to promote overall tendencies to learning rather than to performance raises a fundamental question for American schooling: might we, by systematically altering some of our schooling practices, create more learning-oriented motivational patterns and, thereby, higher achievement?

American researchers have typically studied different goal orientations as if they were individual dispositions, whereas the role of the schooling environment as contextual influences on achievement goal orientations is relatively unstudied. We know that learning goals can be elicited and made differentially salient by situational or instructional demands (e.g. Ames, 1992; Jagacinski and Nicholls, 1984). Several structures of the classroom environment have been found to have an impact on student motivation and are largely controlled by teachers (Rosenholtz and Simpson, 1984). Included among these are the design of academic tasks and activities, the evaluation practices employed and the distribution of authority and responsibility in the classroom (Ames and Archer, 1988; Nelson-Le Gall, 1992, 1993; Resnick, 1995).

The belief that institutional demands and rewards can change psychological belief structures is held intuitively by many educators and lay people. The effects of such institutional features on individual motivational orientations, however, have not been examined directly. Similarly, although research has shown that certain motivational orientations raise performance on particular tasks, it has not shown that these orientations raise overall academic achievement. Working in collaboration with the educators in a number of schools that have decided to try to implement an overall school programme that promotes learning goal orientations and that treats effort, rather than aptitude, as the primary determinant of learning results, we are planning a research programme that will examine four interrelated hypotheses that derive from the arguments we have developed here.

First, we will seek evidence that instructional environments can be created that systematically and in a sustained way evoke learning goals and their associated behaviours. Such environments would, by our hypothesis, be those in which there is a continuous press for all students to engage in strategic learning behaviours, such as testing their own understanding, developing arguments and explanations, providing justifications and adhering to discipline-appropriate standards of evidence and reasoning. Furthermore, an instructional environment that evokes learning goals is likely to be one in which beliefs in each student's capacity to engage in these strategic learning behaviours are communicated both explicitly and implicitly. Finally, an environment that evokes and supports learning goals is likely to be one in which expectations of accomplishment are clear, students understand the evaluative criteria and often judge their own work, and there is clear feedback to students about how they are progressing towards a public standard of accomplishment. Working with our school-based collaborators, we will be building a set of tools for analysing the extent to which these features are present in classrooms throughout the school. These tools will be used both to produce structured observational research data and as a basis for training teachers in ways of organizing their own and their students' work to maximize these features.

Second, we will test the hypothesis that long-term participation in environments that evoke learning goals also changes students' beliefs about what it takes to succeed academically. In our collaborating schools and classrooms, we will measure student beliefs and motivational orientations at several different times during their participation in classrooms that make learning goals salient. This means following students for at least a whole school year and preferably longer. It also makes it desirable to study schools in which entire faculties are creating environments that make learning goals salient. Students would then be spending a greater proportion of their time in such environments, and it would be more likely, therefore, that fundamental belief changes would occur.

Third, we surmise that teachers' capacity to initiate and maintain incremental environments is partly a function of their beliefs about their students' capacities for learning and about their own efficacy as teachers. Using interviews and questionnaires, we will examine teachers' beliefs at different stages of their participation in our collaborative programme. We will then relate teachers' beliefs to their observed instructional activity and to interactions with students in their classrooms.

Fourth and finally, all of these motivational factors are of interest as mediators of student achievement. This means that we must examine a number of indicators of student achievement (e.g. standardized test scores, performance assessments, portfolio results, teacher grades) and relate differences and changes in these indicators to all of the motivational and behavioural data on schools, classrooms, teachers and students.

This is a form of research in which no sharp lines can be drawn between development and research, between our collaborative work with school staffs in developing new school environments and our joint evaluation of their effects. The research is planned as a series of iterative development and study cycles in which social and institutional design principles are actively merged with psychological theory and empirical research methods. Only in such long-term, institutionally based design experiments will it be possible to evaluate possibilities for a radical rethinking of the nature of intelligence and its relation to social beliefs and practices of our society.

References

Ames, C. (1984). Competitive, cooperative, and individualistic goal structures: A motivational analysis. In R. Ames and C. Ames (eds), *Research on Motivation in Education* vol. 1, pp. 177–207. San Diego, CA: Academic Press.

Ames, C. (1992). Classrooms: Goals, structures, and student motivation. *Journal of Educational Psychology*, 84, 261–71.

Ames, C. and Archer, J. (1988). Achievement goals in the classroom: Students' learning strategies and motivation processes. *Journal of Educational Psychology*, 80, 260–7.

Binet, A. and Simon, T. (1905). The development of intelligence in children. *L'Année Psychologique*, 163–91. Also in T. Shipley (ed.) (1961). *Classics in Psychology*. New York: Philosophical Library.

Brown, A. L., Bransford, J. D., Ferrara, R. A. and Campione, J. C. (1983). Learning, remembering, and understanding. In J. Flavell and E. M. Markman (eds), *Handbook of Child Psychology* (4th edn), vol. 3, *Cognitive Development*, pp. 515–629. New York: Wiley.

Carroll, J. B. (1966). Factors of verbal achievement. In A. Anastasi (ed.), *Testing Problems in Perspective*. Washington, DC: American Council on Education.

Cole, M. and Scribner, S. (1974). *Culture and Thought*. New York: Wiley.

Doise, W. and Mugny, G. (1984). *The Social Development of the Intellect*. Oxford: Pergamon Press.

Dweck, C. S. (1988). Motivation. In R. Glaser and A. Lesgold (eds), *Handbook of Psychology and Education*, pp. 187–239. Hillsdale, NJ: Erlbaum.

Dweck, C. S. and Leggett, E. L. (1988). A social-cognitive approach to motivation and personality. *Psychological Review*, 95, 256–73.

Edmonds, R. (1979). Effective schools for the urban poor. *Educational Leadership*, 37, 15–23.

Escalante, J. and Dirmann, J. (1990). The Jaime Escalante math program. *Journal of Negro Education*, 59, 407–23.

Gardner, H. (1993). *Multiple Intelligences: The Theory in Practice*. New York: Basic Books.

Goodnow, J. J. (1990a). The socialization of cognition: What's involved? In J. W. Stigler, R. A. Shweder and G. Herdt (eds), *Cultural Psychology: Essays on Comparative Human Development*, pp. 259–86. Cambridge: Cambridge University Press.

Goodnow, J. J. (1990b). Using sociology to extend psychological accounts of cognitive development. *Human Development*, 33, 81–107.

Guilford, J. B. (1967). *The Nature of Human Intelligence*. New York: McGraw-Hill.

Herrnstein, R. J. and Murray, C. (1994). *The Bell Curve: Intelligence and Class Structure in American Life*. New York: Free Press.

Holloway, S. (1988). Concepts of ability and effort in Japan and the U.S. *Review of Educational Research*, 58, 327–45.

Howard, J. (1991). *Getting Smart: The Social Construction of Intelligence*. Lexington, MA: Efficacy Institute.

Howard, J. (1995). You can't get there from here: The need for a new logic in education reform. *Daedalus*, 124, 85–92.

Jagacinski, C. and Nicholls, J. (1984). Conceptions of ability and related affects in task involvement and ego involvement. *Journal of Educational Psychology*, 76, 909–19.

Lave, J. (1988). *Cognition in Practice: Mind, Mathematics and Culture in Everyday Life*. Cambridge: Cambridge University Press.

Nelson-Le Gall, S. (1990). Academic achievement orientation and help-seeking behavior in early adolescent girls. *Journal of Early Adolescence*, 10, 176–90.

Nelson-Le Gall, S. (1992). Perceiving and displaying effort in achievement settings. In T. Tomlinson (ed.), *Motivating Students to Learn: Overcoming Barriers to High Achievement*, pp. 225–44. Berkeley, CA: McCutchan Publishing.

Nelson-Le Gall, S. (1993). Children's instrumental help-seeking: Its role in the social construction of knowledge. In R. Hertz-Lazarowitz and N. Miller (eds), *Interaction in Cooperative Groups: The Theoretical Anatomy of Group Learning*, pp. 49–68. New York: Cambridge University Press.

Nelson-Le Gall, S. and Jones, E. (1990). Cognitive-motivational influences on children's help-seeking. *Child Development*, 61, 581–9.

Nicholls, J. (1979). Quality and equality in intellectual development: The role of motivation in education. *American Psychologist*, 34, 1071–84.

Nicholls, J. (1984). Achievement motivation: Conceptions of ability, subjective experience, task choice and performance. *Psychological Review*, 91, 328–46.

Peak, L. (1986). Training learning skills and attitudes in Japanese early education settings. In E. Fowler (ed.), *Early Experience and the Development of Competence*, pp. 111–23. San Francisco: Jossey-Bass.

Peak, L. (1993). Academic effort in international perspective. In T. Tomlinson (ed.), *Motivating Students to Learn: Overcoming Barriers to High Achievement*, pp. 41–59. Berkeley, CA: McCutchan Publishing.

Pellegrino, J. W. and Glaser, R. (1982). Analyzing aptitudes for learning: Inductive reasoning. In R. Glaser (ed.), *Advances in Instructional Psychology*, vol. 2, pp. 269–345. Hillsdale, NJ: Erlbaum.

Perret-Clermont, A.-N. (1980). *Social Interaction and Cognitive Development in Children*. New York: Academic Press.

Piaget, J. (1960). *The Psychology of Intelligence*. Peterson, NJ: Littlefield, Adams.

Piaget, J. (1970a). Piaget's theory. In P. H. Mussen (ed.), *Carmichael's Manual of Child Psychology*, vol. 1. New York: Wiley.

Piaget, J. (1970b). *Genetic Epistemology*. New York: W. W. Norton.

Reed, E. (1993). The intention to use a specific affordance: A conceptual framework for psychology. In R. Wozniak and K. Fisher (eds), *Development in Context*, pp. 45–76. Hillsdale, NJ: Erlbaum.

Resnick, L. B. (1995). From aptitude to effort: A new foundation for our schools. *Daedalus*, 124, 55–62.

Resnick, L. B., Saljo, R., Pontecorvo, C. and Burge, B. (1998). *Discourse, Tools, and Reasoning: Situated Cognition and Technologically Supported Environments*. Heidelberg: Springer-Verlag.

Rogoff, B. (1990). *Apprenticeship in Thinking: Children's Guided Participation in Culture*. New York: Oxford University Press.

Rosenholtz, S. and Simpson, C. (1984). The formation of ability conceptions: Developmental trend or social construction. *Review of Educational Research*, 54, 31–63.

Shayer, M. and Adey, P. (1981). *Towards a Science of Science Teaching: Cognitive Development and Curriculum Demand*. London: Heinemann.

Sternberg, R. J. (1977). *Intelligence, Information Processing, and Analogical Reasoning: The Componential Analysis of Human Abilities*. Hillsdale, NJ: Erlbaum.

Sternberg, R. J. and Wagner, R. K. (1986). *Practical Intelligence: Nature and Origins of Competence in the Everyday World*. Cambridge: Cambridge University Press.

Stevenson, H. and Lee, S. (1990). Contexts of achievement: A study of American, Chinese, and Japanese children. *Monographs of the Society for Research in Child Development*, 55, 1 and 2, serial no. 221.

Stevenson, H. and Stigler, J. (1992). *The Learning Gap: Why our Schools are Failing and What we can Learn from Japanese and Chinese Education*. New York: Summitt Books.

Suchman, H. (1992). *Plans and Situated Actions: The Problem of Human–Machine Interaction*. Cambridge: Cambridge University Press.

Terman, L. M. (1916). *The Measurement of Intelligence*. Boston: Houghton Mifflin.

Terman, L. M. (1919). *The Intelligence of School Children: How Children Differ in Ability*. Boston: Houghton Mifflin.

Thorndike, E. L. (1926). *Measurement of Intelligence*. New York: Teachers College, Columbia University.

Thurstone, L. L. (1938). Primary mental abilities. *Psychometric Monographs*, 1 (whole no.).

Tobin, J., Wu, D. and Davidson, D. (1989). *Preschool in Three Cultures: Japan, China, and the United States*. New Haven, CT: Yale University Press.

Vygotsky, L. S. (1978). *Mind in Society: The Development of Higher Psychological Processes* (M. Cole, V. John-Steiner, S. Scribner and F. Souberman, eds). Cambridge, MA: Harvard University Press.

Weiner, B. (1974). *Achievement Motivation and Attribution Theory.* Morristown, NJ: General Learning Press.

Wertsch, J. V. (1985) *Vygotsky and the Social Formation of Mind.* Cambridge, MA: Harvard University Press.

PART 6

MEMORY

CHAPTER 11

MEMORY RESEARCH
Past mistakes and future prospects

Peter Morris

G. Claxton (ed.) *Growth Points in Cognition*, London and New York, Routledge, 1988

'It is a capital mistake to theorise before you have all the evidence. It biases the judgement.'

(Sherlock Holmes in *A Study in Scarlet*, Conan Doyle, 1887)

One major feature of the study of memory throughout much of the past hundred years is that it has proceeded from strong theoretical assumptions that were initially developed upon a very small base of empirical evidence. These theoretical assumptions have then largely driven the subsequent research on memory. The result has been that we have concentrated upon very specialised aspects of memory which may have little relevance to the way memory is used in everyday life. Two examples of this theory-driven research are (1) the assumption that memorising is essentially the developing of new associations, and (2) the short-term and long-term memory distinction. In both cases the theories were developed long before any systematic effort had been made to survey just when and how we use our memories. The associationist account of memory comes with a pedigree stretching back at least to Aristotle, but based always on the speculations of philosophers. I do not want to assert that either of these theoretical examples is wholly misguided, although both can be denied without requiring too much reinterpretation or ignoring of the available evidence. What I do want to point out is that the acceptance of these theoretical positions then determined the framework for many years of experimental research which in retrospect seems blinkered in the questions that it did and did not consider. Once the associationist view was adopted it seemed sensible to introduce the methods that became the stock-in-trade of the verbal learning psychologist who presented lists of unrelated words or nonsense syllables with the object of studying how varying the repetitions, the similarity of the items and so on would influence the learning of new associations. In the study of short- and long-term memory the search was on for the capacity and type of coding in short-term memory, the way information was lost, and so on. To many non-psychologists these seemed strange questions to be dominating the focus of research, but they were the obvious ones to those working in the area, and each new result stimulated a further set of questions within the accepted framework (see Baddeley, 1976, for a good review of both areas of research).

Currently few people studying memory would find much to draw upon from the research on the learning of new associations or that distinguishing between short- and long-term memory, even though both probably captured kernels of truth within their own assumptions. Why? The answer is that more and more people stopped asking questions within the old frameworks and began wondering just what our memories are for. When do we use them? Why do we have them? In this chapter I want to illustrate how the new directions in the study of memory can be seen as filling the gaps and replacing the inadequacies of more traditional approaches to the study of memory.

This re-framing of research by asking about the functions of our memories is well illustrated by Baddeley's research, where he has remoulded the study of short-term memory by asking what role short-term remembering may play, and then elaborating the concept of working memory (e.g. Baddeley, 1983). However, perhaps the best statement of the importance of these questions was made by Neisser (1978) in the opening paper at the first Practical Aspects of Memory Conference. He asked 'What do we use the past *for*?' He was able to produce a list of several different ways in which we use our memories based upon an examination of his own experience. He pointed out, first, that, everyone uses the past to define themselves. Secondly, that one frequently recalls past experiences in search of some sort of self-improvement. Then, on other occasions, personal memories achieve a kind of public importance when, for example, legal testimony is required. Another feature of memory is that we learn many things secondhand through friends, acquaintances and literature. Neisser pointed out that memory is involved in many activities in daily life. We make plans and have to carry them out, we put things down and need to recall where we left them, we are given directions and must follow them to reach our destination, and we meet people and need to pick up the relationship where we left off. In the next section of the chapter I want to enlarge upon the ways in which the associationist, list-learning tradition that arose from the work of Ebbinghaus ignored these important aspects of memory, and how, in recent years, first steps have been taken to rectify this omission. The result has been to make the study of memory vastly more interesting and challenging. Here, however, I want to point out that the limitations imposed by the rigid theoretical positions of the earlier part of the century became obvious only when people began to ask what really happens when we remember things. Neisser's question – What do we use the past for? – directs our attention towards the data that the theories need to explain.

Psychology, in general, is an unusual science in that the leap towards strong theoretical positions and intense study of specialised topics often takes place before very many relevant facts have been discovered. Of course, the idea that all scientific data gathering is theory-driven has been popular in the philosophy of science. In practice, however, the creation of a good theory requires a good supply of facts which will help both to stimulate the theorist's thinking and delimit the range of possibilities she or he has at their command. Most of the important theoretical developments in the natural sciences have followed the acquisition over many years of empirical facts to be explained by the resulting theory. Two famous examples are the way in which Tycho Brahe's observations of planetary movements were necessary for Kepler's calculation of the elliptical movement of the planets, and secondly how Darwin's painstaking collection of evidence led to the development of the theory of evolution. In most sciences it has been fairly clear what the problem is, and what its range and limitations are before useful theories have been developed. In psychology we have often sneered at the collection of empirical generalisations about the way that people behave and it is still common for journals to reject papers that describe interesting empirical observations about memory on the grounds that they make insufficient theoretical contributions. This low regard for the data for which the theories must be explanations has, I believe, seriously hampered the development of psychology.

In the study of memory we seem to be breaking through that disregard for facts which are, in the last analysis, what the subject is about. We are beginning to look at the world of everyday life to see what it is that we have to explain.

We will probably find that before we can produce good, usable theories of the way memory functions in its many roles we will have to develop at least a sketch of a 'natural history' of memory phenomena. Without that we will not be able to choose between competing theories nor develop theories which are truly appropriate. Nor will we concentrate upon what will be really useful in our understanding of the way memory functions.

The fact that we are only now beginning to sketch in the borders of such a natural history is the result of the importance throughout most of this century of the Ebbinghaus tradition.

The Ebbinghaus tradition

It is just over 100 years since Ebbinghaus (1885) published one of the most influential books in experimental psychology. Ebbinghaus' book is fascinating because it reveals the author's interest in a wide range of memory phenomena. It reports, for example, his studies of his own memorising of verses from Don Juan. It would, therefore, be quite wrong to blame Ebbinghaus for all that followed in the tradition which grew out of his initial work. In the years subsequent to the publication of Ebbinghaus' classic there were many important preliminary investigations of real world remembering. For example, Colegrove (1899), collected detailed recollections after 33 years of the situations in which people heard of Lincoln's assassination. Cattell (1895) studied memory for the weather and Stern (1904) was laying the groundwork for research on eyewitness testimony. However, the assumptions underlying Ebbinghaus' main work were ones which fitted so well with those of the behaviourists when the latter came to dominate psychology during the early and middle years of the twentieth century, that the study of memory was for many years based upon the learning of lists of nonsense syllables or unrelated words in laboratory conditions. I want to review the ways in which many of the assumptions of this research have turned out to be misleading, and to see how in recent years there has been a rapid return to those topics which interested Colegrove, Cattell and Stern.

Ebbinghaus' research was based on a strong theoretical position. He followed many philosophers in assuming that learning builds up through the establishment of new associations. Given this assumption, it seemed obvious that the right procedure was to study completely new associations so that the misleading effects of earlier learned associations would not distort the research findings. This philosophy was incorporated into the mainstream study of memory, or 'verbal learning' as it was more respectably called during the behaviourist era. The traditional verbal learning experiment of the 1950s involved the learning of lists of nonsense syllables paired with adjectives. The testing involved presenting for (usually) two seconds the initial nonsense syllable and requiring the subject within those two seconds to report the adjective with which it had been paired. Learning was tedious, slow and easily forgotten. (See, for example, Postman and Keppel, 1969, for examples of some of the best research in this tradition).

Let us look at the factors which such research eliminates or controls and then consider its assumptions and its implications. The use of nonsense syllables and adjectives that have no meaningful relationships within the lists means that prior knowledge and experience is minimised or, if possible, eliminated. Subjects have no interest in what is to be learnt, but this is not regarded by the experimenter as important since in this way possible variations through interest are being controlled. The activity at the time of learning is limited both by the time for which the individual items are presented and by the nature of the material itself. Any memorising strategies which the subjects might attempt to adopt are equally minimised both by the brief presentation and, often, by instructions to the subjects to avoid them. In any case, the material appears so unrealistic that suitable ways of memorising it do not spring to mind. The learning and retrieval conditions and the material to be memorised are standardised and very similar in most of these experiments. Finally, notice how the cues available for retrieval are normally limited to the items with which the word or nonsense syllable was paired and to the conditions (i.e. the same memory drum, the same room), in which the original memorising had taken place.

All this restriction on the conditions of learning was imposed for a very sensible reason. It was not that the experimenters believed that the variables which they controlled were unimportant but rather that they recognised that to understand and experimentally investigate memory processes they needed to control extraneous variables and carefully manipulate the ones which were believed to be important. Nevertheless, the question occurred to most experimental subjects, and even to some experimenters, of whether this devotion to experimental control meant the losing of the metaphorical baby with the extraneous bath of water.

One key assumption of the verbal learning tradition was that there are basic memory processes which were being sampled in the experiments and which could then be identified under more natural conditions. It was unusual for individual differences in memorising performance to be considered. This probably reflected the belief that there were basic memory processes which everyone possessed and which were being carefully unravelled in the controlled experimentation. Unfortunately, as we shall see later in the chapter, both these assumptions of basic memory processes and the unimportance of individual differences were misguided.

Finally we should note implications that follow from the way that the experiments were conducted. They are that memorising is often intentional, and that there are easily discriminable stages of learning and retrieval. So the memory experiments were based upon a clearcut difference between the learning and the retrieval stage.

Criticisms of the Ebbinghaus tradition

The new directions in memory research that have been developing in recent years depend upon reversing most of the Ebbinghaus tradition. One might almost call the new approach the 'Suahgnibbe view', if only it were easier to pronounce!

First, consider the implication that memorising is intentional and involves separate and discrete learning and retrieval stages. The misleading nature of such an implication becomes clear immediately when we ask the question – what do we use our memories for? (Cf. Neisser, 1978, 1982.) Without our knowledge of the past we would not be able to make sense of our present experience nor could we predict what was likely to happen in the future to guide our actions. Once we recognise that our memories are for making sense of the present and for predicting the future it becomes obvious that for them to be of any use they must be continuously encoding new information about our current experience and retrieving any potentially useful information about what has happened to us in the past. Thus, our memories are a continuously exploited resource and the system of memory functioning that we must have evolved will be one which continuously enters new information and is always interrogating what is already stored for suitable, usable past information. When, for example, you are reading this book you are continuously drawing from your memory the meaning of the words, conventions about the way they will be put together and you are interpreting the whole experience through higher order structures which give you a framework for understanding what you read (see, for example, [. . .]; Schank, 1982, and Smyth, Morris, Ellis and Levy, 1987). All this depends upon what you can retrieve from memory. Without your memory you could tell no difference between what you read here and an output from some random letter generator. Also, you will be able to remember details of what you have just read as a spin-off from the process of making sense of the page in front of you. Of course, it still makes sense to consider separately the entering of information into memory and its retrieval from store. However, what is obvious is that those entries into memory which come about through our deliberate attempts to memorise are a very tiny fraction of the actual entries that we will have in memory. Similarly the number of times we retrieve deliberately from memory are tiny compared to those which happen automatically as part of servicing the comprehension processes of the cognitive system. One incidental consequence of this is that there is no fear of overloading memory through deliberate memorisation, perhaps for exams, because the amount that is encoded on these occasions is trivial compared to what is coded automatically with or without our intentions to learn. Another implication of the role of memory in comprehension is that the form in which information is stored must be appropriate to the way comprehension occurs, and be rapidly retrievable. The units of memory (if there are such things) will normally be small packages of information. When we recall longer sequences (tell stories, jokes, give evidence) it will be a matter of stringing together these memory packages, with all the opportunities for errors that this implies, together with the need to mould the whole into a coherent account (e.g. Bartlett, 1932; Neisser, 1981). (For further discussion of the role of memory in cognition, see Smyth *et al.*, 1987.)

There are many specific memory skills

One of the major assumptions of the Ebbinghaus tradition was that the type of memory being studied by the verbal learning, paired associate experiment was sufficiently typical of normal memory processes to mean that the results could be generalised to most other situations. Unfortunately, however, while it may be true that there are certain generalisations which it is reasonable to make about most memory processes, the evidence suggests that there is so much variability in the type of material, the types of processes, the strategies and the processing skills upon which people can draw when they tackle memorising in different situations that the way in which information is entered into memory will often be very different from one situation to another. This makes drawing generalisations about memory very difficult. In other words, the processes that underlie memorising people's faces may be quite different to those used when remembering stories and these again may be different to those for conversations, for intentions to do things, for the geography of the world around us, and so on. Even learning two types of list may involve different sorts of memory processes.

The evidence for the frequent independence of memory abilities between different tasks comes from the study of individual differences. As I pointed out earlier, the investigation of individual differences in memorising was regarded as largely unnecessary for most of the early and middle years of the twentieth century. However, in more recent years it has become more respectable to examine and compare the performance of individuals on different tasks. If the same individuals when tested on a number of tasks turn out to have quite different abilities upon those tasks then it becomes difficult to believe that there is a general memory principle underlying their performance. So, for example, if someone who is good at memorising faces turns out to be no better than average at recalling the plots of stories that they have read and are worse than most people at remembering to do things then, as in other psychometric studies, we should begin to consider these as separate abilities rather than as reflecting one underlying process.

Perhaps the strongest evidence that memory skills are frequently independent came from a large study by Underwood, Boruch and Malmi (1978). They tested 200 students on 31 different laboratory memory tasks. They took special care to make the memory performance measures as reliable as possible since poor reliability is a common feature of many memory tests (see P. Morris, 1984). When Underwood and colleagues factor-analysed their subjects' performance, they found that separate factors emerged for free recall, paired associate learning, memory span, verbal discrimination, spelling ability and vocabulary. These factors seemed virtually independent of each other. Therefore, even for the common laboratory tests it appears that different underlying skills are involved and that there is not some general memory ability which is high in some people and low in others.

Further support for this view that memory skills are task specific comes from several other experiments where people have compared performance on list learning with the memory abilities of people doing more realistic learning tasks. Morris, Tweedy and Gruneberg (1985) found insignificant correlations of 0.26 and 0.32 respectively between the amount that subjects could free recall from a list of common words and either the performance of the same individuals on a quiz about football knowledge or their recall of new football scores which they had just heard. Morris and Morris (1985) reported correlations of less than 0.3 between the narrative free recall by eyewitnesses and the accuracy with which they answered subsequent questions. In both cases one might have expected that those subjects with a good general memory would perform well in all tasks. However, clearly special features about the encoding and retrieval conditions had differential effects upon the individuals in the different tasks.

These small and usually insignificant correlations between the performance of the same subjects in different memory tasks is well illustrated by an unpublished study of mine with Penny Walters. In this experiment 25 students were tested in a variety of different memory tasks. They were initially selected for having been present at an inter-college pool competition within the university. They were tested upon their recall of a particular pool match which they had witnessed, including the appearance of the competitors. Subsequently, they took part in several further tests. The first of these was a measure of their memory span, combining their recall performance both for lists of digits and for lists of letters. Secondly, they were shown a set of common advertisements and were required to recall which ones they had seen after a brief delay. Thirdly, they were presented with a set of photographs of faces and had to identify these faces when mixed with an equal number of distractors. Finally, they were tested on their recall of Bartlett's 'War of the Ghosts' story. While the split half reliability of these tests was reasonably high (0.66–0.85) there were very few significant intercorrelations between performance upon the five different tests. In fact, only that between memory span and recall of the advertisements reach significance with a correlation of 0.57. All other correlations range between 0.06 and 0.24. In other words, how well someone does on one memory task is no predictor of how well they will do on another unless that task is highly similar to the first one.

The independence of the many memory skills has also been suggested by the work of other researchers (e.g. Battig, 1979; Coughlan and Hollows, 1986; and Wilkins and Baddeley, 1978). In general, therefore, when individual differences are studied, it becomes clear not only that they are important but that the assumption that list learning provides a reasonable sample of a basic memory ability is extremely doubtful. Future research on memory will need to take the generality of its findings into account, and some thought will need to be given to ways of identifying the tasks and situations to which a particular memory skill generalises.

The baby and the bathwater

Finally, in our examination of the limitations of the Ebbinghaus tradition let us look at the factors which they chose to control or eliminate. As I described earlier the list-learning paradigm was designed to control or eliminate prior knowledge and experience, interest, variations in the activities at learning, subject strategies, differences in learning and retrieval conditions, the range of material memorised and the types of retrieval cues. Experimental control is essential in research but so is the retention of the thing to be studied. The question arises whether anything of normal memory is left when these variables are controlled in the way they were in laboratory list-learning experiments. Rather than answer the question immediately I want to turn to sketching what I would see as the important factors that influence memory in the world. We will then be able to turn these back to the list-learning experimental conditions and observe whether the list-learning experiment provided a reasonable sample of real world memorising.

Any sketch of the processes that determine memory must begin with the external world. That world contains a wide variety of potential inputs to the human cognitive system. We see events, we listen to conversations, we read books, we watch television and so on. The external world imposes tasks upon us that we have to fulfil. A university lecturer, for example, has to prepare lectures, mark course work assignments and examinations, plan research, guide seminars, supervise practicals and so on. Each task places special demands upon our cognitive system as it attempts to make sense of what is happening and direct our future actions.

In coping with this external world and its current task demands there is continuous internal cognitive activity. Our cognitive systems are always busily processing the input in order to comprehend it, to select a special message from other background information, to identify what is new and how it links with what is old, to devise the ways in which what is happening fits or does not fit our plans, to carry out the specific tasks that the world demands or we wish to impose upon the world and to calculate the implications in general of what we are experiencing. In the process of all this there is a personal context of moods and emotions created by our success and failure.

To achieve the successful processing of the world we draw upon internal resources. We have vast stored knowledge of the meanings of words, of regularities about the world, and of high-level schemas which specify what is likely to happen. We have memories of episodes from the past and we possess control programmes to help direct our processing. These internal resources are what we generally classify as memory and it is these that are in continuous use. They are continuously probed and supply potentially useful information to aid the internal activities of the cognitive system. At the same time, new information as a result of the ongoing processing is stored away in memory alongside previously acquired knowledge. There is, I believe, nothing controversial about that sketch of the processes surrounding memory. Most of them have been the topics of research in recent years (see Smyth *et al.*, 1987, for a review).

If we compare the aspects of the traditional list-learning experiment with this survey of the processes determining memory we quickly see that the list-learning experiment contains almost none of the important factors that determine memory. As a sample of tasks within the world, list learning is extremely rare. Most of our normal memory functions are irrelevant to list-learning experiments and our normal psychological processes are baffled by the abnormal input. In part they are baffled because the internal resources we possess have almost nothing to say about the material being processed. Perhaps, if meaningful words are used, then word meanings can be abstracted from memory. However, these meanings will normally be of little use except as an adjunct of some special-purpose mnemonic strategy such as imaging or making up stories (see, for example, Morris, 1979). The word lists activate no other useful stored knowledge, nothing to do with the schemas that frame our lives, episodes from our lives, no regularities about the world at all (cf. Schank, 1982). It is not, therefore, surprising that this list-learning tradition has told us little about the way that our memories normally work. If you do not put into the experiment what you might wish to study there is no hope of getting out from the result much useable information.

Exploring the low road

In the preface to his book *Memory Observed* (1982) Neisser commented that psychology has followed two routes in the study of memory. Travellers on the high road have hoped to find basic mental mechanisms that can be demonstrated in well controlled experiments. Those on the low road want to understand the specific manifestations of memory in ordinary human experience. Neisser describes *Memory Observed* as 'a kind of guide book to the lower road'. It is certainly a fascinating guide book and highly recommended reading. As we have seen, attempts to study what Neisser calls the high road have led to experimental paradigms which have left out what we would now regard as the important aspects of memory. What happens if we start down the low road and ask what are the main landmarks of memory in everyday life?

In the last few years, as people have begun to study the range of ways that we use memory in everyday life, there have developed many new and interesting research themes. There have been several interesting examples of how, in real life, what we remember is not a simple function of the number of times we experience the stimulus: not, that is, a simple matter of associations building up through frequency. So, for example, an intensive publicity campaign to advertise changes in radio frequencies led to almost no learning by the general public (Bekerian and Baddeley, 1980). People have very poor memories of the details on the coins that they use every day (Nickerson and Adams, 1979). Recently, when I asked 100 students to identify the correct representation of the face of a British 10p coin, 48 of them chose an alternative in which the Queen's head faced in the wrong direction! On the other hand, one experience of a salient event in one's life can lead to memories of many apparently irrelevant details about the situation one was in. Such vivid and detailed memories, sometimes known as flashbulb memories, have re-emerged as a topic for research following the pioneering work of Colegrove (1899) (see, e.g., Neisser, 1982).

One popular topic has been autobiographical memory (Rubin, 1986). Techniques originally used a hundred years ago by Sir Francis Galton, of asking for specific personal memories triggered by cue words, are being applied not only to explore the memories of normal individuals, but also those of the clinically depressed or demented. The study of eyewitness testimony has become a major theme in its own right and, in the process, has restored the study of memory for events which was originally begun by Stern (1904) (e.g. Wells and Loftus, 1984). The context and emotional states under which learning and recall take place have turned out to be major determinants of what people can recall (e.g. Malpass and Devine, 1981; Bower, 1983). There has been fascinating research on the representations that we possess of our geographical surroundings. Distortions in our 'mental maps' seem common, and can perhaps be understood in terms of the activities through which we build up our knowledge (see, e.g., Bartram and Smith, 1984). The permanence and plasticity of our memories have been important research topics. Bahrick (1984a, 1984b) has shown that in some circumstances our memories seem to be resistant to decay or interference, for periods of 25 years or more. On the other hand, Loftus and her associates (e.g. Loftus and Loftus, 1980) have illustrated how easy it is to substitute misleading information during subsequent questioning so that the recall of the original information is virtually impossible except under very special conditions (e.g. Bekerian and Bowers, 1983; Bowers and Bekerian, 1984). Hunter (1985) has reviewed research upon what he calls lengthy verbatim recall. He has shown that the common belief that accurate memory is encouraged in non-literate societies and decays when a written language allows records to be kept and the memory to be supplemented is, in fact, a myth. The reality is that in non-literate societies where there is no record against which to compare memory performance the verbatim accuracy of recall is not what is valued. Recall is for another purpose, for example, the singing of technically sophisticated sagas for the enjoyment of an expert audience or the justification of the present ruler by the construction of an appropriate genealogy.

One major research topic has been the study of remembering to do things. When people are questioned about the memory problems that they have, or the methods that they use to overcome memory lapses (e.g. Harris, 1980; Reason and Mycielska, 1982), it is problems in remembering planned intentions that feature most prominently. Diary studies by Reason and his associates (e.g. Reason, 1984; Reason and Lucas, 1984; Reason and Mycielska, 1982) have helped to locate when such errors occur. The development of models of the processes underlying human slips and lapses has considerable implications for public safety, since many industrial accidents and public transport disasters appear to stem from human errors in the remembering and control of actions (e.g. Reason and Embrey, 1985). Harris (1984) has reviewed the experimental research on remembering to do things which often reflects great ingenuity and inventiveness by the experimenters.

One of the methods initially adopted in the study of everyday memory was the memory questionnaire, asking subjects to indicate their level of memory ability on a wide range of possible areas. Subjects rated how well they remembered people's faces, whether they frequently forgot where they had placed things and so on. The major finding of this research was that while people are consistent in their beliefs about their own memory abilities these beliefs did not seem to match up to the actual performance of subjects in objective attempts to assess their abilities. Herrmann (1984) reviews the poor performance of the memory questionnaires as predictors of actual performance. Elsewhere, (Morris, 1984) I have tried to indicate the many reasons why such questionnaire performance is poor. This lack of general awareness of the strengths and limitations of our own memories makes even more important the careful experimental investigation of everyday memory phenomena.

Finally, in this sketch of some of the recent topics in everyday memory, the importance of the prior knowledge of subjects on the particular type of material to be remembered has been shown to have massive implications for the amount of new information on that topic that they can pick up in one exposure. One example of the influence of prior knowledge on the acquisition of new information is a study by a former postgraduate student of mine (Morris, 1983). Valerie Morris looked at the memory subjects had for details from a video film made up of clips showing part of a football match, a gardening programme, a snooker game and a pop music programme. Her subjects had previously completed a questionnaire on their know-ledge of these topics. She found that the ability to recall new information acquired from the film was very well predicted by the subject's performance on this prior knowledge questionnaire. This was so even though the questions on the film were designed not to be guessable by knowledgeable subjects. She found, for example, that the knowledge about football questionnaire correlated 0.74 with the recall of the questions about the football part of the film.

In a series of experiments I have been interested in the acquisition of new foot-ball scores by individuals from a range of knowledge about the soccer world. In our first study (Morris, Gruneberg, Sykes and Merrick, 1981), we showed that there was a correlation greater than 0.8 between people's general knowledge about soccer and the number of new scores they could correctly recall after hearing the Saturday after-noon results just once. This was so despite the fact that experts are very poor at predicting the likely scores in advance. In a second study (Morris, Tweedy and Gruneberg, 1985) we replicated the finding that general knowledge about football correlates above 0.8 with the number of new scores correctly remembered. One important finding in this experiment was that simulated scores which were designed to be as realistic as possible, but which the subjects knew were in fact constructed by the experimenters, were recalled far differently from the real scores. For those subjects who had least knowledge about football, real and simulated scores were equally well recalled, but as football knowledge increased then the superiority of the recall of real scores steadily grew. While recall of the real scores was unrelated to the recall of a list of words there was a high correlation between the recall of the simulated scores and the free recall word list. The implication was that the attempt to simulate the football score condition failed and that two different skills were involved in the experiment. One involved knowledge of football, the other an ability to free recall lists of words and numbers. I will return to this point in a later section.

The importance of prior knowledge in the memorising of new information would not, perhaps, surprise a devotee of the old verbal learning tradition. In list-learning experiments what was known as 'learning to learn' took place where, as subjects were tested on a series of similar lists, they improved their performance for several of the lists. On the other hand, a central tenet of most of the list-learning research was the importance of interference from similar material. Underwood (1957), for example, demonstrated that the more similar lists a person had learned the quicker that information was lost. This was ascribed to problems with similar information in memory interfering with the items to be remembered. It is important to show that the memorising of new information by experts is not simply improved initially but lost rapidly as would be expected from interference theorists. I was able to show this in a recent experiment carried out with Leslie Edkins. In this experiment subjects with high and low knowledge of soccer studied a list of football scores allegedly coming from the same week ten years earlier. This was chosen to avoid the prob-lems using simulated scores mentioned above. That is, we hoped to 'switch in' the knowledge and interest of the soccer 'experts'. In fact, the fixtures were real but the scores were fictitious and immediately after the presentation of the lists the subjects were informed of this fact. The purpose of this design was to avoid the experts spending more time in the intervening period before test discussing and thinking about the scores. After either twenty minutes or three days recall of the lists was tested. After both time intervals recall was better for the more knowledgeable subjects and there was no sign of an interaction over time. Both groups showed similar declines in the amount recalled. There was therefore no evidence that the better acquisition of information by the knowledgeable subjects was counterbalanced by any more rapid forgetting. Interference theory clearly does not apply to meaningful, interesting material that clicks nicely into a rich, well-developed schema.

Theoretical issues in the nature of the memory representation

The study of memory in everyday life raises many theoretical questions, among the most important of which is the way in which memories are encoded so that they can be retrieved later at an appropriate time. The traditional view that memory is based upon associations has been extended and formalised by cognitive scientists who have developed network models of memory representations that can be simulated on computers. Best developed of these network models is Anderson's ACT theory (e.g. Anderson, 1976, 1983, 1984). Network models, such as ACT, assume that when a new item of information is acquired it is attached appropriately to already existing information so that an interconnected knowledge base is developed which can be explored by activation spreading through the network when information is required. In Anderson's model the information is stored as productions, that is, as condition-action rules which allow for a particular action to take place if the conditions specified by the rule are fulfilled.

Anderson's production system distinguishes between two sorts of memory; declarative memory and procedural memory. Declarative memory is memory for facts while procedural memory involves specifications of what to do. This distinction between what Ryle (1949) called knowing that and knowing how (e.g. that something is a bicycle versus how to ride it) is a widely accepted distinction between the types of information stored in memory. It is worth, however, noting that computer simulations of such knowledge involve similar representations of the production rules themselves: differences occur mainly in the acquisition of the rules and in their execution. Beyond the procedural/declarative distinction there has been more discussion around the possible distinction between episodic and semantic memories. Episodic memories are those for particular personal events while semantic memories store factual knowledge unconnected to the original events which led to the acquisition of the information. Tulving (1983, 1984) has argued that while episodic and semantic memories are interrelated they are sufficiently distinct to justify incorporating separate episodic and semantic memories into models of memory. Prototypical examples of episodic and semantic memories certainly appear very different and can be imagined as serving different functions. An easily accessible semantic memory seems essential for, for example, language comprehension. The reason for the evolution of our ability to remember with considerable detail, often via mental images and re-experienced emotions, events that happened to us in the past is less obvious. Such memories may help in the planning and decision-making that comes with the complex potential for different actions available to human beings. Episodic memory may be a late addition in the evolution of the human species. However, it has been by no means obvious to theorists of memory that the episodic/semantic distinction requires incorporating into their models. Anderson, for example, does not specifically distinguish between the types of memory in his models but it is assumed that differences in the associative network and the types and richness of the associations involved distinguish between memories normally classified as episodic or semantic. Episodic entries retain information about the time and place of their occurrence while semantic information is obtained from nodes in the network where many past experiences have accumulated a large number of associations which specify the meaning of the concepts involved.

In addition to episodic and semantic memory it may be necessary to propose a prospective memory where intentions to act are stored. How our actions are planned and ordered is still relatively poorly understood. However, control systems clearly exist and must be serviced by memory resources. Considerable work needs to be done in unravelling the sort of information that would be required to efficiently serve the many functions of memory. If the cognitive system is composed of many separate but interacting modules (e.g. Fodor, 1983), the form in which the information is stored for use by these modules may differ considerably. For example, the form in which information is stored and used for face recognition may differ considerably from the way it is used for language comprehension and be different again from that used in planning our actions.

Much work remains to be done on the development of and interrelationship between the several types of memory that have been postulated. Do semantic memories develop from the reorganisation of a set of episodic memories or are the processes independent? How are schema developed and what is their relationship to the semantic networks?

The problem in the design and use of any information storage system with a very large capacity such as the human memory is to encode information when it is acquired in such a way that it can be retrieved on the appropriate occasion in the future and to ensure that similar but unwanted information is not also retrieved to confuse or block processing. At some point in the future detailed theories of the process of retrieval must be developed because, while retrieval is the fundamental function of memory, few models of memory have discussed it in sufficient detail to provide a model that could adequately simulate the impressive performance of the human memory system.

Issues arising from the study of everyday memory

Few people will doubt that the study of memory has become much more interesting in recent years. However, the Ebbinghaus tradition had much good sense behind it. How does one develop an adequate theory of memory without experimental control to identify the important variables? It would, I think, be quite wrong to draw as a lesson from the fate of the Ebbinghaus tradition that laboratory research on memory is misguided. On the contrary, I would suggest that we should make every effort possible, to obtain similar degrees of control for the aspects of memory that we study. The problem with the Ebbinghaus tradition was not that memory was studied in the laboratory but that the particular choice of elements to control meant that the type of memorising that took place in the experiments was unrealistic and brought with it none of the features of the real world. As I suggested at the beginning I think that we need a sketch map, a natural history, of when and how memory is used to help us identify important topics. Having done so, however, we need as much experimental control as possible. While modern developments in statistical techniques and in computing have meant that analyses such as multiple regression which were technically beyond the means of many psychologists up to the 1960s are now possible even for undergraduate projects, it still remains necessary whenever possible to undertake experimental control. What we need, therefore, is to bring into the laboratory the very aspects of memory which we wish to study. We need, also, to check that we have got them there once we have brought them in! The Morris *et al.* (1985) study using simulated football scores is a salutary reminder that although one may simulate the real world so that it appears identical in the laboratory we may, if we fail to capture the essential elements, end up studying the wrong thing. We need to continually check that we do really have the important memory skills activated in our laboratory tasks. One means to do this is to use the technique employed in the Morris *et al.* (1985) study. If in one's research one employs a real-world task and a laboratory task that is meant to capture the real world's components, and if the same individuals take part in the experiment then one may check by looking at the individual differences in the two experiments whether the same skill appears to be captured. If one finds that there is little or no correlation in the performance of the subjects in the real-world task and the simulation then it is time to think again about the quality of the simulation. In retrospect, it is surprising how few attempts have been made to check the validity of many psychological experiments developed in the laboratory.

One result of the recognition that what we remember depends very much upon the particular task we are undertaking will be, I think, that memory will be studied much more as a component in particular cognitive processing. Memory is, after all, a resource, a vital helper but not the central character in the cognitive world. It is the act of comprehension and the control of our actions that are central. Ironically, the study of memory may be held up for a while since many of the areas of psychology such as perception, decision-making and planned actions are all still frequently studied in artificial situations which may, as in the case of memory, bear little resemblance to the processing that takes place in everyday life.

Finally, it would be wrong to end a chapter which has been so critical of much early memory research by not pointing out that many useful concepts may be salvaged from the earlier work. We will need many new theories, but, as Baddeley and Wilkins (1984) have pointed out, many of the theoretical concepts from the earlier research may well be relevant to what we now recognise to be more appropriate topics for research on memory. However, which of the theoretical concepts are appropriate and which are not must be tested under the experimental paradigms based upon the use of memory in everyday life.

My conclusion, then, refers back to my initial quotation from Sherlock Holmes. It is a capital mistake to theorise before you have all the evidence, or at least enough evidence, to be sure that your theories are taking you in the right direction. For too long we were unwilling to ask fundamental questions, such as What is our memory for? Things have changed and many new research themes have been the result. However, there remains the danger that each of these themes will develop a life of its own and drift away from the development of general knowledge about memory. We still have a great deal to learn about how we can structure our knowledge of memory and how we can at the same time capture the fundamental memory processes and experimentally control misleading variables. Nevertheless, psychologists are now starting to make statements about memory which people outside the subject recognise as important and valuable for them. For example, there is collaboration between psychologists and the police and psychologists are advising the nuclear industry on ways of improving the memory of its operators. In the prevailing atmosphere where scientists are being asked to justify the expenditure on their research it is fortunate that we are at last, if belatedly, starting to generate findings which have an obvious interest and potential benefit to others than academic psychologists. In the study of memory there are many new directions opening up.

References

Anderson, J. R. (1976), *Language, Memory and Thought*. Erlbaum: Hillsdale, NJ.

Anderson, J. R. (1983), *The Architecture of Cognition*. Harvard University Press: Cambridge, Mass.

Anderson, J. R. (1984), 'Spreading activation', in J. R. Anderson and S. M. Kosslyn (eds) *Tutorials in Learning and Memory*. W. H. Freeman: San Francisco.

Baddeley, A. D. (1976), *The Psychology of Memory*. Basic Books: New York.

Baddeley, A. D. (1983), 'Working memory', *Philosophical Transactions of the Royal Society, Series B*. 302, 311–24.

[. . .]

Baddeley, A. D. and Wilkins, A. (1984), 'Taking memory out of the laboratory', in J. E. Harris and P. E. Morris (eds), *Everyday Memory, Actions and Absentmindedness*. Academic Press: New York.

Bahrick, H. P. (1984a), 'Memory for people', in J. E. Harris and P. E. Morris (eds), *Everyday Memory, Actions and Absentmindedness*. Academic Press: New York.

Bahrick, H. P. (1984b), 'Semantic memory content in permastore: fifty years of memory for Spanish learned at school', *Journal of Experimental Psychology: General*, 113, 1–29.

Bartlett, F. C. (1932), *Remembering: A Study in Experimental and Social Psychology*. Cambridge University Press: Cambridge.

Bartram, D. and Smith, P. (1984), 'Everyday memory for everyday places', in J. E. Harris and P. E. Morris (eds), *Everyday Memory, Actions and Absentmindedness*. Academic Press: New York.

Battig, W. F. (1979), 'The flexibility of memory', in L. S. Cermak and F. I. M. Craik (eds), *Levels of Processing in Human Memory*. Erlbaum: Hillsdale, NJ.

Bekerian, D. A. and Baddeley, A. D. (1980), 'Saturation advertising and the repetition effect', *Journal of Verbal Learning and Verbal Behaviour*, 19, 17–25.

Bekerian, D. A. and Bowers, J. M. (1983), 'Eyewitness testimony: were we misled?' *Journal of Experimental Psychology: Learning and Cognition*, 9, 139–45.

Bower, G. H. (1983), 'Affect and cognition', *Philosophical Transactions of the Royal Society of London, Series B*, 302, 387–402.

Bowers, J. M. and Bekerian, D. A. (1984), 'When will post-event information distort eyewitness testimony?' *Journal of Applied Psychology*, 69, 466–72.

Cattell, J. M. (1895), 'Measurements of the accuracy of recollection', *Science*, 2, 761–6.

Colegrove, F. W. (1899), 'Individual memories', *American Journal of Psychology*, 10, 228–55.

Coughlan, A. K. and Hollows, S. E. (1986), *The Adult Memory and Information Processing Battery (AMIPB)*. A. K. Coughlan: Leeds.

Doyle, A. C. (1887), *A Study in Scarlet*. Ward Lock: London.

Ebbinghaus, H. (1885), *Uber das Gedachtris*. Dunker: Leipzig. (Trans. H. Ruyer and C. E. Bussenius, *Memory*. Teachers College Press: New York, 1913.)

Fodor, J. A. (1983), *The Modularity of Mind: An Essay on Faculty Psychology*. MIT Press: Cambridge, Mass.

Harris, J. E. (1980), 'Memory aids people use: two interview studies', *Memory and Cognition*, 8, 31–8.

Harris, J. E. (1984), 'Remembering to do things: a forgotten topic', in J. E. Harris and P. E. Morris (eds), *Everyday Memory, Actions and Absentmindedness*. Academic Press: New York.

Herrmann, D. J. (1984), 'Questionnaires about memory', in J. E. Harris and P. E. Morris (eds), *Everyday Memory, Actions and Absentmindedness*. Academic Press: New York.

Hunter, I. M. L. (1985), 'Lengthy verbatim recall: the role of text', in A. W. Ellis (ed.), *Progress in the Psychology of Language*, Vol. 1. Erlbaum: London.

Loftus, E. F. and Loftus, G. R. (1980), 'On the permanence of stored information in the human brain', *American Psychologist*, 35, 409–20.

Malpass, R. S. and Devine, P. G. (1981), 'Guided memory in eyewitness identification', *Journal of Applied Psychology*, 66, 343–50.

Morris, P. E. (1979), 'Strategies for learning and recall', in M. M. Gruneberg and P. E. Morris (eds), *Applied Problems in Memory*. Academic Press: London.

Morris, P. E. (1984), 'The validity of subjective reports on memory', in J. E. Harris and P. E. Morris (eds), *Everyday Memory, Actions and Absentmindedness*. Academic Press: New York.

Morris, P. E., Gruneberg, M. M., Sykes, R. N. and Merrick, A. (1981), 'Football knowledge and the acquisition of new results', *British Journal of Psychology*, 72, 479–83.

Morris, V. (1983), *Factors influencing the accuracy of witness reports*. Ph.D. thesis, University of Lancaster.

Morris, V. and Morris, P. E. (1985), 'The influence of question order on eyewitness accuracy', *British Journal of Psychology*, 76, 365–71.

Morris, P. E., Tweedy, M. and Gruneberg, M. M. (1985), 'Interest, knowledge and the memorizing of soccer scores', *British Journal of Psychology*, 76, 415–25.

Neisser, U. (1978), 'Memory: What are the important questions?' in M. M. Gruneberg, P. E. Morris and R. N. Sykes (eds), *Practical Aspects of Memory*. Academic Press: London.

Neisser, U. (1981), 'John Dean's memory: A case study', *Cognition*, 9, 1–22.

Neisser, U. (1982), *Memory Observed*. W. H. Freeman: San Francisco.

Nickerson, R. S. and Adams, M. J. (1979), 'Long-term memory for a common object', *Cognitive Psychology*, 11, 287–307.

Postman, L. and Keppel, G. (eds) (1969), *Verbal Learning and Memory*. Penguin: Harmondsworth.

Reason, J. T. (1984), 'Absentmindedness and cognitive control', in J. E. Harris and P. E. Morris (eds), *Everyday Memory, Actions and Absentmindedness*. Academic Press: New York.

Reason, J. T. and Embrey, D. E. (1985), *Human factors principles relevant to the modelling of human errors in abnormal conditions of nuclear and major hazardous installations*. Report prepared for the European Atomic Energy Community. Human Reliability Associates: Parbold, Lancs.

Reason, J. T. and Lucas, D. (1984), 'Using cognitive diaries to investigate naturally occurring memory blocks', in J. E. Harris and P. E. Morris (eds), *Everyday Memory, Actions and Absentmindedness*. Academic Press: New York.

Reason, J. T. and Mycielska, K. (1982), *Absentminded? The Psychology of Mental Lapses and Everyday Errors*. Prentice-Hall: Englewood-Cliffs, NJ.

Rubin, D. (ed.) (1986), *Autobiographical Memory*. Cambridge University Press: New York.

Ryle, G. (1949), *The Concept of Mind*. Hutchinson: London.

Schank, R. C. (1982), *Dynamic Memory*. Cambridge University Press: Cambridge.

Smyth, M., Morris, P. E., Ellis, A. W. and Levy, P. (1987), *Cognition in Action*. Erlbaum: Hillsdale, NJ.

Stern, W. (1904), 'Wirklichkeitsversuche', *Beitrage zur Psychologie der Aussage*, 2, 1–31. (Trans. U. Neisser, 'Realistic experiments', in U. Neisser (ed.) (1982), *Memory Observed*. W. H. Freeman: San Francisco.)

Tulving, E. (1983), *Elements of Episodic Memory*. Oxford University Press: Oxford.

Tulving, E. (1984), Précis of 'Elements of episodic memory', *The Behavioral and Brain Sciences*, 7, 223–68.

Underwood, B. J. (1957), 'Interference and forgetting', *Psychological Review*, 64, 49–60.

Underwood, B. J., Boruch, R. F. and Malmi, R. (1978), 'Composition of episodic memory', *Journal of Experimental Psychology: General*, 107, 393–419.

Wells, G. L. and Loftus, E. F. (eds) (1984), *Eyewitness Testimony: Psychological Perspectives*. Cambridge University Press: Cambridge.

Wilkins, A. J. and Baddeley, A. D. (1978), 'Remembering to recall in everyday life: an approach to absentmindedness', in M. M. Gruneberg, P. E. Morris and R. N. Sykes (eds), *Practical Aspects of Memory*. Academic Press: London.

CHAPTER 12

CONVERSATIONAL REMEMBERING
A social psychological approach

David Middleton and Derek Edwards

D. Middleton and D. Edwards (eds) *Collective Remembering*, London, Sage, 1990

Relations between discourse and memory

In cognitive psychology, the relationship between discourse and memory is generally seen as an issue of knowledge representation. The aim is to specify what we know about the world, which includes both how to hold a conversation, and also a mental representation of the world that conversations might be 'about'. This latter component would have to include both the general principles by which the world works, and also some sort of memory for particular events, an updatable record that can be drawn upon in talk and comprehension. In our work on conversational remembering, we have been concerned with similar sorts of issues, of how understandings are expressed in talk, but approached in a quite different manner. Rather than looking at how conversational competence is represented cognitively, we are interested in how cognition is represented in ordinary conversations. As far as memory is concerned, the aim is not to specify how putative mental models might represent knowledge and experience, but rather with how people represent their past, how they construct versions of events when talking about them.

This change of perspective has the effect of changing our theoretical concerns. We become sensitive to the pragmatics of communication, to the communicative uses to which people put their representations of experience. People present accounts of past events for all sorts of reasons, amongst which, as Bartlett noted, a concern for accurate and dispassionate accuracy is rather rare. Indeed, from the perspective of communicative pragmatics, dispassionately accurate reporting is merely one of a variety of actions to which talk might be orientated, or even, one of a variety of contentious claims, or positions, which a speaker might adopt with regard to an account. Once we are removed from the confines of some very special and formalized social occasions, such as courtroom testimony and experimental studies of memory, we find that many of the well known psychological distortions of recall, the importation of inferences, schema effects and so on (Bartlett, 1932; Bransford and McCarrell, 1974) come into their own as functional and contextually sensible aspects of ordinary conversation.

It is not only that conversation affords examination of the micro-processes of collective remembering, as these unfold with talk. Larger, societal themes are also available for examination, including historical, ideological and political ones (Billig *et al.*, 1988; [. . .]), educational curricula and modes of thought (Edwards and Mercer,

1987), 'authenticity' in folk traditions and dilemmas of the work-place (Middleton, 1987; 1988). It is a feature of conversation that these themes are not merely available in the discourse for the analyst to discover, available like pebbles on a beach, to be picked up and examined, but rather, are worked on by the participants themselves. In doing education, or reconstructing a Morris dance, or remembering with one's children how they behaved on holiday, or jointly remembering the details of a problematic case as a member of a multi-professional team in the British National Health Service, cultural and ideological themes (even though they may not be named as such) are worked up, illustrated, used and commemorated by participants as part of the pragmatics of speaking.

We began our empirical study of conversational remembering in the time-honoured tradition of psychological research, with a group of undergraduates. We had been conducting a series of practical classes with them, which included Bartlett's serial-reproduction studies (Bartlett, 1932). We had been thinking for some time about the neglected social-cultural dimension of Bartlett's work as represented in his discussions of 'conventionalization' (Crook and Middleton, 1989; Edwards and Middleton, 1987), while also developing an interest in conversation and the analysis of discourse. It seemed to us that the method of serial reproduction was not really social *enough*. In Bartlett's studies, the output from each participant is passed on as the input to the next person in line. This has the methodological advantage of enabling the analyst to study the relationship between input and output, to note the discrepancies and to use these discrepancies as the basis for inferring things about the mental processes or representations that must have intervened – in other words, about the workings of memory.

This methodological advantage is, however, bought at a price. The direction of social influence is all one way, cut and dried, non-interactive. There are no conversations: the 'subjects' have no opportunity to engage with each other communicatively. It occurred to us that, however messy the data might get, there might be an advantage in allowing participants to talk to each other, and to create together, a joint version of remembered events. This might get us closer to the social creation of memory, which Bartlett himself sought. And in any case, unlike Bartlett, we had at our disposal tape-recorders, transcription units and a background of theoretical developments in the analysis of real conversations that the invention of tape-recorders has made possible (linguistic pragmatics, discourse analysis, conversation analysis: for succinct accounts of such developments, see Atkinson and Heritage, 1984; Brown and Yule, 1983; Heritage, 1984; Levinson, 1983; Potter and Wetherell, 1987).

Our procedure was to ask a section of the class to recall together something that they had recently witnessed, and that we would be able, if necessary, to examine independently. They recalled together, in recorded conversation, the feature film *E.T.* Extract 1 is a brief sample of the 35-minute conversation that followed. (Simultaneous speech is bracketed where it begins. & indicates speaker continues speaking. The full account is in Edwards and Middleton, 1986a.)

Extract 1: *Joint recall*

Karen:	well he goes to the fridge to get something to eat first doesn't he with the dog following him
Diane:	yeh that's it
Karen:	mm
Diane:	and he finds him feeding the dog

John:	and then and then he finds the beer
Diane:	and then he finds the beer and what is it there's a link between Elliot and E.T. &
Karen:	Elliott's at school
John:	telepathic link
Diane:	& that whatever happens to E.T. Elliott feels the same effects and E.T. got paralytic [*laughs*] and so E.T. is sort of going
Lesley:	all a bit drunk
Tina:	that's right I remember
Karen:	Elliott is sitting at his school desk and they are doing experiments with frogs are they
Diane:	and he lets all the frogs out
[*General hubbub of agreement*]
Tina:	sets all the frogs out yeh
Lesley:	and what's that little girl that he fancies
John:	it's when he's watching E.T.'s watching television and John Wayne kisses the heroine in the film
Diane:	oh so Elliott kisses her
John:	and then Elliott kisses the little girl

The immediate impression is of a well practised activity which the participants could perform with ease and spontaneity. It was obvious that we were tapping into a familiar discursive practice, in which remembering is done jointly. The participants were skilled at pooling their accounts, dealing with issues of intersubjectivity, with the extent to which versions were jointly held, or disputed, or could be made joint through persuasion and agreement. Specific linguistic devices were identifiable, such as *tags* that signal or invite ratification (doesn't he); *overt agreements* (yeh that's it; that's right I remember); the operation of a *default continuity*, such that each successive contribution was taken to build upon the last as part of the construction of a sequential narrative; the *ratification* through repetition of previous speakers' contributions (and then he finds the beer; sets all the frogs out); *overt requests* for assistance in the joint task (and what's that little girl that he fancies); as well as *metacognitive formulations* of the process of remembering itself (that's right I remember). We shall begin by taking up three of the themes from Extract 1 for further analysis: the nature of context considered as collective memory and understanding; metacognitive formulations (talk about mental processes); and the use of inference and argument in the construction of joint versions of events.

Context as shared understanding

As any conversation proceeds, it does so on the basis of a continuously updated but contentious understanding of what has been said so far, what is understood, what is yet to be resolved. We have argued (Edwards and Mercer, 1987) that this 'context' has to be seen as intersubjective for the participants, rather than existing for the analyst in an objective record, such as in the back pages of a transcript, or in the surrounding circumstances of the speech event. Speakers can only act upon what they understand and remember, and it is a concern to which they address themselves, just what that 'context' at any time should be. Part of this shared context for speaking is a continuously reworked collective memory. In Extract 1, therefore, the joint account proceeds from event to event, each successively marked out and encapsulated in words, each added to the last by a default continuity such that order of mention corresponds to order of event, and each taken by default as jointly held, until some disagreement forces a reformulation, a relocation and a restart (see Edwards and Middleton, 1986a).

In Extract 2 (from Edwards and Mercer, 1989), we have a more institutionalized version of the process, in which a teacher is establishing with her pupils a shared representation of what they have done, and what they will therefore do next. She had earlier got them to suggest some hypotheses about which washing powders might work best, and they were about to put these notions to an empirical test. The teacher's privileged position as arbiter of a legitimate collective account contrasts with the student peer group recalling *E.T.* (Slashes denote pauses; bracketed dots denote undeciphered or omitted talk.)

Extract 2: *Context and collectivity in school*

T: now the other day we were talking about which washing powder was going to wash best and when we began talking about it you gave me some positive firm answers/ [*To Tom*] what made you say what you did say?

Tom: well// we used a popular television things

T: yes erm// well you were thinking about the ones that were advertised on television/ yes/ what did you say first of all? which washing powder did you think was going to wash best?

Tom: Persil

T: [*To Ellie*] what did you think?

Ellie: Persil

T: Persil somebody said Daz/ who was that? [. . .] and you were thinking *then* about what your mothers said.

Pupils: yeh

T: and what your mothers used

Pupils: yeh

T: weren't you? [. . .] then we went on and we looked at what the manufacturers said on the packets about their products and you then thought that which washing powder was going to wash ⎡ best?

Mary: ⎣ Ariel

T: Ariel and what made ⎡ you say that Ariel

Mary: [*interrupting*]   ⎣ it digests dirt and stains [. . .]

T: yes it digests dirt and stains [. . .] [*Turning towards the washing equipment that is laid out on a table*] now when you're staining your fabrics you've got your stains out here// how much stain are you going to use?

Ellie: two blobs// two blobs of five on the cloth.

T: you're going to make two separate areas of five drops not squirts and then [. . .]

The teacher's method is one of elicitation. She builds up a shared account of what everyone has agreed to do, organizing the pupils turns at speaking, so that each child's turn was accorded its position and significance in a teacher-generated list of items. What the pupils omit, she provides, or prompts them to provide. Pupils' contributions are further reworked in the teacher's responses, such that the various washing powders were ones advertised on television, and that the plan was to make 'two separate areas of five drops not squirts'. Each of these reformulations was pedagogically significant. The hypotheses to be tested were derived not merely from the appearance of the products on television, but from advertisers' claims that theirs was best. The point about five separate blobs related to the experimental necessity for controlling for amounts of powder used, so that any observed differences might be attributable to the substances themselves. Clearly, the collective account was driven not only by the teacher's privileged social position, her control of turns at talk, but also from her privileged position in relation to the knowledge at issue. The creation of a collective account served as a medium for the pedagogic socialization of scientific thought and practice. Similarly, in other lessons we observed and video-recorded (Edwards and Mercer, 1987; 1989), teachers routinely made use of lesson summaries to reconstruct what had supposedly happened previously. Through these 'reconstructive recaps', messy findings became neat and orderly, the significance of classroom events became routinely formalized in memorable phrases, errors of scientific method were tidied up and teacher and pupils would collude in the elicited creation of a joint version of what had been discovered, and what it all meant.

Discursive metacognition

We discovered in the *E.T.* study, as elsewhere (Edwards and Goodwin, 1985; Edwards and Mercer, 1987; Edwards and Middleton, 1988; Middleton, 1987; 1988), how metacognitive formulations, rather than occurring merely as reflective understandings or observations that people are able to make about the nature of their mental processes (Flavell and Wellman, 1977), arose in an occasioned manner in particular sorts of discursive contexts. They generally occurred at points where the activity of remembering ran into trouble or difficulty, and especially, at moments when one person's account provoked sudden recognition, or disputation, from another person. There seemed in these data to be evidence of a social-discursive basis for metacognition itself, of the sort hypothesized by various theorists (Mead, 1934; Piaget, 1928), such that the very notion of mind, of mental life, of memory and experience as objects of reflective awareness, is given shape and occasion by discursive practices in which versions are being compared, conjoined and disputed. Indeed, it is possible to suggest a developmental process on the basis of this pattern. The awareness of having and using a 'memory', and the awareness of its properties, may well arise as a matter of difficulty – as a matter of *not* being able to remember something, of being suddenly reminded, of having something on the tip of your tongue, of trying to remember and of trying to square an offered version of events with what another speaker says.

In conversational remembering, therefore, the talk is revealed as more than just a window upon mental processes and metacognitive conceptions. Conversations emerge as a significant *environment* in which such thoughts are formulated, justified and socialized according to how other speakers talk about mental processes. In this sense, we should write not of metacognitive 'awareness', as if it were merely a matter of becoming conscious of the real nature of pre-existing mental processes, but rather, of metacognitive construction – acquiring a conventional vocabulary and discourse for mental life, which is designed to serve the social pragmatics of conversation. Metacognition can be analysed as the development of a culturally shared discourse for making claims about mental processes (cf. anthropological and social constructionist studies, such as Gergen, 1985; Harré, 1983; Heelas and Lock, 1981), for arguing, justifying, accounting to other people for what we claim to know. We shall consider some recorded conversations with children in a later section.

Inference and argument in collective remembering

In experimental studies of memory, much of the interesting stuff of cognition is not visible in the data, but has to be theorized to make sense of the observed discrepancies between input and output. The existence and operation of mental 'schemata', 'scripts', 'models', 'scenarios', 'story grammars' and the related processes of plausible inference through which what people recall is not the same as what they experienced; all have to be inferred by the analyst on the basis of such discrepancies. One of the appealing features of studying conversational remembering is that we often find these processes of sense-making expressed overtly in the talk. When people remember things together, seeking to compare and contrast different accounts, to construct and defend plausible versions or to criticize or doubt their accuracy, they articulate the grounds and criteria for what is remembered. Inferential links are made overtly; plausibility is directly invoked. Furthermore, the articulation of these things occurs in a context that lends them additional significance – the context of communicative pragmatics. That is to say, the criteria for remembering are seen to be contingent upon the action to which the talk is orientated; they are occasioned by the developing context and purposes of conversation. This can be seen clearly in Extract 3 (from Edwards and Middleton, 1986a).

Extract 3: *Inference and argument*

Diane: it's very confusing 'cause there's not really a basic story it's all just the
        fact ⌈ that
Lesley: ⌊ little things that
        ⌈ happen
Diane: ⌊ yeh little things that happen that don't really make that much like er
        they met he met the other children
[. . .]
John: he's trying to explain first of all where he is from do you remember
Diane: yeh he's
Karen: that's after he has met all the ⌈ children because &
John: ⌊ 'cause he says Eli-i-ott like this
Karen: & all the children were there
[. . .]
Diane: so he meets the older boy um because doesn't he bring him in and says
        you know what I told you because before he'd been telling everybody
        that ⌈ he'd &
John: ⌊ that's right
Paul: ⌊ yeh
Diane: & got some sort of monster or whatever
[. . .]
Diane: she dressed him up
Karen: that's right
Diane: 'cause he looks so funny

At the start of Extract 3, the participants were experiencing some difficulty in establishing the precise order of events. Diane and Lesley duly switch to metacognitive mode, and agree that the difficulty resides in the input, the film itself – it lacked something that would normally make sequential remembering easier – 'a basic story'. In the other parts of the extract, the point to note is the speakers' use of the logical operators *so*, and *because* ('cause). For instance, Karen points out that the incident in question has to be placed after *E.T.*'s meeting with the other children, because all the children were now present. This is a recognizable connecting inference, of the sort that psychologists are accustomed to through the work of Bartlett (1932), Bransford (1979) and others. However, this and the other uses of *because*, John's and Diane's, do not merely link events together. In fact, John's and Diane's uses signal no logical connection at all. They appear to be addressed to the developing consensus itself – meaning, not 'this happened because that happened', but 'this version should be accepted by everybody because . . .'. They are used to introduce reminders, particularly memorable images, that can serve as familiar benchmarks for the placing of the more disputable items. John's '(be)cause' follows his 'do you remember' – it argues for why everyone should accept his version of events – a communicative-pragmatic argument, rather than that some events must logically have followed others.

Thus, we find in these data not only inferences that link events to those already established, but also a rhetorical, argumentative basis for the process. Inferences are sensitive to social considerations, framed so as to dispute or forestall alternative accounts, in favour of the one that is being offered. Remembering events is the production of versions of events, which are acceptable in so far as they succeed over other possible, foreseen or actual versions. Again, it is a temptation too strong for us to resist, to ponder the cognitive and developmental implications of this. It again suggests the plausibility of a dialogical basis for human thought (cf. Vygotsky, 1978; 1987; Wertsch, 1985), and specifically, for an origin of self-conscious, metacognitive, and rationalized remembering, from within communicative pragmatics – from within children's conversations and arguments.

Discursive frames

There was, in fact, a rather gross communicative-pragmatic effect at work in these data, but nevertheless, one that is consistently ignored in psychological studies of remembering – namely, the effect of our experimental instructions, or the communicative context generally, in promoting a specific sort of remembering – a particular communicative frame within which everything would be recalled. The participants in our study took it as their task that they should proceed to reconstruct, point by point, in proper sequence, the narrative order of events. Many of the key characteristics of what they recalled, in which order and by which principles of organization, were dictated by this narrative frame. But there were signs of another, alternative frame at work, especially at the end of the session, when, having reached the end of the narrative and of the task proper, the subjects spontaneously carried on reminiscing about what had obviously been a pleasant and interesting experience. We left the tape-recorder running. But now, instead of reconstructing the story in sequential order, they proceeded to dip into it at lots of different points, back and forth, recalling what were, for them, particularly poignant, or significant, 'bits'.

Extract 4: *Selective reminiscences: the good bits*

Diane: it was so sad
Lesley: that little boy was a very good actor
Diane: he was brilliant he really was
Tina: especially at the end when he [. . .]

Karen: he was quivering   ⌈ wasn't he
John: ⌊ how many didn't cry at it
Lesley: [*emphatically*] I didn't and I'm ⌈ proud of it too
                                 ⌊ [*General laughter*]
John: I cried
Karen: I cried most when ⌈ the flower came blooming back into life
Steve: ⌊ wipe my eyes/ [*sarcastically, amidst general laughter*]
             I wept tears
Diane: tell you what got me the bit when he didn't get on the space ship right at
             the beginning
             [. . .] the actual story line was really boring
                ⌈ wasn't it
Karen: | yeh
Lesley: ⌊ yeh dead boring
Tina: it was the effects that did it
[. . .]
Paul: it had some incredible little funny bits in it when he got
               ⌈ drunk and things like that
Lesley: ⌊ yeh
Paul: & but apart from that
Karen: I thought the best bit was when they found him lying there
Diane: yeh [*laughs, followed by general assent and laughter*]
Karen: the most realistic bit was that bit in the middle
Diane: yeh
Karen: when he was lying there he really looked
               ⌈ something that was dead
Diane: ⌊ oh that's right
Lesley: because they'd had such a panic of looking for him before hadn't they
Diane: yeh and it looked so realistic

It was a little disconcerting for us to hear the opinion, agreed explicitly in Extract 4 by three participants without any demurring from the others, that it was precisely these 'incredible little funny bits' that were especially memorable, while the actual story line, which had been so carefully reconstructed for our benefit, was in itself 'boring'. Not only that, but within this new discursive frame, lots of graphic descriptive details were introduced that had earlier been omitted from the narrative. The participants, having satisfied what they assumed to be the formalities of the task, clearly preferred to exchange reminiscences of what was best, worst, funny or incredible – memories based upon personal reactions and evaluations. But again, the data are not reducible merely to the expression of a set of individual reactions. Each reaction and evaluation was offered for general approval or disputation, as a candidate for social comparison, either for general acceptance as shared and ratified, or for marking out the offerer as distinctive. The group members operated with the notion that emotional reactions and evaluations were subject to the same sorts of social processes as simple versions of events. Participants expressed disagreement, agreement, sarcasm and embarrassment at each other's reactions, while generally orientating themselves to the creation of a consensus of evaluation. Diane's final few turns are remarkable in this respect; she was already agreeing with Karen that 'the most realistic bit was that bit in the middle' before she had heard which 'bit' Karen was referring to.

Text and talk

This point about the importance of the communicational setting, or discursive frame, for what is remembered is a general one that goes beyond the confines of the *E.T.* study. It pervades all kinds of communicative remembering, including many experimental designs for individual memory, in which we can take the subjects' performance as communicational – occasioned as a response to the experimenter's instructions. For example, it arose in another study we did with a class of students replicating Bartlett. Here, we were interested in the differences between oral and written communication. A great deal has been written by psychologists, anthropologists and historians about this difference, about the different formal and functional characteristics of speech and writing, and the profound effects upon human thought and intelligence of the invention of writing (for example, Goody, 1977; Havelock, 1976; Luria, 1976; Olson, 1980; Ong, 1971; Scribner and Cole, 1981). For written text, some theorists claim all sorts of wonderful and controversial cognitive effects, from the growth of scientific thought to the creation of logical reasoning. But one point that most writers agree about, is the importance of written text for having transformed how we store and use information – written records can be systematically kept, stored and consulted, doing away with the need always to rely upon verbatim recall. The relation to memory is intriguing. We have a picture in which written text lends itself to verbatim copying, storage and repeated consultation. And yet, when it comes to the experimental study of memory, subjects are invariably presented with small bits, or extracts of written materials, and asked to recall them. It was, in fact, partly the prospect of dealing with spoken language, rather than written text, that had encouraged us to look at conversational remembering. People generally have to rely upon memory for what was said, but can consult the originals for what is written.

We asked our experimental group to try remembering, conversationally, some stories that they had encountered in the practical class the week before (see Edwards and Middleton, 1986b). One member of the group had been absent that week, and was asked to act as a 'scribe', making a written record of the story that the rest of the group then proceeded to reconstruct, talking their way through it, as in the *E.T.* study. Extract 5 shows a brief sample of data from that study. On the left are sections of the recorded conversation, and on the right is what the scribe wrote.

Extract 5: *Text and talk*

	Talk	*Text*
1	'beautiful woman': 'messenger': 'serving wench': 'buxom wench': 'Chinese buxom wench': 'she had big tits'	Serving maid . . .
2	'. . . he meets the mistress who was the most beautiful intelligent . . .': 'what's happened to the purple wine . . . oh sorry purple wine and fornication . . . and he goes inside and they lie down on the couch well eventually chatting her up first they lie down on the couch and drink purple wine and fornicate'	. . . meets mistress. Beautiful and intelligent. Falls instantly in love. Goes in and they lie on couch, they drink purple wine and fornicate

3	'he goes back to the old noble-man's house'	Goes on to nobleman's house.
4	'he decides he quite likes the idea of purple wine and fornication'	Decides he wishes he was back with the woman
5	'. . . so he keeps on organizing, he keeps on talking about visiting his parents when he is going to the house in the forest'	Says he's going home but really goes back to woman in cottage.
6	'. . . in town shopping', 'in the market-place'	. . . in the market.

What interested us were the qualitative differences between the conversation and its written record. The written version was considerably shorter, but was also qualitatively different, tidied up, serialized into a single coherent narrative and contained several interesting transformations and additions to what was said, such as those listed in Extract 5. The rather bawdy conversation was even bowdlerized in the written version, with most of the overt sexual references omitted or rendered euphemistically. Some things are treated as easier to say than to write, and some things are considered more appropriate to written text than to speech. Text is generally 'for the record', more formal, more condensed. Obviously what interested us was that going from speech to writing, we found many of the same phenomena that Bartlett had attributed to the workings of memory – condensations, additions, transformations, the imposition of coherence and so on. But the scribe did not have to rely upon memory. She wrote as the others spoke, and got them to pause, slow down, repeat things and occasionally questioned the accuracy of what she was writing. It was Bartlett without remembering. The effects seemed to be at least partly due to the different communicative conventions of talk and text.

In fact, there is evidence of similar, text-convention effects at work in Bartlett's own data. Extract 6 is from his classic 'War of the Ghosts' study (Bartlett, 1932: 65, 121).

Extract 6: *The War of the Ghosts*

The original
One of the young men said: 'I have no arrows.' 'Arrows are in the canoe,' they said. 'I will not go along. I might be killed. My relatives do not know where I have gone. But you,' he said, turning to the other, 'may go with them.' So one of the young men went, but the other returned home.

Reproduction 2
'No,' they replied, 'we cannot fight, for we have no arrows.' 'There are arrows in the canoe, so come and tarry not.' 'Nay,' replied one of the Indians, 'I shall not come, for if I am killed, my people, who have need of me, will be sore grieved.' Then, turning to his companion, he went on: 'You go. You have no friends, and if aught befall you will not be missed.' 'Aye, go I will,' answered his friend, and bidding him adieu, he joined the men in the canoe; and the other went back home.

The second, reproduced version has clearly acquired embellishments of the sort that Bartlett himself, and subsequent cognitive psychology, has discovered: inferential links that fill in the gaps of narrative coherence, such as the notion that the

Indian who 'went' was his companion's 'friend', and actually got into the canoe, and said goodbye to his companion, and the implication is also spelled out explicitly, that the possession of arrows bears upon whether the two men should go and fight. But in addition to these inferential links, other aspects of the transformation are essentially *literary*. It is imbued with the stylistic conventions of English and Scottish folk songs and tales (bidding adieu, tarrying not, being sore grieved, saying 'aye' and 'nay', and so on). Bartlett's subject was obviously not merely remembering the story. He was *rewriting* it, such that the nature of the remembering was significantly a function of the style of the discourse which constituted it.

Discourse analysis and versions of events

Wertsch (1987) points out that conventional differences in versions of remembered events extend not only to speech and writing, but also to different sorts of written texts, such as police records versus newspaper reports. Indeed, this is a general point that any pragmatic approach to the construction of versions has to recognize; accounts are always designed to accomplish particular pragmatic actions, and will vary accordingly. This means that versions of events cannot be taken merely as windows upon individuals' mental representations, but have to be studied in their social, conversational context. Wertsch's perspective derives from the socio-historical tradition of Soviet development psychology, which originated with Vygotsky (LCHC, 1983; Vygotsky, 1987; Wertsch, 1985). The emphasis is upon the socio-historical construction of mind, a process in which cultural signs (including language) function as mediators of human social activity, and are the major origin of intelligent thought. Language is instrumental; signs are 'mental tools' that work, that mediate understanding of the past in action in the present (cf. Middleton, 1987).

It is not a far cry from this notion of the representational instrumentality of language to seeing versions of events as pragmatically variable accomplishments. Recent sociological and social-psychological developments in discourse analysis (Gilbert and Mulkay, 1984; Potter and Wetherell, 1987) offer an approach to text and conversation in which versions (of events, of persons, of scientific discoveries or whatever) are shown to be not only pragmatically occasioned, but also intrinsically structured and organized to accomplish particular sorts of pragmatic actions. We can illustrate this approach to the investigation of remembering with some recent work by Edwards and Potter (1989).

This study begins with a detailed examination of Ulric Neisser's (1981) classic paper on John Dean's testimony to the Senate Watergate committee. Through a close comparison of Dean's testimony with Nixon's subsequently published 'presidential transcripts' of tape-recorded conversations in the Oval Office, Neisser had been impressed by the extent to which Dean failed to remember all sort of details, and even important elements of the gist of things, while nevertheless managing to convey an accurate impression of Nixon's involvement, at least in the 'cover-up'. In seeking to clarify what Dean actually remembered, Neisser proposes a threefold set of types of accuracy of recall. These are: (a) verbatim recall, (b) gist and (c) repisodic memory. Verbatim recall is word-for-word accuracy; gist is getting the essential features correct despite detailed omissions and errors; repisodic memory is at a still more general level, and consists in doing what Dean did, recalling the overall nature and implications of a repeated series of events, despite lots of gross errors of recall: 'there is usually a deeper level at which he is right. He gave an accurate portrayal of the real situation, of the actual characters and commitments of the people he knew, and of the events that lay behind the conversations he was trying to remember' (Neisser, 1981: 4).

In adopting a discourse-analytical approach (cf. Potter and Wetherell, 1987), Edwards and Potter (1989) argue that people's accounts of past events, before they can be taken as data on the cognitive workings of memory, need to be examined as contextualized and variable productions that do pragmatic and rhetorical work, such that no one version can be taken as a person's real memory. Indeed, what is offered and taken to be an adequate summary, the 'gist' of things, is itself studiable as a participant's accomplishment, a matter for disputation or agreement. Similarly, as we noted earlier, Edwards and Mercer (1987; 1989) have analysed the way that summaries of classroom lessons are used by teachers to reformulate messy and problematical events according to their originally planned outcomes – in effect, articulating classroom events in terms of what 'ought' to have happened. Dean's rememberings can be examined, therefore, in their conversational context, as versions that are designed for the context in which they occur, as warrants under cross-examination for Dean's own essential truthfulness, for his lack of involvement and personal responsibility in the criminal events at issue. Thus, it is part of Dean's account that he was blessed with a particularly good memory for detailed conversation. This was warranted in various ways, including both direct claims, and also the offering of graphic descriptions of place and circumstances:

> ... anyone who recalls my student years knew that I was very fast at recalling information ...
>
> (quoted in Neisser, 1981: 5)

> ... you know the way there are two chairs at the side of the President's desk ... on the left-hand chair Mr. Haldeman was sitting ...
>
> (p. 11)

> I can vividly recall that the way he sort of rolled his chair back from his desk and leaned over to Mr. Haldeman and said, 'A million dollars is no problem.'
>
> (p. 18)

These sorts of accounts served to bolster Dean's claim to an almost verbatim memory of conversations in the Oval Office.

Edwards and Potter (1989) proceed to analyse a series of newspaper accounts of a controversial press briefing given by the British Chancellor of the Exchequer, Nigel Lawson. Amongst the various devices and variances analysed is the sort of empiricist warranting (cf. Gilbert and Mulkay, 1984) of factuality of which Dean made use. Lawson had declared the initially published press accounts of the briefing to be 'a farrago of invention', 'inaccurate, half-baked' accounts which 'bear no relation whatever to what I said' (*Times*, *Guardian*, Tuesday 8 November 1988). The journalists concerned subsequently produced detailed narratives of the events, enriched with the sort of descriptive detail that made John Dean's rememberings so convincing:

> At one point I heard a click, and assumed the tape had run out. It was directly in front of me. When I looked to check, the spools were still spinning. The clicking I heard turned out to be Don Macintyre of the Sunday Telegraph, seated to my right, chewing a pen top.
>
> (*Sunday Mirror*, 13 November 1988)

It was noticeable that these sorts of descriptions occurred only after the issue of accuracy and fallibility of accounts had been raised, and indeed, as with Dean, after the competence and truthfulness of the rememberers had been called into question. Versions of events were constructed rhetorically, as parts of arguments (cf. Billig, 1987).

Conversations with children

We have been speculating about developmental implications – about how children might come to use metacognitive formulations of the workings of memory, how they are inculcated into educated discursive practices and understandings (cf. Walkerdine, 1988), and how they may be socialized in family conversations into ways of representing the past – how to talk about it, what sorts of things are memorable and why. In a further study (Edwards and Middleton, 1988), we collected a set of tape-recordings of family conversations, in which mothers, and sometimes fathers, recorded themselves with their young children – usually pairs of siblings aged between four and six – talking through their collections of family photographs.

Extract 7: *Learning remembering*

Mother: oh look/ there's when we went to the riding stables wasn't it?
Paul: yeh/ er er
Mother: you were trying to reach up and stroke that horse
Paul: where? [*laughs*]
Mother: would you like to do that again?
Paul: yeh
Mother: you don't look very happy though
Paul: because I thought I was going to fall off
Mother: you thought you was going to fall off did you?/ right misery/ daddy was holding on to you so that you didn't// did it FEEL very bumpy?
Paul: yeh
Mother: did it make your legs ache? [*Paul laughs*] Rebecca enjoyed it
Paul: yeh
Mother: she's a bit older wasn't she?/ you were a little boy there

Extract 7 (unpublished elsewhere) is a sample from one of these conversations. It contains many of the features that we have found interesting. Most of the work is being done by Paul's mother – she sets the scene, locating the picture in the context of the past events in which it was taken, a visit to the riding stables. She provides for Paul a description of what he is depicted as doing, and prompts him for an affective evaluation of the past that includes its relevance to the present and the future – 'would you like to do that again?' Paul's apparent unhappiness in the next picture is noted, and he is asked for, and provides an explanation ('I thought I was going to fall off'). Past events and emotional states are treated as essentially rational – they require explanations, motivational accounts for why they occur. Paul's mother recalls that he had been a 'right misery', enquires further about his feelings and reactions and points out that, in contrast, his elder sister had enjoyed herself. This in turn provides an occasion for some developmental comparisons – Rebecca was older, Paul was only a 'little boy' – the implication being that he can expect to react more favourably, like his sister, to future opportunities to go horse riding.

These conversations were used by parents as opportunities for marking past events as significant, recalling children's reactions and relationships, cuing the children to remember them, providing descriptions in terms of which those rememberings could be couched and providing all sorts of *contextual* reminiscences, prompted by the pictures, but of things and events not included within them. Children's identity and relationships change through time, and it is an important part of the developmental process that children come to see themselves as growing and changing, in specified, value-laden ways, within a culturally normative, moral world. This involves making sense of the past, of what one has been, and of the future, what one may become. Family photographs are a powerful mediator of such perspectives, especially when they are taken up in conversation with parents and siblings, and become the basis of comparisons and reactions shared between the people concerned. The children took an especially keen interest in seeing what they and their family looked like in other contexts (such as on the beach, undressed, with mummy bathing topless and daddy with hairy legs), and in recalling what they themselves looked like at an earlier age, reacting mainly with amusement, and making evaluations of the changes, comparing each other and sometimes mocking each other's earlier immaturity. The pictures and the conversational rememberings provided for a kind of family forum in which personal identities, social relationships and the milestones of developmental change could be marked out and interpreted, becoming the basis of an articulated family history.

If remembering is an occasioned activity, done for pragmatic purposes, and sensitive to its social and conversational context, then there is a sense also in which the children are being taught how to remember.

Extract 8: *Inference and argument revisited*

1   With Helen (2 yrs 3 mths) and Sandra (4 yrs 11 mths)
   Mother: . . . who's that?
   Helen: I don't know
   Mother: do you know where you were there?
   Helen: [. . .]
   Mother: whose house were you at there?/ do you recognize . . .
   Sandra: . . . look there's Mummy on a boat/ I didn't go on boat [. . .] 'cause
      look there's ⌈ [. . .]
   Mother: └ oh yes I bet that was in Liverpool when we went on
      the ferry/ ferry boat

2   With Paul (4 yrs 3 mths) and Rebecca (5 yrs 10 mths)
   Mother: do you remember being on this beach?
   Paul: yuk// no
   Mother: don't you/ when we went to Jersey/ on the aeroplane// do you not
      remember that?
   Paul: is that Jersey?
   Mother: mm/ look Rebecca's wearing a hat that says Jersey on it
   Paul: look/ what is that?
   Mother: [. . .] probably a book we were going to go on that/ boat/ or a trip
      down the river/ and we took one or two books to keep you two
      occupied

The examples in Extract 8 (from two different families) are typical of many other such exchanges, in which the children could not recall something, and the mother then proceeded to invoke contextual reminders as an aid to recall. The mothers expressed directly the inferential, reconstructive basis of the process – 'I bet that was in Liverpool', 'probably a book . . .'. And Paul's mother offers him the evidence provided by the picture for concluding that they were on holiday in Jersey – the name of the place was written on his sister's hat. Paul's mother overtly demonstrates how recall (versions of the past) can be justified on the basis of inference and argument.

It is not possible to state definitively from these brief extracts what the children were actually learning; but it seems obvious that these kinds of family conversations are a rich learning environment, in which children's efforts at remembering are taken up by parents in conversation that centres on elaborations and explanations of things, resolving disputes between people, invoking context and using inference to work out and justify particular versions of events. It is an interactive environment, in which the parent takes pains to elicit perceptions, memories and judgements from the children, to examine and elaborate upon them, to contextualize and assign significance to them, in terms of a shared past in which personal identity, family relationships and the landmarks of development can be reconstructed. It is a process that can be well described by Vygotsky's concept of the 'zone of proximal development' [. . .], in which the development of mental processes proceeds within just such a social apprenticeship. The focus of our continuing analysis is upon the developmental implications of the rhetorical organization of family conversations.

Part of what the children are presumably acquiring is discourse itself – a shared way of talking about things, shared reference, shared evaluations, or criteria for evaluation, ways of describing and narrating, the selection of criteria, the offering of more or less interesting or convincing versions. Part of that process is defining what words to name things by. This is, of course, an aspect of most pedagogic transactions, whether children are at home acquiring language and everyday culture, or at school, doing classroom lessons. But it also occurs in adult conversation, as an intrinsic part of putting together common versions of things, where some manner of joint problem solving is involved. This is demonstrated in the difficulties a group of English Morris dancers had in reconstructing a dance which they wished to add to their performance repertoire (Middleton, 1987). Their problem was to re-create an 'authentic' version danced in time to the musical accompaniment. Among the resources they used to achieve this were a cryptic text of dance notation, a vocabulary of terms describing the dance moves and the beat of the dance tune. The reconstruction mainly centred upon the redefinition of the terms they used to describe and announce the moves in the dance. Through argument they improvised the redefinition of the dance terminology and how to fit the problematic moves to the music. The repair and development of the dance and the redefinition of the vocabulary were interdependent in achieving a commonly agreed version, a shared understanding of the dance's movements that would extend beyond any particular performance.

Discourse and cognition

In offering a discourse-analytical approach to remembering, we are not proposing a simple reductionism. The phenomena studied in conversational remembering are not reducible to an account framed in terms of cognitive-neural processes, and neither would such an account be reducible to a description of social-discursive ones. But it is likely that the study of the everyday social-discursive basis of remembering will reveal some ways in which the exclusively individual-cognitive approach to memory can start to seem arbitrary. One of the most obvious benefits is a kind of ecological validity (cf. Neisser, 1982), the study of remembering as people actually do it, addressing the concerns and difficulties of everyday life, including both the ordinary and the extraordinary, rather than when posed in the psychological laboratory with materials and instructions that offer little resemblance to the situations in which remembering is ordinarily done. Indeed, it may be that the amount of control possible in experimental studies is made available only by altering the phenomenon to something which is unrecognizable to everyday practice.

For example, psychological experiments have arbitrarily reified particular aspects of everyday remembering: such as defining memory per se, in terms of a restricted sort of everyday setting in which remembering might be done – the specific communicative context of dispassionate, accurate reporting, usually dealing with materials which have very little personal significance for the rememberer. The experimental approach lends itself most readily to a conception of remembering as involving discrete factors which have separable causal influences upon discrete mental faculties. It is the legacy of Ebbinghaus's (1885) first studies of his own recall of lists of 'nonsense syllables' in preference for materials that might be contaminated by having some ready-made meaning or relevance to the rememberer. As Bartlett (1932) demonstrated, and much of cognitive psychology has done since, those elements of meaning and significance have to be replaced in order for remembering to work in anything like its normal manner. In experimental designs, meaning and context are defined as variables, factors whose effects on the accuracy of recall are manipulable. In the study of discursive remembering, significance and context are intrinsic to the activity, constitutive of it and constituted by it, rather than causally influential upon some other thing called 'memory'.

The individual-cognitive approach conflates method with theory, again producing an arbitrarily limited account of memory. The input–output discrepancy method encourages the notion of memory as being all about the cognitive processes that intervene between input and output – that take place in the time between, and in the space between the ears. Theoretically, this becomes the study of information processing – the method becomes the theory, as input is traced through stages of processing towards output. It is noticeable how the problematical nature of perception is carefully circumvented in memory studies by its incorporation into methodology. The 'original experience' becomes non-psychological, in that it is identified as the 'materials' themselves, the stimulus materials, objectively available for the psychologist and the reader to see. In contrast, the study of discursive remembering deals with output alone. Thus, in the study of teachers' recaps of what has been done in classroom lessons (Edwards and Mercer, 1989), what we have is two discourses at different points in time, each doing constructive work on what everyone is doing, seeing and thinking. The later 'recaps' are reformulations in situated discourse of earlier situated discourse, which is studiable in just the same way. There is no neutral 'input'. As with our study of Dean and Lawson (Edwards and Potter, 1989), the nature of the true original event is precisely the point at issue for the participants, and is studiable as such through their discourse. What we have for comparison is not input and output, but two outputs at different times, serving different communicative purposes, and requiring the same sort of analysis. In our initial investigation of recall of the film *E.T.*, that topic was chosen because we imagined it would be useful, if not necessary, to have recourse to the original experience. In fact, no such recourse was taken, nor felt necessary (indeed, one of us did not see the film until some four years later). Of course, had such recourse been taken, it is not obvious how it would have avoided constructive work on the part of the investigators that would be, from however advantaged a position, of an essentially similar sort to that of the rememberers. With discourse analysis, we do not have to say anything about what has happened in the space or time between – we merely have to deal with a socially occasioned variability from one time to another. The methodological advantage is considerable – like the behaviourists, our analysis remains at all times close to the observable, recorded conversational record. But unlike the behaviourists, we are not shackled with the severe limitations of stimulus–response psychology.

The study of remembering in conversation affords unique opportunities for understanding remembering as organized social action. Reports of past events are studiable as pragmatically occasioned versions whose variability is due not only to the nature and vicissitudes of individual cognition, but to the conversational work that those versions accomplish. Collective versions of past events are available as grounds for justifying current and future action; and because they are so 'useful' it is quite ordinary to find them being reconstructed and contested.

References

Atkinson, J.M. and Heritage, J. (eds) (1984) *Structures of Social Action: Studies in Conversation Analysis*. Cambridge: Cambridge University Press.

Bartlett, F.C. (1932) *Remembering: a Study in Experimental and Social Psychology*. Cambridge: Cambridge University Press.

Billig, M. (1987) *Arguing and Thinking*. Cambridge: Cambridge University Press.

Billig, M., Condor, S., Edwards, D., Gane, M., Middleton, D.J. and Radley, A.R. (1988) *Ideological Dilemmas: a Social Psychology of Everyday Thinking*. London: Sage.

Bransford, J.D. (1979) *Human Cognition: Learning, Understanding and Remembering*. Belmont, CA: Wadsworth.

Bransford, J.D. and McCarrell, N.S. (1974) 'A sketch of a cognitive approach to comprehension', in W. Weimer and D.S. Palermo (eds), *Cognition and the Symbolic Processes*. Hillsdale, NJ: Lawrence Erlbaum.

Brown, G. and Yule, G. (1983) *Discourse Analysis*. Cambridge: Cambridge University Press.

Crook, C. and Middleton, D. (1989) 'Bartlett's significance for a cultural psychology of cognition', paper presented at the Annual Conference of the British Psychological Society, St. Andrew's, Scotland, April.

Ebbinghaus, H. (1885) *Über das Gedächtnis: Untersuchungen zur experimentellen Psychologie*. Leipzig: Duncker & Humboldt.

Edwards, D. and Goodwin, R.Q. (1985) 'The language of shared attention and visual experience: a functional study of early nomination', *Journal of Pragmatics*, 9 (4): 475–93.

Edwards, D. and Mercer, N.M. (1987) *Common Knowledge: the Development of Understanding in the Classroom*. London: Methuen.

Edwards, D. and Mercer, N.M. (1989) 'Reconstructing context: the conventionalization of classroom knowledge', *Discourse Processes*, 12: 91–104.

Edwards, D. and Middleton, D. (1986a) 'Joint remembering: constructing an account of shared experience through conversational discourse', *Discourse Processes*, 9 (4): 423–59.

Edwards, D. and Middleton, D. (1986b) 'Text for memory: joint recall with a scribe', *Human Learning*, 5 (3): 125–38.

Edwards, D. and Middleton, D. (1987) 'Conversation and remembering: Bartlett revisited', *Applied Cognitive Psychology*, 1: 77–92.

Edwards, D. and Middleton, D. (1988) 'Conversational remembering and family relationships: how children learn to remember', *Journal of Social and Personal Relationships*, 5: 3–25.

Edwards, D. and Potter, J. (1989) 'The chancellor's memory: rhetoric and truth in discursive remembering', unpublished mimeo, Loughborough University.

Flavell, J.H. and Wellman, H.M. (1977) 'Metamemory', in R. Kail and J. Hagen (eds), *Perspectives on the Development of Memory and Cognition*. Hillsdale, NJ: Lawrence Erlbaum.

Gergen, K.J. (1985) 'The social constructionist movement in modern psychology', *American Psychologist*, 40: 266–75.

Gilbert, G.N. and Mulkay, M. (1984) *Opening Pandora's Box: a Sociological Analysis of Scientists' Discourse*. Cambridge: Cambridge University Press.

Goody, J. (1977) *The Domestication of the Savage Mind*. Cambridge: Cambridge University Press.

Harré, R. (1983) *Personal Being: a Theory for Individual Psychology*. Oxford: Blackwell.

Havelock, E. (1976) *Origins of Western Literacy*. Toronto: Ontario Institute for Studies in Education Press.

Heelas, P. and Lock, A. (eds) (1981) *Indigenous Psychologies*. London: Academic Press.

Heritage, J. (1984) *Garfinkel and Ethnomethodology*. Cambridge: Polity Press.

LCHC (Laboratory of Comparative Human Cognition) (1983) 'Culture and cognitive development', in W. Kessen (ed.), *Carmichael's Manual of Child Psychology: History, Theories and Methods*. New York: Wiley.

Levinson, S.C. (1983) *Pragmatics*. Cambridge: Cambridge University Press.

Luria, A.R. (1976) *Cognitive Development: its Cultural and Social Foundations*. Cambridge, MA: Harvard University Press.

Mead, G.H. (1934) *Mind, Self and Society*. Chicago: University of Chicago Press.

Middleton, D. (1987) 'Dance to the music: conversational remembering and joint activity in learning an English Morris dance', *Quarterly Newsletter of the Laboratory of Comparative Human Cognition*, 9 (1): 23–38.

Middleton, D. (1988) 'Talking work: argument in co-ordination, commemoration and improvisation in team work', paper presented at University of California San Diego Conference on Work and Communication, 11–15 July.

Neisser, U. (1981) 'John Dean's memory: a case study', *Cognition*, 9: 1–22.

Neisser, U. (1982) *Memory Observed: Remembering in Natural Contexts*. Oxford: W.H. Freeman.

Olson, D.R. (1980) 'Some social aspects of meaning in oral and written language', in D.R. Olson (ed.), *Social Foundations of Language and Thought: Essays in Honor of J.S. Bruner*. New York: Norton.

Ong, W.J. (1971) *Rhetoric, Romance and Technology: Studies in the Interaction of Expression and Culture*. Ithaca, NY: Cornell University Press.

Piaget, J. (1928) *Judgement and Reasoning in the Child*. London: Routledge & Kegan Paul.

Potter, J. and Wetherell, M. (1987) *Discourse and Social Psychology*. London: Sage.

Scribner, S. and Cole, M. (1981) *The Psychology of Literacy*. Cambridge, MA: Harvard University Press.

Vygotsky, L.S. (1978) *Mind in Society*, ed. by Michael Cole, Vera John-Steiner, Sylvia Scribner and Glen Souberman. Cambridge, MA: Harvard University Press.

Vygotsky, L.S. (1987) *Thought and Language*, ed. by A. Kozulin. Cambridge, MA: MIT Press.

Walkerdine, V. (1988) *The Mastery of Reason: Cognitive Development and the Production of Rationality*. London: Routledge.

Wertsch, J.V. (1985) *Vygotsky and the Social Formation of Mind*. Cambridge, MA: Harvard University Press.

Wertsch, J.V. (1987) 'Collective memory: issues from a sociohistorical perspective', *Quarterly Newsletter of the Laboratory of Comparative Human Cognition*, 9 (1): 19–22.

PART 7

COOPERATIVE LEARNING

CHAPTER 13

WHEN AND WHY DOES COOPERATIVE LEARNING INCREASE ACHIEVEMENT?

Theoretical and empirical perspectives[†]

Robert E. Slavin

R. Hertz-Lazarowitz and N. Miller (eds) *Interaction in Cooperative Groups: The Theoretical Anatomy of Group Learning*, New York, Cambridge University Press, 1993

'Class,' said Ms. Cooper, 'it's now time for you to start your team practice. I've given you each a blank outline map of Europe. I'd like you to work with your team-mates to make sure that you and everyone else in your team can recognize the major countries. You'll have the rest of the period to study your maps together. Tomorrow I'll give you a quiz on this material, and any teams that get an average of 90% or better will get Superteam certificates and will be able to go to recess first. Do a good job of explaining to each other; remember, you won't be able to help each other on the quiz, so everyone in your team has to be able to fill out the map correctly. Are there any questions? You may begin work.'

Ms. Cooper's sixth-grade class is studying a unit on the geography of Europe using Student Teams Achievement Divisions (STAD) (Slavin, 1986), one form of cooperative learning. She has taught a lesson on the major countries of Europe and is now giving instructions to the teams on how they are to work together. The teams consist of four to five students who are heterogeneous in performance level, sex, and ethnicity. They remain together for about 6 weeks, and then students are assigned to new teams according to the same criteria.

The instructions Ms. Cooper gives her class seem simple and straightforward enough. Yet she is making profound changes in two of the most important elements of classroom organization: *task structure* and *incentive structure*. Task structure refers to the ways in which the teacher (or students themselves) set up activities designed to result in student learning. Most classrooms use *independent task structures*, in which students are expected to work by themselves, listen to the teacher, or respond to the teacher (Bossert, 1977; Sirotnik, 1982). Yet Ms. Cooper has set up a *cooperative task structure*, in which students are encouraged to work together to help one another learn.

Ms. Cooper is also significantly altering the classroom incentive structure. Most classrooms use a *competitive incentive* structure, in which students compete for a

---

[†] This chapter was written under a grant from the Office of Educational Research and Improvement U.S. Department of Education (No. OERI-R-117-90002). However, any opinions expressed are those of the author and do not represent OERI policy.

limited number of good grades, the teacher's praise and attention, or other rewards. Other classes may use an *individualistic incentive structure*, in which students earn a particular grade if they achieve at a given, pre-established level (e.g., 90% is an 'A' regardless of how many students score at this level). However, Ms. Cooper has set up a *cooperative incentive structure*, in which students can earn certificates and a little extra recess time based on the average score achieved by all members of a heterogeneous team. The particular cooperative incentive structure used by Ms. Cooper emphasizes *individual accountability*, in that the group's success depends on the learning of each group member, as demonstrated on a quiz taken without teammate help. In this situation, the only way the team can succeed is if every member of the group can independently fill out the outline map, so the most effective practice strategy is for students to explain to each other, quiz each other, and continue to work with each other until every team member has the skill. In a cooperative incentive structure lacking individual accountability, students might be rewarded based on the quality of a single worksheet, test, project, or other product.

Although there is a growing consensus among researchers about the positive effects of cooperative learning on student achievement as well as a rapidly growing number of educators using cooperative learning at all levels of schooling and in many subject areas, there is still a great deal of confusion and disagreement about *why* cooperative learning methods affect achievement and, even more important, *under what conditions* cooperative learning has these effects. Researchers investigating cooperative learning effects on achievement have often operated in isolation from one another, almost on parallel tracks, and often describe theoretical mechanisms held to explain achievement effects of cooperative learning that are totally different from the mechanisms assumed by others. In particular, there are researchers who emphasize the changes in incentive structure brought about by certain forms of cooperative learning, whereas others hold that changes in task structure are all that is required to enhance learning. The problem is that applications of cooperative learning typically change many aspects of both incentive and task structures, so disentangling which is responsible for which outcomes can be difficult.

This chapter discusses theories to account for the achievement effects of cooperative learning and examines the empirical data from classroom experiments that inform these theories.

Effects of cooperation: laboratory research

The issue of cooperative versus competitive incentive structures is one of the oldest themes in social psychology (this section is adapted from Slavin, 1983a). Research on this topic was already well developed by the 1920s (Maller, 1929). However, until recently this research was done in brief studies either in social psychological laboratories or, more commonly, in contrived field settings that resemble the laboratory. In this chapter, studies that were implemented over periods of less than 2 weeks in any setting are referred to as laboratory studies. Although these brief studies tend to be too limited in external validity to be useful as evaluations of cooperative learning methods for use in classrooms, they have provided much of the theoretical basis on which the practical cooperative learning programs and research on these programs are based. This chapter does not presume to review the hundreds of laboratory studies on cooperation and competition but summarizes the major findings relevant to building the theoretical base from which research on practical cooperative learning methods derives its conceptual framework.

Effects of cooperation on performance

Despite the many studies conducted to determine the effects of cooperation on performance, these effects are still rather poorly understood. Four reviews completely disagreed on the direction of the effects. D. W. Johnson and R. T. Johnson (1974) summarized the research by stating that cooperation is better than competition or individualization for all but the most concrete, repetitive tasks. In a later meta-analysis, D. W. Johnson, Maruyama, R. Johnson, Nelson, and Skon (1981) suggested that the evidence supporting cooperative incentive structures over competitive and individualistic ones in increasing productivity is so strong that further research on this comparison is unnecessary. However, Michaels (1977) reviewed much of the same literature and concluded that competition is usually better than cooperation for most tasks. Slavin (1977) held that over the brief duration of a laboratory study, cooperation is more effective in increasing performance when coordination of efforts is vital to effective functioning, whereas competition is at least as effective as cooperation when coordination of efforts is not so important. Because most tasks of practical importance (including learning) do not *require* coordination of efforts between two or more individuals, this conclusion was closer to that of Michaels (1977) than to those of D. W. Johnson and R. T. Johnson (1974) or D. W. Johnson *et al.* (1981). However, Slavin (1977) held that over longer periods, growth of social pressures favoring performance in cooperative groups makes cooperation more effective. A similar conclusion was reached by Miller and Hamblin (1963), who postulated that cooperative reward structures were most effective for interdependent (cooperative) task structures but least effective for independent tasks.

To understand the controversy over the laboratory evidence concerning the effects of cooperative incentive structures on performance, it is important to have a causal model linking cooperative incentive structures with enhanced performance. The following sections develop such a model.

Does help help?

The most obvious effect of a cooperative incentive structure should be to get individuals to help one another. This is so apparent that most studies have not measured it, but those that have done so have always found more helping under a cooperative incentive than under an individual or competitive one (Deutsch, 1949a; Slavin, 1980; Johnson & Johnson, 1981). It is obvious that for many tasks, such as carrying heavy loads, taking tests, or solving difficult problems, helping is likely to lead to a better group product. However, although it appears likely that cooperative incentives increase helping among group members, it is not so clear that helping per se always increases performance. Two similar studies illustrate the distinction. Klugman (1944) had small groups of children do arithmetic problems under a cooperative contingency in which the groups received rewards based on the number of problems they could do accurately, with no time limit. He contrasted this condition with one in which children worked for individual rewards based on the number of problems they could work correctly. The group under the cooperative condition got significantly more problems right. In a similar study, DeCharms (1957) found exactly the opposite relationship; the children who worked independently got more correct answers on the arithmetic problems than did those working under the cooperative incentive. There was a critical difference between the studies; Klugman (1944) allowed the children unlimited time, but DeCharms (1957) set a time limit and told his subjects to concentrate on speed. In the Klugman study, students were able to pool their knowledge to improve the performance of all group members; in the DeCharms study, helping was of little value and might have even slowed the subjects down.

Thus, although it is clear that under certain conditions cooperative incentives lead to increased helping behavior, *the degree to which help is valuable for performance depends on the task and outcome measure.* Most of the tasks used in the laboratory research on cooperation, competition, and individualization on which cooperation produces the highest performance are problem-solving tasks on which two (or more) heads are obviously better than one. For example, Miller and Hamblin (1963) gave each of four subjects 3 unique numbers between 1 and 13. The task was to find the missing number. Since the four subjects had 12 numbers between them, they only had to share their numbers to find the missing one, and they did share more readily when they received a group reward based on how fast they could find the answer than when they were in competition to find the answer first, where sharing would simply help others to win. Literally dozens of studies have shown that two or more individuals working together can figure out a maze or a concept underlying a set of numbers or words faster than can individuals working alone (e.g., Lemke, Randle, & Robertshaw, 1969; Gurnee, 1968; Laughlin, McGlynn, Anderson, & Jacobson, 1968). When two or more individuals take a test together, they do better than when they work separately (e.g., Laughlin & H. Johnson, 1966; D. W. Johnson & R. T. Johnson, 1979). Many studies have shown that two or more individuals can solve problems of various kinds better when they work in groups than when they work independently (e.g., Deutsch, 1949a; Hammond & Goldman, 1961; Thorndike, 1938).

On the kinds of tasks used in the studies cited above, groups *obviously* score better than individuals. In the problem-solving studies, groups would have outscored individuals even if more able group members solved the problems by themselves, because the less able group members would have still been assigned the group score. As early as the 1930s, Thorndike (1938) considered the superiority of group to individual problem solving to have been proved and proposed that further research go beyond that rather obvious finding to explore what kinds of tasks groups do best. In fact, in many of the studies cited above, it was assumed at the beginning that groups would outperform individuals, and some issue beyond group versus individual problem solving was the focus of research.

A few studies examined the reasons that groups did better on problem-solving tasks and concluded that they did better simply because they pooled the problem-solving abilities of their members. Faust (1959), Marquart (1955), and Ryack (1965) compared groups that really worked together with 'nominal' groups. The nominal group scores were created by randomly assigning subjects who had actually worked alone to artificial 'groups' and crediting all 'group' members with having solved a problem if any one of them solved the problem. In all three studies, the real groups had much higher scores than the individuals, but not than the nominal groups, suggesting that the real groups had high scores not because of their interaction or motivation but because if any individual could solve the problem their teammates would get credit for it, regardless of their own participation or learning.

Another category of tasks where cooperation is obviously more efficient than competition is when competition is likely to disrupt performance. The classic example is the Mintz (1951) experiment, in which the task was for several individuals to pull cones on strings out of a milk bottle whose neck would permit only one cone to be withdrawn at a time. Under cooperative instructions (get all the cones out as quickly as possible), the individuals arranged to take turns and quickly got all the cones out, but under noncooperative instructions (get your own cone out as quickly as possible), the traffic jam at the mouth of the bottle increased everyone's time. In another study,

Graziano, French, Brownell, and Hartup (1976) gave children stacks of blocks. The children were assigned to groups of three. In a cooperative condition, the children built a tower together and were rewarded based on the total number of blocks in the tower. In a noncooperative condition, children also built a single tower, but they were rewarded based on the number of their *own* blocks they could get into the tower. In the condition in which children were trying to get their own blocks into the tower, the towers fell more often and ultimately included fewer blocks than in the condition in which children were concerned only with increasing the total number of blocks in the tower.

When hindering is a likely outcome of a cooperative task or reward structure, and cooperative instructions or rewards remove the hindering, cooperation will, of course, improve group performance. Many studies comparing cooperation and competition are of this type (e.g., Crombag, 1966; Raven & Eachus, 1963).

Group productivity versus individual learning

The kind of performance of interest in this chapter bears little relationship to building towers of blocks, pulling cones out of bottles, or even problem solving in the sense studied in the experiments just discussed. *Learning* is a completely individual outcome that may or may not be improved by cooperation, but it is clearly not obviously improved by cooperation the way problem-solving performance of the kind described earlier is. Leonard Bernstein and I could write a brilliant concerto together, about twice as good as the average of the concerto he could write and the one I could write working separately (I can barely read music). But how much would we *learn* from working cooperatively? I doubt that Leonard Bernstein would learn much about writing concertos from me, and I might do better to take a course on music than to start by watching a composer write a concerto. The point of this example is to illustrate that *learning is completely different from 'group' productivity*. It may well be that working in a group under certain circumstances does increase the learning of the individuals in that group more than would working under other arrangements, but a measure of group productivity provides no evidence one way or the other on this; only an individual learning measure that cannot be influenced by group member help can indicate which incentive or task structure is best. Learning takes place only between the ears of the learner. If a group produces a beautiful lab report, but only a few students really contributed to it, it is unlikely that the group as a whole learned more than they might have learned had they each had to write their own (perhaps less beautiful) lab reports under an individualistic or competitive incentive structure. In fact, what often happens in cooperative groups that produce a single report, worksheet, or other group product is that the most able group members simply do the work or give the answers to their teammates, which may be the most efficient strategy for group productivity but is a poor strategy for individual learning. There are several studies in which productivity measures were at variance with learning outcomes. Haines and McKeachie (1967) found that psychology students in large discussion groups covered more questions under cooperative incentives than under competitive ones, but the groups did not differ on exams they took by themselves. Smith, Madden, and Sobel (1957) found more ideas expressed in a cooperative discussion group than in a competitively structured group, but there were no differences in recall of the material discussed. D. W. Johnson, R. T. Johnson, J. Johnson, and Anderson (1976) and D. W. Johnson, R. T. Johnson, and Scott (1978) found that students who worked cooperatively and then took a test on which they could help each other performed much better than did students who worked alone and took the tests by themselves.

However, when the tests were given to the cooperative students individually, they did no better than the individual students in one study (D. W. Johnson et al., 1976) and worse than the individual students in the other (D. W. Johnson et al., 1978).

Because it makes sense only at the individual level, learning is a performance measure that resembles 'means-independent' tasks studied in many social psychological laboratory studies. In these studies, the evidence does not clearly favor cooperative incentives (Miller & Hamblin, 1963). The DeCharms (1957) study in which subjects could do little to help one another found no differences between cooperative and competitive incentives. When differences favoring cooperative incentive structures are found on tasks on which helping is forbidden or useless, it is usually because a cooperative incentive is being compared with no incentive at all. Hurlock (1927) found that students worked more arithmetic problems when they worked in teams trying to 'beat' another team than when they simply were asked to work problems by themselves with no incentive. However, when both groups received some reward, cooperative and competitive incentive structures tended to produce equal performance (e.g., Seta, Paulus, & Schkade, 1976) or competition actually exceeded cooperation in effect on performance (e.g., Bruning, Sommer, and Jones, 1966; Scott & Cherrington, 1974; Weinstein & Holzbach, 1972).

In their meta-analysis entitled 'Effects of Cooperative, Competitive, and Individualistic Goal Structures on Achievement,' D. W. Johnson and colleagues (1981) reviewed 122 studies. They concluded that 'the overall effects stand as strong evidence for the superiority of cooperation in promoting achievement and productivity.... Given the general dissatisfaction with the level of competence achieved by students in the public school system, educators may wish to considerably increase the use of cooperative learning procedures to promote higher student achievement' (p. 58). This unequivocal conclusion, based on a substantial difference in effect size favoring cooperative over individualistic and competitive incentive structures, would appear to make the cautions discussed in this chapter concerning the effects of cooperation on learning irrelevant. However, despite the title, only about 40 of the 122 studies reviewed involved comparisons of cooperative and competitive or individualistic methods with *individual achievement* as a dependent variable (see Slavin, 1984). Most of the studies compared group productivity with individual productivity on tasks on which group productivity was obviously more effective, such as jointly solving mazes, number problems, scrambled words, and so on. In one study, the dependent variable was scores in a card game, in which cooperating individuals could share cards to get a higher score (Workie, 1974). One (Bjorkland, Johnson, & Krotee, 1980) involved golf performance, and another (Martino & Johnson, 1979) involved swimming and compared the number of swimming skills gained by two learning-disabled students who learned cooperatively with the number gained by two who learned individualistically. Many of the studies involved building block towers, manipulating apparatus, judging weights, and other tasks minimally related to school achievement (e.g., Gordon, 1924; Graziano et al., 1976; Raven & Eachus, 1963). Of the studies that did involve achievement, many simply found that two or more students who take a test together do better than students who work alone (e.g., Garibaldi, 1979; Hudgins, 1960; D. W. Johnson & R. T. Johnson, 1979; D. W. Johnson et al., 1976; D. W. Johnson et al., 1978; D. W. Johnson, R. Johnson, & Skon, 1979; Laughlin & Bitz, 1975; Laughlin, Branch, & Johnson, 1969). Thus, the net direction of the effects of cooperative, competitive, and individualistic incentive and task structures per se on individual learning is not resolved by the Johnson et al. (1981) meta-analysis (Slavin, 1984).

The purpose of the foregoing discussion was to illustrate the observation that the evidence of the laboratory and brief field studies is inconclusive with respect to the effects of helping on individual learning. Clearly, studies of group productivity or other studies in which working together is obviously more effective than working separately add little to an understanding of how different task structures affect individual learning, and such studies dominate the social psychological laboratory literature on cooperation, competition, and individualization. Because individual learning is an individual task, the most relevant literature for a theory of cooperation and learning would be the studies of other individual tasks that tend to find equal or greater performance under competitive and individualistic conditions than under cooperative conditions. However, learning is not just like typing or coding, either. For certain kinds of learning, discussion under cooperative conditions may improve subsequent individual achievement. For example, discussion of text improves student recall of the text content more than reviewing the text alone (Dansereau, 1985; Slavin & Tanner, 1979). Engaging in controversy over social studies materials apparently improves recall of important concepts (D. W. Johnson & R. T. Johnson, 1979), as does controversy among pairs of nonconservers on Piagetian conservation tasks (Ames & Murray, 1982). Thus, studying in small groups may in itself be more effective than solitary study for some learning tasks, but at this point the laboratory research on this is limited.

Group norms

Helping between group members is not the only means by which cooperative incentive (as opposed to task) structures might influence individual performance. Another mediating variable that could link cooperative incentive structures to increased performance is group member support for whatever helps the group to be rewarded or group norms favoring performance. For example, in Ms. Cooper's class, students encourage one another to learn the geography of Europe because the group's success depends on the individual learning of all group members. These norms are central to Deutsch's (1949b) theory of cooperation and competition, and in his study of cooperating discussion groups he documented their occurrence (Deutsch, 1949a). Thomas (1957) also found that cooperative incentives led to peer norms favoring the performance of tasks that help the group to be rewarded. Slavin (1975) and Slavin, DeVries, and Hulten (1975) found that students in cooperative groups who gained in academic performance also gained in sociometric status in cooperative groups, whereas they lost status in competitive groups. Hulten and DeVries (1976), Madden and Slavin (1983), and Slavin (1978) found that students who had worked in cooperative learning groups were significantly more likely than control students to agree that their classmates wanted them to do their best. These findings indicate that peer norms do come to favor achievement as a consequence of cooperative incentive structures.

If group member norms support performance of tasks that help the group to succeed, it seems logical that this would improve performance on the part of group members. Coleman (1961) found that in schools in which academic achievement helped a student to be accepted by the 'leading crowd,' the brightest students turned their attention more toward doing well academically than they did in schools in which achievement was not so well esteemed by the peer group. Student support for academic goals was also found by Brookover, Beady, Flood, Schweitzer, and Wisenbaker (1979) to be a strong predictor of student achievement, controlling for student background factors. Thus, the evidence supports a conclusion that group member helping on a group task and group member norms supporting performance are consequences of cooperative incentive structures and, under certain circumstances, may increase performance, including learning.

Diffusion of responsibility

Although the effects of group tasks and group norms favoring achievement are likely to have positive or, at worst, neutral effects on performance, there is one effect of cooperative incentives whose net impact is probably to *decrease* performance. This is the problem of diffusion of responsibility. In a cooperative group, it is often possible for individuals to be rewarded even if they themselves made little contribution to the group, or for individuals to fail to be rewarded even though they have done their utmost (Slavin, 1977). Laboratory science groups in which a single lab report is produced are good examples of this problem; some students always seem to find a way to get others to do the work. For this reason, studies in which a single product is made by a group are the most likely to show significantly greater gains in individual learning for competitive or individualistic groups than for cooperative ones (D. W. Johnson *et al.*, 1978; Julian & Perry, 1967). Diffusion of responsibility is highest when group members can substitute for one another in performing the group task. When this is possible, some students are likely to do the minimum, hoping that their teammates will pick up the slack. In theory, diffusion of responsibility should be a very serious problem in cooperative incentive and task structures. According to expectancy theory (Atkinson & Birch, 1978; Kukla, 1972), given a reward of a certain value, motivation is related to the difference between the probability that individuals will be successful if they do their best minus the probability that they will be successful if they do not do their best (Slavin, 1978, 1980). In a cooperative incentive structure, especially one involving a large group, the chances that any group member's extraordinary efforts will make a difference in the group's success is far less than would be the case in an individualistic or a fair competitive structure, where extraordinary effort is more likely to pay off (Slavin, 1977, 1978).

Because cooperative incentive structures are common in adult life (if not in classrooms), societies have worked out many ways to deal with the inherent problem of diffusion of responsibility. These include repeated exhortations to group members about the virtues of cooperation or of doing whatever helps the group to be rewarded. The pep talk before the game is an example of this, as are special televised appeals by the president to conserve energy or to do anything that may not be in an individual's best interests but is in the nation's best interest (a nation is a cooperative incentive and task structure). Another way that groups combat diffusion of responsibility is to have interpersonal sanctions for doing whatever helps the group: Teammates cheer each other on and express norms in favor of practicing and doing one's best. If a girl on a swimming team decides to skip practice or miss an important meet, her teammates are likely to be upset with her (much in contrast to the situation in a classroom, in which skipping school may be tolerated or even encouraged by peers). If group members' performances are visible to the other group members, they are likely to administer a very contingent reward and punishment system to ensure that group members are all doing their best.

In summary, individuals placed under a cooperative incentive are likely to encourage one another to do whatever helps the group to succeed and to help one another with the group task. Cooperative incentive structures are also likely to increase diffusion of responsibility, because each group member's own rewards are no longer dependent on his or her own efforts alone. The effect of group member encourage-

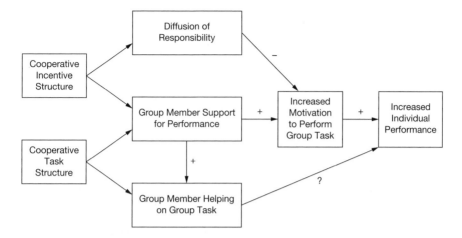

Figure 10 Simple theoretical model of effects of cooperative incentive and task structures on performance. From Slavin (1983a). Reprinted with permission.

ment on performance is probably positive, but the effect of helping may or may not be positive, depending on the kind of task involved. The effect of diffusion of responsibility is to reduce the chances that additional effort will be rewarded and thus is likely to reduce performance. Cooperative task structures are hypothesized to increase performance by increasing helping among group members and by influencing group members to encourage one another to perform the group task.

A model of how cooperative incentive and task structures might affect performance is depicted in Figure 10 (from Slavin, 1983a). Again, there is only one route by which cooperative incentive structures may be definitely assumed to enhance individual motivation and thus individual performance, the route through group member support for performance. Group members' helping one another may or may not improve individual performance, depending on what the task and outcome measures are. Diffusion of responsibility, which increases as group size increases, is hypothesized to have a negative effect on individual motivation (and thus performance).

What is implied in Figure 10 is not, of course, that the net effect of cooperative incentive and task structures on individual performance is zero. What it is meant to convey is that the net effect depends on whether the cooperative incentive and task structures are designed to maximize the positive effects and minimize the negative ones. For example, all of the ways (described earlier) that group members use to reduce the effects of diffusion of responsibility essentially involve accentuating group member support for performance (or negative sanctions for nonperformance). In structuring a group task to increase individual performance, there are many ways to activate group support for performance. Making group member contributions visible and quantifiable makes it possible for group members to accurately identify contributing and noncontributing members. This may be done by making the group reward depend on the sum of the members' individual performances (as in a wrestling or a chess team) or by giving each member a unique subtask (as in an assembly line). Increasing the value of group rewards is likely to increase motivation to apply interpersonal sanctions to motivate members' efforts. The impact of helping can also be influenced by restructuring the task to improve performance under cooperative conditions. This is likely to be the case whenever the group's goal is to produce some product, as in problem-solving tasks or projects. However, when the goal is not a group product but is an individual outcome (such as learning), helping can be made more effective, for example, by training group members in effective tutoring methods or by providing materials that lend themselves to peer learning (see, e.g., Slavin, Leavey, & Madden, 1984). Making the group goal and means of achieving it as clear as possible may also focus group members' efforts on effective helping. Certain learning tasks, such as comprehending technical material (Dansereau, 1985) or acquiring conservation principles (Murray, 1982), seem to lend themselves to cooperative task structures and may not require group rewards at all.

Seen in the light of the model outlined in Figure 10, the results of the laboratory research are no longer inconsistent. As noted earlier in this chapter, when positive effects of cooperative incentive and task structures on performance are found in brief experiments (e.g., Klugman, 1944; Slavin & Tanner, 1979), the tasks involved have tended to be ones where helping is likely to improve performance and group members can easily monitor and thereby reinforce each others' performance. Where competitive or individualistic incentives have produced greater performance, the tasks have tended to be ones on which helping is unlikely to make much difference (e.g., DeCharms, 1957) or individual group members' contributions are difficult to observe or reinforce and individuals may easily substitute for one another in performing the group task (e.g., D. W. Johnson *et al.*, 1978; Julian & Perry, 1967).

Actually, as noted earlier, brief laboratory or field-based laboratory studies are inherently biased against cooperative incentive and task structures. Diffusion of responsibility can occur from the first minutes a group is together. Helping strategies and especially group member support and norms favoring performance are likely to take time to develop. However, although the laboratory research on cooperative incentive and task structures has not produced performance effects that are unambiguous in general direction, it can support an understanding of the conditions under which positive or negative results are likely to be seen.

Alternative perspectives on cooperative learning

The theory outlined in the preceding section is an example of a *motivational* perspective on the achievement of cooperative learning, in that it emphasizes the potential effects of cooperative incentive structures (as opposed to task structures). However, there are several quite different perspectives on cooperative learning. The following sections (adapted from Slavin, 1989) expand on the motivational perspectives and review alternative perspectives, summarize the empirical support for each, and present an integrative theory of cooperative learning and achievement.

Motivational perspectives

Motivational perspectives on cooperative learning focus primarily on the reward or goal structures under which students operate (see Slavin, 1977, 1983a). From a motivationalist perspective (e. g., D. W. Johnson *et al.*, 1981; Slavin, 1983a), cooperative incentive structures create a situation in which the only way group members can attain their own personal goals is if the group is successful. Therefore, to meet their personal goals, group members must both help their teammates to do whatever helps the group to succeed and, perhaps even more important, encourage them to exert maximum efforts. In other words, rewarding groups based on group performance (or the sum of individual performances) creates an interpersonal reward structure in which group members will give or withhold social reinforcers (e.g., praise, encouragement) in response to teammates' task-relative efforts (Slavin, 1983a). One intervention that uses cooperative goal structures is the group contingency (Slavin, 1987), in which group rewards are given based on group members' behaviors. The theory underlying group contingencies does not require that group members be able to actually help one another or work together. The fact that outcomes are dependent on one another's behavior is enough to motivate students to engage in behaviors that help the group to be rewarded, because the group incentive induces students to encourage goal-directed behaviors among their teammates (Slavin, 1983a). A substantial literature in the behavior modification tradition has found that group contingencies can be very effective at improving students' appropriate behaviors and achievement (Hayes, 1976; Litow & Pumroy, 1975).

The motivationalist critique of traditional classroom organization holds that the competitive grading and informal reward system of the classroom creates peer norms opposing academic efforts (Coleman, 1961). Because one student's success decreases the chances that others will succeed, students are likely to express norms reflecting that high achievement is for 'nerds' or teachers' pets. Such work restriction norms are familiar in industry, where the 'rate buster' is scorned by his or her fellow workers (Vroom, 1969). However, by having students work together toward a common goal, they may be motivated to express norms favoring academic achievement, to reinforce one another for academic efforts.

Not surprisingly, motivational theorists incorporate group rewards into their cooperative learning methods. In methods developed by my colleagues and myself at Johns Hopkins University (Slavin, 1986) students can earn certificates or other recognition if their average team scores on quizzes or other individual assignments exceed a pre-established criterion. Methods developed by D. W. and R. T. Johnson (1986b) and their colleagues at the University of Minnesota often give students grades based on group performance, which is defined in several different ways. The theoretical rationale for these group rewards is that if students value the success of the group, they will encourage and help one another to achieve, much in contrast to the situation in the traditional, competitive classroom.

Evidence from practical applications of cooperative learning in elementary and secondary schools supports the motivational position that group rewards are essential to the effectiveness of cooperative learning, with one critical qualification. Use of group goals or group rewards enhances the achievement outcomes of cooperative learning if and only if the group rewards are based on the individual learning of all group members (Slavin, 1983a, 1990). Most often, this means that team scores are computed based on average scores on quizzes that all teammates take individually, without teammate help. For example, in STAD (Slavin, 1986) students work in mixed-ability teams to learn material initially presented by the teacher. Following this, students take individual quizzes on the material, and the teams may earn certificates based on the degree to which team members have improved their own past records. The only way the team can succeed is to ensure that all team members have learned, so the team members' activities focus on explaining concepts to one another, helping one another practice, and encouraging one another to achieve. In contrast, if group rewards are given based on a single group product (e.g., the team completes one worksheet or solves one problem), there is little incentive for group members to explain concepts to one another, and one or two group members may do all the work (Slavin, 1983b).

A recent review of 68 studies of cooperative learning in elementary and secondary schools that lasted at least 4 weeks compared achievement gains in cooperative learning and control groups. Of 43 studies of cooperative learning methods that provided group rewards based on the sum of group members' individual learning, nearly all found positive effects on achievement (Slavin, 1990). The median effect size for the 32 studies from which effect sizes could be computed was 0.30 (30% of a standard deviation separated cooperative learning and control treatments). In contrast, studies of methods that rewarded groups based on a single group product or that provided no group rewards found few positive effects. Comparisons within studies found similar patterns; group goals based on the sum of individual learning performances were necessary to the instructional effectiveness of the cooperative learning models (e.g., Huber, Bogatzki, & Winter, 1982).

Social cohesion perspectives

One theoretical perspective somewhat related to the motivational viewpoint holds that the effects of cooperative learning on achievement are strongly mediated by the cohesiveness of the group, in essence that students will help one another learn because they care about one another and want one another to succeed. This perspective is similar to the motivational perspective in that it emphasizes primarily motivational rather than cognitive explanations for the instructional effectiveness of cooperative learning. However, motivational theorists hold that students help each other learn because it is in their own interests to do so. Social cohesion theorists, in contrast, emphasize the idea that students help group members learn because they care about the group. A hallmark of the social cohesion perspective is an emphasis on team-building activities in preparation for cooperative learning and on processing or group self-evaluation during and after group activities. Social cohesion theorists tend to downplay or reject the influence of group incentives and individual accountability held by motivationalist researchers to be essential. For example, Cohen (1986, pp. 69–70) states that 'if the task is challenging and interesting, and if students are sufficiently prepared for skills in group process, students will experience the process of groupwork itself as highly rewarding. ... [N]ever grade or evaluate students on their individual contributions to the group product.' Cohen's work as well as that of Sharan and Hertz-Lazarowitz (1980) and Aronson (Aronson, Blaney, Stephan, Sikes, & Snapp, 1978) and their colleagues is based more on social cohesiveness theories. Cohen, Aronson, and Sharan all use forms of cooperative learning in which students take on individual roles within the group, which Slavin (1983a) calls 'task specialization' methods. In Aronson's Jigsaw method, students study material on one of four or five topics distributed among the group members. They meet in 'expert groups' to share information on their topics with members of other teams who had the same topic and then take turns presenting their topics to the team. In the Sharan and Hertz-Lazarowitz Group Investigation method, groups take on topics within a unit studied by the class as a whole and then further subdivide each topic into tasks distributed among members of the group. Each student investigates his or her subtopic individually and ultimately presents their findings to the class as a whole. Cohen's adaptation of DeAvila and Duncan's (1980) Finding Out/Descubrimiento program has students take different roles in discovery-oriented science activities.

One main purpose of the task specialization used in Jigsaw, Group Investigation, and Finding Out/Descubrimiento is to create interdependence among group members. In the methods of D. W. Johnson and R. T. Johnson, a somewhat similar form of interdependence is created by having students take on roles as 'checker,' 'recorder,' 'observer,' and so on. The idea is that if students value their teammates (as a result of team-building and other cohesiveness-building activities) and are dependent on one another, they are likely to encourage and help one another to succeed. The

Johnson and Johnson (1986b) work straddles the social cohesion and motivation-alist perspectives described in this chapter; while their models do use group goals and group incentives, their theoretical writings emphasize development of group cohesion through team building, group self-evaluation, and other means more characteristic of social cohesion theorists.

The achievement outcomes of cooperative learning methods using task special-ization are unclear. Research on Jigsaw has not generally found positive effects of this method on student achievement (Slavin, 1990). One problem with this method is that students have limited exposure to material other than that which they studied themselves, so learning gains on their own topics may be offset by losses on their teammates' topics. In contrast, there is evidence that when it is well implemented, Group Investigation can significantly increase student achievement (Sharan & Shachar, 1988). In studies of at least 4 weeks' duration, the Johnson and Johnson (1986b) methods have not been found to increase achievement more than individualistic methods unless they incorporate group rewards (in this case, group grades) based on the average of group members' individual quiz scores (Slavin, 1990).

Research on practical classroom applications of methods based on social cohesion theories provides inconsistent support for the proposition that building cohesiveness among students through team building alone (i.e., without group incentives) will enhance student achievement. There is some evidence that group processing activi-ties such as reflection at the end of each class period on the group's activities can enhance the achievement effects of cooperative learning (Yager, R. T. Johnson, D. W. Johnson, & Snider, 1986). On the other hand an Israeli study found that team-building activities had no effect on the achievement outcomes of Jigsaw (Rich, Amir, & Slavin, 1986).

In general, methods that emphasize team building and group process but do not provide specific group rewards based on the learning of all group members are no more effective than traditional instruction in increasing achievement (Slavin, 1990). One major exception is Group Investigation (Sharan & Hertz-Lazarowitz, 1980; Sharan & Shachar, 1988). However, in this method groups are evaluated based on their group products, which are composed of unique contributions made by each group member. Thus, this method may be using a form of the group goals and indi-vidual accountability held by motivationalist theories to be essential to the instructional effectiveness of cooperative learning.

Cognitive perspectives

The major alternatives to the motivationalist and social cohesiveness perspectives on cooperative learning, both of which focus primarily on group norms and interper-sonal influence, are the cognitive perspectives, which contend that interactions among students will in themselves increase student achievement for reasons that have to do with mental processing of information rather than with motivations. Cooperative methods developed by cognitive theorists involve neither the group goals that are the cornerstone of the motivationalist methods nor the emphasis on building group cohe-siveness characteristic of the social cohesion methods. However, there are several quite different cognitive perspectives.

Developmental perspective. One widely researched set of cognitive theories is the developmental perspective (e.g., Damon, 1984; Murray, 1982). The fundamental assumption of the developmental perspective on cooperative learning is that interaction among children while performing appropriate tasks facilitates learning of critical concepts. Vygotsky (1978, p. 86) defines the zone of proximal development as 'the distance between the actual developmental level as determined by independent problem solving and the level of potential development as determined through problem solving under adult guidance *or in collaboration with more capable peers*' (emphasis added). In his view, collaborative activity among children promotes growth because children of similar ages are likely to be operating within one another's proximal zones of development, modeling in the collaborating group behaviors more advanced than those they could perform as individuals. Vygotsky (1978, p. 86) described the influence of collaborative activity on learning as follows: 'Functions are first formed in the collective in the form of relations among children and then become mental functions for the individual. . . . Research shows that reflection is spawned from argument.'

Similarly, Piaget (1926) held that social-arbitrary knowledge – language, values, rules, morality, and symbol systems – can only be learned in interactions with others. Peer interaction is also important in logical-mathematical thought in disequilibrating the child's egocentric conceptualizing and providing feedback to the child about the validity of logical constructions.

There is a great deal of empirical support for the idea that peer interaction can help nonconservers become conservers. Many studies have shown that when conservers and nonconservers of about the same age work collaboratively on tasks requiring conservation, the nonconservers generally develop and maintain conservation concepts (Bell, Grossen, & Perret-Clermont, 1985; Murray, 1982; Perret-Clermont, 1980). In fact, a few studies (e.g., Ames & Murray, 1982; Mugny & Doise, 1978) have found that pairs of disagreeing nonconservers who had to come to consensus on conservation problems both gained in conservation. The importance of peers operating in one another's proximal zones of development was demonstrated by Kuhn (1972), who found that a small difference in cognitive level between a child and a social model was more conducive to cognitive growth than a larger difference.

On the basis of these and other findings, many Piagetians (e.g., Damon, 1984; Murray, 1982; Wadsworth, 1984) have called for an increased use of cooperative activities in schools. They argue that interaction among students on learning tasks will lead *in itself* to improved student achievement. Students will learn from one another because in their discussions of the content, cognitive conflicts will arise, inadequate reasoning will be exposed, disequilibration will occur, and higher quality understandings will emerge.

From the developmental perspective, the effects of cooperative learning on student achievement would be largely or entirely due to the use of cooperative *tasks*. In this view, the opportunity for students to discuss, argue, and present their own and hear one another's viewpoints is the critical element of cooperative learning with respect to student achievement. For example, Damon (1984, p. 335) integrates Piagetian, Vygotskian, and Sullivanian perspectives on peer collaboration to propose a 'conceptual foundation for a peer-based plan of education':

1   Through mutual feedback and debate, peers motivate one another to abandon misconceptions and search for better solutions.
2   The experience of peer communication can help a child master social processes, such as participation and argumentation, and cognitive processes, such as verification and criticism.
3   Collaboration between peers can provide a forum for discovery learning and can encourage creative thinking.
4   Peer interaction can introduce children to the process of generating ideas.

However, Damon (1984, p. 337) explicitly rejects the use of 'extrinsic incentives as part of the group learning situation,' arguing that 'there is no compelling reason to believe that such inducements are an important ingredient in peer learning.'

One category of practical cooperative methods closely related to the developmental perspective is group discovery methods in mathematics, such as Burns's (1981) Groups of Four method. In these techniques, students work in small groups to solve complex problems with relatively little teacher guidance. They are expected to discover mathematical principles by working with unit blocks, manipulatives, diagrams, and other concrete aids.

The theory underlying the presumed contribution of the group format is that in the exploration of opposing perceptions and ideas, higher order understandings will emerge; also, students operating within one another's proximal zones of development will model higher quality solutions for one another. However, studies of group discovery methods such as Groups of Four (Burns, 1981) find few achievement benefits for them in comparison to traditional expository teaching (Davidson, 1985; L. C. Johnson, 1985; L. C. Johnson & Waxman, 1985).

Despite considerable support from theoretical and laboratory research, practical cooperative learning methods based on developmental or discovery theories have yet to demonstrate their instructional effectiveness outside of the laboratory. However, it is likely that the cognitive processes described by developmental theorists are important as mediating variables to explain the effects of group goals and group tasks on student achievement (Slavin, 1987, 1990). This possibility is explored in the last section.

Cognitive elaboration perspective. A cognitive perspective on cooperative learning quite different from the developmental viewpoint is one that might be called the cognitive elaboration perspective. Research in cognitive psychology has long held that if information is to be retained in memory and related to information already in memory, the learner must engage in some sort of cognitive restructuring, or elaboration, of the material (Wittrock, 1978). One of the most effective means of elaboration is explaining the material to someone else. Research on peer tutoring has long found achievement benefits for the tutor as well as the tutee (Devin-Sheehan, Feldman, & Allen, 1976). More recently, Dansereau and his colleagues at Texas Christian University have found in an impressive series of brief studies that college students working on structured 'cooperative scripts' can learn technical material or procedures far better than can students working alone (Dansereau, 1985; [...]). In this method, students take roles as recaller and listener. They read a section of text, and then the recaller summarizes the information while the listener corrects any errors, fills in any omitted material, and helps think of ways both students can remember the main ideas. On the next section, the students switch roles. Dansereau (1985) found in a series of studies that although both the recaller and the listener learned more than did students working alone, the recaller learned more. This mirrors both the peer-tutoring findings and the findings of Webb (1985; [...]), who discovered that the students who gained the most from cooperative activities were those who provided elaborated explanations to others. In this research as well as in Dansereau's, students who received elaborated explanations learned more than those who worked alone, but not as much as those who served as explainers.

One practical use of the cognitive elaboration potential of cooperative learning is in writing process models (Graves, 1983), in which students work in peer response groups or form partnerships to help one another draft, revise, and edit compositions. Such models have been found to be effective in improving creative writing (Hillocks,

1984), and a writing process model emphasizing use of peer response groups is part of the Cooperative Integrated Reading and Composition (CIRC) program (Stevens, Madden, Slavin, & Farnish, 1987), which has been found to increase student writing achievement. Part of the theory behind the use of peer response groups is that if students learn to evaluate others' writing, they will become better writers themselves, a variant of the cognitive elaboration explanation. However, it is unclear at present how much of the effectiveness of writing process models can be ascribed to the use of cooperative peer response groups as opposed to other factors (such as the revision process itself).

One interesting development in recent years that relates to the cognitive elaboration perspective on cooperative learning is Reciprocal Teaching (Palincsar & Brown, 1984), a method for teaching reading comprehensive skills. In this technique, students are taught to formulate questions for one another around narrative or expository texts. In doing so, they must process the material themselves and learn how to focus in on the essential elements of the reading passages. Studies of Reciprocal Teaching have generally supported its effects on student achievement (Palincsar, 1987).

Practice Perspective.   One perspective on cooperative learning that has rarely been articulated is one based on the idea that cooperative learning increases opportunities to practice or rehearse material to proficiency. Direct instruction theorists (e.g., Brophy, 1979) hold that opportunities to practice are critical determinants of instructional effectiveness. At least one theorist, Rosenshine (Rosenshine & Stevens, 1986), accounts for the success of cooperative learning largely in these terms. Practice explanations make most sense in connection with the learning of skills or information with high memory demands but few concepts, such as spelling and math facts. In fact, two of the only studies to find positive effects from forms of cooperative learning lacking group rewards or individual accountability are two Dutch studies of pair learning in spelling (Van Oudenhoven, Van Berkum, & Swen-Koopmans, 1987; Van Oudenhoven, Wiersma, & Van Yperen, 1987). In this subject, it may be apparent to students that the opportunity to take turns quizzing one another on spelling lists is simply more effective than trying to study alone, and no incentives may be needed.

Classroom organization perspective

One perspective on cooperative learning that has not been identified previously focuses on the ability of students to take responsibility for managing themselves in cooperative groups, freeing the teacher to attend to more essential tasks (such as teaching). For example, in a class using reading groups, students can work with one another on meaningful activities during follow-up time while the teacher is teaching one of the reading groups. This use of cooperative learning is essential to CIRC (Stevens et al., 1987) and Team Assisted Individualization–Mathematics (TAI-Math) (Slavin, 1985). In both of these methods, students work in mixed-ability learning teams while the teacher calls up groups of students at the same performance level for lessons. Back at their desks, the remaining students work together on activities that advance them in the subject. In TAI-Math, they work separately on units, check each other's work, and provide explanations and help. In CIRC, students take turns reading to one another; they locate characters, settings, problems, and problem solutions; they summarize stories to one another; and they practice spelling, vocabulary, decoding, and comprehension skills. Both TAI (Slavin, 1985) and CIRC (Stevens et al., 1987) have been consistently effective in increasing student achievment. The classroom organization aspect of these programs is not directly parallel to the theoretical perspectives described earlier and is not a major theoretical rationale for their effectiveness, but it provides a structure within which motivational, cognitive elaboration, and practice dynamics (among others) can operate.

Use of pairs or peer response groups in writing also takes advantage of the classroom management potential of cooperative learning. By training students to respond to one another's writing, the teacher not only is freed from the impossible burden of responding to several drafts but is also able to spend most of class time communicating with students individually.

Reconciling the six perspectives

The six theoretical perspectives discussed here all have well-established rationales, and most have supporting evidence. All are demonstrably 'correct' in some circumstances, but none are probably both necessary and sufficient in *all* circumstances. Research in each tradition tends to establish setting conditions favorable to that perspective. For example, most research on cooperative learning models from the motivational and social cohesiveness perspectives takes place in real classrooms over extended periods, as both extrinsic motivation and social cohesion may be assumed to take time to show their effects. In contrast, studies undertaken from the developmental and cognitive elaboration perspectives tend to be very short, making issues of motivation moot. These latter paradigms also tend to use pairs, rather than groups of four or more; pairs involve a much simpler social process than larger groups, which may need time to develop ways of working well together. Developmental research almost exclusively uses young children trying to learn conservation tasks, which bear little resemblance to the 'social-arbitrary' learning that characterizes most school subjects; cognitive elaboration research mostly involves college students.

However, these alternative perspectives on cooperative learning may be seen as complementary, not contradictory. For example, motivational theorists would not argue that the cognitive theories are unnecessary. Instead, they would argue that motivation drives cognitive process, which in turn produces learning. It is unlikely that over the long haul students would engage in the kind of elaborated explanations found by Webb (1985) to be essential to profiting from cooperative activity if they had no reason to care about their teammates' learning. Similarly, motivational theorists would hold that an intermediate effect of extrinsic incentives must be to build cohesiveness, caring, and prosocial norms among group members, which could in turn affect cognitive processes. One model of the relationships among the six alternative perspectives is diagrammed in Figure 11 (from Slavin, 1989).

The process depicted in Figure 11 shows how group goals might enhance the learning outcomes of cooperative learning. Provision of group goals based on the individual learning of all group members might affect cognitive processes directly by motivating students to engage in peer modeling, cognitive elaboration, and/or practice with one another. Group goals may also lead to group cohesiveness, increasing caring and concern among group members and making them feel responsible for one another's achievement, thereby motivating students to engage in cognitive processes that enhance learning. Finally, group goals may motivate students to take responsibility for one another independently of the teacher, thereby solving important classroom organization problems and providing increased opportunities for cognitively appropriate learning activities.

From the perspective of the model diagrammed in Figure 11, researchers from outside the motivational perspective are attempting to short-circuit the process to

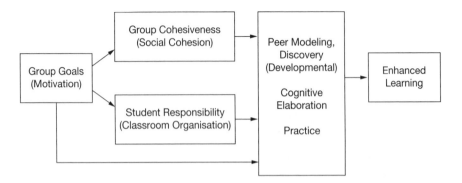

Figure 11 Hypothesized relationships among six perspectives on cooperative learning. From Slavin (1989). Reprinted with permission.

intervene directly on mechanisms identified as mediating variables in the full model. For example, social cohesion theorists intervene directly on group cohesiveness by engaging in elaborate team building and group processing training. The Sharan and Shachar (1988) Group Investigation study suggests that this can be done successfully, but it takes a great deal of time and effort. In this study, teachers were trained over the course of a full year, and then teachers and students used cooperative learning for 3 months before the study began. Earlier research on Group Investigation failed to provide a comparable level of preparation of teachers and students, and the achievement results of these studies were less consistently positive (Slavin, 1989).

Cognitive theorists would hold that the cognitive processes that are essential to any theory relating cooperative learning to achievement can be created directly, without the motivational or affective changes discussed by the motivationalist and social cohesion theorists. This may turn out to be accurate for some school tasks, but at present demonstrations of learning effects from direct manipulation of peer cognitive interactions have mostly been limited to very brief durations and to tasks that lend themselves directly to the cognitive processes involved. For example, the Piagetian conservation tasks studied by developmentalists have few practical analogues in the school curriculum. However, the research on Reciprocal Teaching in reading comprehension (Palincsar & Brown, 1984) shows promise as a means of intervening directly on peer cognitive processes, and long-term applications of Dansereau's (1985) cooperative scripts for comprehension of technical material and procedural instructions seem likely to be successful.

Clearly, much work remains to be done to fully develop a theory to account for cooperative learning effects on achievement and to understand the conditions under which each of the several motivational and cognitive perspectives has explanatory value. Each of the perspectives discussed here contributes to a more complex understanding of how cooperative learning affects student achievement. Until recently, researchers have tended to work on parallel tracks, showing little recognition of work being done in other research traditions on issues related to the achievement effects of cooperative learning. It is now time to look beyond usual disciplinary boundaries to consider more broadly how cooperation among students can enhance their learning.

References

Ames, G. J., & Murray, F. B. (1982). When two wrongs make a right: Promoting cognitive change by social conflict. *Developmental Psychology, 18*, 894–897.

Aronson, E., Blaney, N., Stephan, C., Sikes, J., & Snapp, M. (1978). *The Jigsaw classroom.* Beverly Hills, CA: Sage.

Atkinson, J. W., & Birch, D. (1978). *Introduction to motivation* (2nd ed.). New York: Van Nostrand.

Bell, N., Grossen, M., & Perret-Clermont, A.-N. (1985). Socio-cognitive conflict and intellectual growth. In M. Berkowitz (Ed.), *Peer conflict and psychological growth,* (pp. 88–112). San Francisco: Jossey-Bass.

Bjorkland, R., Johnson, R., & Krotee, M. (1980). *Effects of cooperative, competitive, and individualistic goal structures on golf skills.* Unpublished manuscript, University of Minnesota.

Bossert, S. (1977). Tasks, group management, and teacher control behavior: A study of classroom organization and teacher style. *School Review, 85*, 552–565.

Brookover, W., Beady, C., Flood, P., Schweitzer, J., & Wisenbaker, J. (1979). *School social systems and student achievement.* New York: Praeger.

Brophy, J. E. (1979). Teacher behavior and its effects. *Journal of Educational Psychology, 71*, 733–750.

Bruning, J., Sommer, D., & Jones, B. (1966). The motivating effects of cooperation and competition in the means-independent situation. *Journal of Social Psychology, 68*, 269–274.

Burns, M. (1981, September). Groups of four: Solving the management problem. *Learning, 9*, 46–51.

Cohen, E. (1986). *Designing groupwork: Strategies for the heterogeneous classroom.* New York: Teachers College Press.

Coleman, J. (1961). *The adolescent society.* New York: Free Press.

Crombag, H. G. (1966). Cooperation and competition in means-interdependent triads. *Journal of Personality and Social Psychology, 4*, 692–695.

Damon, W. (1984). Peer education: The untapped potential. *Journal of Applied Developmental Psychology, 5*, 331–343.

Dansereau, D. F. (1985). Learning strategy research. In J. Segal, S. Chipman, & R. Glaser (Eds.), *Thinking and learning skills: Relating instruction to basic research, Vol. 1.* Hillsdale, NJ: Erlbaum.

Davidson, N. (1985). Small-group learning and teaching in mathematics: A selective review of the research. In R. E. Slavin, S. Sharan, S. Kagan, R. Hertz-Lazarowitz, C. Webb, & R. Schmuck (Eds.), *Learning to cooperate, cooperating to learn* (pp. 211–230). New York: Plenum.

DeAvila, E., & Duncan, S. (1980). *Finding Out/Descubrimiento.* Corte Madera, CA: Linguametrics Group.

DeCharms, R. (1957). Affiliation motivation and productivity in small groups. *Journal of Abnormal and Social Psychology, 55*, 22–226.

Deutsch, M. (1949a). An experimental study of the effects of cooperation and competition upon group process. *Human Relations, 2*, 199–231.

—— (1949b). A theory of cooperation and competition. *Human Relations, 2*, 129–152.

Devin-Sheehan, L., Feldman, R., & Allen, V. (1976). Research on children tutoring children: A critical review. *Review of Educational Research, 46*(3), 355–385.

Faust, W. (1959). Group vs. individual problem-solving. *Journal of Abnormal and Social Psychology, 59*, 68–72.

Garibaldi, A. (1979). The effective contributions of cooperative and group goal structures. *Journal of Educational Psychology, 71*, 788–795.

Gordon, K. (1924). Group judgements in the field of lifted weights. *Journal of Experimental Psychology, 7*, 398–400.

Graves, D. (1983). *Writing: Teachers and children at work.* Exeter, NH: Heinemann.

Graziano, W., French, D., Brownell, C., & Hartup, W. (1976). Peer interaction in same- and mixed-age triads in relation to chronological age and incentive condition. *Child Development, 47*, 707–714.

Gurnee, H. (1968). Learning under competitive and collaborative sets. *Journal of Experimental Social Psychology, 4,* 26–34.

Haines, D., & McKeachie, W. (1967). Cooperation versus competitive discussion methods in teaching introductory psychology. *Journal of Educational Psychology, 58,* 386–390.

Hammond, L., & Goldman, M. (1961). Competition and non-competition and its relationship to individual and group productivity. *Sociometry, 24,* 46–60.

Hayes, L. (1976). The use of group contingencies for behavioral control: A review. *Psychological Bulletin, 83,* 628–648.

Hillocks, G. (1984). What works in teaching composition: A meta-analysis of experimental treatment studies. *American Journal of Education, 93,* 133–170.

Huber, G. L., Bogatzki, W., & Winter, M. (1982). *Kooperation als Ziel schulischen Lehrens und Lehrens.* Tubingen, West Germany: Arbeitsbereich Padagogische Psychologie der Universität Tubingen.

Hudgins, B. (1960). Effects of group experience on individual problem solving. *Journal of Educational Psychology, 51,* 37–42.

Hulten, B. H., & DeVries, D. L. (1976). *Team competition and group practice: Effects on student achievement and attitudes* (Report No. 212). Baltimore: Johns Hopkins University, Center for Social Organization of Schools.

Hurlock, E. (1927). Use of group rivalry as an incentive. *Journal of Abnormal and Social Psychology, 22,* 278–290.

Johnson, D. W., & Johnson, R. T. (1974). Instructional structure: Cooperative, competitive or individualistic. *Review of Educational Research, 44,* 213–240.

—— (1979). Conflict in the classroom: Controversy and learning. *Review of Educational Research, 49,* 51–70.

—— (1981). Effects of cooperative and individualistic learning experiences on interethnic interaction. *Journal of Educational Psychology, 73,* 444–449.

—— (1986a). The effect of prolonged implementation of cooperative learning on social support within the classroom. *Journal of Psychology, 119,* 405–411.

—— (1986b). *Learning together and alone,* (2nd ed.). Englewood Cliffs, NJ: Prentice-Hall.

Johnson, D. W., Johnson, R. T., Johnson, J., & Anderson, D. (1976). The effects of cooperative vs. individualized instruction on student prosocial behavior, attitudes toward learning, and achievement. *Journal of Educational Psychology, 68,* 446–452.

Johnson, D. W., Johnson, R. T., & Scott, L. (1978). The effects of cooperative and individualized instruction on student attitudes and achievement. *Journal of Social Psychology, 104,* 207–216.

Johnson, D. W., Johnson, R., & Skon, L. (1979). Student achievement on different types of tasks under cooperative, competitive, and individualistic conditions. *Contemporary Educational Psychology, 4,* 99–106.

Johnson, D. W., Maruyama, G., Johnson, R., Nelson, D., & Skon, L. (1981). Effects of cooperative, competitive, and individualistic goal structures on achievement: A meta-analysis. *Psychological Bulletin, 89,* 47–62.

Johnson, L. C. (1985). *The effects of the "groups of four" cooperative learning model on student problem-solving achievement in mathematics.* Unpublished doctoral dissertation, University of Houston.

Johnson, L. C. & Waxman, H. C. (1985, March). *Evaluating the effects of the "groups of four" program.* Paper presented at the annual meeting of the American Educational Research Association, Chicago.

Julian, J., & Perry, F. (1967). Cooperation contrasted with intra-group and inter-group competition. *Sociometry, 30,* 79–90.

Klugman, S. (1944). Cooperative versus individual efficiency in problem solving. *Journal of Educational Psychology, 34,* 91–100.

Kuhn, D. (1972). Mechanism of change in the development of cognitive structures. *Child Development, 43,* 833–844.

Kukla, A. (1972). Foundations of an attributional theory of performance. *Psychological Review, 77,* 454–470.

Laughlin, P., & Bitz, D. (1975). Individual versus dyadic performance on a disjunctive task as a function of initial ability level. *Journal of Personality and Social Psychology, 31,* 487–496.

Laughlin, P., Branch, L., & Johnson, H. (1969). Individual versus triadic performance on a unidimensional complementary task as a function of initial ability level. *Journal of Personality and Social Psychology, 12*, 144–150.

Laughlin, P., & Johnson, H. (1966). Group and individual performance on a complementary task as a function of initial ability level. *Journal of Experimental Social Psychology, 2*, 407–414.

Laughlin, P., McGlynn, R., Anderson, J., & Jacobson, E. (1968). Concept attainment by individuals versus cooperative pairs as a function of memory, sex, and concept rule. *Journal of Personality and Social Psychology, 8*, 410–417.

Lemke, E., Randle, K., & Robertshaw, C. (1969). Effects of degree of initial acquisition, group size and general mental ability on concept learning and transfer. *Journal of Educational Psychology, 60*, 75–78.

Litow, L., & Pumroy, D. (1975). A brief review of classroom group-oriented contingencies. *Journal of Applied Behavior Analysis, 8*, 341–347.

Madden, N. A., & Slavin, R. E. (1983). Effects of cooperative learning on the social acceptance of mainstreamed academically handicapped students. *Journal of Special Education, 17*, 171–182.

Maller, J. (1929). *Cooperation and competition.* New York: Teachers College, Columbia University.

Marquart, D. (1955). Group problem solving. *Journal of Social Psychology, 41*, 103–113.

Martino, L., & Johnson, D. (1979). The effects of cooperative vs. individualistic instruction on interaction between normal-progress and learning-disabled students. *Journal of Social Psychology, 107*, 177–183.

Michaels, J. (1977). Classroom reward structures and academic performance. *Review of Educational Research, 47*(1), 87–88.

Miller, L., & Hamblin, R. (1963). Interdependence, differential rewarding, and productivity. *American Sociology Review, 28*, 768–778.

Mintz, A. (1951). Non-adaptive group behavior. *Journal of Abnormal and Social Psychology, 46*, 150–159.

Mugny, G., & Doise, W. (1978). Socio-cognitive conflict and structuration of individual and collective performances. *European Journal of Social Psychology, 8*, 181–192.

Murray, F. B. (1982). Teaching through social conflict. *Contemporary Educational Psychology, 7*, 257–271.

Palincsar, A. S. (1987, April). *Reciprocal teaching: Field evaluations in remedial and content area reading.* Paper presented at the annual meeting of the American Educational Research Association, Washington, D.C.

Palincsar, A. S., & Brown, A. L. (1984). Reciprocal teaching of comprehension monitoring activities. *Cognition and Instruction, 2*, 117–175.

Perret-Clermont, A.-N. (1980). *Social interaction and cognitive development in children.* London: Academic Press.

Piaget, J. (1926). *The age and thought of the child.* New York: Harcourt Brace.

Raven, B., & Eachus, H. (1963). Cooperation and competition in means-interdependent triads. *Journal of Abnormal and Social Psychology, 67*, 307–316.

Rich, Y., Amir, Y., & Slavin, R. E. (1986). *Instructional strategies for improving children's cross-ethnic relations.* Ramat Gan, Israel: Bar Ilan University, Institute for the Advancement of Social Integration in the Schools.

Rosenshine, R., & Stevens, R. (1986). Teaching functions. In M. C. Wittrock (Ed.), *Handbook of research on teaching* (3rd ed.), pp. 367–391. New York: Macmillan.

Ryack, B. (1965). A comparison of individual and group learning of nonsense syllables. *Journal of Personality and Social Psychology, 2*, 296–299.

Scott, W., & Cherrington, D. (1974). Effects of competitive, cooperative, and individualistic reinforcement contingencies. *Journal Personality and Social Psychology, 30*, 748–758.

Seta, J., Paulus, P., & Schkade. J. (1976). Effects of group size and proximity under cooperative and competitive conditions. *Journal of Personality and Social Psychology, 34*, 47–53.

Sharan, S., & Hertz-Lazarowitz, R. (1980). A group-investigation method of cooperative learning in the classroom. In S. Sharan, P. Hare, C. Webb, & R. Hertz-Lazarowitz (Eds.), *Cooperation in education.* Provo, UT: Brigham Young University Press.

Sharan, S., & Shachar, H. (1988). *Language and learning in the cooperative classroom.* New York: Springer.

Sirotnik, K. A. (1982, March). *What you see is what you get: A summary of observations in over 1,000 elementary and secondary classrooms.* Paper presented at the annual meeting of the American Educational Research Association, New York.

Slavin, R. E. (1975). *Classroom reward structure: Effects on academic performance, social connectedness, and peer norms.* Unpublished doctoral dissertation, Johns Hopkins University.

—— (1977). Classroom reward structure: An analytic and practical review. *Review of Educational Research, 47,* 633–650.

—— (1978). Student teams and comparison among equals: Effects on academic performance and student attitudes. *Journal of Educational Psychology, 70,* 532–538.

—— (1980). Effects of individual learning expectations on student achievement. *Journal of Educational Psychology, 72,* 520–524.

—— (1983a). *Cooperative learning.* New York: Longman.

—— (1983b). When does cooperative learning increase student achievement? *Psychological Bulletin, 94,* 429–445.

—— (1984). Team assisted individualization: Cooperative learning and individualized instruction in the mainstreamed classroom. *Remedial and Special Education, 5*(6), 33–42.

—— (1985). Team-Assisted Individualization: Combining cooperative learning and individualized instruction in mathematics. In R. E. Slavin, S. Sharan, S. Kagan, R. Hertz-Lazarowitz, C. Webb, & R. Schmuck (Eds.), *Learning to cooperate, cooperating to learn* (pp. 177–209). New York: Plenum.

—— (1986). *Using student team learning: Third edition.* Baltimore, MD: Center for Social Organization of Schools, The Johns Hopkins University.

—— (1987). Cooperative learning: Where behavioral and humanistic approaches to classroom motivation meet. *Elementary School Journal, 88,* 9–337.

—— (1989). Cooperative learning and achievement: Six theoretical perspectives. In C. Ames and M. L. Maehr (Eds.), *Advances in motivation and achievement* (pp. 161–177). Greenwich, CT: JAI Press.

—— (1990). *Cooperative learning: Theory, research, and practice.* Englewood Cliffs, NJ: Prentice-Hall.

Slavin, R. E., DeVries, D. L., & Hulten, B. H. (1975). Individual vs. team competition: The interpersonal consequences of academic performance (Report No. 188). Baltimore: Johns Hopkins University, Center for Social Organization of Schools.

Slavin, R. E., Leavey, M., & Madden, N. A. (1984). Combining cooperative learning and individualized instruction: Effects on student mathematics achievement, attitudes, and behaviors. *Elementary School Journal, 84,* 409–422.

Slavin, R. E., & Tanner, A. M. (1979). Effects of cooperative reward structures and individual accountability on productivity and learning. *Journal of Educational Research, 72*(5), 294–298.

Smith, A. J., Madden, H. E., & Sobel, R. (1957). Productivity and recall in cooperative and competitive discussion groups. *Journal of Psychology, 43,* 193–204.

Stevens, R. J., Madden, N A., Slavin, R. E., & Farnish, A. M. (1987). Cooperative Integrated Reading and Composition: Two field experiments. *Reading Research Quarterly, 22,* 433–454.

Thomas, E. J. (1957). Effects of facilitative role interdependence on group functioning. *Human Relations, 10,* 347–366.

Thorndike, R. L. (1938). On what type of task will a group do well? *Journal of Abnormal and Social Psychology, 33,* 409–413.

Van Oudenhoven, J. P., Van Berkum, G., & Swen-Koopmans, T. (1987). Effect of cooperation and shared feedback on spelling achievement. *Journal of Educational Psychology, 79,* 92–94.

Van Oudenhoven, J. P., Wiersma, B., & Van Yperen, N. (1987). Effects of cooperation and feedback by fellow pupils on spelling achievement. *European Journal of Psychology of Education, 2,* 83–91.

Vroom, V. H. (1969). Industrial social psychology. In G. Lindzey & E. Aronson (Eds.), *The handbook of social psychology* (Vol. 5, 2nd ed.). Reading, MA: Addison-Wesley.

Vygotsky, L. S. (1978). *Mind in society* (M. Cole, V. John-Steiner, S. Scribner, & E. Souberman, Eds.). Cambridge: Harvard University Press.

Wadsworth, B. J. (1984). *Piaget's theory of cognitive and affective development* (3rd ed.). New York: Longman.

Webb, N. (1985). Student interaction and learning in small groups: A research summary. In R. E. Slavin, S. Sharan, S. Kagan, R. Hertz-Lazarowitz, C. Webb, & R. Schmuck (Eds.), *Learning to cooperate, cooperating to learn* (pp. 147–172). New York: Plenum.

Weinstein, A. G., & Holzbach, R. L. (1972). *Effects of financial inducement on performance under two task structures*. Proceedings of 80th Annual Convention of the American Psychological Association. Washington, D.C. APA.

Wittrock, M. C. (1978). The cognitive movement in instruction. *Educational Psychologist, 13*, 15–29.

Workie, A. (1974). The relative productivity of cooperation and competition. *Journal of Social Psychology, 92*, 225–230.

Yager, S., Johnson, R. T., Johnson, D. W., & Snider, B. (1986). The impact of group processing on achievement in cooperative learning. *Journal of Social Psychology, 126*, 389–397.

CHAPTER 14

COLLABORATIVE LEARNING WITH COMPUTERS

Paul Light

P. Scrimshaw (ed.) *Language, Classrooms and Computers*, London, Routledge, 1993

Computers and the individualisation of learning

It has often been held that one of the main advantages of computers in education is that they make it possible to *individualise* the teaching-learning process [. . .]. O'Shea and Self, for example, refer to individualisation and feedback as 'twin gods much worshipped in the computer-assisted learning literature' (1983, p. 70). What does individualisation mean in this context? In its 'strong' form it could refer to a state of affairs in which individual learners each had their own tailor-made curriculum; with content, level and style of learning all being geared to the particular charac- teristics of the individual. In its weaker, but more usual, form it means that, even if all learners are doing broadly the same thing, they can do it at a pace appropriate to their own level of mastery and rate of progress.

The contrast, then, is with the situation of teaching a large class together, where the pace and level have to be pitched at some kind of 'average', which doesn't neces- sarily correspond to that of many (or any) of the individuals concerned. From this point of view, the *ideal* class size would be one, and the ideal teacher-child ratio one to one. This can't economically be achieved with 'real' teachers, so the argu- ment goes, but the computer might make it possible.

From a 'behaviourist' point of view, [. . .] the virtues of individualised tuition can be seen in terms of the possibilities it opens up for generating a gentle 'ladder' of rewarded successes, allowing the child to build up gradually to the desired perform- ance. Within a 'constructivist' framework the individualistic perspective is less explicit, but it is none the less often implicitly present. The dominant image tends to be of the learner as a lone scientist, grappling with problems, testing theories and building models of the world based on experience. Piaget, for example, uses an anecdote about a child (who later became a mathematician) discovering the principles of number conservation while playing alone with pebbles, arranging and rearranging them. If one starts with this perspective on the learning process, it is natural to see the advent of the computer in terms of its potentialities for stimulating and supporting learners in this kind of individual voyage of discovery.

Thus from some points of view the educational ideal might be for all learners to have their own computer, and for them to work on their own projects, at their own level and pace, more or less independently of both teachers and other learners. This potential independence of the machine-based learning process from interaction with other learners has, since the early days of the teaching machine, awoken fears of a dehumanised and dehumanising future for education. As Lepper and Gurtner (1989) remark, the prospect of a classroom in which children spend the day plugged into their own individual desktop computers seems a chilling one to many teachers.

Many of the more negative images of the role of the computer in education associate it with the replacement of warm blooded educational experience, grounded in social interaction, by a cold blooded, technologically controlled learning environment. This is in part an ideological matter, of course, reflecting a tension between on the one hand a vision of education (and indeed of society) as a fundamentally cooperative venture and on the other a vision of education and society framed in terms of individual survival in a competitive world. But it is also, in part at least, a psychological matter. To what extent *can* cognitive or intellectual aspects of development be separated from social–emotional aspects? In this chapter we shall be exploring the thesis that learning in any context is as much a social as an individual process. [. . .] Here we shall be concerned with the claim that what goes on *between learners* can be crucially important to the effectiveness of the learning process. And paradoxically, as we shall see, there is an argument for saying that the advent of the computer could and should lead to greater rather than lesser development of collaborative approaches to learning.

Interaction in learning: observation and description

The worrying image of the socially isolated and withdrawn learner, usually seen as an adolescent hunched over his or her (typically his) computer for hours at a time, still has considerable currency. However, the reality in most cases seems to be very different, both in and out of school. For example, a group of French sociologists (Boffety *et al.*, 1984) have described the rich social culture of the computer clubs and informal, out-of-school networks of computer enthusiasts which have grown up around one French secondary school of which they made an intensive study. They point out that in many ways these groups and networks resembled very closely those which had grown up in the same school around a shared interest in rock music, or in motor cycles.

Within the school curriculum, the simple fact of scarce resources militates against highly individualised work with computers, especially at primary level. The situation may be subject to rapid change, of course, but in a survey of UK primary schools, Jackson, Fletcher and Messer (1986) obtained clear evidence that the predominant pattern was for children to work in pairs or small groups rather than individually at the computer. Although it might seem at first sight that this is simply a reflection of the normal British primary school practice of working in groups, this is not necessarily the case. As many observational studies have indicated (e.g. Bennett, 1987; Galton, 1989) the children working around a table in a typical primary school are typically not working on *joint* tasks but rather on *parallel* ones. By contrast, when they are sent off to have their turn working at the computer they are often engaged in a truly *joint* learning experience, working together on a shared task. Moreover, it is a learning experience in which the teacher may be relatively little involved. Under these conditions, far from reducing the opportunities for group-based and socially interactive learning, computers may actually be associated with an increase in such opportunities.

In the United States, researchers at Bank Street College, New York, took an early interest in the ways in which the introduction of computers seemed to affect the interactive aspects of children's learning (Sheingold, Hawkins and Char, 1984). Sheingold and her colleagues report that when working with computers, students appeared to be interacting more with each other about learning tasks, and calling on each other more for help. In one classroom observation study, for example, they compared sessions in which children were using computers to learn to program in Logo with other, non-computer-based work. Children were free to interact and work together in both situations, but the researchers observed more interaction in the context of the computer-based than the non-computer-based work. This interaction took varied forms, including systematic collaboration, casual 'dropping in', and soliciting help from a more expert learner.

Researchers in Great Britain interested in the use of Logo in school settings have likewise reported that children working in pairs or small groups with Logo typically show high levels of spontaneous, task-related interaction. As Martin Hughes (1990) notes, the early Logo work, influenced heavily by Papert, was concerned with the effect of working with Logo on individual cognitive skills. However, many anecdotal accounts emerging from individual teachers using Logo in their classrooms attested to striking *social* effects. Intensive case study research, such as that conducted by Celia Hoyles and Rosamund Sutherland (Hoyles and Sutherland, 1986, 1989) also strongly suggests that the introduction of Logo programming can have positive effects on children's *socially interactive* learning. Indeed these researchers argue that the advantage of Logo as an approach to teaching mathematics rests in large part on the way in which it provokes and sustains a high level of *discussion* between learners.

The value of discussion and interaction amongst learners in the context of their learning has been endorsed by a succession of educational reports (e.g. Bullock, 1975; Cockroft, 1982) and is given further official sanction by many of the curriculum documents stemming from the 1988 Education Reform Act. Before we go on to look more specifically at research in the field of collaborative computer use, it is worth devoting a little time in the next section to considering *how* exactly discussion and interaction are supposed to confer benefits on children's learning.

Discussion, interaction and learning

There is, as we have already noted, a widespread belief amongst teachers and others concerned with education that discussion and interaction are 'a good thing'. The benefits they are supposed to confer may be at a very general level, and may be as much social as intellectual. For example, Crook refers to the belief: 'that cognitive development involves a necessary coordination of our thinking with that of others in the interests of various kinds of harmony and in the service of various kinds of joint activity' (1987, p. 31). Producing students who are disposed and able to cooperate with one another is a legitimate goal for education, and some research on collaborative learning has focused on its effects on school children's sociability and cooperativeness. However, in this chapter we are more concerned with any direct effects that a collaborative mode of working might have on levels of achievement or learning outcomes.

One problem which arises straight away is whether one should be concerned with effectiveness in terms of how much the learners manage to achieve when working together, or in terms of the learning outcomes for each of the individuals concerned. For example, the title of the Sheingold *et al.* article referred to earlier, 'I'm the thinkist, you're the typist' refers to one particular pattern of interaction they observed. The authors comment that this distribution of roles may have been quite an effective way of 'getting the job done', but was probably not very productive as a learning experience for some of the individuals concerned.

It is worth pausing a little longer over this issue, though. While it is fairly obvious that we don't want to use group achievements as the sole criterion of the quality of a group learning experience, it is not altogether obvious that we should take the opposite tack and concern ourselves exclusively with what each of the learners can do *on their own* as a consequence of the group experience. In the everyday environment, whether of children or adults, most thinking, reasoning and problem solving does go on in groups of one sort or another. For example, we could go back to the Piagetian conception which we introduced much earlier on, of 'the child as scientist', and remark that the implicit conception of the scientist as someone who *individually* grapples with the secrets of nature hardly squares with the realities of scientific work. In this, as in almost all other work contexts, the ability to function effectively in a team is a key qualification for success.

So different questions could be asked about the efficacy of discussion and interaction in learning, depending on the valuation one places on different kinds and levels of learning outcome. It is perhaps an indication of the strength of the individualistic ethos in our society that even in this area, where we are particularly concerned with social processes in learning, educationalists and researchers have tended to take for granted that we should be concerned mainly or exclusively with *individual* learning outcomes. The question thus becomes: what possible mechanisms or processes might lead to better individual learning outcomes when children work together in pairs or small groups at the computer than when they work on their own?

The effects of having a partner (or partners) can be thought of at a number of levels. We might think, for example, about the possibility that having a partner makes the task more fun, or less threatening. We might suppose that partners could pick up ideas from one another, or help each other to remember things. We might attribute particular significance to the role of argument and disagreement in shaping learning, or more simply suppose that just *talking about* the problem to someone else helps us to think about it more clearly ourselves.

Learners will obviously come to any given task with different backgrounds of knowledge and understanding, and perhaps different levels of familiarity or ability relevant to the particular task at hand. In some cases one learner may offer others a comprehensive model to imitate. In others each may be able to contribute different, perhaps partially overlapping subsets of task-relevant information. Using software which calls for the exploration of a wide range of different possibilities, or which imposes a heavy load on memory, one can see fairly readily that 'two heads might be better than one'.

Research has been undertaken on the way in which conflicts or disagreements between partners in a learning experience might affect learning. Willem Doise and colleagues in Switzerland, for example, have highlighted *socio-cognitive conflict* as a key factor (Doise and Mugny, 1984). Basing their work on some of Piaget's tests of children's logical reasoning for 5–7 year olds, they suggest that individuals typically fail because they 'centre' their attention on one aspect of a problem and fail to notice other, equally relevant factors. By bringing together two or three children, even if they are at more or less the same level of development there is a fair chance that their attention will be captured by different aspects of the situation, so that they will come into conflict with one another. For example, in Piaget's most famous task, where the child has to appreciate that the amount of, say, juice remains the same when the juice is poured into a different shaped container, one child may notice that the 'new' jar is fatter while another may notice only that the level is lower. On their own, they would thus draw opposite, and equally wrong conclusions, but Doise observed that in the course of interaction the conflict often resulted in both of the children 'decentering' to a higher level, conserving solution which recognised the validity of both of their points of view. In some circumstances at least, then, two wrongs *can* make a right. Whether this kind of 'socio-cognitive conflict' represents an important general mechanism for learning remains an open question.

Some researchers have focused more on the role of talk itself in facilitating the learning process. For example Celia Hoyles (1985; Hoyles, Sutherland and Healy, 1990) uses the term *distancing* to describe the way in which articulating one's thoughts for someone else can help to sort them out for oneself: 'Talking provokes a representation of one's thoughts – a process which inevitably raises them to a more conscious plane of awareness so that they can become the objects of reflection and modification' (Hoyles, Sutherland and Healy, 1990). She also sees talk as having a *monitoring* role, with learners developing shared plans and then monitoring and checking each other's actions, as well as their own, against the plan.

Where have we got to, then? We saw earlier that there is increasing recognition that interaction between learners can confer advantages in the context of computer-based learning. A number of observational studies lent credence to this view. We have also seen a number of plausible ways in which discussion and interaction *could* facilitate individual learning. You may well be able to come up with some others. However, we have not touched on much in the way of *evidence* thus far. Indeed, it could be argued that our account has been unduly partisan, since we have ignored ways in which *individual* computer use might be seen to have advantages. So at this point we need to return to the question of research evidence, specifically concerned with computers and learning, to see just how consistent that evidence is with the story we have been trying to tell.

Peer facilitation of computer-based learning: the experimental approach

At the heart of any experimental approach in this, as in any other field is the idea of *comparison*. At its simplest, one might want to compare the progress of learners who work alone at the computer and of those who work together. If large numbers of learners are available, and if it is possible to assign them to different learning situations ('experimental conditions') at random so as to get two equivalent groups, then it may suffice just to set up one condition in which students work in, say, pairs (again, perhaps, pairing them at random) and another condition in which students work alone. The outcome could be assessed by 'post-testing' everyone individually to see what they have learned.

One study which comes close to this 'simplest case' was conducted in Israel by Zemira Mevarech and her colleagues (Mevarech, Silber and Fine, 1987). Five classes of 12 year olds used arithmetic drill-and-practice-type Cal software over a month period. A third of them worked individually from the outset. The others worked in pairs, being encouraged to share the keyboard, to help each other, and to discuss and agree solutions. The main point at issue was whether the children who worked together would in fact learn more than those who worked alone.

The only departure from the design outlined above was that the children were paired up, not at random, but on the basis of having similar scores at pre-test. At the beginning of the study, all the children worked alone at the computer on a sample of all the types of items to be learned. They were then grouped into triplets on the basis of having similar scores. One was selected at random from each trio to go into the individual learning condition while the other two formed a pair. This arrangement ensured that, overall, the initial ability levels of those who worked individually were closely comparable with those who worked in pairs, and also that in the pairs there would be no great disparities in ability.

At the end of four months all children again undertook an individual assessment across all the types of items on which they had been working, and this was repeated again some two months later. Both in the immediate and the delayed post-test the children who had worked in pairs showed significantly greater achievement gains than the children who worked alone. It is also interesting to note that a questionnaire-type measure of the children's *anxiety* about mathematics showed that working in pairs alleviated such anxiety, especially of low ability students, significantly more than did the individual mode of working.

Across a range of studies on this issue, results are by no means entirely consistent. Some studies have found a significant advantage of working in pairs, others have not. However, the third possible outcome, that children would do better when working alone at the computer than when working in pairs, does not seem to have been found.

In order to understand why peer facilitation of learning is sometimes found and sometimes isn't, it is necessary to look more closely at the patterns of interaction involved. In some cases it has proved possible to improve conditions for peer facilitation of learning by simple modifications of the software. For example, Light *et al.* (1987) conducted a number of studies using a version of the Towers of Hanoi task. The screen display is shown in Figure 12. The aim of the game is to move the three (or more) 'tiles' from one peg to another (say, from peg number 1 to peg number 3). The two key rules are that only one tile may be moved at a time, and that one must never put a larger one on top of a smaller one. With three tiles, as shown, the optimal solution takes seven moves.

The research design involved random assignment of 8 year olds to individual or paired conditions and random assignment to particular pairings, except that children were always paired with another child of the same gender and from the same school class. The studies, which took place in schools but not as part of regular classes, involved one or sometimes two sessions of practice on the task, followed a week later by an individual post-test for all children, using slight variants on the same task.

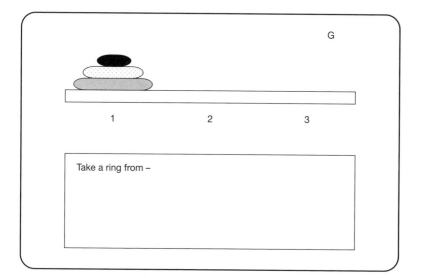

Figure 12 The screen presentation for the microcomputer version of the 'Towers of Hanoi' task.

The first of these studies showed no significant advantage of working in pairs, which was surprising given earlier findings of peer-facilitation with a non-computer version of the task. Observation suggested that in the computer-based version the students tended to just take turns to make moves, or in other cases one of them dominated the whole task. On the previous non-computer version (Light and Glachan, 1985), we had used handles on each side of each 'tile', and with the students sitting opposite one another, we required them *both* to help make each move. So we decided to try to replicate this in the computer version, introducing a 'dual key' constraint, such that each participant had a different part of the keyboard, and *both* had to key in a given instruction before it would be executed. We compared 20 students who worked alone (for a single session of practice), 20 who worked in pairs without the dual key constraint, and 20 who worked in pairs with this constraint. At the individual post-test a week later, there was no difference in the efficiency of solutions for the first two conditions, but significantly more of the children in the third, 'dual key' condition were able to solve the problem in the optimal number of moves.

This kind of study makes it clear that simply putting learners together in front of a computer will not ensure peer facilitation of their learning. Conditions have to be such that they engage both with the task *and with one another* in the course of their learning. The features of the computer itself will not ensure this. On the whole it seems fair to say that microcomputers have been designed with a single user in mind. The keyboard and the mouse are devices which seem naturally adapted to the single user. On the other hand the VDU screen is a readily shareable resource, at least in a pair or small group. What is written or shown on the screen (or pointed out) has a public and shared character (as compared, for example, to what is written in students' own workbooks). The effects of different types of interface device upon patterns of interaction in learning have been little studied as yet, but research in this area would be well worth pursuing. And of course the nature of the *software* in use has a potentially major effect, as we saw in a small way with the 'dual key' study.

The influence of different types of software has been discussed by Crook (1987), for example. On the basis of classroom observations he found that some types of CAL software tend to elicit a great deal of simple turn taking. Others, especially those where the problem is readily perceived and shared but the solution is complex, elicited more interaction. The richest forum for discussion was provided by an adventure game. Crook highlights several points as being in need of more research. These include the issue of individual differences in children's ability on the given task, and the possibility that collaborative modes of working might heighten their awareness of relative ability, with deleterious consequences for the less able children. Crook suggests (p. 36) that this may be particularly true where computers provide very clear and direct trial by trial feedback. Again, the information we seem to need more of concerns the ways in which different types of pairings/groupings (e.g. similar vs mixed ability) interact with different types of tasks/software.

One of the candidates which we considered in the previous section, when we were trying to identify possible 'major ingredients' in profitable interchanges around the computer was simply *talk*. It might be just the fact of having to *talk* about what you are doing as you solve a task which makes learning more effective. Some evidence for this comes from a study by Ben Fletcher (1985) using a specially devised problem-solving task, based on a 'spaceship' game, in which children had to find settings of three 'input variables' which would achieve a specified target for a given 'output variable' (such as the number of passengers carried). Fifty-five children aged between 9 and 11 years were the subjects, working in school but out of the classroom. Eleven children worked on their own, silently. Eleven others worked alone but were encouraged to talk aloud about each decision they made and why they made it (the experimenter was present but did not interact). The rest of the children were formed into eleven groups of three, each group containing children matched in ability in terms of reading age. These children were encouraged to talk amongst themselves and reach consensus decisions. On three of the four performance targets the groups *and* the verbalising individuals performed better (in terms of the number of decisions needed to reach the specified targets) than the silent individuals. Fletcher does not want to argue that *all* the advantage of peer interaction in learning stems from verbalisation, but it does seem that it may be an important factor in at least some cases.

'Working together', in the sense that we have used the expression, has referred to situations in which several students work together in a broadly collaborative fashion. There seems to be a broad consensus that *cooperative* learning situations are likely to be more effective than *competitive* ones. One study which has directly addressed this is reported by Johnson, Johnson and Stanne (1986) in the United States. Seventy-five 11–13 year olds worked on a computer-based geography simulation task, involving mapping and navigation. A third of them worked in an individual condition where, subject to sharing time on the available computers, students worked on their own on the task for 45 minutes a day over a 10-day period. Another third of the students worked *competitively*. They were assigned to groups, usually of four, and were instructed to compete to see who was best. Finally, a third of the students worked *cooperatively*. Again they were assigned to groups of four but were instructed to work together as a group. In all conditions, students filled in individual worksheets every day, on which they received feedback and took a final test. In the 'individual' group they were told that they would be graded against an absolute standard of excellence. In the competitive condition they were to be graded by how well they did relative to others in their group. In the cooperative condition they were told that they would be graded by the average of the scores of the group members on the worksheets and final test. Children in the cooperative condition showed significantly higher levels of achievement, both on a day by day basis and in the final test, than either of the other groups. They also, incidentally, showed less dependence on the teacher and more positive attitudes towards working with students of the opposite sex than students in the other conditions. On the basis of this and other similar studies, Johnson, Johnson and Stanne argue that the *cooperative* organisation of groups, tasks and rewards has a central role to play in the peer facilitation of computer-based learning.

One interesting design feature of the study just described is that none of the students were actually working *on their own*. All were working in the context of a class, the difference between conditions being in the 'ground rules' by which they were working and the way in which individual tasks were organised in relation to one another. In most of the experimental studies we have described, which took place outside the classroom, the 'individual' condition literally involved the student working by him- or herself at the computer with no access to the other students. In classroom terms this is arguably a fairly unrealistic situation.

This point was illustrated, for example, in a study we conducted with 11 and 12 year olds while they began to learn to use the programming language micro-PROLOG (Light, Colbourn and Smith, 1987). The students worked in class groups of eight over a number of sessions. Each group of eight was given access to either two, four or eight microcomputers so that they worked either four, two or one to a machine. We videotaped some of the learning sessions and also tested the students' individual grasp of micro-PROLOG at the end. No overall differences in learning outcome were found between the three conditions. However, when we analysed the videotape it turned out that the amount of task-related *interaction* between students was also very similar across the three conditions. During the learning session, the students were very much left to their own devices, without a lot of teacher input. In these conditions, even when they had a machine to themselves the students tended to engage in a very high level of task-related interaction with their neighbours. The net result was that the amount of interaction was largely unrelated to the number of machines available.

We wouldn't want to claim too much for this one study, but it does serve to highlight the interesting question of how, if at all, changing the level of provision (in terms of the number of computers available), will affect students' learning. The effects may depend, as much as anything, on any indirect effects that the level of resource may have on the organisation of the learning environment, and thus on the interactional context in which learning takes place.

Studies such as the last two we have mentioned also highlight the problem of knowing what is the appropriate comparison or 'control' condition for research in this field. Should we compare, as many studies have done, the pair or group working at the computer on the one hand and the individual working in isolation at the keyboard on the other? Or is it more appropriate to use as a comparison the individual working on his or her own computer but with free access to fellow students?

Faced with this difficulty, one research option we have is to move away from studies which set up different conditions in order to compare them, towards a more 'correlational' approach. If we want to understand whether a particular type of interaction facilitates learning, we can simply observe students in any situation within which such interaction is *possible*, and see if those who spontaneously engage in a lot of it are in fact those for whom the learning outcome is best. In other words, how well does the quality or quantity of interaction *correlate* with successful learning. An advantage of this approach is that it is much easier to employ it in the context of ongoing 'real' learning situations, rather than specially set up experimental ones.

One example of this approach can be found in the work of Noreen Webb and colleagues (Webb, Ender and Lewis, 1986). They observed a group of 30 11 to 14 year olds following a course in BASIC programming. All the students worked in pairs, but at the end they were given an individual test to assess their competence. During the paired learning sessions careful measures were taken of the children's spontaneous verbal and interactive behaviours. Variables which turned out to be related to individual achievement in programming included giving and receiving explanations, receiving responses to questions, and verbalising aloud when typing at the keyboard: in other words, the students who engaged in the highest levels of these interactive behaviours during learning were the ones who scored best on the programming test at the end of the course.

Webb's categories of verbal interaction are in one sense very *non*-interactive, since they are simply counts of how many of various kinds of utterances each child produced or received. They don't really attempt to get at, for example, the level of disagreement or *conflict* involved in the learning experience. Yet as we saw earlier, it has been argued that 'socio-cognitive conflict' lies at the heart of productive peer interaction. What evidence is there that conflict has an important role to play in the context of computer-based learning?

Some evidence, albeit rather crude, comes from a study by Light and Glachan (1985). Twenty pairs of 8 year olds were observed working in pairs on a computer game based on the popular code-breaking peg-board game Mastermind. The frequency of 'conflicts' was scored from videotapes of the interaction – a conflict was defined as a situation where one student put forward a proposition for an entry, the other put forward a counter-proposition, and at least one of them explicitly tried to justify their proposition against their partner's (usually by reference to the feedback given by the computer in respect of earlier entries). Note that conflict in this sense implies disagreement about strategy, and argument, but not necessarily mutual hostility! In most cases such 'conflicts' were embodied in very positive and mutually supportive discussions. It turned out that members of those pairs which showed a high level of such conflict during the learning sessions did significantly better on an individual post-test using the same task.

Clearly, this finding is consistent with the idea that such conflict offers a productive learning experience. But alternatively it could simply reflect the fact that more able children tend to engage in more of this kind of conflict. In this study, fortunately, we were able to exclude this alternative explanation because we had included an individual *pre*-test as well as post-test in the design of the study. By looking back to the pre-test data it was possible to show that those students who engaged in more conflict during the learning sessions were neither significantly more nor less able, at least on this particular task, at the outset.

There is thus some support for the idea that conflict plays an important role in productive learning interactions. But neither the socio-cognitive conflict model nor common sense would suggest that the amount of disagreement will always be a good index of effective learning. What the theory predicts is that disagreement will be effective when it serves the purpose of drawing students' attention to aspects of a problem they might otherwise have neglected and when some *resolution* of the conflict is possible which in some way reconciles the various perspectives involved.

Celia Hoyles and her co-workers have approached the task of analysing the constructive role of discourse in a subtler, more qualitative fashion. Their approach has been to work with much smaller numbers of students – just a few pairs – but to follow their interactions around the computer over a long period of time. Their work (e.g. Hoyles and Sutherland, 1989; Hoyles, Sutherland and Healy, 1990) has been conducted in the context of classroom mathematics work in the secondary school. Using audiotapes of interaction in conjunction with a video record of what was going on on the screen, they have attempted to pick out and examine productive interchanges in detail.

As they see it, the collaborative situation facilitates the generation and articulation of hypotheses about patterns and regularities, and the verbal exchanges help to bridge from a particular pattern detected by one of the children to its generalisation in the form appropriate to the computer environment.

Conflict, as they use the term, occurs when there is any kind of mismatch between what a student is trying to bring off and what the partner, or the computer itself, allows or comprehends. Conflict in this sense, they suggest, may be as much or more a feature of the student-computer interaction as it is of the student-student interaction. The nature of this cognitive conflict and the points at which it arises depend very much on the software in use. But the critical role for discussion between learners comes precisely at the point when this conflict arises: at this point the different perceptions of the problem and of the solution have to be negotiated, made explicit and rendered compatible with the mathematical constraints of the task.

This analysis points up the fact that when a pair of students interact with a computer we may see 'two-way' interaction (between the students) or 'three-way' interaction (involving the students and the computer). One might add, of course, the possibility of 'four-way' interactions, bringing the teacher back into account, though we have been studiously ignoring that dimension in this chapter!

In sum, then, as we have seen, the mid- to late 1980s have witnessed the appearance of a considerable body of research on the way in which learner-learner interactions can facilitate computer-based learning. Taken as a whole this research certainly seems to confirm that what goes on between students working together at the computer can and often does form a very important ingredient of the learning situation. In comparing the efficacy of say, pairs as against individuals, though, this kind of research tends to gloss over all kinds of variations amongst students which may be highly relevant. For example, we have not been able to say much about how group size, or the levels and ranges of ability within groups, affect computer-based learning, nor about how individual temperamental differences affect the way students respond to individual versus collaborative ways of working. Nor have we dealt with the issue of *gender* differences, and how these might be affected by different patterns of computer use. [. . .]

Conclusions: collaborative learning and the computer

As well as being limited in its treatment of individual and group differences, this chapter has been limited in terms of the kinds of software and hardware environments and applications we have discussed. We have considered some of the ways in which the computer can support profitable interaction between learners, working together at the machine, but we have not considered interaction *through* the machine, by networking, conferencing or electronic mail, for example [. . .]. We have not really considered the extent to which the computer might come to act as a *participant* in an interactive process of learning. Intelligent tutoring systems aim to create a tutorial dialogue between the student and the machine which has many of the features of a 'real' social interaction. Some are aimed at more than one learner at a time, while others are being developed which attempt to simulate an 'interactive partner' within the Intelligent Tutoring System itself (e.g. Chan and Baskin, 1988). Developments in these fields may radically change our conception of the role of interaction in computer-based learning in the future.

We opened this chapter by sketching the argument that computers in education could deliver something that the hard-pressed human teacher was rarely able to deliver, namely 1:1 teaching geared sensitively to the needs of the individual learner. We might end it with almost the opposite scenario. From the Plowden Report right through to the National Curriculum documents, the *potential* of collaborative learning in small groups has been recognised. However, in practice schools have not found it at all easy to tap this potential. For example, in 1980 when Galton and colleagues published the ORACLE study, based on extremely detailed observation of primary classrooms, they reported that despite grouped seating arrangements the children almost always worked separately, on their own individual tasks. This was before computers arrived on the scene.

The studies we have considered in the course of the chapter strongly suggest that the use of computers has the potential to enhance collaborative learning. They also confirm that, in the context of computers, this mode of learning can lead to improved outcomes, even when these are judged at the individual level. It may be, then, that the computer can deliver something which other teaching and learning contexts tend to lack – perhaps by providing just sufficient structure, direction and support to the learning process to enable the collaborative learning process to be effectively sustained.

Before accepting such a conclusion too glibly though, we ought to give some thought to the *kinds* of evidence which we have been drawing on. Experimental research has a natural place in academic disciplines such as psychology, but how useful is this kind of research in the practical domain of education? Often, in order to maximise experimental control of the variables, artificial situations are created by researchers. There is a tension between the goal of maximising the 'power' of the experiment (by keeping it as *simple* as possible) and the goal of making the study *valid* in relation to the real contexts of teaching and learning. Researchers are often accused of giving too much attention to the first of these goals and not enough to the second. The old joke about the man looking under a lamp post for a coin which he dropped somewhere else 'because the light is better here' may be all too applicable.

There is, then, plenty of room for scepticism about the usefulness of research. As Heather Govier (1988) points out, teachers are accustomed to relying on their own judgements as experienced practitioners rather than on experimental research. Perhaps the best way for teachers to treat research in this field is as an indication of *possibilities*, and as a stimulus to evaluate or re-evaluate their own experience. And perhaps the best way for researchers to make progress in this field is by working much more closely than in the past with practising teachers. It is notable that a new large-scale research project on groupwork with computers (Eraut and Hoyles, 1988), which will run well into the 1990s, is firmly wedded to the idea of using teachers as co-researchers and drawing all data from the context of 'real' classroom practice.

If studies such as this kind can claim more validity than shorter-term, more controlled experimental research, it is partly because they recognise that in practice learners are exposed to many more influences than simply those of an immediate learning partner. They are part of a larger group: a school, a college, a class, or whatever. We have concentrated in this chapter on a 'micro-social' domain, concerned with interactions between learners in the immediate learning situation. We have largely neglected questions about the organisation of groupwork in the classroom, and the wider social and cultural context within which learning occurs. Even more significantly, perhaps, we have had little or nothing to say about the role of the *teacher* in all this. [. . .]

References

Bennett, N. (1987) 'Cooperative learning: children do it in groups – or do they?', *Educational and Child Psychology*, 4: 7–18.

Boffety, B., Descolonges, M., Daphy, E. and Perriault, J. (1984) 'Rock on Informatique?: pratiques technologique d'adolescence et modes de vie', Paris, Institut National Recherches Pedagogique.

Bullock, A. (1975) *A Language for Life*, London, HMSO.

Chan, T.-W. and Baskin, A. (1988) 'Studying with the Prince: the computer as learning companion', paper presented to ITS-88 Conference, Montreal, June.

Cockcroft, W. (1982) *Mathematics Counts*, London, HMSO.

Crook, C. (1987) 'Computers in the Classroom', in Rutowska, J. C. and Crook, C. (eds) *Computers, Cognition and Development*, New York, John Wiley & Sons Inc.

Doise, W. and Mugny, G. (1984) *The Social Development of the Intellect*, Oxford, Pergamon Press.

Eraut, M. and Hoyles, C. (1988) 'Groupwork with computers', *Journal of Computer Assisted Learning*, 5: 12–24.

Fletcher, B. (1985) 'Group and individual learning of junior school children on a micro-computer-based task', *Educational Review*, 37: 251–61.

Galton, M. (1989) *Teaching in the Primary School*, London, David Fulton Publishers.

Galton, M., Simon, B. and Croll, P. (1980) *Inside the Primary School*, London, Routledge & Kegan Paul.

Govier, H. (1988) *Microcomputers in Primary Education: a survey of recent research*, Economic and Social Research Council Information Technology and Education programme Occasional Paper ITE/28a/88.

Hoyles, C. (1985) 'What is the point of group discussion in mathematics?', *Educational Studies in Mathematics*, 16: 205–14.

Hoyles, C. and Sutherland, R. (1986) 'Using Logo in the mathematics classroom', *Computers and Education*, 10: 61–72.

Hoyles, C. and Sutherland, R. (1989) *Logo Mathematics in the Classroom*, London, Routledge.

Hoyles, C., Sutherland, R. and Healy, I. (1990) 'Children talking in computer environments: new insights on the role of discussion in mathematics learning', in Durkin, K. and Shine, B. (eds) *Language and Mathematical Education*, Milton Keynes, Open University Press.

Hughes, M. (1990) 'Children's computation', in Grieve, R. and Hughes, M. (eds) *Understanding Children*, Oxford, Blackwell.

Jackson, A., Fletcher, B. and Messer, D. (1986) 'A survey of microcomputer use and provision in primary schools', *Journal of Computer Assisted Learning*, 2: 45–55.

Johnson, R., Johnson, D. and Stanne, M. (1986) 'Comparison of computer assisted cooperative, competitive and individualistic learning', *American Educational Research Journal*, 23: 382–92.

Lepper, M. and Gurtner, J. (1989) 'Children and computers: approaching the twenty-first century', *American Psychologist*, 44: 170–8.

Light, P.H., Colbourn, C.J. and Smith, D. (1987) 'Peer interaction and logic programming: a study of the acquisition of micro-prolog', *ESRC Information Technology and Education Programme*, Occasional Paper ITE/17/87.

Light, P.H., Foot, T., Colbourn, C. and McClelland, I. (1987) 'Collaborative interactions at the microcomputer keyboard', *Educational Psychology*, 7(1): 13–21.

Light, P.H. and Glachan, M. (1985) 'Facilitation of individual problem solving through peer interaction', *Educational Psychology*, 5: 217–25.

Mevarech, Z., Silber, O. and Fine, D. (1987) 'Learning with computers in small groups: cognitive and affective outcomes', Second European Conference for Research in Learning and Instruction, Tubingen, W. Germany.

O'Shea, T. and Self, J. (1983) *Learning and Teaching with Computers*, Brighton, Harvester Press.

Sheingold, K., Hawkins, J. and Char, C. (1984) ' "I'm the thinkist, you're the typist": the interaction of technology and the social life of classrooms', *Journal of Social Issues*, 40(3): 49–61.

Webb, N., Ender, P. and Lewis, S. (1986) 'Problem solving strategies and group processes in small groups learning computer programming', *American Educational Research Journal*, 23: 247–61.

PART 8

ACTIVITY THEORY

CHAPTER 15

LOOKING BEYOND THE INTERFACE
Activity theory and distributed learning

David R. Russell

M. Lea and K. Nicoll (eds) *Distributed Learning*, London and New York, RoutledgeFalmer, 2002

Introduction

In this chapter, I first outline some basic principles of activity theory and then explore some ways it has proved valuable for analysing distributed learning, in both schooling and workplace training. Activity theory was developed out of the Russian developmental psychologist L.S. Vygotsky's (1994) cultural–historical approach to learning by one of his two main collaborators, A.N. Leont'ev (1981), beginning in the late 1930s. It has evolved into a major direction in psychology (called 'cultural psychology') and now has adherents worldwide.

Activity theory (AT) [. . .] has for many years been used in studies of human–computer interaction, such as computer interface design and computer-supported cooperative work (Nardi 1996). In the past 5 years, it has begun to be used to understand distributed learning, as technological innovations in education have often 'seemed to be designed to exploit the capabilities of the technology rather than to meet an instructional need', to be technology-driven rather than theory-driven (Koschmann 1996: 83). As a result, instructional designers have often overlooked the cultural and historical aspects of education, focusing instead on individual learners encountering the machine interface (Kapetin and Cole 1997; Leavis 1997; Bakardjieva 1998; Guribye and Wasson 1999).

AT, like many of the other theories in this volume, attempts to go beyond the theories of learning that seem so obvious when teachers or instructional designers look at a person in front of a computer 'learning' the 'material' that appears on the screen. At first glance we imagine, perhaps, an individual responding to stimuli on the screen, internalising 'material' through repetition. In this view, the behaviourist stimulus–response learning theory seems a good enough explanation. Or we imagine, within the mind of the individual looking at the screen, inborn structures of thought being activated, in a communication of ideas between minds, as in idealist theories (like Plato's or Kant's) or structuralist theories (like Piaget's). Yet when we look further back over time, things often seem much less tidy. Some people do not learn at all but turn away from the screen, lacking motivation. Some interpret that 'material' in ways we may not expect (and may not like). People learn (and forget) to different degrees and in different ways, or put that learning to unexpected uses which thwart our object as teachers/designers. Faced with these problems, the old and still-dominant educational theories that focus on individuals are often inadequate to the

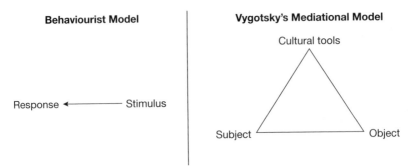

Figure 13 Two models of cognition and learning.

daunting complexity of the task designers of distributed learning face. Distributed learning is often, in a word, messy – despite the seeming simplicity of person–screen–content.

AT understands this complexity as the effect of tool mediation. Human learning, unlike much animal learning, is mediated by cultural tools. Most human learning, from a very early age, is not the simple result of stimuli or inborn cognitive structures, but rather a complex result of our interactions with others mediated by tools in the culture, including language. Vygotsky expanded the behaviourist theory of learning by introducing the concept of tool mediation (see Figure 13). When people encounter some object in the environment, a stimulus, they interpret and act on it not directly, but through the mediation of tools used by others. For example, a child learns to use a ball as part of joint activity – by watching others use the ball in a game, by listening to their words (another kind of tool) and perhaps by becoming involved in the game, the joint activity.

Some instructional designers and educational researchers have found AT useful because it looks beyond the individual learner, the interface and the 'material' to understand the social and material relations that affect complex human learning, people's interactions with others as mediated by tools, including symbols.

AT understands learning not as the internalisation of discrete information or skills by individuals, but rather as expanding involvement over time – social as well as intellectual – with other people and the tools available in their culture. 'The question of individual learning now becomes the question of how that which is inside a person might change over time as a consequence of repeated social interactions with' other people and their tools, including the very powerful tools of words, images and gestures (Hutchins 1995: 290).

If learning with computers is – despite the surface appearance – social and cultural, then we who design distributed learning need to theorise how people use cultural tools to teach and learn, to change and be changed, through our interactions with others. In sum, AT can provide a richly descriptive answer to the question: Why and how do people learn (or fail to learn) using computer networks? AT has been criticised as a 'loose' theory, more valuable for understanding what went wrong than doing predictive work (Nardi 1998; Roschelle 1998). Indeed, AT is less a tight theory than 'a philosophical framework for studying different forms of human praxis as developmental processes, both individual and social levels interlinked at the same time' (Kuuti 1994: 52). AT is a heuristic framework for asking important questions that other theories may not raise so clearly, and for seeing relationships among those questions that may guide design and evaluation.

When we see students encountering course materials via liquid crystal displays, it is easy to forget that there is much more going on. AT helps us remain aware of the intersections with the very dispersed activities and trajectories of the participants engaged in activity together – designers, teachers, students, technicians and others. AT prompts us to ask how we can 're-mediate' our interactions by changing our tools or the ways we share them with others. The questions AT invites us to ask grow out of some basic principles of behaviour, communication and learning. These principles push us to look beyond the interface to wider tool-mediated social interactions.

Basic principles

Although AT is a dynamic and evolving theory, several basic principles are shared by its adherents. Here I draw mainly on Cole's (1996) important book, *Cultural Psychology*.

- Human behaviour is social in origin, and human activity is collective (Cole and Engeström 1993). Human–computer interactions are also social in origin. Even when we are alone in front of a screen, we are in a profound sense engaging in collective activity, although that activity may be widely distributed in time and space, mediated by complex networks of tools.
- Human consciousness – 'mind' – grows out of people's joint activity with shared tools. Our minds are in a sense co-constructed and distributed among others. Our thoughts, our words and our deeds are always potentially engaged with the thoughts, words and deeds of others. Through involvement in collective activity, however widely distributed, learners are always in contact with the history, values and social relations of a community – or among communities – as embedded in the shared cultural tools used by that community or communities.
- AT emphasises tool-mediated action in context. Human beings not only act on their environment with tools, they also think and learn with tools. At a primary level these tools are material, 'external' – hammers, books, clothing, computers, telecommunications networks. But we also fashion and use tools at a secondary or 'internal' level – language, concepts, scripts, schemas. Both kinds of tools are used to act on the environment collectively (Wartofsky 1979). This suggests that distributed learning must take into account *all* the tools people use, not just the computer, as well as the relations among tools of various kinds as they mediate joint activity.
- AT is interested in development and change, which it understands broadly to include historical change, individual development and moment-to-moment change. All three levels of analysis are necessary to understand people learning with computers.
- AT grounds analysis in everyday life events, the ways people interact with each other using tools over time. It looks beyond the student-with-computer to understand the (techno-) human lives we live and their broad potential for learning and growing together.
- AT assumes that 'individuals are active agents in their own development but do not act in settings entirely of their own choosing' (Cole 1996: 104). Individual learners learn, of course, but they do so in environments that involve others, environments of people-with-tools that both afford and constrain their actions. Telecommunications networks always do both.

- As Cole states, AT 'rejects cause and effect, stimulus response, explanatory science in favor of a science that emphasises the emergent nature of mind in activity and that acknowledges a central role for interpretation in its explanatory framework'. Accordingly, it 'draws upon methodologies from the humanities as well as from the social and biological sciences' (Cole 1996: 104). As we shall see, AT studies of distributed learning often combine traditional comparison-group studies with case studies, ethnographic observation, discourse analysis and rhetorical analysis to make sense of – rather than 'control for' – the complexity of human learning mediated by telecommunications networks.

An activity system: the basic unit of analysis

When we look at the myriad people, and the tools and relationships among them that affect distributed learning, it is difficult to know what to focus on, how far to go beyond the learner and the interface. What are we really looking at when we see students attempting to learn with electronic information technology? What, in other words, is the unit of analysis? According to AT, it is not a collection of individuals and stimuli. AT suggests we focus on a group of people who share a common object and motive over time, and the wide range of tools (including computers) they share to act on that object and realise that motive – what AT calls an 'activity system'. The activity system is a flexible unit of analysis (theoretical lens), which allows us to train our gaze in different directions and with different levels of 'magnification' to help us answer the questions that puzzle us. The world is not neatly divided into activity systems. It is up to the researcher or designer to define the activity system based on the purposes of the research study or the design task, to focus the theoretical lens AT provides.

For AT, the activity system – not the individual – is the basic unit of analysis for both cultures' and individuals' psychological and social processes, including learning. As Vygotsky's basic mediational triangle (Figure 13) suggests, any time a person or group (subject) interacts with tools over time on some object with some shared motive to achieve some outcome, one can analyse their interactions as an activity system. We might, for example, view as an activity system a hobby club, a religious organisation, an advocacy group, a political movement, a school, a discipline, a research laboratory, a profession, a government agency, a company – even a group of friends who gather regularly at a pub for conversation (Engeström 1987; Cole and Engeström 1993). But one can also focus the 'lens' more tightly: on activity systems that are part of a larger activity or institution, such as a course of study or a distributed learning design group.

In one sense, an activity system might be thought of as a context for behaviour and learning but not in the sense of something that *surrounds* the individual's behaviour and learning. Rather, it is a functional system of social/cultural interactions that constitutes behaviour and produces that kind of change called learning. In this AT view, context is not a container for a learner, but rather a weaving together of the learner with other people and tools into a web or network of sociocultural interactions and meanings that are integral to the learning. (It is helpful to recall that the word 'text' is from the Greek word 'weaving' – as in 'textile'. In this sense, context is what is 'woven together'.) By viewing context as a functional system rather than a container, the designer of distributed learning can identify behaviours and try to explain their meanings in terms of the activity systems in which they are produced and understood. This is why learning is conceived of as expanding involvement with an activity system(s) (Cole 1996).

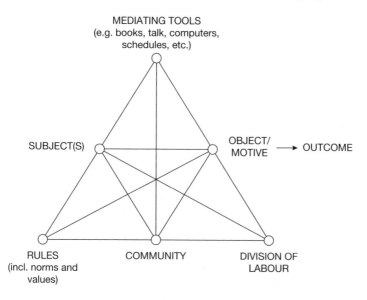

Figure 14 An activity system (Engeström 1987).

Engeström (1987) has developed Vygotsky's basic mediational triangle to represent more fully the essential social relations that teachers and designers need to account for to understand learning (Figure 14). This diagram suggests the various elements of an activity system (the nodes) and their connecting relations (the lines). By understanding joint activity that results in change (learning), we can perhaps ask more effective questions about how an activity functions (or fails to function) for an individual or group – the subject in the diagram.

Let us look first at the elements of an activity system, using Engeström's version, and note the possible relations between them. To illustrate how AT may help us to understand distributed learning, I will refer to a course in media studies I have taught for 10 years and have recently put online. I will view the course as an activity system to help me answer the very broad question: How does distributed learning shape the teaching and learning? (AT analysis, like any other, begins with questions or problems.)

Activity systems have a *subject(s)* – an individual or sub-group engaged in an activity – in this case the students and the teacher. It is crucial to remember here that each of us participates in many activity systems (home, school, work, clubs, political parties, etc.) and each brings a different history of diverse involvements to a particular activity system. One must recognise 'where students are coming from' – their history of previous involvements – to understand their distributed learning. As the subjects (people) engage in some joint activity over time – an activity system – they change (and learn) as they negotiate new ways of acting together. Again, learning is viewed as expanding involvement – social as well as intellectual – with some activity system over time, rather than the internalisation of discrete information or skills. In terms of my course, the re-mediation of distributed learning made it more difficult, in one sense, for the subjects to get to know one another, because the tools for teaching and learning changed from primarily oral to entirely written; however, in another sense, students' postings about themselves on the first day provided a more permanent reference point than first-day introductions in a conventional course. And we often referred back to these. The tool–subject relationship allowed me to see many affordances and constraints, such as these, as the course moved online.

The *object* refers to the 'raw material' or 'problem space' on which the subject brings to bear various tools. This might be the 'object of study' of some discipline (e.g. cells in cytology, literary works in literary criticism) or the object of some production process (automobiles in an automobile company). In my course, it is the 'content': mass media studies. The object is more than raw stimuli; it is a culturally formed object with a history, however short or long. The object or focus of activity implies an overall direction of that activity, a (provisionally) shared purpose or *motive* (e.g. analysing cells or literary works, building and selling automobiles). In my case, the motive is officially learning about mass media studies. Of course, the direction or motive of an activity system and its object may be understood differently or even contested, as participants bring many motives to a collective interaction and as conditions change. Dissensus, resistance, conflicts and deep contradictions are constantly produced in activity systems, as we shall see. Students approach the course with different understandings of media studies and different motives for studying it, as I found out when they responded to my online questions with answers that often made me wonder if they were enrolled in the same course! I had to design interactions to make these differences evident and come to a generally shared understanding of the object – media studies – and the motives for studying it. Again, this was both afforded and constrained by the distributed electronic tools. Moreover, the object/motive of the course for the first 2 weeks unexpectedly became learning to use computers, not the 'content', as students and I (I have to confess) primarily focused our attention on getting used to the interface. What was expected to be a mediational tool, the computer interface, became instead the object – although we were able to work that out in time and focus on the desired object/motive.

Finally, people who use tools act on the object to produce some *outcome*, which may be anticipated or surprising (e.g. research articles in cytology and literary criticism, automobiles made and sold in an automobile company, etc.).

Tools are understood as anything that mediates subjects' action upon objects. Like other species, humans act purposefully to meet biological needs; but unlike other species, human behaviour may differ radically among groups because we use tools, cultural artefacts. (Think of all the different ways of meeting the biological need for shelter in different cultures, in contrast to the bee's hive or the robin's nest.) There are many means (tools) that may be used by humans to achieve a similar outcome – for example, to send a message or teach arithmetic – and how these differ culturally and historically. The use of tools (including writing, speaking, gesture, architecture, clothing, as well as conventional tools) mediates humans' interactions, separating biological motives from the socially constructed – human – objects and motives of activity. And the tools that people in some activity system share and the ways they use them change over time, as they borrow new ways of working together from other activity systems or invent entirely new ways, potentially transforming the activity. Introducing computers, for example, has often changed the activity of teaching and learning, as was the case in my course. But there were many other tools in the course, both physical and conceptual – readings, images, video, theories, questions, and so on which had to be re-thought in relation to the computer tools.

As Engeström has extended the analysis of activity systems (the bottom triangles in Figure 13), we can see the essential elements of the social relations necessary to activity. The subject is (or is part of a larger) *community*, which conditions all the other elements of the system. Although people engaged in the same activity may be separated by great distances, as in distributed learning, or by differences of many kinds – including deep conflicts – if they act together on a common object with a common motive over time, they form a community. In my course, the community was the students and myself. But in a wider sense, we were part of the community of scholars in media studies (in which the students were neophytes), and our reading and writing, collectively and individually, made us interact with that wider community, the discipline. We were linked, electronically through the World Wide Web and e-mail, as well as through print media, to others engaged in mass media studies, beyond the participants in the class. The mediation of the computer allowed us to be in wider and more sustained contact both with examples of mass media (on the web) – the object of study – and with the community of scholars who study it.

Moreover, we see that activity systems also have a *division of labour* that shapes the way the subject(s) acts on the object (and potentially all the other elements of the system). People take on different roles in the activity. In traditional schooling, for example, the labour is divided between a teacher (who teaches) and students (who learn). But new affordances and constraints, arising at any of the other nodes, may change the division of labour. For example, new tools, such as computerised communication, may drive changes that allow the division of labour to change and students to function more as teachers of other students, or even as teachers of the teacher. This happened in our course, often to my surprise. The new tool, the computer, mediated the division of labour in new ways. It allowed students to quickly bring new materials to the attention of the teacher and other students, through links to websites. And, as I mentioned before, it allowed students' comments to remain for inspection and further written discussion. The division of labour moved in such a way that I became (sometimes reluctantly) much more of a facilitator, coordinating the posting and written discussion of various mass media materials the students brought from the web. The re-mediation also made the division of labour more complex in that the software tools allowed groups of students to carry on sustained (and preserved) interactions during the course that would have been impractical without these new electronic tools.

Activity systems always have *rules*, broadly understood not only as formal and explicit but also as unwritten or tacit – what are often called norms, routines, habits and values. These rules shape the interactions of subject and tools with the object. Of course, these rules can also alter, tacitly or explicitly, with changes in other nodes in the system, but the rules allow the system to be 'stabilised-for-now'. The re-mediation of the course through computer tools necessitated a host of new rules and norms. In one sense, it made the rules more explicit, firmer, because they could not be communicated tacitly or negotiated quickly in face-to-face interaction. The norms for 'discussion', largely assumed in the face-to-face classroom, had to be worked out explicitly with the new tool, requiring written procedures for carrying on asynchronous discussion to maintain the subjects' focus on the object and realise the motives of the course. But the re-mediation of the course also allowed certain rules (e.g. schedules and routines) to be built into the interface and become invisible (though less negotiable) for participants.

Contradictions: when people are at cross-purposes

As we have noticed, activity systems we human beings make are constantly subject to change. The version of AT I describe sees these changes as driven by *contradictions* within and among activity systems. An activity system 'is constantly working through contradictions within and between its elements' (Engeström 1987). In this sense, an activity system 'is a virtual disturbance- and innovation-producing machine' (Engeström 1990: 11). A change in any element of the activity system may conflict with another element, placing people at cross-purposes.

Contradictions can emerge between and among any of the elements of the activity system. Let me illustrate this with a different example. One may analyse as an activity system the teachers in my university English department who had over time used web-based teaching materials they created themselves. These tools were very loosely structured, with a range of links among them through which students could access the materials along different paths. Indeed, we valued this flexibility so highly that it became a norm (rule) for teaching. When my department wished to offer distributed learning courses, the university required my department to use a 'distance learning' software program supported by the university's instructional design unit. The program required us to organise teaching materials along a linear 'learning path' which students had to follow in order, lockstep. This produced a contradiction between the activity systems of instructional design and departmental teachers of mass media (see the broken arrow between the object/motive of the two activity systems in Figure 15).

Moreover, contradictions may arise between and among activity systems. Because the required distance learning web program was more complex and time-consuming to use, it required English teachers to turn to an instructional designer from another activity system, the instructional design unit, who was familiar with the software program – but not with our teaching content or methods (object/motive, rules). This new web tool required a new *division of labour* in our teaching, which produced conflict that had to be resolved over time (see the broken arrow between tools and division of labour in Figure 15).

Contradictions may also arise when participants from different activity systems have different objects and motives. For example, the instructional designer's object/motive was the software and its efficient functioning. The object, motive of

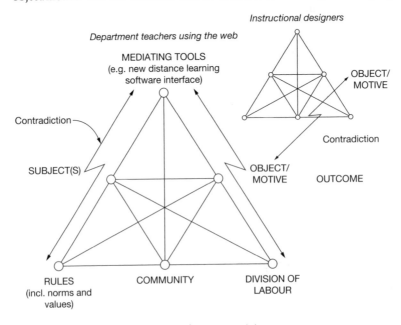

Figure 15 Contradictions within and among activity systems.

the department's teachers was the students' learning about mass media. For teachers, the software was a tool, not an object/motive, and one that we wished to think about as little as possible. This produced a contradiction between the activity systems of instructional design and mass media teaching (see the broken arrow on the right in Figure 15). There was and is a great deal of conflict (pedagogical and political) that we are trying to understand and deal with as we 're-mediate' our teaching using the new software – and the new relationships with people who have a different object and motive.

Zones of proximal development: construction zones for learning

We have seen how AT answers the question: What are we looking at? I now turn to the question: What are we looking for – and hoping to design – in using AT for distributed learning? We are looking for (and designing) times and places where people's involvement in a shared activity with cultural tools can produce that kind of change called learning.

Because the activity systems that form (and are formed by) our lives are dynamic, they constantly present opportunities for learning. Vygotsky called these opportunities 'zones of proximal development' (ZPD), which he defined as the difference between what one could do alone and what one could do with assistance. That assistance might come from teachers, peers, co-workers or others. In these 'construction zones', learning takes place as people using tools mutually change themselves and their tools (Newman *et al.* 1989: 61). People change and learn as they expand their involvement with others in a community, and the tools that community uses in certain ways. In this view, learning is social. What appears first in the social or interpersonal plane is then (perhaps) internalised, appearing on the cognitive or intrapersonal plane. It may then be externalised in future social activity, leading to further change and perhaps learning. It is, in Engeström's (1987) phrase, 'learning by expanding'.

In Vygotsky's classic experiment, for example, an adult asks a young child to fetch a toy (object/motive) from a shelf that is too high for the child to reach without the aid of a stool and a stick placed in the room (cultural tools). When the child cannot immediately reach the toy, she may ask for aid from the adult, who then shows her how to use the tools to reach the toy. A zone of proximal development has formed between what the child could do without and what she could do through social interaction using certain cultural tools (tool, stick, words, gestures).

To extend this basic concept to distributed learning, we might imagine a course that consisted merely of readings posted on the web, compared to a course that provided opportunities for interactions with teachers, other students and perhaps outside experts. It is those human interactions, mediated by a range of tools, that allow zones of proximal development to emerge.

The significance of AT for distributed learning lies in its ability to analyse the dynamic human interactions mediated by computers at both the micro (psychological and interpersonal) and the macro (sociological or cultural) levels to understand – and construct – zones of proximal development. Computers are thus viewed as one tool among many others (architecture, clothing, speaking, writing, money, schedules, etc.) through which knowledge, identity, authority and power relations are continually (re)negotiated. Learning is therefore not a neat transfer of information but a complex and often messy network of tool-mediated human relationships that must be explored in terms of the social and cultural practices which people bring to their uses of the tools they share.

How AT has been used: three examples

I give below three examples of instructional designers using AT to understand and restructure (re-mediate) distributed learning. AT has mainly used qualitative and historical research methods, although all three projects I describe also used some quantitative methods. Space does not permit me to elaborate either. URLs in the references below provide details of each project.

AT in evaluating distributed learning: the Docta Project

A group of Norwegian researchers are using AT to study the design and use of collaborative telelearning scenarios, the Docta Project (2000). For them, AT offers an insight into 'the processes of collaboration, enabling us to identify collaboration patterns and further our understanding of how instructors, students and other learning facilitators organise their learning and work' (Wasson and Morch 1999). For example, Andreassen (2000) followed three graduate students taking teacher training courses at universities in different cities. The students collaboratively used a web-based shared workspace called TeamWave. They had two goals, the first of which was to learn Salomon's (1992) techniques for creating 'genuine interdependence' in work; that is, collaboration where the group can achieve more collectively than individually, as distinct from mere 'cooperation' where the result is merely the sum of individual efforts – 'ganging up on the task'. The second goal was to use 'genuine interdependence' to collaboratively create a web-based learning environment on endangered animal species for primary school science students.

Andreassen (2000) found that the students did not use the software tools to produce genuine interdependence, a 'partnership of collaborating peers', but rather 'ganged up on the task'. They merely 'cooperated' with each other, working individually 'to get the whole task over with as easily and fast as possible', and they did not recognise the potential of the software for creating genuinely interdependent collaboration.

At first glance, this seemed to be the fault of the software (perhaps it was too difficult to learn) or of the students (perhaps they found the task uninteresting, did not get on with each other, etc.). However, using AT, Andreassen traced the failure to *contradictions* within and among activity systems. He was able to discern a deeper set of relationships and a more useful analysis of the problem to guide future efforts.

In the first phase of the project – training on the software – the students did use genuine interdependence to create a zone of proximal development to learn to use the software for collaboration. Early on, the students co-constructed *rules* for interacting, first through e-mail (a tool with which they were familiar) and then through the synchronous 'chat' tool and the asynchronous 'brainstorming' communication tool in the TeamWave program. Using the synchronous chat tool, they scheduled 'chat' meetings, where they decided to create six rooms, each on a different ecosystem, reflecting the interests of the three members. Because the asynchronous brainstorming tool did not automatically indicate the author's name on each posting, they quickly developed a new unwritten rule when one of the students included her name after each sentence: add names to postings (later shortened to initials). In AT terms, they 're-mediated' their interactions using a different tool, and formulated different rules of interactions, which initially proved to be more productive of collaboration in the training phase. Clearly, the software tools were not at fault, since the group created a zone of proximal development for learning, and the students were able to use genuine interdependence to do so.

AT also helped Andreassen understand the change the group experienced as it moved from the first phase – training in the software and in Saloman's guidelines for genuine interdependence – to the second phase – the design of the web learning environment on endangered species. Andreassen analysed these phases as two linked activity systems. The object of the first phase – the software – became a tool for the second phase – the web learning environment.

However, two contradictions appeared in time transition from the training phase to the design phase, which suggested that the cause of the failure lay beyond the software and the participants' willingness to collaborate. First, there was a contradiction between the motive of the activity system of their collaboration and the motives of the activity systems of the different courses in which they were individually enrolled. Although they found the task engaging and the other group members congenial, their collaboration was not part of the regular curriculum of the courses and was not evaluated by the instructors. Little was actually at stake for the students, so as time pressures from these courses and other activities in their everyday lives impinged on the collaboration, they did not maintain a shared *motive* sufficient to engage in 'genuine interdependence', in completing the teaching materials. They lacked 'a common motivational factor, which attainment requires sharing of information, pooling of roles, and joint thinking, might be regarded as important if one is to facilitate a genuine collaboration effort' (Andreassen 2000).

The second contradiction was between *division of labour* and *rules*. In the training phase, the students set up a division of labour based on genuinely interdependent collaboration and rules (scheduling, communication procedures, etc.), where all three students worked on each of the rooms; but in the design phase, time constraints led them to a different division of labour. 'Labour was divided among the members for them to finish individually and the work turned asynchronous.'

> The need to share information was reduced or even diminished. Even though the students acknowledged the value of feedback and agreed to provide it throughout the design activity, this hardly ever happened ... When time division of labour paved the way for individual rather than team work, the new meeting rules, set subsequent to the division of labour, were perceived as inflexible and cumbersome.
>
> (Andreassen 2000)

Although new rules were proposed for synchronous contact, these were never agreed or implemented.

> Although having the same overall object, that of designing the learning environment, one can argue that the students put the main focus on achieving the goals of their individual actions. In other words, the preparation and commissioning of the separate rooms by the individual student took precedence over completing the learning environment as a joint team effort of information sharing, pooling of roles, and joint thinking.
>
> (Andreassen 2000)

Andreassen concluded that the students did not use the software tools to create a zone of proximal development that took advantage of a 'partnership of collaborating peers' for creating the rooms. Neither did they realise the potential of the software for creating interdependent collaboration in qualitatively different zones of proximal development, although the problem was not 'in' the software. AT guided

Andreassen to suggest that the outcome might have been more successful had the activity system of the collaboration been more firmly linked to the activity systems of the courses in their home universities (*motivation*), and had the three participants retained the more collaborative *division of labour* with which they began, using synchronous communication regularly throughout with the *rules* they originally agreed among themselves.

Activity theory in technical training: learning a geographic information system

Spinuzzi (1999) observed a group of 13 third-year university students in Community and Regional Planning, who were taking a course in geographic information systems (GIS). Late in the course, they were learning to use a government computer program that plots traffic accident locations and provides statistics on accidents (e.g. road conditions, injuries, vehicle damage), from data entered by police in their accident reports. The GIS program is called Accident Location and Analysis System (the apt acronym is ALAS). Although the students had become familiar with other GIS programs, they found it extremely difficult to use this program to find information on specific accidents, experiencing numerous 'breakdowns' (points at which they could not proceed without the help of the instructor).

At first glance, the students' difficulties appeared to be caused by the greater complexity of this program as compared to other GIS programs they had learned: more instruction and practice seemed to be the solution. However, using AT, Spinuzzi was able to trace these breakdowns to fundamental contradictions in the interface (tool), which in turn reflected historical contradictions in the whole activity system of accident location and analysis now reflected in the GIS ALAS program. The cultural history of this activity system proved crucial to developing improvements in the GIS ALAS interface to help students and new employees to learn the program. To reduce breakdowns, Spinuzzi had to look beyond training 'in the software', to training in the ALAS activity system, its history and institutional uses.

One breakdown arose when students viewed accidents that appeared to have occurred in cornfields or in houses not on roads. Experienced users knew that the records on which the GIS ALAS system was built were gathered before the invention of computerised maps. Accidents were plotted using less precise paper maps, divided into coordinates. Each accident was given a numerical coordinate, called a 'node', corresponding to the paper maps. In the late 1990s, the system was put on to a computerised GIS map. However, the history of the system had produced a *contradiction* between representations: the old node/coordinates system of locating accidents and the geographic system of the new GIS ALAS program's electronic map. The nodes did not precisely correspond to the electronic map location because of the contradiction. The contradiction between tools for representing accidents, growing out of two historical periods of the activity system of ALAS, led students to mistake the geographic representation for the underlying node system and thus experience breakdowns. The experts knew that one sometimes had to refer to the older, paper representation, or to one's knowledge of the area.

To redesign the software tool to reduce breakdown for learners (whether students or new employees), Spinuzzi proposed that the interface should explain the contradiction and display it directly, by including both node/coordinate and GIS representations. One could then teach students or new users to see the relation between the two. By acknowledging the contradiction rather than trying to bury it in the interface or work around it, the interface would then allow students to expand their involvement with the whole accident location and analysis activity system and negotiate it with fewer breakdowns. It would create new zones of proximal development.

Students also experienced breakdowns in accessing records from pull-down menus. They could not access all the information on a single accident without undertaking numerous steps. Again the cultural history of ALAS reveals why this was so. People from different activity systems use different types of information from the ALAS database: traffic sign designers (accident frequency by location and direction), insurance companies (severity of injury and property damage), road designers (road conditions at accident by location), police (fatality, violation, time), and so on. The interface was designed to provide quick access for users from these different activity systems, each with a different object and motive in using the software tool; while students (or new employees) needed an overview of the shape of individual accident records to understand the structure of the records and the uses of the information. They needed to expand their conceptual understanding not only of the software tool and database, GIS ALAS, but also of the whole accident location and analysis activity system, in its interactions with other activity systems that used portions of the data. They needed the big picture. The AT analysis suggested that software designers should add a function for accessing complete records of individual accidents, as a learning tool, although it would serve little purpose beyond that.

AT's cultural historical analysis guided Spinuzzi in developing suggestions for redesigning not only the software tool – to 'fix' things that seemed to cause breakdowns – but also for redesigning the training process. Both the interface and the training had to take into account the historically evolved complexity of the activity system specially to facilitate learning it – to construct zones of proximal development. Instructional designers must look 'beyond the interface to the activities in which information systems are used' (Spinuzzi 1999: 226).

Activity theory in children's learning: Fifth Dimension after-school program

The Fifth Dimension is an after-school program for disadvantaged children aged 6–14 years, with sites in 12 cities in four countries. Many of the children have great difficulty learning in formal schooling. At first glance, this seemed to be a problem with the children or their family and peer environments. Indeed, the ordinary response of many schools is to require students to spend more time doing school activities, either longer (after school) instruction or additional homework. But using AT, the Fifth Dimension program was able to see ways to 're-mediate' school activities as a mix of activities, some from schooling, some from computer games, some from web-mediated social interaction.

The goal of the Fifth Dimension program is to produce learning outcome desirable in formal schooling within a very different activity system – to re-mediate learning using different tools, object/motive, rules, community and division of labour. From the point of view of the children participating in the program, the object/motive is to play the games together successfully – that is, to have fun. However, the designers of the program have re-mediated the activity of school learning by deliberately mixing activity choices (some school-like some game-like, some creative play) to avoid contradictions in motives. The re-mediated system produced an outcome similar to – often better than – that produced in the activity system of formal schooling.

As Blanton *et al.* (1999) describe it:

> The heart of the Fifth Dimension is a three dimensional maze containing computer games and educational tasks. The maze is divided into twenty 'rooms', and each room provides access to either computer or non-electronic activities. In all, the maze contains over 120 educational and computer games. Children make progress through the maze by completing tasks set for them in each game or activity. Adventure Guides provide directions for how to play games and complete tasks. Children decide on goals, where they will begin their journey in the maze, how long they will stay in a 'room', where they will go next, and how they will complete the tasks in the maze.

A 'real make-believe' Fifth Dimension Wizard, an anonymous electronic entity that 'lives' in the Internet, writes and chats with the children via modem, performing the role of patron.

> The Wizard has a home page, and helps the children gain access to the World Wide Web, where they may display their own creative work. The wizard also affords a locus for conflict resolution, helping to mediate typical power relations between children and adults, and preserving the mobility of expert and novice roles.
>
> (Brown and Cole 1999)

The Fifth Dimension Wizard is in fact operated by the staff, consisting typically of a director and a group of prospective teachers, often second-year university students planning a career in teaching. The staff also give face-to-face guidance and support to children in their progress through the Fifth Dimension maze – and in their learning, of course.

Standard experimental–control group comparisons found that extended participation in the Fifth Dimension program had positive effects on children's learning of cognitive skills, transfer of learning to school settings, computer use and standardised school-administered tests of achievement (summarised in Brown and Cole 1999). Research also found strong evidence that prospective teachers 'transform their beliefs about education away from the belief of learning as a linear process towards a definition of learning as a social process involving active participation of children in socially constituted practices' (Blanton *et al.* 1999). This is remarkable, since previous research has shown that it is extremely difficult to change teacher education candidates' preconceptions of teaching, learning and pupils.

The many studies of the program are based on AT, which provides a useful framework for understanding *how* the changes in the students and their 'guides' occurs. For example, in the study of prospective teachers, the researchers charted the communication flow among three activity systems in which the students were involved: university teacher education, the local school system and the Fifth Dimension program. Researchers constructed a pre- and post-test of attitudes and beliefs towards teaching, learning and pupils based on the different *rules* (norms) obtaining in the three activity systems. The researchers used qualitative methods to follow the prospective teachers as they moved among the three activity systems, noting zones of proximal development that grew out of the contradictions among them. For example, in interacting with children in the programs, prospective teachers encountered moments where children were further along in the Fifth Dimension maze than the teachers – and more familiar with the software tools. The students began to teach them how to perform the tasks. In these zones of proximal development for the prospective teachers, positive changes in attitudes about disadvantaged students' capabilities occurred. It is not surprising that students can teach teachers, but what AT contributes is an analysis of *how* that change in the division of labour occurred (how zones of proximal development were created) and how that change led to a change in attitudes towards disadvantaged students in the circulation of discourse among the three activity systems in which the prospective teachers participated.

The qualitative research on the Fifth Dimension program suggests that distributed learning is best accomplished when it accommodates a diversity of individual interests – in other words, when learners have choices. Moreover – and perhaps paradoxically – distributed learning appears to be most successful when people can better achieve their chosen goals by acting together than by acting alone. Yet creating activity systems where this mutual help in zones of proximal development is possible (or even essential for success) takes a great deal of time, especially in distributed systems where asynchronous or infrequent communication replaces face-to-face. Finally, collaboration does not mean there will be no conflict, only that there are means of resolving – or of constructively using – conflicts to further the learning. Indeed, distributed learning, like all learning, must take into account the fact that people have many different emotions which affect their interactions and their learning.

Conclusion: what AT can and cannot do

I began this chapter by saying that AT can have heuristic value for planning and 'trouble-shooting' redesigns of distributed learning, although it is a 'loose' theory that does not attempt firm predictions. I wish to conclude by posing some questions (following Lewis 1997) highlighted by various triads of nodes (a study that discusses each question is cited for each).

- *Subject–community–objective/motive.* Motivation is particularly difficult to address in distributed learning environments, where participants may not have face-to-face support from teachers or peers. Do individual learners (or subgroups) understand themselves as part of a disciplinary or learning community focused on a common object? Or do they feel disenfranchised, able only to learn discrete information for their own personal motives rather than being engaged in expanding involvement with a community and its activity (zones of proximal development) (Dirckinck-Holmfeld 1995)?
- *Subject–tools–object.* What tools do subjects bring to bear on the object of the learning, both those tools the course provides *and* those which subjects might bring from their previous involvements in other activity systems? This is a particular problem for distributed learning, as the computer is such a pervasive tool that it may crowd out others, or make them less visible (Fifth Dimension).
- *Subject–tools–community.* How do the computerised tools (such as group-ware) afford – and constrain – students and teachers in forming a community where differences can be negotiated and mutual support (ZPDs) constructed? If some students use e-mail while others employ a different asynchronous tool, different communities may form among the students (Lewis and Collins 1995).
- *Subject–rules–community.* How do participants understand (and agree upon or dissent from) the interactional rules (norms) of the activity system, especially when (as in distributed electronic learning) there is no face-to-face communication to clarify and negotiate those rules? This is particularly difficult in distributed learning because participants may bring different assumptions – often unconsciously so – about ways of working (Andreassen 2000).

- *Subject–community–division of labour.* How will the teaching–learning labour in distributed electronic learning be divided (and renegotiated) in the community, when members of that community bring different histories and skills to the activity (Hoyles *et al.* 1994)? If the division of labour is exclusively teacher/individual students, then opportunities for creating community (and new zones of proximal development) are diminished.
- *One activity system interacting with others.* What other activity systems are participants engaged in which might create contradictions that afford or constrain their learning? How can teachers and others learn about these in the absence of face-to-face interaction (Spinuzzi 1999)?

These questions suggest only some of the many that AT analysis can highlight for designers of distributed learning environments. Because AT is a flexible framework (albeit complex), and compatible with many [. . .] other theories [. . .], it is helpful in understanding what happens when students encounter course materials via liquid crystal displays. AT makes it hard to forget that there is much more going on – dispersed activities and trajectories of the participants engaged in activity together, whether designers, teachers, students, technicians or others. Where we are at cross-purposes, we must ask how we have come to be that way, and how we might use those contradictions to experience each other in more human and productive ways. By focusing on various relationships among participants and their tools, AT prompts us to ask better questions for designing distributed learning environments and understanding and evaluating where and why they work or break down. If something unexpected – or messy – happens when people use those environments, AT can provide analytical lenses to understand what has occurred, and perhaps use it productively for teaching and learning.

References

Andreassen, E.F. (2000) Evaluating how students organise their work in a collaborative telelearning scenario: an activity theoretical perspective. Masters dissertation, Department of Information Science, University of Bergen, Norway. Online at: http://www.ifi. uib.no/docta/dissertations/andreassen/.

Bakardjieva, M. (1998) Collaborative meaning-making in computer conferences: a sociocultural perspective, in M. Bakardjieva, T. Ottmann and I. Tomek (eds) *Proceedings of ED-MEDIA/ED-TELECOM 98.* Charlottesville, VA: Association for the Advancement of Computing in Education.

Blanton, W. E., Warner, M. and Simmons, E. (1999) The Fifth Dimension: application of cultural-historical activity theory, inquiry-based learning, computers, and telecommunications to change prospective teachers' preconceptions. Online at: http://129. 171.53.1/blantonw/5dClhse/publications/tech/effects/undergraduates.html.

Brown, K. and Cole, M. (1999) Socially shared cognition: system design and the organization of collaborative research. Online at: http://129.171.53.1/blantonw/5dClhse/ publications/tech/cognition.html.

Cole, M. (1996) *Cultural Psychology.* Cambridge, MA: Harvard University Press.

Cole, M. and Engeström, Y. (1993) A cultural-historical approach to distributed cognition, in G. Salomon (ed.) *Distributed Cognitions: Psychological and Educational Considerations.* Cambridge: Cambridge University Press.

Dirckinck-Holmfeld, L. (1995) Project pedagogy as a foundation for computer-supported collaborative learning, in B. Collins and G. Davies (eds) *Innovative Adult Learning with Innovative Technologies.* IFIP Transactions A-61. Amsterdam: Elsevier.

Docta Project (2000) Design and use of collaborative telelearning artifacts. Department of Information Science, University of Bergen, Norway. Online at: http://www.ifi.uib. no/doct/index.html.

Engeström, Y. (1987) *Learning by Expanding: An Activity Theoretical Approach to Developmental Research*. Helsinki: Orienta-Konsultit Oy.

Engeström, Y. (1990) *Learning, Working, and Imagining: Twelve Studies in Activity Theory*. Helsinki: Orienta-Konsultit Oy.

Guribye, F. and Wasson, B. (1999) Evaluating collaborative telelearning scenarios: a socio-cultural perspective, in B. Collins and R. Oliver (eds) *Proceedings of Educational Multimedia: Hypermedia & Telecommunications 1999 (EdMedia '99)*. Charlottesville, VA: Association for the Advancement of Computing in Education.

Hoyles, C., Healey, L. and Pozzi, S. (1994) Groupwork with computers: an overview of findings, *Journal of Computer Assisted Learning*, 10(4), 202–15.

Hutchins, E. (1995) *Cognition in the Wild*. Boston, MA: MIT Press.

Kapetin, V. and Cole, M. (1997) Individual and collective activities in educational computer game playing. Online at: http://129.171.53.1/blantonw/5dClhse/publications/tech/Kaptelinin-Cole.html.

Koschmann, T. (1996) Paradigm shifts and instructional technology, in T. Koschmann (ed.) *CSCL: Theory and Practice of an Emerging Paradigm*. Mahwah, NJ: Lawrence Erlbaum.

Kuuti, K. (1994) Activity theory as a potential framework for human–computer inter-action research, in B. Nardi (ed.) *Context and Consciousness: Activity Theory and Human–Computer Interaction*. Cambridge, MA: MIT Press.

Leont'ev, A.N. (1981) *Problems of the Development of Mind*. Moscow: Progress Publishers.

Lewis, R. (1997) An activity theory framework to explore distributed communities, *Journal of Computer Assisted Learning*, 13(4): 210–18.

Lewis, R. and Collins, B. (1995) Virtual mobility and distributed laboratories: supporting collaborative research with knowledge technology, in B. Collins and G. Davies (eds) *Innovative Adult Learning with Innovative Technologies*. IFIP Transactions A-61. Amsterdam: Elsevier.

Nardi, B. (ed.) (1996) *Context and Consciousness: Activity Theory and Human–Computer Interaction*. Cambridge, MA: MIT Press.

Nardi, B. (1998) Activity theory and its use within human–computer interaction (response to Roschelle), *Journal of the Learning Science*, 7(2): 257–61.

Newman, D., Griffin, P. and Cole, M. (1989) *The Contraction Zone: Working for Cognitive Change in School*. Cambridge: Cambridge University Press.

Roschelle, J. (1998) Activity theory: a foundation for design (review of Nardi), *Journal of the Learning Science*, 7(2): 241–55.

Salomon, G. (1992) What does the design of effective CSCL require and how do we study its effects? *SIGCUE Outlook (Special Issue on CSCL)*, 21(3): 62–8.

Spinuzzi, C. (1999) Designing for lifeworlds: genre and activity in information systems design and evaluation. Ames, IA: Iowa State University. Online at: http://english.ttu.edu/spinuzzi/spinuzzi-dissertation.pdf.

Vygotsky, L.S. (1994) *The Vygotsky Reader* (edited by V. der Veer and J. Valsiner). Oxford: Blackwell.

Wartofsky, M. (1979) *Models: Representation and the Scientific Understanding*. Dordrecht: Reidel.

Wasson, B. and Mørch, A. (1999) DoCTA: design and use of collaborative telelearning artefacts. Online at: http://www.ifi.uib.no/staff/barbara/papers/edmedia99.html.

PART 9

BEHAVIOUR MANAGEMENT

CHAPTER 16

AN ECOSYSTEMIC APPROACH TO EMOTIONAL AND BEHAVIOURAL DIFFICULTIES IN SCHOOLS

Paul Cooper and Graham Upton

Educational Psychology, Vol. 10, No. 4, 1990

In this chapter the authors describe an ecosystemic approach to emotional and behaviour problems in schools. It should be stressed, from the outset, that the article is of a theoretical nature and intended as a stimulus to further discussion and research. An account of the historical development of the approach is presented, along with examples of its application, in an attempt to identify the potential value of such an approach to teachers and schools. It is suggested that:

1   The ecosystemic approach offers new ways of conceptualising behaviour problems in schools, which are based on the view that human behaviour is developed and maintained through interactional processes.
2   The ecosystemic approach described by the present authors, offers teachers a new range of strategies for dealing with emotional and behavioural problems, which emphasise collaborative approaches to problem solving and the central importance of individuals' phenomenological interpretations in the development of solutions (though not, necessarily, the phenomenological approach of *all* involved individuals).
3   The ecosystemic approach offers specific and practical measures which may lead to the enhancement of the overall effectiveness of schools, stressing as they do the power that is derived from the appreciation of differing, sometimes conflicting, personal perspectives on situations, and the importance of giving consideration to human individuality. This approach not only offers assistance to students and their teachers but also has important implications for relationships among staff and between staff and parents.

There is, as yet, an absence of substantial research evidence to support the effectiveness of the ecosystemic approach in schools. It is hoped that this chapter will begin to suggest a direction which such research might take. Already there are reports from America of the use of ecosystemic approaches by school staff. Molnar & Lindquist (1989) have recently described a range of intervention strategies and given examples of their use by American school personnel (teachers, counsellors and psychologists) who have received brief in-service training in the techniques. The foundation of the ecosystemic approach, however, lies in the field of family therapy, the literature on which abounds with case study examples of the successful use of intervention strategies based on interactional principles with families where presenting conditions include eating disorders, sexual dysfunction, violent behaviour, bed-wetting and obsessional behaviour.

Before delineating the approach proposed by the present authors, it is necessary to describe its origins. It is important to stress from the outset, however, that we are not proposing any kind of simplistic analogy between the classrooms and the family. Our approach draws on family therapy sources, but is informed by a specifically educational perspective, which emphasises the distinctive qualities of the school/classroom situation and the existing specialised skills of teachers. We must also emphasise that we do not suggest that practising teachers can or should develop the level of skill and expertise possessed by trained family therapists. We are suggesting, however, that it might be possible for teachers to make profitable use of systemic insights, and particular intervention techniques which follow from these insights, in their everyday interactions with students, students' parents/families and colleagues.

An important aspect of this article relates to our concern to place the ecosystem approach within the humanistic tradition of British education which emphasises the need for schools to be run on democratic, person centred lines, with their ultimate goal being the development of autonomous, self-directing individuals. We argue that teachers, and consequently schools, in order to be 'effective', must give prominence to humanistic principles in their daily practice (Cooper, 1989). Our approach can also be seen in the context of the current concern for increased school effectiveness, as exemplified in the recent Elton Report on discipline in schools (DES, 1989), and in the increasingly important role of teachers as guardians of children's rights, as a consequence of the 1989 Children Act (Bridge and Luke, 1989).

The origins of the ecosystemic approach

(a) Systemic theory and recursive causality

The ecosystemic approach to human behaviour is founded on the notion that the origins and purposes of human behaviour are essentially interactional. Human beings are neither wholly free, in an existential sense, to behave as they choose, nor is their behaviour wholly determined by environmental forces. Human beings exist as strands in a social web that can be likened to a biological ecosystem in which individual organisms' behaviour and development is both constrained by and a constraining force upon the behaviour and development of other organisms, interaction with whom is essential for fulfilment of survival needs. From an ecosystemic viewpoint, human behaviour is the product of ongoing interaction between environmental influences and internal motivations which derive from prior (mainly social) experience. Furthermore, the overarching, twin human needs for a recognised personal identity and a sense of social belonging make the social group (or 'system') the central focus of human activity, to the extent that individuals' personal needs and motivations are often subordinate to those of the group as a whole. The potential for conflict, both interpersonal and intra-personal, in such circumstances is obvious. All group members depend upon the group to supply particular needs, thus the maintenance of the group is paramount, even if its maintenance requires the sacrifice of one of its members.

The theoretical origins of this view of human behaviour rests in the work of Ludwig von Bertalanffy (1950; 1968) and Gregory Bateson (1972; 1979), and in the clinical practice of pioneer family therapists, such as Selvini-Palazzoli *et al.* (1973), Minuchin (1974), and de Shazar (1982; 1985). Von Bertalanffy is responsible for the original formulation of 'General System Theory' (von Bertalanffy, 1950; 1968). This theory argues that the physical and social sciences can be seen to share a common concern with analysing data in systemic terms A key tenet of General System Theory is that simplistic notions of causation are inadequate and that living organisms share the characteristic of purposiveness, by which they act upon stimuli rather than simply responding to stimuli in a unilinear manner. Thus causation is seen in terms of circular configurations (referred to by Bateson [1979] as a 'recursive'), characterised by the cybernetic concept of 'feedback', whereby the goals of the system (including the maintenance of the system itself) are achieved through resisting stimuli which are directed toward the system's goals (negative feedback) and through promoting and encouraging stimuli which serves the system's goals (positive feedback). The inter-connectedness of elements within a system also means that change in any part of the system will reverberate throughout the system. Family therapy techniques are based on these principles.

(b) Family therapy

Bateson was among the first to apply a systemic approach to the realm of mental health and family functioning. Bateson *et al.* (1956) published a highly influential paper which reported the presence of recurrent patterns of communication in the families of diagnosed schizophrenics, which, they argued, served to promote and maintain the symptomatic behaviour. A central concept introduced in this paper is that of the 'double bind', which describes the way in which so called schizophrenic individuals were observed to be required by their families to fulfil contradictory demands, the fulfilment of any one of which represents the breaching of another (e.g. behaving with hostility toward the symptomatic individual, then behaving in a loving manner when the individual responds negatively to the initial hostility). In short the symptomatic individual is placed in a 'no win situation' in which the outwardly irra-tional behaviour, characteristic of schizophrenia, can be interpreted as a rational response to the double bind. The motivation for placing and maintaining the symp-tomatic individual in this situation is that it provides the family as a whole with a stable communication pattern which masks other family pathologies (e.g. a decaying marital relationship) which threaten the survival of the family system. The schizo-phrenic individual is socially constructed by the family group (with his or her unwitting compliance) as a problem which deflects attention from other difficulties and also provides a focus of activity which the family can share without engaging in conflict which may threaten its survival. Thus the double bind can be viewed in terms of a strategy which promotes what the family perceives as manageable conflict, in place of what is perceived as unmanageable conflict. Manageable conflict is encouraged (positive feedback) whilst unmanageable conflict is avoided (negative feedback).

The logical consequences of this formulation is that symptomatic behaviour, (e.g. schizophrenia) becomes an integral part of family functioning and particularly of interactional patterns in the family. It therefore follows that the unit of treatment, in such situations, should be the family of the symptomatic individual, rather than that individual alone (as in traditional psychiatric practice). It is this contention which forms the basis of the practice of family therapy.

The perspective offered by the present writers draws on three major approaches to family therapy (Speed, 1984), each of which emphasises particular elements in the ecosystem of family dysfunction (that is, a particular range of influences on interac-tional events). These approaches are not mutually exclusive and are often combined by therapists. The aim of therapy is always to promote positive change in the family system which enables the family to function effectively and without the need for the destructive interactional patterns that have grown up around the symptomatic individual. Each therapeutic model offers a systemic analysis of interpersonal interaction in families and together they provide us with a range of analytical tools for developing systemic analyses of classrooms and other interactional systems.

The first of these approaches to family therapy is that provided by the Milan group (Selvini-Palazzoli *et al.*, 1973; Selvini, 1988), which advocates that therapists should focus on those conflicts which the family system is attempting to avoid. Milan therapists, therefore, devote considerable energy to the development of systemic hypotheses which account for symptomatic behaviour in terms of family functioning. The purpose of the therapy is to bring these conflicts to the surface and devise behavioural strategies which the family can perform in order to resolve them.

The second approach is referred to as the Structural approach (Minuchin, 1974). Here the emphasis is on family structure. It is argued that a major source of family dysfunction is to be found in inversions and distortions in the family hierarchy (e.g. where the child in a nuclear family takes on a parental role and becomes the key decision maker). These distortions lead to contradictions between actual and expected behaviour, with family members overtly claiming to act in accordance with a family structure (e.g. claiming that the parents are the key decision makers) which their actions covertly distort. An important structural concept is that of 'boundary', which describes the degree of separation between members of a system (e.g. family). Where boundaries are too rigid, members become 'disengaged' from one another and communication between members is diminished. Where boundaries are too weak, 'enmeshment' develops and members become incapable of achieving the necessary distancing they require for the development of their individual roles and identities. Structural therapy aims to restore the family system to a more appropriate structure which asserts the appropriate hierarchical and boundary relationships.

The third approach is referred to as Strategic therapy. Strategic therapy places particular emphasis on the interactional sequences which surround and maintain the symptomatic behaviour (Watzlawick, *et al.*, 1974; Madanes, 1981), and more recently, on areas of family functioning in which problems are dealt with successfully, with a view to adapting successful problem solving behaviour to less tractable problems (de Shazer, 1982; 1985; Molnar & de Shazar, 1987). The key tenet of this approach is that change in any part of an ecosystem produces change throughout the system. Strategic therapists focus on specific situations in which problem behaviour occurs (or does not occur) and their aim is to devise strategies which family members can use which give negative feedback to problem behaviour and encourage the development of new and sustainable patterns of interaction. Some strategic therapists (e.g. Madanes, 1981) argue that by giving families strategies which lead them to make behavioural changes, family members are led into a process which forces them to confront underlying, masked conflicts. Essentially, however, strategic therapists are less overtly concerned with uncovering these masked conflicts (unlike Milan therapists), preferring to focus on specific situations in which problem behaviour is manifest.

The challenge faced by all systemic family therapists is to help families to establish new interactional patterns which 'fit' the family system and so appear to the family members to be appropriate to their needs. It might even be said that family therapists do not attempt to impose solutions upon their client families. Instead they seek to activate patterns of interaction which are already available, though hitherto unexplored or simply dormant, in the existing family system. This is a particularly difficult task, because the systemic nature of interactional patterns means that they have a self perpetuating, circular (i.e. 'recursive') quality, in which cause and effect cannot be objectively isolated. Individuals, caught in such patterns, which they feel to be destructive, often feel powerless to effect change, believing their own behaviour to be rational and inevitable. Strategic therapists often locate problem maintaining behaviour in that very behaviour which family members have devised as problem solving behaviour. The therapist is, therefore, often attempting to lead family members to a point where they will dispense with a pattern of behaviour which has developed in relation to particular circumstances pertaining to the family. This gives rise to the essential character of systemic therapy, which is that it promotes change through the use of non-lineal (and often indirect) intervention strategies. These non-lineal strategies do not overtly challenge problem behaviour, but rather seek to change the behaviour by rendering it ineffective in the eyes of family members, with the result that they dispense with the behaviour of their own choice. This often involves readjusting family members' perceptions of their behaviour through the prescription of tasks which lead clients to a new perspective on their behaviour. Such readjustment, however, can only be successfully achieved when the therapist is able to frame the new perspective in terms of the family members' personal systems of meaning; that is, family members have been shown how, according to their own values and perceptions, such a readjustment is called for.

There is much overlap between the three main approaches, and practicing therapists often combine elements from different approaches (Hoffman, 1981). It has been suggested that some of the apparent theoretical disagreements between the groups can be attributed to the different client groups with which each school of therapy chooses to work (Speed, 1984). The Milan group, for instance, worked most often with the families of individuals with life threatening or severely psychotic conditions (e.g. schizophrenia, anorexia), whilst strategic therapists tend to work with more common disorders, such as bed wetting, marital disharmony and sexual dysfunction which, though apparently mundane by comparison, are often equally intractable. For our purposes there is a number of principles under which the various approaches to family therapy unite:

1   The aim of therapy is to promote positive change in situations characterised by interactional patterns (i.e. patterns of feedback and reinforcement, by which particular behaviours are perpetuated or suppressed) which are harmful to one or more of the family members.
2   This makes the interactional system the focus for intervention, rather than any individual member, since it is the system which functions to maintain the undesired situation.
3   Successful change depends upon the quality of 'fit' between the chosen intervention and the existing pattern of family functioning (i.e. the intervention must be an alternative pattern of behaviour which is perceived by the family or family subsystem as viable).
4   Accurate knowledge of the pattern of family functioning is only achieved by a therapist who is willing and able to form a cooperative relationship with family members and is, in effect, able to 'join' with the family to create a therapeutic system which facilitates the exposure of the interactional patterns surrounding problem behaviour and the perceptions and personal meanings underlying them.
5   The need for the therapist to control personal bias and to achieve both a detached and deepened understanding of the family situation is facilitated by the use of a therapeutic team, the presence of which is often hidden behind a two-way mirror during therapy sessions. This results in the generation of additional and often divergent perceptions of what is observed. This 'poly-ocular view'

(de Shazer, 1985) promotes creativity which is necessary for the generation of appropriate interventions.

6 Once an appropriate intervention is put into action, the feedback mechanisms in the family system take over and thus a new interactional pattern is established. The therapist is no longer required, having facilitated a positive solution which utilises the family's inherent capacity for self regulation.

The term 'ecosystemic'

We choose the term ecosystemic (after de Shazer, 1982; Molnac & Lindquist, 1989) with extreme care. The most common use of the word 'ecosystem' is as a term to describe the interdependence of living things in the natural world. The chief characteristic of an 'ecological' perspective is a concern for the way in which small changes in any part of the ecosystem have consequences which are amplified throughout the global environment (e.g. for economic and social reasons, pesticides, offering short term protection for crop yields, may force pests to adapt and develop resistance to the pesticides, and this in turn will require the continual development of new crop strains and ever more potent pesticides, placing concomitant pressures on economic, social and natural resources). This concept of interdependence and recursive causation is central to the approach to human interaction described here, which stresses the ways in which human systems constantly adapt in order to minimise the destructive effects of change, and in so doing create new patterns of interaction.

This is a different view from that associated with the term 'systems approach', as proposed by social theorists such as Parsons (1951). Such theorists espouse a mechanistic view, seeing human behaviour as being constrained by the social system, to the extent that action by the individual is seen to be ineffectual. From such a viewpoint, systems change is only achieved through the exercise of power by groups of individuals, or by individuals with a disproportionate share of power.

An application of systems theory to school behaviour problems has been proposed by Burden (1981), whose view is heavily influenced by functionalist explanations and a model of causation which is both lineal and unidirectional:

> [a systems approach] does not dispute that some problems may well stem from within an individual child or from within an individual teacher, but seeks to understand how the explicit and implicit organizational structure of a school affects the perception and behaviour of its pupils in a way that leads them to be seen as problematical or disruptive by those faced with the task of maintaining that structure.
>
> (p. 35)

Burden is here stressing the constraining effect of the institutional environment. The view we propose emphasises the ability of individuals to influence systems in ways that produce positive and predictable change, even in the face of apparent resistance from the system. This is not to say that we do not recognise and accept the power of the institution to influence behaviour. We do, however, find contentious Burden's assertion that:

> ... a piecemeal approach centred on problems is nonsensical when seen within the framework of such organizational complexity, since the intricate relationship of parts cannot be treated out of context of the whole.
>
> (p. 31)

We suggest that system theory allows any ecosystem to be entered at several different levels, one of which, in the case of schools, may be the institutional level. Other levels might include the classroom, the tutorial group or an interactional dyad. There is the potential for change effected at a lower level to resonate at other points throughout the system. For example, a pupil from an ethnic or religious minority may contravene a school rule, as a result of wearing clothing which is prescribed by her religion or culture but proscribed by the school rules. If this pupil refuses to comply with the school rules conflict may develop which results in either a change in the school rules or the development of alternative schooling arrangements for other children of the same minority. Either way, the actions of an individual can be seen to have a resonance throughout the larger system. Systemic processes operate at all levels in interactional systems, potentially allowing each element within a system, however small, to change the entire system. We suggest that the term 'ecosystemic' best describes this multi-faceted quality of interactional systems.

An ecosystemic approach to school behaviour problems

A significant proportion of the work of family therapy is concerned with childhood behaviour problems. It is not surprising, therefore, that in recent years many family therapists (particularly in America) have begun to focus some of their attention on the school system as a factor in family difficulties which manifest themselves in childhood behaviour problems. Lindquist *et al.* (1987) suggest that school related problems are best characterised in one of three ways, as: (a) a problem in the family that disturbs the school; (b) a problem at school that disturbs the family or (c) a problem at school that does not disturb the family.

Smith (1978), Worden (1981) and Okun (1984) all describe ways in which students' problem behaviour in school can sometimes be related to difficulties in the family system, particularly in terms of 'triangulation'. Triangulation describes a relational triad in which two members form an alliance against the third. This can take the form of an overclose relationship (what structural therapists call 'enmeshment') between a student and parent, at a time when there is marital disharmony. The student is oversensitised to the anxieties of one parent and the object of the other's hostility. The student's symptomatic behaviour (e.g. disruptive behaviour at school) serves as a diversion for the family in times of parental disharmony and creates the circumstances which enable the parents to behave as an apparently 'normal' family (i.e. with parents cooperating in reaction to stress apparently created by their child's misbehaviour at school) with the student's misbehaviour in school serving as a rationalisation for the over-closeness in the parent–child relationship. In these circumstances the major source of family disharmony (the parental dyad) is left unacknowledged and attention is focused on the student's behaviour. Another important family-school triangle is the parent–child–teacher triangle (Okun, 1984; Guerin & Katz, 1984), in which a parent–child conflict is displaced to the teacher–student relationship. In these circumstances school based intervention is unlikely to achieve a lasting solution, and family therapy is called for. Worden (1981) suggests that a child's behaviour problems in school can often be seen as an indication of a clash of values or roles between the two systems. Hsia (1984) describes how families' often paralysed response to the highly disturbing symptoms of school phobia can be indicative of underlying family difficulties which serve to sustain and promote the child's phobic reaction. In all of these cases, family interactional patterns are serving to maintain the students' symptomatic behaviour. The focus of intervention in these circumstances, therefore, becomes the family of the symptomatic student, rather than the student alone.

In Britain, Dowling & Osborne (1985) have developed what they describe as a 'joint-systems' approach to a wider consideration of the school ecosystem, seeing the school as an important influence on the pupils' behaviour. They, therefore, advocate that family therapists act as consultants to the school system as well as the family system, as appropriate. Taylor & Dowling (1986) and Dowling & Taylor (1989) describe the setting up of an outreach service, whereby a group of family therapists make themselves available, on a regular basis to parents and teachers by basing themselves on school premises. Campion (1985) also advocates the training of British educational psychologists in family therapy techniques as a means of bringing families and schools into closer harmony.

Most recently, in America, Molnar and Lindquist (1989) have described a school focused approach, which involves classroom teachers and other school personnel using systemic techniques in the normal course of their work. Molnar & Lindquist's work is particularly apposite at the present time in Britain, coming as it does in the wake of the Elton Report (DES, 1989), since it takes as its focus the need to provide teachers with techniques for dealing with oppositional pupil behaviour of the type identified as being most prevalent in the national survey commissioned by the Elton Committee (Gray & Sime, 1989). These behaviours are termed 'oppositional' because they represent deliberate and repeated infringements of classroom rules which teachers impose in order to create, what they believe to be, the necessary conditions for effective teaching and learning to take place.

The main problem with the types of behavioural difficulties described here is their persistence and apparent resistance to the approaches which teachers most commonly use to oppose them (e.g. reasoning, punishment, ignoring, detention, discussion, withdrawal, referral to another teacher, withdrawal of privileges [see Elton Report, p. 240]). These (essentially 'lineal') approaches, far from changing the problem behaviour, can serve to maintain and promote the behaviour they seek to alter. The ecosystemic approach of Molnar & Lindquist, however, seeks to offer teachers the means to change the problem behaviour, not by challenging the behaviour overtly, but by utilising the systemic principles which sustain interactional patterns. One of the major aims of their approach is to assist teachers in redefining oppositional behaviour in terms which lead both teacher and perpetrator to see the behaviour as cooperative or positive, rather than oppositional or negative. The perpetrator is deprived of a barrier against which to kick by being presented with a new and undesired rationale for the negative behaviour. The behaviour, therefore, loses its original effect and is made redundant (this point is exemplified in the section headed 'intervention').

The very act of developing a new perception of the negative behaviour can itself remove the teachers desire to change the behaviour though, more often, it is the projection of this new perception which leads the pupil toward a conscious decision to change the behaviour pattern. Thus, the pupil's determination to behave according to his/her own value system and not to be merely obedient to the teacher's wishes, is employed by the teacher as a means of controlling the pupil's behaviour. For this reason the approach has been referred to as employing 'judo' principles (Mandel *et al.*, 1975). The key point is, however, that behaviour problems are resolved without loss of face and without the pupil surrendering behavioural autonomy. This makes the approach particularly appropriate to classrooms in which qualities of autonomy and self direction are valued pupil traits which may be threatened by approaches to problem behaviour which demand the pupil's open surrender of autonomy in subservience to the teacher's authority.

As yet, there are no published examples of the use of such interventions in British schools. There is, however, a growing number of reports and articles describing the successful use of such strategies in American schools. Mandel *et al.* (1975) describe the successful use of such techniques with EBD pupils in a special school who swear, and are belligerent towards teachers. Others describe the successful use of such techniques in mainstream schools, with pupils who present physical aggression toward other pupils (Brown, 1986), tantrum behaviour (Amatea, 1988), fighting, in-school truancy, depression with suicidal tendencies (Williams & Weeks, 1984) and school phobia/school refusal (Hsia, 1984). Molnar & Lindquist (1989) also describe the use of these techniques with a wide range of behaviour problems encountered in mainstream schools, such as, lack of attentiveness, chronic gossiping, apparent inability to settle down to work, failure to complete homework and classwork assignments, talking out of turn, interrupting the teacher and belligerence toward teachers and pupils. They also describe instances in which teachers employed the techniques successfully with problematic colleagues.

Key components of the ecosystemic approach to school behavioural problems

Below is an exposition of some of the key features of the ecosystemic approach to school behaviour problems (see also, Upton & Cooper, 1990):

1   *Problem behaviour in the classroom does not originate from within the individual who displays the behaviour, but is a product of social interaction.*
2   *Interactional patterns may be conceptualised in simple or complex ways.* The simple analysis is confined to here and now situations, and will define a student's negative behaviour in terms of the interactions which immediately surround this behaviour. A complex analysis will take into account factors in the wider ecosystem and explore purposes which the here and now behaviour might serve in other, related ecosystems. Such an analysis may relate oppositional behaviour in the classroom to interactional patterns in the student's family.
3   *The cause of any instance of problem behaviour is part of a cyclical chain of actions and reactions between participants.* Each event in the interactional chain is both a cause of ensuing events and the effect of preceding events. Student classroom behaviour which is defined as 'problematic' is always goal directed, and, from the student's viewpoint, it is understandable, rational, and above all, necessary. What appears problematic to the teacher may well be the solution to a problem for the student, for a subsystem in the classroom or school, or the student's family. Attempts to directly oppose goal directed behaviour inevitably meet with resistance and can, therefore, help to encourage the problematic situation to continue. The repeated use of failed solutions in this way is often characteristic of apparently intractable systemic problems.
4   *Intervention, based on an ecosystemic analysis must recognise the contribution made to the interactional events surrounding a problem, by ALL participating parties.* This emphasises the reflexive quality of the ecosystemic approach, which requires teachers to analyse their own behaviour and its relation to the perceived problem. Teachers can only influence their students by eschewing confrontational approaches and entering into a cooperative relationship with them in which the 'problematic' behaviour is reconstructed in terms which are meaningful to both the student and the teacher (and members of significant subsystems, such as family members, other students, school personnel, where appropriate) and which

reveal one or more of the following things: (a) the goals served by the behaviour; (b) the inappropriateness, for the student, of the goals that are or may be served by the behaviour; and (c) alternative/more effective means of achieving the goals which the behaviour is perceived to serve.

In constructing a picture of a problem situation it is necessary for the teacher to establish awareness of his/her phenomenological interpretation of the situation and to set this against those of others involved, particularly students. The teacher must identify in specific behavioural terms: (a) the precise nature of the problem as s/he sees it, in terms of repeating behavioural patterns, the times, places and individuals involved; (b) possible positive interpretations of the problem behaviour; and (c) how the situation will be different when improvement begins and after the problem is solved. This involves the teacher in a degree of self analysis, in which evidence for the existence of the problem is amassed and scrutinised, along with the teacher's behavioural expectations. Molnar & Lindquist (1989) describe this process as 'sleuthing'. A vital component of the process involves the teacher in seeking perspectives on the situation other than his/her own; particularly those of the students involved. Molnar & Lindquist suggest that teachers be alert to students' use of figurative language in their descriptions of problematic situations. Since it is through figurative language that we make personal sense of the reality around us, it follows that teachers will communicate more effectively with students if they make use of their own figurative language and use this as an exploratory tool in defining situations from the students' viewpoint. (It would seem to us also, that this recognition of the importance of students' viewpoints has important implications for patterns of classroom interaction, which suggest links between the ecosystemic approach and humanistic approaches to education, which will be briefly discussed in the conclusion to this chapter). Teachers must also be constantly alert to positive changes, however apparently insignificant, which occur in the classroom ecosystem whether or not they appear to be related to the problem situation. Such minor changes may give rise to hitherto unthought of solutions.

Intervention

The chief characteristic of recurring problem situations is their apparent self-perpetuating inevitability. Individuals believe themselves to be behaving in the only rational way that is possible in the given circumstances. For instance, a teacher reprimands a pupil who disobeys her. The pupil responds to the reprimand with abuse. The teacher reprimands the pupil further; the pupil abuses the teacher further and so on. Each is driven by the conviction that not to confront the other's reprimand/abuse, is to accept the unacceptable. A distinguishing characteristic of ecosystemic intervention is the use of 'divergent explanations of problem behaviour' (Molnar & Lindquist, 1989, p. xv). Such divergent explanations seek to redefine problem situations so that conflict (or resistance) is seen as cooperation. This tenet holds true in any social ecosystem, whether it be (for example) the interactional dyad of the pupil and teacher, the mesosystem (i.e. the interaction among systems) of family and school, super-power and super-power.

As has already been noted, behaviour which functions to maintain an individual's symptomatic condition can often be seen, from a systemic viewpoint, to be serving a goal elsewhere in the system. Power & Bartholomew (1985) present a case study, involving a student with learning and behaviour difficulties, in which parent–school enmity was seen to be a predominant factor. After a period of sustained conflict between the school and the family, a family therapist was brought in as consultant. The therapist developed the following interpretation of the situation. The student was seen by his teachers to be underachieving and his parents appeared to be using their son's difficulties as a diversion from their marital problems. The parents were able to unite with one another in their concern for their son's problems and this helped to prevent marital break-up. Consequently, the parents had a vested interest in maintaining their son's difficulties and did so by opposing the school's efforts to solve their son's problems, through, for instance, over-protectiveness and encouraging him not to complete homework assignments. Teachers at the school responded to what they saw as family collusion, by being unsympathetic toward the student and making unrealistic demands upon him. The school–family relationship was seen to be characterised by a pattern of symmetrical interaction, 'that is, one in which each party responds to what the other is doing in a similar way' (p. 223). Such relationships are founded on constant competition for the dominant position. Thus, in the present case, the teachers' suggestion that the student's school problems were related to the family circumstances would be met by the counterclaim that the teachers were not working effectively. It is the nature of such relationships to escalate, leading to deeper entrenchment on both sides, with each party undermining the efforts made by the other to help the student. The chief loser here, ironically, is the student.

Clearly, such a conflictual situation would be unlikely to produce a solution to the student's difficulties. The consultant family therapist proposed an intervention which sought to convert this relationship into a complementary relationship. A complementary relationship is characterised by non-competitive interaction, so that, for instance, dominance is met with passivity, anger with appeasement and so on. The consultant persuaded the school personnel to be compliant with the parents' views at the next meeting, and to adopt a subordinate role. When, during the meeting, the parents became hostile toward the school staff, the social worker took up the parental position and presented it in an exaggerated form, suggesting that their son should be relieved of all pressures in class. The parents responded to this in a conciliatory manner and for the first time they suggested that 'the teacher did have the right to place some expectations on the students in her class' (p. 226). This was a point at which the parents and staff were in agreement for the first time. The deadlock was broken and an opportunity to develop a collaborative relationship was established. The eventual outcome of this case was that the parents and the school personnel agreed to recognise the primacy of each other in their respective domains. The teachers agreed not to pressurise the student in class and, instead of setting specific home-work tasks in addition to classwork, they agreed to allow him to take uncompleted classwork tasks home. It was agreed that whether he completed the tasks at home was a matter for the parents to decide and the school would simply award the appropriate grade without placing any pressure on the student. By allowing the student to take classwork home, the school was enabling the parents to control the pressure their son was placed under. This newly collaborative relationship between the school and the family also led to their accepting advice from a psychologist on aiding their son with stress management. Thus the student's therapeutic needs were met, as were the parents' needs for a collaborative activity with one another (i.e. as a diversion from their marital difficulties) and the school's position was also validated.

A key feature shared by ecosystemic intervention strategies and demonstrated in the above example, is that, when they succeed, individuals change their behaviour and become more cooperative with others, whilst retaining their sense of control over their own behaviour. For example, the parents in the above example, when faced with an overly compliant response, found that it was necessary, for their own purposes, to support the school position, and soften their dominant stance. They stated that they wanted the school to place a certain amount of pressure on their son, even though this had been a major source of disagreement earlier. This point emphasises the ecosystemic idea that it is the patterns of interaction among people which maintain problematic situations, rather than the situation which appears to be the focus of the problem. The purpose of ecosystemic intervention techniques is to offer participants the means to break out of destructive cycles of interaction, through the creation of new cycles. This is demonstrated repeatedly by Molnar & Lindquist (1989), in their exemplification of ecosystemic techniques for classroom teachers and other school personnel.

The archetypal ecosystemic technique, described by Molnar & Lindquist, is that of 'reframing'. The technique is based on four basic propositions: (i) we behave in accordance with the way in which we interpret problem situations; (ii) there are often many different but equally valid interpretations of any given situation; (iii) if we change our interpretation we can change our behaviour; and (iv) change in our behaviour will influence the perceptions and behaviour of others.

For example, a teacher may seek to reprimand a student, in order to prevent him or her from repeatedly talking out of turn. The student, however, might persist with the deviant behaviour regardless of the increasing severity of the reprimands. Without knowing what that pupil's perception of the situation is, the teacher is still able to effect change in the ecosystem by changing her own perceptions and behaviour. The teacher's behaviour is clearly based on the interpretation that talking out of turn is a deviant act. The reframing technique requires the teacher to seek a new, plausible and positive interpretation of the behaviour, through the process of 'sleuthing' (see above) and then to behave in strict accordance with this. For it is essential that the reframing be feasible and believable in the eyes of the pupil. Such an interpretation might be that the student often interrupts the teacher in order to seek clarification for particular points made by the teacher. The behaviour is now defined as a positive service to the class as a whole.

For the intervention to be effective, the teacher must behave in strict accordance with the reframing. In order to do this the 'symptom prescription' technique (Molnar & Lindquist, 1989) might be used. This involves the teacher encouraging the student to perform the symptomatic behaviour in revised circumstances. The teacher might suggest to the student that she or he increase the frequency of interruption in order to optimise the value of the service it provides.

The successful outcome of such an intervention would be that a situation of conflict has now become one of cooperation. As with the antagonistic parents referred to above, the apparent concession by a former adversary may give rise to complementary concessions. On the other hand, it could be said that control of the problematic behaviour has now passed from the student to the teacher. Where the behaviour may have been perceived in the past as means by which the student gained control over the teacher (by 'winding him or her up') it has now become a means by which the teacher exerts control over the student. In any event talking out of turn is now redundant as a tool for engaging in conflict. To do so now is, in fact, perceived as an act of cooperation. The likelihood is that the student will cease the behaviour and possibly take up another form of behaviour which achieves the initial goal of the interrupting behaviour.

Molnar & Lindquist provide many examples in which interventions of this sort succeed and they repeatedly suggest, on the basis of anecdotal reports of teachers using such approaches, that the seed of cooperation that is planted in such situations often has a transforming effect on the quality of interpersonal relationships involved. Students with whom teachers have experienced difficulty in forming cooperative relationships become more amenable and generally much easier to get along with. Such observations require careful consideration and experimental scrutiny. As they stand, however, these observations suggest a number of interesting hypotheses as to the effect of ecosystemic approaches on the social climate of the classroom which would seem to be in line with research which has shown the considerable influence of teacher expectations on pupil performance and behaviour (e.g. Hargreaves *et al.*, 1975).

In order to demonstrate this approach, an observational study, conducted by one of the present authors in an English special school, will be presented. This study will be used: (i) to demonstrate an ecosystemic analysis of classroom behaviour and (ii) to indicate intervention strategies that might arise from such an analysis. It should be stressed that this is a theoretical demonstration. Whilst the classroom events described were actually observed, the interventions were not applied and were not communicated to the teacher involved. It should also be stated that the authors (both of whom are experienced school teachers and educational researchers) recognise the classroom events described here to be of an extreme nature. This lesson contained by far the worst examples of classroom disharmony observed throughout a four week period in which the researcher visited three schools. These events are not typical of the daily life of schools in Britain and must not be considered as such. This extract is presented because we believe it to illustrate, graphically, certain key issues in the ecosystemic approach, which appear, in a less heightened form, in classrooms throughout the education system.

A case study

The following interactional sequence was observed in a special school for pupils of secondary age with emotional and behavioural difficulties. The school operated a behavioural programme by which pupils could obtain privileges in accordance with their performance on a range of criteria which was constructed in consultation with pupils and formalised in terms of a 'contract'. Teachers passed on the pupils' contracts to one another when lessons changed and at the end of each lesson teachers awarded each pupil a mark (out of ten) for his or her performance in accordance with the contract terms. The lesson involved a group of four third year boys who were taught by an experienced special needs teacher who had been at the school for approximately six months. The teacher had given the pupils a worksheet to complete. All four pupils had been working fairly calmly for several minutes when the following sequence look place. Throughout the sequence the teacher maintained the outward appearance of calmness and composure and employed a calm and patient voice. (Names and other analytically irrelevant details have been altered).

['*P*' refers to 'Pupil'; *P1* is also referred to as 'Carl', '*T*' refers to 'Teacher']

P1: [puts pen down emphatically] I'm not doing this, it's boring.

P4: Yeah, it's boring.

T: [Calmly] If you are not on task you are going to lose points. You may get a nought.

[P4 pushing worksheet away, turns to P3 and they begin a conversation]

P1: [pushing worksheet on floor, fiercely] I don't care. I'm not doing this boring, shit work. [gets out of seat and makes for the classroom door, which he opens].

T: If you go out of the room, you will get a nought on your contract. [T gives P1 a stern look, to which he responds with an impish grin, as he stands provocatively, holding the handle of the open door; looking as if he might step out of the room at any time]

T: Sit down Carl and do your work.

[P1's grin fades to an aggressive scowl, as he moves away from the doorway and begins to roam the classroom with apparent aimlessness.]

T: Sit down Carl, or I'll have to give you a nought.

P1: Balls!

T: If you're off task, I have to give you a nought; you know that.

P1: Fuck off!

T: Carl, I want you to get on with your work.

P1: Fuck off, you bitch.

[P2 looks up from his work occasionally to see what is going on, but continues to work for the most part. P3 is by turns working and scuffling with P4, who has not resumed working. P3 and 4 stand up as if to fight.]

T: [to P's 3 and 4] Okay you two, you're off task; that's going to be nought, unless you get back to it.

[P3 and P4 exchange conspiratorial grins. They make as if to square up to one another. They sit down. P4 kicks a chair, sending it loudly spinning across the room. Meanwhile P1 has returned to the door; has opened it, and is hanging out of the doorway into the corridor.]

P1: I'm fucking off!

T: I've told you, if you go out of the classroom, you're going to get nought on your contract.

P1: So. If I want to go, I go. You can't stop me.

T: [to P1] If you don't do the work now, you'll have to do it later, at home. [NB this is an established practice within the school]

P1: Fuck off.

[P1 starts to roam the room again. P4 picks up his worksheet, screws it up and throws it. The missile hits P1, who retrieves it and throws it. The teacher is in the line of fire, and is hit]

P1: [looking genuinely surprised and apologetic] Sorry miss! [T gives P1 a stern look. P's 2, 3 and 4, snigger silently, behind the T's back] I didn't mean it to hit you. [P's 2, 3, and 4 are now seated; apparently working].

T: Right, that's a nought for you Carl. [Writes on a piece of paper]

P1: That's not fair!

T: What do you expect?

P1: Fucking cow! Bitch!

[P1 sits down and angrily starts to write on a sheet of paper, which he then violently destroys]

P1: I'm not doing it. It's rubbish. [scatters torn fragments over the floor]

T: You're just going to have to do it later.

P1: Fuck Off! [P1 stands up and kicks his chair hard against the wall. He starts to walk around the room again. T deals with a query from P3 about the worksheet. P1 goes over to P4; they start to tussle; this time a little more seriously than before. T interposes herself between them.

T: [firmly] Stop that!

P4: [Sits down] Give us another worksheet then.

[P1 is still standing in front of the teacher, in a confrontational stance. There is a sense of mockery in the stance, but only just. T walks away from P1. P1 follows, muttering barely audible swear words, the most audible of which is 'fuck'. T does not react. P1 bumps into teacher]

P3: Ooh! Carl's going to rape miss! [P's 2 and 4 laugh]

P1 [to P3] Fuck off, you cunt! Fuck off!

[There is a loud noise in the corridor. P1 goes to the door and opens it.]

T: [Sharply] Don't go out there! I told you ...

P1: Fuck off! I'm not staying here! [He leaves the room and does not return.]

This interactional sequence illustrates the principle of circular causality in that the teacher and Carl repeatedly challenge one another in an attempt to assert their individual definitions of the situation. At which ever point we choose to punctuate this interactional sequence we can identify both Carl's behaviour as a cause of the teacher's behaviour and the teacher's behaviour as the cause of Carl's behaviour. Both are attempting to assert their will over the other and to avoid giving in to the will of the other. The teacher's choice of control strategies appears to be based on the assumption that she is in a position of authority over Carl. From the start, it is clear that Carl does not accept this definition of the situation. Carl's determination to assert his refusal to recognise the teacher's authority stimulates the teacher to continued attempts to assert her authority (through the use of commands and threats), which in turn stimulates Carl to further displays of resistance and so on, in a relentless circle of assertion and counter-assertion. This circle of causation rapidly develops into an escalating spiral (symmetrical escalation, see above), which is exemplified by Carl's increased use of verbally offensive language (swearing and insults) and provocative posturing ('roaming' behaviour, standing in the doorway, confrontational stance), with a corresponding escalation in the teacher's assertion of authority (at first threatening sanctions calmly, then firmly, and finally applying one of the threatened sanctions).

Both the key actors in this sequence attempt to influence one another's behaviour in a *lineal* manner, that is, they appear to perceive one another's behaviour in terms of 'either/or logic' (de Shazer, 1985). They see only the alternatives of accepting or rejecting the behaviour of the other. An ecosystemic approach recognises that, in a self perpetuating situation such as this, neither alternative is appropriate, since both alternatives produce conflict which is unacceptable to one or other of the parties involved. What is required, in such a situation, is for one of the parties to behave differently but in a way which still appears to be rational to both parties.

In the present example an appropriate systemic technique might be that of 'reframing'. The art of reframing is to produce an alternative meaning for a particular behaviour which is equally convincing to all those involved in the interaction. In the present example, opportunities for reframing are offered to the teacher by those aspects of Carl's behaviour which she clearly perceives to be oppositional. For instance, when Carl first leaves his seat and goes to the door as if to leave, the teacher immediately responds with a threat of punishment. The teacher is, therefore, implying that she frames Carl's behaviour as oppositional. A suitable reframing might involve defining Carl's behaviour not as a sign of assertiveness but rather as an expression of vulnerability and, as such, a stimulus for sympathy rather than punishment. The teacher might suggest to Carl that whilst such behaviour is normally forbidden, that Carl's special vulnerability and sensitivity to the classroom situation make his desire to leave understandable and his inability to control this urge worthy of sympathy. The teacher may even go on to suggest that Carl's behaviour serves a positive function for the teacher ('positive connotation of function', Molnar & Lindquist, 1989) in that it reminds the teacher of the need to take particular care when dealing with a pupil as specially sensitive as Carl clearly is. The teacher may also suggest that the behaviour reveals a positive motive ('positive connotation of motive', ibid.) in that it leaves the teacher free to devote more time to the remaining pupils and so reveals a tendency toward a self-sacrificing nature; a trait which exemplifies Carl's sensitivity to others' needs. Another approach might be for the teacher to suggest that Carl leave the room at other times during the lesson for a period specified by the teacher ('symptom prescription', Molnar & Lindquist, 1989).

In selecting an appropriate intervention, it is essential that the teacher take into account the pupil's likely response to the chosen intervention. On the basis of the present example, for instance, it would seem that Carl is unlikely to wish to behave in ways that make him appear 'vulnerable' or 'sensitive' (i.e. this would run counter to the aggressive 'macho' image he projects), whilst the unsettled and excitable behaviour he exhibits make such an explanation feasible. Furthermore, once the teacher has made such a case and behaves in accordance with the reframing, the pupil is faced with the alternatives of continuing his current pattern of behaviour, and so supporting the reframing, or ceasing the behaviour pattern and so confounding the teacher's reframing. Either way, the teacher has gained ascendancy. If the pupil continues to misbehave he is merely proving the teacher right and allowing her to express empathy and understanding. If the pupil ceases to misbehave, then the teacher's strategy has led to restoration of order. Given the tendency of such oppositional pupils as Carl towards assertiveness (Mandel *et al.*, 1975) it is more likely that he would seek to take the latter course.

From an ecosystemic viewpoint, the intervention strategies outlined above would gain particular force from the fact that they would represent a change in the interactional pattern. The present extract, coincidentally, offers an example of the power of such an unexpected change. When the worksheet-missile inadvertently strikes the teacher, Carl is suddenly apologetic, and refers to the teacher, for the first time, as 'miss'.

The intervention hypothesised above might be termed a 'simple' ecosystemic intervention (Upton & Cooper, 1990) in its avoidance of any inquiry into the motivations of the participants. Though, of course, a teacher working autonomously would intervene only after having subjected her phenomenological construction of the situation to critical scrutiny and with consideration of what is known of the student's viewpoint. A more complex intervention, which might be necessary if classroom-based intervention proved ineffective, would entail a more detailed enquiry, possibly by a family therapist. In conversation with the teacher involved, after this lesson, the researcher remarked with admiration on the teacher's self control and display of patience. The teacher responded to this by saying that she was able to behave in this way because she firmly believed that such a conflict situation did not represent a problem for her but was rather a problem internal to the student. She believed that all she could do in such circumstances was to remain patient and firm but that it was outside her capability to change such situations. She remarked, philosophically, that at other times she seemed to get on quite well with Carl. This had been one of those occasions when Carl was in one of his moods.

Unfortunately, Carl was unavailable for interview, as staff felt that he required a cooling period. It is important to note, however, that Carl's condition, for several hours after this event, is best described as distraught. It was suggested by members of staff, however, that Carl's reaction might be related to what was generally perceived to be his lack of respect for women. It was noted that he was in the care of his single mother who staff felt was easily manipulated and bullied by her only son. Whilst the teacher's negative framing of the situation would support the feasibility of the intervention proposed above, the information relating to Carl's background might indicate that the problem be tentatively characterised as 'a problem in the family that disturbs the school' (Lindquist *et al.*, 1987), and thus appropriate for a joint systems approach (see above).

Conclusion: towards a new educational perspective

An ecosystem approach seeks to define behaviour problems in schools in terms of the interactional systems which maintain and promote behaviour. This approach rejects ways of conceptualising behaviour problems which see the problem in terms of quality or defect of the individual. As such, the ecosystemic approach is in keeping with the wealth of research evidence which describes the ways in which schools and teachers unwittingly engage in the construction of 'deviant' pupils (Keddie, 1971; Sharp & Green, 1975; Hargreaves *et al.*, 1975; Reid, 1985). These and other writers argue that it is the quality of interpersonal interaction between teachers and pupils in many of our schools, that produces students who are disaffected and who actively resist their teachers in return for what they see as the degradation and ill treatment that characterises the daily routines in many schools (Hargreaves, 1967; Rosser & Harré, 1976; Woods, 1976; Tattum, 1982; Schostak, 1983). These writers draw on the testimony of pupils to make the case that disruptive behaviour in schools can often be seen as a rational response to intolerable circumstances.

The ecosystemic approach offers a mechanism for analysing and changing interactional patterns that can be employed by individuals at the dyadic level, as well as at larger institutional levels. The vital importance of the school–family interactive system which has long been seen as an important area for development in British education, particularly in relation to learning and behavioural difficulties (DES, 1978; Reynolds & Sullivan, 1979; Galloway, 1985; Galloway & Goodwin, 1987; DES, 1989), is also recognised by this approach and practical measures for overcoming some of the difficulties encountered in this area are suggested.

In these important areas the ecosystemic approach can be seen to indicate avenues for research and application. It is envisaged that such work would provide a valuable addition to that which is already being done by some advocates of behavioural approaches (e.g. Wheldall & Merrett, 1984; Wheldall *et al.*, 1983; Wheldall, 1987; Wheldall & Glynn, 1989), who are concerned to promote the development of learning environments which are more responsive to the needs of school students, through the sensitisation of teachers and parents to the influence they can have on the behaviour of students.

In looking to the future of the ecosystemic approach and its application to British education we see certain important contextual factors of which account must be taken. The first is what we see as the humanistic tradition of British education, which can be traced back to the early writings of A.S. Neill (Neill, 1916), through the child centred movement of the 1960s (DES, 1967), the development of student initiated learning approaches (Barnes, 1976), and into the contemporary concern for democratic schooling (Fletcher *et al.*, 1985; Harber & Meighan, 1989). In a recent micro-sociological study, Cronk (1987) has shown how a humanistic approach to classroom behaviour problems can lead to an improvement in students' classroom behaviour and lesson involvement. Central to Cronk's approach is the importance attached to the sharing of phenomenological constructs of the classroom situation, between pupils and teachers. This clearly relates to Molnar & Lindquist's (1989) concept of sleuthing. We suggest that the effectiveness of such sleuthing, the aim of which is to gain an understanding of students' phenomenological worlds, would be enhanced if the sleuths were trained in some of the counselling skills of humanistic psychology, which involve the development of empathy through the exercise of skills, such as active listening, reflection and paraphrase (Rogers, 1980; Mearns & Thorne, 1984). The absence of empathic understanding between teachers and students would seem, from a reading of the literature on school behaviour problems referred to above, to be a major factor in the development and maintenance of behaviour problems. The use of empathy by teachers would add to the reflexive quality of the ecosystemic approach with regard to teacher behaviour, by encouraging teachers to continually analyse the experience of school from the student's standpoint.

A second contextual matter relates to the role of the mainstream classroom teacher in British schools. Concern has been expressed in recent years about the way in which support staff, delegated to mainstream schools to act as consultants to mainstream teachers in the support of pupils with special educational needs, have been increasingly used by mainstream schools in the role of peripatetic specialist teachers. Galloway & Goodwin (1987) have suggested that this situation has had the reverse effect to that of its original intention and has resulted in the de-skilling of mainstream teachers in the special educational needs area. This can be seen in the broader context of increased specialisation in the teaching force, in which teachers' roles become evermore precisely defined in terms of specialist skills and responsibilities. Galloway (1985) has suggested that the pastoral effectiveness of some schools has been undermined by the development of separate pastoral systems which have the twin effects of identifying certain teachers as having specialist pastoral responsibilities, whilst excluding other 'non-specialist' teachers from the performance of pastoral functions. In the face of such tendencies toward 'de-skilling' we suggest that the ecosystemic approach offers skills which mainstream teachers could develop through INSET, as Molnar & Lindquist (1989) have suggested.

Whilst the examples of ecosystemic interventions described by Molnar & Lindquist would appear to be well within the capabilities of appropriately trained mainstream teachers, those joint systems interventions which involve school and family, would clearly remain within the province of the specialist family therapist. We would suggest however, that the training of teachers in ecosystemic approaches will make teachers more aware of the potential value of family therapy and, therefore, more likely to seek the support of family therapists, in the context of the type of outreach model described by Taylor & Dowling (1986) and Dowling & Taylor (1989).

Molnar & Lindquist (1989) provide a range of techniques which they claim can be easily assimilated by teachers who can use them autonomously and to great effect. One of the key features of the ecosystemic approach is a recognition of the power that can be derived from different perspectives on a situation. With this in mind, it would seem that the ecosystemic approach might develop in the context of staff support groups (as recommended by the Elton Committee) with access to a specialist family therapist (and/or educational psychologist trained in family therapy) who would perform the dual roles of professional supervisor and training consultant. Peer group support would facilitate the development of new perspectives on difficult situations and have valuable social implications for teachers, who often feel professionally isolated in these matters. The availability of a specialist consultant would also help teachers decide when it was appropriate to hand cases over to specialist therapists. The effectiveness of this approach, however, still needs to be established, as does the feasibility of staff-peer support groups, as mentioned here. Clearly, the next step in developing the ecosystemic approach in a British context will involve research into these areas.

References

Amatea, E. (1988) Brief systemic interventions with school behavior problems: a case of temper tantrums, *Psychology in the Schools*, 25, pp. 174–183.

Barnes, D. (1976) *From Communication to Curriculum* (Harmondsworth, Penguin).

Bateson, G. (1972) *Steps to an Ecology of Mind* (New York, Chandler).

Bateson, G. (1979) *Mind and Nature: a necessary unity* (New York, Dutton).

Bateson, G., Jackson, D., Haley, J. & Weakland, J. (1956) Towards a theory of schizophrenia, *Behavioural Science*, 1, pp. 251–254.

Bridge, S. & Luke, S. (1989) *Blackstone's Guide to the Children Act 1989* (London, Blackstone).

Brown, J. (1986) The use of paradoxical intervention with oppositional behavior in the classroom, *Psychology in the Schools*, 21, pp. 77–81.

Burden, R. (1981) Systems theory and its relevance to schools, in: B. Gillham (Ed.) *Problem Behaviour in the Secondary School* (London, Croom Helm).

Campion, J. (1985) *The Child in Context: family systems theory in educational psychology* (London, Methuen).

Cooper, P. (1989) Respite, Relationships and Re-Signification: A Study of the Effects of Residential Schooling on Pupils with Emotional and Behavioural Difficulties, with Particular Reference to the Pupil's Perspective, *Unpublished Ph.D. thesis*, University of Birmingham.

Cronk, K. (1987) *Teacher–Pupil Conflict in Secondary Schools* (Lewes, Falmer).

de Shazer, S. (1982) *Patterns of Brief Family Therapy: an ecosystemic approach* (New York, Guilford Press).

de Shazer, S. (1985) *Keys to Solution* (New York: Norton).

DES (1967) *Children and their Primary Schools (Plowden Report)* (London, HMSO).

DES (1978) *Special Educational Needs (Warnock Report)* (London, HMSO).

DES (1989) *Discipline in Schools (Elton Report)* (London, HMSO).

Dowling, E. & Osborne, E. (1985) (Eds) *The Family and the School* (London, Routledge & Kegan Paul).

Dowling, E. & Taylor, D. (1989) The clinic goes to school: lessons learnt, *Maladjustment and Therapeutic Education*, 7(1), pp. 24–29.

Fletcher, C., Caron, M. & Williams, W. (1985) *Schools on Trial* (Milton Keynes, Open University Press).

Galloway, D. (1985) Pastoral care and school effectiveness, in: D. Reynolds (Ed.) *Studying School Effectiveness* (London, Falmer).

Galloway, D. & Goodwin, C. (1987) *The Education of Disturbing Children* (London, Longman).

Gray, J. & Sime, S. (1989) *Teachers and discipline*: a report for the committee of enquiry into discipline in schools by Sheffield University (Appendix D of the Elton Report, *op. cit.*).

Guerin, P. & Katz, A. (1984) The theory in therapy of families with school related problems: triangles and a hypothesis testing model, in: B. Okun (Ed.) *Family Therapy with School Related Problems* (Rockville, CO, Aspen).

Harber, C. & Meighan, R. (1989) (Eds) *The Democratic School* (Ticknall, Education Now).

Hargreaves, D. (1967) *Social Relations in a Secondary School* (London, Routledge & Kegan Paul).

Hargreaves, D., Hester, S. & Mellor, F. (1975) *Deviance in Classrooms* (London, Routledge & Kegan Paul).

Hoffman, L. (1981) *Foundations of Family Therapy* (New York, Basic Books).

Hsia, H. (1984) Structural and strategic approaches to school phobia/school refusal, *Psychology in the Schools*, 21(3), pp. 360–367.

Keddie, N. (1971) Classroom Knowledge, in: M. Young (Ed.) *Knowledge and Control* (London, Collier-Macmillan).

Lindquist, B., Molnar, A. & Brauchmann, L. (1987) Working with school related problems without going to school: considerations for systemic practice, *Journal of Strategic and Systemic Therapies*, 6(4), pp. 44–50.

Madanes, C. (1981) *Strategic Family Therapy* (San Francisco, CA, Jossey-Bass).

Mandel, H., Weizmann, F., Millan, B., Greenhow, J. & Speers, D. (1975) Reaching emotionally disturbed children: 'judo' principles in remedial education, *American Journal of Orthopsychiatry*, 45(5), pp. 867–874.

Mearns, D. & Thorne, B. (1988) *Person Centred Counselling in Action* (London, Sage).

Minuchin, S. (1974) *Families and Family Therapy* (Canterbury, Harvard University Press).

Molnar, A. & de Shazer, S. (1987) Solution focused therapy: towards the identification of the therapeutic task, *Journal of Marital and Family Therapy*, 13(4), pp. 349–358.

Molnar, A. & Lindquist, B. (1989) *Changing Problem Behavior in Schools* (San Francisco, CA, Jossey Bass).

Neill, A.S. (1916) *A Dominie's Log* (London, Herbert Jenkins).

Okun, B. (1984) Family therapy and the schools, in: B. Okun (Ed.) *Family Therapy with School Related Problems* (Rockville, CO, Aspen).

Parsons, T. (1951) *The Social System* (Glencoe, Free Press).

Power, T. & Bartholomew, K. (1985) Getting uncaught in the middle: a case study in family-school system consultation, *School Psychology Review*, 14(2), pp. 222–229.

Reid, K. (1985) *Truancy and School Absenteeism* (London, Hodder and Stoughton).

Reynolds, D. & Sullivan, M. (1979) Bringing schools back in, in: L. Barton & R. Meighan (Eds) *Schools, Pupils and Deviance* (Nafferton, Nafferton Books).

Rogers, C. (1980) *A Way of Being* (Boston, Houghton-Mifflin).

Rosser, E. & Harré, R. (1976) The meaning of trouble, in: M. Hammersley & P. Woods (Eds) *The Process of Schooling* (London, Routledge & Kegan Paul).

Schostak, J. (1983) *Maladjusted Schooling* (Lewes, Falmer).

Selvini, M. (1988) *The Work of Mara Selvini-Palazzoli* (New York, Aronson).

Selvini-Palazzoli, M., Boscolo, L., Cecchin, G. & Prata, G. (1973) *Paradox and Counterparadox* (New York, Aronson).

Sharp, R. & Green, A. (1975) *Education and Social Control* (London, Routledge & Kegan Paul).

Smith, A. (1978) Encountering the family system in school-related problems, *Psychology in the Schools*, 15(3), pp. 379–386.

Speed, B. (1984) Family therapy: an update, *ACPCP Newsletter*, 6(1), pp. 2–14.

Tattum, D. (1982) *Disruptive Pupils in Schools and Units* (Chichester, Wiley).

Taylor, D. & Dowling, E. (1986) The clinic goes to school: setting up an outreach service, *Maladjustment and Therapeutic Education*, 4(2), pp. 90–98.

von Bertalanffy, L. (1950) The theory of open systems in physics and biology, *Science*, 3, pp. 25–29.

von Bertalanffy, L. (1968) *General System Theory* (New York, Brazillier).

Upton, G. & Cooper, P. (1990) A new perspective on behaviour problems in schools: the ecosystemic approach, *Maladjustment and Therapeutic Education*, 8(1), pp. 3–18.

Watzlawick, P., Weakland, J. & Fisch, R. (1974) *Change: principles of problem formation and resolution* (New York, Norton).

Wheldall, K. (Ed.) (1987) *The Behaviourist in the Classroom* (London, Allen & Unwin).

Wheldall, K. & Glynn, T. (1989) *Effective Classroom Learning* (Oxford, Blackwell).

Wheldall, K. & Merrett, F. (1984) *Positive Teaching: the behavioural approach* (London: Allen & Unwin).

Wheldall, K., Wheldall, D. & Winter, S. (1983) *Seven Supertactics for Superparents* (Windsor, NFER/Nelson).

Williams, J. & Weeks, G. (1984) The use of paradoxical techniques in a school setting, *American Journal of Family Therapy*, 12(3), pp. 47–57.

Woods, P. (1976) Having a laugh: an antidote to schooling, in: Hammersley & Woods, *op. cit.*

Worden, M. (1981) Classroom behavior as a function of the family system, *School Counsellor*, 8(3), pp. 178–188.

Educational Psychology
An International Journal of Experimental Educational Psychology

EDITORS
Kevin Wheldall, *Macquarie University, Australia*
Richard Riding, *University of Birmingham, UK*

Supported by an International Editorial Board

Educational Psychology provides an international forum for the discussion and rapid dissemination of research findings in psychology relevant to education. The journal places particular emphasis on the publishing of papers reporting applied research based on experimental and behavioural studies. The journal also publishes periodical literature reviews.

The aim of the journal is to be a primary source for articles dealing with the psychological aspects of education ranging from pre-school to tertiary provision and the education of children with special needs. The prompt publication of high-quality articles is the journal's first priority.

This journal is also available online. Please connect to www.tandf.co.uk/online.html for further information.

To request a sample copy please visit: **www.tandf.co.uk/journals**

SUBSCRIPTION RATES
2003 – Volume 23 (5 issues)
Print ISSN 0144-3410
Online ISSN 1469-5820
Institutional rate: US$1049; £541 (includes free online access)
Personal rate: US$216; £135 (print only)

Carfax Publishing
Taylor & Francis Group

For further information, please contact Customer Services at either:
Taylor & Francis Ltd, Rankine Road, Basingstoke, Hants RG24 8PR, UK
Tel: +44 (0)1256 813002   Fax: +44 (0)1256 330245 Email: enquiry@tandf.co.u
Website: www.tandf.co.uk
Taylor & Francis Inc, 325 Chestnut Street, 8th Floor, Philadelphia, PA 19106, US
Tel: +1 215 6258900 Fax: +1 215 6258914 Email: info@taylorandfrancis.cor
Website: www.taylorandfrancis.com

cedp